by Franz Schurmann

THE ECONOMIC STRUCTURE OF THE YUAN DYNASTY
IDEOLOGY AND ORGANIZATION IN
COMMUNIST CHINA

with Orville Schell

THE CHINA READER

* IMPERIAL CHINA: *The Decline of the Last
Dynasty and the Origins of Modern China
The 18th and 19th Centuries*

** REPUBLICAN CHINA: *Nationalism, War, and
the Rise of Communism   1911–1949*

*** COMMUNIST CHINA: *Revolutionary Reconstruction
and International Confrontation   1949–1972*

with Peter Dale Scott and Reginald Zelnik

THE POLITICS OF ESCALATION IN VIETNAM

by Nancy Milton with Naomi Katz

FRAGMENT FROM A LOST DIARY

People's China

*Social Experimentation,
Politics,
Entry onto the
World Scene*

1966 through 1972

4 *The China Reader*

*Edited, annotated,
and with introductions
by DAVID MILTON,
NANCY MILTON,
and FRANZ SCHURMANN*

People's China
Social Experimentation, Politics, Entry onto the World Scene
1966 through 1972

RANDOM HOUSE, New York

Library of Congress Cataloging in Publication Data

Main entry under title:

The China reader.

Vol. 4 compiled by D. Milton, N. Milton, and F. Schurmann.
Bibliography: v. 4, p.
CONTENTS:—1. Imperial China: the decline of the last dynasty and the origins of modern China; the 18th and 19th centuries.—2. Republic of China: nationalism, war; and the rise of Communism; 1911–1949. [etc.]
1. China—History—Addresses, essays, lectures.

Library of Congress Cataloging in Publication Data

I. Schurmann, Herbert Franz, comp. II. Milton, David, 1923–   comp.
DS735.S43   951.05   66-21489
ISBN 0-394-48426-6

Manufactured in the United States of America

98765432

First Edition

Grateful acknowledgment is made to the following for permission to reprint previously published material:

Joseph Alsop: For "The Soviet Buildup on China's Frontier" by Joseph Alsop, from *San Francisco Chronicle*, December 6, 1972; and for "Peking's Awesome Underground City" by Joseph Alsop, from *San Francisco Chronicle*, December 1, 1972. Copyright © 1972 by Joseph Alsop.

The China Quarterly and Marianne Bastid: For "Economic Necessity and Political Ideals in Educational Reform During the Cultural Revolution" by Marianne Bastid, from *The China Quarterly*, Number 42 (April–June, 1970), pages 16–45.

Eastern Horizon: For "For Use, Not For Profit" by Joan Robinson, from *Eastern Horizon*, Volume XI, Number 4 (1972), pages 6–15.

*TO THOSE IN EVERY COUNTRY WHO
STORMED THE HEAVENS IN THE 1960's*

Mao Tse-tung to Anna Louise Strong in August 1946:

To start a war, the U.S. reactionaries must first attack the American people. They are already attacking the American people—oppressing the workers and democratic circles in the United States politically and economically, and preparing to impose fascism there. The people of the United States should stand up and resist the attacks of the U.S. reactionaries. I believe they will . . .

Although the Chinese people still face many difficulties and will long suffer hardships from the joint attacks of U.S. imperialism and the Chinese reactionaries, the day will come when these reactionaries are defeated and we are victorious. The reason is simply this: the reactionaries represent reaction, we represent progress.

Mao Tse-tung to Edgar Snow in December 1970 (Mao's remarks are in paraphrase):

But between Chinese and Americans there need be no prejudices. There could be mutual respect and equality. He said he placed high hopes on the peoples of the two countries. If the Soviet Union wouldn't do (point the way), then he would place his hopes on the American people. The United States had a population of more than 200 million. Industrial production was already higher than in any other country and education was universal. He would be happy to see a party emerge there to lead a revolution, although he was not expecting that in the near future.

In the meantime, he said, the foreign ministry was studying the matter of admitting Americans from the left, middle and right to visit China. Should rightists like Nixon, who represented the monopoly capitalists, be permitted to come? He should be welcomed because, Mao explained, at present the problems between China and the U.S.A. would have to be solved with Nixon. Mao would be happy to talk with him, either as a tourist or as President.

PREFACE

While Volume IV of the *China Reader* appears in 1974, all the work except for the introduction was completed at the end of 1972. We have added a short appendix on the Tenth Congress of the Chinese Communist Party held in early August 1973, and the introduction refers to events of 1973. But Volume IV as such covers China during the six years from 1966 through 1972.

Readers will note two forms of romanization for Chinese names and terms. The romanization generally used in English is the Wade-Giles system. But the Chinese also have their own romanization that is used exclusively within China. Since English-language publications from China still frequently use Wade-Giles renderings as well as the Chinese romanization, however, we decided not to standardize usage, but to append a romanization chart. We also call readers' attention to the common practice of omitting the Wade-Giles mark for the aspirate (as in *ch'i*).

Readers may also note an occasional discrepancy of one day in various dates. This is due to the difference of time zones between China and the United States. Again we found it difficult to standardize all dates.

While Chinese scientific work continued during the Cultural Revolution, evident in their successful synthesis of insulin, we have not included any selections on science in this volume. We felt that this volume should stress the political and social issues that were so important during the period 1966 through 1972.

We wish particularly to thank Mr. Chi-ping Chen of the Center for Chinese Studies of the University of California,

Berkeley, for good-naturedly helping us with our incessant requests for materials.

David Milton
Nancy Milton
Franz Schurmann

October 3, 1973
San Francisco

CONTENTS

INTRODUCTION

When President Nixon arrived in Peking on February 21, 1972, it had already become clear that world politics had changed fundamentally since 1966, when the first three volumes of the *China Reader* appeared. Then, China and America seemed on the verge of war. In 1972 a rapprochement between China and America was underway despite the intensification of the American bombing of Indochina. During those six years much has happened in China, America, and the rest of the world to alter fundamentally the pattern of world politics prevailing since the end of World War II. Events in China and China's role in the world have been major factors in those changes. Thus we felt the time ripe to put together Volume IV of the *China Reader* series to document those six important years. But unlike the earlier volumes, this volume gives prominence to the Chinese view of events. The Chinese have a powerful and practical view of the world and of themselves, from which much can be learned.

Volume III of the *China Reader* was entitled *Communist China.* That Volume IV is entitled *People's China* should not imply that China is no longer Communist. In giving titles to the previous three volumes, the editors sought to characterize each period with what was most striking politically. Thus, the first volume referred to China as an empire, the second to China as a republic, and the third to the fact that the Chinese Communist Party was—and remains—China's guiding political body. The present editors felt, however, that both external and internal developments during the years covered in this volume make the title *People's China* particularly appropriate. The Chinese never use the term "Communist China," and their recent new world role has accustomed Americans to the use of the name the Chinese give themselves, "People's Republic of

China." But we also believe that the Cultural Revolution, the most important internal event in China during those six years, reaffirmed a fundamental principle of the Chinese Revolution: that in the long run there can be no politics without the participation of the people.

Though the waves of the Cultural Revolution have subsided and though many old political forms have reappeared, we believe that the Cultural Revolution made clear to all in China that no politics, however smoothly managed by an elite party or bureaucracy, are invulnerable to social forces. This is a basic tenet of Chinese political thinking whose roots go far back into Chinese philosophy and whose substance now is formed by the Marxism-Leninism that the Chinese hold as their central world view. Furthermore, the Chinese believe that social forces are ultimately the basis for all politics throughout the world. However much their entry onto the world scene was motivated by their relationships to the superpowers, America and Russia, the Chinese see themselves as on the side of the great majority of peoples, nations, and countries in the world. How China's entry into the world scene is related to the Cultural Revolution, which appeared to direct China's energies inward, is still a mystery to most people. However, a link is indicated by the fact that the Chinese make analogies between the pretensions of the superpowers to dominate the world and those of their own authoritarian leaders prior to the Cultural Revolution to dominate China.

This Chinese view of politics explains the structure of this book. We begin with society, then go on to politics, and end with foreign affairs.

The 700 million people of China who must live and prosper essentially from resources China herself offers remain the core fact of all fundamental politics in China. No nation can prosper unless it develops its resources, but the Chinese have felt that people too must develop through new social institutions. In many ways, China's social institutions are more advanced than its economic development, which has suffered from severe external and internal constraints during the quarter-century existence of the People's Republic. It is this that made us chose the communes as the opening subject of this reader, and to entitle the beginning section "Great Social Experiments."

The conviction that broad experimentation is essential to social progress is an integral part of contemporary Chinese political thought. As a member of the Shanghai Revolutionary Committee at the height of the Cultural Revolution said to two of us during a discussion concerning China and America: "We think that a society that is motionless like a stagnant pool is unhealthy. When the water is moving turbulently the society is moving ahead."

Over 80 percent of China's population is rural—its 20 percent urban population is greater than that of all Japan. One need only look at comparably big nations such as India, Brazil, or Indonesia, for example, to see what could have happened if China's liberation had not come in 1949. While the advanced urban sector might have leaped forward as it has in Brazil, the mass of the peasantry would have remained in rebellion-breeding stagnation. Though in the 1950's there were some leaders in China who advocated developing wherever feasible and taking care of the rest of the country later, Mao Tse-tung never departed from the conviction that the peasants—all half billion of them—who had given Chinese Communism victory had to move ahead as well as the city people. The communes now constitute the core social structure in the villages, as visitors can see from the lively participation of the poorest of their members. The communes are much more than collective farms which pool labor and share gains. With their various levels, they are a framework in which people function politically to voice their interests, economically to produce and consume, and socially to form a community beyond that of family and neighbors.

We have followed the section on communes with one on the economy. As our introductions and selections indicate, the Chinese economy has far to go before it reaches the levels of the advanced nations. During the 1960's the Chinese made "self-reliance" their guiding policy in economic development. That this policy was to a large extent motivated by foreign actions— the cut-off of Soviet aid, the looming American threat in Indochina, and finally Soviet deployments on their northern borders—is now clear from the fact that, with a change in the international climate, they are willing to go beyond self-reliance. China must now accelerate its heavy industrial development in order to keep pace with population growth and satisfy the rising expectations of its people. To do so it must import capital goods, technology, and finished products from abroad. The sources of those imports have to be the developed economies of the world. But if the trends toward peace in Eastern Asia and in the world as a whole should vanish, self-reliance has given the Chinese the option of seeking a different road for their economy—one which may not produce affluence but will assure survival.

The most important social experiment to come out of the Cultural Revolution was that of the revolutionary committee. Elite administrative habits of powerful party committees in factories, offices, and schools were increasingly excluding people from meaningful participation in decision-making. The revolutionary committees arose as representational people's bodies to take over decision-making for the party committees. At present it appears as if the party committees, many of which were swept away by the Cultural Revolution, have returned and preempted the work of the revolutionary committees. As old cadres criticized during the Cultural Revolution return, so do old political forms. Little is said today in China about the Paris Commune model of political organization, which at the beginning of the Cultural Revolution electrified people. Then it seemed as if the Chinese were moving from a "vanguard" to a people's council concept of organization—namely from a centralized leadership by the party to leadership by workers' "soviets" as in the early days of the Russian Revolution. But with their characteristic dialectical habit of never abandoning an opposite even when vehemently attacking it, during the entire period of the Cultural Revolution, the Chinese continued to stress the leadership role of the Communist Party. And as the Cultural Revolution ebbed, that role was reasserted in the rapid re-formation of party committees.

But as happens with so many of China's experiments, the seeds remain in the ground to germinate again at some time in the future. Unless one believes that man's centuries-old dream of self-government has now finally been buried by the bureaucratic imperative of complex modern societies, then popular forces demanding political representation and participation will erupt again. If Mao is convinced as to anything, it is to this capacity of large bodies of people to rise up with hurricane-like force, often when least expected by rulers.

The hurricane force that arose with the Cultural Revolution came from China's youth, largely in the cities. The issue is indicated by our mild-sounding word "education." But in China education has connotations different from those in our country. For centuries, education was the channel through which the young gained power, wealth and prestige, the channel through which the young succeeded their elders. For over a decade now the subject of "successors" has been widely discussed, and was written into the Party Constitution adopted at the Tenth Party Congress (see Appendix, p. 632). Succession in China means far more than who succeeds to the top leadership. In fact, the key question is who shall constitute the millions—but not tens or hundreds of millions—who will assume the key jobs of society. That these jobs should not be channels for personal power, wealth, and prestige was what much of the Cultural Revolution was about. But that education remains a channel for succession in China is a fact that the Cultural Revolution could not alter. There are still few universities in China and limited numbers of secondary schools. Whosoever gains entry into them can expect good opportunities in life. That the Chinese in 1966 felt the wrong kinds of people were gaining entry to higher education is indicated by the fact that entrance exams were abolished at the very beginning of the Cultural Revolution. But exams are coming back in China, and significantly, this question once again is at the center of domestic political debate.

Education also has another fundamental meaning different from that in America. The Chinese have always regarded education as a way of infusing values into the young. That education should be a marketplace in which "ideas are exchanged" never made sense to them. They believe that the values inculcated by education are decisive in determining the kind of leadership the nation will get years hence. Much of the ideological struggle that seemed so obscure to outsiders yet made sense to people in China was over the issue of what values should govern the educational process. One concept vehemently attacked during the Cultural Revolution was the notion that the educated would become the political elite, much as is the case in the Soviet Union, or as was the case for centuries in old China. The Chinese themselves admit that elitism is far from being eradicated.

That the Chinese have done some remarkable things in the field of health is apparent from the lively interest in Chinese medicine the acupuncture vogue aroused. But the American proclivity for viewing medicine in technological ways has prevented people from understanding that the key to the Chinese approach to medicine is social. Health is a matter of the individual body, but the path to health must involve other people. For the Chinese, as important as the doctor who administers medical knowledge is the social context in which healing must occur.

Readers reading this introduction and then perusing the volume will note a theme which goes through both: the fact that what is social, what makes people act, work, and live as a group is always at the core of Chinese political thinking. But at the same time, the Chinese are convinced that individuals are so different, so strongly willed that effort is constantly required to keep the group together. No conception of China was ever more offensive and more utterly wrong than that of the "blue ants" propagated some years ago. Not leveling of individual differences but fitting them all into a working social context is a major function of education and the moral and ethical values it teaches.

Some in the West have assumed that ideology in China served a never-ending quest for liberation in which individuals and suppressed groups could finally exercise their full human faculties. "Dare to rebel" was one of the key slogans of the Cultural Revolution, and in the Party Rules adopted at the Tenth Party Congress, special safeguards were written in for dissident opinions. For Mao Tse-tung, as the teacher of the Chinese Revolution, progress for individuals, classes, and the world can only come through turmoil in which people free themselves again and again from fetters. But at the same time, there is a positive content to their ethical teaching, best expressed in the widely known slogan: "Serve the people." If old values are overthrown, new ones must be gained, or else "anarchism" ensues. The "spirit of communism" expresses more than the need for human liberation. It includes those values people must have if they are eventually to live in communal society, which is what the word communism means.

The subjects of the first part of this volume are all in what the Chinese, following Marxist usage, call the substructure. That of the second part, the Cultural Revolution, relates to the superstructure: namely the political realm, which always has its roots in the substructural realm of society. The subjects of the first part are mundane in that matters social are usually so, but the Cultural Revolution was hardly mundane. It erupted in the late spring of 1966 with vehement denunciations of "demons and monsters," went through a succession of fierce struggles, and finally, in 1971, led to the downfall of Lin Piao, who since 1966 had been the leader of China second only to Mao himself. What this part shows is that since 1966 struggle has gone on within the highest ranks of the leadership, and the Tenth Party Congress foresaw a continuation of similar struggles well into the future. In this volume, we stress the early years of the Cultural Revolution and say little about the Ninth Party Congress (adding material on the Tenth only in the appendix). We have done so because it was in those years that millions of people participated in the struggles, whereas what went on later was within the highest councils, unreflected by corresponding struggles among the people. This is not to deny the importance of those mysterious power struggles, as against Lin Piao and Ch'en Po-ta, but to indicate that the legacy of the Cultural Revolution which years hence will be remembered by people in China will, in our estimation, be that of the first years when people struggled over but also experimented with power.

There is a widespread opinion among foreign China watchers that the Cultural Revolution was but a violent temper tantrum that allowed accumulated resentments to blow off, but once these were blown off, normality in the form of the political structure that prevailed before May 1966 quickly returned. Certainly with the perspective of the late summer of 1973, when this introduction was written, much evidence would lend credence to such a belief. A remarkable number of old leading cadres bitterly criticized during the Cultural Revolution, notably Teng Hsiao-p'ing, have returned to prominence. Many political structures disbanded during the Cultural Revolution—as, for example, the Communist Youth League and the trade unions—

have been resuscitated. The army, which did so much of the administrative work during the Cultural Revolution, has withdrawn from civil affairs and is once again concentrating on its military roles. So the Party in its well-known form is back in power, and the Tenth Party Congress sanctioned its leading role. The more it changes, the more it stays the same—as the oft-quoted French saying goes.

But is it or could it be the same? Never has the historical clock been turned backwards, because conditions keep changing so much that even an apparent turning back is a change. One thing that has changed, trivial as it may seem, has been the impersonality with which all political processes were clothed, in the Russian fashion. The doctrines of party organization espoused by Liu Shao-ch'i—along with Lin Piao still excoriated as archenemy of the Chinese Revolution—held that while struggle may go on within the Party, the Party itself had to appear as a solid fortress monolithic to all outside. The Cultural Revolution broke down those ramparts, and since then a stupefying array of people have appeared on the scene, named and visible in one fashion or another. Unbelievably long lists of people participating in political functions are published. We offer one explanation—that those same social forces which erupted from below during the Cultural Revolution have achieved some kind of representational reflection within the complex structure of China's leadership. Under Liu Shao-Ch'i, the Party was seen as a vanguard for all the proletariat but not as representing them. Today, after all the turmoil the Party has been through, it still sees itself as the vanguard—that is, the leadership-giving instrument of the society—but it also has come to represent the social forces more so than was the case earlier.

Perhaps the revolutionary committees have left an imprint on the Party as it emerged from the Cultural Revolution. The revolutionary committee was not a vanguard but a representational body; like a "soviet," it represented the people in the unit, say factory or office. Perhaps the party now is, deliberately or not, seeking a path which will fuse its vanguard role of the past with the representational role of the revolutionary committees. The character of the Ninth Party Congress indicated continuing struggle, as evident later in the denunciations of Lin Piao and Ch'en Po-ta. But the character of the Tenth Party

Congress shows the presence of a wide array of forces each of which played a role—left, center, or right—during the Cultural Revolution.

What about Lin Piao? What about Ch'en Po-ta? People always seem fascinated by politics embodied in an individual, and few questions excited China watchers in 1971 and 1972 more than these. During the Tenth Party Congress, Lin and Ch'en were openly accused of being counterrevolutionary renegades, and Lin, together with his wife and son, was additionally accused of having attempted the assassination of Mao Tse-tung. In 1966 it appeared that Lin Piao, commander of the armed forces, had sprung to Mao's assistance, when threatened with plots led by P'eng Chen and Liu Shao-ch'i. That same year the only other prominent figure to second Mao was Chou En-lai, leader of China's government. And in the Tenth Party Congress, Chou gave the chief political report, indicating a position of preeminence in the country.

The demise of Lin Piao can be explained as symbolizing the withdrawal of the army from civil affairs, and that of Chen Po-ta as symbolizing the defeat of ultra-left forces which sought to monopolize their newly acquired power. But such abstract explanations seem unsatisfying for the downfall of these two men who at one time appeared to incarnate much of the spirit of the Cultural Revolution. The lurid Chinese contention that Lin Piao planted a bomb under a train carrying Mao Tse-tung does not arouse much credence abroad. While the Chinese stress Lin's intrigues against Mao, they also indicate that he was opposed to the new line in foreign policy, specifically the opening to America. In foreign policy, Lin Piao stood for a stance of isolationism with armed preparedness, like that of Albania. China maintains its stance of armed preparedness but has become a major actor on the world scene, forming new relationships going far beyond the old isolationism, particularly with the United States. As Watergate has shown Americans, there remains much mystery about politics at the highest levels of a country, and only future historians will be able to provide clearer answers to the questions posed by Lin Piao's downfall.

Lin Piao years earlier was regarded as a symbol of the Chinese army, as a strategist of world revolution, and as one of the leaders of the Cultural Revolution. Though several leading generals fell along with Lin, no great convulsions shook the Chinese army. The Chinese believe the world revolutionary process which they also call the "great troubles" continues. And the Chinese vehemently defend the achievements of the Cultural Revolution, its legacy having been determined for history well before September 12, 1971, when Lin Piao died.

The fate of Lin Piao forms a link between the earlier and later phases of the Cultural Revolution, and also between the second and third parts of this volume. From 1966 to early 1969, the Chinese were preoccupied with internal struggles, foreign affairs, including the war in Indochina, being relegated to the background. In March 1969, however, foreign affairs once again intruded into the Chinese political scene, but from a direction few in the world would have presumed likely. In March 1969 Chinese and Soviet armies fought a small but real war along the frozen banks of the Ussuri River, the easternmost boundary between the two countries. Though that episode might seem minor compared to the massive violence practiced by the Americans in Indochina, allegedly to halt "Chinese expansionism," since 1969 the war in Indochina has gradually come to wind down, while the tension between China and the Soviet Union has mounted, so much so that in 1973 there were alarums in the Western press about a possible Soviet attack on China. Lin Piao allegedly died in a plane crash in Mongolia, a country tightly linked to the Soviet Union, where sizable Soviet armies are stationed. Since Lin's death was followed by a series of Chinese policies which saw the United States as a possible counterweight to the immense Soviet military forces concentrated on the northern Chinese borders, one can presume that Lin's attitudes toward the Soviet Union and the United States were major obstacles to the evolution of those policies.

Following the Chinese belief that all politics springs from a social base, we have placed foreign affairs last in this volume. But any reading of the earlier volumes of the *China Reader* indicates that ever since 1840, foreign powers have deeply affected broad sectors of China's internal life. Since that time the Chinese have suffered a series of attacks from abroad that even when successfully resisted cost the Chinese dearly. War has been the tangible link between foreign and domestic affairs. Viewing the accelerating pace with which the two superpowers, America and Russia, are piling up arms, Mao Tse-tung and Chou En-lai can hardly be faulted for holding that "great troubles" will continue to erupt in the world, that there is constant danger of a new world war, and that China may yet again become the target of external attack.

There are only two countries which could launch an attack against China: the United States and the Soviet Union. In the mid-1960's, when Volume III was written, the greatest danger seemed to be that of a war between China and the United States. The Indochina war many times approached China. As late as the spring of 1972, American planes were bombing close to the Chinese border, and if some of the contingency plans reported in the *Pentagon Papers* are to be believed, the possibility of the raids crossing the border was always there. When American troops invaded Cambodia, Mao Tse-tung warned of the danger of a new world war, and that warning forms the first item in our selection. That he then meant the danger from America is clear, but it is even more clear now that he equally meant the danger of war from the Soviet Union.

As we indicate in Part III, the Chinese were convinced that the war in Indochina was "waning," even though at times it flared up again. They seemed equally convinced that the danger from the Soviet Union was "rising."

Few matters in world politics seem so puzzling to Americans and many other peoples as the conflict between two great nations which were once so tightly linked in alliance and friendship. Only a few years back nothing would have seemed so improbable as a spectacular visit to Peking by President Richard Nixon, earlier one of America's leading anti-Communists, followed by a relationship some commentators, like Joseph Alsop, have called an informal alliance between China and America. Yet if two decades earlier China "leaned towards" the Soviet Union, in the early 1970's it was leaning towards America as a counterweight to the Soviet threat.

We have indicated that extirpation of the Russian model from China's political and social life was one of the chief goals of the Cultural Revolution. Were there also men, cliques, and groups beholden to the Russians, as the Chinese alleged of Liu Shao-ch'i and his followers during the Cultural Revolution and alleged about Lin Piao during the Tenth Party Congress? It is difficult for outsiders to believe, yet Premier Chou En-lai, now widely regarded as one of the greatest statesman in the world, explicitly stated so. But believable or not, the Chinese make a further case about Russia which is based on fact and not on allegation. They point to the immense and growing deployments of Soviet troops on their long common frontier. And they took the Nixon Doctrine that America was withdrawing from eastern Asia seriously, despite the continuing war in Indochina. Even in the mid-sixties America was a distant enemy, but Russia was close, only three hundred miles or so from Peking, and only four hundred miles from the Chinese nuclear test sites in Sinkiang.

We begin our review of China in the world with Cambodia and end with China's underground shelters to protect the Chinese from nuclear attack. Will there be war between China and the Soviet Union? Or will the dangers pass and some form of hostile but nonviolent coexistence come into being? If the question of war or peace was central to Volume III, it remains so for this volume, except that Russia has replaced America as China's principal enemy.

—David Milton,
Nancy Milton, and
Franz Schurmann

October 3, 1973

I. Great Social Experiments

⤢ When the Cultural Revolution broke out, the common reaction in America was one of horror: law and order was breaking down; gangs of radical students were attacking respected officials; a mad leader, trying to recapture his revolutionary youth, was plunging his country into chaos. Five years later, the praises of China pour out of the busy typewriters of the many American visitors, some of whom only shortly before had written in the above vein. What was madness five years before is now admired as the frontier spirit which we had a century ago. What was collapsing into bloody civil war five years ago (or was imprisoned in totalitarian tyranny a decade ago) now became one of the most exciting, most successful societies in the world. Was it Chuang-tzu who dreamt he was a butterfly or a butterfly who dreamt he was Chuang-tzu? Did China change or was it the magic wand of publicity?

Much has changed in the New China from year to year, but much has not. What has not changed is China's character as a revolutionary country. Revolution in China has the same connotation as the word "progress" used to have in America. It means constant efforts to elevate the conditions of life of all citizens and unceasing struggle against recurrent relapses back into injustice, inequity, and inequality. The Chinese believe growth comes through struggle, and struggle means experimentation.

During the early 1950's, when the Chinese were following Russian models, they were already uncomfortable with the idea of planning superstructures and wanted to get back to the experimental tradition they had so successfully developed during the Yenan period. When they collectivized, they took the idea from the Russian experience, but then went through a trial-and-error process which finally culminated in the present-day communes. Experimentation does not mean ad hoc espousal of something new and exciting, as is often the case in America. The Chinese are conservatives when it comes to principles, namely those of Marxism-Leninism, and even the most radical of experiments they attempt are within the Marxist-Leninist framework. They hold that man's proper social existence is collective, not individualistic. They maintain that man is a political being and must serve the people, not escape into privatism. They believe in fighting enemies and in taking up arms to do so. Experimentation means trying various ways to build socialism.

In terms of the transformation of society, the Chinese have gone through three great periods. From 1949, the year of Liberation, until 1958, they pulled a chaotic country together with powerful organizational structures and started China on the road to industrialization. In 1958 the Chinese launched their Great Leap Forward, which materially and spiritually transformed the countryside. In 1966 they unleashed their Cultural Revolution, which aimed at changing the nature of governmental power. During that first period, when Russian models dominated virtually everything they did, they appeared to believe, as did the Russians, that organization plus industry added up to socialism. The Chinese built heavy industries as fast as they could, neglected consumer-goods industries, and regarded agriculture mainly as a source of savings for heavy industrialization. As their growth rate soared, they received plaudits both from the Russians and from tough-minded American economists. But the Chinese were dissatisfied as they saw a widening gap between the advancing industrial sectors and a socially and economically stagnant agriculture. The Yenan period, as an experiment in the liberated society of the future, had taught them development must be comprehensive, must bring all sectors up and not just some chosen few, and above all, must be in the interests of the poor peasants as they themselves see them and not as seen by planning theorists. Or, as one of our selections says, "Mao Tse-tung has always recognized that the easiest way to fall from power is to get on the wrong side of the Chinese peasant" (p. 81).

The Great Leap Forward was an extraordinary experiment in the transformation of an entire society. Even those of us who were sympathetic with the experiment could not escape the effects of the prevailing derision with which Western experts and media reviled the Great Leap Forward. Some even called it the Great Leap Backwards. As experiment after experiment faltered, the jeers intensified. The backyard steel program was little more than massive waste in the eyes of most economists, and the urban communes seemed a blind attempt to impose a simple village life on a complex city. But the loudest chorus of failure was directed against the rural communes, and the loudest voices were often those of the China experts. The communes had to fail because the Chinese were failing to recognize that all peasants produce only for self, and not for public interest. The Soviet experience had demonstrated that the most productive agriculture was on the private plots, and the collectivized sector registered disaster upon disaster. China would be no different.

As foreign visitors returned to China in large numbers in 1971, the communes had been in existence for thirteen years. Everywhere, as the visitors could see for themselves, the communes formed the backbone of rural life. As two of us who have lived in China can testify, the peasants in the communes are among the liveliest, healthiest, and most humor-loving people in the country. Until the difficult year of 1972, China had enjoyed ten years of good harvests. How much of this success was due to good weather and how much to the communes is difficult to say, but during this time the experiment which began in 1958 went through several twists and turns until it arrived at its present form, which the Chinese show with such pride to visitors. In fact, they are more willing to show the poorer communes, which have moved very far from their earlier state as miserable villages, than the richer ones, which often were based on prosperous villages to begin with.

The basic forms of the commune, as they originated in 1958 and were modified in 1960, have remained: a production team of some score households or a hamlet that works together on the fields; a production brigade that is essentially a village or several hamlets; and the commune itself, grouping together several brigades. The twists and turns that have taken place over the last years have been about the commune's relationship to the government on the one hand, and to its members on the other. The approach that the Chinese now ascribe to Liu Shao-ch'i held that a mix of centralized control by the state with private plots was the best basis on which to advance agricultural output. This is essentially the Russian approach to their *kolkhozy*. Liu proposed to exercise such control through state-directed investment in the communes and by something akin to the old Russian machine tractor stations (central machinery pools belonging to the state from which farms could borrow implements). Mao Tse-tung's approach stressed self-reliance. The communes, and not the state, must generate their own investment funds. They must acquire their own machinery. The state would negotiate contracts for delivery of farm products, not impose obligatory quotas. And as a substitute for the private plots, Mao proposed that each peasant household be allowed to retain its own food reserves from the collective product. Moreover, households can purchase manufactured products through supply and sales cooperatives attached to the communes rather than by cash purchases from proceeds of goods hawked in the city markets. Liu was essentially a centralizer in the Russian tradition, and Mao a decentralizer in the Yenan tradition. Mao was convinced that if the peasants were masters of their own productive destiny, they would perform. Liu feared the chaos that would ensue if the wise guiding hand of the state were not present to direct the peasants.

No question has more concerned the Chinese than that of what we in the West call motivation or incentives. The society from which China was liberated was a stagnant society in which people did the minimum. China today is an activist society in which it is presumed that man is happiest when he can do many things. There is no meditation in China. Marxism-Leninism teaches that man most fulfills himself when he is an active public creature. The Russians were also obsessed with the problem of motivating a people historically considered inert (in the fashion of the famous lazy anti-hero Oblomov). Their solution was competitive material incentives. The Chinese have never felt that material incentives alone were the solution, nor have they disdained material incentives. There never was a debate as between "moral" and "material" incentives in China. Rather, the Chinese hold that if the social conditions in which men live are correct and if they have a flexible, growing consciousness ("correct world view," as the Chinese call it), then men will be motivated to perform. Questions of wages, salaries, work points, or other remuneration can then be resolved on a practical basis.

We present a selection on the Tachai commune which many foreigners have visited and which the Chinese consider a model for rural living and working, and equitable remuneration. They believe that correct social arrangements among the members, coupled with a highly developed, informed, and flexible consciousness, have resulted in satisfactory production as well as a satisfactory wage system. For the Russians motivation begins with wages. For the Chinese it ends with wages.

During the urban turmoil of the Cultural Revolution, little seemed to be happening in the rural communes beyond the provision of shelter to millions of Red Guards tramping through the countryside. The Cultural Revolution was a revolution of the superstructure, by which Marxists mean the political system or the governing institutions. Since the communes were the substructure—that is, society and economy proper—they were not directly involved in the struggles. But if the "capitalist roaders" had won out in the Cultural Revolution, the communes today would be rather different from what they are. In earlier years, one of the most common manifestations in the countryside was the mobilization of millions of peasants to do socially necessary labor. Western observers generally regarded this with a mixture of horror and admiration—after all, unlike other backward countries, the Chinese were getting things done. Prior to the Cultural Revolution, a "socialist education campaign" was underway in the countryside which many saw as the precursor of a new mobilization. But there was no mobilization. Self-reliance is the opposite of mobilization. For a brief time in the late 1960's, self-reliance went to such an extreme that the phrase "75,000 China's" was heard, meaning that each of the 75,000 communes constituted a self-contained entity. That phrase is no longer heard because China is recentralizing from earlier extremes of decentralization. With recentralization, some of the mobilizational policies of the past may also be returning, but the principle of self-reliance and local effort has become an integral part of the Chinese rural scene.

During the early 1960's the Chinese set forth a range of

economic priorities which were the exact reverse of those in the early 1950's. First came agriculture, then light industry, and last heavy industry. For the Russians such priorities were heresy and idiocy, simply serving to show that Mao was unconcerned about people's welfare so long as he could tinker with their souls. How could any society develop economically without masses of steel plants? The Chinese went even further than reversing the sacrosanct Russian economic priorities: they propounded the notion that agricultural output could not rise unless the social arrangements in the commune were correct. Ten years of good harvests would indicate that there is something right about the communes, aside from good weather. Maybe there is an old traditional strain in this Chinese concern for proper social arrangements. One of the best-known ancient wisdoms in China is the admonition first to "rectify oneself, then to arrange one's family, and thereby one can gain the world." But it would be short-sighted to see the Chinese approach as merely "Chinese," without implications for others. As the economist Carl Riskin has pointed out, even Western economists have abandoned the carrot-and-stick theory of worker motivation. And the recent discovery by American students of business that paternalism is the source of the Japanese economic miracle shows that academics are beginning to recognize what ordinary people have long known—that while people need money to live, far from all will work just for more money.

What is the state of the Chinese economy that Mao Tse-tung was convinced would turn out all right if the social experiments succeeded? Experiments have to be simple and clear-cut to be attempted, but their results will always be complex. There is nothing simple about the Chinese economy. Like Chinese civilization itself, the Chinese economy is intricate, subtle, and intriguing—so intriguing, in fact, that for two decades, despite the American embargo on trade with China, businessmen throughout the world, including Americans, were dreaming of vast new trade with China, despite the not always encouraging economic and political indications coming from China. The Chinese have released virtually no statistical data on the performance of their economy since the late 1950's, and the few figures that have been released hardly satisfy the economists' enormous appetite for data. Visitors' impressions, talks with

Chinese officials, and the laborious analyses of the Chinese economy performed by external intelligence agencies add up to the following picture of the Chinese economy: it has done very well in the production and distribution of food products; it has produced a surprising volume of consumer goods both for domestic consumption and for export; it lags in heavy industrial development.

A decade ago, virtually the only question economists wanted answered from their studies of the Chinese economy was: How do the Chinese come off in their growth rates compared to other countries, or, more crudely put—who's ahead in the race? What was most annoying about the Chinese (and other socialist countries) was that they refused to calculate the "services" component of what we call the Gross National Product and so allow a "real" evaluation of their economic performance. For us, "services" are jobs with measurable (presumably) inputs and outputs. For the Chinese, "services" are what all of society is about. The notion of calculating the economic input of a Mao Tse-tung Thought study session—which, as even hostile observers now admit, helps to imbue people with a work ethic—would appear laughable to the Chinese. But equally laughable is the whole Western obsession with "who's ahead." One of our selections notes that China's industrial growth rate for 1971 was between 15 and 20 percent, its agricultural growth rate was some 3 percent, and its overall increase in national income some 10 percent. The performance is satisfactory, but not spectacular by Japanese standards.

Unlike the Russians, who simply divide their economy into two vast sectors (industry and agriculture), the Chinese divide their economy into three sectors (heavy industry, light industry, and agriculture). Heavy industry consists of enterprises the state considers vital for economic development and national defense. Light industry consists primarily but not exclusively of consumer-goods industries. And agriculture, of course, is the farm economy. While agriculture is the primary source of savings for the economy as a whole, it is also the prime supplier of raw materials to light industry. Light industry produces for both domestic consumption and export; from the latter, China earns vital foreign exchange. The state lays a heavy tax burden on light industry's profits, which are high due to the wide gap between the prices of raw materials and those of the manufactured products. The government invests its income in heavy industry and such other enterprises deemed vital for development and defense.

One of the most important principles that the Cultural Revolution finally embedded in the Chinese economy was that of self-reliance in finding capital, equipment, and raw materials. In return for considerable freedom in determining their own production plans, rural communes and light industrial enterprises must generate their own resources for new investment. Except in strategic industries, the government everywhere encourages local initiative. But this has not resulted in the kind of "market socialism" which operates in Yugoslavia or which Dubček sought to introduce into Czechoslovakia. As Joan Robinson points out (p. 50), Chinese enterprises accept the discipline of an administratively imposed pricing system (though flexibility is built into the pricing system, as it is into everything else in China). There has been no market-induced inflation in China since Liberation in 1949, and the Chinese, watching the downs of the dollar and the ups of the yen and the mark, boast of their renminbi as one of the most stable currencies in the world. Keeping the balance between unit initiative and overall control must surely be one of the most difficult tasks of the Chinese administrative system. The administration that supposedly broke down during the Cultural Revolution seems to have gone on functioning despite the shambles it reportedly (from Hong Kong sources) was in—prices remained stable; food supplies were generally plentiful; and while industrial production and exports dropped, the declines were far from catastrophic and far less than in 1960–61.

People have been interested in the Chinese economy for a variety of reasons. While a few economists tried to build econometric models with the skimpy data available, others were ultimately concerned with the military capabilities of the economy. Businessmen have been interested in trade potential. Radicals saw Chinese socialism as an exciting new approach to economic development. But lately, as our selection from *Fortune* implies, a different kind of interest has arisen, particularly among Americans. Americans are no longer so certain that they are the best of the best in the areas of the economy, technology, and organization for which they felt they had particular talents and callings. Japan has done astoundingly well in the economy; other countries are invading that field of scientific-technological research and development which America once thought was its exclusive preserve; and our superb organization has produced too many discomforting signs of alienation, conflict, and breakdown. It is China's achievements in producing social cohesion along with satisfactory economic development (and not either/ or, as is the case in other developing nations) which is intriguing many Americans, including economists.

But it would be an error to portray the Chinese economy as a smashing success, a model for all to follow. The last to suggest that would be the Chinese themselves. They keep on repeating tirelessly to all their visitors that China is still a poor country with an immense population, that it still lacks a solid industrial foundation. But now, they believe, is the time for China to begin that rapid development which they postponed earlier so that the social and political questions could be resolved. The Chinese are now saying: We do not have enough steel. Development will require vast new construction programs, which require an expanding steel industry. At the same time, China must accelerate its imports of capital goods from abroad. The Chinese have traditionally been trade-oriented, and remain so. But they are also careful in developing new trade ties, and above all, will never become so dependent on one source of supply as they were on the Soviet Union in the 1950's.

No one can write about China's great social experiments without considering the experiments in revolutionary administration which occurred during the Cultural Revolution. During the early 1960's the general Western reaction was that the Great Leap Forward had failed, and the Chinese would finally settle down to reality and forget all those schemes about things like communes. Now, in the aftermath of the Cultural Revolution, one hears the same comments, often from those same pundits. Having had their fling in the 1960's, the Chinese are now settling down. No one now speaks of the "Paris Commune" ideas of the Cultural Revolution, and it is hard to say exactly what the situation is with the revolutionary committees. Many old cadres, including some who were bitterly attacked as capitalist roaders, are back at their old desks. New Party com-

mittees have been formed. Some see signs of a new conserva-
tism in China—for example, in the new interest in ancient
archaeology. The Great Leap Forward did not produce that
material plenty it had promised, but it planted seeds, some of
which eventually grew into trees of solid size. The Cultural
Revolution has also planted seeds, and one can only wait to
see what comes of them.

Three things that happened during the early months of the
Cultural Revolution were to set the guidelines for the political
experiments of the entire period. First were the open, direct,
and unequivocal attacks on the highest Party officials. Second
was the entry of the masses (primarily students) into the
hitherto closed sanctum of Central Committee proceedings in
July. And third was the formation of the first revolutionary
committee in early 1967. Prior to these first attacks on high
Party officials (the president of Peking University, Lu P'ing, and
at that time Peking first party secretary, P'eng Chen, once
rumored to be a possible successor to Mao), leading officials had
often been indirectly criticized by the heaping of abuse on their
subordinates (as in the 1957 antirightist campaign). But during
the Cultural Revolution, the highest officials, including the
President of the Republic, Liu Shao-ch'i, were directly criticized
and toppled from power. While external observers were obsessed with the struggle for power, the Chinese people were
being taught that periodic cultural revolutions in which an entire stratum of bureaucratic power-holders would be swept
from society were essential for a society to remain alive and on
a progressive course.

The entry of the masses into the Central Committee sessions
was the initiation of the mass politics that characterized the entire Cultural Revolution. It was raucous, confused and ever-
shifting, drawing everyone into the political arena. It was public
democracy at work at its best, its most mediocre, and its worst.
One thing it was not: a political process going on behind closed
bureaucratic doors with occasional bland, reassuring com-
muniqués to "inform the people." This open character of the
Cultural Revolution explains the vehemence with which Liu
Shao-ch'i's works, particularly his famous volume on the training of Party members, were attacked. Liu's volume was a training manual which exhorted Communists to be dedicated, disci-

plined, and unafraid to voice their opinions, but only *within* the Party. The Russian tradition of separating the power-holders from the people was frontally attacked during the Cultural Revolution, and while socialist democracy may still be only a promise in China, the idea has been launched, as was that of the communes during the Great Leap Forward.

It was the novel phenomenon of the people entering directly into the political process which explains why at this time the Chinese were fascinated with the Paris Commune of 1871. In 1971 the century anniversary of the Paris Commune was celebrated with great fanfare in China, although the political emphasis was somewhat different than in 1966. The word "commune" has a long history in Chinese communism, one that goes back to the Canton Commune of 1927: it signifies the direct seizure and exercise of power by the people and the organization of disciplined bodies under leadership to protect that power. In 1958 the adoption of the word "commune" for the new rural collectivities was meant to imply that the peasants had created and were administering them. In that surge toward democracy unleashed by the Cultural Revolution, the Chinese found in the Paris Commune just the model sanctioned by the Marxist tradition which they wanted. Marx was caught by surprise when the communards seized Paris, but he quickly hailed them—a political flexibility highly pleasing to the Chinese, and to Mao in particular. While the people of Paris were building proletarian power, a traitorous bourgeois government in Versailles was haggling with the Prussian enemy for lenient terms which would allow the bourgeois democracy in Versailles to triumph and the Paris revolution to be smashed. But while the urban setting of the Paris Commune and the struggle between the two 1871 French lines seemed so similar to their own Cultural Revolution, what particularly intrigued the Chinese was the fact that the communards, having seized power, began to construct their own people's organizations and government, and armed themselves in self-defense, not as vigilantes but as a regular army.

The most important organizational formation to come out of the Cultural Revolution was the revolutionary committee. The revolutionary committee was in theory a representative body of people in a particular unit (like a school or a factory or an office) who had seized power from a party committee ruled by capitalist roaders. Soon the revolutionary committees came to supplant party committees in every organization. Starting as isolated grass-roots bodies, they spread like wildfire and eventually supplanted the party committees at the level of provincial government. The party committee was a branch of the Chinese Communist Party, one which in principle was supposed to be responsible to the people as well as loyal to higher echelons. In fact, as was claimed during the Cultural Revolution, the party committees had become ruling bodies—all centralism and no democracy. They were seen as emanations of the top Party officials, their personal power instruments. The revolutionary committee was the opposite. It was a body which arose from below and was supposed to be truly representative of the people and subject to their political will.

Forming revolutionary committees was one of the most arduous, painful, and sometimes violent political processes which went on in China during the Cultural Revolution. As Americans should remember from their own formative period, democracy is a messy process. Various models began to be propagated, notably the seizure of power in Shanghai (see pp. 289–315) and the "triple alliance," on which basis revolutionary committees in Heilungkiang were formed. The "triple alliance" seemed like a sensible format for the construction of a revolutionary administration: one third of the members would be activists who had surged forth from the people during the struggles; one third would consist of "old cadres," who had broken with the capitalist roaders but had had years of experience in running a complex organization; and one third would consist of People's Liberation Army soldiers who provided the backbone of the organization, gave it its Maoist spirit, and formed the link with the country as a whole. The rationale behind the revolutionary committees was that the initiatives would come from the people, while the old cadres would fit the unit into the overall national context.

The actual history of the revolutionary committees has been rather different from what was intended. As factional fights hampered action, soldiers came to play a predominant role. After the Ninth Party Congress in the spring of 1969, a new process of reconstituting party committees began. Unlike the arduousness of the process of forming revolutionary committees, the party committees were reestablished with surprising speed. Many old cadres simply came back to their desks, including some who had been bitterly attacked during the Cultural Revolution. As the party revived, the army began to phase out of administration, a process accelerated by the demise of Lin Piao and some of China's top generals. In China, the pendulum has always swung from democracy to centralism and then back. So it is not surprising that some of the pre–Cultural-Revolution forms have returned.

As the ferret eyes of the China watchers search for every bit of bureaucratization as a sign that the "moderates" are back in power and the Chinese are becoming more "normal" (meaning "like us"), one has to ask honestly whether they may not be right. Was the Cultural Revolution a glorious but brief episode, a deviation from the norm willed by Mao but not capable of being sustained? Mao has several times alluded to the possibility that China could go revisionist despite one or many cultural revolutions. Is the pile-driver relentlessness of bureaucratic growth inevitable? Mao's bet is that it is not, due to his conviction that the world will be one of trouble, mess, and confusion (what the Chinese call *lùan*), and not of peace and harmony. Bureaucracies make the opposite bet that they will be able to keep the lid on and themselves in power. But whatever the case, the Cultural Revolution will rank among those great democratic happenings that periodically rekindle hope in men.

The Cultural Revolution first erupted in Peking University when teachers and students put up *ta-tzu-pao* (*dazibao*) attacking President Lu P'ing, were subjected to the channeling maneuvers of the "work teams," and then erupted into the Red Guard phenomenon, which began with university students and soon spread to colleges and high schools. After final exams had been suspended, all the universities were closed. Teachers continued to receive their salaries, but no one taught. Exceptions were made for scientific-technical personnel working in national security areas. During the summer and autumn of 1966, entire classes embarked on what some American newspapers called the "children's crusade"—millions of students began walking through China visiting villages and famous revolutionary sites, not as individual tourists but with their classmates.

By the end of the year, students were urged to return to school and carry on the revolution in the classroom. The idealism of 1966 and early 1967 then turned into the campus factionalism of 1967. By late 1967 the turmoil had ended as worker-peasant propaganda teams entered the universities and restored discipline.

That there was an educational crisis in China was easier for outsiders to accept in view of the vast student upheavals that had occurred at the same time in Japan, West Europe, and America. For all the differences in social systems, what happened in Peking's universities was often strikingly similar to what happened at Berkeley, at Tokyo, at Vincennes, at the Free University of Berlin, and at many other schools. And while university administrators are breathing a sigh of relief that the turmoil has passed, most people who work in education know that something has happened in a field concerned with something so elusive as teaching, learning, and researching. While the elementary and intermediate schools in China are now fully functioning, as of early 1973 the universities there are still in a state of indecision. Scientific and technical learning has made the most rapid comeback, since course content is determined by what the Chinese themselves call "world standards." There is no Lysenkoism in China—no ideological theories of nature's workings. What the Chinese learn in their microbiology courses is the same that Americans learn, and often from the same journals. But it is a different matter in the Chinese equivalent of the social sciences and the humanities.

During the fever heat of the Cultural Revolution, the Chinese read little but newspapers, wall posters, and *Quotations from Chairman Mao*. No book was printed for general circulation except the *Quotations*, and book stores featured virtually nothing but bright red heaps of the little red book. If one takes Mao's principle of firmness in principle and flexibility in practice and uses it to explain this literary phenomenon, one might say that the little red book contained the simple principles, but the immense amount of ephemera—written in different styles, often outrageous like American underground newspapers, ranging from bombast to simple literary gems—reflected the ever-changing reality of Chinese politics. The fact is that there was a great deal of exciting material to read in China in those days.

One can probably never find out how much this avalanche helped raise the general level of consciousness of the people, but the material was poured out in every corner of China. The quantity was helpful to foreign collectors, who amassed great quantities in Hong Kong and Tokyo.

Without books, it is hard to imagine education. As the schools began to reopen, the easiest kind of book to bring out once again was one which contained the basic knowledge of elementary and intermediate education. But university education requires more complex books, and the Chinese are still not sure which books should be assigned in their various curriculums. Assigning a book for a class is considered a serious political matter in China. Not having a "marketplace of ideas," they cannot accept a laissez-faire regime in book assignments. But books are coming back into vogue. Aside from the Marxist classics, several Chinese classics have been republished, and other books will soon come off the presses. The Chinese are now being urged to study history, archaeology, and foreign languages. Westerners must remember that education has been the core of Chinese civilization for two thousand years. Whereas our word for civilization implies "cities," theirs contains the Chinese word for "writing."

As with everything else, the Chinese will allow the new forms of university education to grow slowly. Before the Cultural Revolution, a university degree, for all the proletarian propaganda, conferred much the same kind of elite status it does in capitalist countries. The Cultural Revolution broke that elitism but also broke the education. The old Confucian ideal held that the educated man must above all else be a model to others, and even today the phrase "to make oneself a model" (*i-shen tso tse*) is widely used in China. The Chinese couldn't possibly conceive of a higher education which "exposes students to all sorts of ideas." There must be a purpose to education, and until they have achieved some unanimity on what that is, they will move forward slowly with the revival of university education.

Concerning elementary and intermediate education, the consensus in China is far greater, and so the problem of educational reform is less difficult. Even in the schools of the pre-1949 liberated areas, the Communists always stressed educational policies that would keep the students close to the people and would combine learning with work; they hoped to provide at least an elementary education for all children in the country. However, when the Cultural Revolution began, accusations were mounted against the capitalist roaders that in concentrating on quality education, they had left vast residues of illiteracy in the country, particularly among the poorest strata of the population. The centralized system of education was blamed, and a new policy enunciated the fostering of what in America would be called community control of the schools. Since elementary schools are often attached to a production unit, workers in that unit began to exercise greater control over teachers and courses. Thus the powers over teacher assignments were invested in the local revolutionary committees rather than in the Peking Ministry of Education. The assumption was that self-reliance and local control would make for better and more widespread education. Since schools are regarded as miniature versions of the larger society, students do work such as they will later be doing in factories and on farms. Manual labor is highly stressed in China, as is military drill. Not only are students instilled with a sense of national pride, but they are taught they must be prepared to defend their country and its revolution.

Traditionally the Chinese have felt that education and learning should pervade the entire community, though in Confucian practice, only a tiny minority monopolized its skills. Before the Cultural Revolution, a division-of-labor atmosphere reigned, with education regarded as a special skill worked out in pedagogical institutes and supervised by the Peking Ministry of Education, much as is the case in the Western European countries, Japan, and of course, the Soviet Union. The Cultural Revolution, however, moved the pendulum back toward a closer relationship between school and community. So by going beyond the Soviet-style approach, the Chinese, in one of their amazing swings of the dialectic, have also returned to a concept of schooling closer to their own cultural tradition.

If education played a prominent part in traditional Chinese culture, so did medicine. As it did in ancient Greece, medicine formed part of the classic Chinese tradition of learning. But while traditional medicine does not exist in the West—since newer scientific advances are always supposed to supersede outmoded practices—it not only exists in the countries of Eastern

Asia, but after passing through a period during which it was disdained, it has been developing along lively new paths. The Chinese are among the most practical-minded people in the world. Their attitude toward traditional medicine is not fetishistic or nationalistic, but simply a common-sense awareness of the fact that it seems to have demonstrable therapeutic value. This is particularly true of acupuncture, which after Nixon's 1972 visit to China, has enjoyed a flurry of attention in the West. But the fascination for acupuncture is due more to the voracious American appetite for learning new "techniques" than to a real concern as to how the Chinese have tackled health problems in their own country. For the Chinese that is the main story, and acupuncture simply one of their many trial-and-error methods which turned out to be successful.

China's health problems at the time of Liberation in 1949 were so staggering that few Americans can imagine them. Suffice it to say that the average life expectancy was under thirty-five years. As is the case in most other poor countries, the main sources of disease and death in China were bad sanitation, bad hygiene, and lack of the most basic immunizations and medical care. With that extraordinary organization the Chinese so quickly established after Liberation, they swept through the entire country cleaning up the filth, sanitizing public facilities, inoculating people, instructing them in basic child care, killing pests (such as flies and sparrows), and most of all convincing people that disease was not a natural disaster. As a result, China's death rate dropped to levels not that far below Western and Japanese levels. Predictably, that resulted in a vast surge of population growth, which the Chinese are now combating with a vigorous and well-organized birth-control campaign.

What is not sufficiently realized in America is that while the Chinese still have many pathologies left from their legacy of poverty, they are also facing many of the same health problems as the advanced countries. As Chinese doctors who have visited America have indicated, they are eager to learn all the advanced medical techniques and theories they can. Chinese libraries are well stocked with international medical literature. That research and development in medicine was not halted during the Cultural Revolution is indicated by the synthesis of insulin which the Chinese achieved during that period. The technical approach of the Chinese to health and medicine is what it has been since the Liberation: a mixture of advanced Western methods with traditional practices. Since the Cultural Revolution, however, there has been a change in the human approach. The barefoot doctors are not simply paramedical personnel sent down to treat peasants, but trained medical people, one of whose main tasks is to teach the people basic medical knowledge. What the Chinese destroyed was the image of a begowned doctor, replete with degrees on his walls, surrounded by terrifying apparatuses, performing incisions on a drugged patient who was told he had to be "helped" (to use a favorite American term) by a knowledgeable expert. The Chinese have at times ridiculed expertise, but the term "expert" is back in good repute. What they have attacked is the authoritarian arrogance of the doctor (as well as that of all others in positions of power and authority). The task of the barefoot doctor, whether that person is a simple medical technician or a renowned doctor, is to explain to patients and other people what (s)he is doing while at the same time giving the best medical care possible.

The entire Cultural Revolution was about consciousness, about people knowing, and the Chinese have taken that directly into the field of health and medicine. Science and technology are complex, but that is no reason why they cannot be explained in simple terms. And if renowned doctors and medical researchers have to explain what they are doing, that is no reason why, in the long run, their research and skilled practice should suffer. That during the Cultural Revolution the pendulum perhaps swung too far toward mass participation is indicated by the renewed Chinese emphasis on "expertise." Some foreigners visiting China lament the state of the universities, the lack of research, and so on. As with their heavy industry, the Chinese know they have sacrificed some things in medicine for the sake of achieving proper social arrangements. But, as Mao has said several times, the Chinese feel they eventually must catch up with and surpass world levels in science and technology.

In compiling this section on great social experiments, we could have chosen material on many other areas of experiment in a society that has decided to revolutionize its entire feudal and bourgeois legacy. But as we were finishing the work, we realized that we had failed to cover what in the long run may be regarded by future historians as the greatest experiment of all in People's China, that being what the Chinese call "changing one's outlook," and what in Western circles is regarded as an attempt to change man himself. The Chinese, as Marxists, hold that human relations cannot become equitable unless the material foundations of those relationships change in more equitable directions. But for Mao, while that has been a necessary condition for the achievement of socialism, it was never sufficient. Unless people's consciousness or people's outlook changes, then socialism cannot be achieved. Socialism must be built on spiritual as well as material foundations—thus the frequency with which Mao uses the word "spirit" in his writings. Therefore, we decided to entitle this section of the Introduction "The Spirit of Communism."

The Chinese believe that learning and relearning is possible throughout one's life. The main setting for such adult learning is the group study sessions, in which virtually everyone participates. During the Cultural Revolution, throughout China one could see small groups of people "studying" with their little red books. Some Westerners felt these sessions resembled Bible-reading meetings, and generally thought there was something quasi-religious about the cult of adoration for Mao. Mao himself said to Edgar Snow that he was not happy about this, although the cult may have served a purpose at the time. Indeed, after 1969 the plethora of Mao objects rapidly vanished from China, leaving his public image increasingly that of "teacher," by which, as he also told Snow, he would like to be remembered in history. Study sessions are lively and spirited; everything is discussed, ranging from the aphorisms in the red book to, more recently, foreign affairs, material for which comes from the "News for Reference," their digest of the world press.

During the Korean War, Americans were electrified by a satanic new device of personality manipulation which was called "brainwashing" and which the Chinese reportedly were practicing on American prisoners of war. Subsequently, calmer research revealed that these were really "thought-reform" sessions featuring intensive criticism and self-criticism. Similarities were soon seen between thought reform and certain psychotherapeutic practices in America. But the term "thought reform" was dropped during the Cultural Revolution, most likely because of its authoritarian tone. In contrast to the 1950's, when thought reform was often an intense process in which participants' thought was broken down and then rebuilt along new lines, study today seems more relaxed, more in the nature of what it is supposed to be: group learning.

But while the Chinese have abandoned the psycho-manipulative techniques of thought reform, they are as concerned as ever with changing human behavior. One of the most widely propagated slogans during the Cultural Revolution was *tou-szu, p'i-hsiu,* meaning "Fight privatism and criticize revisionism." In line with the general theme of self-reliance, each person must initiate the process of changing behavior by oneself, and the first step is combating any withdrawal into private concerns. The Chinese, both as Confucians and as communists, are convinced that the road to spiritual health lies in being a full social and political being. The American drug culture with all its fantasy wanderings through the head is not only incomprehensible to the Chinese but reminds them of their own opium-sodden past. "Criticizing revisionism" means one must engage in class struggle, which since the Cultural Revolution, means primarily the fight against revisionism: the phenomenon of authoritarian arrogance masquerading as socialism, the practitioners of which range from the corrupt Soviet Union to "limelighters" within the ranks of the revolution.

Two behavioral manifestations the Chinese singled out for intensive struggle during the Cultural Revolution were authoritarianism and what we in America would call discrimination. When the Chinese denounced the Liu Shao-ch'i line as "the capitalist road," the image conjured up was that of a powerful boss giving orders to flunkies, who scurry about deferentially doing the boss's bidding. Following the ancient mandarin tradition and a newer tradition of the Soviet-style party apparatchik, entrenched power began to supplant true leadership in the command posts of authority. But as the old capitalist roaders began to fall, new limelighters appeared, shouting the slogans of the left, more left than the left, and always anxious to be in the limelight. The purge of the "ultra-left" in China has to be explained in power political terms, and many of those purged were sincere revolutionaries and not limelighters (as undoubtedly were many of the capitalist roaders). But as exemplary personalities, as models, limelighters—whether of the left, center, or right—were bad, and such behavioral tendencies had to be eradicated. The Chinese believe passionately in leadership, but not in domination. Whether mandarin, apparatchik, or entrenched professional, the Chinese want to rid themselves of that mentality.

Not just during the Cultural Revolution, but throughout their whole revolutionary history the Chinese Communists have constantly fought to reduce the manifold discriminations and inequalities inherent in their society. The essence of Confucianism was inequality, which two millennia of practice turned into hundreds of discriminatory levels, putting some on top and others in the middle or on the bottom. The Chinese Communists are not egalitarians nor anarchists. They believe in leadership, and they accept wage differentials. Some people have more power, live better, and enjoy more prestige than others in China. While the Chinese are not happy about many of the inequalities that remain, they are not so disturbed as one might imagine. But what offends the Chinese is the perpetuation of inequality beyond the requisites of leadership and socially necessary role. During the Cultural Revolution, it was discovered that high cadres sent their children often in chauffeur-driven limousines, to special, privileged schools. That the Chinese saw as the formation of a new class and smashed it. But feudalism and capitalism had left countless residues of such class barriers: city people over country people; men over women; old over young; prestigious over ordinary citizens; Chinese over nationalities; North Chinese over South Chinese; educated over uneducated; and so on. Nothing more offended the Communists than the arrogant Confucian discrimination against women, and the liberation of women (through the "Marriage Law") was one of the first acts of the new revolutionary government. While women's liberation has been a major concern of the Chinese, it is not regarded as a special and separate movement apart from the movement to eradicate all these manifold forms of discrimination.

In February 1973 Alain Bouc, the *Le Monde* correspondent, reported from China: "Today the accent is on 'rectification,'

'consolidation,' and 'readjustment' after seven years of fairly
erratic experiment and cultural revolution in all fields" [*The
Guardian* (Manchester), February 17, 1973]. The pendulum is
swinging from struggle back toward unity, as it has so often
in the history of Chinese Communism. Experiments and struggle are by their nature often erratic until some consensus is
reached that one must cease experimenting and go on to work
for one's goals. But as the Cultural Revolution (as well as earlier mass movements) revealed, the struggle was over what
those goals should be. In 1949 the Chinese finally rejected the
capitalist model of development, and in 1966 they rejected the
Russian model. In the process of rejection and creation, they
have come up with their own road to socialism, adequate to
their conditions and, they believe, of instructive value to others.

1. COMMUNES

There is no other American whose life was for so long a part of the history of modern China and its revolution as Anna Louise Strong. In 1925 she was one of the few Western correspondents admitted to Canton during the Hong Kong strike, and two years later, reporting on the Revolution of 1927, she attended the first meeting of the revolutionary Wuhan government and witnessed the historic Hunan peasant uprising which Mao Tse-tung had predicted earlier that year. (See *China Reader,* Volume III.) These events were the beginnings of China's long revolution, and from this brief but powerful encounter, Anna Louise Strong was to develop a commitment which would endure until her death in Peking in 1970, at the age of eighty-four.

From the time of her first visit until the late 1940's, Anna Louise Strong returned to China from her base in Moscow at several historically decisive moments. In 1947 Mao Tse-tung, then in the caves of Yenan, granted her the now immortalized "paper tiger" interview, in which he predicted the soon-to-be-realized Communist victory of 1949. The next decade was a harsh one for this veteran reporter of revolutions—arrested and deported by the Soviet Union in 1948, she returned to the United States and was rehabilitated by Khrushchev in 1955. Anna Louise Strong left America for the last time in 1958 and returned to China at the age of seventy-two. Her intermittent association with the Chinese revolution, particularly in Yenan, had long before convinced her that the Chinese Communists were evolving new and significant forms of social organization, and fresh political approaches, all quite different from those she had experienced in Moscow. It was this challenge quite as much as her affection for the Chinese people which drew her back to China.

Within the walls of the garden compound that was her Peking home, Anna Louise Strong maintained to the very end of her life her intense interest in the great social experiments of the new China. Those Chinese and American friends who

went weekly to have lunch or dinner in her serene, high-ceil-
inged old apartment brought with them news of that vital
world, and from their stories and her own journeys in China,
she questioned, selected, and analyzed. During her measured
strolls in Peking's ancient and elegant parks, she was recognized as the lady of the "paper tiger" interview, Chairman
Mao's American friend, and even small children greeted her
as such.

Although she was interested in everything that happened in
China, America, and the rest of the world, in the half-century
since her observation of the Hunan peasant uprising, she had
retained a particular interest in the future of China's 500,000,-
000 peasants. She was extremely knowledgeable in her grasp of
agricultural questions and passionately interested in the same
matters which absorb the Chinese themselves—in grain yield,
irrigation projects, rural electrification. Her return to China in
1958 coincided with the establishment of the people's communes, and she went immediately to investigate that monumental experiment, so euphorically greeted in China and so
reviled abroad. In 1964 she updated her 1958 study of the
communes and discussed the test of the communes during the
three hard years of 1959 through 1962. We include here the
closing chapter of *The Rise of the Chinese People's Communes
—And Six Years After.* It includes an excellent explanation of
the original organizational structure of the communes and of
some of the developments and changes which had come about
in the intervening years of trial and error.

In the now nearly one decade since that chapter's writing, the
structure of the communes remains basically the same, but the
communes are no longer considered experiments. Clearly the
powerful social, economic, and political foundation of rural
Chinese society, they are remarkable not only for such tangible
achievements as resolving the food problems of centuries,
but for bringing to the stagnation of Chinese village life
an energy and confidence apparent to even the most uncom-
mitted of visitors. Anna Louise Strong often spoke to several
of us about the possibilities of the communes as exciting new
forms of social organization able to bypass the concomitant evils
of industrialization plaguing the advanced world. The evolution
of the communes continues to bear out many of these hopes.

Increasingly, they are not only economic, but political, social, and even military units, and increasingly, they are units of local control, determining for themselves problems of capital investment, education, and social services. Whether the communes suggest answers to the rest of the world is, of course, problematical, but for China, it is clear that they are among the most successful and potentially significant of the post-revolutionary period's great social experiments.

All visitors to China have an opportunity to visit a few communes and see for themselves this gigantic success story, and everywhere they hear about Tachai, the production brigade which has become a model for the whole country. It is indicative of the revolutionary ethos that still permeates the struggle in the Chinese countryside to bend nature to man's will that Tachai is representative not of rich and prosperous brigades, but of poor and backward ones. The story of Tachai is a Sisyphean tale of the efforts of a village of poor peasants, cursed with a heritage of bleak and rocky land, to transform it into the fertile terraces which today draw visitors from around the world. The selection on Tachai is typical of the many stories about that model commune circulating in China, and Chen Yung-kuei is widely known throughout China.

★   ★   ★

ANNA LOUISE STRONG*
Some Closing Comments

It seems time for some comments on the communes. They form the base of China's rural life today but are badly understood abroad. A Latin American friend just back from Cuba tells me that people everywhere asked about the communes, and many

* Anna Louise Strong, *The Rise of the Chinese People's Communes— And Six Years After* (Peking: New World Press, 1964), pp. 216–28.

thought they had failed and been abandoned. When U.S. press and Khrushchev both sneer at communes, what are Cubans to believe?

So it must be said flatly:

First, the communes exist; they arose in 1958 and are now in their sixth year; with every year they have grown stronger and more adapted to their tasks.

Second, they exist in basically the same form in which they appeared, which was hailed by the Communist Party's resolution in Wuhan in December 1958 as "a new social organization fresh as the morning sun above the broad horizon of East Asia." They survived three years of the worst natural disasters of the century, which struck when the communes had just been organized and were still hardly stabilized and hence most vulnerable. Foreign critics try to blame the bad crops on the communes, but the Chinese know that, while some mistakes of some communes in some areas added to the difficulties, the communes basically were the force that saved the country, preventing disasters from becoming widespread famine.

Changes of course have occurred in the communes; all living forms change. What is surprising and what I only realized recently is that none of the changes make it necessary to retract a single paragraph of the first Party resolutions that described the communes in 1958. "The Rise of the Chinese People's Communes," which forms the first part of this book, was written and originally published in early 1959. To my surprise the only significant change I had to make for this edition was to put a footnote to the 1958 grain statistics, which were long ago admitted to be wrong. The basic form and basic aims remain.

Even more, the communes not only still fulfill the description and purposes outlined in 1958 by the two historic resolutions of the Chinese Communist Party—in Peitaiho on August 29, 1958 and in Wuhan in December of the same year—but they still embody all the aspirations which the peasants at that time expressed in their wildest dreams.

The view that men by community organization can prevail over heaven was expressed in the ringing peasant slogan, "Man's will, not heaven, decides." This is still the profound faith, but is sought more clearly in terms of years of steady mechanization, more fertilizer and increased water control. The women still seek freedom from the ancient household drudgery and find it in the fact that the commune's processing of grain relieves the farm-wife from substituting for the donkey at the old dizzy task of dragging the heavy grinding stones around and around. Other household drudgery is lessened by the increasing electrification and the better handling of water, which no longer has to be carried so far on shoulder-poles. Nurseries and kindergartens maintained by the communes are also a liberation for the women. Only the public dining rooms which in 1958 swept the rural areas have been greatly diminished, for the family kitchens were found to be needed, especially in the north where the same heat cooks and warms the home, but public meals for nurseries, kindergartens, schools, workshops and seasonally for field gangs still lighten the household burden, and collective kitchens are organized on a small scale by neighbors, a tendency likely to increase.

Even the shout for "free grain" which in late 1958 swept the rural areas, expressing the faith that famine was conquered, and that now in the communes nobody would ever starve—a demand which most peasants at the time felt more essential than even their own personal wages—was never really given up. For while the actual free distribution of grain led to much waste and was soon stopped, usually within a few months, it is replaced today by a careful handling of a "welfare fund" to ensure that nobody in the "team" shall lack food.

Since each change in the commune, made by its members for improvement, has been greeted abroad as a "liquidation," I shall sum up briefly what the Chinese People's Commune was, and is, how it differs from all other forms of farm collectivization, and what the changes were in the past six years.

Some attacks first describe the commune incorrectly and then attack the form they have described. Khrushchev's attacks are of this type; probably the first open criticism of China he ever expressed was his remark to Senator Humphrey in late 1958 which sneered at the commune as a form which had been tried in the Soviet Union and failed. The communes that existed in the U.S.S.R. in early days were, as I myself saw them and as everyone knew them, a type of collective that held property in common with equal distribution to all; they were highly thought of theoretically but had to be dropped as "premature." Attributing this equalitarian form to China, Khrushchev then attacks it as a departure from Marxism-Leninism, etc., etc. But the Chinese Communists never advocated that equalitarian form.

People's Communes in China arose, not as an experiment in equalitarianism, but as a merger of agricultural cooperatives to create a larger unit for better control of the rural environment, and especially, but not exclusively, for water control and irrigation. In early 1958 most of China's more than half billion peasants were in 740,000 agricultural cooperatives with an average membership of 160 families. When the year ended, they had merged into 26,000 communes, usually on the scale of a township, with an average of several thousand families. (The number of communes subsequently fell, for a brief period, to 24,000 as a result of some mergers. Still later it increased threefold by subdivision in some provinces to fit local conditions, but the commune throughout remains the form which merges all the cooperative farming in the country, and to which practically all peasants belong.)

This original merger took place in 1958 in a great drive of peasant enthusiasm based on the realization that the cooperatives were not big enough to handle irrigation projects, in which every canal was at the expense of somebody's land but that, by pooling resources and making joint plans, they could "conquer nature" and insure that nobody in the future need starve. This was a sound hope and it has proved true.

A second feature of the communes, in addition to size, is its wider function. It assumed the handling, not only of agriculture but of local industry, commerce, education, home defense on a township scale. One of the "excesses" that occurred was that some communes, in enthusiasm, launched too many local industries, using up resources and labor wastefully in occupations not suited to their area. One commune in Honan boasted of making synthetic rubber from sweet potatoes; there were many such inventive ideas. Hence one of the natural changes was that they eventually dropped many of the small industries but expanded occupations and enterprises correlated with agriculture, such as livestock, orchards, forestry, the grinding of grain, processing of peanuts into edible oil, sugar refining, local truck transport and the making of farm implements and machinery.

The third aspect of the Chinese People's Commune, in which

it differs most sharply from all other forms of farm collectivization anywhere, is that it combines government power with production. The commune is both the upper level of the combined farming cooperatives and also the lowest level of state power at township level. The peasants of the township survey the total resources of their township and have the state power to use them.

This is still the basic difference of the Chinese communes from all other forms of farm collectivization. What first recommended it locally was that improvements like local roads, reservoirs and irrigation canals could be done with authority at once by local initiative. One husky commune chairman from Manchuria told me in 1958 when I asked who paid for local roads: "Nobody pays for roads. We just make them!" He was utterly unaware of cost accounting; the peasants have learned much about it since. But basically, while roads and irrigation projects are always planned with the county and even with the province for large constructions, the smaller projects are really "just made" by the peasants whose villages they serve. The merging of commune with "state power" also gives authority and connections with upper branches of government, in seeking priorities for electrification and pumps.

The Chinese believe that this merger at basic level will also enable an easier transition to communism when the time comes. The form of farm collectives practiced in the U.S.S.R. and elsewhere creates a duality in which the collectives are separate from the state. The state power may favor the collective and control it by law, but a contradiction of interests remains which will some day have to be bridged. In China, state power is inside the organization at township level. As the commune's economic strength increases, so does the share of the state within it. This, it is believed, will make possible a future transition to "ownership by the whole people" with less contradiction. Still later, the commune itself may survive as a basic cell in a communist society.

These three basic characteristics of the Chinese People's Commune were given by the first resolutions of the Communist Party in 1958; they still remain. It was also specified in those resolutions that, in the distribution of income, the basic principle should be payment for work done, and any diversion of funds for other purposes, such as an accumulation fund or "free supply," should be strictly limited. In practice this at first was not always done.

For the first demand that swept the country with enthusiasm was that everyone should be fed, that the hunger of generations should be conquered at last. This, as described at the time in the accounts that now make up the initial chapters of this book, took the form of "free grain" in public dining rooms; in many places "free dishes" of other kinds were added and competitions arose as to the number of "free services," from tailoring to barbering and theater tickets. In some places—Kwangsi among others—competitions took place among husky young men as to who could eat the most grain.

Some people in China today tend to avoid mentioning these "excesses." But I myself agree with an old peasant in Kwangsi who said: "We just had to do it once, just once in order to break down the centuries in which every family concentrated on its own small plot." When foreign critics in malice express the hope that the Chinese Communists will now "let the peasants" drift back to their ancient ways of agriculture, I think of this old man in Kwangsi.

For the Big Leap in 1958 and the communes with it broke the "old ways of farming" forever. A new type of peasant awoke to life, conscious of collective power. No peasant that I meet wants to go back. He wants to go forward; he wants various adjustments and changes. He does not want the old feudal, medieval village, most of whose people were illiterate. Foreign comments describe China's rural areas as "80 per cent illiterate with antediluvian tools"; this is no longer true. Most peasants under thirty read and write and take an interest in their country and the world. Illiteracy is higher in older-age groups, but the overall percentage is now very low.

While it is true that very primitive tools still remain, and the ancient shoulder-pole has not everywhere given place even to the wheelbarrow, much less to motor power, the urgent needs of irrigation and water control are already covering much of the countryside with high-tension lines and power pumps. Mechanization of agriculture for one-fourth of earth's people is a long task, requiring much investment of cash with labor; but with the pressure of the communes behind it, this advances fast.

What then are the changes in the communes in the past six years? I must preface this by stating how changes take place. People abroad seem to think that somebody in Mao Tse-tung's office sends them out as binding decrees. Nothing of the kind. Neither the origin of the commune nor any of its changes began as a decree by the state or even as a resolution by the Communist Party. The rise of the communes was a mass movement which the Party summed up and promoted. The first Party resolution about it was issued on August 29, 1958 when 30 per cent of the peasants had already formed communes; the second resolution in Wuhan in December, with the modest title "Some Questions Concerning the People's Communes," was adopted after 99 per cent of the peasants had joined.

Most of the changes came similarly, by local actions to meet local problems, followed at intervals by a summary or analysis from the Central Committee or perhaps merely a reference in the *People's Daily*, noting that such practices had appeared and making comments about them. Any summing-up by the Central Committee, any "suggestion" made with approval of the *People's Daily*, at once became a strong indication to all the Party members that this was a policy to be regarded with favor. In no case were they legally binding or passed as laws. The final word in every commune lies with its members.

Roughly one may say that in the past six years the most obvious change was the tripling of communes in number with consequent reduction in size; the most spectacular event was the brief adoption of "free grain" which in some places never occurred, in others lasted from a few months to a year; the most important change politically is the decentralization of the "accounting unit" which at first tended to be the commune as a whole, but quickly became its larger subdivision, the "production brigade," and by 1962 was in most places transferred to the smaller subdivision, the "production team."

None of these changes took place suddenly or universally. In Canton I learned with surprise that even the tripling of communes by subdivision into smaller units was not at all general throughout China, but largely confined to mountainous areas with minority nationalities where difficult communications and different languages made smaller commune-townships better. Thus in Kwangtung Province the number and size of communes had hardly changed, but in Kwangsi, its neighbor province, there had been only 1,000 communes in 1958 and there are now nearly 10,000! The "tripling of communes" is not general but an average.

The chief change I saw in the communes in 1964 in visits near Canton was the increase in prosperity, confidence and especially in better accounting since my last visits in 1962. The change to the "team" as accounting unit concentrates responsibility for production and distribution in one place, the original natural village, the oldest, most stable unit in the countryside where everybody knows everybody else. This "team" averages 20 to 40 households, and seldom goes above 100. When the early cooperatives developed, they had their limits in this village; when the higher forms appeared, the village remained one of its "production teams" but the distribution of income was made at the higher level, which even then led to contradictions between production and distribution that are now resolved.

This is the change that is held abroad to have "liquidated the commune," "retreating" further back even than the higher cooperatives to "local initiative" and hence, it is assumed, towards capitalism. In China it is held to have affirmed more clearly the "socialist" principle of "to each according to his work." It gives each small village full control of and responsibility for its own produce. The small team "owns" the crop, divides it, pays the taxes; these, incidentally, are much smaller now than in 1962, being only some five per cent of the basic crop. This small team has been throughout the unit that handled production; it now regains, in most communes, the right to dispose of its own crops.

The immediate result of this change was to make a clear distinction between the "better-off" teams and the "hard-up" teams. The backward villages are pinpointed by their own accounting. This enables the backward villages to analyze the source of their troubles, and it enables the commune and brigade to come to their assistance, by helping them change their conditions and methods, and raise their income by their own efforts, instead of glossing over their backwardness by sharing the crops of better teams. Thus we saw that in Hsinhua Commune, of 98 teams that had been originally "hard-up" with a lower than average crop, 96 had advanced with the help of the commune so that by 1963 they were level with the average and some even surpassed the average. The commune form of organization is admirably adapted to give such aid, not primarily by donations, whose effect is transient, but by helping the teams to learn from each other, and increase their own skills.

Finally, just as the small team can be more readily and intimately helped by the commune than by government aid from higher levels, so the individually "hard-up" families can, at the present stage of production, be helped more effectively and with greater justice by the small village team. The villagers all know each other from long experience of working together. They are the best judges of the reasons why any particular household is in difficulties, whether this is due to illness, or a large number of dependents, or just plain laziness. The small team, controlling the joint crop of the village, is in the best position to apply the remedy.

A striking example of this is the crop distribution in 1963 by the Yangho Team of East Flower Commune, as reported in *China Reconstructs* for June 1964 by Chang Yen, who spent some time in the village and attended discussions at several levels. Here we see clearly how the team is able to combine the basic principle of paying each worker according to his work with the equally basic principle that nobody shall be allowed to starve.

The Yangho Team has 57 families. In the past its land was subject to flood and the peasants could not count on more than a single crop. In the "old society" most of the poorer peasants were continually in debt to the landlord and moneylender. So it is not surprising that when East Flower Commune was organized in 1958, half of the families in Yangho were in debt to their cooperative. In the next five years, through the water-conservation work done by the commune and the consequent double-cropping and release of labor for side occupations, the income of the members steadily grew. After the 1962 harvest, only six households were in debt to the team; after the 1963 harvest, only two.

In 1963 Yangho Team had an excellent crop plus additional income from side occupations which was equal to that from the crop. After selling one-third of the grain to the state and setting aside for seed, fodder and taxes, which, as usual now in this area, were only five per cent of the gross income, Yangho, in general meeting, voted a small per cent to the Welfare Fund and another small per cent to the accumulation fund and "divided the rest among its members in proportion to the work each had done." Each member then could draw this income partly in grain and partly in cash. In grain he could draw up to the total needs of his household, as reckoned by ages, sex and general activities; the rest he drew in cash.

This strict observance of the principle of paying according to work gave a relatively large income to households whose labor power was large and whose dependents were few, but they were not entitled to draw in grain any more than the normal food consumption of their household; they took their gains in cash. At the other extreme, a household with only one able-bodied worker and many small children or in which the bread-winner had been incapacitated by illness, might find that all the work done was not enough to care for the household properly. In that case the Welfare Fund came to its aid. The Welfare Fund exists so that nobody in the team, for whatever cause or misfortune, should lack the basic guarantees of food, clothing, shelter, education and care of health.

Yangho Team considered the plight of the "hard-up" families, first in a small conference with the needy households to learn their needs, then in a preliminary committee and finally in the general meeting of the team. Three different cases are instructive.

We first take a widow with three small children who had been "on welfare" and in debt to the cooperative for several years but who, when the second crop was counted in 1963, found that through the general rise in the value of the "work-day," she had earned enough to buy the grain for her family till the next crop, with 66 yuan in addition in cash. The team leader suggested that 66 yuan ($26.40) might not be enough for miscellaneous expenses till the next accounting—this comes twice a year in teams with a double crop—and that the Welfare Fund might still assume part of the cost of her children's grain.

The widow refused the aid. "I have a house that costs me nothing," she said. "I have now all the rice we need. I have a private plot with vegetables and also a pig and chickens. We will get by on 66 yuan and be glad to be out of debt."

This left two families to consider as "hard-up" and needing aid. The first was that of Kao, a widower with an aged father and two children in primary school. Kao was known to everyone as a conscientious worker but so slow that his total workpoints were not enough to support his household. The moment his case was mentioned, everyone agreed that the Welfare Fund should advance Kao grain for his children. Kao replied, with tears in his eyes: "The commune is our unbreakable rice-bowl."

The final problem was Mrs. Lo, whose husband worked in another county and apparently sent no money for her and the two children. Mrs. Lo was known as an idler. The team leader reported that he had tried hard to find any kind of work that she would do properly; he had even given her work to do at home. But after the grain that she needed for herself and the children was balanced against her work, she still owed the team 66 yuan. Mrs. Lo's case aroused conflicting views; it was referred to the general meeting.

The general meeting was a huge turnout. It passed rapidly through the reports of the year's gains, which most people knew already: a rice yield of 1,306 catties per *mou*, more than double that of 1957; an average income per household of 780 yuan ($312). Then argument grew hot over Mrs. Lo. The women especially denounced her. When an easygoing old man argued that the crop was good and "nobody would notice it if we give grain for Mrs. Lo's children," a woman retorted that "all the women would notice it if an idler gets as good treatment as a hard worker." To treat idlers like honest workers would, she said, be bad for everyone's morale. The matter was finally settled by giving Mrs. Lo a public criticism and warning her to work better in the coming year, but giving her grain for the children from the Welfare Fund since "in no case must we hurt the children."

Thus was the eternal problem of the idler in the collective handled by Yangho Team. At the present stage of production, when agriculture is still largely done by hand, it is clearly better that such problems be handled by the small unit, the local village which is long acquainted with all parties, and which can most effectively reconcile two great principles on the reconciliation of which all collective life depends: the principle that each worker shall receive according to his labor, and the principle that nobody in the collective, not even the idler, and especially not the idler's children, shall be deprived of the necessities of life.

We have seen that the Chinese People's Communes still exist, that they continue to fulfil the basic aims for which they were called into being in 1958, that the changes which they have undergone in these six years have been for the purpose of more efficiently fulfilling those aims. In the three hard years of unusual natural disasters, the communes saved the country: first by their constructions of water-conservation works which, even when only partly finished, resisted the first shock of drought or flood; then by the forms of mutual aid that they made possible; and in the final emergencies by acting as channels of state relief so that communities were held together and people did not scatter to beg and die along the roads. Many Chinese experts believe that without the communes, the disasters of the three hard years would have lost millions and possibly tens of millions of lives.

We have seen that the communes still have the power to mobilize labor on a large scale for public improvements and that they do it today more accurately and with better accounting than in the first enthusiasm of the Great Leap of 1958. Through their double nature, as a cooperative form that is also government at township level, the communes can even mobilize labor effectively and economically on the scale of eleven counties, as in the reconstruction plans of the East River Basin. We have also noted that in the tremendous increase of water-conservation facilities of Kwangtung Province, only 30 per cent of the cost was born by the province, since the communes were able to mobilize the labor on the basis of each locality building for its own prosperity. Thus the annual costs of irrigation, and of all similar improvements, remains low for all time to come.

In 1958 when the enthusiasm for the Great Leap was at its height, a Chinese leader surprised me by saying: "We think the commune is a good form for us; but it will take ten years of testing to make sure."

The Chinese leaders are not hot-heads; they weigh their enthusiasms against the difficulties and the facts. Six years have gone by in which the communes have faced many hardships, made some mistakes and some adjustments and scored great successes. With each year they have become an ever-stronger section of the forces that remake the Chinese land.

More than this, they have proved able to build a collective form that cherishes and develops the initiative of the individual, and that educates and disciplines individuals to seek the collective good. Thus they move consciously towards that distant goal which today, prosaically or combatively, is called communism, which men in many lands and many ages have sought by many names in many ways, and which Chinese in the long past foresaw as the "Great Harmony" of men with nature and with their fellow-men.

CHIA WEN-LING*
The Story of Tachai

Before liberation, no one more than thirty *li* away had ever heard of this poor hill village. Tachai only had 800-odd *mu* of land scattered in plots over seven gullies, eight ridges and one slope at the foot of Tiger Head Mountain. The two largest plots were no more than five *mu* each, the smallest less than one tenth of a *mu*. The soil on the high, stony hills was as hard as iron, swept dry by parching winds. Even in an exceptionally good year, the grain yield per *mu* was no more than 140 catties. Most of this went to one landlord and three rich peasants. Forty-eight of the village's sixty-four households were poor or lower-middle peasants, thirty of them had been working outside as hired hands, thirteen of them had to go out begging. Tachai's people lived on chaff and wild plants. Although it lay only ten *li* from Hsiyang, the county town, nobody but tax collectors went there.

In August 1945 the red flag of liberation at last came to Hsiyang. The great storm of land reform began. Chen Yung-kuei and others led by the Party overthrew the landlord and seized back the land. The paupers had stood up.

But they were wretchedly poor. What path should Tachai

* Chia Wen-ling, taken from *The Seeds, and Other Stories* (Peking: Foreign Languages Press, 1972), pp. 168–93.

take after land reform? Two diametrically opposed answers were given. One was to get organized and take the path of socialist collectivization. This was the path pointed out by Chairman Mao: **"Without socialization of agriculture, there can be no complete, consolidated socialism."** The other was the continuation of individual farming by each family. This was the capitalist road advocated by the hidden traitor Liu Shao-ch'i: "There can be no collectivization of agriculture until industrialization has been carried out."

Tachai's liberated peasants kept stubbornly to Chairman Mao's teachings. Chen Yung-kuei consistently refuted the fallacious theories of Liu Shao-ch'i. "During the war against Japan," he said, "we relied on hand grenades and locally made land mines to defeat the Japanese with their modern guns and heavy artillery. During the War of Liberation, we relied on millet and rifles to wipe out Chiang Kai-shek's eight million troops equipped by U.S. imperialism. Now that we're building socialism, why must we have machines before we can collectivize agriculture? If we wait for machines before starting to build socialism, that will hold everything up." Then he added, "If the liberated peasants continue their individual farming, how are they different from their position in the old society? When men are united, they can move mountains. If we want to free our children and future generations from poverty, we must organize together and take the road of socialist collectivization pointed out by Chairman Mao." He talked things over with Tachai's poor and lower-middle peasants; they launched into mutual aid and cooperation.

Some well-to-do middle peasants, however, thought the paupers would "take advantage" of them, and they did their best to defeat them. They got together a group of men of their own sort, and some of the best farmhands among the poor peasants, and formed the Stout Fellows' Team. In fact, though they called themselves a mutual-aid team, each continued to farm on his own. Because Chen Yung-kuei was a strong man in his thirties, they got him to join them. But Chen Yung-kuei was determined to take the cooperative road. He disapproved of the way they excluded most of the poor and lower-middle peasants, so he withdrew from the team. He organized the nine households left out, including four men over fifty and five boys aged eleven to sixteen, into a genuine mutual-aid team. They called it the Old and Young Team.

This gave rise to a good deal of talk. Well-to-do middle peasants sniggered, "Those old men in Chen Yung-kuei's team are on their last legs, and the youngsters don't know the first thing about farming. We shall soon see some fun!" Some put on a show of sympathy and said, "Fancy a husky fellow, a first-rate farmer, working himself to the bone with that bunch of old crocks and kids! Chen Yung-kuei must be out of his mind."

But neither jeers nor soft soap could shake Chen Yung-kuei. They only made him more determined to run his team well. Although the Old and Young Team was short of draught animals, tools and manpower, its members saw eye to eye and worked with a will. By going all out for a year they got a good harvest—a higher yield, in fact, than the Stout Fellows' Team. This indisputable fact convinced the people of Tachai of the advantage of getting organized. That winter forty-nine of the village's sixty-seven households joined Chen Yung-kuei's Old and Young Team.

In the spring of 1952, Chen Yung-kuei and his teammates were eager to turn their mutual-aid team into a cooperative of the semi-socialist type.

Chen Yung-kuei made over a dozen trips to the county town to relay the demand of Tachai's poor and lower-middle peasants to start a co-op, but the county authorities dared not allow this because they were under the thumb of Liu Shao-ch'i and his agents in Shansi Province. Not until 1953, when the surging tide of agricultural cooperation was sweeping the whole country, did they grant a grudging permission.

Chen Yung-kuei's team was a large one, of forty-nine households, but the county would not allow more than thirty households in a cooperative. Since none of the team members wanted to go back to individual farming, Chen Yung-kuei, elected as chairman of the co-op, kept two sets of accounts, one for thirty households and a secret one for forty-nine. When the time came to share out the autumn harvest, the county cadres discovered this and gave them a dressing down. Nevertheless, the co-op's average yield that year went up to 237 catties per *mu*. This strengthened the co-op members' faith in collectivization and they drew up a ten-year plan for building up their barren mountain region. Relying on their collective strength, they made up their minds to wipe out Tachai's poverty and backwardness. . . .

Summer, 1963. Tachai's crops had grown thick, lush and green. The commune members rejoiced at the prospect of a good harvest. As far as yield was concerned, Tachai had already surpassed the average reached along the Yellow River. Now they determined to raise more than eight hundred catties per *mu.*

Then the unforeseen happened. The worst rain and flood in a century brought terrible ruin.

From August second to eighth, the rain poured down steadily. In this single week Old Man Heaven deluged the district with the equivalent of the entire rainfall of 1962. No sterner test had ever confronted the people of Tachai. . . .

The downpour finally stopped, but the weather remained capricious. Chen Yung-kuei and the other cadres hastily called a meeting and discussed the problem of the villagers' housing. Having settled this, he hurried off to inspect the fields. The floodwaters had attacked like wild beasts—the damage was fearful! The flood had caused landslides, whole fields had been washed away, buildings had collapsed, cave houses had fallen in. The arable land in the gullies which had taken ten years to build up had been washed away. Most of the land on the hills had lost outer borders. In some places the subsoil had shifted, the earth had gaped open, the crops were lying flat. There had been over a hundred houses and over a hundred cave houses in the village. Seventy per cent had collapsed, leaving the villagers homeless, the livestock without shelter. Not even old men in their eighties could recall such a calamity.

Could the people of Tachai overcome such a serious catastrophe? What could they rely on to overcome it? Chen Yung-kuei called meetings to discuss these questions carefully. Some commune members said that since Tachai had done its bit for the country by selling the state over 1,758,000 catties of grain in the eleven years since cooperation, now that they were in trouble the state ought to help them. A few cadres felt that a loan would lessen the ideological problems and facilitate their work. Most of the members, however, were against asking for relief. They said that Tachai Brigade would not have existed if not for liberation. If Chairman Mao and the Party hadn't led them along the road of collectivization, if the state hadn't backed them up, Tachai couldn't have done anything for the country.

Old Party member Chia Chin-tsai said firmly: "We can walk this road ourselves, without being propped up. Let the state keep its relief for those who really need it."

This increased Chen Yung-kuei's determination not to apply for relief. But how to turn belief in self-reliance into mass action? How to spur the villagers' revolutionary drive? He pondered these questions carefully in the fields, at meals, and when lying in bed. Eventually he summed up the masses' arguments for self-reliance as ten reasons for not asking for state relief—ten big advantages.

1. It was in the interest of the state. Money was needed to build up the country. If Tachai did without state aid, that was equivalent to aiding the state and the building of socialism.

2. It was in the interest of the collective. Overcoming difficulties by their own efforts would further reveal the strength of their collective economy and make the villagers love the collective more.

3. It was good for the cadres. Self-reliance would temper them and force them to use their brains more.

4. It was good for the commune members. It would overcome any idea of depending on others and would spur them to strive hard and work tirelessly.

5. Overcoming the disaster by their own efforts would greatly strengthen the determination of the poor and lower-middle peasants and deflate the arrogance of the class enemy.

6. It was good for the socialist emulation campaign for overtaking and learning from the advanced and helping the backward.

7. It was good for developing production.

8. It was good for maintaining the honor of being an advanced unit.

9. It was good for unity.

10. It was good for training successors. . . .

This analysis helped the villagers to see things in the right light. Their unanimity led to united action. With Chen Yung-kuei giving the lead, old and young, men and women set to work. In the short space of five days they propped up 250 *mu* of seedlings which had been flattened out, and most of these grew well after being manured. Next, as life became more settled, they started rehabilitating the fields, collecting fertilizer and preparing to sow winter wheat, so as to ensure a good harvest the next year.

Old Man Heaven went on making trouble, as if bent on testing the determination of the people of Tachai. Tachai was hit by six more calamities: two hurricanes, a hailstorm, a severe frost, spring flooding and summer drought. But the villagers, like men of iron, relying on their own hands, won through one calamity after another. . . .

[In 1964] Tachai had the biggest harvest in its history, with an average yield of 826 catties per *mu* and a total output of over 620,000 catties, 200,000 more than the previous year. . . .

In the past Tachai had used the labor management system of recording work points. There were over a hundred different farming jobs, and a set number of work points was fixed for each. They tried this for several years, but it did not work out well. After studying Chairman Mao's works the brigade members felt that they could improve the system by relying on their political consciousness. So Tachai had started a system of reckoning according to pace-setters. Each said what he felt he deserved and the other discussed his appraisal. After the introduction of this new system, more people turned out to work and efficiency went up. In 1962, the year before they adopted this system, the average number of workdays for everyone— men and women, full-time and part-time workers—was 250. It increased in 1963 to 260; in 1964, to 280. The brigade members thoroughly approved of this method. It put political consciousness, not work points, in command. It embodied the principle of "to each according to his work" and was simpler and more rational than the complicated work-point quota system.

★   ★   ★   ★   ★

2. THE ECONOMY

While Western economists like to present various national economies in terms of aggregate performance, shown by elaborate data graphs or input-output tables, the Chinese have made that impossible in their own case by releasing virtually no statistics on their economy over the last decade and more. National security considerations have been a main factor in this statistical secrecy, understandable inasmuch as one of the overriding reasons for the widespread professional interest in the Chinese economy was to measure its military capabilities. Moreover, as the severe attacks against the academic economist Sun Yeh-fang during the Cultural Revolution showed, the Chinese seem suspicious of the policy implications of academic economics. But as the statistical shrouds are beginning to lift and new forms of economic writing are appearing, it might be well to remember that China has a rich, complex, and sophisticated economic tradition, as befits one of the oldest trading nations in the world. The point is that their traditional economic experiences make them conceive of the economy much as one might conceive of a family or any other human community: full of different forces, clashing trends, unexpected changes, intricacies and grossnesses at the same time. The classic simplicity and elegance of economic analysis do not appeal to the Chinese, nor does its policy implication of carefully laid out plans which economic units are then supposed to carry out.

As with everything else, the Chinese hold that the economy begins with man, and not with the abstractions of capital, land, and labor. If the social arrangements within which people work and their motivations are correct, then capital, land, and labor can be activated to perform efficiently and effectively for the public good. Thus, we have chosen for our first selection one by Joan Robinson, a founder of Keynesian economics in the early 1930's, a teacher at Cambridge University in England, and a student and friend of People's China for a decade and a half. One has to remember how deeply rooted the concepts of "economic man" and "the market" are in Western economics to understand the implications of Joan Robinson's discussion of incentives and of pricing. Western economists by and large believe prices are either administratively set by "command" (as in Russia) or are shaped by market forces. The Chinese have neither a command economy nor market socialism, and while their system is not yet fully understood abroad, they have achieved equitable and satisfactory economic performance without inflation.

The second selection by Louis Kraar could not and would not have been written before 1971. While its rough-gruff, sometimes sardonic, tone differs from that of Joan Robinson, the picture he presents of the Chinese economy is not that different from that of other visitors nor from that which Joan Robinson has been presenting for over ten years. The economy works, and the Chinese work—that is a main theme of the article. Some years back, the Americans discovered the Japanese economic miracle where the work ethic of Japanese workers seemed to be a main factor in Japan's success. Now Americans have discovered another East Asian nation with a work ethic. This comes at a time when American managers are deploring the deteriorating work habits of their own people. The article presents impressions of various farms and factories Kraar visited, and those microcosmic impressions coincide with what one knows of the economy as a whole.

Lastly we present a considerably abridged selection from the *1972 Yearbook of the Far Eastern Economic Review*, which sums up the state of the Chinese economy in 1971. The author is probably Leo Goodstadt of the *Review*, a trained economist and a careful student of the Chinese economy. The *Far Eastern Economic Review* is oriented to businessmen with very practical interests in economies, quite different from the more theoretical, or policy-oriented interests of the economists. The selection takes the main sectors of the Chinese economy, makes some general comments on trends, provides examples, and states the issues that are being contested. Like any business journal, it gives one a sense of the diversification of the economy. Economies do not change that fast, so the trends of 1971 can be used to judge trends in subsequent years.

★   ★   ★

*JOAN ROBINSON**
For Use, Not for Profit
A Report on a Recent Visit to China

INDUSTRY

In China now, as far as the state sector is concerned, that is to say the whole of regular industry and commerce, there are no individual monetary incentives for anyone. Formerly there was a system of bonuses, copied from the Soviets; this was swept away during the Cultural Revolution at the demand of the workers. The workers said: It is true that some get more money income with bonuses, but then others get less. The system was so complicated that no one could work out what was due to him, and anyway the whole conception seemed to them insulting, particularly special bonuses for what everyone should regard as his duty, such as care in avoiding accidents. They objected also to group bonuses which went to the welfare fund of individual enterprises. If the welfare fund is necessary, it ought to be assured. Now there is a national scale of wage rates (with some regional variation), no piece rates or overtime pay, and the payment into the welfare fund is a regular proportion of the wage bill (generally 11 per cent) which is reckoned as part of the cost of production of output.

The national wage scale is in eight grades, with lower rates for apprentices and higher for technicians. The individual's grade depends upon length of service, skill and "political attitude," that is, diligence, unselfishness, helpfulness, willingness to take on the awkward jobs and so forth. There is evidently a certain negative monetary incentive in the desire not to miss promotion to a higher grade, but it seems that promotion in the ordinary way is more or less automatic. During the Cultural

* Joan Robinson, "For Use, Not for Profit: A Report on a Recent Visit to China" in *Eastern Horizon*, Vol. XI, No. 4 (1972), pp. 6–15.

Revolution due promotions were forgotten; in August 1971 there was a ruling that, over the lower grades, promotions were to be made on a regular plan. Workers in the third grade or below who had been at work before 1957 must be raised to the fourth grade; those in the second grade who had been at work before 1960 should be raised to the third grade, and so forth. The period of work of an apprentice counted toward his promotion and so did a period of service in the army.

The additional pay had to be back-dated to July 1971, so that individual workers would not suffer by delay in an enterprise that took a long time to work out. A delay of nine or ten months made quite a lump of new purchasing power and caused a spurt of demand, when it came, for such things as bicycles and sewing machines, but supplies were available.

Apprentices (like students) get an allowance which enables them to live (often in dormitories provided by the enterprise) with not more than 6 *yuan* a month of pocket money—but clothes are provided.

There must be a manual of wage grades, for light and heavy industry in the various regions. It is not easy to make out the details from casual inquiries. Wages are highest in Shanghai; higher in heavy industry than in light industry. There is equal pay for equal work, but more women traditionally are in light industry and commerce. The general range is from 30 *yuan* per month to 104 *yuan*. Technicians get more. In heavy industry in the Northeast, where the average wage was 62 *yuan* per month, technicians were getting 147 *yuan*.

Arguments in favor of still smaller differentials that came up during the Cultural Revolution have been dismissed as ultra-Left. On the other hand, the recent promotions for lower-grade workers required some "political education" of workers in the top grades who got no benefit from it.

There are no longer any bonuses to individual workers for inventions or technical improvements, but the encouragement to initiative is stronger than before. A triple unit of workers, technicians and cadres concerned with management is set to work whenever snags appear or whenever a worker has a bright idea, to solve problems or improve design and operation of equipment.

There are no bonuses for managers and no pecuniary advantage from success to an enterprise as a whole. The management of an enterprise has been allotted a certain number of workers, technicians and cadres and receives the appropriate wage fund. Prices of materials and products are all given in the plan. Prices include a proportion of profits. Good management, economy and high output per head increase the total profit. Total profit is handed over to the state (that is to the city or province) without distinction between planned and super-planned profit. A failure to achieve planned profit, unless for some acceptable reason, obviously, is not good for a manager's reputation, but it does not directly affect anyone's personal income.

It seems that the movement since the Cultural Revolution in China is in the exact opposite direction from the economic reforms in the Soviet sphere. The tendency of the proposals associated with the name of Liberman, the abortive reforms of Ota Šik and some actual methods in use in Hungary are based on the conception of giving more independence and financial responsibility to the management of the individual enterprise and using profitability of production as the criterion of success. The claim for these schemes is that they improve efficiency by breaking out of the rigidity and overcentralization of Soviet-style planning.

Breaking out of that system can no doubt produce striking immediate improvements, but "market socialism" seems to run into a fundamental objection, quite apart from the erosion of socialist morality that monetary incentives bring about. The difficulty is connected with the determination of prices. When the enterprise has the right to fix the prices of its own products, much of the waste and irrationality of the market must follow —imperfect competition, advertisement, catering to tastes of the higher-income families and neglecting the needs of the poorer ones. In Yugoslavia, giving the workers of each enterprise a direct interest in its profits worked wonders as far as the internal efficiency of management was concerned, but it fails to give them an interest in providing employment for others or in evening up the level of development between regions. Moreover, it gives them the same interest as capitalist firms have in pricing their goods on the principle of charging what the traffic will bear.

The Chinese regard "putting profits in command" as "taking the capitalist road." Insofar as the profit criterion was used, under the influence of Liu Shao-ch'i, it led to anomalies. (Here, of course, profit does not mean the expected rate of return on investment, but an allowance for profit in the final price of products.) Enterprises were not allowed to fix their own prices, but so long as they had an interest in the level of profits and were instructed to maximize profits, the composition of output for an enterprise was influenced by the ratio of profit to prime cost (wages, materials, power, etc.) for different items rather than by the composition of demand—say demand from the communes for small rather than heavy tractors or from households for children's clothes rather than grown-up sizes. It is impossible to work out such a delicate system of profit ratios as to get exactly the desirable product mix. A policy of going forward from the system in force before the Cultural Revolution toward putting the market in complete command (as under the proposals of Ota Šik) was rejected in the "struggle against revisionism."

Under the system now in force, the prices of all outputs and inputs are given to the enterprise; its plan of production is worked out in consultation with higher authorities; carrying it out depends on self-respect and public spirit, or, as the Chinese put it, on the high level of political consciousness of the workers.

This system avoids the problem which is tormenting the planners in the Soviet sphere—that is, how to make use of their now considerable industrial productive capacity to supply consumption goods to consumers that they actually want to consume. So long as initiative and economic power lie with the producer, the enterprises are accustomed to produce what suits them and throw it on to the market. Now that the Soviets have arrived at potential affluence, they are at a loss how to make use of it.

China did not wait for potential affluence to devise a system that takes account of the consumer's needs and tastes.

Representatives of the Department of Commerce at every level who are in charge of retailing provide the services of a wholesaler. They are concerned in the process of planning for light industry and so can influence the composition of output to fit the consumer's preferences reported from the shops, and they keep a finger on the pulse of the overall relation of demand to supply so that, when output has expanded relatively to total expenditure, some prices can be cut. The prices chosen to be cut is a matter of policy—recently the chief benefit has gone to medicines, which are selling now at 20 per cent of the prices ruling in 1950. (So long as industry yields profit overall, it does not matter that some commodities are sold at a loss.)

The shops take trouble to serve consumer needs; pharmacies provide first aid for simple cases; in the city, when the night shift from a big factory comes off at 1 A.M., local shops are open; in the country, the village shop (still formally a supply and marketing cooperative, but actually supplied by the Commerce Department) sends shoulder-loads of goods up to the mountains when commune members are camping beside their work.

The system of controlling light industry through wholesaling began when the "national capitalists" in the coastal cities were instructed to continue producing after Liberation. They were supplied with raw materials and given contracts to produce finished goods, mainly textiles. After 1956 they were absorbed into the state-private system and came fully into the sphere of the planned economy.

The method of operating through contracts is still widely used. For instance, the Department of Commerce of a city makes contracts for fruit and vegetables with surrounding communes. The deal is made in overall wholesale terms between the city and the commune, and then broken down into detailed day-by-day deliveries from each particular team to each shop or street-side stall. Formerly, say, tomatoes had a short season and were dumped onto the public all at once. ("We used to think," said a commune spokesman, "what we produce, they have to eat.") Now, production is staggered out over as long a season as possible (a "greenhouse" is used which consists of a sheet of plastic stretched between two banks of earth). With cold storage, apples are on sale all over the country all the year round.

Manufactured consumer goods are also dealt with by means of contracts. The contract, say for a textile factory with the Department of Commerce, specifies design, quality and delivery dates for three months' output. The weaver, in turn, has a contract for yarn, and so forth. The finished goods are allocated to particular shops. An enterprise that fails to fulfill its contract has to compensate the purchaser.

In some provinces, operating through contracts has been superseded by what is regarded as a more satisfactory method. The Department of Commerce, say of a city, knows the planned output of the local factories, and it knows what has been allocated for local consumption; it has had a hand in framing and agreeing to the plan. The staff of the department is divided into companies concerned with different groups of commodities; the companies purchase the planned quantities of the various commodities (balancing overfulfillment with deficiency, or adjusting the plan as required) and pass the goods to the shops.

There has been a great drive to diversify local production to make each area as self-sufficient as possible. The city of Shenyang in the Northeast, a highly specialized center of heavy industry, formerly imported from outside its municipal boundary 70 per cent of its agricultural and manufactured consumer goods. During the Cultural Revolution, mainly by mobilizing women as workers and by encouraging suburban communes to diversify production, they reversed the proportions and now provide 70 per cent for themselves.

It is not only through the operation of the Department of Commerce that Chinese planning establishes consumer's sovereignty over supplies. The individual enterprises also concern themselves to cater to the tastes of the public. The enterprise gets information from the shops directly about customers' opinions and sends some workers and cadres to serve behind the counter where its products are being sold. It encourages the public to write in their complaints and suggestions. It sends workers into the country and to the army to ask about requirements. It exchanges designs with other enterprises in the same line and collects samples from abroad. Since the public can only choose between what already exists, it is up to the enterprise to carry out research (for instance, a textile factory is working on the properties of synthetic fibers) and try out new designs. From time to time there is an exhibition sale of newly produced goods in a department store.

The Export Corporations operate independently of the Department of Commerce. They select particular factories to send samples to the biannual Export Fair and place contracts according to the foreign orders received. There is evidently some push and pull between the Corporations and the Department. For the best quality products, they have to work it out somehow; and give the orders to the producers; exports (and foreign aid) are a sacrifice for the population, for there is nothing of which the home market could not absorb more if it were available.

The general principle of this system is that the workers and the management of an enterprise are concerned with efficiency and quality of production, but have nothing to do with sales.

I have often discussed this problem of consumer's sovereignty under socialism with economists from Eastern Europe. I find that they cannot conceive how the Chinese system could work. Certainly, it is a necessary condition for such a system that individuals have no pecuniary interest in production, for as long as income or bonuses depend on sales, there is an irresistible temptation for the producer and the retailer to fix up schemes to exploit the public and share the swag, and the Chinese system depends upon a high level of morality (or "political consciousness") in every sphere from top to bottom. If this has been lost in Eastern Europe, it cannot be recovered merely by changing the relations between commerce and industry. But the Chinese communists are not at all sentimental; they do not rely on morality alone. They rely on the fact that the mass of the workers, who in the nature of the case have nothing to gain from corruption, can see what is going on and, especially since the Cultural Revolution, are alerted to their rights and their duty to keep it clean.

AGRICULTURE

In agriculture, for the individual, or rather the family, economic incentives are still strong, but they operate at the collective level as well as individually; the individual's share in the income of his group depends on the number of work points to his credit, while the value of the work point, in kind and in cash, depends on the production of the group. The team—

workers from round about fifty neighboring households—is generally the basic accounting unit. There are some brigades which were successful as cooperatives from 1956 or before and now carry on as collective units; I came across one case where the whole commune was the accounting unit; this was a historical accident; one large cooperative, which refused to split up, was created in 1956, and the commune was formed in 1958 by accretion around it.

Various systems of work points are in use; sometimes different teams in the same commune use different systems, according to the level of political development that they have reached. The most approved system is used in the famous brigade of Tachai. Everyone registers simply by the half-day worked; at a single annual reckoning, everyone is awarded marks by his companions, from 10 to 6. The number of days worked is then multiplied by his mark and so his total of points allotted. Some teams use the Tachai system but with the difference that the adjudgment of marks is made quarterly or monthly. A modified Tachai system is the "pace setter." In each team, one member is chosen for 10 marks and the rest judge themselves in relation to his performance. Before the Cultural Revolution mainly strength and hard work were taken into account; now there is more stress on "political attitude."

Another method is to allot marks in advance to individuals and require the team to reassess them at the end of each month according to how they have done. The old system, a kind of job evaluation, is still in use in some areas. A points-price is set on each task; this may be given to a group; the group then distributes the points amongst its members, or it may be given to an individual.

The advanced communes use a points-price for special jobs, such as building or driving carts. These work out as slightly more remunerative than ordinary agricultural tasks. Moreover, when jobs are being allotted to team members, the most exacting have to be given to the best workers, who have the highest marks. Thus there is some element of job evaluation even in the most advanced system.

The fact that the income received for a work point depends on the produce that a team gets from its own particular area of land prevents a negative response of work forthcoming to rising income. Most people, if they are free to choose, prefer to do less work as earnings per unit of effort rise. With the work-point system, slacking by any individual is doing wrong to his neighbors by checking the rise in the value of the work points that all will get. The individual is not free to please himself, he is kept up to the mark by his neighbors. This is another way in which Chinese institutions have been devised in such a way to support political motivation instead of pulling against it. Peasants are taught to feel that they are working for the nation, for the revolution and for all the oppressed people of the world, but they are clearly and obviously doing good for themselves at the same time. . . .

THE BALANCE OF TRADE

The basic characteristic of the Chinese economy is that 80 per cent and more of the population, organized in communes, is responsible for feeding and housing itself. The surplus provided by the communes feeds the rest of the population and provides raw materials (particularly cotton) to industry.

The rest of the economy acquires the surplus from agriculture in four ways: from the agriculture tax, quota sales of crops, above-quota sales, and through the free market. (There are also state farms which are organized on the same basis as industry. I did not have an opportunity to get information about them but I had the impression that, considering how lavishly they are mechanized, they do not compare favorably with the most progressive communes.)

The agricultural tax was instituted after the land reform while cultivation was in the hands of private peasants. It was assessed on the basis of the normal productivity of each *mou* of land, amounting at that time to about 14 per cent of gross output. When cooperatives and communes were formed, the liability to tax went with the land; the liability was converted for cash crops into money payments equivalent to the grain in the original assessment. As output per *mou* has grown, the proportion of tax has automatically fallen; it is now said to be about 6 per cent of gross output on the average of the country as a whole; in some provinces it is about 4 per cent and in particular districts less than 2 per cent.

In some areas, the original assessment, made in 1953, is still

in force; in others reassessments were made in 1961 or 1964.
The method of reassessment was explained to me in a county
near Shanghai where some communes were enjoying a much
higher level of income than others because they were selling
vegetables to the city. The overall tax rate was reckoned to be
7.7 per cent at the time that the change was made. Each brigade
reported its average income over the past three years. Money
income was reduced to the equivalent in grain and 7.7 per cent
of the national quantity of grain was taken and divided by the
area of cultivable land of the brigade. This gave the tax assessment per *mou* in terms of grain, to be paid in money at the
standard price of grain.

The burden of tax is still uneven between teams and between
communes. There seems to have been a directive in 1971 to
readjust the tax burden, while leaving the total payment for
each county unchanged. In one county that I visited, the readjustment had been made, taking progressive proportions of
income per head in each team. In other provinces, nothing was
known about it. The tax is remitted in case of natural calamities. Some provinces count only 80 per cent of the tax revenue
so as to leave a margin for meeting revisions.

In some provinces, there is a surcharge on the agricultural
tax of 12 per cent or 16 per cent, which goes to the county.
In others, the county keeps 5 per cent of the tax, and in others
again, the county passes on the whole tax to the provinces.

The agricultural tax provides less than 10 per cent of national
revenue and it might be argued that all this fuss and complica-
tion is not worthwhile, but for the ordinary run of communes
delivering the tax grain after the harvest has become symbolic;
it is made the occasion of a festival, with drums and flags.

The main source of the deliveries from the communes to the
rest of the economy, far and away more important than the
others, is quota sales. Sales are made at fixed prices, which
have been raised from time to time but never lowered. Each
team or brigade agrees to its annual production plan and its
quota of sales. Formerly the quota was related to average output of the last three years; during the Cultural Revolution the
recalculations were not made everywhere. In 1971 a set of
quotas has been agreed and is not to be changed for five years.
No one could say what is expected for 1976.

The general principle in setting quotas is that each team should have enough to feed its members. Rich communes are selling a large proportion of their output and the poorest are selling little, or even receiving subsidies. This is the key to the apparent harmony of the Chinese economy compared to other developing countries, whether in the socialist or the market sphere. The surplus from agriculture, necessary for the growth of industry, is taken from those that find it least painful to part with it, and, indeed, from those who nowadays are eager to sell in order to buy more from industry.

Teams who offer to sell more than their quota of grain receive a 30 per cent premium on the price. The fixing of the quota for five years means that most teams can look forward to increasing over-quota sales as productivity rises. In some cases they are advised to build up stock instead of selling the extra grain or to use it to expand animal husbandry.

(Every household, team and commune is building up stocks of grain, and each commune has an emergency reserve, not to be used except in case of war or severe natural calamities.)

Cash crops, such as cotton, are sold on the basis of quotas but without a premium for above-quota sales. The trade in vegetables, fruit and meat with the commerce department is conducted in terms of contracts, not quotas. There is no problem of ensuring supplies as the communes are eager to get contracts which provide an opportunity to earn money all the year round.

The private markets are now quite a minor source of supply. Before the Great Leap they were said to provide 12 per cent of total retail sales; now the estimate is 2.5 per cent.

The counter-flow of purchases by agriculture from industry is partly from households and partly from brigades and communes.

As we have seen, there is a great circulation of money within a commune. Money comes in to the teams for sales of grain. The team as such pays a contribution to the commune; it pays for fertilizer and for services such as tractor plowing and it may contribute out of its accumulation fund to schemes of development. The major part of the team's money income is distributed to households as payment for work points. The households pay a small fee for having their grain processed, for electric light, for building and so forth; part of their purchases from the retail shops are for local products such as fruit or sauces, while most are "imported" from state or collective industry.

The brigades and the commune make money from the services they provide to their members and from "exports" from their industries. They purchase fertilizers, electric power, machinery, and equipment and materials for their industries.

Over and above the agricultural tax, agriculture contributes to the national revenue in respect to the element of tax and profit in the prices of the manufactured goods that are purchased by communes and by households. Prices of fertilizer and agricultural machinery are kept low as a matter of policy. Over the years since 1962 the terms of trade have shifted in favor of agriculture, as the prices of the main crops have been slightly raised and the prices of many manufactures appreciably cut.

THE NEW MAN

The success of the Chinese economy in reducing the appeal of the money motive is connected with its success in economic development. When everyone has enough to eat today and hope of improvement tomorrow, when there is complete social security at the prevailing level of the standard of life and employment for all, then it is possible to appeal to the people *to combat egoism and eschew privilege.* It would not make much sense to the workers and peasants, say, in Mexico or Pakistan. No doubt there are individuals in China with the temperamental itch for money, just as there are some people in the West who do not care about it. Individual temperaments are molded by the setting in which they find themselves. The enormous pressure to commercialize every aspect of life in our society is substituted in China by an even stronger pressure the other way, and "human nature" seems to fit it just as well, indeed better, since the Chinese seem to be much less neurotic than us. In any case, for the time being at least, Chinese economic policy appears to be working more successfully than in any other planned economy, let alone in the so-called developing countries in the toils of the world market.

LOUIS KRAAR*
I Have Seen China—And They Work

Soon after entering China, a visitor begins to see that its methods of running the economy are different from those of any other nation. Throughout the rest of the world, in both industrialized and underdeveloped countries, the basic thrust of development is to substitute capital for labor. In China, this is a secondary theme. At every level, China mobilizes its abundant resources of labor—from a population that amounts to nearly a quarter of mankind—to compensate for a scarcity of capital.

In the South China countryside I saw farmers wading barefoot through brilliant green rice paddies to toss handfuls of fertilizer. Along roadways, men and women pull carts or pedal trishaws heaped with grain, petroleum drums, or scrap metal. Neighborhood workshops organize every able-bodied person not otherwise employed. One group of housewives in Canton (or Kwangchow, as the Chinese call it) takes oily rags that industrial plants have used to wipe machinery, cleans them, and returns both the cloths and the extracted oil for reuse.

BLURRED AUTHORITY

The dedication and discipline required for all this exertion are fostered by a relentless process of indoctrination, which stresses psychic rather than material rewards for individuals. Workers are endlessly exhorted to show their revolutionary zeal by increasing production. The ubiquitous thoughts of Chairman Mao Tse-tung are supposed to provide the motivating doctrine, and the rigorous programs of Maoist study for the entire work force

* Louis Kraar, "I Have Seen China—And They Work" in *Fortune* (August 1972).

do appear to give most Chinese a strong sense of purpose. But they try to apply the often vague or ambiguous doctrines in ways that yield practical results. The Pearl River Paper Mill, for instance, follows the Maoist principle of relying on ordinary workers to help devise technical improvements, but one of the managers emphasizes: "Only the rational ideas are accepted. Before adopting anything, we first make experiments."

Management, the Chinese claim, is in the hands of the "broad masses." Every factory and farm is nominally controlled by a "revolutionary committee" of workers, party members, and Army personnel. Administrators and engineers now work closely with those on the assembly line. And while China operates its economy according to a state plan, central controls are sufficiently loose to allow each factory's committee considerable autonomy in setting its own targets for producing goods, raising capital, and building production equipment. Some Chinese are more equal than others, of course, but the system of participatory management seems to give everyone at least the sense of helping to shape basic decisions. It also provides a typically Asian forum for smoothing over conflicts and disagreements through lengthy discussions.

The blurring of formal structures of authority is facilitated by a pervasive egalitarianism. Official titles and other status symbols are avoided. In this ostentatiously classless society, a boss wears the same drab, baggy garb as laborers, and is officially ranked only as a "responsible person." There is also a remarkable degree of equality in consumption. The Chinese share a lean, but gradually improving, standard of living. Austere housing and nearly free medical care are generally available. Workers do not own automobiles, but neither do factory directors.

Within this egalitarian atmosphere, the system often demands hard toil and seems to evoke remarkable diligence. I watched some 1,500 young men and women "volunteers" from Shunte County's agricultural communes patiently wielding little steel hammers mounted on long, thin bamboo staves to break up stones for a new power and irrigation project. The workers are repeatedly told they are "the masters of the country," and loudspeakers set up around the torrid work site blare out strains of Chinese revolutionary symphonies to inspire sweaty efforts.

"The people cannot wait for machines, so we use our own hands and indigenous tools," explains a ranking "responsible person" attired in plain cotton work clothes. Although the project was begun only last year, it was able to draw as many as 5,000 peasants during slack periods in farm work and now is well on the way to completion.

In keeping with a national policy to rely on local factories, ten generators for the power project have been built and installed by the county's own small electrical-machinery workshop. At the factory I found a dark, hot, noisy, Dickensian atmosphere. Two men wearing ordinary work fatigues, cloth gloves, and gauze masks hand-carry a bucket of molten steel clear across the shop to pour into sand molds. Women patiently wind each electric coil. The workers proudly show production machines they pieced together from scrap and castoffs of larger plants.

A network of these small, local industries supplements major factories and helps provide jobs for the endless tide of young people entering the labor force. In Canton's Bao Gong neighborhood, I visited a group of residents who have set up a household facility for assembling semiconductor diodes used in electric meters. Two people were trained at a large state-run factory and then instructed others. Bao Gong operates thirteen other simple cooperatives that serve as the Maoist equivalents of subcontractors to larger plants. Also, small rural factories make a variety of products for their own communities. This dispersal of industry is in keeping with Maoist doctrine, but it also serves important practical purposes. It eases burdens on China's weak transportation system, and it restrains the flow of peasants into urban centers.

EXTRA EFFORTS FOR THE REVOLUTION

Throughout the Chinese economic system, a great deal of rationality is mingled with the abstract thoughts of Chairman Mao. Managers make use of such practical concepts as cost and even profit. I particularly noticed this at the Kwangchow Bicycle Plant, where workers in a series of converted old machine shops are increasingly mechanizing the production process. Kuo

Chiang-swea, vice chairman of the factory's revolutionary committee, explained the moves in terms that any capitalist counterpart could appreciate: "Our Kapok brand twenty-eight-inch model is now very popular in the countryside, but our production cost is still higher than other factories." To expand output and reduce unit costs, the plant has designed its own equipment for electroplating and spray-painting parts. (Young women workers, however, still must put ball bearings into the wheel assemblies by hand.) The improvements have shaved production costs by 6 percent to about $32 per bike; consumers pay a standard state-fixed price of about $47.

Vice Chairman Kuo and his comrades receive no extra financial reward for extra efforts. Salaries are set by government on an industry-wide basis, and since the recent Cultural Revolution, bonuses and overtime pay have been eliminated. "We do not improve efficiency for the purpose of increasing our own wages, but consider it more of a contribution to the socialist revolution," Kuo maintains.

Careful accounting is made of costs and receipts at the bicycle plant. It must pay "fraternal factories" for tires and a few other parts the plant cannot produce. "Yes, we make a profit," the vice chairman reported with undisguised satisfaction. Last year the plant earned about $3 million. It was not clear whether the concept of profit took account of depreciation or simply represented income minus outgo. In any event, higher authorities allowed the plant to keep $120,000 for investment in new equipment. The rest of the profit was turned over to the state. China (unlike even the Soviet Union) levies no personal or corporate income taxes, and earnings of industries constitute a major source of government revenue.

The workings of the Chinese economic system are visible on a larger scale at the Kwangchow Heavy Machine Tool Plant. At the entrance a billboard proclaims in bold red letters, "Unite to win even greater victories." Within the huge, fenced compound, 5,000 employees work in three shifts turning out equipment for mining, petroleum refineries, chemical plants, and sugar mills. Along with keeping industrial production going around the clock, the factory maintains agricultural plots for raising pigs and growing vegetables, dormitories for unmarried workers, eating facilities, and an array of anti-aircraft guns discreetly shrouded in canvas. And it serves as a center for subtle group dynamics and political action—directed toward motivating workers to increase output.

Members of the factory's revolutionary committee greeted me at the doorway of a hulking, grayish brick administration building and led the way down its gloomy corridors, past roomfuls of clerks clicking off accounts on abacuses. In a conference room, portraits of Marx, Engels, Lenin, Stalin, and Mao looked down sternly from the white plaster walls. Two young women in pigtails quickly padded over the concrete floor to pour tea. They were factory workers and they sat down and joined the discussion.

Chang Chow-kwong, a member of the committee, explained the fundamental management philosophy. "Before the Cultural Revolution," he said, "directors and engineers managed production. Now we rely on the broad masses of the people—the workers, who are masters of the country." Politics, he went on, plays a commanding part in motivating the workers. "We use Mao Tse-tung's thoughts to educate the workers and staff members to grasp revolution and promote production."

ENGINEERS AGAINST THE MASSES

Behind these incessantly repeated stock phrases lies a complex system that does allow a lot of worker participation in management. All important decisions for the plant are made by the factory's revolutionary committee, a supposedly representative "leading body" of twenty-one workers, eight party members, and two Army men. Administrators and engineers, including all committee members, are expected to spend a full day each week performing manual labor. "In this way, they're more closely linked with the masses," claims an administrator. In less doctrinaire terms, the practice thrusts managers into continuing contact with the realities of the production process.

Workers, moreover, fully discuss every management problem with representatives of the revolutionary committee before any decision is reached—a procedure that helps laborers identify with the broader aims of the plant and quietly smothers disagreements. Ordinary workers also participate in other managerial duties, such as helping to supervise financial operations and quality-control measures. Some even serve alongside engineers in the development of new production machinery and techniques. The so-called "technical innovation teams" help the plant to make the most of its meager resources. One workshop, for instance, assembled a metal-planing machine from scrap steel and spare parts, including the gears of an old truck. "We have a shortage of big equipment and our mechanical level is still not high," a technician said, "so we combined modern and indigenous methods."

The machine-tool plant adopted cooperative management after a siege of political action during the Great Proletarian Cultural Revolution, the disruptive ideological rumble that went on from 1966 to 1969. As factory officials recall, the plant plunged into an intense period of "struggle and mass revolutionary criticism" in 1967. Taking their cue from the nationwide movement, workers held countless meetings, wrote polemical articles, and plastered workshops with posters—all to denounce "the revisionist line that depends on a few experts to run the factory."

The antirevisionists concentrated bitter attacks on the five engineers who until then had solely managed all production processes. "They would not accept the rational suggestions of the workers," says a staff member who participated in the upheaval. "The initiative and creativeness of the broad masses of workers could not be brought into play."

Management responsibility shifted to the revolutionary committee in March, 1968. One incident that workers now like to recount is how they rebelled against rules the engineers established in the stainless-steel workshop—rules that forbade casting operations without the presence of technicians, at night, or on windy or rainy days. Once those restrictions were dropped, the plant found it could easily increase output of stainless steel because casting could be done at any time.

During the radical reform drive, which Mao instigated to shake up China's bureaucratic elite, many party officials and engineers were removed from managerial positions to spend six months to a year as ordinary laborers in the plant. Since this "re-education" they have returned to management—but with new obligations. "Every week I spend one day in the workshop," explains the former vice director, Hwang Siang. "Before the Cultural Revolution, we were supposed to do manual labor, but frankly I did not do it as often as now. Since the establishment of the revolutionary committee, we adhere to this as a system."

Hwang, who has worked in the machine-tool factory for twenty-two of his fifty-seven years, is now vice chairman of its management committee. Although back in a top executive slot, he wears gray cotton work clothes and sandals without socks. He pointedly refers to his "worker origin." As he recalls the turmoil of 1967, counterrevolutionary elements "instigated people to stop production." Management found a remedy: "These people were deceived, so we carried on education to raise their consciousness."

The Army's presence undoubtedly helped the learning process too. When the Cultural Revolution got out of hand, Mao ordered the People's Liberation Army to move into every enterprise and restore order. Though inconspicuous, the military men still exercise widespread authority—at the Kwangchow machine-tool plant, among other places. The "most responsible person" at the plant, and its chairman, is an Army representative whom I was never able to meet. Confronted with this apparent contradiction in the principle of management by the masses, a member of the committee blandly says: "We can learn what we don't know through practice. After the chairman came to the factory, he integrated himself with the broad masses."

IN MEMORY OF MAO

The broad masses as well as the integrated chairman participate in the factory's most crucial decision, the setting of the annual production target. This process involves a combination of participatory democracy and Communist political manipulation. In the third quarter of the year the municipal revolutionary committee that governs Canton proposes a tentative draft target for the machine-tool plant. This initial plan allows ample leeway for the factory to gain status by enlarging the production goal. In 1970, for instance, the municipal committee recommended a 30 percent increase in output over the previous year. Through a series of discussions in the workshops, employees at the machine-tool plant realized that improved equipment could enable them to expand output 100 percent. The revolutionary committee surveyed the shops to make sure the goal was realistic and then accepted it. The plant overfulfilled the higher target. That, anyway, is how people there tell the story now.

Once the production goal is officially set, the factory committee mounts a relentless effort that draws together national pride, Maoist ideology, and practical production advice to mobilize the work force. "We take measures to guarantee fulfillment of the targets," says Lu Yuan-mei, the slight, articulate woman who is No. 2 in the administrative department. She wears the same loose-fitting trousers and jacket as male colleagues—and seems a bit more self-confident than most of them. "Every month," she says, "we give the production targets to workers in different shops. Simultaneously, we let them know the significance of fulfilling the targets. We explain that it's not only to build up our own country, but that they have an international duty to support revolution." Each production line also gets specific guidance on its part of the production process.

In practice, this approach appears to prod the work force into giving its utmost effort. In the plant's No. 1 Workshop—which Chairman Mao personally inspected sixteen years ago—a team was recently ordered to develop a new vertical lathe for production of mining equipment. The workers were fed elaborate explanations of how important their tasks would be in supporting the vital growth of China's iron and steel industry. Higher-ups endowed the lathe with special significance by proclaiming it a factory monument to mark the anniversary of Mao's visit. A few model workers, it is said, became so fired up with the mission that they stayed on the job for twenty hours at a stretch.

"THE SWEETNESS OF TODAY"

Political manipulation to inspire worker effort is a pervasive and insistent aspect of life in China. Even the songs I heard children singing in the factory kindergarten promote the ideals of unselfish devotion to the state and the satisfaction of hard work. Upon joining the machine-tool plant at sixteen, new workers divide their first month equally between workshop duties and special classes. The young people are drilled in Maoist principles and given down-to-earth lectures by older workers who recall their own personal hardships in pre-Communist China. "These young people know nothing of past sufferings," maintains Comrade Lu. "Veteran workers let them know the sweetness of today through comparisons with life before liberation."

Workers who reveal inadequate "class-consciousness" by showing up late at the factory or performing jobs poorly are singled out for special treatment. Older workers visit their homes to provide what is called "patient ideological education." In practice, this amounts to a fierce form of political and social pressure that never lets up until the errant employee falls into line. Committee members profess to find it beyond belief that boredom and apathy are a problem in some American factories.

Psychological prodding is also built into the routine of every production team. Members of a team work together in the shop forty-eight hours a week and spend the compulsory four and a half hours a week studying together. The study sessions review Maoist works, discuss current events, and devise specific means for meeting production targets. Leaders try to relate all of this to the tasks at hand. Peking's admission to the United Nations, for example, served as a rallying point for urging the factory toward greater efforts to show that China was a nation worthy of the support it received. The factory's well-staffed political department guides the study groups in party policies and provides topical material. Every worker seemed completely conversant with details of the Shanghai communiqué issued at the end of President Nixon's visit to China. The political department also seeks out examples of model workers and glorifies their accomplishments—both as a reward to the individuals and as an example for others to emulate.

With all these vigorous nonmaterial incentives acting upon the Chinese, material incentives are decidedly modest. As part of a national wage raise gradually extending to all factories, the average pay at Kwangchow Machine Tool recently rose by $1.20 a month, to $26.80. On that income a worker subsists on a level that cannot by any means be considered dire poverty. For one thing, he pays no income taxes or major medical expenses. What's more, the Chinese pricing system (along with rationing of essential foods and cotton cloth) assures that salaries readily cover necessities and leave a surplus for saving to buy the relatively expensive consumer durables, such as a bicycle or radio. The average worker with a family pays about $2 monthly rent, including water and electricity, about $6 for food, and the simple people's costume that almost everyone wears costs only a few dollars. Shops are well stocked with textiles and basic household goods at low prices that have largely remained steady for a decade. A sewing machine or bicycle, on the other hand, costs slightly under two months' wages. Even so, the spread of consumer goods is clearly visible—village homes with sewing machines, teen-agers taking snapshots with Chinese-made cameras, workers with shiny new Shanghai brand wristwatches.

Despite the egalitarian tone, there are significant inequalities in pay. At the machine-tool plant, new employees start at $16 per month, an experienced hand gets about $39, and Vice Chairman Hwang $59.60. He seemed perfectly willing to tell me his salary in a room filled with lower-paid workers. Factory managers say that the long-term goal is to make the pay scale more nearly equal.

There is an even greater disparity of incomes between industrial workers and peasants, who constitute 85 percent of the population. The collective farms pay members according to their contribution and some intangible measure of ideological development; cash incomes sometimes run as low as one-sixth of factory wages, but peasants supplement earnings by raising much of their own food and gaining extra "work points" through participation in other commune efforts. On a larger scale, Peking's currently moderate economic strategy is to provide agriculture with larger amounts of fertilizer and farm machinery. State prices on these items were slashed last year, while farmers received more for peanuts, sugar cane, and other cash crops. Eventually, the Chinese figure, bigger inputs of modern farm technology will raise peasant incomes. And the government is banking heavily on small rural industries to make the means more readily available.

LEAP FORWARD TRACTORS

In Shunte County, a lush farming area in the Pearl River Delta of Kwangtung Province, a network of small manufacturing plants turns out much of the equipment used on the agricultural communes. "We're carrying out the revolutionary spirit of self-reliance," asserts Chiu Tan, an official in the county's industrial department. These county manufacturing units are helping to modernize agriculture by closely gearing operations to the particular needs of the locality.

One plant has mobilized 520 workers—nearly half of them women—to make water pumps, crop sprayers (described as "artificial rain makers"), and other farm equipment. The factory has just started assembling ten-horsepower Leap Forward brand "walking tractors." They are so called because farmers walk the machines through fields for plowing. The ten people's communes in the county provide a captive market for the plant's machinery. But the Chinese have their own form of consumerism. Under a policy launched during the Cultural Revolution, local plants must make certain their products are completely acceptable to commune customers. "At first, our tractors were not up to the standard," acknowledges a county official. The first batch drew complaints from peasants that the plowing-depth controls tended to stick; the factory recalled the tractors to work out the kinks and is now finally ready to assemble a hundred units this year.

Although the local factories use fairly primitive methods (such as hand-forging metal parts), they obviously help spread the use of modern equipment throughout the countryside. Farm machinery, electric generators, and water-control equipment can be seen in wide use at the county's communes. At Lo Lui People's Commune, most of the 17,000 households have electricity, its leaders claim, and a day's observations around the 12,000-acre spread indicate that this is probably true.

The commune—once pushed as a giant basic production unit—is now mainly an administrative center with a market and small processing facilities. Lo Lui, for instance, cultivates silkworms and sends cocoons to a county factory for processing into thread. Actual farming is performed by "production teams" in each village, where peasants cultivate collectively held land as well as tend their smaller privately owned plots. At lunch in the cottage of one peasant family, my host noted that much of the food came from his private plot, and the commune even lends initial capital to households that want to raise their own animals. These deviations from the strict collective system were found to be necessary to increase food production. Communal mess halls and backyard steel furnaces, pushed by Peking during its disastrous and ill-managed Great Leap Forward phase of 1958–60, are no longer part of commune routines.

LIKE A BIG FAMILY

But discipline and sacrifice of personal aspirations to state goals are still very much in evidence, as I discovered in long discussions with several peasant families. Wu Chen-chu, a twenty-seven-year-old peasant in the No. 6 Production Team of the commune's Lu Nan Production Brigade, shares with his sister an austere but immaculately clean three-room brick cottage. Sitting in his whitewashed bedroom, which doubles as the living room, he maintains, "Our lives have been getting better and better." But Wu's daily routine is still far from easy. Each morning he rises at six and works in collective fields for four and a half hours. He returns home for a lunch of fish, rice, vegetables, and eggs, and is free to cultivate his own crops for a while. In midafternoon he returns to collective duties for several more hours. His sister works in the commune's silkworm-cultivation center.

Their combined annual cash earnings come to about $440, which is supplemented by fruits, vegetables, chickens, and pigs raised on the land around their home. Questioned about personal ambitions, Wu professed none beyond service to the state. "I'm a farmer and a commune member. Without the country, which is like a big family, what am I?"

This is a characteristic voice of the new China. It is a voice so remote from traditional American values that a visitor from the United States cannot fully grasp the Maoist system, much less judge it. The Chinese dedication to rigorous toil to build up their country certainly seems admirable—all the more so because in the United States affluence has so widely eroded the will to work and pride in manual labor. It's clear, however, that most Chinese have no alternative but to respond to the constant pressures for arduous effort.

Despite deep differences in values and economic systems, the Chinese are making a determined effort to carry out the directive of Premier Chou En-lai that China and the United States should "learn from each other." Everyone from party leaders down to young factory workers and peasants has thoroughly studied the joint communiqué issued at the close of President Nixon's visit. Individual Chinese are groping toward trying to learn from the United States even though their knowledge of it is even more hazy than Americans' knowledge of China. At the Kwangchow Heavy Machine Tool Plant, a revolutionary committee member told me apologetically: "I'm very sorry now that we still don't understand each other well, so it's hard to say what we should learn from you." And it's hard for an American visitor to say what we should learn from China.

FAR EASTERN ECONOMIC REVIEW 1972 YEARBOOK*
Survey of the Chinese Economy

ECONOMY

China entered a new phase of national development in January 1971 with the start of the fourth five-year plan. This important step in China's development should have led to dramatic changes in the mood and policies of every sector of the economy. In practice, the year was marked by orderly progress which suggested a desire for consolidation rather than a dramatic leap forward. This sentiment was natural enough since the basic guidelines for economic growth—agriculture as the base (with top priority for grain), simultaneous development

* *Far Eastern Economic Review 1972 Yearbook*, pp. 143–54.

of both large and small industries and the creation of self-
sufficient industrial and farming communities across the nation
—were proclaimed first in late 1969.

Refinements of this policy—self-reliance in finding capital,
equipment and raw materials for production and expansion; a
central government warning that the state could not afford to
subsidize agriculture and that industry would have to be responsible for providing a large proportion of its own machines because the capital equipment sector already was overstrained—
had come in 1970. Thus 1971 saw the push forward of China's
economy along a path which had become apparent in the previous two years. . . .

The priorities of the new five-year plan were not spelled out
officially. During the year a switch in emphasis to heavy industry—iron, steel, coal, cement, electric power, chemical fertilizer
and machinery—was marked, even when produced in small village plants ("the five small industries"). Chekiang Province in
April listed these elements of the new plan very clearly: "Agriculture is the issue of first importance . . . industry mainly involves the production of coal, iron and steel. We must grasp
steel as the key link. In developing the steel industry we should
proceed from the mining of ores and the development of [coal]
mines." In May, Anhwei Province announced specifically: "The
fourth five-year plan calls for the quicker development of the
metallurgical industry. This demands a large increase in ore
production."

However, considerable debate arose on the question of expanding this particular sector of the economy. Some—in
Anhwei, for example—argued that opening up mines to exploit
local mineral resources was not as difficult as building processing plants and therefore did not deserve top priority. This
theory was attacked at both national and provincial levels, sug-
gesting the expansion of the economy had advanced so rapidly
that existing coal and iron ore resources had been stretched
to the limit by steel demands from the capital equipment
sector. . . .

The biggest area of discord created by the new priority for
steel and the industries which supported this sector was the
conflict over the status of electronics. The *People's Daily* in
May struck out at those who saw China's industrial revolution
beginning with a breakthrough in electronics. "Electronics plays

an important part in economic construction and national defense," the paper said. But it added that iron and steel must come first as these industries provided the raw materials for the growth of the electronics sector. . . .

The industrial front—and the whole of the economy to varying degrees in 1971—was subject to conflicting pressures from the central government. The basic issue was control over economic development. Almost every statement on the establishment of a new Communist Party committee called for the strengthening of party (and thus Peking) control over economic policy. . . .

The problem of local versus national interests remained unsettled in 1971. Peking constantly urged local officials to give the state's needs top priority. Yet Mao's command to respect local initiative was reprinted regularly. The spate of denunciations of those who were satisfied with meeting only local needs pointed to an unresolved dispute between the ministries in Peking and the men on the spot. A Peking article on the search for new minerals spotlighted the clash between the two sides: "It is imperative to concentrate our efforts to ensure fulfillment of the state plan's priority projects . . . before general and local ones." The article attacked the idea of centralizing power in the hands of national ministries and called for "the correct policy of delegating administrative power to the local authorities." But it went on to blast "decentralization.". . .

However, the peasants had been encouraged to start local industries on a large scale. Thus, a large proportion of the Chinese economy was not under Peking's direct supervision. According to statistics released by the central government in September, plants "not attached to the central industrial departments" accounted for 40 per cent of national output of cement and 50 per cent of China's production of chemical fertilizers—two key industries.

These undertakings came under provincial, county, commune or production brigade control. Their development was actively encouraged by Peking in preference to large plants on the grounds of cheapness, adaptability to local needs and speed of return on investment. However, the plants seemed to fit only indirectly into the national plan, and their profits and assets were controlled by the lower-level administrative unit which had financed them. . . .

A difficulty was the labor shortage. The Ministry of Fuel and Chemicals had to emphasize the need to ensure mining did not draw labor away from the fields in the peak cultivation months. Workers and peasants should be mobilized for industrial activities in their slack months.

The *People's Daily* explained the correct strategy here and implied the country had become thoroughly confused on how to keep a balance between farming and local industry: "Labor should not be transferred at random from the frontline of agricultural production . . . when local industry has developed, it is possible to manufacture some of the more modern technical equipment urgently needed in agricultural production. This will save more labor in farming."

The peasants were to expand their local factories without reducing the amount of labor needed to maintain bumper harvests. Large numbers should be shifted out of the fields only when local factories had produced the machines to replace manual labor. Still, the problem of how much labor to allocate to local industry, what crops to grow and how dominant food grains should be in the peasant economy remained issues for debate throughout 1971. . . .

General performance by the economy looked good on the basis of the percentage figures of increased output released by the authorities during the first three quarters of 1971. After allowing for the seasonal slackening in growth rates during the second quarter, when attention switched to farming to pick up sharply again in the next quarter before National Day (October 1), it seemed that China in 1971 might chalk up an industrial growth rate of between 15 per cent and 20 per cent over the previous year with about 3 per cent in agriculture (because of poor weather). On the whole, the economy in 1971 ought to have achieved at least the same rate of increase in national income—10 per cent—as it experienced in 1970 according to Japanese government estimates of China's economic performance.

FINANCE

China's financial situation makes sense only in the context of its national planning framework. The system of direct state control of major industries and those plants for which it provides capital—plus the establishment of output quotas for enterprises not directly under Peking's supervision—means normal methods of analyzing a country's financial performance do not apply. The efficiency with which resources are allocated, the amount set aside for saving and new investment, the return on capital and the volume of consumption all are supposed to be under tight central control.

It became clear during 1971 that a great deal of confusion reigned on the planning front, and the degree of financial direction was far less than Peking thought desirable. At the root of this problem was the chaotic state of the planning mechanism, which had been engulfed in the Cultural Revolution's tide. The various economic ministries during the year began to display greater willingness to publish instructions to the country and to map out guidelines. This trend was particularly evident in the case of the State Planning Commission. Yet the difficulties in getting a grip on the economy remained considerable for Peking. . . .

The actual mechanics of Chinese planning was a matter of guesswork during 1971. In July, for instance, the Ministry of Agriculture and the First Ministry of Machine-Building jointly sponsored a conference for southern China on mechanization of rice cultivation. This showed Peking was in contact with the lower levels of the administration. At the same time, state plans for farming and other sectors of the economy had been mapped out and quotas transmitted to the various communes and factories. In Heilungkiang Province, a July broadcast referred to the need to adapt the state plan to local conditions. But a contradiction in the planning system was apparent in this province (and in many others): during the previous month, the *Heilungkiang Daily* had called upon each level of the local administration to draw up "unified plans and overall arrangements to make a success of industrial, agricultural and all other work." The amount of freedom to ignore the plan or to argue about targets set by the center seemed significant. . . .

An article during the summer in the *People's Daily* suggested that in some instances the state plan was not conveyed directly to the unit concerned but was revealed only to the cadre assigned to take charge of the project. The paper made it clear that targets put forward by the state often strained capacity to

the limits. According to a February article in the same newspaper, the masses were supposed to play a direct part in filling
out the details of a factory's plan for the year. However, man-
agements often were reluctant to entrust this task to the workers on the ground that far too many opinions would have to be
absorbed into the planning process.

But Peking preferred this mass approach as it forced workers
to be responsible for meeting the targets they had proposed and
compelled management to explain clearly the instructions from
the upper echelons. This policy seemed sensible enough. But
Peking said the masses were far from infallible and exposed
the workers of one Heilungkiang area in March who had
erected a blast furnace without working out where the necessary raw materials would come from. The peasants of one
Kwangsi commune wrote a letter to a national daily confessing
they had bungled mining operations by setting up small pits
without any regard for planning. However, when plants failed
to meet their state quotas—as in the case of a newly-equipped
steel plant in Hofei—the blame generally was placed on poor
leadership standards. . . .

As in 1970, commerce remained a complex issue. One school
of thought apparently favored the use of markets and prices as
a means of encouraging production. Peking slapped this idea
down by arguing that national planning was the correct way
to balance supply and demand, with prices playing a secondary
role. The main point made by the government was that "putting
prices in command" would encourage the output of goods on
the basis of the profits they offered rather than on national
needs. . . .

Peking appeared to maintain its pressure on districts and
units to go in for self-financing. A Honan county discussed how
profits from mining had financed the purchase of agricultural
equipment, the electrification of the villages and the establishment of small processing factories. Indeed, part of the problem
in exercising any financial supervision was the multiplicity of
overlapping units which owned or managed concerns—all the
way down from national enterprises to production brigade
workshops, with various industrial plants, and provincial or
district economic bureaus all enjoying considerable degrees of
autonomy. The extent of this lack of supervision of the way

money was being used became apparent following an article which related how the capital had only just begun to introduce budgetary controls and conventional accounting systems during 1971 into the construction industry.

The banking system was encouraged to spread its wings in 1971 and take a positive part in helping plants to overcome their production problems. *Red Flag* reported in February how a branch of the People's Bank in Liaoning Province had helped a factory in need of capital for expansion to sort out its inventories and to collect back debts. It reduced the credit required from Rmb 1 million to Rmb 300,000. The same article praised efforts to bring the workers into the process of controlling the use of funds and stocks. In the countryside, according to the *Shensi Daily* in April, the employment of peasants in supervising the activities of financial organizations led to the discovery of various malpractices. One problem was the notion banks were actively supporting production if they increased the volume of credit to enterprises. According to Hunan Province in the spring, this led to an alarming upsurge in the lending volume. The correct path was for bank staff to enter such enterprise seeking loans and to go through the undertaking with a fine-toothed comb to uncover every idle resource on the premises, a policy which seemed to meet with considerable success. In Chekiang Province, the People's Bank in June helped factories to reduce the amount of waste items thrown away, showing how it could be employed by other plants. Shensi Province in August described how a bank branch had succeeded in setting up a fertilizer factory as a result of exploiting the by-products of local industry.

Throughout the year, in fact, a vigorous anti-waste campaign was carried out on two fronts. The first concerned the volume of idle stocks held in factory warehouses. Sinkiang region held a conference which explicitly linked the battle to uncover unused resources to the success of the five-year plan. Peking, apparently short of capital to finance new projects, believed tighter control of stocks would cut down the demands made on the national treasury and release goods deteriorating in factory stores for exploitation by new enterprises. . . .

Tighter accountancy procedures, with workers and professional accountants combining to keep the books, were urged throughout China during the whole of 1971. Several areas showed a fear of paying attention to accounting procedures in case this led to allegations that profits were the main concern of management—a charge which had toppled many cadres between 1966 and 1969. And members of the labor force often seemed to resent the formalities of proper accounting. . . .

A strong effort was made to tighten control over rural fairs, the free markets in which peasants were able to sell goods made in their spare time. A Szechwan provincial report in September indicated this work was not popular with cadres and was essentially a question of ensuring reasonable and stable prices. The failure to eradicate rural fairs and free markets was an indication of the strength of peasant resistance to interference with their cash incomes. Shanghai told of an attempt to ensure local cadres did not use their status to obtain credit facilities improperly.

When these bits and pieces were put together, the overall picture was one of a central government hard-pressed for resources to sink into economic development and forced to grab at every chance to reduce the amount of cash and materials allocated to economic undertakings. At the same time, the amount of credit created by the banking system seemed to have reached a ceiling. There was pressure to prevent any further loan demands on the banks. . . .

National revenue still was highly limited, with 90 per cent of the budget coming from the profits of state enterprises. As the government pointed out, agricultural taxation had been slashed from 12 per cent in 1953 to a mere 6 per cent by 1971. The country had no personal taxes. Peking explained that while the peasants were getting 90 per cent more for their products than in 1950, the retail price of agricultural goods had remained quite stable since 1958. The price paid by the peasants for fertilizers, insecticides and diesel oil had dropped by between one third and two thirds since 1950. The cost of this "buy dear, sell cheap" policy, said Peking, was borne by the state.

However, Peking's burdens were eased by the slow growth of wages. Average annual earnings of workers and staff (excluding "those who started working in the last few years") was Rmb 650, a 50 per cent rise over 1952 according to official statistics. The gap between the top and the bottom of the salary scale—at 600 per cent—was low, said Peking. Although industrial wages deliberately had been set low to reduce the gap between urban workers' living standards and those of the peasants, rent, water and electricity cost only 4 per cent to 5 per cent of a family's income.

Some efforts were made during 1971 to raise the quality of life in both town and country. The textile industry made a substantial increase in the number of colors in which fabrics were printed, following complaints by the public about drab clothing. Village stores and city department stores reorganized work hours to suit customers.

TRADE

Peking did not define its foreign trade targets for 1971. The clues which emerged in various official statements on foreign commercial relations about China's trade policy for the period of the fourth five-year plan were highly confusing. In December 1970 the appointment of a new Minister of Foreign Trade, Pai Hsiang-kuo, was announced. Although this move indicated foreign trade had a special importance in Peking's eyes as this ministry was one of the first to be normalized after the Cultural Revolution chaos, Pai appeared an unimpressive man for a job which had vital economic and diplomatic implications for China. A former district commander in Kwangtung province, he continued to wear his army uniform on official occasions. Despite his lack of any known qualifications for the job, foreigners who came in contact with him both at home (the visit of Australian Opposition leader Gough Whitlam in July) and abroad (on his visit to Ceylon in January) described him as astute, self-assured and very well briefed.

The same contradiction became apparent when two counties in March denounced themselves for having put "exports in command" of the local foreign trade bureau while eyewitness accounts from another district in the same province indicated Mao-study classes had been drastically reduced in a plant producing for export. In May, the light-industry ministry said one advantage of the growth of its sector of the economy was the opportunity it provided for expanding exports, a statement repeated in late September.

The Chinese were ready to sell advantageously on world

markets when they had adequate supplies apparently. But in February imports were said to be of considerable value, as models to be collected by the nation's commercial organizations from overseas and then imitated (with suitable modifications) by domestic industry.

However, it was a constant cause for pride during 1971 that Chinese industry was able to replace foreign production techniques with its own designs, for which impressive productivity was claimed. The industries concerned ranged from steel (in February) to petroleum (in September). The *People's Daily* made a special point of attacking those in the shipbuilding industry who admired foreign techniques and felt they could be copied directly. The article implied dissatisfaction in some quarters with Chinese technological standards and significant pressure to purchase from abroad equipment of the most modern design. . . .

While Chinese policy on foreign trade displayed a certain hesitation and a number of contradictions, the picture was very different in the outside world. Foreign nations queued for the right to deal with Peking. In June, the United States finally abandoned its ban on all commerce and financial dealings with China. Non-strategic goods were freed from embargo, and United States dollars, it was revealed in the previous month, could be used in financing deals with any countries including China. The requirement that 50 per cent of grain exports from the United States be carried in American bottoms was also dropped.

In August, Washington opened the door to the use of Export-Import Bank financing of trade with Peking. Chinese trade corporations and other official commercial bodies reacted coolly to the news from Washington. While representatives of such major American concerns as Boeing were able to hold face-to-face talks with Peking's representatives in Hong Kong (with staff from China Resources Company), the basic line laid down by Peking was that China would not enter directly into contracts with the United States. However, reliable reports indicated Chinese interest in token purchases of wheat, tobacco, jet aircraft and transport equipment from America, possibly to be arranged through third parties. . . .

The overall impression was of a China anxious to increase its contacts with foreign countries and to use trade as part of its diplomatic strategy in finding new friends. Its foreign aid program and its willingness to engage in serious consultations with foreign business representatives at the highest level in a relaxed and frank mood showed how China had settled down on the foreign trade front since 1966. Nevertheless, the Chinese responsible for external trade were categorical in explaining China would never allow the total of foreign trade to become a significant factor in the country's national income.

Both in private and in public statements, Peking recalled how hamstrung it had been after the 1958 Great Leap collapsed, followed by three disastrous harvests when the Russians pulled out their technical teams and equipment and broke their trade contracts.

The Canton trade fair was held as usual in April and May. Many overseas businessmen felt the trade fair was being downgraded. They got the impression that direct dealings with prominent business corporations abroad and trade ministries overseas as more and more countries established diplomatic relations with Peking were undermining the fair's usefulness. But indications were that the autumn fair in Canton would be even bigger than the spring occasion, and some traders were forecasting a large rise in China's exports of industrial crops and greater interest in machinery imports. Yet the arrangements under way to permit the Danes and the Austrians, for example, to hold industrial exhibitions in China showed the Canton fair was likely to become a less unique trading opportunity than it had been in the past.

AGRICULTURE

Mao Tse-tung has always recognized that the easiest way to fall from power is to get on the wrong side of the Chinese peasant. During 1971, a running battle was fought by Peking and the provincial administrations to hold back the "ultra-leftists" who wanted to abolish all private property in the countryside. These extremists sought to end communal ownership, by the peasants, of land and machinery plus rural factories, to abolish private plots, to forbid peasants to raise livestock on a household basis,

to end the system of using villages or parts of a village community (production teams) as the basic economic unit in farming and to pay wages on the basis of need rather than results. . . .

The *People's Daily* in February had ordered the nation to
make no changes in the existing commune organization and
declared that the regulations governing the villages and their
enterprises remained unchanged even after the Cultural Revolution, since they had been framed by Mao himself. The issue
came up repeatedly during 1971. In Hunan the debate centered
on whether pigs should be kept on a commune or a household
basis. In Kwangtung, one county abolished payment on the
work-point system and "pursued absolute egalitarianism" to the
detriment of the local economy.

The *People's Daily* in mid-year attacked these trends as
"ultra-leftist" and at the same time attacked those who reduced
peasant incomes to bolster commune investment funds. The
Fukien Daily in July made a similar point, warning the province
to leave enough grain in the peasants' hands for their family
needs. In the same month, the *Hunan Daily* suggested Peking
was afraid of interfering with the existing economic setup in
the countryside not only because of the damage the abolition of
communal ownership and spare-time private enterprise would
do to peasant morale but because the villagers were bored with
policy debates. . . .

The central government seemed confident the country had
enough food to meet all its needs. It claimed national self-
sufficiency in September and commented that grain was imported only to make it possible to provide food assistance to
other nations. Some local reports criticizing officials for general
unconcern about the autumn harvest because their needs had
been met by a bumper spring output indicated the rural population did not feel any sense of insecurity about the food situation.

Still, the widespread reports of unfavorable weather meant
the chances of agriculture doing significantly better than the
bumper year of 1970 had to be discounted. It may have been
significant too that leftist pressure to "socialize" the peasants
was stoutly resisted: weather problems were hardly the best
background for radical reforms of the village economy. Also
noteworthy was the decline in complaints about peasant reluctance to meet the state's procurement targets for grain, a

marked feature of 1969 and 1970. Discipline in the communes may have improved considerably during 1971, yet the authorities may have felt it unwise to press the peasants too hard for more grain while the autumn harvest remained in doubt.

China had moved well forward in the previous two years in building up its defenses against natural disasters, and in the struggle to modernize agriculture. Although some areas still preferred the "imperial calendar" in planning their work instead of adjusting to the new schedules demanded by modern hybrid seeds, the pressure to adopt scientific farming techniques seemed to yield promising results. Kiangsi Province in May explained how seed varieties had to be chosen carefully to meet the requirements of local soils and microclimates. This message was repeated by other areas. . . .

Mechanization was credited with helping to maintain yields under adverse natural conditions. The main impetus for introduction of machinery to the land was the labor shortage, which made new arrangements essential in 1971 to free women from other work to take part in cultivation. The more intensive cultivation techniques demanded by scientific farming and the demands of rural industry for workers affected the volume of labor for tilling the soil.

Peking reported in September that 90 per cent of the nation's counties had set up plants to manufacture and repair farm machines. More than two-thirds of the country's major administrative units had full-scale farm machinery industries, and China had more than 1,000 types of agricultural machines. Local factories—mainly small-scale—accounted for about 80 per cent of all farm equipment manufactured in China. Also, the state had built and renovated its own large farm equipment plants. Although Peking stressed that districts were expected to finance their own mechanization, loans were made available to poorer units to help them speed mechanization.

INDUSTRY

China's industrial field saw rapid progress through 1971. While such debates as the relative merits of electronics versus steel caused heartache in some quarters, the general thrust of factory activity was strongly upward. Peking's main concern was to bolster supplies of raw materials—a difficult task. . . .

For the new five-year plan, steel output was a major factor in determining the ultimate success of the development program. Key plants such as Anshan reported steady increases in output. The important Penchi Iron and Steel Corporation illustrated in mid-year how it had built up the range of products it supplied from its own resources for the manufacture of steel, rolled steel and pig iron. It claimed large breakthroughs in its output of coke, refractory bricks, limestone and sulfuric acid. From Shanghai came reports of 150 new varieties of shaped steel tubing.

The picture in the coal industry was similar. The Fushun and Funghsiang mining bureaus claimed they had made substantial reductions in production costs while pushing output to new levels. Kirin Province reported mines which managed to make astonishing economies in the amount of electricity consumed with no adverse effects on the rate of output growth.

Mass campaigns to open new coal deposits led to a burst of enthusiasm for digging coal (often open cast) in provinces as far apart as Chekiang and Kwangtung. In coal the emphasis was on self-sufficiency. The key consideration was the elimination of fresh strains on China's overloaded transport system. It was clear that if small rural plants had to import coal from far away, havoc would result on the railways and roads.

While heavy industry replaced electronics as the glamor sector during 1971, the reports on manufacturing activities across the country showed that many industries were sharing in the general boom. A typical list of products in which large increases were recorded in Kweichow almost duplicated the lists from Kiangsu and Szechwan: cement, fertilizers, machine tools, hand-operated tractors and textiles.

The petroleum industry claimed a particularly successful year. Quotas for the year were considerably higher than in 1970 but were nevertheless completed ahead of schedule. This industry was one in which investment in new plant apparently went mainly to large and medium undertakings in contrast to the rest of the economy. In September, Peking stated it no longer was dependent on foreign supplies. Also, China's oil industry had developed its own technology and allowed the creation of a modern petrochemical industry, according to Peking, turning out synthetic rubber, plastics, synthetic fibers and industrial chemicals.

As in 1970, innovations were heavily stressed by the central government and provincial authorities. The range of bright ideas transformed into new products was considerable. In Liaoning, for instance, success was claimed in substituting superior-strength nodular iron for high-grade alloy steel in manufacturing reduction gears for tractors. In a Hunan metal factory, a workshop claimed to have boosted efficiency 48-fold by changing its grinding techniques. The Paochi Steelworks in Shensi Province reported in July that it had managed to finish construction of equipment for producing large-diameter tubes for only Rmb 1.5 million compared with the Rmb 18 million imported equipment would have cost to do the same job.

While coordination between plants was not so prominent a feature in official propaganda, the degree of cooperation between plants and factories—even different areas—seemed to continue at a high level. Shanghai, for example, told how the low-alloy silicon steel needed for bicycles was produced by two steel plants and a cycle factory working together. They managed to slash the trial production period of the metal from one to two years down to sixty days.

Local industry was heavily emphasized, mainly because of Mao Tse-tung's instructions on the basic strategy for diversifying China's industrial centers and combining units of all sizes to contribute to the maximum possible growth. Small factories, the government insisted in September, were cheap to build, quickly brought into production and able to take advantage of even small deposits of raw materials. Kwangtung Province claimed the ability to build a commune blast furnace for Rmb 100. Total costs including ancillary equipment capable of turning out "several tens of tons of cast and pig iron" annually were estimated at only Rmb 2,000.

The range of products turned out by rural industry was impressively wide. In Shansi Province the list included felt, blankets, wool yarn, salt, paper and detergents. The capacity of manufacturing centers in the countryside to meet the peasants' needs was shown in an August report on how industry should support agriculture. One county in Hopei Province built in five months a sulfuric acid plant with an annual capacity of 8,000 tons; it doubled production of phosphoric fertilizer to 20,000 tons a year by improving the existing chemical plant. It claimed by late 1971 to have turned out almost one million parts for tractors and motor engines, more than 4,000 farm machines, some 3,000 machines and engines, 150,000 agricultural tools and 22,000 tons of chemical fertilizer in the previous three years. . . .

One special feature of the year was the greater readiness to admit the value of technical skills in manufacturing. While attacking the political views of technicians reared in the pre-cultural revolution universities, Peking in May demanded they should not be afraid to point out when production plans were contrary to scientific knowledge; they should be ready to engage in research despite the feeling that "technical work is dangerous"; and they should again exploit whatever foreign knowleuge was useful to China. In fact, the importance of trained technicians in development was admitted frequently. . . .

TRANSPORT

For Chinese transport in 1971, nothing was more trying than economic success. The domestic transport system was hardpressed by the demands placed upon it by a healthily expanding economy.

The volume carried in 1970 on China's railways and inland waterways had already exceeded the 1969 totals by more than 20 per cent, according to Chinese claims. With China's industrial and agricultural output continuing to climb, railway freight volume rose in the first five months of 1971 by 15 per cent over 1970's corresponding period, stretching to the utmost the railway system's ability to cope. Coastal and river shipping to May 1971 was some 20 per cent more than in the previous twelve months, and the government's giant Yangtze River Transport Company declared a 35 per cent gain in freight. . . .

Most important, Peking pushed a major campaign to lay new railway trackage. In accordance with the program to disperse industry geographically, new railways had priority over the double-tracking of prevailing railway lines. Development was so strong that it seemed it might reach the budgetary limits. By the end of May, 55 per cent of 1971's planned investment for railway building had been expended.

The dispositions of new railways remain China's secret except to U.S. and Soviet spy satellites, but word has leaked of four important new spur lines in the south: the Hwa-Foo railway running 140 kilometers through Anhwei province; the An-Wei line, spanning the 50 kilometers between An-loo and Wei-chia-tien in Hupeh; the Ping-Mei spur extending in northern Kwangtung from the main north-south trunk line across to the town of Mei-ling-kwan; and from there a new line will connect eventually with Kanchow in Kiangsi Province.

To traffic its enlarged system, China placed special importance on the output of its own locomotive industry, though Peking felt compelled to pursue a modest program of imports. Seventy French and German locomotives were scheduled to join domestic models on the rails within a year, and in June Peking ordered an additional fifty French diesels.

In 1970, the various transport services were absorbed into a giant new Communications Ministry. The new ministry's program for better coordinating the movement of merchandise helped to explain why there had been no repetitions of early 1971's minor transport crisis, when goods awaiting shipment overcrowded warehouses. Strong efforts were made to ensure that those vessels and vehicles which in previous years were empty on return runs now were fully loaded, and a campaign was underway to cut sharply into loading times. Management of warehousing in some places was centralized.

In road construction, stress was placed on rural areas, where transport remained a severe problem. Even after a major road-building campaign in Shansi Province, fully 10 per cent of the province's agricultural communes were without truck roads. In some of the hillier sections of the country, footpaths still provided the only links between townships. In 1971, the provinces endeavored to expand rural bus lines.

Motor-vehicles production rose. Every province except Tibet could manufacture its own vehicles, in line with the drive for regional self-sufficiency. Coordination of efforts improved.

Changchun No. 1 Motor Vehicle Plant, China's first and largest, supplied half the provinces with major sets of molds, enabling many to move more efficiently into mass production.

China's international transport outlets expanded greatly during the year as the winds of diplomacy shifted dramatically in Peking's favor. In April the United States announced that American vessels and aircraft could carry Chinese cargoes between non-Chinese ports, and that foreign-registered U.S.-owned vessels could call at Chinese ports. Making transport to and from China generally more convenient, President Nixon also ended almost all restrictions on American oil companies providing U.S. fuel to ships or aircraft proceeding to or from China. . . .

★   ★   ★   ★   ★

3. REVOLUTIONARY ADMINISTRATION

The basic experience of revolutionary committees is this—
they are threefold: they have representatives of revolutionary
cadres, representatives of the armed forces, and representatives of the revolutionary masses. This forms a revolutionary
"three-in-one" combination. The revolutionary committee
should exercise unified leadership, eliminate redundant or
overlapping administrative structures, follow the policy of better troops and simpler administration and organize a revolutionized leading group which keeps in contact with the masses.

Mao Tse-tung (1967)

For nearly half a century the Chinese Communists have experimented with the construction of new political institutions to
replace the shattered structure of the old order. Revolution
brings about an explosion of political participation by millions
of people who for the first time in their lives enter the political
realm. The history of the Chinese Communist Party largely deals
with the efforts to mobilize new groups into politics and with the
creation of new political institutions. Mao was one of the first
Chinese political leaders to recognize the new institutions of
peasant power in the peasant associations of Hunan in 1927.
After an investigation of the peasant movement, he wrote:
"With the collapse of the landlords, the peasant associations
have now become the sole organs of authority and the popular
slogan 'All power to the peasant associations' has become a
reality."

The process of creating new political institutions is a long
one. New structures of government created by the early American colonists were in the process of development for more than
a century before they became the basis of the revolutionary government after 1776. In China, the process of creation of new
political structures still continues, and the Cultural Revolution
represents only the latest stage in the long history of the mobilization of wider and wider political participation by the

Chinese people. As the most intense and sophisticated political experiment in the history of the revolution, the Cultural Revolution, with all its successes and failures, will influence the development of Chinese political institutions in the decades ahead.

Inheriting the concept of the vanguard political party from Lenin, the Chinese utilized this instrument to forge the coalition of workers, peasants, and intellectuals that took power in 1949. After the victory of the revolution, the seventeen-million-member Chinese Communist Party organization exercised leadership of the nation through a network of highly disciplined and hierarchically structured party committees. During the 1950's and early 1960's, this efficient party apparatus took on many of the characteristics of the Soviet Communist Party. Loyalty to the party took precedence over any other consideration and all other institutions of power became the administrative subordinates of the party. After the death of Stalin, Mao and other Chinese leaders became more and more disenchanted with the policies pursued by Stalin's successors. Growing disagreement on the line of the international Communist movement finally led to the break between the two largest Communist parties in the world, the withdrawal in 1960 of Soviet technicians from China, and sharp attacks by the Chinese on the Soviet model of socialism.

It was within this context that Mao led the criticism of what the Chinese considered to be the restoration of capitalism in the Soviet Union. By the restoration of capitalism, the Chinese meant not a return to private ownership of industry, but the growth of new elites and a new bureaucratic class which through the arbitrary use of political power had succeeded in establishing a new system of domination and exploitation of the people.

By the middle of the 1960's, Mao had reached the conclusion that if it were led by the wrong people, a Communist party exercising a monopoly of political power might be transformed into a fascist party; rule in the interests of the many could be converted into rule in the interests of the few. Mao's writings and speeches from this period made it clear that he believed loyalty to the revolution and the masses had to take precedence over the more parochial loyalty to the party organization. In Mao's view revolutionaries existed outside the party as well as within the party, and in some cases, people outside the party were even more revolutionary. Mao was searching for a formula to prevent the transformation of the leading organs of state power from servants of society into masters of society.

One formula for the prevention of new elite formations was promulgated very early in the Cultural Revolution—continuous mass participation in politics and mass supervision over ruling officials. The Paris Commune of 1871 would provide the political model for the formation of new permanent revolutionary institutions. In the selections we have included portions of a long article published in March 1966, entitled "The Great Lessons of the Paris Commune." This and other articles outlining the structures of new political institutions which might guarantee the future of the revolution were to the Chinese people what the Federalist Papers had been to the American people in the last quarter of the eighteenth century. The key provisions of the Paris Commune that were underlined by the Chinese press in 1966 were:

1. A system of direct election and recall of public officials.
2. The setting of a low maximum salary for officials.
3. Mass checkup on the work of the commune and its members.
4. The organization of a network of basic-level mass organizations which would meet frequently to review higher decisions, and where activists could make proposals or advance critical opinions on social and political matters.

As the giant Cultural Revolution unfolded, attempts were made to realize the commune formula of permanent mass organs of power. However, factionalism, a general lack of unity, the historic tendency to consolidate control at the center, and the general complexity of the mass movement undermined the realization of the Paris Commune system of popular direct organs of power. By February 1967 the idea had been all but abandoned by the leaders of the Cultural Revolution. Chou En-lai admitted in a speech to representatives of rebel organizations that the Paris Commune election system required "the integration of the revolutionary organizations with the masses of the people," the rehabilitation of the rightists, the isolation of the "ultra-leftists," and the unity of 95 percent of the masses and the cadres. The premier added that China was far from having reached that stage.

The next best thing was to create a new organ of power that hopefully would unite the revolutionary masses, the cadres, and the army. This new political institution was the revolutionary committee, constructed on the foundation of a three-in-one combination of revolutionary cadres, revolutionary masses, and representatives of the People's Liberation Army. Our selection on this new political structure sheds some light on the function, purpose, and operation of the revolutionary committee. Revolutionary committees and other administrative organs, particularly in factories, took as their program of operation the Constitution of the Anshan Iron and Steel Company, which had been written by Mao Tse-tung in 1960. This constitution stipulated the following five basic principles: "Keep politics firmly in command; strengthen the party leadership; launch vigorous mass movements; institute the system of cadre participation in productive labor and worker participation in management, of reform of irrational and outdated rules and regulations, and of close cooperation among cadres, workers, and technicians; and go full steam ahead with the technical revolution." To this was added the slogan, "Fewer troops and simpler administration."

It is too early to draw definitive conclusions on the future role of the revolutionary committee. The questions of interest will be: how much power do the new committees exercise; how representative are they; and what is their relationship to the newly rebuilt party committees. Apparently the Chinese are attempting to retain the vanguard party concept while at the same time searching for means of mass control of this vanguard. One conclusion well warranted is that it is unlikely that after three years of intensive mass participation in politics the Chinese people will quickly forget concepts of democratic participation in political life.

★　　★　　★

CHENG CHIH-SZU*
The Great Lessons of the Paris Commune—
In Commemoration of Its Ninety-fifth Anniversary

The Proletariat Which Has Seized Power Must Prevent the Transformation of Its State Organs from Servants of Society into Masters of Society. High Salaries and Multiple Salaries for Concurrently Held Posts Must Be Abolished Among All Cadres Working in Proletarian State Organs, and These Cadres Must Not Enjoy Any Special Privileges

How to prevent degeneration of the state organs of the dictatorship of the proletariat? The Paris Commune took a number of exploratory steps in this matter, and adopted a number of measures which, tentative as they were, had most profound and far-reaching significance. These measures provide us with important revelations.

Engels said: "Against this transformation of the state and the organs of the state from servants of society into masters of society—an inevitable transformation in all previous states— the Commune made use of two infallible means. In the first place, it filled all posts—administrative, judicial and educational —by election on the basis of universal suffrage of all concerned, subject to the right of recall at any time by the same electors. And, in the second place, all officials, high or low, were paid only the wages received by other workers. The highest salary paid by the Commune to anyone was 6,000 francs. In this way an effective barrier to place-hunting and careerism was set up, even apart from the binding mandates to delegates to representative bodies which were added besides."

* Cheng Chih-szu, in *Peking Review*, No. 16 (April 15, 1966), pp. 23– 29 (translated from an article in *Red Flag*, No. 4, 1966).

The masses were the real masters in the Paris Commune. While the Commune was in being the masses were organized on a wide scale and they discussed important state matters within their respective organizations. Each day around 20,000 activists attended club meetings where they made proposals or advanced critical opinions on social and political matters great and small. They also made their wishes and demands known through articles and letters to the revolutionary newspapers and journals. This revolutionary enthusiasm and initiative of the masses was the source of the Commune's strength.

Members of the Commune paid much attention to the views of the masses, attending their various meetings and studying their letters. The general secretary of the Commune's Executive Committee, writing to the secretary of the Commune, said: "We receive many proposals every day, both orally and in writing; some are from individuals and some are sent in by the clubs or sections of the International. These are often excellent proposals and they should be considered by the Commune." The Commune, in fact, seriously studied and adopted proposals from the masses. Many great decrees of the Commune were based on proposals by the masses, such as abolishing the system of high salaries for state functionaries, canceling arrears of rent, instituting secular education, abolishing night work for bakers, and so on and so forth.

The masses also carefully checked up on the work of the Commune and its members. One resolution of the Communal club of the third arrondissement said: "The people are the masters . . . if men you have elected show signs of vacillation or stalling, please give them a push forward to facilitate the realization of our aims—that is, the struggle for our rights, the consolidation of the Republic, so that the cause of righteousness shall triumph." The masses criticized the Commune for not taking resolute measures against the counter-revolutionaries, deserters and renegades, for not carrying out immediately the decrees it passed, and for disunity among its members. For example, a letter from a reader appeared in the April 27 issue of *Le Père Duchêne* saying: "Please give members of the Commune a jolt from time to time, ask them not to fall asleep, not to procrastinate in carrying out their own decrees. Let them make an end to their private bickering because only by unanimity of view can they, with greater power, defend the Commune."

The provisions for the replacing and recalling of elected representatives who betrayed the interests of the people were not empty words. The Commune did, in fact, deprive Blanchet of his position as a member of the Commune because he had been a member of the clergy, a merchant and a secret agent. He had smuggled himself into the ranks of the National Guard during the siege of Paris and had sneaked into the Commune under a false name. The Commune deprived Cluseret of his position as a military delegate in view of the fact that "carelessness and negligence on the part of the military delegate nearly led to the loss of Fort Issy." Earlier, the traitor Lullier had also been dismissed and arrested by the Central Committee of the National Guard.

The Paris Commune also resolutely did away with all the privileges of state functionaries, and in the matter of salaries it made an important reform of historic significance.

We know that states ruled by the exploiting classes invariably offer their officials choice conditions and many privileges so as to turn them into overlords riding roughshod over the people. Sitting in their high positions, enjoying lucrative salaries and bullying the people—such is the picture of officials of the exploiting classes. Take the period of the French Second Empire: the annual salaries of officials were 30,000 francs for a deputy to the National Assembly; 50,000 francs for a minister; 100,000 francs for a member of the Privy Council; 130,000 francs for a Councillor of State. If someone held several official posts at the same time, he received multiple salaries. Rouher, for instance, a favorite of Napoleon III, was at once a deputy to the National Assembly, a member of the Privy Council and a Councillor of State. His yearly salary amounted to 260,000 francs. A skilled Parisian worker would have to work 150 years to earn this amount. As for Napoleon III himself, the state treasury gave him 25 million francs a year; with other state subventions, he had a yearly income of 30 million.

The French proletariat detested this order of things. Even before the founding of the Paris Commune, it demanded on many occasions that the system of high salaries for officials be abolished. With the founding of the Commune, this long-time wish of the working people was realized. On April 1, the famous decree was issued that the highest annual salary paid to any functionary should not exceed 6,000 francs. The decree stated: Before, "the higher posts in public institutions, thanks to the high salaries attached to them, were the object of solicitation and given out as a matter of patronage." But "there should be no place for either sinecures or high salaries in a truly democratic republic." This sum of 6,000 francs was equivalent to the wage of a skilled French worker at the time. According to the eminent scientist Huxley, it was just a little less than a fifth of what a secretary to the London metropolitan school board received.

The Paris Commune forbade its functionaries from getting paid for multiple posts, and the decision of May 19 said: "Considering that under the system of the Commune, the remuneration attached to each official post must be sufficient to maintain the well-being and dignity of the one who carries out its functions ... the Commune resolves: It is forbidden to give any extra remuneration for functioning in more than one post; officials of the Commune, who are called upon to serve in other capacities in addition to their usual one, have no right to any new remuneration."

At the same time as the Commune abolished high salaries and forbade salaries for multiple posts, it also raised the lower salaries so as to narrow the gap in the salary scale. Take the post office for example: the wages of the low-salaried employees were raised from 800 francs to 1,200 francs a year, an increase of 50 per cent, while the high salaries of an annual 12,000 francs were cut by half, to 6,000. In order to ensure the livelihood of low-salaried personnel, the Commune also forbade by express provision all monetary deductions and fines.

Members of the Commune were models in carrying out its regulations regarding the abolition of privileges, high salaries and multiple salaries for those occupying several posts. Theisz, a member of the Commune in charge of the post office, should have received a monthly salary of 500 francs according to regulations, but he would agree to take only 450. General Wroblewski of the Commune voluntarily gave up his officer's pay and refused to move to the apartment offered him at the Elysée Palace. He declared: "A general's place is with the troops."

The Executive Committee of the Paris Commune also passed a resolution abolishing the rank of general. In its April 6 resolution, the committee said: "In view of the fact that the rank of general is incompatible with the principles of democratic organization of the National Guard ... it is decided: the rank of general is abolished." It is a pity that this decision failed to be carried out in practice.

The leaders of the state received wages which were equivalent to that of a skilled worker; they had the obligation to do more work but no right to receive more pay, still less to enjoy any privileges. This was an unprecedented thing. It truly translated into reality the catchword of "cheap government"; it removed the aura of "mystery" and "particularity" from the so-called conduct of state affairs—a means employed by the exploiting classes to fool the people. It turned the conduct of state affairs simply into one of a worker's duties and transformed functionaries into workers operating "special tools." But its great significance lay not only in this. In the matter of material rewards, it created conditions for preventing the degeneration of functionaries. Lenin said, "This, combined with the principle of elective office and displaceability of all public officers, with payment for their work according to proletarian, not 'master-class,' bourgeois standards, is the ideal of the working class." He added, "The abolition of all representation allowances, and of all monetary privileges to officials, the reduction of the remuneration of *all* servants of the state to the level of '*workmen's wages.*' This shows more clearly than anything else the *turn* from bourgeois to proletarian democracy, from the democracy of the oppressors to that of the oppressed classes, from the state as a '*special force*' for the suppression of a particular class to the suppression of the oppressors by the *general force* of the majority of the people—the workers and the peasants. And it is on this particularly striking point, perhaps the most important as far as the problem of the state is concerned, that the ideas of Marx have been most completely ignored! ... The thing done is to keep silent about it as if it were a piece of old-fashioned 'naïveté.' "

And this is exactly what the leading clique of Khrushchev revisionists has done: They have completely ignored this important experience of the Paris Commune. They chase after privileges, make use of their privileged status, turn public activities into opportunities for personal gain, appropriate the fruits of the people's labor and receive incomes that are tens of times, or even over a hundred times, greater than the wages of ordinary workers and peasants. From political standpoint to mode of living, these people have turned their backs on the working people and imitated what the bourgeoisie and the bureaucrat-capitalists do. In an attempt to strengthen the social basis of their rule they also use high salaries, high awards, high fees and stipends and other diverse methods of making money to raise up a highly paid and privileged stratum. In an attempt to corrode with money the revolutionary will of the people, they talk wildly about "material incentives," saying that rubles are "powerful locomotives," and that they should "use rubles to educate people." Compare the Khrushchev revisionists' activities with the "naïveté," as they see it, of the Paris Commune and one can see clearly what is meant by servants of the people and masters of the people, what is meant by state organs being turned from servants of society into masters of society. "Do you want to know what this dictatorship looks like?" Engels wrote. "Look at the Paris Commune. That was the Dictatorship of the Proletariat." Similarly, we can say: Do you want to know what a degenerated dictatorship of the proletariat looks like? Then look at the "state of the whole people" of the Soviet Union under the rule of the Khrushchev revisionist clique.

The Proletariat Should Be on Guard Against the Enemy's Phony Peace Negotiations While He Is Really Preparing for War, and Employ Revolutionary Dual Tactics to Deal with Counter-Revolutionary Dual Tactics

The Paris Commune bequeathed us great and inspiring lessons. Many are positively valuable; others offer the lessons of bitter experience.

Leadership of the Commune was shared by the Blanquists and Proudhonists. Neither were revolutionary parties of the proletariat. Neither understood Marxism or had experience in leading the proletarian revolution. Impelled forward by the proletariat, they did certain things correctly, but because of their lack of political consciousness they also committed many mistakes. One of the chief of these was that they fell victim to the enemy's peace negotiations fraud while he was really preparing for war. They had the enemy pinned to the wall but they failed to press home their victorious attack and wipe him out. They let the enemy gain a breathing space under cover of his sham peace negotiations and in that time he was able to reorganize his forces for a counterattack. They had the chance to expand their revolutionary victory, but they let it slip through their fingers. . . .

While Versailles was sharpening its knives, Paris was casting votes; while Versailles was preparing for war, Paris was holding talks. The result was that the Versailles banditti with their butchers' knives entered Paris. They shot captured Commune members and soldiers; they shot refugees who sought sanctuary in churches; they shot wounded soldiers in hospitals; they shot elderly workers, saying that these people had caused repeated uprisings and were hardened criminals; they shot women workers, saying that they were "women incendiaries," and that they resembled women only "when they are dead"; they shot child workers, saying that "they'll grow up into insurgents." This carnage which they called "hunting" lasted throughout June. Paris was filled with corpses, the Seine was a river of blood and the Commune was drowned in this sea of blood. More than 30,000 people were massacred and over 100,000 people were incarcerated or forced into exile. This was the return Versailles gave Paris for her "benevolence" and "magnanimity." This was how it ended its trick of false peace talks and real war preparations. This was a bitter lesson written in blood. It teaches us that the proletariat must carry the revolution through to the end; that fleeing bandits must be pursued and destroyed, that drowning rats must be beaten to death; that the enemy must not be given a chance to regain his breath.

If it can be said that ninety-five years ago, most of the members of the Paris Commune failed in time to see through Thiers' plot of fake peace talks and real war preparations, and that this was mainly because of lack of sufficient experience and understanding, then today, when the Khrushchev revisionists are doing everything they can to serve U.S. imperialism's fake peace and real aggression, it is certainly not a matter of lack of understanding. The Khrushchev revisionists have gone over completely to a renegade position and are collaborating with the U.S. imperialists in the attempt to strangle the revolutionary movement of the proletariat and the national-liberation movement by counter-revolutionary dual tactics. However, the times are progressing, people are progressing, and the revolution is progressing. The revolutionary people are learning better and better how to use revolutionary dual tactics to oppose counter-revolutionary dual tactics, and how to carry the revolution through to the end. The imperialists, revisionists and all reactionaries together with all their varieties of counter-revolutionary dual tactics will finally be thrown by the people into the garbage bin of history lock, stock and barrel.

Commemorating the twenty-first anniversary of the Paris Commune, Engels wrote: "Let the bourgeoisie celebrate their 14th of July or their 22nd of September. The festival of the proletariat everywhere will always be March 18."

Today, as we mark the festival of the proletariat—the ninety-fifth anniversary of the Paris Commune uprising—a look at the world shows a great revolutionary situation where "The Four Seas are rising, clouds and waters raging; The Five Continents are rocking, wind and thunder roaring." History has fully borne out the prediction Marx made ninety-five years ago when he said: "But even if the Commune is crushed, the struggle will only be postponed. The principles of the Commune are eternal and cannot be destroyed; they will declare themselves again and again until the working class achieves its liberation." "The Paris Commune may fall, but the Social Revolution it has initiated, will triumph. Its birth-stead is everywhere."

PEOPLE'S DAILY*
Revolutionary Committees Are Fine

The spring breeze of Mao Tse-tung's thought has reached every corner of our motherland. The revolutionary committees which have come into being one after another stand like red flags fly-

* Peking Review, No. 14 (April 5, 1968), pp. 6–7 (translated from People's Daily, March 30, 1968).

ing in the wind. To date, revolutionary committees have been established in seventeen provinces and municipalities and in one autonomous region. More are in the preparatory stage in other areas. Vast numbers of units at the grass-root levels have set up their own revolutionary committees. This is a significant indication of the fact that the situation in the great proletarian cultural revolution is excellent and is getting even better. This is a magnificent act in the struggle for all-round victory in this revolution.

When the newborn revolutionary committees appeared on the eastern horizon a year ago, our revered and beloved leader Chairman Mao, with his great proletarian revolutionary genius, pointed out with foresight: **"In every place or unit where power must be seized, it is necessary to carry out the policy of the revolutionary 'three-in-one' combination in establishing a provisional organ of power which is revolutionary and representative and enjoys proletarian authority. This organ of power should preferably be called the Revolutionary Committee."**

Our great leader Chairman Mao again recently pointed out: **"The basic experience of revolutionary committees is this— they are threefold: they have representatives of revolutionary cadres, representatives of the armed forces and representatives of the revolutionary masses. This forms a revolutionary 'three-in-one' combination. The revolutionary committee should exercise unified leadership, do away with redundant or overlapping administrative structures, have 'better troops and simpler administration' and organize a revolutionized leading group which is linked with the masses."** Chairman Mao's brilliant directive sums up the experience of revolutionary committees at all levels and gives the basic orientation for building revolutionary committees.

The "three-in-one" revolutionary committee is a creation of the working class and the masses in the current great cultural revolution. Chairman Mao teaches: **"We must have faith in and rely on the masses, the People's Liberation Army and the majority of the cadres."** The "three-in-one" revolutionary committee is the organ which organizationally knits closely together the three sides pointed out by Chairman Mao after having summed up the experience of the masses, so as more effectively to meet the needs of the socialist economic base and the needs of consolidating the dictatorship of the proletariat and preventing the restoration of capitalism.

The "three-in-one" revolutionary committee is a great creation of the hundreds of millions of the revolutionary masses that appeared in the course of their struggle to seize power from the handful of Party people in authority taking the capitalist road. It has shown enormous vitality in leading the proletariat and the revolutionary masses in the fight against the class enemy over the past year and more.

This "three-in-one" organ of power enables our proletarian political power to strike deep roots among the masses. Chairman Mao points out: **"The most fundamental principle in the reform of state organs is that they must keep in contact with the masses."** The representatives of the revolutionary masses, particularly the representatives of the working people—the workers and peasants—who have come forward en masse in the course of the great proletarian cultural revolution are revolutionary fighters with practical experience. Representing the interests of the revolutionary masses, they participate in the leading groups at various levels. This provides the revolutionary committees at these levels with a broad mass foundation. Direct participation by the revolutionary masses in the running of the country and the enforcement of revolutionary supervision from below over the organs of political power at various levels play a very important role in ensuring that our leading groups at all levels always adhere to the mass line, maintain the closest relations with the masses, represent their interests at all times and serve the people heart and soul.

This "three-in-one" organ of power strengthens the dictatorship of the proletariat. **"If the army and the people are united as one, who in the world can match them?"** The great Chinese People's Liberation Army is the main pillar of the dictatorship of the proletariat and a Great Wall of steel defending the socialist motherland. The revolutionary "three-in-one" combination carries our army-civilian unity to a completely new stage. In its work of helping the Left, helping industry and agriculture, exercising military control and giving military and political training, the People's Liberation Army has made big contributions over the past year and more and has been well steeled in the process. As a result of the direct participation of P.L.A.

representatives in the work of the provisional organs of power at all levels, our dictatorship of the proletariat is better able to withstand storm and stress, better able to smash the intrigues by any enemy, whether domestic or foreign, and play a more powerful role in the cause of socialist revolution and socialist construction.

Revolutionary leading cadres are the backbone of the "three-in-one" organs of power. They have rich experience in class struggle and are a valuable asset to the Party and people. By going through the severe test of the great proletarian cultural revolution and receiving education and help from the masses, they were touched to the soul and remolded their world outlook further. The combination of the revolutionary leading cadres and representatives of the P.L.A. and of the revolutionary masses in the revolutionary committees makes them better able to carry out Chairman Mao's proletarian revolutionary line, grasp and implement the Party's policies, and correctly organize and lead the masses forward. At the same time, veteran cadres and young new cadres work together in the revolutionary committees, learn from each other and help each other so that, as Chairman Mao teaches, **the veterans are not divorced from the masses and the young people are tempered.** Organizationally, this guarantees the work of training successors to the proletarian revolutionary cause.

This "three-in-one" organ of power has absolutely nothing in common with the overstaffed bureaucratic apparatus of the exploiting classes in the old days. It has an entirely new and revolutionary style of work of its own and it functions in a way which is beneficial to the people. The "three-in-one" revolutionary leading body brings together the P.L.A. "three-eight" working style,* the laboring people's hard-working spirit and our Party's fine tradition of maintaining close contact with the masses. **"Remain one of the common people while serving as an official."** Maintain **"better troops and simpler administra-**

---

* The Chinese People's Liberation Army, under the leadership of Chairman Mao, has fostered a fine tradition. This fine tradition is summed up by Chairman Mao in three phrases and eight additional characters, meaning firm, correct political orientation; a plain, hard-working style; flexibility in strategy and tactics; and unity, alertness, earnestness and liveliness.

tion," and drastically reform old methods of office and administrative work. Have a small leading body and a small staff, as certain revolutionary committees have begun doing, so that there is no overlapping or redundancy in the organization and no overstaffing, so that bureaucracy can be prevented. In this way, the style of hard work, plain living and economy is fostered, corrosion by bourgeois ideology is precluded; and the revolutionary committee becomes a compact and powerful fighting headquarters which puts proletarian politics to the fore and is full of revolutionary enthusiasm and capable of taking prompt and resolute action.

In order to become genuinely revolutionary headquarters with proletarian revolutionary authority, the revolutionary committees should hold fast to the general orientation for the struggle, consistently direct the spearhead of attack against China's Khrushchev and the handful of other top Party persons in authority taking the capitalist road and their agents, distinguish the contradictions between ourselves and the enemy from contradictions among the people, carry on revolutionary mass criticism and repudiation, continue to consolidate and develop the revolutionary great alliance and the revolutionary "three-in-one" combination and constantly sum up experience and draw lessons. It is precisely in the storm of class struggle that the revolutionary committees in many places are being consolidated.

Of all the good things characterizing the revolutionary committees, the most fundamental is the creative study and application of the thought of Mao Tse-tung and the doing of this well. Revolutionary committee members are outstanding P.L.A. commanders and fighters, revolutionary leading cadres and representatives of the revolutionary masses who have been assessed and selected by the broad masses in the course of the struggle. The highest demand which they put upon themselves is to be loyal to Chairman Mao, to the thought of Mao Tse-tung and to Chairman Mao's proletarian revolutionary line. We hope that all the leading members of the revolutionary committees will continue to regard studying, carrying out, spreading and defending Chairman Mao's instructions as their most sacred duty. The revolutionary committees should see to it that Chairman Mao's instructions are transmitted most promptly and accurately so that the masses of workers, peasants and soldiers are imbued with the thought of Mao Tse-tung, and so that it is translated into the conscious action of the masses and becomes an inexhaustible source of strength in transforming the world.

The revolutionary committee is something new which has emerged in the course of the revolutionary mass movement and it is continuing to develop. It should be cherished and supported by all revolutionary comrades. As for the shortcomings and mistakes which are inevitable in the course of its growth, we should make well-intentioned criticism so as to help it keep on making progress and improving. It is necessary to be on guard against and expose plots by the class enemy to shake and subvert the revolutionary committees either from the Right or the extreme "Left." All personnel of the revolutionary committees should resolutely implement Chairman Mao's proletarian revolutionary line, carry out his latest instructions in an exemplary way, make strict demands on themselves, have a correct attitude to themselves and to the masses, conduct constant criticism and self-criticism and pay the closest attention to wiping out any vestige of being divorced from the masses.

The revolutionary "three-in-one" provisional organs of power which have sprung up all over the country will lead the proletariat and the revolutionary masses in establishing proletarian authority and in playing a vital revolutionary role in the momentous struggle to win all-round victory in the great proletarian cultural revolution.

★   ★   ★   ★   ★

4. EDUCATION

The great debate over education during the Cultural Revolution, although wider in scope than earlier discussions, was nothing new for the People's Republic of China. Disagreement over educational policy was closely tied to the debate over economic policy, and as such, had been part of a "two-line struggle" since the 1950's.

In 1949 the Chinese Communists faced many new tasks (banking, for example), but education was an area in which they had had considerable experience. The Yenan model of the 1940's—specifically the experience of K'ang Ta, the Communist university of the liberated areas—was to many, Mao Tse-tung in particular, the touchstone of what socialist education should be. The governing principles of K'ang Ta were to combine labor and study, theory and practice, thus uniting mental and physical labor to create a new type of cultured worker and soldier. The schools of the Yenan type produced their own food, tools, clothes, and housing, and refined the Red Army technique of "officers teaching soldiers, soldiers teaching officers, and soldiers teaching each other."

The First National Educational Work Conference of December 1949 stated that "the education of New China should use the educational experiences of the old liberated areas, should absorb the useful experience of the old education, and should make use of the experience of the Soviet Union." By the mid-fifties, however, full-scale emulation of the Soviet educational system was the dominant trend. Political education and student participation in physical labor were reduced or eliminated for intensive academic study, the end result of which would be the creation of a technological elite through specialized education —the foundation, in essence, of the Soviet strategy for economic development.

During the late fifties and early sixties, Mao put forth a number of counterproposals, recommending the reduction of academic courses, the use of locally prepared and relevant teaching materials, the introduction of a shortened five-year primary system, and diversified schools run by the local communities. Thus, on the eve of the Cultural Revolution, there were in China both the Soviet-style schools and the Mao experiments, and in addition, traditional methods and materials remaining not only from the Kuomintang period, but also from the ancient and tenacious Confucian heritage. In 1968 a Chinese educator said to us, "Our school system has been a mishmash of Confucianism, Deweyism and Sovietism." The widespread charges of elitism circulating during the Cultural Revolution, however, were evidence that narrow academic specialization was the prevailing tendency.

In her article, Marianne Bastid discusses the criticisms raised against the dominant system of education, focusing both on problems of elitism and capacity. Overspecialization, it seemed, was not merely producing a privileged class of specialists, but specialists too narrowly trained to serve the interests of a country whose main occupation was still a widely diversified agriculture. Ms. Bastid describes many of the events of the Cultural Revolution which centered around questions of education, and some of the results of that historic movement. She quotes from Mao Tse-tung's "directive" of July 1968 on the reform of colleges of science and engineering, in which he calls on them to "take the road of the Shanghai machine-tools plant in training technicians from the workers and peasants with practical experience . . . who should return to production after a few years of study." We include here from the *People's Daily* a report on the Shanghai plant which was taken as a model and studied throughout China. Although it is still difficult to know how many of the educational reforms suggested by the Cultural Revolution have been incorporated into the present educational system, it is clear that this model for the training of technical personnel is by now well-established.

Marianne Bastid discusses the peasants' dissatisfaction with the highly structured state-controlled rural schools. Demands for primary schools designed to deal flexibly with local problems of seasonal work patterns, family responsibilities, geographical location, and relevance of teaching materials resulted in much rural experimentation during the Cultural Revolution. The *Red Flag* article on the Sungshu Primary School demonstrates how one production brigade in a mountainous area of southern Liaoning took over the running of their schools in accordance with their own needs. Now, "There are no classrooms," they state. "Instead, heated mud and brick beds in the brigade members' houses, thatched sheds of the production teams, smithies and places under trees and on the banks of a stream are all . . . classrooms."

In the cities, changes have not been so dramatic, for the problems were not so acute. One of the major complaints of the peasants was that village schools had been modeled too rigidly on urban schools. The most significant change in urban primary and secondary schools seems to be the closer relationship with local factories and an increased stress on practical work. Tillman Durdin writes of his visits to schools in major cities and of what has changed and what has remained the same.

The final selection is a theoretical article from the *People's Daily* of October 1972 dealing with the question so fiercely debated in the course of the Cultural Revolution—that is, the correct relationship between politics and vocational work. Politics for the Chinese is used very broadly to mean questions of ideology, social morality, and correct social relationships. The article is a clear and unrhetorical summary of much of the impassioned experimentation of the preceding periods, and discusses the inadequacies of "the teaching of pure knowledge" on the one hand, and "politics may overrule anything else" on the other.

It is impossible to state definitively which aspects of China's educational reform are likely to remain. The same questions which have been debated throughout the last few decades will no doubt be raised again, for the difficulties of maintaining a system which is both "red" and "expert" are not small ones, particularly as China's initial industrialization expands. As the final article indicates, however, the experience of the Cultural Revolution has brought about a widespread awareness of the pitfalls of both extremes of the contradiction and a heightened sophistication in dealing with them.

★   ★   ★

MARIANNE BASTID*
Economic Necessity and Political Ideals in Educational Reform During the Cultural Revolution

Educational reform has been one of the important issues raised during the Cultural Revolution, not merely because it belongs to the realm of culture but, more important, because it bears on the question of "cultivating revolutionary successors" and on the shaping of the whole future of China. . . .

CRITICISM AGAINST THE OLD SYSTEM OF EDUCATION

The "old" educational system under attack was essentially the system as it existed in 1965. Criticism against it was launched at the very beginning of the Great Proletarian Cultural Revolution in June 1966. . . . They come under three headings: the inadequacy of school enrollment; the contents and methods of education; and the general orientation of the old system, dealing with who goes to school, what is taught at school and what the schools are intended for.

The main criticism against the inadequacy of school enrollment was that children from poor and lower-middle peasant families were barred from the greater part of the educational ladder. Ostracism of workers' children occurred, it seems, only at the middle school, college and university level. The direct responsibility for the exclusion of those children has been imputed first to various institutional features of the schools, such as the examination system and age limits. The entrance examination to middle schools and universities is a subject of

* *China Quarterly*, No. 42 (April–June 1970), pp. 16–30, 34–45.

major concern in towns. The entrance examination to primary school was a feature of well-known or special institutions in urban areas but it existed also for some schools in the countryside, and the injustice of the system has been severely attacked. But peasants were more concerned about the rules on age limits, which excluded a lot of youngsters from elementary or advanced educational opportunities, and about the promotion examinations, which eliminated a number of "slow" children, most of them sons and daughters of the poorest. Actually it is the marks system with its corollaries of promotion and repeating that has come under the fiercest, steadiest and most united attack, as the key stratagem which excluded children of the working class. The marks system has been attacked on ideological grounds. It is pointed out that this system puts intellectual culture, self-interest and advancement above anything else, thus endangering socialism. However, the theoretical foundation of this system—the underlying assumption that it is possible to measure accurately the value of an individual and place it on a scale—has hardly been analyzed and questioned. In fact, the complaints against the marks system are basically economic: the existence of tuition fees makes the matter crucial. In every report from the countryside, it is stressed that children from poor and lower-middle peasant families simply cannot afford to repeat a class, something which is almost inevitable with the marks system. This grievance is thus related to the general complaint against tuition fees and the cost of education, which are viewed by a majority of peasants as a clear discrimination against their children. While this issue is often omitted in reports from the cities, it is always raised in those from rural areas, and in a number of cases it is the first charge against the old system. A common additional charge is that the school is located too far away, so that the children cannot get there on foot, while their families cannot afford to pay boarding fees. . . .

Criticisms of the contents and methods of education stress the length of studies, the heavy curriculum, the bookishness, and the abstruse and smothering character of the teaching with its emphasis on cramming and memorizing. The six-year primary and the six-year secondary courses are said to be excessive, especially since much of what is taught is superfluous and over-elaborate. Staggering under heavy homework, students are said to rise early and go to sleep late. They stay indoors, ruining their health or becoming short-sighted. Tied down to books, they stagger from concept to concept and lose all real power of analysis. The prominence given to academic culture leaves no time for politics and, above all, no time for the study of the thought of Mao Tse-tung. . . .

On the key issue of the general orientation of the educational system, two different accusations are put forward. One is the charge of cultivating an elite. The system, it is claimed, fostered a promotion-conscious mentality. Liu Shao-ch'i is charged with having spread the reactionary tenet "to study in order to become a mandarin." As the Yenan middle school in Tientsin put it:

> In the revisionist view . . . the aim should be to cultivate people capable of serving as cadres, engineers, *hsien* magistrates and even secretaries of provincial committees, that is to cultivate parasites and revisionist seedlings divorced from the practice of the Three Great Revolutions, class struggle, struggle for production and scientific experience.

Another report said:

> Bourgeois say: if graduates just become ordinary workers, what is the use of having colleges? They declare that their purpose in running universities is to turn out highly trained "experts," such as scientists, engineers, lawyers, economists, administrators, whom they regard as the "elite" of society, superior to the working people.
>
> The bourgeois system serves to maintain the rule of the capitalist class over the working people and make science, technology and arts its monopoly.
>
> China is a state where the working people are the masters; it is inconceivable that the working class should run colleges to turn out people who look down upon physical labor and the laboring people. Of course the working class requires its own intellectuals who master science, technology and other knowledge, but in the first place, schools and colleges should turn out true revolutionaries who are faithful to the cause of the working class and who always remain one with the working people. . . .
>
> The Soviet Union provides a lesson: its universities pro-

duce a privileged stratum of bourgeois intellectuals who are the "elite" of society sitting on the backs of the working people. . . .

The issue at stake is that of producing people who gain a higher status through education and consequently feel and behave as superiors.

The other charge, which is uttered by different people, does not focus on elitism but on capacity. It could be summed up thus: the old system turns out an elite which is incompetent and useless. Peasants say: "The more they go to school, the more stupid they become." There is a whole folklore of racy anecdotes featuring the palefaced, thin, dogmatic, dissatisfied graduate versus the quick-minded, efficient, hard-toiling, open-hearted "local expert," who spent a short time in a less sophisticated school but grasps better the thought of Mao Tse-tung. He cannot grow Michurin apples or Caucasian maize, but he knows all about rice and wheat; he works himself instead of giving orders; he listens to the villagers and helps them.

In cities and towns, protests are mainly against the notion of "elite" itself. This accounts for the radicalism of some reform proposals which suggested nothing less than the wholesale abolition of schools. Although these proposals were dismissed later on as "anarchist," they suggest a widespread sense of guilt, even of anti-intellectualism, among young Chinese intellectuals, not unlike some recent attitudes of their western brothers.

In rural areas the issue tends to focus rather on inefficiency, incapacity, waste of time, money and talent. Education is described as an investment which does not yield interest.

The criticism against the old educational system thus mixes up economic and political motives, with, however, the latter predominant. These political motives account for the deliberate darkening of the pre-1966 education picture, which is obvious to anyone who is acquainted with Chinese schools before the Cultural Revolution. By 1965, Chinese education was very far from being a mere copy of Soviet or American bourgeois education. As will be seen below, most of the educational experiments brought in by the Cultural Revolution had been tried under various forms in Yenan or during the Great Leap Forward, and not all of them had been discontinued. It would be a travesty of the facts to regard all Chinese students, or even teachers, prior to 1966 as a host of petty mandarins with their hands in their sleeves. In education, as in other matters, there has been a long struggle between the revolutionary line and the revisionist line, and according to many reports, the latter has not always prevailed. If the general critique against the educational system holds true, it must be understood as often being directed against mere intentions or tendencies. The picture is deliberately drawn in black colors, as is frequently the case in campaigns designed to arouse powerful reactions.

REFORM PROPOSALS

The number and variety of educational reform proposals show that powerful reactions were indeed aroused. From the Chinese press it can be seen that these reform proposals fall into four stages, following directives given from the top by Chairman Mao or the Central Committee.

Before February 1967, when the call to "resume classes to make revolution" was launched, few detailed reform projects appeared. Some tentative proposals were made in early June 1966 with the decision of the Central Committee on 13 June to reform the entrance examination and postpone admission to universities. But soon after those who made them were accused of revisionism and reformism. One of the charges brought against the work teams in early August was that they tried to divert the students from politics by asking them to discuss educational reform. Only guiding principles were given, incorporated in documents dealing with other questions. Such is the paragraph relating to students in the text where Chairman Mao calls on the country to become a big school of revolution and the tenth of the Sixteen Points, which is almost identical. The two texts ruled that the control of the bourgeoisie over the schools be ended, that the curriculum should be shortened and revolutionized, that students should also learn agriculture, industry and military science and that they should criticize the

114   PEOPLE'S CHINA

bourgeoisie. Greeted with enthusiasm, these directives helped to
intensify the attack against the old system and its supporters.
During this period, however, the focus was on general political
issues, and no proposal for the carrying out of the new pedagogical principles received publicity.

After the great revolutionary exchanges of the summer and
autumn of 1966, from 1 December, the Central Committee and
the State Council repeatedly called for students and teachers
to return to their schools. On 4 February 1967, the Central
Committee issued a draft regulation on the resumption of
courses in all primary schools after the Spring Festival, and on
19 February another document was issued for the middle
schools. On 7 March 1967, three important documents were
published. One was an editorial in the *People's Daily* entitled
"Primary and Middle Schools Resume Classes to Make Revolution." It called for the continuation of the Cultural Revolution
inside the schools, developing the criticism and struggle against
reactionaries by studying Chairman Mao's Quotations and the
Cultural Revolution documents, as well as some science and
language courses. This summons was ascribed to the Central
Committee, which also issued a circular entitled "Draft Regulations Governing The Great Proletarian Cultural Revolution
Currently Under Way in Universities, Colleges and Schools—
For Discussion and Trial Implementation." Everybody, it said,
should be back in their unit before 20 March and should
undergo short-term military and political training; leniency
should be shown, except to people in authority taking the
capitalist road and reactionary academic authorities; students
and teachers should unite and create an organ of power to
lead the Cultural Revolution; the Red Guards should be consolidated and rectified. The third document was a directive
from Chairman Mao. It was published by the *People's Daily*
only on 8 March 1968, although it was based on the experience
of the Yenan middle school in Tientsin, an account of which
appeared on 21 March 1967 in the *Tientsin jih-pao*. Its wording
has similarities to that of the Draft Regulations of the Central
Committee; to some it may seem only a later version of the
regulations, but the directive adds a very important point: the
role of the army—which had in fact intervened in the Yenan
middle school experience. It reads:

... The army should give political and military training in the
universities, middle schools and the higher classes of primary
schools, stage by stage and group by group. It should help in
reopening school classes, in strengthening the organization,
in establishing a leading organ of the three-in-one alliance
and in carrying out the task of struggle-criticism-transformation. It should first make experiments at selected points and
acquire experience and then popularize it step by step. . . .

The admonishments from the top left room for a fair amount
of initiative. The only obligation of the young people was to
get out of the streets and go back to school, an order which
many obeyed with reluctance. During this period, until the end
of October 1967, the reform proposals dealt mainly with the
organization of power within the schools. Experiments and
suggestions were made regarding the achievement of the Great
Alliance, whether on the basis of the various militant organizations inside the school or on that of the teaching classes. Some
further opinions were expressed on the setting up of school
revolutionary committees with the help and participation of the
People's Liberation Army.

In the heated political struggle of the spring and summer of
1967, educational change could not progress smoothly. A
"black wind of anarchism" blew everywhere. On 25 October
1967, the *People's Daily* had to reiterate more earnestly the
call to resume classes. This time, however, the editorial quoted
the paragraph relating to students in Chairman Mao's directive
of 7 May 1966:

> Students, while taking studies as the main task, should learn
> other things as well, namely, besides learning literature they
> must also learn industry, agriculture and military science,
> and they must also criticize the bourgeoisie. The duration of
> the course of study must be shortened and education must be
> revolutionized. The situation in which bourgeois intellectuals
> rule our schools cannot be allowed to continue.

This instruction sets the aims of the educational reform. The
editorial insisted that this reform could not be achieved without actually teaching and studying. It commented:

> . . . In the process of resuming classes to make revolution,
> teachers and cadres should constantly remind themselves that

the work in which they are engaged has a great bearing on the cultivation of successors to the proletarian revolution. They should have the courage and determination to thoroughly criticize the old educational system and completely break out of their own bourgeois world outlook. They should realize that they are both educators and educated and that their students are wiser than they in many respects. They must go to the students, mingle with them, establish a new socialist type of teacher-student relationship. . . .

The directive and the editorial are especially noteworthy on two points: one is the contents of education, the other one is the question of world outlook and attitude, particularly of teachers. As far as the contents are concerned, school-training should give young people several strings to their bows. In a way it amounts to a dismissal of the notion of *chuan*, usually translated as "expert." However, one should remember that *chuan* in Chinese does not mean "expert" or "skilled" so much as "specialized" in one single field. Dedication to the study of a narrow technique does not necessarily imply proficiency in its application. Peasants and workers mentioned hundreds of cases where highly trained personnel stumbled over technical problems which they themselves finally succeeded in solving by discarding the blind worship of dogmatic rules and principles. Besides, in China as elsewhere, employment planning is difficult. If young people cannot, and above all will not, do jobs which do not fall exactly within their special domain, the economic balance and progress might be endangered. Without a doubt, too many academic scientists and technicians have been trained in recent years. Not infrequently a university graduate in physics or chemistry would be found holding some desk job in a big city administrative office. This was due not only to bureaucratic aberrations. The fact was that the massive effort started in 1958 to enroll more students in the scientific departments had not been completely discontinued, while the rate of industrialization launched by the Great Leap Forward had been much slowed, and the basic orientation of education had moved from people's science to specialists' science. The countryside was in desperate need of more, and more professional, manpower, but new trainees were too learned, and equally too ignorant, to be of real use. At the same time, the already overstaffed urban industry could not absorb them all.

Versatile people were and still are needed, but versatile in concrete things. There is no idea of a reversion to the mandarin type of education—general abstract knowledge without expertise. The required study of industry, agriculture and military science, besides specialization in a particular subject, is to be understood as thoughtful work experience in those activities to familiarize the student with some of their basic principles. The value of such an education in a country where a rural economy prevails and remains largely nondifferentiated, is self-evident. It meets the criticism voiced by the villagers who want the hydraulic engineer sent to them to be able to tell rice from wheat in the fields, and to lend a hand in repairing a machine.

But the question is one of moral and mental attitude even more than of variety or practicality of the students' intellectual equipment. Young people must be accustomed to adapt themselves to any situation and make the best of it. They should be open-minded, perceptive and active. Their cardinal virtue ought to be intellectual humility. All this depends on the "proletarian world outlook" as opposed to the "bourgeois world outlook," which means serving the collective interests of the majority instead of the self-interest of an elite. The "bourgeois" scientist may show humility in front of his colleagues, in order to transcend them later on, but not in front of ordinary people. Experience in industry and agriculture at the basic level is meant to develop a proletarian world outlook in the students' minds, giving them not only a sense of reality and relativity useful to any intellectual worker, but also a personal feeling for society with its contradictions and struggles. Military instruction is intended to develop physical endurance, to teach some of the skills of the People's Liberation Army, and even more its spirit. Upon the transformation of the teacher himself lies much of the fate of revolutionary education, as it is he who sets a living example to his students and can influence them deeply. The intention is by no means to cultivate "political parrots," as spiteful critics word it—in any case Chairman Mao says that students must take studies as their main task. Neither is mystic idealism the aim, but real efficiency to achieve a rate of modernization which cannot be truly and fully brought about by revisionist bourgeois education.

The democratic basis of the educational revolution was stressed in an injunction from Mao broadcast on 2 November:

The proletarian revolution in education should be carried out by relying on the mass of revolutionary students, teachers and workers inside the schools, by relying on the activities among them, namely those proletarian revolutionaries who are determined to carry the Great Proletarian Cultural Revolution through to the end.

The late October and early November 1967 directives stirred up new reform proposals focusing on the general organization of school work. Several tendencies appeared. One was to suggest rebuilding the school like an army with its battalions and companies, minutely scheduled periods of drill, study and productive work, military virtues and discipline. The teacher should play the role of an ordinary soldier among the pupils and, like a company cadre in the army, should make revolution and work together with the pupils. Another trend rejected compulsory methods and showed a strong reluctance to rebuild a system. As a group from Peking Normal University put it:

> From the bourgeois point of view, system means authority and compulsory methods should be adopted to make pupils study. From the proletarian point of view, the human factor and politico-ideological work come first while system is secondary and auxiliary. Only by arousing people's initiative and consciousness is it possible to teach and study well.

Along these principles the practice of promotion and repeating could be abolished. Instead of an entrance examination, one could combine recommendation with selection. Spare-time school students would be admitted to higher institutions, without age limit, and eventually in another than the first year. The curriculum should be flexible.

Others, flaunting the banner of "to rebel is justified," maintained that to resume classes to make revolution was "slave-mentality," the 7 March directive being "patchy reformism, not revolution but reaction." The great alliance they called the "big hodge-podge," and the three-in-one combination the "three-in-one conglomeration." Criticism and repudiation of the revisionist line, they said, were divorced from class struggle, disregarded state affairs and had nothing in common with the rebels. Schools, and especially universities, should be abolished;

students and teachers would be distributed among communes and factories.

Judging by the relentless criticism against them, these last opinions, which were branded as anarchist, seem to have been fairly widespread. This fact partly accounts for the stress on military example and discipline, particularly from March 1968 on, as well as for the call on the workers and peasants to help reform teaching and do the ideological work. While enforcing discipline, however, a careful attempt was made to point out the difference between "proletarian discipline" and the "organization discipline" of the bourgeoisie, the former being one willingly accepted and consciously obeyed. Participation of workers and peasants in school affairs remained informal except in a few places, but the idea of unceasingly seeking their advice on educational matters, and entrusting them with the leadership of students' and teachers' manual labor and ideological transformation was put forward as a way of abiding by Chairman Mao's directives.

The fourth stage in the reform projects started in late July 1968, and soon brought to the fore the rural schools. On 22 July 1968, the *People's Daily* published a "recent" directive from Chairman Mao:

> It is *still* necessary to have universities; here I refer mainly to colleges of science and engineering. However, it is essential to shorten the length of schooling, revolutionize education, put proletarian politics in command and take the road of the Shanghai machine-tools plant in training technicians from among the workers and peasants with practical experience and who should return to production after a few years of study.

This statement settled the upper level of the new fabric. It put an end to disputes on the expediency of running institutions of higher education. The Shanghai machine-tools plant experience showed that engineers and technicians directly promoted from among workers with practical experience were more efficient than university graduates. Their training was faster and therefore cost less. They were generally more progressive, more concerned with common interest, less tied down by pride and prejudice. Consequently, the plant staff suggested that, while continuing the practice of promoting technicians directly from among the workers, young workers who had graduated from lower or higher middle school and who had two to five years' experience of work should be selected to study in the universities and colleges. University graduates should never be immediately appointed as cadres but serve first as ordinary workers, to get a "certificate of ability" from the peasants and workers. Later on, according to practical needs, some might take part in technical work while still doing fixed periods of manual work, others continuing to be workers and peasants. Though stressing the shortcomings of university graduates, the Shanghai machine-tools plant report was far less harsh about formal education than many other documents. There was no suggestion that the direct promotion of workers was the best possible method for getting technicians. Light and shade was introduced into the text itself by the use of such expressions as "relatively," "rather more," "generally." The report ushered in the rehabilitation of basic theoretical studies which by this time were supported also by the first workers' propaganda teams sent to the school.

Very soon, however, attention was transferred from the upper level of the educational system to its base, as it would have been difficult to build a new system from the top down. In his article "The working class must exercise leadership in everything," published on 25 August, Yao Wen-yuan conveyed three "recent" directives from Chairman Mao, one of which applied especially to education:

> In carrying out the proletarian revolution in education it is essential to have working-class leadership; it is essential for the masses of workers to take part and, in cooperation with Liberation Army fighters, bring about a revolutionary "three-in-one" combination, together with the activists among the students, teachers and workers in the schools who are determined to carry the proletarian revolution through to the end. The workers' propaganda teams should stay permanently in the schools and take part in fulfilling all the tasks of struggle-criticism-transformation in the schools, and they will always lead the schools. In the countryside, the schools should be managed by the poor and lower-middle peasants—the most reliable ally of the working class.

Immediately an increasing number of reports came out on rural schools run by brigades. On 14 October the *Red Flag* stated:

> It seems that it is quite possible that the rural areas can realize more speedily than the cities Chairman Mao's thinking on the proletarian revolution in education. This is because the superiority of the poor and lower-middle peasants can be established more easily in the schools there. It offers new proof of the pressing need to send Mao Tse-tung propaganda teams of workers, with fighters of the People's Liberation Army participating, to the schools in the cities.

The importance of these documents of the summer 1968 lies in the fact that they keep the idea of a whole system of schools as a distinct institution performing a definite task in the state, and that they suggest a new type of leadership in education. Consequently, a number of specific reform proposals sprang up, relating to every aspect of the educational system: curriculum, leadership inside the school, links of the school with the society and the state. Comparatively few of these projects relate to institutions of higher learning. There were, however, suggestions about moving the technical colleges to the places for which they were supposed to train people—agriculture institutes to the countryside, polytechnical institutes to the factories —and integrating them with *collective* production. Instead of working together in a separate workshop or field (as was generally the case previously during the manual work period), or even on the school grounds, the students would be scattered among ordinary workers and share their regular work. Others insisted, on the contrary, that the right solution was that each department or institute should establish its own factory, as in 1958. As to the departments of humanities, one finds little more than general statements that they must be integrated with society. . . .

From abstract general concepts the educational reform proposals have thus developed towards very practical measures, the main features of which are to give control of the schools to those who are going to use their products, and to make these products fit for the service expected of them. It should be pointed out how far this approach is from the idea of "student power" as it appeared in the youth revolt in other countries. In China, students have certainly won through the Cultural Revolution the right to express their opinion; they are represented on the schools' revolutionary committees. But it has been felt that to substitute student authority for the authority of teachers and cadres is nothing more than to replace an older elite by a younger elite: it runs against the very principles of socialist revolution. . . .

IMPLEMENTATION OF REFORM

The situation appears to be very different in the cities and in the countryside. Although all city schools interrupted their courses, this was not such a general phenomenon in the countryside. In the cities, army teams entered the schools in February and March 1967, and the workers' propaganda teams came in from the end of July 1968. There was no such uniformity in the villages: soldiers were stationed in an extremely limited number of schools, at very variable dates: workers scarcely came in, except in special cases, such as suburban commune schools; the seizure of power in schools by peasants took place sometimes as early as March 1967, sometimes as late as September 1969. Besides, people in the countryside know what they need. It is far less clear in the cities. It is not by accident that no draft regulations have yet come out for urban schools. Of course the urban schools can train people according to the needs of the countryside, but are these needs exactly the same as those in the cities? Should the very sophisticated schools which existed in Peking, Shanghai, Tientsin, Nanking and Canton be abolished? On the other hand, if urban schools train urban personnel and are only linked with factories or city organizations, will this not perpetuate the tendency of towns to specialize in industry, and the differences between town and country?

The implementation of educational reform displays a very wide local variety. As it was of precisely excessive standardization that the old system was accused, there has been no preordained plan uniformly applied. Experiments are conducted at various points; their results are used in some of the reform proposals; interpreted and adapted, they are also the starting point of new experiments in other communities. This sensible approach is a current method in Communist China, it bears the authority of Chairman Mao's theory of knowledge and practice, and was again advocated by him for use in education in his directive of 7 March 1967. . . .

Rather than describing how the few schools for which we have extensive data have carried out the Cultural Revolution, it seems better for the purpose of this discussion to pass over the details of the power struggle inside the various institutions and point out only, from a wider number of sources, the general features of the educational achievement of the Cultural Revolution.

In the administrative reorganization of the schools, no effort has been spared to do away with any independent staff specializing in educational management, and to reduce as far as possible the number of full-time teachers. A Lanchow middle school, for example, had 59 teachers before the Cultural Revolution; 24 have been retained part-time; among the new teaching staff, made up by adding soldiers, workers and peasants, only four teach full-time, all of them veteran workers. Where no such radical solution could be applied, in order to prevent the remaining full-time teachers from forming any kind of bureaucratic organization or specialized group, they are blended with other elements, namely workers, peasants and soldiers who keep a foot in another reality outside the school walls. The school Party branch is scarcely mentioned. In one case, it was put under the leadership of the Party organization of the factory which managed the school. In another, members of the workers' propaganda team have entered the school Party organization. Large schools set up a revolutionary committee in which people from outside participate in a variable ratio. In cases when the school is run by a given community—factory, commune, neighborhood—some of those outside members belong to the community revolutionary committee concerned, which leads the school revolutionary committee. If the school is under the joint management of several communities, there might be above the school revolutionary committee, a leading body composed of representatives of the school and of the various organizations involved. As to very large institutions, such as universities, it is not yet clear how they are to be managed above the level of their own revolutionary committee. Small schools usually do not have a revolutionary committee but are managed by given communities. Sometimes they are directly under the community revolutionary committee concerned, which can appoint some of its members to deal with daily school problems, even to form an educational leading group from people inside and outside the school, while retaining supreme control. Sometimes people from the school staff are elected to join the community revolutionary committee. Sometimes the community appoints an educational revolutionary committee or leading group which is responsible for school matters. It is composed of a majority of people who keep their regular job in the community, and a few teachers and students.

Those steps break through a rigid concept of division of work, and put forward a new praxis for the management of state affairs—the necessity of an Education Ministry has even been questioned. Bureaucracy is replaced by something called the "leading group" (ling-tao pan-tzu). Lin Piao is mentioned as the father of the notion, with the following quotation: "The leading group is very important because it stands for political power." The leading group is composed of a diversified personnel whose members are noted for their dynamism and the trust put in them by others. It is still too early to know if and how the body is to be renewed. The important and new point at the moment is the idea of general initiative, responsibility and concern. Previously, initiative, responsibility and concern were in fact rather the monopoly of Party members; now they are entrusted and put forward as a duty to other people also. The change may mean a great deal for the countryside, where Party members were relatively scarce at the grass-root level. . . .

As far as the enrollment of students is concerned, there is no doubt that many children from poor families in rural areas have now been given the opportunity to receive some education. All kinds of arrangements are provided by the brigades: itinerant teachers, part-time schooling, new schools, abolition or reduction of tuition fees and no age limit. In some places the children can take to school their baby sisters or brothers and even the cows. A system of recommendation is widely applied for admission to middle schools, the size of which has often increased. Moreover, some rural schools take in educated youth for short-term training on special subjects. It seems that many of the city primary school graduates, who were unable to enter middle school, have been sent to the countryside. The same applies to middle school graduates. In July 1968 and July 1969, numerous articles praised those young people who left the cities to settle in villages. Once in the countryside, it seems that in some places these youths still get some kind of formal instruction. When they left, they knew they were going for several years; now the stress is on "being a peasant one's life long"; but it may well be that after a two- or three-year stay some of them will be selected for admission to the universities. As university courses are definitely going to be shortened to two or three years, and enrollment increased, there will probably be no fewer university graduates in 1972 than if college students had been regularly enrolled and had accomplished the five- or six-year course since 1966. As to the quality of the future graduates, it is worth pointing out that the long full-time course system has not given such outstanding results either in China or in other countries that the new system may not give better ones.

Anyway, the standards of "scholarly achievements" are altered as exemplified in the contents of the curriculum. Mao Tse-tung's thought is put first, which can account for both the diversity and common trends of the programs set up by individual schools. Furthermore, there are interpretations according to the spirit and interpretations according to the letter, with more or less emphasis on the exclusive use of Mao's writings as the textbook. In some places, characters are learned in the *Quotations*; language courses are taught on the basis of the *Three Well-known Essays*; each chapter, each paragraph of a mathematics course is introduced by an excerpt from Mao. Elsewhere, though Mao's writings are always the basic material of instruction, the balance is different. Political education is sought through regular meetings for criticizing and repudiating the revisionist line. Workers and poor peasants are invited to give lectures on class struggle. The general knowledge courses are linked to class struggle and production struggle. In arithmetic, the questions deal with exploitation in the old times and the yield of the fields. Fundamentals of physics and chemistry are taught on the basis of the experience of pupils with machines or fertilizers. They first learn the "how" by using the implements, then the "why" through lectures by their teacher. Students receive regular military training both in drill and discipline, from the PLA and the militia. Manual labor, with emphasis on agricultural work, is integrated into the curriculum. In rural schools and some factory schools, these activities are often run in order to reap a profit. But warnings are uttered against the danger of an excessively utilitarian and mechanistic conception: to do manual work does not teach industry; students must not be used as additional unqualified manpower. Some schools organize manual labor in a very enlightened way, both to help the students in mastering skills and knowledge, and to give them social experience and political consciousness by participating in collective tasks together with ordinary workers.

However, whatever may be the good will and conviction of workers, teachers and students, the regulation of manual labor depends much on material conditions. In many rural schools, the schedule is equally divided between manual labor and formal teaching. Some theoretical knowledge is taught, it is true, while working, and labor is intended to keep up the revolutionary spirit of the youth, but its high ratio is an economic necessity to support the school and enable poor children to attend it. At the other end of the scale, the low ratio— often a half-day a week—of manual labor in large city schools does not inevitably mean a lack of proletarian faith. First, these institutions can afford it: their financial situation and that of their pupils is not so difficult. Second, the very organization of urban economy compels these schools to reduce the proportion of manual labor: for the time being, Peking factories cannot accommodate all the city pupils and students half-time. Even when conditions are at their best—for instance, if the school is a dependency of the factory—equal division between labor and classes does not seem the ideal. Let us take the case of the Lanchow foundry middle school. It resumed courses with three days work and three days classes a week. After a period of experiment, the class-time has increased to four days, including twenty-four periods of class among which twelve are devoted to Mao Tse-tung's thought, four to fundamentals in industrial work, four to revolutionary literature and art, two to military and physical culture, two to flexible studies. Rural schools insist that they compile their teaching material themselves according to local needs. There is evidence, however, that this task is also carried on by commissions which act for a larger area.

Teaching "by enlightenment" is considered to be true revolutionary pedagogy, but it is acknowledged that, at least in the primary school when pupils do not know anything, teaching "by infusion" is necessary. Some schools hold examinations— not "trapping" ones: the questions are given beforehand— others do not. There is no attempt to stuff the brain as during the Great Leap Forward, when for the sake of revolution the language students had to learn the dictionary by heart; on the contrary, the key phrase is "little but well." Nevertheless, educators would like to see precisely defined the political, cultural and scientific level to be reached by their students. . . .

To many observers the originality of the current educational revolution is questionable. It is true that part of the criticism recently voiced was brought forward in 1964 and 1965, though not so harshly and radically. Pedagogy "by enlightenment," examinations with open books, "little but well," living study and living use of Mao Tse-tung's thought, opening the schools to workers', poor and lower-middle peasants' children, shortening the courses, integrating them with practice and manual labor were commonplaces—some of these principles were put into operation, but the process was slow, hampered by many psychological obstacles. As in other fields, the reform, which was sponsored by Chairman Mao, met overflowing verbal compliance and little practical support. The Cultural Revolution has not entirely removed the obstacles, but it has certainly shaken their foundation, thus opening the way to a really new education. After such a huge shock, even if people are not completely remolded, there are certain things which they dare not do any more. It is only through revolution that the intended reform could be achieved. The Cultural Revolution type of education resumes the mass line of the Yenan period and of the Great Leap Forward. Even without going back to the *Report of an Investigation into the Peasant Movement in Hunan,* the emphasis on *min-pan* (run by the people) is a feature from the years 1943–45. When criticism of current education was developed in 1944, transfer of authority from professional educators, decentralization, integration of education with the social and economic life of the village had been implemented to cope with the failings of a too elitist system. Such have also been the trends in 1957–59. However, despite common goals and methods, the present situation is different. Realism has been learned from past experiments. Never had the question of power over education been so thoroughly clarified. Furthermore, the average cultural level of the country is considerably higher than in 1958, not to speak of 1944, which accounts for a wider awareness of a broader range of problems, and for less shortage of spare teachers. This means that although enlightened statesmen draw up the educational directives, the official statement that it is primarily the workers and poor peasants who are behind the reforms may, this time, not become a fiction. Thus, instead of the dualistic system into which previous attempts degenerated, an education could emerge which gives equal rank to everyone by cultivating "laborers with socialist consciousness and culture."

The priority given to ideology is not a priority to pure abstract theory. On the other hand, economic necessity has doubtless prompted a number of criticisms, proposals and measures in the educational field, though educational reform as a whole cannot merely be considered as a solution of budget difficulties. The reform meets concrete political ideals. Those ideals could be summed up through a quotation from a Liberation Army fighter as the need to create revolutionary public opinion:

> . . . We must create revolutionary public opinion in a big way . . . To create revolutionary public opinion in a big way means spreading vigorously Marxism-Leninism and Mao Tsetung's thought. . . .
>
> The course of the struggle in the Great Proletarian Cultural Revolution has shown us that once Chairman Mao's latest instructions and the various combat orders issued by the proletarian headquarters with Chairman Mao as its leader and Vice-Chairman Lin as its deputy are brought to the notice of the proletarian revolutionaries and the broad revolutionary masses, and translated into their conscious action, they will yield inexhaustible strength that carries all before it. . . . Don't entertain the thought that to create public opinion is something intangible, and we can do with or without it,

while production is something solid and it will do to grasp production alone. Actually this is not so. Theory is not anything intangible, because spirit can be translated into matter. If "solid" things are not led by "theory," they also cannot be well grasped, and would go astray in the direction of capitalism. The more we are strained in production, the greater is the need to create revolutionary public opinion in a big way and to surmount all kinds of difficulties with revolutionary drive.

The struggle for production can be successful only in a real political society, where the majority of people are concerned and are able to understand and even share in decisions related to the collective life. The advent of such a political society requires the suppression of the elite which monopolized state power, giving the illusion of the existence of a political society but actually usurping the rights and also the duties of the people below. To eradicate the roots of any established elite, the youth must be trained to be versatile, responsive to concrete challenge and unconceited. That does not prevent society from having leaders, but one motto of the "leading group" will be dynamism: they must "dare" to innovate, not content themselves with what is already established.

PEOPLE'S DAILY*
The Road for Training Engineering and Technical Personnel

PROFOUND CHANGE RESULTING FROM THE GREAT PROLETARIAN CULTURAL REVOLUTION

The Shanghai machine-tools plant is a large factory famous for its production of precision grinders. Its technical force of more than 600 engineers and technicians is made up of people from three sources: 45 per cent of them are from the ranks of the

* *People's Daily* (July 22, 1968), pp. 2a–9a.

workers, 50 per cent are post-liberation college graduates and
the remainder are old technicians trained before liberation.
The tempest of the great proletarian cultural revolution has
brought about a profound change in the ranks of the technicians
who work at the plant. . . .

ROAD FOR TRAINING ENGINEERING
AND TECHNICAL PERSONNEL

The young technicians up to thirty-five years of age at the plant
come from two sources: college graduates (numbering some
350, of whom one tenth are postgraduates or graduates of colleges abroad) and technical personnel promoted from workers
(numbering around 250, a few of them having studied for
several years at secondary technical school). The facts show
that the latter are better than the former. Generally speaking,
the former are more backward in their ideas and are less competent in practical work, while the latter are more advanced
ideologically and are more competent. At present, the overwhelming majority of the technical personnel of worker origin
have become the technological backbone and approximately
one tenth of them are capable of independently designing high-
grade, precision and advanced new products. The chief
designers of six of the ten new precision grinding machines
successfully trial-produced in the first half of this year are
technical personnel of worker origin.

Selecting technical personnel from the workers is the road
for training proletarian engineers and technicians.

There is a sharp contrast between two technicians of about
the same age who have different experiences:

One is a Shanghai college student who, after graduation,
spent one year studying a foreign language. Then he went
abroad for further study, and four years later, was there granted
the title of "associate doctorship." In 1962, he went to work
as a technician in the laboratory of the grinder research department of the plant. Although he has studied for over twenty
years, he has not made one significant achievement in scientific
research because his theoretical studies were divorced from
practice and he failed to integrate himself well with the
workers.

The other is a worker who began as an apprentice at the age of fourteen. At eighteen, he was sent to a technical school for machine building in Shanghai where he studied for four years. In 1957, he began to work as a technician in the same research department. He was the chief designer of a huge surface grinding machine which was successfully trial-produced in April of this year. The machine is up to advanced international standards and is urgently needed to advance China's industrial technology. It fills in a blank in the country's manufacture of precision grinders. . . .

Why do technicians of worker origin develop more quickly and make greater contributions?

The most important reason is that they have profound proletarian feelings for Chairman Mao and the party and, in their advance along the road of science and technology, they seek neither fame nor reward, and defy all danger and difficulty to reach their objective. They bear in mind the teachings of Chairman Mao and constantly strive to overtake the imperialists, revisionists and reactionaries in pace and quality. They always look for ways to economize for the state and they arrange things to suit the convenience of the workers. Some young intellectuals, however, who had been poisoned by the revisionist educational line, were for a long time divorced from the bench and the workers, chased bourgeois fame and wealth and achieved nothing. . . .

The contrast between technicians of worker origin and the old bourgeois intellectuals who were poisoned by personal fame and wealth is even more striking. A bourgeois "expert" spent eight years designing a grinder and wasted a large amount of state funds, while not succeeding; but he accumulated some "data" as his capital for his own reputation and wealth. The workers say: "How can we expect such a person to care a lot for our new society?"

Chairman Mao says: "The fighters with the most practical experience are the wisest and the most capable." In their long period of work at the bench, the technicians of worker origin accumulate considerable practical experience which becomes linked with theory after they have studied for a few years in spare-time general or technical school. Thus a leap forward in knowledge is achieved and soon they become capable of independent scientific research and designing. This is a very important reason for their rapid maturing. When they study, they have specific problems in mind; therefore they understand and apply quickly what they learn. . . .

Before they become one with the workers, college-trained technicians are deficient in practical experience, have book knowledge divorced from practice, and are therefore scarcely able to achieve anything. A few college-trained technicians of this type once designed an internal thread grinding machine. The workers followed their blueprints but could not assemble it. Later, some workers with rich practical experience reprocessed some of the parts and the machine was then able to be assembled.

The combination of the revolutionary spirit—daring to think, to act and to make a breakthrough—with a strict scientific attitude is an essential prerequisite if technicians are to scale the heights of science and technology. A person's world outlook as well as his practical experience is of vital importance in achieving this combination. Many technicians of worker origin, unfettered by an urge for personal fame or material gain and rich in practical experience, dare to break down fetishes and superstitions and break through all unnecessary restrictions and are the least conservative in their thinking. . . . Some technicians trained in technical schools do not pay attention to their own ideological remolding. They are prone to be concerned with their own gains and losses, and fear to lose face or give up their airs of knowing it all. At the same time, because they have accommodated themselves to many regulations and restrictions, it is not easy for them to break down old fetishes and superstitions and evolve new technologies. Some of them say: "The more books one reads, the heavier the yoke becomes, and as a result, one loses the spirit of a pathbreaker."

If faced with a choice between graduates from colleges or graduates from secondary technical schools, the workers in the Shanghai machine-tools plant prefer students from the secondary technical schools, because the technical school students are less cocksure, have more practical experience, and are less bound by foreign conventions, though they may have less book knowledge. Quite a number of students in this category have made much more rapid progress than students from colleges. For example, the design of two highly efficient automatic production lines was the work of a couple of 1956 graduates from secondary technical schools.

THE ORIENTATION FOR THE REVOLUTION IN EDUCATION AS SHOWN BY THE PLANT

An analysis of the different types of engineering and technical personnel at the Shanghai machine-tools plant and the roads they have taken shows us the orientation for the revolution in education. . . .

On the basis of Chairman Mao's thought on education and the practical experience of the plant, the workers and technicians put forward the following opinions and ideas in respect to the revolution in education:

First, as Chairman Mao points out, schools must train workers "with both socialist consciousness and culture" and not "intellectual aristocrats" who are divorced from proletarian politics, from the worker and peasant masses and from production, as the revisionist educational line advocated. This is of cardinal importance if we are to prevent the rise of revisionism. Comrades at the Shanghai machine-tools plant are of the opinion that the past practice of college graduates working as cadres in factories or in the countryside right after leaving school was wrong. Integrating themselves with the workers and peasants and participating in productive labor is the important way for young students to remold their world outlook and gain practical technical knowledge. Therefore, they propose that college graduates should first work as ordinary laborers in factories or in the countryside. They should get "qualification certificates" from the workers and peasants. Then, according to the need of the practical struggle, some can take up technical work while participating in labor for a certain amount of time. The others will remain workers or peasants.

Second, school education must be combined with productive labor. Chairman Mao says: "Our chief method is to learn warfare through warfare." In the case of some technical personnel at the Shanghai machine-tools plant it was seen that one serious drawback of the old educational system was that theory was divorced from practice and scholasticism was enforced so that the students became bookworms, and the more they read the more foolish they became. Only by taking part in practice can one grasp theory quickly, understand it profoundly and apply it creatively. Workers and technicians at this plant advance the idea that schools should invite experienced workers to teach so that workers appear on the classroom platform. Some courses can be given by workers right in the workshops. There was a young technician who worked in a research institute after he had graduated from college. All day long, he pored over books, trying to digest theory and learn foreign languages. Since he was divorced from practice, he felt more and more frustrated. In the initial stage of the great cultural revolution, he went to learn from some experienced workers in the machine-tools plant where he worked at the bench. Things were quite different. . . .

Third, as to the source of engineering and technical personnel, they maintain that, apart from continuing to promote technicians from among the workers, junior and senior middle school graduates who are good politically and have two to three or four to five years of experience in production, can be picked from grass-roots units and sent to colleges to study. Every condition exists for this to be done. Take the Shanghai machine-tools plant, for example. Most of its workers have acquired a level equivalent to or above junior middle school education. The advantages in selecting such young people to go to college are as follows: first, they have a comparatively high political consciousness; second, they have a certain competence in practical work and are experienced in production; and third, junior and senior middle school graduates average about twenty years of age after they have taken part in labor for several years. A few years of higher education then fits them for independent work at the age of twenty-three to twenty-four. As it is now, after being assigned to their work posts, college graduates generally have to undergo two to three years of practical work before they are gradually able to work independently. Therefore, the selection of young intellectuals with practical experience for college training is in conformity with the principle of achieving greater, quicker, better and more economical results.

Fourth, on the question of reforming the present technicians in the plant and raising their level, they point out that large numbers of school-trained technicians have for a long time been poisoned by the revisionist educational line and the revisionist line in running enterprises. In addition, there is a group of pre-liberation-trained technicians. Though some of them are patriotic and hard-working, do not oppose the party and socialism, and have no illicit relations with any foreign country, there are many unsolved problems in their world outlook and style of work. The factory should hold aloft the great banner of revolutionary criticism in line with Mao Tse-tung's thought, and organize these technicians for active participation in revolutionary mass criticism and repudiation in accordance with the policies laid down in the "decision of the Central Committee of the Chinese Communist Party concerning the great proletarian cultural revolution." This will enable them thoroughly to repudiate the fallacies of "experts should run the factories" and "putting technique first" as well as "going slow" and "servility to things foreign" which China's Khrushchev trumpeted. It will also enable them thoroughly to repudiate the bourgeois ideas of seeking fame and wealth. The factory should, at the same time, help these technicians to integrate themselves with the workers and link theory with practice by organizing them to work, group by group, as rank-and-file workers for periods, or by arranging for them to work frequently at the bench while remaining technicians.

RED FLAG *

A Primary School Where Poor and
Lower-Middle Peasants Hold Power

There is a new-style rural school—Sungshu primary school—in a mountainous area in southern Liaoning Province. Fostered and run by the poor and lower-middle peasants and following Chairman Mao's proletarian line in education, it has developed in a healthy way. Majestic and towering as a pine tree, it has

* *Red Flag*, December 1968, pp. 12–16.

taken deep root in the hearts of the poor and lower-middle peasants.

POOR AND LOWER-MIDDLE PEASANTS' AGE-LONG DESIRE FOR EDUCATION REALIZED

The Sungshu production brigade of the Chienyi commune in Yingkow County where this primary school is located has 231 households scattered around two gullies, five ridges and along the banks of a river. In the area of the adjoining five production brigades there was only one school in the old society. Of its 53 pupils, Sungshu had only two; one was the child of a landlord, the other of a rich peasant. At present, among the poor and lower-middle peasants in the production brigade who are above the age of thirty-five, 70 per cent are illiterate.

Because of the domination of the revisionist educational line after Liberation, a "regular" primary school was set up about four kilometers from the Sungshu brigade with state funds. In accordance with the regulations, tuition and book fees were demanded, or else firewood, grain and so forth were required under the pretext that the pupils should work their way through school. In addition, overstrict demands were made concerning what pupils should wear. The indignant poor and lower-middle peasants say: "That kind of a school is run just to keep out our sons and daughters." Up to 1964, more than 45 per cent of school-age children in this brigade couldn't go to school.

In 1964, the poor and lower-middle peasants were overjoyed to hear Chairman Mao's instruction: "Permission should be given to the people's communes and production brigades to run schools, if conditions exist," and other teachings of his on revolution in education. They decided to set up a school by themselves. However, someone remarked: "It's just child's play for peasants to run schools. It will be gone with a mere gust of wind." Even a cadre tried to frustrate the peasants' efforts behind their backs.

The poor and lower-middle peasants refused to be taken in. Elderly poor peasant Li Sheng-wen said: "Chairman Mao has instructed us to set up schools and we must do it!" Other peasants said: "We peasants should run schools of our own because we know what type of people our children should be trained into." In this way they started the school which now has 155 pupils in four grades and which is divided into seven classes. By now over 90 per cent of the school-age children are attending the school. When the school was started in 1964, it had only one class of fourteen pupils.

POOR AND LOWER-MIDDLE PEASANTS
GRASP POWER COMPLETELY

Since Sungshu primary school was set up, power has been grasped by the poor and lower-middle peasants. In its initial stage, a "committee for running the school" was established under the brigade party branch committee. It is now the "committee for the revolution in education," which is set up under the leadership of the brigade's revolutionary committee and has the participation of the poor and lower-middle peasants. This committee grasps the power in personnel, culture and finance in the school.

How have the poor and lower-middle peasants managed the school in the past four years?

The poor and lower-middle peasants selected reliable people as teachers from among educated young people who returned to the countryside. In the past, many bad elements sneaked into the teachers' ranks in the "regular" schools. The poor and lower-middle peasants put forward their opinions, but these were never accepted. They said angrily: "We have selected the livestock breeders. Why can't we select the teachers?" So when it came to their running the school, they chose every teacher after extensive consultations and careful observation and investigation. Returned educated young people to be chosen teachers must have good class origin, high political consciousness, and a good record in collective productive labor, and must have deep class feelings toward the poor and lower-middle peasants. "We feel at ease when we put our children in the care of teachers we selected," the poor and lower-middle peasants said.

They changed the teaching content and the teaching methods thoroughly. Following Chairman Mao's teaching that it is essential to "revolutionize education," the poor and lower-middle peasants abolished the rules and restrictions laid down by the revisionist line in education. When teaching material was unavailable, they themselves compiled and mimeographed the textbooks. The first lesson was "Long live Chairman Mao." They discarded all the feudal, bourgeois and revisionist trash from the old textbooks, and added lessons in Chairman Mao's works, class education and production skills, thus carrying out Chairman Mao's teaching that "teaching material should have local character."

They closely link the teaching with reality. The pupils attend classes half the day, participate in labor the other half-day, and regularly take part in public activities. During the busy farming season, the curriculum gives way to production. For lessons in class education and production skills, either the pupils take their lessons outside the classrooms or poor and lower-middle peasants are invited to give lectures so that they can occupy the lecturer's platform. The teachers regularly organize the pupils in the higher forms to teach those in the lower forms. Classes and forms in the last few years were increased without adding to the number of teachers, and the quality of teaching improved steadily. The teachers have become the organizers of school education, social education and home education, and a lively atmosphere of conscientious teaching and study has set in.

The poor and lower-middle peasants discussed and decided school expenses and teachers' pay. The teachers were paid according to the work-point system, whereby their work was recorded daily and they were paid for it according to prevailing standards, just like the commune members. The poor and lower-middle peasants say: "Teachers like these think like us. They are like members of our families in their actions, too."

Chairman Mao recently pointed out penetratingly: "In the countryside, schools and colleges should be managed by the poor and lower-middle peasants—the most reliable ally of the working class."

The poor and lower-middle peasants of the Sungshu production brigade say: "Only when we ourselves hold power in running schools in the countryside can they be run well. If the bourgeois intellectuals usurp power, they are bound to make a mess of our schools." . . .

There are no classrooms. Instead, heated mud-and-brick beds in the brigade members' houses, thatched sheds of the production teams, smithies and places under trees and on the banks of a stream are all their classrooms. There are no desks and benches. They use boxes, broken mangers, and old tables and stools. They set up the school simply, and established four teaching locales for eight production teams so that the children of the poor and lower-middle peasants can study at the locale near their homes.

Moreover, irrational conventions have all been thrown aside. Pupils who have to do domestic chores can bring younger brothers or sisters to class. They also can come late and leave early, or they can attend classes on a seasonal basis. Children are enrolled without age restriction. Two women team leaders attend the school during slack farming seasons so that they can study Chairman Mao's works still better.

For the pupils, taking part in productive labor is a fundamental course. Manual labor—such as digging medicinal herbs, collecting tree seeds and cutting firewood—has been carried on over a long period so that the pupils can cover the cost of their studies by their own productive labor. In its four years, the school has not collected any money from the pupils. And it spent no money from the state prior to the great cultural revolution. This is a sharp contrast with the so-called "regular" schools in the vicinity. The poor and lower-middle peasants say proudly: "In our style of work, we are just like Yenan." . . .

During the expansion of Sungshu primary school the three women teachers were reeducated by the poor and lower-middle peasants. Our great leader Chairman Mao recently pointed out: "The majority or the vast majority of the students trained in the old schools and colleges can integrate themselves with the workers, peasants and soldiers, and some have made inventions or innovations; they must, however, be reeducated by the workers, peasants and soldiers under the guidance of the correct line, and thoroughly change their old ideology. Such intellectuals will be welcomed by the workers, peasants and soldiers." The teachers of Sungshu primary school have integrated with the poor and lower-middle peasants during the past four years and have made outstanding achievements.

When Hsu Ching-fang, daughter of a poor peasant, entered the dilapidated shed serving as the classroom for the first time and saw the three-legged desk, the bourgeois school she had once attended sprang to mind and she thought she would do better to work in the fields. At this moment the old poor peasant Li Sheng-wen told her of the bitterness of the life under oppression and exploitation and lack of schooling in the old society. He encouraged her to bring credit to the poor and lower-middle peasants. Some other poor and lower-middle peasants sent her *Serve the People* and other brilliant works of Chairman Mao's.

All this educated her and she made up her mind to serve the poor and lower-middle peasants her whole life. In the past few years she has frequently joined the poor and lower-middle peasants in doing physical labor, learning from them and taking them as her teachers. She teaches and learns at the same time and is a teacher and a student at one and the same time. She said from her heart: "The poor and lower-middle peasants are my good teachers." The masses affectionately called her "fine daughter of the poor and lower-middle peasants."

In 1967 the brigade decided to give each of the three women teachers a subsidy of thirteen *yuan*. They all refused, saying: "We are also members of the commune. We don't want to get extra money." The poor and lower-middle peasants said with pleasure: "With such schools and such teachers, future generations will not change color."

TILLMAN DURDIN*
Schools Retain Many
Conventional Subjects

> CANTON, China, May 6—*The changes that have been made in primary and secondary schooling in China do not appear to be as drastic as official publicity has depicted them.*

A visit to one model middle school in Peking and questioning about lower-level education there and elsewhere show that much of the conventional teaching system remains.

* Tillman Durdin, from *The New York Times Report from Red China* (New York: Avon Books, 1972), pp. 280–282.

At the Peking No. 2 Secondary School, for example, mathematics, languages, physics, chemistry, history, geography, physical education and public affairs—a kind of civics course—form a basic part of the curriculum just as these subjects did before the Cultural Revolution and just as they do in secondary schools in the West.

These courses are taught insofar as possible through use of maxims and philosophy of Mao Tse-tung, and, in addition, there are separate courses in political education, basic farming and revolutionary art and culture that have political indoctrination as their main objective. However, the teaching of basic general knowledge is obviously a major preoccupation of the school.

And discipline is back in vogue. A new student body of 1,500 boys and girls had replaced the youngsters who from late 1966 until late 1968 had no regular classes. During that period, pupils were free to rampage in and around Peking while hauling principal and teachers before "struggle" meetings at which they were denounced for so-called revisionist ideas and practices.

The former students have been sent off to work in the countryside or in factories, and their successors are obviously under firm control of the school authorities, who, oddly enough, include the same teachers as before. Now, however, military men stationed in the school see that things run properly.

Ma Yu-shan, who was principal of the school in 1966, no longer holds that post, which has been abolished, but is a member of the Revolutionary Committee that now runs the school. He gives the impression of still having a strong voice in school affairs.

This is not to say that broad changes have not been made. For one thing, the No. 2 Secondary School, as a junior middle school, has moved into studies formerly confined to senior middle schools.

This is in conformity with the new plan that provides for five years in primary school instead of the former six and for five years instead of six in junior and senior middle school. Under the new plan senior middle school graduates at the age of fifteen and sixteen go to work in factories or in farms for a couple of years and then, if found suitable, go on to a university for two to three years.

In addition the Maoist content of all studies, to say nothing of those courses especially designed to indoctrinate, is now all-embracing. In the two foreign languages taught in the school, French and English, lessons are made up of quotations from Chairman Mao.

"Unissons-nous pour remporter des victoires encore plus grandes!" ("Let us unite to achieve even greater victories!") a French class repeats in unison after their teacher. Across the hall, a class in English declaims, "Be resolute! Fear no sacrifice and surmount every difficulty to win victory!"

The teacher in a Chinese language class uses a Mao poem extolling the heroism of the Chinese Red Army during the Long March that the Communist forces made in 1934–35 in their war against Kuomintang troops. In a geometry class, a Mao quotation on the wall advises students they "must deduce the rule from objective conditions, not merely to sum up but to guide actions."

The school is also more Maoist now in the way the students combine class studies with practical work. Each student must spend three hours a day for one month in a shop making metal and wooden chairs or performing the painstaking task of processing tiny disks into diodes for use in precision meters or transistor radios.

The school produces 30,000 diodes a month for electronics plants. The factories pay 12 cents per diode, but the money goes to the school, not the students.

Classes meet for thirty-one weeks. There are eight weeks of vacation during which there are periods of military training, four weeks spent learning work in a factory, four weeks spent learning work on a farm and a week of so-called summing up during which certain students are singled out for their class records and political understanding.

The new primary schools and senior middle schools follow a pattern similar to that of the No. 2 Secondary School, but officials acknowledge that the new schools at both primary and secondary levels are still experimental.

The new system has not been generally adopted yet in Peking, and in Shanghai officials questioned said that the city was still experimenting with the system.

One problem is trying to cram the material that formerly was covered in twelve years into ten years. Another is that workers and peasants long past usual primary school age and without any schooling are now admitted to classes in which they study alongside much younger pupils. This involves disparities of learning speed and difficulties in the relationships of students.

PARTY BRANCH OF CHANGCHIAK'OU MUNICIPAL NO. 22 MIDDLE SCHOOL*
Strengthen Teaching of Basic Knowledge and Fundamental Theories

Correctly Handle the Relationship between Political Education and Intellectual Education and Strengthen Teaching of Basic Knowledge

How to handle correctly the relationship between political education and education in cultural knowledge in the course of teaching is an important problem in the struggle between the two lines. Swindlers of the Liu Shao-ch'i type at one time disseminated "vocational work in command" and opposed the putting of proletarian politics over vocational work and at another time advocated "politics may overrule anything else" and frenziedly abolished the putting of vocational work under the command of proletarian politics. These two tendencies have occurred in teaching. But at the present stage, the interference comes on the main from the "Left."

Some comrades hold that putting politics in command of teaching of cultural knowledge means devoting more time to teaching politics, and subsequently they devote very little time to teaching cultural knowledge and even substitute politics for cultural knowledge. Some teachers do not put Mao Tse-tung's thought in command of the teaching of cultural knowledge but separate them from each other, so that politics has not been put in command and teaching of cultural knowledge has been

* Party Branch of Changchiak'ou Municipal No. 22 Middle School, from *People's Daily* (August 15, 1972), (SCMP 10/30–11/3/72, 72-44).

impeded. Some teaching materials have been compiled in a one-sided way, attention being paid to ideological education exclusively to the neglect of teaching of basic knowledge.

In order to handle correctly the relationship between political education and education in cultural knowledge, it is necessary to solve the problem of method but the most important thing is to solve the problem of understanding.

A language teacher of our school once selected two essays written by the students: One had a clear theme, its contents were pruned appropriately and it was written in a practical style; the other did not have a clear theme but was filled with political slogans and empty talk. The teacher compared and criticized these two essays in class with the object of making the students learn from the former essay. In the course of comparison, however, some students said that the latter essay "had a clear political viewpoint." A debate took place in the class. Fearing that he would commit the mistake of "letting politics be overruled," he tried to compromise and said that each of these two essays had its own strong points.

We learn deeply from this incident that the key to solving the problem of understanding lies in clearly distinguishing between the two lines.

First, to distinguish between the grasp of basic knowledge and fundamental training under the command of politics on one side and the so-called teaching of pure knowledge on the other side.

Education conducted in middle school is fundamental education which is aimed at making the students learn basic knowledge and carry out fundamental training. In the past, teaching of basic knowledge and conduct of fundamental training were regarded as "teaching of pure knowledge" but they practically aimed at conducting bourgeois education. Criticizing teaching of basic knowledge and fundamental conduct training of the past does not mean to weaken basic knowledge and fundamental training but to eliminate the bourgeois ideology in teaching instead. To achieve this end, we lead the teachers to eliminate the pernicious influence of revisionism in various links of basic knowledge and fundamental training. We encourage the teachers to put themselves under the guidance of the correct thinking and to strengthen basic knowledge and fundamental training regarding such aspects as teaching material, method of teaching, preparation of lessons, delivery of lessons, criticism and correction of assignments done by the students, and giving of instruction outside the school. After making this distinction and acquiring a clear guiding thought, the teachers have a clear orientation to follow in grasping basic knowledge and fundamental training and will work energetically. This year, we have conscientiously grasped the work of eliminating the misuse of characters and have acquired remarkable results in this concern.

Second, to distinguish between the putting of politics in command of vocational work and the fallacy that "politics may overrule everything else."

In the course of conducting line education, we studied profoundly Chairman Mao's teachings, "Politics is the commander, the soul," "The relationship between being red and being expert, between politics and vocational work, constitutes a unity of opposites," and "The tendency of paying no attention to politics must be criticized. We should oppose armchair politicians on the one hand and 'practical men' who have lost their bearing on the other," and came to understand that: The relationship between politics and vocational work can only be the relationship between the commander and the commanded. Putting the proletarian politics in command of vocational work means adhering to the unity between politics and vocational work and aims at turning proletarian politics into life-blood for all branches of vocational work. This does not mean that vocational work is not needed. Instead, it means doing various branches of vocational work with greater success and making vocational work serve proletarian politics better under the guidance of Chairman Mao's revolutionary line. In the sphere of teaching, this means applying the stand, viewpoint and method of Marxism, Leninism and Mao Tse-tung's thought in teaching socialist culture lessons well, so that the students can raise their ideological consciousness, acquire cultural knowledge and become laborers who have socialist consciousness and culture.

Correctly Handle the Relationship between Theory and Practice. Strengthen Teaching of Fundamental Theories.

How should we strengthen teaching of basic knowledge and fundamental theories and improve the quality of teaching? The bourgeoisie runs a school by taking the road of "three separations," whereas the proletarian target of training students has determined the combination of teaching with the three great revolutionary movements. We have conscientiously implemented the principle of integrating theory with reality in the course of teaching.

In order to change the conditions of "three separations" in teaching in the past, we have since 1968 followed Chairman Mao's "May 7 Directive," perseveringly run the schools with open doors, carried out activities of learning from workers, peasants and army men, opened channels in various fields for linking teaching with the three great revolutionary movements, thereby creating conditions for integrating theory with reality. But running a school with open doors does not mean that theory has been integrated with practice. To handle correctly the relationship between theory and practice, we also must take a firm hold of the line education.

We once took a tortuous path in handling this problem. At the beginning, we suggested that factories operated by schools should adopt top-flight techniques; students going to the factories must learn to master a kind of special skill; the farms operated by the schools must achieve self-sufficiency in grain within three to five years; anybody who talked about book knowledge in class should be considered as "restoring the old." The phenomena of conducting teaching behind closed doors were changed in the main, but other phenomena emerged: Much time was devoted to labor, social activities were frequent, and numerous methods were adopted to link classroom teaching with reality in a far-fetched way; little time was devoted to teaching fundamental theories conscientiously and the students learned very little knowledge. Some teachers elected to teach only those lessons which had contents easily linked with reality, and they skipped the fundamental theories. Later, during the campaign to criticize the ultra-"Left" ideas spread by swindlers of the Liu Shao-ch'i type, some comrades had another view. They said: "The students should take study as their main task. They must sit down to study well and should no longer wander about." As a result of the influence by this idea, they were not so enthusiastic in running factories and building the farms; they seldom went out of the school to learn lessons and invited workers and peasants to come to teach lessons, and the school was again left in solitude.

In view of these two tendencies, we held a line study class. Through study, we understand that: The two tendencies in handling the relationship between theory and practice are precisely a reflection of the struggle between the two lines. It is a "Left" deed to put forth impractical demands and ask other people to do what is impossible (impossible at least for the time being); failure to integrate theory with reality where conditions permit is a comeback of the pernicious influence of the "three separations." Summing up historical experience makes us understand that in order to handle correctly the relationship between theory and practice, we must proceed from the goal of training and the practice of fundamental education in middle schools. On the one hand, we must make strenuous efforts to teach and learn well the fundamental theories of the courses specified in the curricula; on the other hand, we must adhere to the principle of integrating theory with reality, and make the broad masses of teachers and students bring their subjective activity into play and create conditions for integrating theory with reality where possible. But we must oppose the formalist and pragmatist tendencies.

To handle correctly the relationship between theory and reality, we must also pay attention to drawing two demarcation lines:

First, we must draw a demarcation line between teaching of theoretical knowledge by proceeding from reality on the one side and "taking the books as the center" and regarding practice lightly on the other side.

A controversy once took place when a mathematics teacher taught the "ordinary method of extracting the square root." Some comrades held that the workers could solve the problem of extracting square root in the course of production by looking it up from a mathematics table and they basically didn't have to work the operations step by step as taught in books, and the method and principle of extracting the square root as taught in books was saying that the square root table showed the results exclusively which might be referred to when necessary in the course of production, but in a school, the students must make clear the principle and learn the method, and teaching such a lesson should not be regarded as separating theory from reality. We supported the latter opinion and organized type teaching. Our consensus was that we must know not only the facts but also how these facts were arrived at, and explaining the basic principle and basic method clearly meant creating conditions for the students in integrating theory with reality.

Second, we must draw a demarcation line between "laying emphasis on study" and teaching lessons behind closed doors.

"Laying emphasis on study" does not mean teaching lessons behind closed doors. We drew lessons from the setback which occurred in a former course leading from running a school with open doors to running a school behind closed doors. While strengthening teaching of fundamental theories, we adhered to the principle of running a school with open doors and upheld the unity between theory and practice.

In the past few years, we basically had a plan for the "major subjects" and a system for "supplemental courses," thereby guaranteeing enough time for teaching lessons and accomplishing the task of the "supplemental courses" according to schedule. The atmosphere of study in the small classrooms became stronger and stronger and the road of study in the big classrooms became broader and broader. The formation of a tie between the teaching research group and the factory operated by a school promoted the combination of teaching and production and of theory and reality.

Party Branch of Changchiak'ou Municipal
No. 22 Middle School

★　★　★　★　★

5. HEALTH

The problem of the development of large-scale modern health services carries with it fundamentally the same harsh choices involved in all economic development—that is, the possibility, on the one hand, of the training of a relatively small number of specialists who will form the basis of a professional cadre, or, on the other hand, the widespread dissemination of less specialized medical care. For the Chinese Communists, who in 1949 inherited both the staggering medical problems of a huge, undernourished, war-worn population and an infinitesimal corps of medical personnel, the approach, as in all fields, was to use the resources that existed, both traditional and modern, and to "walk on two legs." The new government undertook gigantic popular campaigns in sanitation, immunization, and public health education, and at the same time, set in motion the slower development toward a first-rate modern medical establishment. Dr. Joshua Horn, a British surgeon who practiced medicine in the People's Republic for fourteen years, describes at the beginning of his selection the inherited problems and some of the early steps towards their solution.

By the mid-fifties, the results were already impressive. Many of the basic public health problems were well on the way to being solved. Within another decade, however, by the mid-sixties, a consistent pattern of development was becoming apparent. As medical schools and teaching hospitals steadily continued to be built up in the major cities, so the historically familiar pattern of all industrializing nations began to assert itself. The best research facilities were in the cities, thus attracting the foremost researchers; the finest equipment was concentrated in urban hospitals; the greatest number of medical students were assigned there, and by the time Mao Tse-tung issued his June 1965 "Instructions on Public Health Work," the situation was as he, in his characteristically direct and satiric way, described it. The 15 percent of the Chinese population who lived in the cities were receiving virtually all of China's still insufficient medical care.

Dr. Horn's vivid descriptions of the work of the rural medical teams of which he was a member show the concrete response to the problem. Dr. Horn's team of Peking medical volunteers was in fact organized in April of 1965, before Mao's "Instructions" were issued, but the medical initiatives of that period all demonstrate an increased awareness of the inadequacies of rural medical care. Horn's discussion of the training and work of the peasant volunteers which began late that same year is a good microscopic view of a phenomenon which through the impetus of the Cultural Revolution has developed greatly since that time. The "barefoot doctors" of the last few years are not paramedical personnel in the usual sense of the word, nor are they highly trained personnel. They represent perhaps a "third" way between two highly differentiated approaches to medical care.

In "The Human Services in China," Victor and Ruth Sidel, both of Albert Einstein College of Medicine, New York, present a knowledgeable overall view of these services as they appeared to some of the first American visitors of the medical and social-work professions to visit China since 1949. The Sidels discuss such questions as mental health and infant care within the context of Chinese community organization and political ethos. In China, there is no separating the problems of birth control or immunization from the larger matters of local political and neighborhood organization, and the Sidels approach their investigation of the human services with this awareness. They state in the final sentences of their article: "They [the Chinese] are asking questions and experimenting with answers that are very different from ours. And they are experimenting in ways through which, it seems to us, an admirable compatibility between stated political goals and ideals and human service practice has been achieved."

★   ★   ★

MAO TSE-TUNG*

Instructions on Public Health Work:
A Talk Given to Medical Personnel on June 25, 1965

Tell the Ministry of Public Health that it only works for 15 percent of the entire population. Furthermore, this 15 percent is made up mostly of the privileged. The broad ranks of the peasants cannot obtain medical treatment and also do not receive medicine. The Public Health Ministry is not a people's ministry. It should be called the Urban Public Health Ministry or, the Public Health Ministry of the Privileged or even, the Urban Public Health Ministry of the Privileged.

Medical education must be reformed. It is basically useless to study so much. How many years did Hua T'o [a third-century physician] study? How many years did Li Shih-chen of the Ming Dynasty study? Medical education does not require senior middle school students, junior middle school students or graduates of senior elementary school. Three years are enough. The important thing is that they study while practicing. This way doctors sent to the countryside will not overrate their own abilities, and they will be better than those doctors who have been cheating the people and better than the witch doctors. In addition, the villages can afford to support them. The more a person studies, the more foolish he becomes. At the present time the system of examination and treatment used in the medical schools is not at all suitable for the countryside. Our method of training doctors is for the cities, even though China has more than 500 million peasants.

A vast amount of manpower and materials have been diverted from mass work and are being expended in carrying out re-

* Mao Tse-tung, translated in *Current Background*, No. 892 (October 21, 1969), p. 24.

search on the high-level, complex, and difficult diseases, the so-called pinnacles of medicine. As for the frequently occurring illnesses, the widespread sicknesses, the commonly existing diseases, we pay no heed or very slight heed to their prevention or to finding improved methods of treatment. It is not that we should ignore the pinnacles. It is only that we should devote less men and materials in that direction and devote a greater amount of men and materials to solving the urgent problems of the masses.

Another odd thing. Is it because, when making an examination, they are afraid they will give others their own diseases that doctors without fail always wear gauze masks, irrespective of what disease they might have? I think the main reason is that they are afraid the other persons will infect them. This must be dealt with on an individual basis. This above all creates a barrier between the doctor and the patient.

We should keep in the cities those doctors who have been out of school for a year or two and those who are lacking in ability. The remainder should be sent to the countryside. . . ., the four clearances were taken care of and basically concluded. But medical treatment and public health work in the countryside were not concluded! In medicine and health, put the stress on the rural areas!

*JOSHUA HORN**
From *Away With All Pests*

HEALTH AND THE PEASANTS

To understand the present, it is necessary to view it against the past.

China has always been a predominantly agricultural country

* Joshua Horn, *Away With All Pests* (New York: Monthly Review Press, 1969).

with four fifths of her people living in the countryside and yet it is no exaggeration to say that before Liberation most of China's peasants had virtually no access to modern medicine and very scant access to traditional medicine. Modern-type doctors congregated in the towns, where there was money to be made. Traditional doctors, widely regarded as the highest authorities in all matters pertaining to science and art, were closely linked with the landlords and officials. Many of them lived in the county towns, and their scarcity value in the villages enabled them to charge fees which were beyond the reach of the mass of poor peasants. Their herbal remedies were often very expensive, for it was held to be self-evident that cheap medicines were ineffective in comparison with dear ones.

Some traditional doctors were prepared to visit villagers in their homes without payment, but others demanded a fee and suitable transportation, which, in the area I am familiar with, involved a retinue of guards with either a comfortably saddled mule or donkey, or a sedan chair and bearers. Traditions had to be observed. Custom demanded that a visiting doctor must be wined and dined with an unspecified but clearly understood degree of luxury before seeing the patient. If he had traveled far or if the weather was bad, he had a right to expect hospitality in accordance with his station for as long as he desired. All this was only possible for the landlord class, and ordinary peasants could only call a doctor through the good offices of the landlord. If a peasant reinforced his supplications with adequate material inducements, his landlord might consent to call a doctor, ostensibly to see a member of his own household, but actually to see the peasant. Here too, there were binding unwritten conventions. Things had to be so arranged that it would appear that only because the doctor had an observant eye had he noticed the plight of the patient hovering in the background, and only because he had a compassionate heart, had he consented to treat him. The landlord host, basking in the reflected glory of the doctor, despite a display of custom-decreed protests, would munificently pay his fee. The reckoning came later and might plunge the peasant into debt for many years to come.

In view of these crippling financial and social burdens, it is not surprising that although many traditional doctors developed great skill in diagnosis and treatment and although some unreservedly placed their skill at the service of the people, the peasants looked elsewhere for relief from their suffering.

In many villages, a peasant with a flair for acupuncture or manipulation would gradually acquire a reputation and would be called in to treat the sick. Often he would train his son, who, in turn, would extend his skill by learning to recognize and infuse wild medicinal herbs. Although these village "doctors" were illiterate and were despised by the professional traditional doctors and although the medicine they practiced was crude and rudimentary, they did a certain amount of good and created the social climate for the subsequent training of true peasant doctors.

Superstitious practices were widespread. Witch doctors, usually unkempt semi-demented women with an awe-inspiring appearance, attributed illness to ghosts, devils and evil spirits which they tried either to exorcise or placate. Placation involved sacrifices of chickens or other luxuries which the poverty-stricken people couldn't afford, while the evil spirits could only be exorcised by incantations and weird antics, which, if they did not frighten the spirits, certainly frightened the patient and the spellbound onlookers.

Many harmful superstitions were associated with childbirth. In some areas women had to give birth unaided in a shed or outhouse; in others, mother and child were kept in a darkened room for several weeks after delivery; elsewhere, the baby could not be dressed for the first month of life, and after that could only be wrapped in old rags. Ignorant gamps often attended at childbirth, and their practice of biting through the umbilical cord and applying cow dung to the stump caused many babies to die of tetanus, a disease which, because of its commonness and time of onset, came to be known as "nine-day illness."

Poverty and ignorance were reflected in a complete lack of sanitation as a result of which fly- and water-borne diseases such as typhoid, cholera, dysentery, took a heavy toll. Worm infestation was practically universal, for untreated human and animal manure was the main and essential soil fertilizer. The people lived on the fringe of starvation and this so lowered their resistance to disease that epidemics carried off thousands every year. The average life expectancy in China in 1935 was stated to be about twenty-eight years. Reliable health statistics for pre-

Liberation China are hard to come by but conservative estimates put the crude death rate in times of peace at between thirty and forty per thousand and the infantile mortality rate at between 160 and 170 per thousand live births. The plight of the women and children was bad beyond description. The men had to have what grain there was, to give them strength to work in the fields. The women, especially those who stayed at home to look after the children, ate only thin gruel, grass and leaves. They were so ill-nourished that by the time they reached middle age, they were toothless and decrepit. Many adolescent girls, lacking calcium and vitamin D, developed softening and narrowing of the pelvic bones, so that normal childbirth became either impossible or so dangerous that 6 to 8 per cent of all deaths among women were due to childbirth. Babies were breast-fed for three or four years, for no other food was available. This threw a heavy strain on the mothers, and also resulted in child malnutrition and such vitamin-deficiency diseases as rickets and scurvy. There were no preventive inoculations against infectious diseases, and from time to time epidemics of smallpox, diphtheria, whooping cough and meningitis swept through the countryside with devastating results. Lice and poverty went hand in hand, and with them louse-borne diseases such as typhus fever. Military occupation and the licentiousness of the landlords and local gentry spread venereal diseases among the people and no treatment was available. The prevalence of tuberculosis can be gauged from the fact that in 1946 60 per cent of all applicants for student visas for study abroad were found to be suffering from this disease.

FIRST STEPS
Such was the public health situation in the rural areas which the People's Government inherited in 1949. It is against this background that subsequent developments have to be seen. I have not exaggerated the enormity of the medical tasks confronting the new regime and its corps of medical workers, but by omission have understated them.

Writing in 1948, Dr. Winfield, an American who had spent thirteen years in China, wrote: "Many of her most common causes of illness and disease are rooted in the very structure of her overcrowded peasant society."

Since Liberation, the population has increased considerably

but the health situation has been transformed, showing that "overcrowding" was not an important factor.

One of the first steps taken after Liberation was to unite the available medical workers. At this time, the number of modern doctors was certainly much less than one per 100,000 of population, nearly all of them in a few big cities, whereas there were several hundred thousand traditional doctors who enjoyed the confidence of the people. Accordingly, in August 1950, the first National Health Conference was convened and Mao Tsetung issued a call for unity between traditional and modern doctors.

Whatever they lacked in modern scientific knowledge, there was no doubt that traditional doctors, properly organized, could make a valuable contribution to the protection of the health of the people. It would have been the height of folly and irresponsibility to discard this force before there was something better to replace it. Moreover, as already described, subsequent developments have proved that the modern has a lot to learn from the old and that a combination of the two can open up paths impossible for either alone.

Within two years of Liberation, Chinese volunteers were helping the Koreans to repel U.S. aggression and it became necessary to mobilize the people to protect their health from the dangers arising from the use of germ warfare in Korea. A patriotic health campaign was promoted in response to this need. Tens of millions of people of all ages, guided by sanitary workers who supplied the know-how and the necessary materials, waged a war of extermination against the "four pests"— flies, rats, bedbugs and mosquitoes.

The unprecedented success of this campaign has been acknowledged by many Western observers. In many parts of the country, flies were virtually eliminated: an astounding feat in the fly-ridden Orient and one which could only be accomplished by an unusually united and responsive population.

However, the control of flies and other insects requires a long-term, not a temporary, campaign, and therefore, after the Korean conflict, the Patriotic Health Campaign remained a permanent part of the Chinese people's war against disease. In the villages it is now closely integrated with the hygiene and sanitary work of the mobile medical teams.

For many years after Liberation, the main effort in developing health services was concentrated in the towns. There were many reasons for this, some of which were valid, while others, during the great scrutiny of the Cultural Revolution, are being reexamined and sharply criticized.

It was urgently necessary to train more doctors, and this necessitated the building of new medical schools and teaching hospitals in the cities. More than fifteen times as many doctors graduated between 1949 and 1964 than in the preceding twenty years. In 1963, 25,000 doctors graduated and I believe that China is now turning out more medical workers than any other country in the world. The curriculum for traditional doctors is being standardized and schools of traditional medicine have been established. Medical research has made great progress, and some first-class laboratories have been built, equipped and staffed.

At the same time, the rapid development of industry and the corresponding growth in the urban population made it essential to provide medical services for industrial workers and their families. By 1964, the number of urban hospital beds had increased tenfold.

All this explained, or was alleged to explain, the concentration of available medical resources in the towns rather than in the country. . . .

FACING THE COUNTRYSIDE

Since China is a vast country which is emerging very rapidly from a state of extreme backwardness, it is inevitable that there should be unevenness in both the speed and direction of progress.

In order to avoid the dangers of misrepresentation and oversimplification, I confine this chapter to my personal experience of the new rural medical services in a county on the northern fringe of Hopei Province. This is one of the poorer parts of China where the terrain is mountainous, communications poor and the climate hard. For more than a decade, it was part of the puppet Japanese state of "Manchukuo" and it still bears scars of colonial oppression and devastation. Certainly there are many parts of China where things are much better, where the climate is kinder, the terrain more hospitable and where the establishment of a rural health service has made greater progress. Equally certainly, there are other areas which have not yet reached this level. While the situation which I shall describe may not represent conditions throughout China, it does not exaggerate but probably understates the advances which have been made since the Chinese Communist Party formulated its health policy of orientation towards the countryside.

The new policy is being put into effect in a number of different ways, the most important of which is the sending of mobile medical teams from the towns to the countryside.

MOBILE MEDICAL TEAMS

In April 1965 my hospital in Peking called for volunteers to organize a medical team to serve a rural area a few hundred miles away in northern Hopei. Within six months it comprised 107 nurses, laboratory workers, administrators and doctors of all specialties and levels of seniority. It is intended that in the near future at least one third of the hospital staff shall be working with the mobile team on a rotation basis, and this proportion will increase later. This team serves twelve People's Communes with a total population of about 80,000 persons. It is divided into three medical brigades, each based on a central clinic which serves the surrounding three or four Communes and is responsible for smaller clinics in selected production brigades. Doctors in the small clinics regularly visit every village within a specified area and are available for emergency calls. All the villages are linked by telephone.

The medical brigade centered on the Four Seas clinic, which serves about 15,000 peasants scattered over a large, mountainous area, has a complement of thirty-five, some stationed in the central clinic and the remainder organized into six small groups based in different villages. Most villages can only be reached on foot or by riding donkeys over stony paths.

The members of the small groups in the outlying villages either live together in peasant cottages which also serve as clinics, or they lodge separately with villagers. In either case they usually eat with villagers, paying for meals at a standard rate. When they are traveling round the outlying villages and it is impossible for them to return to base at night, they stay with peasants, sharing the same *kang* (a raised platform of brick or baked mud which usually runs the whole length of the room; it is heated by the use of a stove and serves as a bed) and helping to carry water and collect firewood for the household.

At least once a week, and more often during the busy farming seasons, the medical workers join the peasants in manual labor in the fields.

The usual period of service with the mobile team is one year, all its members are volunteers, and a balance is maintained between new graduates and experienced doctors and between the different specialties. Whatever their original specialty, while they are in the countryside, doctors are expected to undertake any kind of medical work. To equip them for their new life and new work, they receive a preparatory course of training before leaving the city.

They get eight days' home leave every two months with free transportation and they are paid their normal Peking hospital salaries while in the countryside. Many of them apply to extend their tours of duty but usually this is not possible since their colleagues in Peking are anxious to replace them. Some volunteer to settle down permanently in the countryside; twelve doctors from my hospital have done so since the scheme started eighteen months ago.

In addition to general mobile medical teams, there are also specialized teams according to local needs and resources. In this area, for example, there is a mobile eye, ear, nose, throat and dental team which spends a month in each People's Commune in turn. There is also a birth control team.

SIX TASKS
The mobile medical teams have six tasks:

Task One

The first task is to provide preventive and therapeutic services in the area served and, in accordance with policy, preventive work is given priority. All children are immunized against infectious diseases by a traveling inoculation team which visits the villages whenever primary immunization or "booster" doses

become due. Before Liberation only vaccination against smallpox was available for the rural population and this involved a
journey to the county town and the payment of about ten
pounds of grain. Now immunization is free and, to express
their appreciation and also to encourage the children to regard
the doctors as friends rather than enemies, the villagers make
the inoculation team's visit a festive occasion, welcome it with
drums and cymbals, gaily decorate the cottage where the injections are to be given and congregate to share the fun. If, not-
withstanding this psychological preparation, a child objects to
the benefits about to be conferred on him, a pockmarked elder
is produced for his education and then there is usually no
trouble.

Smallpox, typhoid, diphtheria, infantile paralysis and whooping cough have now practically disappeared from this area and
recently Chinese medical scientists have developed a method of
active immunization against measles which has greatly reduced
its incidence and severity. All children receive oral BCG against
encephalitis and infectious meningitis.

Another aspect of preventive work in the countryside is the
prevention of water-borne diseases. Drinking water in the villages comes from wells, rivers or springs which can easily be
contaminated with disease-producing germs. The first step was
to win the active support of the people, for without this nothing could be done. Lectures illustrated by posters and lantern
slides were given and a microscope was set up near a contaminated water source so that the peasants could themselves see
the germs swimming about in the water. An old Chinese saying
holds that one seeing is worth ten thousand hearings. Once
they were convinced that they had been swallowing millions of
microorganisms, they cooperated wholeheartedly.

A village near the Four Seas clinic had only one well and outbreaks of intestinal infection there were common. An investigating group from the mobile medical team found that the
water was heavily contaminated. The mouth of the well opened
at ground level and was surrounded by mud and excreta which
were washed into the well whenever it rained. Moreover, as
many peasants regretfully affirmed, not a few piglets and chickens had fallen into the well, never to be seen again. The team
suggested building a low wall around the mouth of the well,

covering it with removable wooden boards and paving the surrounding soil with stone slabs. The peasants agreed and, working together with the doctors and nurses, soon had the job done. After this, outbreaks of intestinal infection gradually ceased and a few weeks later the peasants could see that there were no more wriggling germs in the water. Drums and gongs to celebrate victory over the tiny enemy! And the word got around that these young doctors sometimes knew what they were talking about and that it might be worthwhile to listen to their advice. . . .

Sometimes it is impossible to make water safe at the source and then it must be sterilized after it has been collected. Since this region lacks coal and the accumulation of brush wood is labor consuming, boiling is not practicable and chlorination is often used instead. Water is stored in large earthenware urns and bleaching powder, which is issued free, is added to reach a chlorine concentration of from one per cent to three per cent which sterilizes the water without excessively affecting its taste.

A very important aspect of preventive work concerns the disposal of human and animal excreta. This is not a schistosomiasis area but feces can spread diseases in three ways. Firstly, by contaminating drinking water it can spread water-borne diseases. Secondly, it can provide a breeding place for flies which carry the germs of dysentery and gastro-enteritis. Thirdly, it can spread hookworm and roundworm for, if untreated feces containing worm eggs is used as fertilizer, the crops will be contaminated with eggs which will grow into mature worms after being swallowed. The mobile teams urge the peasants to use leakproof, covered latrines and they themselves have constructed many prototypes about two feet long, one foot wide and one foot deep, lined with bricks or with stones bound with lime and covered by a wooden board. When the peasants appreciate their advantages, they are widely adopted and in some villages every house now has its own latrine.

When the latrines are emptied, the excrement, mixed with animal dung, is treated by a simple process of high-temperature composting. A mixture of equal parts of dung, earth, water and straw is piled into a specially prepared pit in which vertically placed sheaves of maize provide ventilation. Gradually, the temperature of the compost rises high enough to kill harmful worm eggs and make it safe for use as fertilizer. After high-temperature composting, the manure becomes lighter in weight and easier to spread while its effectiveness as fertilizer is enhanced.

In the northern mountainous region where I worked, lice elimination is also part of the preventive work carried out by the mobile medical teams, for lice can spread typhus fever. This is one of the activities where the duties of the health workers and of the Patriotic Health Campaign overlap. The mobile team supplies the know-how and the materials while the actual work is carried out by volunteers working under the local committee of the Patriotic Health Campaign. In this region, lice are only a problem in the cold weather when the peasants wear padded clothes and sleep under quilts which are not easily washed. A delousing team, equipped with sprayers and a solution lethal to lice, visits every cottage while the peasants are working in the fields and thoroughly sprays the quilts and straw mats covering the *kang*. The peasants habitually sleep on the heated *kang* covered by quilts and so the same night the delousing team returns and sprays their padded clothing. The procedure is repeated three times at weekly intervals and this greatly reduces the number of lice even if it does not completely eliminate them.

Another example of preventive work is the prevention of goiter, which formerly affected most adults in some villages. The main cause, lack of iodine in the drinking water, has now been remedied by adding an iodine compound to table salt. As a result goiter is now less common and in time it will disappear.

The therapeutic or curative work carried out by the mobile teams takes place at three levels; in the central clinics, in the small village clinics, and in the homes of sick villagers.

The Four Seas central clinic, which was completed in May 1966, comprises several single-storied brick buildings. It does not yet have electricity or running water but these will soon be laid on. It is linked with the surrounding communes by good roads and receives patients at any time. Very low fees, which can be waived when necessary, are charged and paid into the clinic funds.

Most kinds of blood tests can be carried out and in its first six months, 138 operations including radical excision of tuberculous lesions of the spine, intestinal obstruction, Caesarian section, removal of the gall bladder, hernia and appendectomy were performed there. A few years before, none of these operations could have been performed in the countryside, the patients would have gone without treatment and many of them would have died.

Although the therapeutic work at the next level, in the small village clinics, is on a modest scale, its value should not be underestimated. These clinics, housed in typical three-room peasant cottages, use one room for clinical examination, one for minor surgery and midwifery, and one as a pharmacy. Patients are seen at any time of the day or night, the staff consisting of three or four doctors and nurses from the mobile medical team and a few traditional doctors. Originally the traditional doctors conducted private practice, directly charging fees for their services. Then they amalgamated to form group practices which were still essentially of a private nature. Next they formed collectives, paid their fees into a common fund and drew fixed salaries. The advent of the mobile team increased the scope of their work but lowered its profitability because the fees charged by the mobile team were much lower than their own. To solve this problem, the mobile team members now also pay their receipts into the common fund of the traditional doctors who, in return, have lowered their charges to the mobile team level. This means, in effect, that a Peking municipal hospital is subsidizing medical services for peasants some hundreds of miles away, for it still pays the salaries of mobile team members. This cannot be a permanent arrangement and the method of remuneration of traditional doctors in the village clinics must undergo further change. One possibility which is being discussed is for the People's Communes to incorporate the village clinics and either pay their medical workers fixed salaries, or enroll them as commune members and allocate them work points in the usual way. The only final solution is a free comprehensive medical service for all, but this is not yet feasible. One of the important lessons of the new health policy is that by relying on the socialist consciousness and enthusiasm of medical workers, and by training local personnel, it is possible in China to improvise a rural health service very cheaply during the course of building up the country. It will not take many years before a comprehensive free health service is available for all.

The third level of the therapeutic service is in the villagers' own homes and even in the fields while they are working. This is certainly the most novel and possibly also the most important aspect of therapeutic work in the rural areas. Team members stationed in the cottage clinics are responsible for weekly or twice-weekly visits to every village in the neighborhood. The villagers know the approximate time of the doctor's arrival and with traditional Chinese courtesy wait for him at the entrance to the village. Everybody knows everybody else in these villages and it is not necessary to inquire far to find out who is sick, where he lives and what his symptoms are. As the doctor goes from cottage to cottage he collects an ever-growing retinue of followers and "advisers," mostly children who give the proceedings a charming atmosphere of informality. The mountain folk are wonderfully generous and warm-hearted and though their possessions are meager they lavish hospitality on their visitors. . . .

One might argue that it is not an efficient way of using doctors, when there are so few of them, to let them spend hours tramping from village to village seeing a handful of patients. But that would be a one-sided viewpoint, for it would take no account of the tremendous stimulus to morale which these domiciliary visits give to the peasants who constitute 80 per cent of China's total population. Nor would it allow for the fact that were it otherwise, the doctors could not know how the majority of their fellow countrymen live and work. Nor would it recognize that unless a peasant is really incapacitated, he prefers to put up with aches and pains and go on working rather than take a day off to go and see a doctor. Nor would it take into account the fact that the mobile medical teams are pioneering the rural medical service of the future.

Mobile team members based on the village clinics carry medical boxes with them so that they can dispense medicines on the spot. In the surgical field, at first they performed only minor operations but, with increasing experience, they undertook major emergency operations and later, nonemergency major operations performed in the villagers' own cottages. This saves the peasants much money and trouble and the results have been very good. Although hygienic conditions in the cottages are poor, the post-operative infection rate is certainly no higher and may even be lower than in modern, air-conditioned hospitals.

One mobile team of eye surgeons, working in the south of China, performed more than a thousand eye operations without a single case of infection.

Elsewhere I describe some operations which have been successfully performed in peasants' cottages in this isolated mountainous region. The examples given could be multiplied many times.

The Second Task

The second of the six tasks is to train auxiliary medical personnel from among the local people. It is this aspect of their work that I personally consider to hold the key to future advances.

China, like many other countries, needs many more doctors and needs them quickly. China, like *all* other countries, needs doctors who are completely devoted to the welfare of the ordinary people, who understand them, who are not separated from them by barriers of cash or class and who can serve both their immediate and their long-term needs.

I am convinced that after a period of trial and error, the policy of training medical workers from among the local population can meet both of these needs for China.

Since the concept is a new one and is still in an experimental stage, the methods and objectives of training vary greatly from province to province but the objective everywhere is to train one peasant doctor for each production brigade, one volunteer sanitary worker for each production team and enough midwives to ensure that every peasant woman giving birth is helped by a person of some professional competence.

Since there are some seventy thousand People's Communes in China and every Commune is divided into production brigades which are in turn subdivided into production teams, it is clearly intended to train many hundreds of thousands of medical workers.

I shall again write only about my personal experience in one particular area.

Peasant Doctors

In the area served by the Four Seas clinic, the training of peasant doctors started in November 1965 after the autumn harvest had been reaped and the grain was safely in the granaries. Each of the thirty-two production brigades in the area held meetings to select candidates for medical training, giving preference to intelligent youths with three years of secondary school education who had shown concern for the collective interests. Only two girls were selected because of a natural reluctance to train people who might leave their villages when they marry. The thirty-two candidates went to Four Seas clinic where they were interviewed by their prospective teachers and they studied there until the following April when they returned to their villages in time for the spring sowing.

Throughout their period of training, emphasis was placed on developing those Communist qualities so stressed by Mao Tsetung, of selfless service to the people, of limitless responsibility in work and of perseverance in the face of difficulties. The intention was not merely to impart medical knowledge, but to evolve a new kind of socialist-minded rural health worker who would retain the closest links with the peasants and be content to stay permanently in the countryside.

For the first two weeks they studied anatomy and physiology, dissected pigs, and attended lectures illustrated by models and lantern slides. After this introductory course they learned the elements of bacteriology and pathology in the mornings and clinical medicine and hygiene in the afternoons. They learned to identify germs in contaminated water and to recognize the eggs of worm parasites in excreta. They learned how to make drinking water safe, how to treat night-soil, how to sterilize needles and syringes and how to give injections. They learned how infectious diseases are spread and how to diagnose them. They accompanied their teacher doctors on their rounds, learned the use of the stethoscope, how to take a medical history, how to diagnose common diseases and how to detect the signs of serious illness. They examined patients who came to the clinic and discussed their findings with the doctor in charge. They concentrated on a few diseases commonly seen in the neighborhood, and on the use and dosage of some forty drugs. They memorized fifty acupuncture points and the symptom complexes which they control and they practiced the technique of acupuncture. Each student was issued a well-illustrated book specially written for peasant doctors.

They studied hard and enthusiastically. Late at night, they read aloud to each other by the uncertain light of oil lamps, discussing problems and never hesitating to consult their teachers with whom they lived as equals and with whom they shared the day-to-day household chores, in addition to nursing the patients.

As the winter went by and the frozen streams began to thaw, the students gained in confidence and initiative. They took turns being on night duty, welcoming patients who came from afar with a hot drink and a friendly greeting, and making a preliminary examination before calling the doctor.

Five months is a very short time in which to learn the rudiments of medicine but these students learned more in five months than I would have thought possible. They learned fast because their studies were practical and combined theory with practice, because they were determined to justify the trust put in them by their own folk and because, although young, they were mature working men, disciplined and capable.

While studying, they were credited with the number of work points which they would have earned if they had remained in their villages. Tuition and accommodation were free; they brought grain with them and went home for more when necessary.

In the spring when they returned to their brigades, they were issued with medical boxes, resumed work in the fields, but also looked after the health of their fellow peasants. Their medical work was unpaid but if it resulted in a loss of work points, these were made up. They supplied drugs at cost price, using the money to replenish their stocks and getting more when needed from the brigade cashier.

I spent many hours talking, walking and working with Wang Sheng-li, a twenty-eight-year-old peasant doctor in training. He is a slightly built, intelligent, earnest young man who models himself on Dr. Bethune. He told me that he was determined to master his new profession and to use his skill unstintingly in the service of his fellow peasants. He wore a Red Guard armband and described how the Cultural Revolution in his village was sweeping away superstition and other obstacles to the advance of socialism, changing bad habits and replacing them by beneficial ones. The old custom of giving mothers nothing to

eat but gruel for three months after childbirth had been criticized and now mothers were given eggs, fish and bean curd. A
nearby temple had been stripped of unsuitable paintings and
converted into a children's nursery. He was intensely interested
in politics, read the newspapers avidly, listened to the radio and
was never without his little red book of quotations from the
writings of Mao Tse-tung which he cited frequently and aptly.

I joined him and Dr. Chen, a consultant physician and one
of Wang's teachers from the previous winter, on their weekly
round of patients. Young Wang told Dr. Chen about his diagnosis and treatment and listened eagerly to his comments. Im-
pressed by the accuracy of Wang's observations, I asked him
to tell me about his recent surgical experiences. He thought for
a moment and then told me of four surgical emergencies he had
dealt with in the last few weeks.

"The first one," he said, "was Old Gao, a carpenter over in
Ten Family Inn village. His wife telephoned to say that a
wooden chest which he had been making had fallen on him a
few hours before and that he seemed to be in a bad way. I went
over to see him and found him groaning and moaning and rolling all over the *kang*. I couldn't count his pulse rate since I had
gone straight from the fields and didn't have my watch with me
but it was certainly faster than mine and I had been hurrying.
His belly was as hard as a board. I always have my medical box
with me so I got out my blood pressure apparatus and measured
his blood pressure. As far as I could make out, the high pressure was only 60 m.m. but I'm not very good at measuring the
blood pressure, and I might have been wrong. Then I listened
to his belly with my stethoscope. I knew that I should hear
some gurgling noises showing that the intestines were working
normally but I couldn't hear a thing. That made me think that
he must have burst something inside his belly and that the best
thing to do was to get him to the Four Seas clinic as quickly as
possible. It's not very far and Old Gao's son and myself took
turns at carrying him on our backs, but by the time we had
gone half way, he was shouting that he couldn't stand the pain
so I gave him an injection of pain killer. The pain killer worked
well and we got to Four Seas before sunset."

Dr. Chen took up the story. "We operated on him that night
and found that young Wang was quite right. He had torn a hole

in his large intestine and there was nearly a pint of blood in the abdomen. It might have been better if Wang had called us out rather than bring Old Gao in because although it's not very far, it's a long way for a sick man and it's rough going. Anyway, he did very well and is back at work now.". . .

The provisional plan is for peasant doctors to have at least three periods of full-time teaching at yearly intervals. As I write, the land is again in the grip of winter and the thirty-two peasant doctors who started their training last year have reassembled at the Four Seas "medical school" for their second course of study.

The method of study is different from what it was last year because the teachers now have experience in training peasant doctors and because the requirements of the students are different.

Last year they studied only commonly seen diseases, but this year they systematically study all the diseases of particular organs. For example, last year when learning about lung diseases, they only studied bronchitis, emphysema and asthma while this year they are learning about pneumonia, pleurisy, tuberculosis and lung cancer.

Last year they studied anatomy and physiology as a whole in a short, concentrated, superficial course. This year they are re-studying it in relation to diseases of particular organs. When they study lung diseases, they also revise and deepen their knowledge of the anatomy and physiology of the lungs.

Last year diseases were studied at random; this year they are grouped together according to specialties such as medicine, surgery, gynecology, ophthalmology.

Last year it was not always possible to find actual patients to illustrate their theoretical studies, but this year their teachers know where to find examples of diseases related to lectures given that day.

This year the practical work is conducted mostly in the students' own villages but the students also visit Peking's teaching hospitals and see advanced medical techniques in use. Although it will be many years before these village doctors have access to the latest medical techniques, it is valuable for them to have some knowledge of the level which one day they must reach and surpass.

I know that some educationalists in the West view this kind of experiment with apprehension and talk of the dangers of "lowering standards." They should realize that before Liberation, when the handful of medical students in the Rockefeller-endowed Peking Union Medical College had higher standards and a longer course of study than medical students in England or America, this did not benefit the Chinese peasants, for the overwhelming majority of them enjoyed no medical services of any kind. Chairman Mao quotes an old Chinese saying to the effect that what is needed is not more flowers embroidered on the brocade but fuel in snowy weather.

The training of peasant doctors makes it possible not only to increase rapidly the available medical personnel in China's countryside, but also, in the long term, to produce a better type of doctor than orthodox methods of training can do. It is much more than a temporary expedient. Whatever gaps a peasant doctor may have in his medical knowledge can be made good as he gains experience or by joining refresher courses in city hospitals. His uniquely valuable characteristic is his closeness to his patients. They are his own folk and there is mutual trust and confidence between them. The results of his work are constantly tested in practice in such a way that he can learn immediately both from success and failure. He is both a peasant and a doctor and cannot sink into narrow professionalism or become mentally divorced from the people he serves.

In addition to training peasant doctors, the mobile teams also train sanitary workers and midwives. The former, who receive two weeks' training in basic first-aid and sanitary work, continue to work mainly as peasants but are also available for minor injuries and for ensuring that the water protection and night-soil disposal procedures initiated by the mobile teams are maintained and extended. They are issued with first-aid materials and a few drugs for minor ailments.

The latter are usually village girls in their twenties, although some are older and are themselves mothers. They are given a few weeks' practical and theoretical instruction in the principles of midwifery and accompany the doctors when they conduct prenatal examinations and deliveries. Their duties are to anticipate difficulties in childbirth by regular prenatal examinations and to assist women who have previously had normal deliveries.

In case of difficulty, they call on the mobile team for help. Although they cannot become expert midwives after a few weeks' training, that can be remedied by further experience and repeated courses. They are undeniably a big improvement on the ignorant, unhygienic gamps whom they replace. I spoke to several mothers who had been delivered by these newly trained midwives and they were well satisfied. One of them said, "Childbirth used to be a dangerous ordeal but now we approach it with a light heart, knowing that we and our babies will survive." The population in her village had doubled since Liberation because of the phenomenal reduction in infantile and maternal mortality and the complete disappearance of the tragic necessity, for so long imposed by poverty and hunger, of doing away with baby girls at birth.

The Third Task

The third task is to make the Party's policy of planned parenthood become a reality in the Chinese countryside.

This is not a nationwide policy, for some national minority areas such as Tibet, Inner Mongolia, and parts of Yunnan are, as a result of centuries of poverty, disease, and oppression, dangerously underpopulated. Here the policy is to improve conditions and gradually to build up the population.

To make planned parenthood available to all, it is necessary first to educate the people to understand its advantages and secondly to provide them with the means of achieving it. The mobile teams carry out both these tasks.

I attended an evening lecture on hygiene and birth control illustrated by an old-style magic lantern using a pressurized paraffin lamp. The village hall was packed and, although children were nominally excluded, they couldn't resist the fascination of the brightly lit colored lantern slides. At first they peered through the windows and then, as the pressure on window space grew, they infiltrated into the hall until they became a majority of the audience.

After dealing with such mundane subjects as night-soil disposal, fly control and food protection, the speaker, a doctor from the mobile team, described the anatomy and physiology of the male and female organs of reproduction. An animated filmstrip showed the process of penetration of the sperm into the ovum and a gasp of astonishment greeted the spectacle of the fertilized ovum dividing and redividing until it looked first like a raspberry and then like a curled-up tadpole.

Then he described various methods of contraception, discussed their advantages and disadvantages and passed around contraceptive appliances for inspection. At this point the children lost interest and filed out, admonished by their parents to go straight home.

He spoke of the advantages of planned parenthood, showing that limitation of families to two or three children was in the interests of the children, of their parents and of the country; that mothers would be better able to look after their children; that schools would be less crowded; that mothers would be able to play a bigger part in producing wealth for the benefit of all; and that mother and child would be healthier and happier.

He urged the women to discuss it among themselves and with their husbands.

When he had finished, the barrage of questions showed that the women were deeply interested in the new possibilities opening up for them.

Subsequently, I asked many village women what they thought of family planning and their answers revealed two conflicting, but perfectly understandable, trends. One was that in the past they had been too poor to raise children, many had died at birth or starved to death and those who survived had gone hungry, naked and unlettered. Now that there were food and schools for all, and life was pleasant and secure, why should they restrict their families? This view was warmly supported by grandparents steeped in the Confucian tradition that many grandchildren brought them honor, prosperity and social security.

The other trend was to welcome the idea of planned parenthood and to appreciate its advantages but sometimes to doubt whether it was possible.

The propagandists first try to win the support of the peasants' own organizations, especially the women's organizations, for once this has been done the idea usually gains acceptance.

The means of contraception are provided free by the State and specialized family-planning mobile teams have been organized for propaganda and instruction in the technique of birth control. Many methods are in use but none are ideal. A large-scale trial of the contraceptive pill is in progress but it is too early to be certain that it is free from risk. The intrauterine device is fairy satisfactory in towns but in the countryside, among women who do heavy manual labor, it has been found to have disadvantages.

Research work, propaganda and practical work go hand in hand and I am sure that, before long, Chinese women in town and countryside will be able to control the size and spacing of their families according to their wishes.

The Fourth Task

The fourth task is to cooperate with and raise the level of the medical services which existed in the countryside before the mobile teams arrived on the scene.

Developments in the Four Seas Clinic illustrate this. The clinic was established by the county government in 1952 with a staff of one traditional doctor and one pharmacist. Later they were joined by other traditional and middle-grade doctors but they were professionally isolated and their accommodations and equipment were poor. The advent of highly trained members of the mobile team, and of doctors from Peking who have settled down in the countryside, has made an enormous advance possible. They work together as a team, learning from each other and consulting on difficult problems. The newcomers contribute their knowledge of modern medicine and the original clinic members their knowledge of local conditions and of traditional remedies. The old shacks in which they originally worked have been replaced by a large brick building with accommodation for twenty-five patients, an operating room, an out-patient department, a laboratory where biochemical and blood tests can be carried out, and a library of medical books and journals. It has become, in effect, a small modern rural hospital serving fifteen thousand people.

The same kind of progress, on a more modest scale, can be seen in the little village clinics. The old fee-paying system and the last vestiges of private practice are disappearing. Even tiny clinics like the one in Pearl Spring village have a microscope and apparatus for blood-testing. The original staff there exchange experiences with their colleagues from Peking and refresher courses are arranged for them in leading Peking hospitals.

The Fifth Task

The fifth task is to cooperate with and assist the Patriotic Health Campaign, a mass movement which originally concentrated on eliminating flies, bedbugs, rats and mosquitoes. Under the stimulus of the mobile medical teams, its work now includes lice elimination, water control, food protection and the safe disposal of night-soil. In several villages, Patriotic Health Campaign activists, working in cooperation with mobile medical team members, have used simple, indigenous methods to install running-water systems and bathhouses. Through the Patriotic Health Campaign, the mobile teams are linked directly with the villagers.

The Sixth Task

The sixth task is for members of the mobile medical teams to utilize the opportunity of a year in the countryside, in close contact with the peasants, to deepen their understanding of the laboring people, and to change their thinking in such a way that they fit better into the new society and become more effective in building socialism.

Though this task is less concrete than the other five, an understanding of it is one of the keys to understanding New China.

A basic tenet of Marxism is that the thinking of people and their moral values are determined by the kind of society in which they live and by their status in that society.

It is sometimes assumed that the moral values of one's own day and age have, with slight modifications, always existed; that they are inborn, part of "human nature," fixed and unchangeable. However, a backward glance shows that this is not so.

In ancient Greece, many slave owners doubtless considered themselves to be enlightened and humane men. They may well have been so according to the standards of their time, but time moved on, society changed and with it men's thinking, so that today slavery is viewed with abhorrence.

In European feudal society, the ruling class considered it right and proper not only that peasants should till their fields, but that they should be serfs tied to their lord's land and, in many places, that the lord should have the right of the first night. Few would defend these rights today.

The capitalist society, in which I was born and bred, fosters the conviction that it is a law of nature that some should live off the labor of others, that some should be rich and some poor, that some should own factories and hire others to work in them, that black people should toil to keep white people in luxury, that the driving force in society should be self-interest.

What slave society, feudal society and capitalist society have in common is that the dominant world outlook in each of them is selfishness.

When the revolution triumphed in 1949 and China started to build socialism, it was relatively easy to change the economic structure of society. But the cataclysmic upheaval by which one class overthrew another was merely the first step on the long road to the society of the future. There remained the much more difficult and protracted task of changing the standpoint, thinking, morals and habits of millions of people so that much of what had seemed natural in the old society would seem unnatural and hateful in the new, and what had seemed impossible in the old society would become desirable and entirely possible in the new.

This process of change, known in China as ideological remolding, is difficult for everyone but especially so for those who in the old society were accustomed to leading a soft life and enjoying special privileges.

Two thousands years of feudalism in China implanted a deep-rooted contempt for the unlettered peasants in the minds of the intellectuals.

Mao Tse-tung, recalling his own student days, wrote: "I began life as a student and at school acquired the ways of a student. . . . At that time I felt that intellectuals were the only clean people in the world, while in comparison workers and peasants were dirty. I did not mind wearing the clothes of other intellectuals, believing them clean, but I would not put on clothes belonging to a worker or peasant, believing them dirty. But after I became a revolutionary and lived with workers and

peasants . . . I came to know them well . . . I came to feel that
. . . in the last analysis the workers and peasants were the clean-
est people, even though their hands were soiled and their feet
smeared with cow dung. . . ."

The sixth task given to the mobile medical teams is, by mix-
ing closely with the laboring people and sharing in their struggles for a better life, to initiate a similar change in their own
thinking, so that they can take the first step towards ideological
remolding.

Most of China's doctors and nurses have had little or no contact with peasants. When I joined a mobile team myself, I expected that the process of adjustment from the soft city life to
the hard life of the villages would be difficult for them. But I
was often surprised to see how quickly my colleagues settled
down. Within a few short weeks most of them were enjoying
enormous meals of coarse grain which they would never have
looked at in Peking, participating enthusiastically in heavy manual labor and feeling thoroughly at home with the peasants.
I expressed my surprise to a rather pampered young woman
doctor whose airs and graces had earned her the doubtful title
of "Shanghai miss." She said, "Yes—I'm surprised too. Before
I came down here I thought I'd never be able to live on millet.
It's so hard and my stomach has always been delicate. But
funnily enough it seems to agree with me. For the first few
weeks, life here was really very difficult. The brick *kangs* were
terribly hard to sleep on, I had a horror of lice, the latrines disgusted me and I hated the idea of eating from the same bowl
as the peasants. Now I have got used to all these things. I sleep
much more soundly than in Peking, lice are nothing to be afraid
of and the peasants are so kind and generous that I feel
ashamed of my squeamishness. After all, why should I be so
choosy? These peasants work from dawn to dusk almost every
day of the year producing food for all of us. They don't make
a song and dance about it. They are unselfish and are happy to
be making their contribution to our country. Now that I have
got used to living in the countryside, my heart seems to be
warmer, the paths seem broader and the meals more appetizing
than any I have eaten before.". . .

Dr. Wang, an overseas Chinese from Indonesia, told me
about an outbreak of impetigo of the scalp among children in

the village where he was stationed. "Quite a number of children were affected," he said, "so I issued penicillin ointment to the mothers and told them to apply it three times a day. However, the disease continued to spread and I discovered that most of the mothers were out working in the fields and that they were not applying the ointment regularly. They had told the children to rub it in but the youngsters couldn't do it thoroughly. So I applied it myself and they soon got better. Before I came to the countryside, I would have considered it beneath my dignity to spend my time rubbing ointment into children's heads. But here it's just a division of labor. The mothers work in the fields to produce food for us all and I, if I am to be fully responsible, as Dr. Bethune was, should personally make sure that their children are properly treated."

Another doctor told me of a bitter lesson he had learned when he had treated a little boy suffering from meningitis. "When I arrived at the cottage, the parents were overjoyed," he said. "They looked on me as a savior and I felt like one. I assured them that I would soon have their son out of danger but, in spite of working all night, he died very early the next morning. I didn't know what to say to the parents. On the one hand I wanted to console them, but on the other hand I wanted to shield myself. After a mental struggle I decided to tell them that they had called me too late. Just then they came into the room and saw that their child was dead. They were terribly distressed but without hesitation they took me by the arm and started consoling me, telling me that I had worked very hard and had done my best and that I shouldn't take it too hard. I felt so ashamed that tears ran down my checks. You see, we doctors are always concerned about our reputations and, although we do the best we can for our patients, we don't really feel that we are from the same family. But these peasants regard us in the same way as they do their own family. They consoled me when their own child died but I was prepared to tell them that they had called me too late. Here in the countryside we treat their physical ailments and they, without knowing it, treat our ideological ailments."

I would not like to give the impression that ideological remolding, in the sense in which the Chinese use the word, is an easy process which can be accomplished by reading books, by solitary introspection, by generating a surfeit of good intentions or by roughing it in the countryside for a year or two.

On the contrary, it is a lifelong process which, above all, necessitates identification with the struggles of the laboring people to transform the world.

Some mobile team members who seem to make progress while they are in the countryside relapse when they return to the towns. Others never really succeed in learning to "talk the same language and breathe the same air" as the peasants; they regard their sojourn in the villages as a penance to be endured in the interests of their future.

But, taken by and large, the great majority benefit considerably. They get to know and to like the peasants; become more desirous of serving them wholeheartedly and better able to do so; they start to get rid of their selfishness, their competitiveness and their feelings of superiority.

They start to become the kind of socialist-minded, versatile, resourceful medical worker which China needs in hundreds of thousands.

The sixth task of the mobile medical team is, therefore, the key to the accomplishment of the other five.

RUTH AND VICTOR SIDEL*
The Human Services in China

When we arrived in China for a month's visit at the invitation of the Chinese Medical Association, we brought with us a number of preconceptions. Although we knew that most of China's people lived in rural areas, our image of China was one of teeming, poor, and therefore frightening cities. We expected, too, a highly regimented, monotonous society, unrelieved by variety or experiment. Although we knew that the Cultural

*Ruth and Victor Sidel, "The Human Services in China," *Social Policy*, March/April 1972, pp. 25–34.

Revolution had changed some things, we expected to be alienated by a managerial and Communist party elite with chauffeurs and the Chinese equivalent of the Russians' dachas. We also expected to find a worship of Mao bordering on religious fanaticism. And we expected to find an overwhelming and, to us, highly distasteful military presence. What we actually found in September and October 1971 was very different. China is predominantly rural, and our lasting impression is of a vast countryside, green and heavily planted. Its cities are mostly carless, clean, and unhurried, with little or no sign of boredom, cynicism, or irritability. And its people, its great masses of courteous, enormously hard-working people, surprised us immediately, as we realized that the general uniformity of their dress in no way made them either faceless or anonymous. Indeed, we grew more sensitive to faces and their expression, rather than the quirks of clothing and manner that usually stand out among Westerners.

We began to explore China through the Chinese. We found a country with a deep sense of mission and history. A nation trying to be daringly experimental, uncompromisingly doctrinaire, and unconstrainedly pragmatic. In the last few years it has become "democratic" in an antielitist, antihierarchical way that would shock corporate Russians as well as corporate Americans. Above all, it has become the center of some extremely strong beliefs about man and the world—that the highest end of the individual is selfless service to the people; that the people, working together, can do almost anything; and that politics should be total, in fact, should suffuse every aspect of life.

Just how seriously many Chinese take those beliefs—and how with their widespread literal acceptance those beliefs form the intellectual keystone of the country's huge structure of social services—was demonstrated to us daily, if not hourly, as spokesman after spokesman—in hospitals, kindergartens, factories, communes, and government offices—expressed to us the importance in their work of Mao Tse-tung and his thoughts. . . .

No less important is the Chinese faith in learning by doing and in learning precisely what is needed—no more, no less— to do any given job. Perhaps crucial to the whole complex edifice is an unceasing effort to combat rivalry and careerism

and to foster cooperation and teamwork. The People's Liberation Army, for example, is visible everywhere, but in an
essentially helpful role—part Civilian Conservation Corps and
VISTA, part U.S. Public Health Service, part management
consultants. No doubt other Army members, or even the same
ones we saw at other times and places, are practicing marching
or whatever it is that armies do to prepare for (or, as the
Chinese put it, "against") war. But the visible role, by the
tradition of Mao's 8th Route Army, was one of service.

In almost all of our meetings with health professionals and
other service people, paraprofessionals and nonprofessionals
were present and encouraged to speak up without any formality
or awe of authority. A medical professor, the head of a commune hospital, a "barefoot doctor," a midwife—each would
carry himself with a calm assurance that left us with a strong
overall feeling of easy comradeship and genuine equality. . . .

Participation, mutual involvement, the breaking down of
tendencies toward isolation or exclusiveness, the closing of the
gaps between the city and the country, the intellectual and the
laborer—these are the key notions in China's human services
system. From preschool age children are taught to help one
another and to do things together. Even after retirement the
aged are given important responsibilities. Public health campaigns for such things as mass immunization are carried out
by direct contact among neighbors. In medical colleges the
entrance requirements that once favored the children of the
bourgeoisie have given way to the active recruitment of students
from communes and factories. In psychiatric care, too, the
Chinese try to bring the resources of the entire community
into play; in fact, at no point in the system is the importance
of communal activity better exhibited than in its response to
mental illness.

MENTAL HEALTH

The Chinese conception of good care for mental illness is a
blend, like their medicine, of old and new and individual and
collective techniques, with the whole held together by the daily
study of Mao Tse-tung's thought. Indeed, the watchword of the

entire enterprise is Mao's "Let us heal the wounded and rescue the dead"; and the framework of community effort toward the goal—what it turns out to be in practice is a powerful community mental health design. Seven essential components are involved in this system:

Collective help. Patients are organized into divisions and urged to take part in the hospital's operations and to take care of one another—the older cases of the newer ones, the milder cases of the graver ones. Group discussions and study sessions also are heavily emphasized.

Self-reliance. Mental patients are encouraged to "struggle against their disease" and to investigate it in order both to understand themselves and to prevent a relapse. Accordingly, each patient makes continuing efforts at self-criticism and self-analysis based on such non-Freudian principles as Mao's philosophy and the Marxist dialectic.

Physical therapy. Patients with more serious disorders receive chlorpromazine (Thorazine), a calming agent widely used in American psychiatry. Acupuncture is also used experimentally "for relief of excitement." But electroshock and insulin shock therapy have been abandoned.

"Heart-to-heart talks." A psychiatrist meets with patients at regular intervals, individually and in groups, to discuss their problems candidly and guide them through the process of self-investigation.

Community ethos. Through deep involvement with one another, members of the community at large are relied on to provide support and stability for the mentally troubled, both preventively and after discharge, when a patient is considered to be of "great concern" to his family, his neighbors, and his fellow workers.

Follow-up care. After a patient leaves the hospital, he is examined periodically—usually every two weeks at first, then once a month—either at the hospital's outpatient department or through home visits by a doctor or a nurse. The patient is often maintained on medication, though with smaller doses.

The teachings of Mao. Running like a thread through the whole mental health system is the thought of the Chairman—not only slogans or inspirational material, but also difficult philosophical essays such as "On Practice." The point is "to arm the mind to fight disease," to conquer hallucinations and paranoiac ideas, for example, by learning to "recognize a fact" and distinguish the subjective from the objective.

In the psychiatric department of the Third Teaching Hospital attached to the First Peking Medical School, we got to see the process in action. After being shown some of the patients' rooms—they were furnished only with beds and bureaus and had political posters on the walls—we were brought into the patients' clubroom. There the patients spend much of their time—playing ping-pong, listening to the radio, watching television, preparing bandages and medicines as occupational therapy, and conducting study sessions on Mao's thought. A meeting had been called for our benefit, and a small group of patients, dressed in pajamas and striped robes, gathered around a table to tell us "how I use Chairman Mao's thought to conquer difficulties."

The first patient was a man in his early thirties who had been diagnosed as a paranoid schizophrenic. His paranoia centered on his wife. "I was suspicious of my wife," he said. "I insisted that she wanted to divorce me, but she said that she didn't." After being persuaded to enter the hospital by his family and fellow workers, he gradually began to recognize that something was wrong with him mentally. He had, he said, to make a class analysis of the causes of his disease. At last, he said, he realized that the trouble was within himself, that his subjective thinking was not objectively correct. He was too self-interested, he said, but if he could put the public interest first and his own interest second, he would resolve the contradictions and his thinking would be correct again.

Another patient who spoke was a woman in her twenties, a graduate of junior high school, whose main symptom was auditory hallucinations. She said she had heard a voice asking, "What's below your pillow?" and had come to the "ridiculous" conclusion that it was a "biological radio apparatus" placed there by a special agent investigating her. She became agitated, she said, hearing loud speeches in her mind and suffering severe headaches. On entering the hospital, she said, medication had relieved her headaches, but not her hallucinations. Now, she said, she still hears the voices, but she quickly recognizes they don't really exist as a result of an investigation based on the works of Mao. The investigation she compared to a pregnancy; the solution of the problem to delivering a baby. She said that she was receiving acupuncture, drugs, and herb medication, that she was considering what was happening around the world in her studies, and that she had faith that she would continue to improve and finally be completely cured.

While the patients were telling us of their problems and treatment, forty or fifty others were seated around the room, most of them listening attentively. When the session was finished a chorus of men and women arose and sang for us. The singers were directed by a patient and accompanied by a violinist. On the whole the performance was similar to those we had seen elsewhere, with dancing and clapping as well as singing and with every word and gesture intended to convey a revolutionary meaning.

Later we had a long conversation with psychiatrists at the hospital. We were told that commitment always came through persuasion rather than force. The first days after admission were made less difficult by having long-time patients take the new people in hand and help them get accustomed to the surroundings and the regimen of treatment. There is no charge for hospitalization, only for food. Family members may visit a patient twice a week, and when he goes home they, along with his "lane" neighbors and fellow workers, are expected to take an interest in his problems and give him moral support. Usually, the doctors said, a patient goes back to the same job, although sometimes he is given work with less mental strain in the same setting. In any event he can be certain during his hospitalization that there is a job waiting for him.

In the Shanghai Mental Hospital we found much the same ideas and practices. The presence of Mao was all-pervasive. In a study group of eleven patients, two of the patients, serving as propagandists of Mao's thought among the other patients (a task that rotates through the wards), were wearing red armbands. The psychiatrists at this hospital said that more than half of their patients were schizophrenics. They see little suicide, depressive psychosis, or postpartum depression, and illness among teenagers is rare. Almost half of their patients are between the ages of twenty and thirty. The average duration of stay is seventy days and the relapse rate—according to a few simple ward studies in which "relapse" was defined as readmission or outpatient treatment—was below 20 percent.

There was laughter when we asked about Freud. He has had no influence since the revolution of 1949, the psychiatrists said. They have studied Pavlov, but felt he has had limited influence. What, then, in a socialist environment, was the basis of such a disorder as schizophrenia, which the doctors indicated was the most prevalent form of psychosis in China? They felt that there were predisposing factors at work within the patient himself. "Extrinsic factors work through intrinsic factors," one said. The socialist system is extremely beneficial to mental health, they said, because in general it eliminates objective contradictions between the individual and society.

It is hard to assess the respective weight of the various elements that comprise the Chinese mental health system—are features such as the use of groups, medication, or heart-to-heart talks primary, or is the thought of Chairman Mao essential? In any case the strong community base, the follow-up after release, the enlisting of family and fellow workers as part of the postcare team seem important even as American mental health practice, too, gives greater emphasis to community approaches. In essence the entire Chinese society is consistent with a sound community mental health approach: mutual dependence of patients and self-reliance is encouraged rather than dependence on the hospital; the mentally ill are not stigmatized and isolated, but rather are thoroughly integrated into the community life. The social consequences of mental illness, i.e., loss of job, loss of family supports, loss of role in community— things that contribute to chronicity—are not characteristic of modern China.

COMMUNITY ORGANIZATION

In *Deschooling Society* Ivan Illich points out that the poor have always been "socially powerless," but that modern poverty has made them "psychologically impotent" as well by forcing them to rely on institutions that in turn create a greater dependence rather than self-reliance. Certainly China is still a poor nation by most standards, but to us the people did not look "poor"; they did not exhibit any of the apathy and despair that we have come to associate with poverty in the United States. Perhaps it is because they each have the feeling that they play a role in the shaping of their own and their community's life. For within the context of Chinese communism—and there is no doubt that the Party sets policy and tone at all levels —we saw people acting with the obvious confidence and satisfaction of those who know that what they do will make a difference.

Indeed, to get a sense of how it feels to live and work in China one must grasp the way the Chinese community is divided and subdivided from the center of power out to the edges, in their phrase, to "the workers, peasants, and soldiers."

China has twenty-two provinces (including what the Chinese call the "unliberated province of Taiwan"), five autonomous districts in which national minority groups live, and three autonomous cities—Peking, Shanghai, and Tientsin—each of which is directly under the central government rather than the province in which it is situated. The cities are divided into neighborhoods or "streets," the lowest level of local government, and the streets are often further divided into "lanes," small block-like units of 1,500 to 8,000 people that have no official status but are important in the routine daily business of each community.

Chao Yang, a workers' villa or community in Shanghai, provides an example of local urban government. An area of low brick apartment buildings with grass and some trees in front —something like certain sections of Brooklyn—it has a population of 68,000 people, which makes it a "street" with a formal governmental structure. Most of the adults are employed at local textile factories. Two thousand children are enrolled in seven nurseries and kindergartens, 15,000 children in fourteen primary schools, and 13,000 children in seven middle schools. Within the community is a post office, a bank, a library, a cinema, a cultural station, a health station, barber shops, tailor shops, repair shops, restaurants, public baths, public gardens, vegetable, meat, and fruit markets, a swimming pool, and eight branch department stores.

The governing body of the villa is the Chao Yang Revolutionary Committee, which has twenty-one members—one from the People's Liberation Army, six "cadres" (political representatives, usually Communist Party members), and fourteen from the mass. All of the representatives of the mass live within the villa; only some of the cadres do. The day-to-day government of the villa is carried out by a standing committee of the revolutionary committee, consisting of nine members from the revolutionary committee, including the Army member. Except for one retired worker, who receives a pension from his former place of work, the members of the standing committee are full-time, paid workers. The villa is subdivided into eight lanes, each of which has a revolutionary committee that is considered a mass organization rather than a formal governmental structure.

One lane we visited has 8,000 people, who are further subdivided into 52 groups. A group usually consists of the inhabitants of a single building, and each group elects a leader and a deputy leader, who are generally retired workers and are not paid. The group will nominate candidates for the lane revolutionary committee, and the leaders then choose members of the committee from the nominees, "consulting with the mass" about the choice until everyone is satisfied. In the most recent election in this lane there were 68 candidates for the 38 seats on the committee.

The group leaders have numerous responsibilities: organizing the social services for the area; mediating quarrels; organizing retired workers to provide education for youth about the "bitter past"; performing health work; and organizing retired workers and housewives into groups for study of Mao's thought.

A cadre described the kinds of social services that the leaders perform. If mother and father are working and one of the children gets sick, the group leaders will arrange for medical care for the child. Of if the husband is working outside the area and the wife delivers a baby, the leaders will arrange for her to have help in buying food and other items. When there are quarrels within or among families, the leaders gather everyone together to consider how Mao's thought applies to the problem. Everyone participates—the aged, "little Red Guards," and workers. An entire building might participate. "By studying Mao's thought," the cadre said, "one can determine who is right and who is wrong, objectively. It is very rare that this does not solve the problems."

Although the lane committee has responsibility for social services, it was stressed that people could not rely on the revolutionary committee to do everything for them. "Self-reliance" is considered an important character trait; this no doubt accounts for some of the decentralization. Institutions have been decentralized to "raise up the initiative" of the mass as well as to make institutions responsive to those they serve.

HEALTH CARE

The community organization of health care offers an example of how these intricately interwoven groups and groups within groups can be directed toward a goal transcending all of them. Every local subdivision is organized for health care. For instance, the director of the health center in Silvery Lane in Hangchow—a stooped, leathery-faced elderly "housewife" with several teeth missing—is also a cadre and the "responsible member" (chairman, really, but the Chinese feel that term sounds too inflexible) of the lane revolutionary committee. She works full-time at all three of her jobs and receives no pay. Under her on the organizational chart on the wall of the health station are six cadres who are responsible, respectively, for general affairs, prevention, treatment, propaganda, organization, and administration. All of the cadres are housewives except for the cadre in charge of prevention, a doctor from the street health center.

The responsibilities of the lane health station are treatment of minor illnesses, health education (which the Chinese call "health propaganda"), immunization, and birth control. Silvery Lane consists of thirteen "blocks," and the number of health workers in each block ranged from two to seven. The health workers were all housewives, 80 percent of whom have other jobs. All were volunteers. They were trained by doctors and other health workers from the street health stations.

The immunization process shows how intimately the health workers become involved in their neighborhood's activities. Every child has a card with his immunization record on it. When it is time for that child to have another inoculation, the cadre from his block and the health worker visit the family (the distances are very small) to inform them, and the child is then brought to the health center for the shot. If it is not convenient for the child to be brought to the health station, the inoculation is occasionally given by the health worker in the home. Through recruitment of health workers from each lane and through close coordination between the health workers and the lane cadre, every child's health can be attended to.

From the 1920s on, Mao and his followers have been dedicated health reformers. In the twenty-three years since the Chinese Communists took power they have made extraordinary efforts to improve the quality of the nation's health care and to extend its benefits throughout the society. From our observations as well as those of several other recent visitors, China can point to a series of concrete advances.

The number of people receiving some form of modern medical care—including such regular preventive measures as inoculation, sanitation regulation, and health education—has increased enormously, from a small fraction of the population to essentially everyone.

Venereal disease (and along with it the institution of prostitution), drug addiction, and alcoholism have been overcome at a time when they are rising throughout the West and, at least in the case of V.D., in Poland and the Soviet Union, too.

The incidence of parasitic and infectious diseases has so far declined in Shanghai that now, as in many Western countries, cancer and cardiovascular diseases have become the principal causes of death. . . .

The Chinese cite various evidence of the success of their health measures. In the neighborhoods we visited records showed that more than 90 percent of the children had been inoculated against tuberculosis (BCG vaccination), diphtheria, whooping cough, tetanus, polio, measles, meningitis, and encephalitis. Careful records are kept of the contraceptive devices in use among the women in each area as well as of the birth rate. In one Hangchow lane we visited, the birth rate was 5.9 per 1,000; for the entire city of Shanghai it was 6 to 7 per 1,000. Compared to the birth rate for the United States (17 per 1,000), this is a remarkably low figure; compared to that of our poor urban areas such as the South Bronx, where the figure is about 25 per 1,000, it is almost unbelievable. The birth rate in rural areas of China is still high—three to four times that of the cities—but overall the Chinese appear to be making progress.

Another great change in the Chinese health care system has occurred in the medical schools. Reopened in 1970 after having been shut down during the height of the Cultural Revolution, the medical schools are now run by revolutionary committees that decide on the size of the classes and select students from candidates put forward by factories or communes. The selection is based on ideological commitment and physical fitness as well as academic ability. The curriculum is intended to turn out clinicians rather than researchers—indeed, the publication of research papers and medical journals in China is still suspended —and all but about one-quarter of the three-year term is spent out of the classroom in practical training of one kind or another.

After graduation the students who are chosen to specialize are sent to a specialty hospital where, like the psychiatrists we met, their training is deemed complete not through examinations, but through the agreement of their colleagues that they are ready. Such flexibility, while it raises the possibility of a good man's being held back by personal or political disagreements with his associates, is all but sure proof against the traditional professional methods that the Chinese have been combating in the last few years.

By far most of the new doctors return to the factories or communes that first chose them as candidates for medical training. No doubt they feel a sense of obligation to those who gave them an opportunity to excel in a difficult field as well as a desire to help others; these feelings are extremely important as motivation since the top income they can expect to get throughout their careers is not much higher than that of other workers in the society.

CHILD CARE AND TRAINING

In the years since the Cultural Revolution, one of whose aims was to root out the last remnants of bourgeois class ideas, the early care and training of Chinese children has been transformed into a system meant not only to impart knowledge, but also to implant philosophical and cultural values in the nation's young. As Yung Ping, a cadre in a Shanghai nursery and an official of the China Welfare Federation, expressed it: "Our goal is to train children by means of socialist education and socialist culture to be successors to the socialist cause."

From their earliest days in preschool classes Chinese children are taught the substance of Mao's "Three Constantly Read Articles"—to love the workers, the peasants, and the soldiers, to love physical labor, to be selfless, to help the revolution everywhere, and to feel that no sacrifice, even death, is too great to "serve the people." Enthusiastic teachers communicate those ideals with films, television, stories, songs, dances, books, posters, and dolls. Before long, the teachers say, the children learn through interaction in class to be kind to one another and to be responsible for one another.

"If a child falls down," one cadre in a nursery school said, "he does not ask the teacher to help him." The teacher has taught the other children to help him brush off. "By three years old," the cadre said, "the children are buttoning the buttons down the back of each other's jackets." Cooperation, not competition, is the mode, and the group rather than the individual is the focus.

As an example of this is practice, we watched one day as two teachers in a Pai Hai kindergarten showed slides and told the story of Norman Bethune to twenty-six six-year-olds. That Bethune, a doctor from Canada, came to China to help the Chinese was an instance of internationalism. His devoted care of the people was the highest form of selflessness. And his making with his own hands of the medical tools he lacked exemplified self-reliance. After the teachers and students had pronounced in unison a quotation of Mao's on Bethune, one of the teachers asked: "What did you learn from the story?" One child answered: "The spirit of mutual help." And another: "How he treated the patient and only cared about the patient and not himself and mixed with the mass." And still another: "That he donated his own blood to patients." Then the teacher brought it down to them: "If you found a sick child, what would you do?" The answer: "I would get medicine for him and get water for him." (The child did not say he would

go and look for a doctor, but told how he would try to be
of help himself.)

The classrooms in the school were large and sunny, with
the lower portion of each concrete wall painted dark green—
perhaps to prevent fingerprints—and the upper portion white.
On the walls were pictures of Mao and posters showing scenes
from revolutionary operas or movies, sometimes of a military
character with a soldier, for example, aiming his rifle at the
enemy. The children sit at desks or four to a table, and the
teacher usually stands in front of the class, joining wholeheartedly in the singing and clapping. Very few toys were in
evidence, with the exception of squeaky rubber dolls, about
three to five inches tall, that portray the different professions
—barefoot doctors, peasant, soldier, and the like.

The books used to teach reading are revolutionary in content as well. They are small and paperbound—it is a comic-
book format, but adults are often seen reading them—with
action-filled pictures and narrative at the bottom of the page.
One we saw was about guerrillas, a man and a boy, victoriously fighting the Japanese. Another was a biography of Lenin,
and a third was about an Army doctor who heroically cares for
her patients. A fourth was about a peasant who was hurt in
the war, but recovered and returned to his commune, where
he worked hard and became a leader.

But teaching youngsters the ideals of Mao is only one of the
revolutionary goals of these preschool institutions; another is
liberation of the mothers. "Women used to worry about how
to run a family and serve a husband, but now our great ambition is to make revolution," says Chen Hui-cheng, a staff member of the Canton branch of the All China Medical Association.
Clearly institutions for the care of preschool children are essential if women are going to "make revolution," and three principal types have been developed. From fifty-six days old, when
the mother's maternity leave ends, until seven years old, when
almost all of the children go on to primary school, the children
of China can attend a nursing room (up to one and a half), a
nursery (from one and a half to three), a kindergarten (from
three to seven).

Nursing rooms exist in most factories or other places of

work. They facilitate the mothers' return to productive work and the breast-feeding of their infants. Women are encouraged to breast-feed, and nearly all do until the baby is from one to one and a half years old, when he is weaned directly to the cup and stops coming to the nursing room. The mother is free to stop her work and nurse her baby twice during the day; supplementary bottles are used when necessary. The nursing room is staffed by women in white coats, who are referred to as "aunties," an affectionate term used for female adults in general. They have had no special training in caring for infants, but the "most patient, most responsible" women among the workers are chosen to care for the babies.

The nursing rooms provide the infants with an early experience of collective living. The rooms are somewhat dark, filled with masses of cribs, and oddly quiet, considering the outcry that such a number of babies might make. Indeed, the relative absence of crying among Chinese infants is something that many recent visitors have observed. The Chinese themselves see nothing unusual in it, however, and offer no explanations. The nursing rooms are equipped with cribs, individual playpens, occasionally a playpen for two children, rocking horses, and a few toys. The family supplies the clothes and the quilt for the baby. In general the "aunties" don't pick the babies up if they do start to cry; instead, they rock them in bamboo carriages that may hold one or two children. Pacifiers are not used. Toilet training begins in the nursing room, collectively, between twelve and eighteen months. After breakfast and lunch the children are seated on white enamel potties in an effort to establish regularity. And within a month or two, the Chinese say, the children usually learn.

At the age of one and a half the children may enter a nursery or may be cared for by grandparents. Sometimes their mothers may care for them, but this seemed to be a rare occurrence. There are two kinds of nurseries and kindergartens—"part-time," meaning open just during the day, and "full-time," meaning open all day and all night. Part-time nurseries are far more common than full-time ones. Both nurseries and kindergartens are organized at every level of society. They are run in the cities by the municipal government and district government, the street committees, the lane committees, and, in the case particularly of nurseries, by factories, hospitals, and scientific institutes. In the country nurseries and kindergartens are run by the communes at each level of organization. Some factories are virtually self-contained communities. The Third Textile Mill of Peking, for example, employs 6,000 workers and provides living quarters for 2,000 families, dining halls, a nursing room, a nursery school, a kindergarten, a primary school, and a middle school.

SUMMARY

It is difficult, of course, to judge how well the principles so explicit in the social services we observed in the areas we visited are working out in practice throughout a vast country like China. And we can only wonder, of course, where it goes from here. Can a society attempting to base itself explicitly on altruism and on the spreading of education and other advantages equitably through the "mass" provide sufficient incentives for the technological and industrial development needed to protect itself adequately in a hostile world? In the long-run are the Chinese sacrificing "quality" for "quantity," or lowering the standards of performance in their attempt to provide meaningful tasks for everyone? Can the current enthusiasm last after the current long-revered leaders die?

Clearly, such questions are impossible for us to answer. First, all of us have learned too much since the 1920s to say, as Lincoln Steffens did of the Soviet Union, "I have seen the future, and it works." The most that we can say is, "We have seen some aspects of China's present, and they are very exciting." Second, as the Chinese themselves would admit, they have just gone through one Cultural Revolution whose results are not yet fully apparent, and they will probably need such revolutions intermittently to keep the original goals alive.

Finally, the answers are deeply buried in the cultural history of China and—even if we understood it and its relevance, which we do not—specific lessons for Western societies would be hard to draw. Suffice it to say that the Chinese are still groping for ways to build a society in which people collectively and individually can reach the fullest potential and gain the greatest measure of fulfillment. The Chinese do not claim to have found the solution. But they are asking questions and experimenting with answers that are very different from ours. And they are experimenting in ways through which, it seems to us, an admirable compatibility between stated political goals and ideals and human service practice has been achieved.

★   ★   ★   ★   ★

6. SPIRIT OF COMMUNISM

When *The New York Times'* James Reston wrote a column titled "New China: A Sink of Morality," he spoke for many subsequent visitors who also find in China America's lost Protestant ethic. It is sometimes argued by others, residents of the old China, that the Chinese have always been courteous, industrious, and frugal, and that this enormous society mysteriously imbued with virtue is really just a well-organized extension of the old Confucianism. The new China has indeed had powerful cultural traditions to call upon, but these traditions also had their negative side—the concern with one's family to the exclusion of the larger society; the callousness to the suffering of strangers; the tyranny of the old over the young, of men over women. A story widely discussed in Peking while two of us were living there will perhaps illustrate the essence of the change.

The Summer Palace on the outskirts of Peking, the luxurious folly of the last Empress Dowager, who built it with monies allocated for an imperial navy, is now a popular playground. In summer the huge lake, with its arched marble bridges, is alive with swimmers and rowers, and in winter its precarious icy surface swarms with skaters. Inevitably, as on all natural lakes used for skating, there are a few accidents. The remarkable aspect of one much-publicized accident was not that a young man fell through the ice and was rescued, but that literally dozens of skaters and bystanders rushed to his aid and in the process also went through the thin ice. All were saved by helping one another and attributed their survival to the thought of Chairman Mao.

What was the meaning of this rather strange incident? Would it not have been more sensible, we asked our Chinese friends, for one or two people, preferably expert swimmers, to take the responsibility for the rescue rather than run the risk of an unnecessary mass tragedy? To view the matter in such a way, they told us, was to miss the whole point. In the old society, no one would have attempted to save the victim of an accident. One's responsibilities were to his own family. Who would care for them if one should drown trying to help a stranger? The remarkable thing about the incident described was that many people had so changed their world outlook that they had reflexively acted to save an unknown person.

Mao's conviction that it is possible and essential to remold man in this way has taken hold of the thinking of the Chinese people. The objective world must be changed by creating more equitable social and economic relations between people, but beyond that, the subjective world of human thought must also be transformed to create a new kind of human being whose outlook is selfless and social. Without this, there is no possibility of creating the better future world the Chinese envision. It is for this reason that we call this section "Spirit of Communism." The Chinese believe that to build the material base for a society of equality is far less difficult than to create this communist spirit. We feel it is appropriate that all of the selections included are statements by the Chinese themselves rather than Western interpretations, for the description of the transformation of the spirit of a people is best done by those who experience it.

In her candid discussion of women's liberation in China, Soong Ching-ling, Vice-President of the People's Republic since 1949, describes the legal, economic, and social changes which have permitted the Chinese woman to break loose from her ancient proscriptions, but she also describes the restrictions which remain; these, she states, arise primarily from backward ideas. Backwardness to the Chinese consists not only of the tyranny of the oppressor, but also the passivity of the oppressed. "Only when the feudal-patriarchal ideology is eradicated can we expect sexual equality to be fully established." Thus, the oppression of one group by another—be it of women by men, "people" by bureaucrats, rural people by urban people—is seen as part of a total problem, the remains of an ideology of stratification, which must be understood and consciously rejected. In his 1965 interview with André Malraux, Mao stated: "Equality is not important in itself; it is important because it is natural to those who have not lost contact with the masses." Seen in this way, it is easier to understand what the Chinese mean when they speak of the necessity of developing a "proletarian world outlook." If all people develop a proper sense of commitment to the needs of the whole, then the needs of any one unequal group will necessarily be met.

The second selection is a theoretical approach to the question of how one actually does remold oneself. It is based on Mao's popularized statement of dialectics that "one divides into two." The thinking of everyone, it states, is made up of contradictory aspects in a constant state of struggle: "We must pay complete attention to the process of each quantitative change, vigorously combat self-interest on each specific question, and, as in fighting street by street, capture the positions of self-interest in our minds one by one."

The other articles are all examples of the practical application of these theoretical principles. The first deals with the problem of "limelight mentality," a phenomenon of serious proportions during the period when new and young leadership came into prominence during the Cultural Revolution. It is a mentality not unfamiliar to those outside China. The term is taken from a passage in Mao's little red book in which he refers to people who are "after fame and position and want to be in the limelight." This is an example of the way in which the little red book was utilized during the Cultural Revolution, as a way of raising a specific problem into the realm of the general morality.

The article describing the new rules for the working style of the Shantung Revolutionary Committee is a refinement of this morality into actual regulations for those in positions of leadership. The commonsensical approach should be clear anywhere. The regulations begin: "It is forbidden to heap praise on members of the revolutionary committee."

The final selection goes into the inverse side of the problem of inequality—the creation of an hereditary elite. It is a warning to Communist cadres not to raise their children as a privileged class, but to "let our children plunge into the class struggle in society. They must go into the midst of workers, peasants and soldiers so as to weather the storm and see the world." It is not merely the ideas of privilege cherished by the ruling classes of other eras which must be smashed, but also those of the new ruling class. This was a theme running through the

Cultural Revolution and stressed once again each time new forces were swept into positions of leadership. The question of special privileges for the children of cadres generated intense public feeling, for those who had been less than equal by birth had a powerful sensitivity to the creation once again of a group more than equal by birth.

★   ★   ★

SOONG CHING-LING*
Women's Liberation in China

History has proved that Women's Liberation in China—women obtaining equal status with men—began with the democratic revolution, but will be completed only in the socialist revolution.

What is the democratic revolution? It is a revolution to overturn the feudal rule of a landlord class, a revolution participated in by the people at large under the leadership of a political party. It first took place in China in 1911, when a monarchy was overthrown, the emperor—the biggest landlord in the entire land—was dethroned, and the aristocracy was dispersed. But this revolution was not completed until 1949 when, at about that time, the land of all big landlords was confiscated. Peasants and landlords were hostile to each other. The former participated in the revolutionary movement in 1927, and only after a long period of class struggle did they succeed in overturning the latter.

What has the overturning of the landlord class to do with the Women's Liberation Movement? In the spring of 1927, our great leader Chairman Mao Tse-tung clearly gave us the correct explanation: **"The political authority of the landlords is the backbone of all the other systems of authority. With that over-**

*Soong Ching-ling, *Peking Review*, No. 6 (February 11, 1972), pp. 6–7.

turned, the clan authority, the religious authority and the authority of the husband all begin to totter. . . . As to the authority of the husband, this has always been weaker among the poor peasants because, out of economic necessity, their womenfolk have to do more manual labor than the women of the richer classes and therefore have more say and greater power of decision in family matters. With the increasing bankruptcy of the rural economy in recent years, the basis for men's domination over women has already been weakened. With the rise of the peasant movement, the women in many places have now begun to organize rural women's associations; the opportunity has come for them to lift up their heads, and the authority of the husband is getting shakier every day. In a word, the whole feudal-patriarchal system and ideology is tottering with the growth of the peasants' power." Needless to say, before the democratic revolution, the women in China were in various ways oppressed and exploited. Women of the richer classes and even the majority of the poorer classes were occupied in their homes and had no social occupation. Women workers, especially the domestic ones, received very low wages. Indeed very few women had any economic independence! Meantime, very few girls were enrolled in schools. The women graduates by and large returned to their homes. Only a very few became teachers in primary schools and girls' middle schools.

The pace of the Women's Liberation Movement closely followed the advance of the democratic revolution. Women's status in China was raised by 1930, on the eve of the war against Japanese aggression. There were already at that time colleges and even middle schools where coeducation was established. Women graduates, quite a number of them, were employed as teachers, doctors and nurses. Most of the graduates from Christian missionary schools and colleges, however, did not take up any occupation, but remained in their families to become "social vases," then a nickname for those who were busy with social entertainments but had no profession of their own. These women, married or single, free from feudal etiquette, became social toys and bourgeois parasites. At this time, there were many women working in textile industries, but they were under capitalist exploitation, receiving low wages and suffering from poverty.

At the end of the war against Japanese aggression and occupation, the Chinese people under the leadership of the
Chinese Communist Party accelerated the revolutionary movement. Thus numerous women threw themselves into all kinds
of revolutionary work, and some of them joined the military
services. They gained their economic independence. Party
members devoted themselves to propaganda work, in villages
and factories. Many of them were women graduates from middle schools. By doing their work, women won equal status with
men. They were very active in the land reform movement and
helped to do away with the land ownership of the big landlords. They eagerly devoted themselves to their various tasks
and with self-sacrificing spirit fulfilled the orders given by the
Party. It was upon the basis of this democratic revolution that
the Chinese people could and did initiate the present socialist
revolution.

When in October 1949, with the defeat of the Japanese
military forces, with the Chiang Kai-shek dictatorship overthrown, with the imperialistic foreign agents cleaned out, the
People's Republic of China was proclaimed, and our democratic
revolution came to its conclusion. From that time, our socialist
revolution began. At the very beginning of the present regime,
the Minister of Justice and the Minister for Public Health were
both women. Many other women entered government services
in Peking as well as in the provinces. In the administration of
various public utilities, there was no lack of women cadres.

Within the last twenty years, more and more women have
enlisted in the army, navy and air forces. They voluntarily
entered these services after having passed a physical examination. More and more women entered agricultural work, herding,
mining, metal-working, hydraulics, communications, transportation, industry, business, retailing, and various other public
services. Since 1966, the first year of our Cultural Revolution,
which is a part of the socialist revolution, the number of women
doctors and nurses has greatly increased. In very recent years,
in a few large cities, all healthy women under forty-five have
been given work in manufacturing, commerce, communications,
transportation, and other services for the people. Middle school
graduates, girls as well as boys, have been assigned to work
in factories, fields and shops. Whatever men can do in these

services women can do just as well. By and large, every woman who can work can take her place on the labor front, under the principle of equal pay for equal work. A large majority of the Chinese women have now attained their economic independence.

If we ask, however, whether the Women's Liberation Movement in China has come to its end, the answer is definitely no. It is true that the landlord system has been abolished for nearly twenty years, but much of the feudal-patriarchal ideology still prevails among the peasants or rather farmers. This ideology still creates problems in the rural areas and some of the small towns. Only when the feudal-patriarchal ideology is eradicated can we expect sexual equality to be fully established.

In order to build a great socialist society, it is necessary to have the broad masses of women engaged in productive activity. With men, women must receive equal pay for equal work in production. Today, in our country, there are people's communes in rural places where women receive less pay than men for equal work in production. In certain villages, patriarchal ideas still have an effect. Proportionately more boys than girls attend school. Parents need the girls to do household work. Some even feel that girls will eventually enter another family, and therefore it would not pay to send them to school. Moreover, when girls are to be married, their parents often ask for a certain amount of money or various articles from the family of the husband-to-be. Thus the freedom of marriage is affected. Finally, as farmers want to add to the labor force in their families, they look forward to the birth of a son, while that of a daughter is considered a disappointment. This desire to have at least one son has an adverse effect on birth control and planned births. A woman with many children around her naturally finds it too difficult to participate in productive labor. Another thing hampering a working woman is her involvement in household work. This prevents many women from full, wholehearted participation in public services.

From the present situation, it is not difficult to understand that genuine equality between the sexes can be realized and the Women's Liberation Movement ended when and only when, led by a Marxist-Leninist political party, the process of the social transformation of society as a whole is completed, when the exploiting class or classes are exterminated, and when the feudal-patriarchal and other exploiting-class ideologies are completely uprooted.

PEOPLE'S DAILY*
Look at Oneself in the Light of
One Dividing into Two

> A Quotation from Chairman Mao
> *Marxist philosophy holds that the law of the unity of opposites is the fundamental law of the universe. This law operates universally, whether in the natural world, in human society, or in man's thinking. Between the opposites in a contradiction there is at once unity and struggle, and it is this that impels things to move and change.*
> —*"On the Correct Handling of Contradictions among the People" (February 27, 1957)*

The unprecedented great proletarian cultural revolution is one that touches people to their very souls. All proletarian revolutionaries must not only dare to touch others' souls, but their own.

Now that the proletarian revolutionaries are in power, we must give still greater importance to the question of the correct approach to oneself. This means we must, as Comrade Lin Piao has pointed out, look at ourselves in the light of the law of "one divides into two."

Everything is divisible according to the law of "one divides into two." Chairman Mao constantly stresses the universality and absoluteness of contradiction. He says: "Marxist philosophy holds that the law of the unity of opposites is the fundamental law of the universe. This law operates universally, whether in the natural world, in human society, or in man's thinking. Between the opposites in a contradiction there is at once unity

* *People's Daily* (July 19, 1968).

and struggle, and it is this that impels things to move and change."

Since the cultural revolution has now developed to a new stage, one of great revolutionary criticism and struggle, every comrade must pay absolute attention to the contradictory aspects in his thinking. He must conduct a vigorous ideological struggle to remold his thinking and, in this way, propel himself and the revolution forward.

Is there any comrade whose thinking and work have no contradictory aspects? There are often pairs of opposites in our minds: proletarian ideas and bourgeois and petit-bourgeois ideas; materialism and idealism; dialectics and metaphysics; right and wrong; achievements and shortcomings, and so forth. Of these pairs, the most essential one is the contradiction between the bourgeois and the proletarian world outlook, the contradiction between self-interest and public interest.

Public interest and self-interest cannot peacefully coexist. Chairman Mao says: "In any given phenomenon or thing, the unity of opposites is conditional, temporary and transitory, and hence relative, whereas the struggle of opposites is absolute." The outcome of the struggle is the transformation of opposites by one eating the other. Therefore, in the struggle between two opposing ideologies, either public interest eats self-interest or the other way around, and there can be no third way.

We must not allow even a speck of the dust of self-interest to enter our minds, or the contradiction will move in the opposite direction.

The outcome of the struggle between such opposing aspects of a contradiction as public interest versus self-interest shows itself indeed in the transformation of one's entire world outlook. Yet it develops through the accumulation of a series of changes on specific questions. The transformation of one's entire world outlook takes final shape precisely through the transformation of opposites on many partial questions. Since our aim is to accomplish a qualitative change from nonproletarian to proletarian ideology, we must pay complete attention to the process of each quantitative change, vigorously combat self-interest on each specific question and, as in fighting street by street, capture the positions of self-interest in our minds one by one.

Chairman Mao teaches us: "In given conditions, each of the

two opposing aspects of a contradiction invariably transforms itself into its opposite as a result of the struggle between them. Here, the conditions are essential. Without the given conditions, neither of the two contradictory aspects can transform itself into its opposite."

Every comrade should consciously strive to create conditions that will bring good results in the transformation of the contradiction and, at the same time, to prevent and avoid conditions that will bring bad results. In order to do so, it is most essential to make earnest efforts to study Chairman Mao's great works and the theory, line, principles and policies set forth by him on the great proletarian cultural revolution, with great emphasis on application, especially on the remolding of one's own subjective world in the mighty storm of class struggle through the practice of struggle in the great proletarian cultural revolution. At the same time, it is necessary to keep in close contact with the masses, listen to their criticism humbly, and engage in strict self-criticism. Only in this way can one steel oneself into a truly thoroughgoing proletarian revolutionary.

Chairman Mao teaches us: "We must learn to look at problems all-sidedly, seeing the reverse as well as the obverse side of things. In given conditions, a bad thing can lead to good results and a good thing to bad results."

An achievement is a good thing. It encourages us to advance with still greater confidence. However, if we only see our achievements without guarding against the contradictory aspect and become self-conceited, we will be dizzy with success and fall all over ourselves. That is why the achievements of some comrades become the starting point for error instead of still greater victories.

To look at oneself according to the law of "one divides into two" means that one must make revolution against one's own subjective world as well as the objective world. Comrade Lin Piao instructs us: "We must regard ourselves as an integral part of the revolutionary force and, at the same time, constantly regard ourselves as a target of the revolution. In making revolution, we must also revolutionize ourselves. Without revolutionizing ourselves, we cannot succeed in making this revolution."

Contradiction is universal and eternal. Even in classless Communist society or after ten thousand years, there will still be contradictions in everyone's mind, though these contradictions will be different in nature from those of the present. Therefore, there will still be a need to approach oneself correctly, constantly look at oneself according to the law of "one divides into two," pay full attention to the contradictory aspects in one's thinking, and ceaselessly carry on the struggle in which one eats the other. This struggle will never end, because the change and movement of the objective reality, the objective world, and hence the process of man's knowledge of truth through practice, will never end.

In this brilliant essay "On the Correct Handling of Contradictions among the People," Chairman Mao teaches us: "The working class remolds the whole of society in class struggle and in the struggle against nature, and at the same time remolds itself. It must ceaselessly learn in the course of its work and overcome its shortcomings step by step, and must never stop doing so.". . .

WENHUI PAO*
Completely Discredit the "Limelight" Mentality

The "limelight" mentality is another enemy confronting proletarian revolutionaries. In the present new situation, this dangerous enemy must be struck down in order to forge grand alliances according to work units, departments and systems.

The "limelight" mentality finds expression in many forms. Examples:
—Unless I take charge, grand alliances and the seizure of power cannot be realized.
—Where there is a chance to make an impression, we will put our name there; where there is limelight, we will be there too.
—We won't speak unless we can say something sensational.

*SCMP No. 3897 (March 6, 1967).

—The smaller the number of people participating in certain work the better.

—If you seize a mountain stronghold, I shall seize a bigger one.

Those who are imbued with the limelight mentality are invariably obsessed with the "me first" mentality and the "small group" mentality, being a typical expression of individualism. Sharply criticizing those who are imbued with the "limelight" mentality, Chairman Mao said: "What are these people after? They are after fame and position and want to be in the limelight. Whenever they are put in charge of a branch of work, they assert their independence. With this aim, they draw some people in, push others out and resort to boasting, flattery and touting among the comrades, thus importing the vulgar style of the bourgeois political parties into the Communist Party."

Those who are obsessed with the limelight mentality know nothing about the Great Proletarian Cultural Revolution. They rise in rebellion for the sole purpose of "self-interest" because they are for the bourgeois world outlook.

The limelight mentality deals direct blows to the great alliance of proletarian revolutionaries. When people are only interested in giving prominence to their own small groups, they will inevitably reject other revolutionary organizations. If they espouse the doctrine of "me first," they will naturally strike blows at others. They want only to do those things that will do them credit and insist on tackling those jobs that put them in the limelight. Thus, they are bound to ignore the revolutionary interests of the proletariat and place themselves in opposition to other revolutionary organizations. Where the limelight mentality is found in a revolutionary organization, its members, so to speak, have sand particles in their eyes. If this is not put right, people with sand particles in their eyes may lose their sight, eventually finding themselves in the same plight as a blind man in the saddle of a blind horse approaching a deep pond in the middle of the night.

Haven't we come upon cases in which some organizations which are seriously obsessed with the limelight mentality have not hesitated to engage in political speculations? In order to startle others on the impulse of the moment, some people have gone so far as to bombard the CCP Central Committee's Cultural Revolution Group and bombard proletarian headquarters, thus committing grave mistakes. Shouldn't we be serious in learning from this painful lesson?

In defense of their limelight mentality, some people have often confused the limelight mentality with revolutionary heroism. In fact, there is nothing in common between the two, because the essence of the former is individualism while that of the latter is collectivism. For the sake of their own personal interests, those who are dominated by the limelight mentality stretch out their hands as far as possible. But when the revolution demands that they give up their personal gains, they become so timid that sometimes they even turn deserters.

On the other hand, revolutionary heroism promotes the spirit of charging and seizing enemy strongholds for the revolution and generates great courage when the interests of the Party are at stake, to the point of sacrificing all one has. Those who espouse revolutionary heroism truly become proletarian revolutionaries, while those imbued with the limelight mentality will never understand what is meant by revolutionary heroism.

In work units which have completed the seizure of power, revolutionaries who exercise power all the more should guard against the emergency of the limelight mentality. This is because the people will acclaim us in our moment of victory which provides bourgeois ideas a good chance to influence and corrupt us. At such a moment, we should never feel elated and never permit self-interest to swell our heads. For if we are hit by the shell of the limelight mentality, we shall collapse in the midst of compliments heaped on us by those with ulterior motives, or we shall unconsciously follow the footsteps of those bourgeois power-holders and go down the wrong path.

The petite bourgeoisie and the bourgeoisie constitute the social foundation for fostering the limelight mentality. This is because the old China was largely populated and in this sense dominated by the petite bourgeoisie. Therefore, to completely discredit the limelight mentality, we have to undergo hard struggle. In the present great cultural revolution, our ultimate goal is to make a clean sweep of all bourgeois and petit-bourgeois "isms." Since the limelight mentality has come to the fore during this great revolutionary period, we should avail ourselves of the opportunity to rally all proletarian revolutionaries and stamp it out.

At present, many revolutionary organizations in Shanghai are taking steps to rectify themselves. Vast numbers of comrades are giving consideration to ways of conforming to the needs of the new situation and energetically putting revolutionary organizations in good order. They are studying ways of regrouping the revolutionary ranks from the bottom to the top according to work units, departments and systems—in this way more extensively forging grand alliances with the Left as the nucleus. As those organizations of a municipal character will shortly accomplish their historical tasks, the persons in charge of these organizations should ardently and energetically forge new grand alliances under the new situation. It will be very dangerous for these people to continue cherishing the limelight mentality and to entrench themselves in their original "mountain strongholds" without any thought of giving up their positions. We hope that all our comrades-in-arms who are in the ranks of proletarian revolutionaries will examine themselves to find out whether the limelight mentality is found in revolutionary organizations. If it is, we should resolutely discredit it!

PEOPLE'S DAILY*
New Working Style for Shantung Cadres

The *Jen-min Jih-pao* today carries the ten regulations of the Shantung Provincial Revolutionary Committee on cadres' style of work. . . .

The committee, a provisional organ of power of the "three-way alliance" type, is made up of representatives of the revo-

* *People's Daily* (June 23, 1967), translated in *SCMP* No. 3968, 1967, pp. 11–12.

lutionary mass organizations, revolutionary leading cadres and representatives of the army units stationed in the locality. . . .

All the members of the committee must take the lead in the study of Chairman Mao's works, and make the study of Chairman Mao's works a necessary, systematic and daily task.

It is imperative to study over and over again such great teachings of Chairman Mao's as "Our point of departure is to serve the people wholeheartedly and never for a moment divorce ourselves from the masses," and "The comrades must be helped to remain modest, prudent and free from arrogance and rashness in their style of work. The comrades must be helped to preserve the style of plain living and hard struggle."

It is imperative to practice criticism and self-criticism regularly, to revolutionize ourselves ideologically and in our work, working style and our way of life. We must remain ordinary working people at all times, resolutely oppose preferential treatment given us and any ways that divorce us from the masses.

For this purpose we prescribe the following provisions:

(1) It is forbidden to heap praise on members of the revolutionary committee. Big-character posters and slogans praising members of the committee are forbidden. In cases where such posters and slogans are put up, efforts should be made to persuade the people to have them covered over immediately.

(2) No member of the committee should make a public speech on behalf of the committee unless it is discussed collectively beforehand by the committee.

(3) There should be no formal welcome or send-off and no applauding at the arrival or departure of members of the committee at mass gatherings. Without permission of the committee, its members may not be photographed or filmed.

(4) Members of the committee must devote a definite amount of time to doing physical labor.

(5) Members of the committee are not allowed to present gifts in their own name or accept gifts.

(6) Generally, the names of committee members should not appear in the press. Where it is necessary for their names to be printed in a newspaper, this must be done according to the stipulations set out by the Party Central Committee.

(7) Members of the committee should live a plain life. Ex-

travagance is forbidden. They are not allowed to use motor cars belonging to the organization for private purposes. They should pay attention to economy when using cars on public business.

(8) Members of the committee should set aside a certain amount of time for interviews with people and should personally deal with letters from the people.

(9) With an attitude of willingness to be the pupils of the people, members of the committee should go among the masses regularly and call fact-finding meetings and forums to invite people's opinions and criticisms.

(10) The Revolutionary Committee should undertake periodical rectification campaigns (once every two months or so). Some representatives of the mass organizations should be invited to participate in each rectification campaign as and when necessary.

KUANG-MING DAILY*
Let Children Weather the Storm and See the World

In ancient China there was a story called "Ch'u Che Advises Empress Dowager of Chao." The story concerned the rule by an Empress Dowager of the Kingdom of Chao in the period of the Warring States. At that time, the Kingdom of Chao was intensely attacked by the Kingdom of Ch'in, and she appealed to the Kingdom of Ch'i for help. The Kingdom of Ch'i was willing to send troops only if she would let her young son, Prince Ch'ang An, be held as a hostage in Ch'i.

The Empress Dowager of Chao was extremely fond of her young son and reluctant to part with him. Suggestions from many ministers were all turned down by her. At that time, a minister by the name of Ch'u Che asked to see the Empress Dowager. From ordinary affairs he went on to discuss how, at the time of the foundation of the Kingdom of Chao, the Em-

* *Kuang-ming Daily* (June 1, 1967), translated in *SCMP* No. 3961.

peror of Chao had made his sons and grandsons princes. However, these sons and grandsons either lost their states while they were still alive or their states were destroyed by their own sons and grandsons when they inherited them. The same was true of other states. The reason for this was that these persons, while enjoying a high position, had rendered no service, and had enjoyed high emoluments without working for them. They also possessed too much power.

Ch'u Che pointed out to the Empress Dowager: Now you have raised the status of Prince Ch'ang An, bestowed on him a large tract of fertile land, and vested him with great power. Yet you do not require him to render services to his country. By so doing, you have planned for him only on a short-term basis and not on a long-term basis.

Having convinced the Empress Dowager, Ch'u Che handed over her young son to the Kingdom of Ch'i as a hostage. Troops were promptly dispatched by the Kingdom of Ch'i.

This story reflected the redistribution of property and power within the landlord class in the early period of the replacement of the slave system by the feudal system. Such a redistribution was carried out in various forms: wars and palace coups, etc. That was what was meant by "the kindness of a princely man is lost after five generations."

We Communists represent not the exploiting classes but the proletariat and the laboring people. However, after the victory of the revolution, if we do not pay attention to making exacting demands on our younger generation, they too will degenerate and may undertake capitalist restoration. By then the property and power of the proletariat will be recaptured by the bourgeoisie.

The succeeding generations of the revolution are an asset to the people, the future of the mother country. It is a glorious duty of us revolutionaries to train our children into strong and reliable successors to the proletarian revolutionary cause. This is a duty we should discharge toward our Party and the people.

Our great leader Chairman Mao has taught us: "The question of training successors to the proletarian cause, fundamentally speaking, is a question of whether we have people to succeed to the Marxist-Leninist revolutionary cause initiated by the older proletarian revolutionaries; a question of whether or not the leadership of our Party and state will continue to be mastered by proletarian revolutionaries; a question of whether our children can continue to advance along the correct road of Marxism-Leninism; and a question of whether or not we can successfully prevent the appearance of the Khrushchev-type revisionism in China. In short, this is an extremely crucial question bearing on the destiny of our Party and State. This is a task for the proletarian cause for a hundred years, a thousand years, and ten thousand years."

The bourgeoisie cultivates its successors according to the bourgeois world outlook. We proletarians cultivate our successors according to the proletarian world outlook.

Throughout the entire historical period of proletarian dictatorship, the struggle between the proletariat and the bourgeoisie for the minds of the younger generation is always an important content of the class struggle. On the question of what kind of successors our cadres' children are to be trained into, there is likewise a sharp struggle between the two lines.

The top Party person in authority taking the capitalist road and a small band of counter-revolutionary revisionists instill into the minds of our young generation, particularly the cadres' children, the bourgeois ideas of special privileges. They spread the fallacy of "one being naturally Red." They preach the reactionary theory of blood heritage in a vain attempt to push the innocent youngsters into the mire of revisionism. In the course of the great proletarian cultural revolution, the children of cadres who have not been properly educated are led astray. This is a serious lesson we must remember.

Chairman Mao has taught us in these terms: "We communists should weather the storm and see the world. This storm is a great storm of mass struggle. This world is a big world of mass struggle."

We the broad masses of revolutionary cadres must, in accordance with Chairman Mao's teachings, let our children plunge into the class struggle in society. They must go into the midst of workers, peasants and soldiers so as to weather the storm and see the world and take workers, peasants and soldiers as their teachers. They should temper themselves in the great furnace of the struggle between the two lines. They should roll over a thousand times in the mud of the masses, so that they may gradually understand the feelings and thoughts of the laboring people. In this way, they may think what the laboring people think, love what they love, and hate what they hate. Thus they may be trained into laborers with socialist consciousness and culture.

We must be responsible toward the revolution, toward the people, and toward the offspring of the revolution. To make exacting demands on our children is to care for them. In order that no revisionism will appear in our country and our posterity will forever be loyal to Chairman Mao, the Party and the people, we should be constantly concerned with the succeeding generation politically and ideologically. We do not truly love our children but ruin them by looking upon them as private property and pampering them materially.

The most important and basic point of educating the next generation is to continuously instill the thought of Mao Tse-tung in their minds. We should teach them from childhood to read Chairman Mao's works, listen to his words, and act according to his instructions. We must conduct class education among them, arm their minds with the class viewpoint, and let them know how laboring people in society once lived painfully under suppression of landlords and capitalists and how the older revolutionaries won the socialist state and today with their blood and lives. Besides, we should make it clear to them that they will have to pay a great price for the defense and consolidation of the proletarian dictatorship, and that they are children of the people and are brought up with the blood and sweat of the laboring people. In this way, they may forever remember that the laboring people are their parents.

We cadres should also pass the glorious traditions of the revolution to succeeding generations and leave with them as heirlooms the "rural styles of work" and "guerrilla tactics," so that they may get rid of bourgeois ideas of special privileges and sense of superiority, and forever preserve the features of the laboring people and the austerity of the Red Army and the old 8th Route Army, who ate nothing but millet and wore straw sandals. Only thus will our youngsters weather the storm, endure hardships and become staunch revolutionary fighters capable of carrying heavy burdens.

So far as cultivation of our children into revolutionary successors is concerned, there is still one more point which must not be overlooked, namely, we revolutionary cadres must set ourselves as examples and combine teaching by words with teaching by personal example. We must make ourselves models to the younger generation politically, ideologically, in action and in style of work.

Chairman Mao says: Veteran cadres performed meritorious services in the past. But they must not rest content with this. They must temper and reform themselves in the midst of the great proletarian cultural revolution and render new meritorious services.

All revolutionary cadres must answer this great call of Chairman Mao. The people have given us positions and authority and have also paid us handsome "emoluments." If we do not render new services but fail to preserve our revolutionary integrity, can we live up to the expectation of the Party and the people? Can we make ourselves revolutionary models to the younger generation?

The revolution is a big melting pot. In the practice of this violent struggle of the great proletarian cultural revolution, revolutionary youngsters have been tested and tempered. This is of extremely far-reaching significance to the cultivation and training of millions upon millions of successors to the proletarian revolutionary cause. How valuable will the next few decades be to the future of the mother country and the future of mankind! The present generation of youngsters will with their hands build the mother country, hitherto poor and blank, into a mighty socialist country and will take part in the struggle to bury imperialism. Their task is heavy and their journey is long. It is necessary for us to educate our youngsters to dedicate their lives to the fulfillment of this great historical mission!

Prophets of imperialism, on the basis of the changes that have taken place in the Soviet Union, have pinned their hope on "peaceful evolution," on the third or fourth generations of the Chinese Communist Party. We must make this imperialist prophecy totally bankrupt.

★   ★   ★   ★   ★

II. The Cultural Revolution

From 1966 to 1969, the world watched in astonishment as millions of Chinese threw themselves into a tumultuous movement aimed at transforming the institutions of the most populous nation in the world. For the first time in modern history, a chief executive called upon his people to struggle against the ruling party which he had helped found and put in power. Thomas Jefferson recognized the recurrent necessity to rekindle the revolutionary flame. In 1787 he wrote to a friend, giving his views on the outbreak of the famous Shays' Rebellion: "God forbid we should ever be twenty years without such a rebellion." But it is Mao who must be given the credit for being the first modern head of state to attempt to institutionalize mass political rebellion as a permanent feature of the national polity.

The Great Proletarian Cultural Revolution gave prominence to the political concept of uninterrupted revolution. Mao Tsetung's ideas on guerrilla and mass revolutionary war are well known, but his notion of uninterrupted revolution as inherent in all social development has until recently received less attention. During a remarkable interview with André Malraux, then French Minister of Culture, in the late summer of 1965, Mao stated: "What is expressed in that commonplace term 'revisionism' is the death of the revolution. What we have just done in the army must be done everywhere. I have told you that the revolution is also a feeling. If we decide to make of it what the Russians are now doing—a feeling of the past—everything will fall apart. Our revolution cannot be simply a stabilization of the past."

In this simple statement, Mao was expressing the concepts that would provide the ideological thrust for the mass campaign which erupted one year later in all the main urban centers of China. In essence, the Cultural Revolution was a nationwide rejection of the Soviet model of socialism and a daring experiment with a new philosophy of continuous revolution. Mao declared that two or three cultural revolutions should be carried out in every century.

Mao, the master of military strategy and the author of the famous statement "political power grows out of the barrel of a gun," always understood that class struggle, whether violent or nonviolent, is, in the last analysis, a political process governed by reasoning and persuasion. World outlook, as he made clear to foreign visitors during a talk included in our selections, cannot be imposed on anyone. It was clear to those of us who could observe the Cultural Revolution that it was a gigantic debate involving millions of participants. Despite sporadic violence, which in a few cases could have led to civil war, the Cultural Revolution in the main followed Mao's dictum that this new type of political struggle should be conducted by reasoning and argument—not by force.

The Chinese Cultural Revolution was in fact a real struggle for political power by political actors participating at every level of government and administration in the country. At the same time, the movement was a prolonged, pervasive educational and ideological campaign to raise the political consciousness of both leaders and led. Many of the Western "China watchers" residing in Hong Kong during the course of the Cultural Revolution, reported and analyzed this historic movement in one-dimensional terms; it was, they said, simply a classical power struggle among leaders. Unable or unwilling to comprehend the dual nature of this massive movement of popular participation unfolding in China, ignoring the forest as they counted the trees, these outside observers concentrated on elite studies, violent confrontations, and added up lists of demoted or promoted leaders. As a result, they were unable to understand the historic impact of the Chinese Cultural Revolution on a modern world plagued with the problems of bureaucratization, political passivity, and routinization of public life. For those of us who were fortunate enough to be on the scene during those tumultuous years, the confusion and occasional violence appeared as inevitable imperfections of a new system of mass political interaction. There is every reason to expect that in the future the new concepts generated by the Chinese Cultural Revolution will overshadow the events that produced them.

Mao understood that the goals of the movement could not be met simply through the removal of officials from office. He underlined the dual nature of the revolution when he said that the main *purpose* of the Cultural Revolution was to "solve the problem of world outlook and eradicate revisionism," while the main *task* was to struggle against the "capitalist roaders" in the Party. "If world outlook is not reformed, then although two thousand capitalist roaders are removed in the current great cultural revolution, four thousand others may appear next time." (See page 261 of the selections.)

Following Mao's own characterization of the Cultural Revolution, we will first discuss the ideological foundations of the movement as represented in the attempt to change world outlook, and then will conclude with some remarks on the political struggle. It is not possible in a brief essay to give an inclusive summary of what the Chinese mean by Mao Tse-tung Thought, but it is possible to touch upon a few central ideas which have had a profound impact upon the Chinese people.

The Chinese have made it very clear that what they call Mao Tse-tung Thought is more than just the ideas of one man. (The Chinese changed Mao Tse-tung's Thought in the English translation to Mao Tse-tung Thought to make clear that they meant more by the phrase than just the ideas of Mao.) Mao Tse-tung Thought represents a summation of Chinese revolutionary experience over a period of four decades. Mao Tse-tung Thought is not a closed system of philosophy or a fixed doctrine; rather, it is a series of concepts and formulations based on the essential principles of Marxism-Leninism. It is as much a method of problem-solving as it is a theory. Besides a number of political theories based on years of Chinese revolutionary experience, three basic concepts fundamental to Mao Tse-tung Thought are: the theory that all social development is based on class struggle; public interest takes precedence over private interest; and history is made by the masses. These concepts were translated during the Cultural Revolution into slogans mastered by every Chinese citizen, as, for example, "Never Forget Class Struggle"; "Serve the People"; "Fight Self—Repudiate Revisionism"; and "Trust the Masses."

Maoist political concepts are infused with ethical content, a combination derived from traditional Chinese thought and certain aspects of Marxism. The Chinese world outlook, although recognizing that social systems are based on historical context and technological development, puts great stress on the subjective nature of man's consciousness. Mao Tse-tung Thought is thus in philosophical opposition to concepts of Western social science, which in a determinist vein place man in the passive state of being molded by and responding to objective outside forces. Following similar assumptions, Soviet Marxism stresses that socialist forms of production will automatically create men with socialist consciousness. The Chinese take a much more dialectical view of the relation between man and his environment, and have put new emphasis on the subjective side of Marxism. They of course proclaim that the economic base acts on the social superstructure, but they also hold that under certain circumstances, man's consciousness can transform the economic base either progressively or regressively. In short, socialist nations may return to a state of capitalism if socialist consciousness lags behind the relations of production. Mao has been the first leading Communist statesman to suggest that a Communist Party in power can turn into an exploiting party and reintroduce class oppression. The theoretical and practical question that he asked his colleagues before the Cultural Revolution was "What do we do if we develop revisionism in the Central Committee?" His answer was political revolution from below.

Mao Tse-tung Thought as a methodology of action is flexible, pragmatic, and capable of absorbing new concepts. The Chinese engage in a great deal of practice before they attempt to sum up experience and formulate theory to guide future work. They are therefore able to refine past formulations, cast out outmoded concepts, and constantly come up with new guidelines, slogans and programs based on a few basic and unalterable principles. In certain periods, the Chinese hammer away at basic principles with such intensity that outsiders, who do not understand that these periods will be followed by others of flexible and pragmatic application of the principles, believe them to be hopelessly dogmatic. Whether outsiders think them dogmatic or opportunistic, the Chinese see no contradiction between these two different kinds of periods. History and circumstance require one at one time and another at another time. The Cultural Revolution was a period when the Chinese leaders concentrated efforts to inculcate the basic principles of their philosophy into the whole population. In the post-Cultural Revolution period, Mao Tse-tung Thought was deemphasized and the Chinese inaugurated a campaign to study the classic works of Marx and Lenin.

Mao Tse-tung Thought was promulgated as the ideological foundation for the politics of the Cultural Revolution; the effort was made to turn China into "a great school of Mao Tse-tung Thought." While the political struggle involved the discovery and removal of the capitalist roaders, the ideological struggle established criteria for remolding the consciousness of the whole nation. Every Chinese was called upon to "make himself the target of the revolution," to struggle against his own selfish interests and to place the public interest before private interest. Future leaders were to be judged by whether they were devoted to serving the people and had rid themselves of material and power incentives.

It is precisely the flexibility and the generality of Mao Tse-tung Thought that make it difficult at times for the Chinese to operationalize Maoist theory. Disputes arose as to what in every concrete instance constituted the correct interpretation of the general line. However, Mao Tse-tung Thought provided the ground rules of the political process. Without those rules, and the deeper consensus they represented, the Chinese would never have been able to mediate factional disputes that in other times and places would have torn an entire society apart.

Significantly, the publicly defined struggle between the two lines was named the struggle between the proletarian line and the bourgeois revisionist line. By "revisionism" the Chinese clearly meant Soviet Russian revisionism, and to emphasize the point they named Mao's chief opponent, Liu Shao-ch'i, "China's Khrushchev." By this move, the struggle on the international front was clearly linked to the greatest domestic political conflict in the history of Chinese Communism.

By 1965, the Chinese Communist Party was a multimillion-member party apparatus patterned after the Communist Party of the Soviet Union and controlled by Liu Shao-ch'i, the First Vice-

Chairman of the party, Teng Hsiao-p'ing, the First Secretary of the Central Committee, and P'eng Chen, Mayor of Peking and a member of the powerful Political Bureau. Throughout the industrial sector of the economy, Soviet-type rules, regulations, and methods prevailed. Education was to a large extent influenced by Russian, American, and Confucian concepts. In Chairman Mao's view, these were the types of social structures which had led to a new class and elitist regime in the Soviet Union, and if they were not altered, they would produce the same result in China. The Russian factor, then, bears an important relationship to the domestic politics of China during the Cultural Revolution. It was the attempt to avoid the Russian bureaucratic road that provided the raison d'être of the Great Proletarian Cultural Revolution.

A major factor cited by the Maoists for the political divisions among the Chinese leadership was the existence of two geographically separated Party organizations during the long years of revolutionary war. One was the ruling party created by Mao and the veterans of the Long March in the Liberated Areas. Maintaining close ties with the peasantry, the Communist Party in the liberated areas was able to establish a popularly based regime with broad support from the people. In the White Areas under Kuomintang terror, Liu Shao-ch'i and other Communist leaders built an underground party organization that was based on secrecy and rigid hierarchical discipline. Two opposing styles and methods of leadership emerged after liberation in 1949. During the Cultural Revolution, Yenan was held up to the nation as the model for emulation; a shadow was cast on the history of the underground Party organization that had developed in the areas controlled by the Kuomintang and the Japanese.

Liu Shao-ch'i and other leaders representing the urban tradition, favoring an industrial-type approach to problems of the rural economy, and reflecting the planners' bias for orderly advance, soon came into conflict with the Maoist wing of the Party which had led the revolution to victory by the arousing of the peasant masses. From an early date, Mao had favored comprehensive development of the economy, a development strategy seeking the maximum arousal of the population for an assault on backwardness.

During the Cultural Revolution, detailed and documented

facts concerning the policy struggles at the top during the 1950's were widely disseminated. In the early years of the first decade of Communist power, Liu is reported to have prevented the peasants in Shansi Province from forming mutual-aid teams to pool their resources in a rudimentary form of agricultural cooperation. Liu appears to have felt that the peasants were proceeding too soon and too rapidly toward forms of collective agriculture. Mao reversed the policy and supported the peasants' spontaneous move toward low-level forms of agricultural cooperation. Historical evidence supports the conclusion that Liu stood for a policy of increased agricultural production through mechanization while Mao stood for a policy of arousing the masses for collective effort, although apparently Liu had been won over to Mao's view during the second half of the 1950's.

During the Cultural Revolution, in a discussion concerning the advantage of private over collective methods of production, Teng Hsiao-p'ing, the First Secretary of the Party, was reported by Red Guard publications to have once stated, "Black cats or white cats—as long as they catch mice, it's all right." During the "hard years" (1959–1962)—when mistakes made during the Great Leap Forward, droughts and floods, and the withdrawal of Soviet aid combined to bring about an agricultural crisis, Liu encouraged the expansion of private plots and the return to a free market in the countryside.

Chou En-lai, in a talk with foreigners in Peking in 1968, revealed that Mao had believed that the answer to food shortages during the "hard years" and the consequent discontent among the peasantry would be to allow the peasants to keep more of their own grain, thus encouraging production without increasing private landholding. Whatever the merits of the arguments about which Chinese leader stood for which policy during the first decade of Communist rule, it is clear that Mao has been the foremost representative of the poor peasants—the shock troops of the revolution. He has been consistent in his belief that industrialization could not be achieved by exploiting the very class that had made the revolution. The Maoists have always understood that a return to private farming would lead rapidly to a new polarization in the countryside between the rich and the poor.

The conflict between Mao and Liu increasingly revolved

around the inroads made by Soviet Russian methods on the pattern of organization and ideology in the Party, the Army, the economy, and education. By 1966 Mao had been isolated and was unable to control the decision-making apparatus of the Party, now in the hands of Liu Shao-ch'i, Teng Hsiao-p'ing, and P'eng Chen. Discussing the period of the early sixties, Mao said, "They treated me like a Buddha, but no one listened to what I had to say."

Mao's isolation from the decision-making organs of the Party and government had occurred gradually. In 1958 he had relinquished the role of Chairman of the Republic in favor of Liu Shao-ch'i, ostensibly for reasons of health and his desire to be freed for theoretical work. Whether he resigned voluntarily or was forced out of the position is a matter of historical debate, but a year later at the Lushan Conference, he launched an attack on his opponents in the Party. P'eng Teh-huai, then Minister of Defense, had openly opposed the whole Maoist development strategy, including the communes and the Great Leap Forward. Mao, in a sharp rebuttal, threatened that if his policies were overthrown he would return to the hills to mobilize a new peasant army to fight those in power. As a result of this sharp counterattack, Mao was able to muster a majority of votes, enough to remove P'eng Teh-huai and place the army in the hands of Lin Piao, who was an enthusiastic supporter of Mao's policies.

Although most of the top leaders voted with Mao on this occasion, at the 1962 Plenum three years later, Mao accused leading members of the Central Committee of attempting "to reverse the verdict on P'eng Teh-huai," and issued a call for a renewal of class struggle. P'eng Teh-huai thus became a symbol of opposition to Mao.

The unresolved question of P'eng Teh-huai provided the issue for the opening struggle of the Cultural Revolution. An article commissioned by Mao and written by Yao Wen-yuan appeared in a Shanghai newspaper during the month of November 1965. The essay was a critical attack on Wu Han, a historian and Deputy Mayor of Peking, who had written a play in 1961 called *The Dismissal of Hai Jui*. The play was about an honorable imperial governor during the Ming Dynasty who had been unjustly dismissed from office by the emperor. It is distinctly in the Chinese historical tradition to utilize historical subjects for current political debate, and Mao and others had quickly recognized that the play was about the dismissal of P'eng Teh-huai and that the emperor in the play represented Mao.

Strange as it may seem, the article commissioned by Mao was turned down by every official publication in Peking. The fact that Mao, the father of the Chinese Revolution, was unable to get an article published in the capital of the country underlined his lack of power within the Party organization he had helped to found. Yao Wen-yuan's essay was published in Shanghai in November 1965 and was reluctantly reprinted with editor's notes shortly afterwards in Peking. Using classical guerrilla tactics, Mao had begun his attack on a small isolated enemy. Within a year he had enlarged the area of struggle into a massive campaign to "remove those in authority taking the capitalist road."

Realizing that he was opposed by the majority of leaders in the Central Committee, Mao proceeded cautiously from the summer of 1965 to prepare public opinion for a struggle that he must have realized might well reach the level of civil war. Unable to influence the tightly controlled party structure, Mao turned to the army and the masses as the base for his new revolution. Unless the social basis for a mass rebellion had existed, Mao would not have been able to spark the social upheaval which erupted a year later, a factor often ignored by outside observers of the Cultural Revolution.

Lin Piao, one of the great military heroes of the Chinese Revolution, had by 1965 rebuilt the army as a model revolutionary organization. It was the army which had compiled the little red book of Mao quotations, and it was the national army newspaper, *Liberation Army Daily*, which became the vehicle for Mao Tse-tung Thought. It soon became clear that the army newspaper and the national Party newspaper, the *People's Daily*, were disseminating opposing political lines. In April 1966 Mao scored an initial victory when the *Liberation Daily* seized control of the editorial content of the *People's Daily*. It was then possible to launch a massive and coordinated ideological campaign for the Cultural Revolution.

While the evolving Cultural Revolution appeared to be moving on its own track and foreign policy issues were not discussed except for generalities, foreign and domestic events were closely linked, as they always had been. Armed intervention by the United States in the civil war in Vietnam, followed by the massive bombing of North Vietnam in February of 1965, posed a serious threat to Chairman Mao's plan to initiate a campaign for revolutionary renewal on the domestic front. Throughout 1965, a debate over foreign policy occurred among the Chinese Communist leadership. Edgar Snow reported that on his trip to China in 1970, he was told that in the winter of 1965 Liu Shao-ch'i stood for the reactivization of the Sino-Soviet alliance in order to meet the American threat on China's southern border.

Lo Jui-ch'ing, Chief of Staff of the Chinese People's Liberation Army, published a major theoretical article in May 1965 stating that China was prepared to send troops to fight side by side with the people of Vietnam "when they need us." Warning the United States that China was prepared for war, the article scoffed at U.S. nuclear strength by reminding the United States that its monopoly of nuclear weapons had been broken many years ago, and that "now other countries have the bomb." The article, by implication, invoked the Soviet as well as the Chinese nuclear deterrent.

It was clear that an important section of the Chinese leadership was leaning toward military action to counter the American threat to Vietnam and China. Mao appeared to believe that the struggle against revisionism must have priority over any other issue and was consistently opposed to sending the army outside the borders of China. Mao, who wished to use the army as a political base for his domestic revolution, undoubtedly realized that by sending the Chinese army to Vietnam, his political opponents, by one stroke, would have taken the army out of domestic politics. Any joint action with the Soviet Union against the United States might well have resulted in the establishment of Soviet naval and air bases on Chinese soil and would have enormously increased Soviet influence on China's internal political affairs. Mao and Lin Piao stood for a policy that sought to avoid confrontation with the United States while excluding Soviet influence in China's internal politics.

In September 1965 Lin Piao's famous programmatic document, "Long Live the Victory of People's War," was published.

Spelling out the Maoist strategy for world revolution, this manifesto linked all revolutions and peoples' struggles throughout the world in one global crusade to destroy American imperialism, piece by piece. But it was underlined that if a revolution were to succeed, it must rely on its own forces, even under circumstances when all outside aid might be cut off. The lesson the Chinese wished to convey was that their revolution had been successful by following a policy of self-reliance, and hopefully other revolutions could be victorious by following the same strategy.

In November 1965 Lo Jui-ch'ing was removed as Chief of Staff. Mao had succeeded in establishing control over military and foreign policy so that he might proceed to unfold his internal program for the rejuvenation of the revolution.

The Cultural Revolution entered a new stage in the late spring and early summer of 1966 with the Maoist capture of the Peking propaganda apparatus and the overthrow of the Peking City Committee of the Party. P'eng Chen, Mayor of Peking and member of the Political Bureau, Lo Jui-ch'ing, Chief of Staff of the Army, Lu Ting-yi, Chief of the Propaganda Section of the Central Committee, and Yang Shang-k'un, a member of the Secretariat of the Central Committee, were publicly denounced as counterrevolutionaries during this period. Apparently, Liu Shao-ch'i and other leading figures in the Party hoped that some compromise with Mao might be reached. But Mao was in no mood for compromise; he was determined to carry through a revolution regardless of the costs.

In editorial after editorial, the *People's Daily*, now controlled by the Maoist forces, declared that all class struggles are essentially political struggles and that unless the representatives of the bourgeoisie were swept out of the Party, China would suffer the same fate as the Soviet Union, where the "Khrushchev revisionist clique" had usurped the leadership of the party, army, and government. The Cultural Revolution was understood from the beginning to have a far greater scope than criticism of cultural affairs; it was to be a struggle for political power.

Chairman Mao was calling upon the Chinese Communist Party to lead a struggle against itself, and it proved to be a task that the Party would not or could not carry out. While Mao remained in the South during the early summer months of

1966, the leadership of the mass movement was entrusted to Liu Shao-ch'i, Teng Hsiao-ping, and the Secretariat of the Central Committee. Following a policy which had been utilized in earlier mass movements, the Peking Party leaders sent out "work teams" of senior Party cadres to lead the mass movement at the universities and other urban organizations. The work teams understood their task as protecting the Party organization and directed their attack against nonparty intellectuals and "bourgeois academic authorities." Students and nonparty individuals or rank-and-file Party members who criticized senior party officials were branded by the work teams as "counterrevolutionaries." In effect, the mass movement was suppressed and the main targets of what the students referred to as "the fifty days of white terror" were rank-and-file activists and rebels.

Mao suddenly appeared in Wuhan in mid-July and made his dramatic swim across the Yangtze River. After proving his fitness and making the point that he was not too old to lead another battle, he returned to Peking in triumph, and threw his support to the student rebels. Lashing the Party bureaucrats for having suppressed the mass movement, Mao plunged into the Eleventh Plenum of the Central Committee where he was able to eke out a majority vote to demote Liu Shao-ch'i and to promote Lin Piao as his successor and "closest comrade in arms." Those Party leaders who had suppressed the mass movement were accused of following the "bourgeois reactionary line" in opposition to Chairman Mao's "proletarian revolutionary line." From this point on, the Cultural Revolution engulfed the nation in what was to become the most complex and confusing political movement in modern Chinese history.

The Chinese Communist Party failed to give leadership to the mass movement. At the very top, Chairman Mao, Defense Minister Lin Piao and Premier Chou, together with a hand-picked Cultural Revolution Group—including Mao's wife Chiang Ch'ing, his secretary Ch'en Po-ta, and a handful of young intellectuals and a few old party veterans—took over leadership of the nation. Acting in the name of the Central Committee, this small group of leaders directed the army, the government, and the mass movement. Party Committees from the provincial, county, and city levels were suspended after it became evident that they could not be relied on to give direction to the mass movement. Thousands of newly organized Red Guard and rebel organizations mounted the political stage, and it was these organizations which enacted the politics of the Cultural Revolution.

Western observers on the whole reported unfavorably on the emergence of millions of young Red Guards as a major political force in the nation's politics. Some journalists compared the movement to the Children's Crusade of the Middle Ages, and others exhibited a new-found sympathy with old Communists who were under attack from rebellious youngsters. There have been only a few periods of history when uncontrolled mass democracy has held sway for long periods of time; the first year of the Cultural Revolution was one of those periods. Based on the firsthand observation of two of the editors, the early period of the Red Guard movement in Peking was a period of exuberance, vitality, and confusion. Peking Red Guard organizations, made up of middle school and university students, exhibited remarkable discipline and indiscipline, maturity and foolishness, sophistication and naïveté. One Red Guard group did, as the Western press reported, suggest to Premier Chou En-lai that the rules governing traffic lights be changed so that red would mean go and green would mean stop, because it was more revolutionary. But they also agreed with the Premier when he pointed out that this suggestion might not be practical. The fact of the matter is that the student Red Guards spread the concepts of the Cultural Revolution to the whole country and proved themselves to be remarkable organizers and propagandists. The oldest son of one of the editors marched with one Red Guard middle school unit from Peking to the Yellow River, a distance of five hundred miles, and spent a month on the way working in a coal mine in lower Hupei Province. According to his report, the miners were friendly to the students and eager to learn about the political movement in Peking. Other groups succeeded in antagonizing factory workers, who felt that they did not need the students' advice on how to conduct their own political movement.

In the long run, the student movement became unmanageable because of factional quarrels, but the factionalism might have been more manageable if the leaders of the movement had themselves been able to set an example of unity, which they were unable to do by the summer of 1967. The first stage of the Cultural Revolution was led by the students, the subsequent stages, by the army and the workers. During the three years of the Cultural Revolution millions of students traveled extensively throughout the country, and in the long run, this factor may have contributed to the country's unity as the youth came to understand the diversity and the immensity of their homeland and abandoned parochial notions characteristic of a country consisting largely of peasant villages.

While the Red Guards spread the concepts of rebellion to the general populace, the entrenched Party bureaucracy resisted the popular movement to smoke out the "capitalist roaders." Party functionaries openly or secretly organized their own mass organizations to protect themselves and oppose the true rebels. During the early period of the work teams, mass organizations which supported the Party work teams and the old cadres were labeled as "royalist" organizations. These organizations collapsed when the rank-and-file members became conscious that these groups were opposed to Chairman Mao's line. Later, when the nation split into two or more contending groups in every organizational unit, each proclaiming that it supported Chairman Mao, it became more difficult to distinguish those rebel groups representing the true revolutionaries. Often the disputes concerned a disagreement over which cadres or Communist functionaries were the revisionists taking the capitalist road. Recognizing the difficulties inherent in the politics of the Cultural Revolution, Mao stated:

> In the past, we fought North and South; it was easy to fight such wars. For the enemy was obvious. The present Great Proletarian Revolution is much more difficult than that kind of war. The problem is that those who commit ideological mistakes are all mixed up with those whose contradiction with us is one between ourselves and the enemy, and for a time it was hard to sort them out.

The problem was to discover who exactly constituted the "capitalist roaders" in each organization, and often the mass organizations disagreed on which were the good and which the bad cadres. Often by painstaking investigation and research, the masses were able to analyze and correctly evaluate their leaders, but in many cases cadres who had long revolutionary records and whose errors were minor were incorrectly labeled as enemies. In some organizations, cadres who had been able to cover up their bad records were able to "hoodwink the masses" and slip through the net.

Mao had perhaps hoped that the Communist Party would take the lead in cleaning its own house, but the hope was soon dashed. In Shanghai, the old entrenched Party leaders used every tactic to dupe and confuse the masses. Strikes instigated by plant managers and by party officials paralyzed industry, transport, and shipping in the early weeks of January 1967. Attempts were made by the officials still in power to bribe the workers with wage increases and bonuses, and these actions soon emptied the treasuries of the main factories in the city. Rebel leaders, recognizing the plot to buy off the working class in an attempt to protect the positions of the old officials, rallied tens of thousands of students and workers to keep the power plants, factories, and docks working. In effect, the rebel workers and students had seized power in a revolutionary uprising. Seizing control of the main newspaper in Shanghai, the Rebel Workers' headquarters issued a series of editorials and manifestos calling upon the population of China's largest city to rally to the cause of the revolution and the nation. Mao hailed the new revolutionary seizure of power in what was called the "January Storm," and cited the action of the Shanghai workers in seizing control of the factories, newspapers, and municipal government as the model of action for the whole nation.

A new stage of the Cultural Revolution had arrived—the seizure of power from below. Mao astounded the world by calling upon hundreds of millions of Chinese to seize power from the very organization which he had devoted forty years of his life to construct. But his idea was not to destroy the Communist Party; instead, his hope was for a renewal of the revolutionary spirit and the reconstruction of an organization which he felt had been losing its revolutionary purpose. Mao had not become an anti-Communist as the Soviet press asserted. Rather he was urging the nation "to carry through the revolution to the end."

Consolidation of the new revolutionary power in Shanghai proceeded smoothly. A new Revolutionary Municipal Committee was organized under the leadership of Mao's trusted lieutenants, Chang Ch'un-ch'iao and Yao Wen-yuan; a great alliance of the separate citywide mass organizations was formed; and factionalism, if not completely ended, was brought under control. The Shanghai formula did not meet with such success in the rest of the country. Perhaps this was so because no other part of the country possessed a class force as disciplined, mature, and historically conscious as the Shanghai working class. Another factor working against the complete success of the new strategy of "power seizure" in the rest of the country was that the opposition changed its tactics to meet the new situation: working through the rebel organizations, the members of the opposition joined the ranks of those establishing new revolutionary committees. Again the problem of sorting out the good and bad cadres became almost insuperable.

By the spring of 1967, all organizations waved the banner of Mao Tse-tung Thought and many used "the red flag to oppose the red flag." The real politics of the Cultural Revolution, the struggle of concrete groups for concrete political power, was cloaked by revolutionary rhetoric. By the summer of 1967, it became increasingly difficult for the leaders in Peking, who were themselves divided, to find an orientation for the mass movement which could unite the majority behind clear-cut goals and objectives. The last two years of the movement reflected the pendulum swings from right to left as a society in convulsion went through the process of synthesizing a number of new ideas and institutions. Mao had proclaimed that ninety-five percent of the cadres and functionaries of the Communist Party were good, but it was difficult for those down below to reinstate thousands of officials who had been so severely criticized. The division among the top leaders during the storms of the mass movement and even after its conclusion reflected a disagreement on how many and which cadres to reinstate in their former positions.

China's Cultural Revolution was led by a new coalition of

leaders, and as in other great world revolutions, this coalition split in the revolutionary storm. In the summer of 1967, following the suppression of the right-wing mutiny in Wuhan, an ultra-left wave swept over the country. In Peking, a faction of leaders belonging to the Central Cultural Revolution Group organized a massive student movement to overthrow Premier Chou En-lai and seize power for themselves. Mao, deciding that the revolutionary storm was now threatening disintegration of what remained of the state structure, stood firmly behind Premier Chou and with the help of Lin Piao and the army smashed the group known as the "ultra-left." The recalcitrants of the Cultural Group were arrested, and in the fall of 1967 the Army was called upon to enter the universities and other organizations to mediate the factional struggle.

Armed only with their little red books of Mao quotations, these remarkably disciplined political soldiers entered the schools, universities, and factories to give ideological guidance to the warring factions. Many soldiers were hurt attempting to mediate the mass struggles. A campaign was launched to achieve the great alliance of rebel factions through criticism and self-criticism. Every Chinese was encouraged to regard himself as "both the motive force and target of the revolution." The national slogan during this period was to "fight self and criticize revisionism." Nevertheless, it took another two years to achieve unity and to begin the process of rebuilding the shattered party and state structure. The Chinese would probably be the first to say that the job of transformation is yet unfinished.

Perhaps Mao Tse-tung's greatest disappointment was the failure of the Cultural Revolution to produce a united group of leading revolutionary successors. The fall of Chen Po-ta in 1970 and the death and disgrace of Lin Piao in 1971 removed the two most prominent leaders of the Cultural Revolution. Undoubtedly there were groups in China who believed the Cultural Revolution had gone too far and others who felt that it had not gone far enough. But Mao himself has made it clear that the future is never guaranteed. It depends upon what the next generation does with it.

Although invented in Europe, revolutionary politics have now been creatively developed by the Chinese and other revolutionary Asian peoples. China has dared to experiment with new political forms and has been willing to pay the price for its experiments. Whether or not she has found the answer to the problem which the West has come to recognize as the bureaucratization, routinization, and decay of social and political structures, there are few who can deny that China has boldly confronted some of greatest social problems of the modern age.

NOTE ON SELECTIONS

A virtual Niagara of written and oral expression poured out during the three years of mass political upheaval in China from 1966 to 1969. Every urban organization in China, from the smallest bakery to the state ministries, was flooded with locally printed newspapers, speeches of national leaders, and directives from the Central Cultural Revolution Group and the Military Affairs Commission of the Chinese Communist Party. Thousands of personally written wall posters covered the walls of every public building, and often when all available space had been used, the posters were hung on wires stretched across dining halls and meeting rooms. The most important of these posters were copied and printed for distribution throughout the country. Peking, reverberating under the sound of a thousand loudspeakers operated by a thousand organizations, was constantly besieged with new proclamations, new arguments, and new developments.

Confronted with the mountain of material spawned by the Chinese Cultural Revolution, we have selected those documents, speeches, and editorials which we feel reflect the main political and ideological currents at each stage of the movement. In the main, the selections are arranged in chronological order, except in those instances where a document of a later date throws light on an earlier period.

A word of caution is in order concerning the informal speeches and talks of national leaders that we have chosen to include in the selections. Hundred of these informal talks by the top leaders of the country, often taking place in the middle of the night, attempted to give direction to a movement that was constantly changing and frequently chaotic. Notes of these talks were taken by participants and afterwards printed up by rebel organizations. It was common practice for traveling rank-and-file rebels to recopy the transcripts of these informal talks and then distribute them in other parts of the country. In the haste of copying, characters were often dropped or copied incorrectly, and in other cases, whole paragraphs were either lost or edited out. Nevertheless, in one version or another the main meaning of the leader's opinion and instructions penetrated the nation to influence the complex struggle at every turn of events.

We have included a few of these informal speeches which were distributed throughout China during the Cultural Revolution because despite minor inaccuracies, they had a profound effect on millions of Chinese. No longer possessing an organized party apparatus for the transmission of line and instruction, the leaders of the Cultural Revolution had to rely on the editorials of the *People's Daily* and the *Liberation Army Daily* to give direction, line, and orientation to the mass movement. By necessity, the editorials were couched in general and often ambiguous language. Arguments occurred between factional groupings over the exact meaning of the editorials and how to translate them into action. Thus, informal speeches by the leaders became the instrument for refining the general line and coping with the specifics of Chinese politics in every city and province.

Chairman Mao's talk with a visiting Albanian Military Delegation in August 1967 was widely distributed throughout China; two of us first read it in Peking at that time. In this talk, Mao outlines his concept of the history and development of the Cultural Revolution. He divides the movement into four stages: a mobilization stage, a stage for correcting the orientation, and two stages, beginning with 1967, which involve the seizure of power from below. We have organized our selections around these stages, taking the liberty to subdivide the stages to include particular political developments and adding a final fifth stage of the movement which involved the consolidation and rebuilding of the Chinese Communist Party. We have included a subsection on Mao and another on Liu Shao-ch'i since they were the main protagonists of the political conflict and deserve special attention; we have also put together a special subsection covering the "Wuhan Incident" and the "ultra-left" wave which crested in the late summer of 1967 and ended one entire phase of the Cultural Revolution.

Western readers, new to Chinese political culture, will no doubt find a few of these documents arduous reading. Nevertheless, we hope that the reader will absorb some of the color and the drama of a movement which inspired tens of millions to mount the Chinese political stage.

1. MAO TSE-TUNG—
THE LEADING REBEL

The following selections provide a clue to Mao's success as a popular mass leader and demonstrate the dynamic quality of his personality and political style. Mao's conversations with his niece and his informal talks on education were widely distributed among Chinese students in the early months of the Cultural Revolution. His critical views on formal academic instruction were shared by a substantial proportion of the Chinese student body and reflect the outlook of many students in the West as well. Issued with official approval, these documents encouraged a spirit of rebellion among the youth. Wang Hai-jung, a niece of the Chairman, was a student of English at the First Foreign Languages Institute in Peking before the Cultural Revolution. This school is the largest language university in China and the institution where two of the editors taught for a number of years. During the Cultural Revolution, Wang Hai-jung was a cadre in the Foreign Ministry and an active participant in the mass movement. She is now an assistant Foreign Minister, accompanied the Chinese Delegation to the United Nations in New York in 1971, and was present at the high-level talks between Henry Kissinger and top Chinese leaders in 1972 and 1973.

"Twenty Manifestations of Bureaucracy" was an internal document released to the public some time in 1967. It is characteristic of the Chairman's pungent, satirical style of speech and writing; it demonstrates his ability to transmit important ideas in an earthy, simple, and lively manner.

★　★　★

MAO TSE-TUNG
Quotations

"The tree may prefer calm, but the wind will not subside."

—A favorite saying of Chairman Mao.

Marxism consists of thousands of truths, but they all boil down to the one sentence, "It is right to rebel." For thousands of years, it had been said that it was right to oppress, it was right to exploit, and it was wrong to rebel. This old verdict was only reversed with the appearance of Marxism. This is a great contribution. It was through struggle that the proletariat learned this truth, and Marx drew the conclusion. And from this truth there follows resistance, struggle, the fight for socialism.

—Mao Tse-tung
From a speech at the Rally of People of All Walks of Life in Yenan to Celebrate the Sixtieth Birthday of Stalin

MAO TSE-TUNG
Chairman Mao's Conversations with his Niece, Wang Hai-jung*

1

HAI-JUNG: Class struggle is very acute in our school. I hear that reactionary slogans have been found, some written in English on the blackboard of our English Department.

CHAIRMAN: What reactionary slogans have been written?

HAI-JUNG: I know only one. It is, *"Chiang wan sui."*

CHAIRMAN: How does it read in English?

HAI-JUNG: "Long live Chiang."

CHAIRMAN: What else has been written?

HAI-JUNG: I don't know any others. I know only that one.

CHAIRMAN: Well, let this person write more and post them outdoors for all people to see. Does he kill people?

HAI-JUNG: I don't know if he kills people or not. If we find out who he is, we should dismiss him from school and send him away for labor reform.

CHAIRMAN: Well, so long as he doesn't kill people, we should not dismiss him, nor should we send him away for labor reform. Let him stay in school and continue to study. You people should hold a meeting and ask him to explain in what way Chiang Kai-shek is good and what good things he has done. On our part, you may tell why Chiang Kai-shek is not good.

CHAIRMAN: How many people are there in your school?

HAI-JUNG: About three thousand, including faculty and staff members.

CHAIRMAN: Among the three thousand let us say there are seven or eight counterrevolutionaries.

HAI-JUNG: Even one would be bad. How could we tolerate seven or eight?

CHAIRMAN: You shouldn't be all stirred up by one slogan.

* Mao Tse-tung, Joint Publications Research Service (JPRS), U.S. Department of Commerce 52029 (December 21, 1970).

HAI-JUNG: Why should there be seven or eight counter-revolutionaries?

CHAIRMAN: When there are many, you can set up opposition. There can be teachers in opposition. Only they should not kill.

HAI-JUNG: Our school has realized the class line. Among the new students 70 percent are workers and sons and daughters of poor and lower-middle farmers. Others are sons and daughters of cadres and heroic officers and men.

CHAIRMAN: How many sons and daughters of cadres are there in your class?

HAI-JUNG: In addition to myself, there are two, while others are the sons and daughters of workers and poor and lower-middle farmers. They do well. I learn much from them.

CHAIRMAN: Are they on good terms with you? Do they like you?

HAI-JUNG: I think our relationship is good. I find it easy to associate with them and they find the same with me.

CHAIRMAN: That's good.

HAI-JUNG: But there is the son of a cadre who doesn't do well. In class he doesn't listen attentively to the teacher's lecture and after class, he doesn't do homework. He likes to read fiction. Sometimes he dozes off in the dormitory and sometimes he doesn't attend the Saturday afternoon meeting. On Sunday he doesn't return to school on time. Sometimes on Sunday when our class and section hold a meeting, he doesn't show up. All of us have a bad impression of him.

CHAIRMAN: Do your teachers allow the students to take a nap or read fiction in class?

We should let the students read fiction and take a nap in class, and we should look after their health. Teachers should lecture less and make the students read more. I believe the student you referred to will be very capable in the future since he had the courage to be absent from the Saturday meeting and not to return to school on time on Sunday. When you return to school, you may tell him that it is too early to return to school even at eight or nine in the evening; he may delay it until eleven or twelve. Whose fault is it that you should hold a meeting Sunday night?

HAI-JUNG: When I studied at the Normal School, we usually had no meeting Sunday night. We were allowed to do whatever we liked that night. One day several cadres of the branch headquarters of the League (I was then a committee member of the branch headquarters) agreed to lead an organized life on Sunday night but many other League members did not favor the idea. Some of them even said to the political counselor that Sunday was a free day and if any meeting was called at night, it would be inconvenient for us to go home. The political counselor eventually bowed to their opinion and told us to change the date for the meeting.

CHAIRMAN: This political counselor did the right thing.

HAI-JUNG: But now our school spends the whole Sunday night holding meetings—class meetings, branch headquarters committee meetings or meetings of study groups for party lessons. According to my calculation, from the beginning of the current semester to date, there has not been one Sunday or Sunday night without any meetings.

CHAIRMAN: When you return to school, you should take the lead to rebel. Don't return to school on Sunday and don't attend any meeting on that day.

HAI-JUNG: But I won't dare. This is the school system. All students are required to return to school on time. If I don't, people will say that I violate the school system.

CHAIRMAN: Don't care about the system. Just don't return to school. Just say you want to violate the school system.

HAI-JUNG: I cannot do that. If I do, I will be criticized.

CHAIRMAN: I don't think you will be very capable in the future. You are afraid of being accused of violating the school system, of criticism, of a bad record, of being expelled from school, of failing to get party membership. Why should you be afraid of so many things? The worst that can come to you is expulsion from school. The school should allow the students to rebel. Rebel when you return to school.

HAI-JUNG: People will say that as the Chairman's relative, I fail to follow his instructions and play a leading role in upsetting the school system. They will accuse me of arrogance and self-content, and of lack of organization and discipline.

CHAIRMAN: Look at you! You are afraid of being criticized for arrogance and self-content, and for lack of organization and discipline. Why should you be afraid? You can say that just because you are Chairman Mao's relative, you should follow his instructions to rebel. I think the student you mentioned will be more capable than you for he dared to violate the school system. I think you people are all too metaphysical.

2

ON ONE OCCASION CHAIRMAN MAO
DISCUSSED THE PROBLEM OF STUDY

HAI-JUNG: People now are against reading classical works. But the son of a cadre in our class devotes all his time to reading them. All of us are busy practicing speaking English, but he is reading the *Hung Lou Meng* [*Dream of the Red Chamber*]. We are all critical of his reading this novel.

CHAIRMAN: Have you ever read *Hung Lou Meng*?

HAI-JUNG: Yes, I have.

CHAIRMAN: Which character do you like in this novel?

HAI-JUNG: None.

CHAIRMAN: *Hung Lou Meng* is worth reading. It is a good book. We should read it not for its story but as history. It is a historical novel. Its language is the best in classical fiction. The author, Ts'ao Hsueh-ch'in, has made a lively portrayal of Feng Tzu. The characterization of Feng Tzu is excellent. You won't be able to do the same. If you don't read *Hung Lou Meng*, how could you know about feudal society? Before you read *Hung Lou Meng*, you should know these four sayings: "The Chias are not false. They use white jade to build a hall and gold to make a horse." [This refers to the Chia family.] "The A Fang Palaces spread for three hundred li, but they could not accommodate a Shih." [This refers to the Shih family.] "The Eastern Ocean lacks a white jade bed, but the Dragon King invites the King of Ch'in Ling to visit him." [This refers to Feng Tzu's family or the Wang family.] "What a big snow in this year of plenty—pearls cheap like earth and gold like iron!" [This refers to Hsueh Pao-chi's family.] These four sayings summarize the story of *Hung Lou Meng*.

CHAIRMAN: Have you read Tu Fu's long poem "The Northward March"?

HAI-JUNG: No. It is not in *T'ang Ssu San Pai Shou* [*Three Hundred Poems of T'ang*].

CHAIRMAN: It is in *T'ang Ssu Pi Tsai* [*Another Anthology of*

T'ang Poetry]. (The Chairman took out the book, turned to that poem and told me to read it over and over again.)

HAI-JUNG: What problems should I pay attention to when I read this poem? What precaution should I take against its influence?

CHAIRMAN: You are always metaphysical. Why should you take precaution? No. You should receive some influence. You should go deep in it and then emerge from it. Read it over and over again but not necessarily memorize it.

CHAIRMAN: Are you required to study the Holy Bible and Buddhist sutras?

HAI-JUNG: No. Why should we read them?

CHAIRMAN: How can you do translations or handle foreign affairs if you do not study the Holy Bible and Buddhist sutras? Have you read *Liao Chai* [*Stories from the Strange Studio*]?

HAI-JUNG: No.

CHAIRMAN: *Liao Chai* is worth reading. It is well-written. The fox spirits in *Liao Chai* are kind-hearted. They voluntarily help mankind.

CHAIRMAN: How do you say *"chih shih fen tze"* [intellectual] in English?

HAI-JUNG: I don't know.

CHAIRMAN: You have studied English for half a year. You are a *chih shih fen tze* yourself and yet you don't know how to say it in English.

HAI-JUNG: Let me look it up in the *Chinese-English Dictionary*.

CHAIRMAN: Look it up. Is there such a term?

HAI-JUNG: (After leafing the pages of the dictionary) Too bad. There is no such term in your *Chinese-English Dictionary*. It has only the term *chih shih,* but no *chih shih fen tze*.

CHAIRMAN: Let me take a look. (I handed the dictionary to the Chairman.) You found *chih shih,* but no *chih shih fen tze*. This dictionary is useless. It is short of many words. When you return to school, ask them to compile a better *Chinese-English Dictionary*. It should have all political terms and there should be sentences to illustrate the use of each word.

HAI-JUNG: How can our school compile a dictionary? We have neither time nor personnel to do it.

CHAIRMAN: There are many teachers and students in your

school. Why should you doubt their ability to compile a dictionary? Let this dictionary be compiled by your school.

HAI-JUNG: All right. I will transmit your order to our leadership when I return to school. I think we can perform this task.

MAO TSE-TUNG*
Chairman Mao Discusses Education

(February 13, 1964)

TALKS WITH PARTY LEADERS AT SPRING FESTIVAL
CONCERNING EDUCATIONAL WORK

"Today I want to talk to you about education. Today industry has made great progress and I believe that education should also have some reforms. However, education as it now is still leaves much to be desired.

"Period of schooling may be shortened.

"[The Government] may organize a women's militia or women's corps so that girls sixteen or seventeen years of age may experience a military life for six months to one year. I think those seventeen-year-olds may also serve in the Army.

"There are at present too many curricula that drive people to death. Students at primary and middle schools and colleges are living in a tense environment everyday. Their eyes are getting more near-sighted day by day because the school facilities are bad; lighting conditions are poor.

"Curricula may be reduced by half. It won't do to have students having no cultural recreation, such as swimming and sports.

"Historically, the highest graduates of the Hanlin Academy were not very outstanding. Li Pai and Tu Fu were neither

* Mao Tse-tung in *Current Background*, No. 891 (October 8, 1969), pp. 42-44.

Chinshih nor Hanlin. Han Yu and Liu Chung-yuan were only second degree Chinshih. Wang Shih-fu, Kuan Han-ching, Lo Kuan-chung, Pu Sung-ling and Chao Hsueh-chin were neither Chinshih nor Hanlin. All those who were awarded the degrees of Chinshih or Hanlin did not succeed.

"Among the emperors of the Ming Dynasty, only Ming Tai Chu (accession 1368 A.D.) and Ming Cheng Chu (accession 1403 A.D.) were successful. One of them could not read and the other could read only a few words. Later in the reign of Chia Ching (1522–1566 A.D.), intellectuals came to power. This led to no good. The nation was badly ruled. Those who read more books could not make good emperors and were harmful to the welfare of the people. Liu Hsiu was only a grand secretary and Liu Pang a big bag of wind, yet both were excellent emperors of the Han Dynasty.

"The current examination methods contain many surprises, unusual questions and difficult problems. They are designed to deal with the enemy, not the people. These types of examinations were used in the old days in the writing of the eight-legged essays. I do not approve of them and think that they should be completely remolded. I suggest taking some sample examination problems and having them published. Let the students study and do them with open books. For example, we might consider preparing twenty questions about *The Dream of the Red Chamber*. If a student can correctly answer questions and if some of the answers are good and creative, he may be given 100 points. If he answers all 20 questions and the answers are correct but are ordinary without creative thinking, he should be given 50 or 60 points. In examinations, students should be allowed to whisper to each other and to hire others to take the examinations for them. If your answer is right, I copy yours. Copying is good too. In the past, whispering and hiring of examinees were done on the sly. Now let them be open. When I cannot do what you have done, then let me copy. It should be allowed. We should experiment with this system.

"Teachers giving lectures should allow the students to fall asleep. If the lecture is no good, it makes no sense to force others to listen. Listening to distasteful things with eyes opened wide is worse than sleeping in the class. Sleeping may help one to recover from fatigue. Students should be given the choice of not listening to monotonous lectures.

"The present methods are detrimental to talented men and youths. I do not think that people should study so much. Examinations are designed for dealing with the enemy. They poison people to death and should be abolished." . . .

"Actors, actresses, poets, dramatists and writers should be driven out of the cities and all of them should be sent down in groups to the rural areas and factories. They should not always stay in offices. If they do so, they can write nothing. Only when you go down to the rural areas should you be provided with rice.

"Li Shih-chen of the Ming Dynasty personally went to search for herbs in the countryside for a long time; Chu Chung-chih did not attend any middle school or college. Confucius was brought up in a poor peasant family. He was once a shepherd and never attended a college. At one time he was a trumpeter playing at funerals. He also practiced accounting, learned to play string instruments, shoot arrows and drive carts. Since he came from the masses, he knew the pains of the masses. Later on, when he served as an official in the State of Lu, he became a great intellectual and was alienated from the activities of the masses. This was probably so because he employed Tze Lu as his bodyguard who kept the masses away. Our policies are correct, but the methods are wrong. The current duration of schooling and curricula and the teaching and examination methods must all be reformed. All of them are very detrimental.

"Gorky attended school for only two years; his knowledge was gained entirely through his own efforts. Benjamin Franklin of America sold newspapers when he was young. James Watt, the inventor of the steam engine, was a laborer." . . .

"We should not read too many books. We must read Marxist books but not too many of them. A few dozen of such books will suffice. Reading too many books will lead the readers to take opposing views and to become bookworms, dogmatists or revisionists.

"Confucian teachings do not contain any instruction on industry and agriculture. Therefore, students of Confucius exercise their limbs less and know no names for grains. We must do something about this problem." . . .

"The problem now is that there are too many courses and too many books that overload the students. It is not necessary that all subjects have to be tested. For instance, middle school stu-

dents should learn a little logic and grammar without being
subjected to any test. They will comprehend these in time when
they are engaged in practical work. It is enough for them to
know what is grammar and what is logic."

MAO TSE-TUNG*
Chairman Mao Discusses Twenty Manifestations of Bureaucracy

1. At the highest level there is very little knowledge; they
do not understand the opinion of the masses; they do not
investigate and study; they do not grasp specific policies; they
do not conduct political and ideological work; they are divorced
from reality, from the masses, and from the leadership of the
party; they always issue orders, and the orders are usually
wrong; they certainly mislead the country and the people; at
the least they obstruct the consistent adherence to the party
line and policies; and they can not meet with the people.

2. They are conceited, complacent, and they aimlessly discuss politics. They do not grasp their work; they are subjective
and one-sided; they are careless; they do not listen to people;
they are truculent and arbitrary; they force orders; they do not
care about reality; they maintain blind control. This is authoritarian bureaucracy.

3. They are very busy from morning until evening; they
labor the whole year long; they do not examine people and
they do not investigate matters; they do not study policies;
they do not rely upon the masses; they do not prepare their
statements; they do not plan their work. This is brainless, mis-
directed bureaucracy. In other words, it is routinism.

4. Their bureaucratic attitude is immense; they can not have
any direction; they are egoistic; they beat their gongs to blaze
the way; they cause people to become afraid just by looking at

* Mao Tse-tung, JPRS (49826) No. 90, February 12, 1970.

them; they repeatedly hurl all kinds of abuse at people; their work style is crude; they do not treat people equally. This is the bureaucracy of the overlords.

5. They are ignorant; they are ashamed to ask anything; they exaggerate and they lie; they are very false; they attribute errors to people; they attribute merit to themselves; they swindle the central government; they deceive those above them and fool those below them; they conceal faults and gloss over wrongs. This is the dishonest bureaucracy.

6. They do not understand politics; they do not do their work; they push things off onto others; they do not meet their responsibilities; they haggle; they put things off; they are insensitive; they lose their alertness. This is the irresponsible bureaucracy.

7. They are negligent about things; they subsist as best they can; they do not have anything to do with people; they always make mistakes; they offer themselves respectfully to those above them and are idle towards those below them; they are careful in every respect; they are eight-sided and slippery as eels. This is the bureaucracy of those who work as officials and barely make a living.

8. They do not completely learn politics; they do not advance in their work; their manner of speech is tasteless; they have no direction in their leadership; they neglect the duties of their office while taking the pay; they make up things for the sake of appearances. The idlers [e.g., landlord] do not begin any matters, but concentrate mainly upon their idleness; those who work hard, are virtuous, and do not act like the officials are treated poorly. This is the deceitful, talentless bureaucracy.

9. They are stupid; they are confused; they do not have a mind of their own; they are rotten sensualists; they glut themselves for days on end; they are not diligent at all, they are inconstant and they are ignorant. This is the stupid, useless bureaucracy.

10. They want others to read documents; the others read and they sleep; they criticize without looking at things; they criticize mistakes and blame people; they have nothing to do with mistakes; they do not discuss things; they push things aside and ignore it; they are yes men to those above them; they pretend to understand those below them, when they do not;

they gesticulate; and they harbor disagreements with those on their same level. This is the lazy bureaucracy.

11. Government offices grow bigger and bigger; things are more confused; there are more people than there are jobs; they go around in circles; they quarrel and bicker; people are disinclined to do extra things; they do not fulfill their specific duties. This is the bureaucracy of government offices.

12. Documents are numerous; there is red tape; instructions proliferate; there are numerous unread reports that are not criticized; many tables and schedules are drawn up and are not used; meetings are numerous and nothing is passed on; and there are many close associations but nothing is learned. This is the bureaucracy of red tape and formalism.

13. They seek pleasure and fear hardships; they engage in back-door deals; one person becomes an official and the entire family benefits; one person reaches nirvana and all his close associates rise up to heaven; there are parties and gifts are presented. . . . This is the bureaucracy for the exceptional.

14. The greater an official becomes, the worse his temperament gets; his demands for supporting himself become higher and higher; his home and its furnishings become more and more luxurious; and his access to things becomes better and better. The upper strata gets the larger share while the lower gets high prices; there is extravagance and waste; the upper and lower and the left and right raise their hands. This is the bureaucracy of putting on official airs.

15. They are egotistical; they satisfy private ends by public means; there is embezzlement and speculation; the more they devour, the more they want; and they never step back or give in. This is egotistical bureaucracy.

16. They fight among themselves for power and money; they extend their hands into the party; they want fame and fortune; they want positions, and if they do not get it they are not satisfied; they choose to be fat and to be lean; they pay a great deal of attention to wages; they are cozy when it comes to their comrades but they care nothing about the masses. This is the bureaucracy that is fighting for power and money.

17. A plural leadership cannot be harmoniously united; they exert themselves in many directions, and their work is in a state of chaos; they try to crowd each other out; the top is

divorced from the bottom and there is no centralization, nor is there any democracy. This is the disunited bureaucracy.

18. There is no organization; they employ personal friends; they engage in factionalism; they maintain feudal relationships; they form cliques to further their own private interest; they protect each other; the individual stands above everything else; these petty officials harm the masses. This is sectarian bureaucracy.

19. Their revolutionary will is weak; their politics has degenerated and changed its character; they act as if they are highly qualified; they put on official airs; they do not exercise their minds or their hands. They eat their fill every day; they easily avoid hard work; they call a doctor when they are not sick; they go on excursions to the mountains and to the seashore; they do things superficially; they worry about their individual interests, but they do not worry whatsoever about the national interest. This is degenerate bureaucracy.

20. They promote erroneous tendencies and a spirit of reaction; they connive with bad persons and tolerate bad situations; they engage in villainy and transgress the law; they engage in speculation; they are a threat to the party and the state; they suppress democracy; they fight and take revenge; they violate laws and regulations; they protect the bad; they do not differentiate between the enemy and ourselves. This is the bureaucracy of erroneous tendencies and reaction.

★　★　★　★　★

2. MOBILIZATION FOR REBELLION

During the first week of June 1966, a series of editorials published in the *People's Daily*, now controlled by the followers of Mao, provided the ideology and rationale for the mass movement which was to become the Great Proletarian Cultural Revolution. These manifestos, two of which are included in the selections, were to the Cultural Revolution what Tom Paine's *Crisis Papers* and *Common Sense* were to the American Revolution. Studied and discussed word for word by groups and individuals all over China, these editorials mobilized public opinion for the mass struggles ahead.

As we have said, Mao's talk to the group of visiting Albanian military officers, which we have included as our last selection in this subsection, sheds light on Mao's own conception of and strategy for the revolution which he had launched.

★   ★   ★

PEOPLE'S DAILY*
Sweep Away All Monsters

An upsurge is occurring in the great proletarian cultural revolution in socialist China whose population accounts for one-quarter of the world's total.

For the last few months, in response to the militant call of the Central Committee of the Chinese Communist Party and Chairman Mao, hundreds of millions of workers, peasants and soldiers and vast numbers of revolutionary cadres and intellec-

* *The Great Socialist Cultural Revolution* (Peking: Foreign Language Press, 1966), pp. 1–6 (translated from *People's Daily*, June 1, 1966).

tuals, all armed with Mao Tse-tung's thought, have been sweeping away a horde of monsters that have entrenched themselves in ideological and cultural positions. With the tremendous and impetuous force of a raging storm, they have smashed the shackles imposed on their minds by the exploiting classes for so long in the past, routing the bourgeois "specialists," "scholars," "authorities" and "venerable masters" and sweeping every bit of their prestige into the dust.

Chairman Mao has taught us that class struggle does not cease in China after the socialist transformation of the system of ownership has in the main been completed. He said:

> The class struggle between the proletariat and the bourgeoisie, the class struggle between different political forces, and the class struggle in the ideological field between the proletariat and the bourgeoisie will continue to be long and tortuous and at times will even become very acute. The proletariat seeks to transform the world according to its own world outlook, and so does the bourgeoisie. In this respect, the question of which will win out, socialism or capitalism, is still not really settled.

The class struggle in the ideological field between the proletariat and the bourgeoisie has been very acute right through the sixteen years since China's liberation. The current great socialist cultural revolution is precisely a continuation and development of this struggle. The struggle is inevitable. The ideology of the proletariat and the ideology of all the exploiting classes are diametrically opposed to each other and cannot coexist in peace. The proletarian revolution is a revolution to abolish all exploiting classes and all systems of exploitation; it is a most thoroughgoing revolution to bring about the gradual elimination of the differences between workers and peasants, between town and country, and between mental and manual laborers. This cannot but meet with the most stubborn resistance from the exploiting classes.

In every revolution the basic question is that of state power. In all branches of the superstructure—ideology, religion, art, law, state power—the central issue is state power. State power means everything. Without it, all will be lost. Therefore, no matter how many problems have to be tackled after the conquest of state power, the proletariat must never forget state power, never forget its orientation and never lose sight of the central issue. Forgetting about state power means forgetting about politics, forgetting about the basic theses of Marxism and switching to economism, anarchism and utopianism and becoming muddle-headed. In the last analysis, the class struggle in the ideological field between the proletariat and the bourgeoisie is a struggle for leadership. The exploiting classes have been disarmed and deprived of their authority by the people, but their reactionary ideas remain rooted in their minds. We have overthrown their rule and confiscated their property, but this does not mean that we have rid their minds of reactionary ideas as well. During the thousands of years of their rule over the working people, the exploiting classes monopolized the culture created by the working people and in turn used it to deceive, fool and benumb the working people in order to consolidate their reactionary state power. For thousands of years, theirs was the dominant ideology which inevitably exerted widespread influence in society. Not reconciled to the overthrow of their reactionary rule, they invariably try to make use of this influence of theirs surviving from the past to shape public opinion in preparation for the political and economic restoration of capitalism. The uninterrupted struggle on the ideological and cultural front in the sixteen years from liberation up to the current exposure of the black anti-Party and anti-socialist line of the "Three-Family Villages," big and small, has been a struggle between the forces attempting restoration and the forces opposing restoration.

In order to seize state power, the bourgeoisie during the period of the bourgeois revolution likewise started with ideological preparations by launching the bourgeois cultural revolution. Even the bourgeois revolution, which replaced one exploiting class by another, had to undergo repeated reversals and witness many struggles—revolution, then restoration and then the overthrow of restoration. It took many European countries hundreds of years to complete their bourgeois revolutions from the start of the ideological preparations to the final conquest of state power. Since the proletarian revolution is a revolution aimed at completely ending all systems of exploitation, it is still less permissible to imagine that the exploiting classes will meekly allow the proletariat to deprive them of all their privileges without seeking to restore their rule. The surviving members of these classes who are unreconciled will inevitably, as Lenin put it, throw themselves with a tenfold furious passion into the battle for the recovery of their lost paradise. The fact that the Khrushchev revisionist clique has usurped the leadership of the Party, army and state in the Soviet Union is an extremely serious lesson for the proletariat throughout the world. At present the representatives of the bourgeoisie, the bourgeois "scholars" and "authorities" in China are dreaming precisely of restoring capitalism. Though their political rule has been toppled, they are still desperately trying to maintain their academic "authority," mold public opinion for a comeback and win over the masses, the youth and the generations yet unborn from us.

The anti-feudal cultural revolution waged by the bourgeoisie ended as soon as it had seized power. The proletarian cultural revolution, however, is a cultural revolution against the ideology of all exploiting classes. This cultural revolution is entirely different in nature from the bourgeois cultural revolution. It is only after the creation of the political, economic and cultural prerequisites following the capture of state power by the proletariat that the broadest road is opened up for the proletarian cultural revolution.

The proletarian cultural revolution is aimed not only at demolishing all the old ideology and culture and all the old customs and habits, which, fostered by the exploiting classes, have poisoned the minds of the people for thousands of years, but also at creating and fostering among the masses an entirely new ideology and culture and entirely new customs and habits —those of the proletariat. This great task of transforming customs and habits is without any precedent in human history. As for all the heritage, customs and habits of the feudal and bourgeois classes, the proletarian world outlook must be used to subject them to thoroughgoing criticism. It takes time to clear away the evil habits of the old society from among the people. Nevertheless, our experience since liberation proves that the transformation of customs and habits can be accelerated if the masses are fully mobilized, the mass line is implemented and the transformation is made into a genuine mass movement.

As the bourgeois cultural revolution served only a small number of people, i.e., the new exploiting class, only a small number of people could participate in it. The proletarian cultural revolution, however, serves the broad masses of the working people and is in the interests of the working people who constitute the overwhelming majority of the population. It is therefore able to attract and unite the broad masses of the working people to take part in it. The bourgeois individuals who carried out the enlightenment invariably looked down upon the masses, treated them as a mob and considered themselves as the predestined masters of the people. In sharp contrast, proletarian ideological revolutionaries serve the people heart and soul with the object of awakening them, and work for the interests of the broadest masses.

The bourgeoisie, with its base selfishness, is unable to suppress its hatred for the masses. Marx said:

> The peculiar nature of the material it [political economy] deals with, summons as foes into the field of battle the most violent, mean and malignant passions of the human breast, the furies of private interest.

This also holds for the bourgeoisie when it has been overthrown.

The scale and momentum of the great proletarian cultural revolution now being carried on in China have no parallel in history, and the tremendous drive and momentum and boundless wisdom of the working people manifested in the movement far exceed the imagination of the lords of the bourgeoisie. Facts have eloquently proved that Mao Tse-tung's thought becomes a moral atom bomb of colossal power once it takes hold of the masses. The current great cultural revolution is immensely advancing the socialist cause of the Chinese people and undoubtedly exerting an incalculable, far-reaching influence upon the present and future of the world.

The stormy cultural revolution now under way in our country has thrown the imperialists, the modern revisionists and the reactionaries of all countries into confusion and panic. At one moment, they indulge in wishful thinking saying that our great cultural revolution has shown that there are hopes of "a peaceful evolution" on the part of China's younger generation. A moment later, they become pessimistic, saying that all this has shown that Communist rule remains very stable. Then again, they seem to be fearfully puzzled, saying that it will never be possible to find genuine "China hands" who can promptly pass accurate judgment on what is taking place in China. Dear sirs, your wishful thinking invariably runs counter to the march of the history. The triumphant progress of this great and unparalleled cultural revolution of the proletariat is already sounding the death knell not only of the remnant capitalist forces on Chinese soil, but of imperialism, modern revisionism and all reaction. Your days are numbered.

Illuminated by the great Mao Tse-tung's thought, let us carry the proletarian cultural revolution through to the end. Its victory will certainly further strengthen the dictatorship of the proletariat in our country, guarantee the completion of the socialist revolution on all fronts and ensure our successful transition from socialism to triumphant communism!

PEOPLE'S DAILY*
We Are Critics of the Old World

The rapid and vigorous development of China's great proletarian cultural revolution is shaking the world.

Some people say, "The 700 million Chinese are all critics."

Irrespective of who says this, and whether it makes them happy or unhappy, this saying reflects the fact that China's broad masses of workers, peasants and soldiers and revolutionary cadres and revolutionary intellectuals, using as their

The Great Socialist Cultural Revolution (Peking: Foreign Language Press, 1966), pp. 18–21 (translated from *People's Daily*, June 8, 1966).

weapon the thought of Mao Tse-tung, have started to criticize the old world, old things and old thinking on an unprecedented scale.

We criticize the system of exploitation, the exploiting classes, imperialism, modern revisionism, all reactionaries, landlords, rich peasants, counter-revolutionaries, bad elements and Rightists.

We criticize the representatives of the bourgeoisie and bourgeois "scholars and authorities."

We criticize the bourgeois conception of history, bourgeois academic theories, pedagogy, journalism, and theories of art and literaure, and all bad plays, films and works of literature and art.

In sum, we criticize the old world, the old ideology and culture, and old customs and habits which imperialism and all exploiting classes use to poison the minds of the working people, we criticize all non-proletarian ideology, all reactionary ideology which is antagonistic to Marxism-Leninism, to Mao Tse-tung's thought.

Why should we criticize all this?

We do this because it is absolutely necessary for the consolidation of the dictatorship of the proletariat and the building of socialism and communism, and it corresponds to the laws of historical development. Lenin held that after the overthrow of the bourgeoisie, for a long period its strength surpasses that of the proletariat, and that, particularly in the field of ideology, for a long time it still remains predominant and very stubborn. And it uses this in every way to make ideological preparations and get public opinion ready for the restoration of capitalism. This is fully illustrated by the sharp and protracted struggles on the ideological and cultural front between the two classes and two roads in the seventeen years since the liberation of China, and especially by the struggle between the bourgeoisie plotting a restoration and the proletariat opposing a restoration, a struggle which of late has come to the fore.

Chairman Mao told us long ago that everything reactionary is the same: if you don't hit it, it won't fall. This is also like sweeping the floor; as a rule, where the broom does not reach, the dust does not vanish of itself. This applies to everything in the world. We want to build the new world so we must destroy the old; we want to create the new ideology and culture of socialism and communism so we must subject the old bourgeois ideology and culture, and the influence they exert, to thoroughgoing criticism and clear them out.

The essence of Marxism-Leninism is critical and revolutionary. Its essentials are to criticize, to wage struggle and make revolution. What we practice is the militant philosophy of dialectical materialism. Struggle is life. As we go forward along the correct path of struggle, our fighting power will grow and we will be better able to advance our great cause.

Chairman Mao has often emphasized that "there is no construction without destruction, no flowing without damming and no moving forward without a holding back." Destruction here means criticism, means revolution. Destruction necessarily calls for reasoning, and reasoning is construction; destruction comes first, and in the course of it there is construction. The formation and development of Marxism-Leninism and Mao Tse-tung's thought have taken place in the incessant struggle to destroy the ideological system of the bourgeoisie. Chairman Mao says:

> What is correct always develops in the course of struggle with what is wrong. The true, the good and the beautiful always exist in comparison with the false, the evil and the ugly, and grow in struggle with the latter.

Who is to be counted on in making criticism? We must count on the broadest masses of the people, on the workers, peasants and soldiers, the revolutionary cadres and the revolutionary intellectuals. During the revolutionary war, the masses of people used arms to criticize the old world and seize power; since victory, they have been using criticism as their weapon against all the evils left over by imperialism and the landlord and bourgeois classes. Only when all the 700 million people take up Mao Tse-tung's thought, the sharpest of all weapons, to make criticism can there be a clean-up on the broadest scale of the dust left hidden by the bourgeoisie in every corner and a thorough uprooting to the greatest depth of the ideology of

the exploiting classes which have been in a monopolistic and
dominant position for the past thousands of years. Only when
the broadest masses master the proletarian world outlook and
criticize the bourgeois world outlook, master Marxism-Leninism, Mao Tse-tung's thought, and criticize revisionist ideas,
will there be the guarantee of China's socialist revolution being
carried through to the end and of its step-by-step transition
from socialism to communism.

The fact that "700 million people are critics" is stupendous,
it is an epoch-making event. This in itself shows that the thinking of our 700 million people has been emancipated, that they
have risen to full height and that they are no longer slaves of
the old culture and old ideas of imperialism and the exploiting classes. It is not at all accidental that our 700 million people have become critics. It is something new that has arisen
in the conditions of the dictatorship of the proletariat. It is
something new, born of the brilliance of Mao Tse-tung's
thought. It is a new phenomenon, an inevitable product of the
integration of Mao Tse-tung's thought with the broad masses
of workers, peasants and soldiers. It represents the great
awakening of the Chinese people.

The birth and deepening of any great revolutionary movement is inevitably preceded by a gigantic struggle in the ideological field and heralded by a great ideological revolution. In
the history of the proletarian revolution, every major polemic
has been the prelude to and signal for a revolutionary leap
forward. In China, each of the many major polemics in the
ideological field in the seventeen years since liberation has
blazed the trail for the locomotive of revolution. The great cultural revolution now under way, on a scale never known before,
necessarily foreshadows a development of the socialist revolution by leaps and bounds and a new big leap forward in China's
socialist construction.

Once the people have risen, the enemy falls. In China, the
broad masses of workers, peasants and soldiers, the revolutionary cadres and revolutionary intellectuals have risen, and the
representatives of the bourgeoisie and the bourgeois "scholars
and authorities" will fall. In the movement of criticism that is
developing on an unprecedentedly wide scale in the tremendous
cultural revolution, a great new era is now emerging on the

horizon, an era in which the whole of the 700 million Chinese people are people of wisdom.

Let us welcome this great new era with open arms.

MAO TSE-TUNG*

Excerpts from *A Talk by Chairman Mao with a Foreign [Albanian] Military Delegation*

I said at a rally of seven thousand people in 1962 that the struggle between Marxism-Leninism and revisionism had not yet come to a conclusion, that it was quite probable that revisionism would win while we would lose. We reminded everyone of the possibility of defeat in order to help everyone's vigilance against revisionism and to strengthen the effort to oppose and prevent revisionism. As a matter of fact, the struggle between the two classes and two lines has always existed in the Party. That cannot be denied. Being materialists, we of course should not deny it. Since the rally, the struggle between the two classes and two lines in our Party has assumed the expression of struggle between " 'Left' in form but Right in essence" and counter " 'Left' in form but Right in essence," between opposition to the existence of class struggle and the emphasis on the existence of class struggle, between steering a middle course and the bringing of proletarian politics to the fore, etc. All this has been discussed in appropriate documents before.

Today your country has sent here a military delegation to learn about our great cultural revolution. I want to talk about my views on this problem.

Our great proletarian cultural revolution should begin with Yao Wen-yuan's criticism of *Hai Jui's Dismissal from Office* in the winter of 1965. At that time some departments and areas

* Mao Tse-tung (August 31, 1967), translated in *SCMP*, No. 4200 (June 18, 1968), p. 2–7.

of our country were dominated to such an extent by revisionists that they were watertight and could not even be penetrated with a needle. At that time I suggested that Comrade XX should organize the writing of criticism against *Hai Jui's Dismissal from Office.* But nothing could be done even in this Red city, and so it had to be done in Shanghai. When the essay was completed, I read it three times and thought it would do basically. So I let Comrade XX have it published. . . .

After the publication of Comrade Yao Wen-yuan's essay, it was reprinted in most newspapers in all parts of the country, but newspapers in Peking and Hunan did not carry it. Later I suggested that the essay be published in booklet form, but my suggestion was opposed and never acted on.

Comrade Yao Wen-yuan's essay was only a signal for the great proletarian cultural revolution. So we especially supervised the formulation of a May 16 Circular at the Center. This was because the enemies were very sensitive. They would act as soon as they saw the signal. Of course we must also act.

The Circular clearly raised the question of struggle of line. At that time most people disagreed with me. Sometimes I was all alone. They said that my ideas were out of date. So I had to bring my views to the eleventh plenary session of the CCP Eighth Central Committee for discussion. Through the discussion I was able to secure the consent of slightly more than half of those present. . . .

After the eleventh plenary session of the Party's Eighth Central Committee, the focal point was on the criticism against the bourgeois reactionary line in the three months of October, November and December 1966. That openly provoked contradictions within the party. . . .

With regard to policy and strategy, the great proletarian cultural revolution may roughly be divided into four stages:

The period from the publication of Comrade Yao Wen-yuan's essay up to the eleventh plenary session of the CCP Eighth Central Committee may be regarded as the first stage. It was primarily a mobilization stage.

The period from the eleventh plenary session of the CCP Eighth Central Committee to the January Storm may be regarded as the second stage. It was primarily a stage for correcting the orientation.

The power seizure in the January Storm and the revolutionary great alliance and three-in-one combination may be regarded as the third stage.

The fourth stage began with the publication of Ch'i Pen-yu's "Is It Patriotism or National Betrayal?" and "The Essence of Self-cultivation Is Betrayal of the Proletarian Dictatorship."

The third and fourth stages are both concerned with the question of power seizure. The fourth stage, however, involves ideological seizure of power from revisionism and the bourgeoisie. Therefore it is a crucial stage of decision for the struggle between the two classes, two roads and two lines. It is the main theme. . . .

It was desired to bring up some successors among the intellectuals, but now it seems a hopeless task. As I see it, the intellectuals, including young intellectuals still receiving education in school, still have a basically bourgeois world outlook, whether they are in the Party or outside it. This is because for seventeen years after the liberation the cultural and educational circles have been dominated by revisionism. As a result, bourgeois ideas are infused in the blood of the intellectuals. So revolutionary intellectuals must successfully reform their world outlook at the crucial stage of the struggle between the two classes, two roads and two lines, or they may head in a direction opposite that of the revolution.

Here I'll ask you a question: Tell me, what is the object of the great proletarian cultural revolution? (Someone answered that it was to struggle against the capitalist roaders in the Party.) The struggle against the capitalist roaders in the Party is the principal task, but not the object. The object is to solve the problem of world outlook and eradicate revisionism.

The Center has repeatedly stressed the importance of self-education, because a world outlook cannot be imposed on anyone, and ideological remolding represents external factors acting on internal factors, with the latter playing the primary role. If world outlook is not reformed, then although two thousand capitalist roaders are removed in the current great cultural revolution, four thousand others may appear the next time. We are paying a very high price in the current great cultural revolution. The struggle between the two classes and two lines cannot be settled in one, two, three or four cultural revolutions, but the results of the current great cultural revolution must be consolidated for at least fifteen years. Two or three cultural revolutions should be carried out every hundred years. So we must keep in mind the uprooting of revisionism and strengthen our capability to resist revisionism at any time.

Here I wish to ask you another question: What are capitalist roaders? (No reply) Capitalist roaders are power-holders who follow the capitalist road. During the democratic revolution they took an active part in the fight against the three big mountains. But in the fight against the bourgeoisie after the nation-wide liberation, they were not so enthusiastic. They actively took part in the war against local tyrants and in the redistribution of land, but they were not so enthusiastic when it came to collectivization of farming after the nationwide liberation. They do not take the socialist road, but they now hold power. Isn't it right to call them power-holders who take the capitalist road?

When a veteran comes face to face with a new problem, he will resolutely take the socialist road if he has the proletarian world outlook, but if he has the bourgeois world outlook, he will take the capitalist road. That is why we say the bourgeoisie will want to reform the world according to the bourgeois world outlook. Some people who have made mistakes of orientation and line in the great proletarian revolution also try to excuse themselves by saying that veteran revolutionaries have met new problems. But since they have made mistakes, it shows that these veteran cadres have not yet thoroughly reformed their bourgeois world outlook.

From now on, veteran cadres will yet have to meet with many more new problems. To insure that they will resolutely follow the socialist road, they must bring about a proletarian revolution of their mind. I'll ask you this: How do you think we shall change concretely from socialism to communism? This is an important question for the country and for the whole world.

I say that the revolutionary spirit of the revolutionary young generals is very strong. That is very good. But you cannot go up on the stage yet. If you go up on the stage today, you will be kicked off of it tomorrow. These words were used by one of the

Vice Premiers as if they had been his own. That is very wrong. The problem in dealing with the revolutionary young generals is one of bringing them up. It is not right to pour cold water on them when they make certain mistakes.

Some people say that election is very good and very democratic. I think election is only a civilized term. I myself do not admit that there is any true election. I was elected a People's Deputy for Peking District, but how many people are there in Peking who really understand me? I think the election of Chou En-lai as Premier means his appointment as Premier by the Center. Some people say that the Chinese people deeply love peace. I don't think they love peace so much. I think the Chinese people are bellicose.

In dealing with cadres, we must first of all believe that more than 95 percent of them are good or comparatively good. Our confidence cannot be separated from this class viewpoint. Revolutionary cadres and those who want to make revolution must be protected. They must be protected without fear and liberated from their mistakes. Even those who have followed the capitalist road should be allowed to make revolution when after prolonged education they have corrected their mistakes.

Those who are really bad are not many. They form at most 5 percent of the masses and one or two percent in the Party and CYL. The inveterate capitalist roaders are only a small handful. But we must hit at this small handful as the main target, because their influence and poison is deep and great. So their overthrow is the principal task of our current great cultural revolution.

Bad men among the masses cannot be more than 5 percent, but they are scattered and therefore ineffectual. Five percent of them would total 35 million. If they were formed into an army and opposed us in an organized manner, then they would really be a problem deserving our attention. However, they are scattered everywhere and ineffective. So they cannot be the main target of the great proletarian cultural revolution.

All the same, we must sharpen our vigilance, particularly at crucial stages of the struggle, when it will be necessary to prevent bad men from infiltrating our ranks. Therefore the revolutionary great alliance should be conditioned by two prerequisites—one is destruction of self and establishment of devotion to public interest, and the other, struggle. An alliance without struggle will not be effective.

The fourth stage of the current great cultural revolution is a crucial stage of the struggle between the two classes, two roads, and two lines. So more time should be set aside for mass criticism and repudiation. This question is being discussed in the Central Cultural Revolution Group. Some think the suitable time is the end of this year, others favor May next year. But the matter of time must also be subject to the law of class struggle.

★   ★   ★   ★   ★

3. BOMBARD THE HEADQUARTERS—
"CORRECTING THE ORIENTATION"

In the summer of 1965 Mao stated to André Malraux, "I am alone with the masses. Waiting." One year later, Mao was no longer waiting, but acting. During the early summer months of 1966 he remained out of Peking while top leaders of the Party organization, who were subsequently ousted, sent out "work teams" of senior cadres to seize control of the Cultural Revolution. By directing their attack against the student rebels who had dared to criticize Party officials, the work teams suppressed the mass movement. The student Red Guards later referred to the months of June and July as the "fifty days of white terror."

Suddenly, on July 16, the seventy-three-year-old Mao appeared at the city of Wuhan and made his famous swim across the Yangtze River. The event was not publicized until ten days later when all the major newspapers celebrated the event with banner headlines and pictures. The symbolism of this event was not lost upon the Chinese people. Since rumors had been circulating about Mao's fragile health, the phenomenal swim (even if helped by a fifteen-mile-per-hour current) showed that he was fit and ready to plunge into the political struggle against his enemies. He returned to Peking, and from then on was at the center of the stage of the rapidly developing political movement.

Mao immediately held a series of talks with leading members of the Central Committee of the Party. Excerpts from one of these talks, included as our first selection, reveal Mao's anger at the suppression of the mass movement and his determination to reverse the direction of events. After excoriating his colleagues for their fear of the masses and advising them to "make trouble to the end," Mao moved fast to prevent his enemies from controlling the impending Eleventh Plenum of the Chinese Communist Party.

When the members of the Central Committee filed into the meeting of the Eleventh Plenary Session, they were confronted with a big-character poster written by Mao himself. Chosen as our second selection, Mao's poster, titled "Bombard the Head-quarters," was immediately understood by all the delegates as an attack on Liu Shao-ch'i, Teng Hsiao-p'ing, and other prom-inent leaders of the powerful party apparatus.

After a struggle, Mao was able to win a slight majority for his revolutionary program. The Plenum demoted Liu Shao-ch'i, who in 1958 had been designated as Mao's successor, and ele-vated Lin Piao, the Minister of Defense, to the post of Deputy Chairman of the Chinese Communist Party. Lin was officially proclaimed as "Chairman Mao's closest comrade in arms and successor."

The sixteen-point decision issued by the Central Committee, which we have included in its entirety, represented the pro-grammatic document of the Cultural Revolution and laid out the ground rules for the mass movement. Stating that the "out-come of this great cultural revolution will be determined by whether or not the Party leadership dares boldly to arouse the masses," the sixteen-point decision was soon outmoded by events. In fact, in many areas the Party organization refused to lead an attack upon itself, and it was only by reliance on mass organizations outside the Party that the new national leaders in Peking were able to carry on a revolution against the "capi-talist roaders" in the Party.

"Rebellion: The Soul of Mao Tse-tung's Thought," is one of the most famous early big-character posters. Frequently quoted, this colorful manifesto reveals the extent to which Mao's poetry, Peking opera, and Chinese literary tradition influenced the romantic and often anarchistic temper of the young Chinese Red Guards. Lin Piao's speech on November 3, 1966, included as our last selection, was directed to one million young Red Guards who had made the pilgrimage to Peking to affirm their support for the new revolution. From August to December 1966 eight such giant rallies of a million or more Red Guards were held in the giant T'ien An Men square in Peking. Mao appeared at each one of these mass demonstrations, since the Red Guards who had traveled from all over China to Peking, often on foot, refused to leave the city until they had seen the Chairman in person.

★   ★   ★

MAO TSE-TUNG*
Chairman Mao Talks to
Central Committee Leaders

Chairman Mao: Nieh Yuan-tzu's big-character poster of "May 25" is a declaration of the Chinese Paris Commune of the sixties of the twentieth century. Its significance surpasses the Paris Commune. It is beyond us to write this kind of big character poster. . . .

I am speaking to everyone. The young people are the main force of the cultural revolution. They must be fully mobilized.

After returning to Peking I was most distressed. Some schools have quietly closed their doors, some have even suppressed the student movement. Who wants to suppress the student movement? Only the Pei-yang warlords. It is anti-Marxist for the Communist Party to fear the student movement. Some claim every day that they follow the mass line and serve the people, but actually they follow the bourgeois line and serve the bourgeoisie.

The [Youth] League Central Committee should stand on the side of the student movement, but it is actually on the side suppressing the student movement.

Who are opposed to the great cultural revolution? They are the U.S. imperialists, the Soviet revisionists, the Japanese revisionists and the reactionaries.

Under the pretext of "drawing a dividing line between insiders and outsiders," some fear the revolution, and they cover up the posters which have been put up. This situation cannot be tolerated. It is an error in direction and must be changed at once. All conventions must be smashed.

We should trust the masses and be their pupils before we can be their teachers. The current great cultural revolution is

* Mao Tse-tung (July 21, 1966), translated in *Current Background* No. 891, pp. 58–59.

an earth-shaking event. Can we or do we dare undergo the test of socialism? This aims in the final analysis to wipe out classes and reduce the three great differences.

Opposition—particularly to the "authoritarian" ideology of the bourgeoisie—is destruction. Without such destruction, socialism cannot be established. We must carry out struggle, criticism, and transformation.

It won't do just to sit in an office and listen to reports. We should rely on and have faith in the masses, and make trouble to the end. Be prepared for the revolution coming over your own head. Leaders of the Party and the government and responsible comrades of the Party must be so prepared. Presently, we must carry the revolution through to the end. By tempering and remolding ourselves in this field, we can catch up with others. Otherwise, we can only stay outside.

Some comrades are very ferocious when they struggle against other people, but they are unable to wage struggle against themselves. They will never be able to pass the test in this way.

When you are told to kindle a fire to burn yourselves, will you do it? After all, you yourselves will be burned.

Some comrades answer in this way: We are ready. If we are incompetent, we'll quit. We'll live and die as communists. A life of sitting on a sofa in front of an electric fan won't do.

It won't do to lay down conventions for the masses. Seeing that the students were on their feet, Peking University laid down conventions and glorified this as "putting things on the correct track." Actually things were led astray.

(Someone said: Some schools pinned the counterrevolutionary label on students.) Chairman Mao said: The masses are put in the opponent camp in this way. Have no fear of bad people. How many bad people are there after all? The majority of students are good people.

(Someone asked: What should we do if our archives were thrown into disorder in a confusion?) Chairman Mao said: Who are you afraid of? Those who are bad will prove they are bad. Why should you be afraid of the good people? Replace the word "fear" with the word "dare"; it is necessary to prove whether you will ultimately be able to pass the test of socialism.

No person who suppresses the student movement will come to a good end.

MAO TSE-TUNG*
Mao's Big-Character Poster

BOMBARD THE HEADQUARTERS—
MY FIRST BIG-CHARACTER POSTER

(August 5, 1966)

"China's first Marxist-Leninist big-character poster and Commentator's article on it in *Renmin Ribao* (*People's Daily*) are indeed superbly written! Comrades, please read them again. But in the last fifty days or so some leading comrades from the central down to the local levels have acted in a diametrically opposite way. Adopting the reactionary stand of the bourgeoisie, they have enforced a bourgeois dictatorship and struck down the surging movement of the great cultural revolution of the proletariat. They have stood facts on their head and juggled black and white, encircled and suppressed revolutionaries, stifled opinions differing from their own, imposed a white terror, and felt very pleased with themselves. They have puffed up the arrogance of the bourgeoisie and deflated the morale of the proletariat. How poisonous! Viewed in connection with the Right deviation in 1962 and the wrong tendency of 1964 which was 'Left' in form but Right in essence, shouldn't this make one wide awake?"

* Mao Tse-tung, *Current Background* No. 981 (October 8, 1969). Translated from *Peking Review* No. 33 (August 11, 1967), p. 5.

THE CENTRAL COMMITTEE OF THE CHINESE COMMUNIST PARTY*
Decision Concerning the Great Proletarian Cultural Revolution
(Adopted on August 8, 1966)

1. A NEW STAGE IN THE SOCIALIST REVOLUTION

The great proletarian cultural revolution now unfolding is a great revolution that touches people to their very souls and constitutes a new stage in the development of the socialist revolution in our country, a stage which is both broader and deeper.

At the Tenth Plenary Session of the Eighth Central Committee of the Party, Comrade Mao Tse-tung said: To overthrow a political power, it is always necessary first of all to create public opinion, to do work in the ideological sphere. This is true for the revolutionary class as well as for the counter-revolutionary class. This thesis of Comrade Mao Tse-tung's has been proved entirely correct in practice.

Although the bourgeoisie has been overthrown, it is still trying to use the old ideas, culture, customs and habits of the exploiting classes to corrupt the masses, capture their minds and endeavor to stage a comeback. The proletariat must do the exact opposite: it must meet head-on every challenge of the bourgeoisie in the ideological field and use the new ideas, culture, customs and habits of the proletariat to change the mental outlook of the whole of society. At present, our objective is to

* *Decision of the Central Committee of the Chinese Communist Party Concerning the Great Proletarian Cultural Revolution* (Peking: Foreign Languages Press, 1966), pp. 1–13.

struggle against and overthrow those persons in authority who are taking the capitalist road, to criticize and repudiate the reactionary bourgeois academic "authorities" and the ideology of the bourgeoisie and all other exploiting classes and to transform education, literature and art and all other parts of the superstructure not in correspondence with the socialist economic base, so as to facilitate the consolidation and development of the socialist system.

2. THE MAIN CURRENT AND THE TWISTS AND TURNS

The masses of the workers, peasants, soldiers, revolutionary intellectuals, and revolutionary cadres form the main force in this great cultural revolution. Large numbers of revolutionary young people, previously unknown, have become courageous and daring pathbreakers. They are vigorous in action and intelligent. Through the media of big-character posters and great debates, they argue things out, expose and criticize thoroughly, and launch resolute attacks on the open and hidden representatives of the bourgeoisie. In such a great revolutionary movement, it is hardly avoidable that they should show shortcomings of one kind or another; however, their general revolutionary orientation has been correct from the beginning. This is the main current in the great proletarian cultural revolution. It is the general direction along which this revolution continues to advance.

Since the cultural revolution is a revolution, it inevitably meets with resistance. This resistance comes chiefly from those in authority who have wormed their way into the Party and are taking the capitalist road. It also comes from the force of habits from the old society. At present, this resistance is still fairly strong and stubborn. But after all, the great proletarian cultural revolution is an irresistible general trend. There is abundant evidence that such resistance will be quickly broken down once the masses become fully aroused.

Because the resistance is fairly strong, there will be reversals and even repeated reversals in this struggle. There is no harm in this. It tempers the proletariat and other working people, and especially the younger generation, teaches them lessons and gives them experience, and helps them to understand that the revolutionary road zigzags and does not run smoothly.

3. PUT DARING ABOVE EVERYTHING ELSE AND BOLDLY AROUSE THE MASSES

The outcome of this great cultural revolution will be determined by whether or not the Party leadership dares boldly to arouse the masses.

Currently, there are four different situations with regard to the leadership being given to the movement of cultural revolution by Party organizations at various levels:

(1) There is the situation in which the persons in charge of Party organizations stand in the van of the movement and dare to arouse the masses boldly. They put daring above everything else, they are dauntless communist fighters and good pupils of Chairman Mao. They advocate the big-character posters and great debates. They encourage the masses to expose every kind of ghost and monster and also to criticize the shortcomings and errors in the work of the persons in charge. This correct kind of leadership is the result of putting proletarian politics in the forefront and Mao Tse-tung's thought in the lead.

(2) In many units, the persons in charge have a very poor understanding of the task of leadership in this great struggle, their leadership is far from being conscientious and effective, and they accordingly find themselves incompetent and in a weak position. They put fear above everything else, stick to outmoded ways and regulations, and are unwilling to break away from conventional practices and move ahead. They have been taken unawares by the new order of things, the revolutionary order of the masses, with the result that their leadership lags behind the situation, lags behind the masses.

(3) In some units, the persons in charge, who made mistakes of one kind or another in the past, are even more prone to put fear above everything else, being afraid that the masses will catch them out. Actually, if they make serious self-criticism and accept the criticism of the masses, the Party and the masses will

make allowances for their mistakes. But if the persons in charge don't, they will continue to make mistakes and become obstacles to the mass movement.

(4) Some units are controlled by those who have wormed their way into the Party and are taking the capitalist road. Such persons in authority are extremely afraid of being exposed by the masses and therefore seek every possible pretext to suppress the mass movement. They resort to such tactics as shifting the targets for attack and turning black into white in an attempt to lead the movement astray. When they find themselves very isolated and no longer able to carry on as before, they resort still more to intrigues, stabbing people in the back, spreading rumors, and blurring the distinction between revolution and counter-revolution as much as they can, all for the purpose of attacking the revolutionaries.

What the Central Committee of the Party demands of the Party committees at all levels is that they persevere in giving correct leadership, put daring above everything else, boldly arouse the masses, change the state of weakness and incompetence where it exists, encourage those comrades who have made mistakes but are willing to correct them to cast off their mental burdens and join in the struggle, and dismiss from their leading posts all those in authority who are taking the capitalist road and so make possible the recapture of the leadership for the proletarian revolutionaries.

4. LET THE MASSES EDUCATE THEMSELVES IN THE MOVEMENT

In the great proletarian cultural revolution, the only method is for the masses to liberate themselves, and any method of doing things in their stead must not be used.

Trust the masses, rely on them and respect their initiative. Cast out fear. Don't be afraid of disturbances. Chairman Mao has often told us that revolution cannot be so very refined, so gentle, so temperate, kind, courteous, restrained and magnanimous. Let the masses educate themselves in this great revolutionary movement and learn to distinguish between right and wrong and between correct and incorrect ways of doing things.

Make the fullest use of big-character posters and great debates to argue matters out, so that the masses can clarify the
correct views, criticize the wrong views and expose all the
ghosts and monsters. In this way the masses will be able to
raise their political consciousness in the course of the struggle,
enhance their abilities and talents, distinguish right from wrong
and draw a clear line between ourselves and the enemy.

5. FIRMLY APPLY THE CLASS LINE
   OF THE PARTY

Who are our enemies? Who are our friends? This is a question
of the first importance for the revolution and it is likewise a
question of the first importance for the great cultural revolution.

Party leadership should be good at discovering the Left and
developing and strengthening the ranks of the Left; it should
firmly rely on the revolutionary Left. During the movement
this is the only way to isolate the most reactionary Rightists
thoroughly, win over the middle and unite with the great majority so that by the end of the movement we shall achieve the
unity of more than 95 per cent of the cadres and more than
95 per cent of the masses.

Concentrate all forces to strike at the handful of ultra-reac-
tionary bourgeois Rightists and counter-revolutionary revisionists, and expose and criticize to the full their crimes against the
Party, against socialism and against Mao Tse-tung's thought so
as to isolate them to the maximum.

The main target of the present movement is those within
the Party who are in authority and are taking the capitalist road.

The strictest care should be taken to distinguish between the
anti-Party, anti-socialist Rightists and those who support the
Party and socialism but have said or done something wrong or
have written some bad articles or other works.

The strictest care should be taken to distinguish between the
reactionary bourgeois scholar despots and "authorities" on the
the one hand and people who have the ordinary bourgeois academic ideas on the other.

6. CORRECTLY HANDLE CONTRADICTIONS AMONG THE PEOPLE

A strict distinction must be made between the two different types of contradictions: those among the people and those between ourselves and the enemy. Contradictions among the people must not be made into contradictions between ourselves and the enemy; nor must contradictions between ourselves and the enemy be regarded as contradictions among the people.

It is normal for the masses to hold different views. Contention between different views is unavoidable, necessary and beneficial. In the course of normal and full debate, the masses will affirm what is right, correct what is wrong and gradually reach unanimity.

The method to be used in debates is to present the facts, reason things out, and persuade through reasoning. Any method of forcing a minority holding different views to submit is impermissible. The minority should be protected, because sometimes the truth is with the minority. Even if the minority is wrong, they should still be allowed to argue their case and reserve their views.

When there is a debate, it should be conducted by reasoning, not by coercion or force.

In the course of debate, every revolutionary should be good at thinking things out for himself and should develop the communist spirit of daring to think, daring to speak and daring to act. On the premise that they have the same general orientation, revolutionary comrades should, for the sake of strengthening unity, avoid endless debate over side issues.

7. BE ON GUARD AGAINST THOSE WHO BRAND THE REVOLUTIONARY MASSES AS "COUNTER-REVOLUTIONARIES"

In certain schools, units, and work teams of the cultural revolution, some of the persons in charge have organized counterattacks against the masses who put up big-character posters criticizing them. These people have even advanced such slogans as: opposition to the leaders of a unit or a work team means opposition to the Central Committee of the Party, means opposition to the Party and socialism, means counter-revolution. In this way it is inevitable that their blows will fall on some really revolutionary activists. This is an error on matters of orientation, an error of line, and is absolutely impermissible.

A number of persons who suffer from serious ideological errors, and particularly some of the anti-Party and anti-socialist Rightists, are taking advantage of certain shortcomings and mistakes in the mass movement to spread rumors and gossip, and engage in agitation, deliberately branding some of the masses as "counter-revolutionaries." It is necessary to beware of such "pickpockets" and expose their tricks in good time.

In the course of the movement, with the exception of cases of active counter-revolutionaries where there is clear evidence of crimes such as murder, arson, poisoning, sabotage or theft of state secrets, which should be handled in accordance with the law, no measures should be taken against students at universities, colleges, middle schools and primary schools because of problems that arise in the movement. To prevent the struggle from being diverted from its main target, it is not allowed, under whatever pretext, to incite the masses or the students to struggle against each other. Even proven Rightists should be dealt with on the merits of each case at a later stage of the movement.

8. THE QUESTION OF CADRES

The cadres fall roughtly into the following four categories:
  (1) good;
  (2) comparatively good;
  (3) those who have made serious mistakes but have not become anti-Party, anti-socialist Rightists;
  (4) the small number of anti-Party, anti-socialist Rightists.

In ordinary situations, the first two categories (good and comparatively good) are the great majority.

The anti-Party, anti-socialist Rightists must be fully exposed, refuted, overthrown and completely discredited and their influence eliminated. At the same time, they should be given a chance to turn over a new leaf.

9. CULTURAL REVOLUTIONARY GROUPS, COMMITTEES AND CONGRESSES

Many new things have begun to emerge in the great proletarian cultural revolution. The cultural revolutionary groups, committees and other organizational forms created by the masses in many schools and units are something new and of great historic importance.

These cultural revolutionary groups, committees and congresses are excellent new forms of organization whereby the masses educate themselves under the leadership of the Communist Party. They are an excellent bridge to keep our Party in close contact with the masses. They are organs of power of the proletarian cultural revolution.

The struggle of the proletariat against the old ideas, culture, customs and habits left over by all the exploiting classes over thousands of years will necessarily take a very, very long time. Therefore, the cultural revolutionary groups, committees and congresses should not be temporary organizations but permanent, standing mass organizations. They are suitable not only for colleges, schools and government and other organizations, but generally also for factories, mines, other enterprises, urban districts and villages.

It is necessary to institute a system of general elections, like that of the Paris Commune, for electing members to the cultural revolutionary groups and committees and delegates to the cultural revolutionary congresses. The lists of candidates should be put forward by the revolutionary masses after full discussion, and the elections should be held after the masses have discussed the lists over and over again.

The masses are entitled at any time to criticize members of the cultural revolutionary groups and committees and delegates elected to the cultural revolutionary congresses. If these members or delegates prove incompetent, they can be replaced through election or recalled by the masses after discussion.

The cultural revolutionary groups, committees and congresses in colleges and schools should consist mainly of representatives of the revolutionary students. At the same time, they should have a certain number of representatives of the revolutionary teaching and administrative staff and workers.

10. EDUCATIONAL REFORM

In the great proletarian cultural revolution a most important task is to transform the old educational system and the old principles and methods of teaching.

In this great cultural revolution, the phenomenon of our schools being dominated by bourgeois intellectuals must be completely changed.

In every kind of school we must apply thoroughly the policy advanced by Comrade Mao Tse-tung of education serving proletarian politics and education being combined with productive labor, so as to enable those receiving an education to develop morally, intellectually and physically and to become laborers with socialist consciousness and culture.

The period of schooling should be shortened. Courses should be fewer and better. The teaching material should be thoroughly transformed, in some cases beginning with simplifying complicated material. While their main task is to study, students should also learn other things. That is to say, in addition to their studies they should also learn industrial work, farming and military affairs, and take part in the struggles of the cultural revolution to criticize the bourgeoisie as these struggles occur.

11. THE QUESTION OF CRITICIZING
BY NAME IN THE PRESS

In the course of the mass movement of the cultural revolution, the criticism of bourgeois and feudal ideology should be well combined with the dissemination of the proletarian world outlook and of Marxism-Leninism, Mao Tse-tung's thought.

Criticism should be organized of typical bourgeois representatives who have wormed their way into the Party and typical reactionary bourgeois academic "authorities," and this should include criticism of various kinds of reactionary views in philosophy, history, political economy and education, in works and theories of literature and art, in theories of natural science, and in other fields.

Criticism of anyone by name in the press should be decided after discussion by the Party committee at the same level, and in some cases submitted to the Party committee at a higher level for approval.

12. POLICY TOWARDS SCIENTISTS, TECHNICIANS AND ORDINARY MEMBERS OF WORKING STAFFS

As regards scientists, technicians and ordinary members of working staffs, as long as they are patriotic, work energetically, are not against the Party and socialism, and maintain no illicit relations with any foreign country, we should in the present movement continue to apply the policy of "unity, criticism, unity." Special care should be taken of those scientists and scientific and technical personnel who have made contributions. Efforts should be made to help them gradually transform their world outlook and their style of work.

13. THE QUESTION OF ARRANGEMENTS FOR INTEGRATION WITH THE SOCIALIST EDUCATION MOVEMENT IN CITY AND COUNTRYSIDE

The cultural and educational units and leading organs of the Party and government in the large and medium cities are the points of concentration of the present proletarian cultural revolution.

The great cultural revolution has enriched the socialist education movement in both city and countryside and raised it to a higher level. Efforts should be made to conduct these two movements in close combination. Arrangements to this effect may be made by various regions and departments in the light of the specific conditions.

The socialist education movement now going on in the countryside and in enterprises in the cities should not be upset where the original arrangements are appropriate and the movement is going well, but should continue in accordance with the original arrangements. However, the questions that are arising in the present great proletarian cultural revolution should be put to the masses for discussion at the proper time, so as to further foster vigorously proletarian ideology and eradicate bourgeois ideology.

In some places, the great proletarian cultural revolution is being used as the focus in order to add momentum to the socialist education movement and clean things up in the fields of politics, ideology, organization and economy. This may be done where the local Party committee thinks it appropriate.

14. TAKE FIRM HOLD OF THE REVOLUTION AND STIMULATE PRODUCTION

The aim of the great proletarian cultural revolution is to revolutionize people's ideology and as a consequence to achieve greater, faster, better and more economical results in all fields of work. If the masses are fully aroused and proper arrangements are made, it is possible to carry on both the cultural revolution and production without one hampering the other, while guaranteeing high quality in all our work.

The great proletarian cultural revolution is a powerful motive force for the development of the social productive forces in our country. Any idea of counterposing the great cultural revolution to the development of production is incorrect.

15. THE ARMED FORCES

In the armed forces, the cultural revolution and the socialist education movement should be carried out in accordance with the instructions of the Military Commission of the Central Committee of the Party and the General Political Department of the People's Liberation Army.

16. MAO TSE-TUNG'S THOUGHT IS THE GUIDE TO ACTION IN THE GREAT PROLETARIAN CULTURAL REVOLUTION

In the great proletarian cultural revolution, it is imperative to hold aloft the great red banner of Mao Tse-tung's thought and put proletarian politics in command. The movement for the creative study and application of Chairman Mao Tse-tung's works should be carried forward among the masses of the workers, peasants and soldiers, the cadres and the intellectuals, and Mao Tse-tung's thought should be taken as the guide to action in the cultural revolution.

In this complex great cultural revolution, Party committees at all levels must study and apply Chairman Mao's works all the more conscientiously and in a creative way. In particular, they must study over and over again Chairman Mao's writings on the cultural revolution and on the Party's methods of leadership, such as *On New Democracy, Talks at the Yenan Forum on Literature and Art, On the Correct Handling of Contradictions Among the People, Speech at the Chinese Communist Party's National Conference on Propaganda Work, Some Questions Concerning Methods of Leadership* and *Methods of Work of Party Committees.*

Party committees at all levels must abide by the directions given by Chairman Mao over the years, namely that they should thoroughly apply the mass line of "from the masses, to the masses" and that they should be pupils before they become teachers. They should try to avoid being one-sided or narrow. They should foster materialist dialectics and oppose metaphysics and scholasticism.

The great proletarian cultural revolution is bound to achieve brilliant victory under the leadership of the Central Committee of the Party headed by Comrade Mao Tse-tung.

PEKING RED GUARDS*
Long Live the Revolutionary Rebel Spirit
of the Proletariat

Revolution is rebellion, and rebellion is the soul of Mao Tse-
tung's thought. We hold that tremendous attention must be
paid to the word "application," that is, mainly to the word
"rebellion." Daring to think, to speak, to act, to break through,
and to make revolution, in a word, daring to rebel, is the most
fundamental and most precious quality of proletarian revolutionaries. This is the fundamental principle of the proletarian
Party spirit! Not to rebel is revisionism, pure and simple!

Revisionism has been in control of the school for seventeen
years. If we do not rise up in rebellion today, when are we
going to?

Some bold people who were against rebellion have, today,
suddenly turned coy and shy, hemming and hawing incessantly
about us being too one-sided, too high and mighty, too rude,
and going too far.

All this is rank nonsense! If you are against us, then say so.
Why be bashful about it?

Since we want rebellion, the matter has been taken out of
your hands! We are going to make the air thick with the
pungent smell of explosives. Toss them over, grenades and
stick bombs together, and start a big fight. "Sympathy," "all-
sidedness," out of the way!

You say we are too one-sided? What then is your all-sidedness? Your all-sidedness looks like "two combining into one,"
eclecticism.

You say we are too high and mighty? We are "high and

* Peking Review, No. 34 (Sept. 9, 1966), pp. 20–21.

mighty." Chairman Mao has said: "And those in high positions we counted no more than dust." We are going to strike down not only the reactionaries in our school, but the reactionaries of the whole world too. Revolutionaries consider the transformation of the world is their task. How can we not be "high and mighty"?

You say we are too rude? We should be rude. How can we be soft and clinging towards revisionism or go in for moderation in a big way? To be moderate towards the enemy is to be cruel to the revolution!

You say we are going too far? To put it bluntly, your "avoid going too far" is reformism; it is "peaceful transition." You are day-dreaming! We are going to strike you down to the dust and keep you there!

And there are some who are scared to death of revolution, scared to death of rebellion. Sticklers for convention, obsequious, curled up inside your revisionist shells, as soon as there is a whiff of rebellion in the air, you get nervous and afraid. Recently, heartless censures have every day been poured into your ears and, daily, your hearts beat with fear. Don't you feel it insufferable? Hasn't life become unbearable?

Revolutionaries are Monkey Kings, their golden rods are powerful, their supernatural powers far-reaching and their magic omnipotent, for they possess Mao Tse-tung's great invincible thought. We wield our golden rods, display our supernatural powers and use our magic to turn the old world upside down, smash it to pieces, pulverize it, create chaos and make a tremendous mess, the bigger the better! We must do this to the present revisionist middle school attached to the Tsinghua University, make rebellion in a big way, rebel to the end! We are bent on creating a tremendous proletarian uproar, and hewing out a proletarian new world!

Long live the revolutionary rebel spirit of the proletariat!

Red Guards
Middle School Attached to
Tsinghua University
June 24, 1966

LIN PIAO*
Comrade Lin Piao's Speech at the Peking
Mass Rally to Receive Revolutionary
Teachers and Students from
All Over China

(November 3, 1966)

Students, Comrades and Red Guard Fighters:

With boundless love and infinite loyalty for our great leader Chairman Mao, you have come to Peking in the new nationwide upsurge of the great proletarian cultural revolution to see Chairman Mao and to exchange revolutionary experience. On behalf of Chairman Mao and the Central Committee of the Party, I extend my warmest welcome to you!

Chairman Mao is extremely happy to receive you today. This is the sixth time in two months or more, including National Day, that Chairman Mao has received revolutionary students and teachers and Red Guards from all over the country. Chairman Mao is the greatest proletarian revolutionary; he is always with the masses, has full confidence in them, shares weal and woe with them and wholeheartedly supports the revolutionary mass movement. Chairman Mao has set the most glorious example for all comrades in our Party and for the youger generation.

The present situation of the great proletarian cultural revolution is excellent! The gigantic, vigorous mass movement is developing in depth with each passing day. A tremendous change has taken place over the whole face of society and in the mental outlook of the people. The great thought of Mao Tse-tung has become more extensively disseminated and has gone deeper into the minds of the people. As a result of Chairman Mao's call "to take a firm hold of the revolution and pro-

* Lin Piao, Peking Review, No. 46 (Nov. 11, 1966), pp. 10–11.

mote production," the cultural revolution has stimulated the revolutionization of people's thinking and spurred extremely rapid development in industrial and agricultural production and in science and technology. The recent successful guided missile-nuclear weapon test is a great victory for Mao Tse-tung's thought and a great victory for the proletarian cultural revolution!

The Eleventh Plenary Session of the Eighth Central Committee of the Chinese Communist Party announced the victory of the proletarian revolutionary line represented by Chairman Mao and the bankruptcy of the bourgeois reactionary line. In the past two months and more, the correct line of Chairman Mao has been put before the broad masses and has been grasped by them, and criticisms have been made of the erroneous line. The broad masses have really translated into action Chairman Mao's call to "pay attention to state affairs." This is an extremely fine thing. It is an important guarantee that the great proletarian cultural revolution will be carried through to the end.

Chairman Mao's line is one of letting the masses educate and emancipate themselves. It is the line of putting "daring" above everything else and of daring to trust the masses, to rely on them and to arouse them boldly. It is the application and a new development of the Party's mass line in the great cultural revolution. It is the line of the proletarian cultural revolution.

The bourgeois line is one of opposing the mass line, of opposing the education and emancipation of the masses by themselves, of repressing the masses and opposing the revolution. This bourgeois reactionary line directs the spearhead of struggle against the revolutionary masses, and not against the handful of Party members in authority who are taking the capitalist road, and all the ghosts and monsters in society. It uses various ways and means to incite the masses to struggle against each other, and the students to do the same.

The proletarian revolutionary line of Chairman Mao is as incompatible with the bourgeois reactionary line as fire is to water. Only by thoroughly criticizing and repudiating the bourgeois reactionary line and eradicating its influence can the line of Chairman Mao be carried out correctly, completely and thoroughly.

Under the guidance of Chairman Mao's correct line, the broad revolutionary masses of our country have created the new experience of developing extensive democracy under the dictatorship of the proletariat. By this extensive democracy, the Party is fearlessly encouraging the broad masses to use the media of free airing of views, big-character posters, great debates and extensive exchange of revolutionary experience to criticize and supervise the Party and government leading institutions and leaders at all levels. At the same time, the people's democratic rights are being fully realized in accordance with the principles of the Paris Commune. Without such extensive democracy, it would be impossible to initiate a genuine great proletarian cultural revolution, effect a great revolution deep in the minds of the people, carry out the proletarian cultural revolution thoroughly and completely, eradicate the roots of revisionism, consolidate the dictatorship of the proletariat and guarantee the advance of our country along the road of socialism and communism. This extensive democracy is a new form of integrating Mao Tse-tung's thought with the broad masses, a new form of mass self-education. It is a new contribution by Chairman Mao to the Marxist-Leninist theory on proletarian revolution and proletarian dictatorship.

International historical experience of the dictatorship of the proletariat has demonstrated that without carrying out a thoroughgoing, great proletarian cultural revolution of this kind and without practicing such extensive democracy, the dictatorship of the proletariat will be weakened and will change in essence, while capitalism will stage a comeback by various means and the exploiting classes will once again ride on the backs of the people.

Such extensive democracy must be thoroughly practiced not only between the leadership and the masses; it is also absolutely necessary to carry it out thoroughly among the masses themselves and between all sections of the masses. Unless there is such extensive democracy among the masses themselves and unless they are good at mutual consultation, at listening to dissenting views, at presenting facts and reasoning things out, at using their brains to ponder problems, they cannot possibly educate and emancipate themselves, achieve the purpose of developing the ranks of the Left, uniting the great majority and

isolating the handful of bourgeois Rightists, and fully carry out
the line of the great proletarian cultural revolution put forward
by our great teacher Chairman Mao.

Chairman Mao supports you comrades traveling on foot to
exchange revolutionary experience, the advantages of which
are widespread contact with the masses, contact with all aspects
of the life of society, and a deeper understanding of class
struggle in socialist society. It provides better opportunities to
learn from the workers and the peasants and to propagate Mao
Tse-tung's thought on an even broader scale. All this is very
useful for the revolutionary teachers and students to have a
better understanding of Mao Tse-tung's thought and the correct
line of Chairman Mao. Of course, this kind of traveling on foot
for the exchange of revolutionary experience must be undertaken in a planned and organized way and must be well
prepared.

The Central Committee of the Party is convinced that, with
the experience gained in the last few months, the great proletarian cultural revolution will in the days to come make still
better progress and attain still greater success!

March forward under the great banner of Mao Tse-tung's
thought!

Long live the victory of the line of Chairman Mao!

Long live the victory of the great proletarian cultural revolution!

Long live the Chinese Communist Party!

Long live Chairman Mao! Long life, long, long life to him!

★   ★   ★   ★   ★

4. THE JANUARY STORM—
SEIZING POWER FROM BELOW

Shanghai, the cradle of the Chinese Communist revolution, possessing the largest and most politically experienced working class in the nation, was the site of the Cultural Revolution's most important victory in January 1967. It was then that the Shanghai working class united to seize power from the old bureaucratic Party organization in an action that became the model for the whole country. The following selections tell the dramatic story of the Shanghai uprising.

By October 1966 only a few thousand rebels existed out of a total of one million industrial workers in the city. Shanghai workers had always been highly politicized and were loyal to the Communist Party. It was logical, therefore, that the Shanghai workers would approach with caution any call for an attack on officials of a party which they had supported over the years with so much sacrifice and enthusiasm.

Nevertheless, by December 1966, 60,000 workers responded to Chairman Mao's call and joined the Workers' Rebel Headquarters, while an equal number of workers supported the "royalist" or conservative Workers' Red Militia, an organization built by the functionaries of the old Party machine. Clashes between the two groups were frequent, but by the end of December a wholesale defection by the members of the conservative organizations ensued, and the collapse of the Workers' Red Militia followed.

It was at this point that the Party officials in the old Shanghai Municipal Committee, plant managers, heads of bureaus under siege by the rebels, and district Party chiefs counterattacked, using methods that caught Mao and his colleagues in Peking completely unawares. First, the old entrenched Communist cadres, who were skilled organizers, initiated a movement among their followers in the now-defunct Workers' Red Militia to demand wage increases and foment strikes throughout the city. Second, those holding power in the city opened up the municipal and industrial coffers to grant millions of yuan in wage increases, bonuses, and grants in an all-out attempt to buy off the Shanghai working class. The action was surprisingly American in character. Factories were closed, railroads and shipping were paralyzed, and serious power shortages plagued the greatest industrial city in China.

The revolutionary rebels responded to the crisis by in effect seizing power. Rank-and-file workers and students manned ticket booths at the railway stations, factory workers stood triple shifts in the industrial plants, and thousands of volunteers appeared at the docks to help unload cargo. New institutions of power were hastily created in the classic revolutionary pattern. The remarkably high level of revolutionary consciousness achieved by the masses of Shanghai was demonstrated when the hoodwinked workers voluntarily returned the money illegally dispensed by the old Shanghai bureaucrats. At mass meetings organized throughout Shanghai, the guilty functionaries were forced to stand with head bowed as the workers showered them with paper money until the enemy stood knee-deep in the shameful currency.

Mao, watching the situation in Shanghai closely, recognized that the workers in Shanghai had in fact seized power; he was the first to name what had happened "a power seizure from below." Included in our selections is Mao's speech to the Cultural Group and his instruction to Lin Piao and the army to support the revolutionary left, which indicate that the old revolutionary leader had lost none of his skill in grasping revolutionary opportunity in the storms of crisis politics.

The selections chosen include the historic "Message to All Shanghai People" published by the major Shanghai newspaper *Wenhui Pao* shortly after its seizure by the rebel forces. The new revolutionary organ became one of the most influential newspapers in China throughout the remaining years of the Cultural Revolution. Chang Ch'un-ch'iao's speech to the Anhwei delegation, recalling the Shanghai January Storm in which he played a leading part, will undoubtedly remain as a key historic document of the 1967 January seizure of power. Both Chang and Yao Wen-yuan helped to provide the leadership necessary to the Shanghai Maoist victory, and it is no accident that these two men still remain as powerful leaders in post-Cultural Revolution China.

"On the Proletarian Revolutionaries' Struggle to Seize Power," published in the famous *Red Flag* Number 3, 1967, will stand as one of the key programmatic documents of the Cultural Revolution. Commissioned and partly written by Mao Tse-tung, the editorial summed up the Shanghai experience and elevated these lessons to strategy for the new stage of the movement in the rest of the country. Stating that the seizure of power from the capitalist roaders "is not effected by dismissal and reorganization from above, but from below by the mass movement," the Chairman now called for a mass uprising to dislodge recalcitrant bureaucrats wherever they might be found. For a number of reasons, the strategy of power seizure was never to be as effective in the rest of the country as it had been in Shanghai. Lack of experience, the absence of a mature working class, and the scarcity of skilled leaders dictated compromise settlements which often failed to guarantee stable new organs of power. Shanghai perhaps came the closest to producing the new revolutionary successors that Mao was searching for.

★   ★   ★

SHANGHAI WENHUI PAO*
Take Firm Hold of the Revolution, Promote Production and Utterly Smash the New Counterattack Launched by the Bourgeois Reactionary Line

—Message to all Shanghai people

[*Renmin Ribao* **Editor's Note:** The Message to All Shanghai People," published in the *Shanghai Wenhui Pao* on January 5, 1967, is an extremely important document. It holds high the great red banner of the proletarian revolutionary line represented by Chairman Mao and sounds a clarion call to continue the vigorous counter-offensive upon the bourgeois reactionary line. It resolutely responds to Chairman Mao's great call to take firm hold of the revolution and promote production and raises the current key question in the great proletarian cultural revolution. This question does not just concern Shanghai alone but the whole country as well.

With the growth of the revolutionary forces in Shanghai, the *Wenhui Pao* and *Jiefang Ribao* (*Liberation Daily*) have appeared as two completely new and revolutionary newspapers. They are products of the victory of the proletarian revolutionary line over the bourgeois reactionary line. This is a great event in the history of the development of the great proletarian cultural revolution in China. This is a great revolution. This great event will certainly play a tremendous role in pushing

---

*A declaration of the Shanghai Workers' Revolutionary Rebel General Headquarters and ten other revolutionary mass organizations, in *The Great Proletarian Cultural Revolution in China*, No. 10 (Peking: Foreign Languages Press, 1967), pp. 5–10.

ahead the development of the movement of the great proletarian
cultural revolution throughout east China and in all the cities
and provinces in other parts of the country.]

Under the guidance of the proletarian revolutionary line represented by Chairman Mao, the great proletarian cultural revolution has won tremendous victories in the mass movement over
the last few months in the criticism of the bourgeois reactionary
line. We have entered the year 1967 to the sound of militant
songs of triumph. It was pointed out in the New Year's Day
editorial of *Renmin Ribao* and the journal *Hongqi*: "1967 will
be a year of all-round development of class struggle throughout
China. It will be a year in which the proletariat, united with
other sections of the revolutionary masses, will launch a general
attack on the handful of Party persons in authority who are
taking the capitalist road, and on the ghosts and monsters in
society. It will be a year of even more penetrating criticism
and repudiation of the bourgeois reactionary line and elimination of its influence. It will be a year of decisive victory in
carrying out the struggle [to overthrow those in authority who
are taking the capitalist road], the criticism and repudiation
[of the reactionary bourgeois academic 'authorities' and the
ideology of the bourgeoisie and all other exploiting classes] and
the transformation [of education, literature and art and all other
parts of the superstructure not in correspondence with the socialist economic base]." In other words, it will be a year in
which the bourgeois reactionary line will totally collapse and
disintegrate completely, a year in which the great proletarian
cultural revolution will win a great, decisive victory.

The broad revolutionary masses of Shanghai have also won
an initial victory in the struggle to criticize and repudiate the
bourgeois reactionary line implemented by a handful of people
within the Party in the Shanghai area and have carried the
struggle to a deeper and broader new stage.

The mass movement of the great proletarian cultural revolution in our Shanghai factories is surging forward vigorously,
smashing through all resistance with the might of an avalanche
and the force of a thunderbolt. We, workers of the revolutionary rebel groups, follow Chairman Mao's teachings most closely

and resolutely carry out **the policy of "taking firm hold of the revolution and promoting production" advanced by Chairman Mao himself. Chairman Mao teaches us: "Political work is the life-blood of all economic work."** We of the revolutionary rebel groups clearly understand that if the great proletarian cultural revolution is not carried out well, we will lose our orientation in production and slide back in the direction of capitalism. What we ourselves have experienced in the course of the great proletarian cultural revolution has increasingly proved to us that only if the great proletarian cultural revolution is carried out well, will production develop on a still greater scale. Any idea of counterposing the great cultural revolution to the development of production is erroneous.

However, a handful of Party persons in authority who are taking the capitalist road and those who obstinately adhere to the bourgeois reactionary line have a bitter hatred for the great proletarian cultural revolution. They have been trying by every means to resist **the policy of "taking firm hold of the revolution and promoting production" put forward by Chairman Mao.** Their schemes and devices may be summarized in the following ways:

At the beginning of the movement, they used the pretext of "taking firm hold of production" to repress the revolution and oppose taking firm hold of the revolution. When we workers of the revolutionary rebel groups wanted to rise up in revolution and criticize and repudiate the bourgeois reactionary line, they used the tasks of production to bring pressure to bear on the workers and tagged us with the label of "sabotaging production." Did they really want to "take firm hold of production"? No, they wanted to defend their own positions and attempted to obstruct our revolution. We exposed their schemes and rose up bravely in rebellion.

Then they resorted to another trick, that is, they played with high-sounding revolutionary words, giving the appearance of being exceedingly "Left" in order to incite large numbers of members of the Workers' Red Militia Detachments whom they have hoodwinked to undermine production and sabotage transport and communications under the pretext of going north to "lodge complaints." They did this to attain their aim of undermining the great proletarian cultural revolution and the dictatorship of the proletariat. More recently, a handful of reactionary elements were even plotting to cut off water and electricity supplies and bring public transport to a standstill. We must drag out these reactionary elements and exercise proletarian dictatorship over them, punish them severely and never allow them to succeed in their criminal schemes.

Comrade revolutionary workers! Go into action at once! Resolutely carry out **the policy of "taking firm hold of the revolution and promoting production" advanced by Chairman Mao!** We, workers of the revolutionary rebel groups, must become models in **"taking firm hold of the revolution and promoting production."** We must serve as the vanguards and the backbone not only in taking firm hold of the revolution, but also in promoting production. Our city of Shanghai, China's biggest industrial producer, plays an extremely important role in the overall economic life of the country. But lately, in many factories and plants, it has occurred that some or even the majority of the members of the Workers' Red Militia Detachments have suspended production and deserted their posts in production. This runs directly counter to the stipulation by the Party Central Committee on taking firm hold of the revolution and promoting production and directly affects the people's livelihood and the development of national economic construction. Our revolutionary rebel workers, bearing in mind the teachings of Chairman Mao, have stood our ground in the face of this adverse current, have given proof of our high sense of revolutionary responsibility, and, under extremely difficult conditions, have shouldered all the production tasks of our factories and plants, thus dealing a telling blow against the handful of Party persons in authority who are taking the capitalist road, and smashing their big plot by which they attempted to thwart the revolution through sabotaging production. The actions of these workers are correct and splendid! All of us comrades of the revolutionary rebel groups should learn from them. **Chairman Mao teaches us: "We should support whatever the enemy opposes and oppose whatever the enemy supports."** We, workers of the revolutionary rebel groups, have the lofty aspiration, the determination and the strength to do still better in both revolution and production and to carry out **Chairman Mao's great call for "taking firm hold of the revolution and promoting production."**

The broad sections of our class brothers of the Workers' Red

Militia Detachments who want to make revolution! **"Taking firm hold of the revolution and promoting production" is a policy put forward by Chairman Mao,** a policy stressed time and again by the Party Central Committee, an important policy which guarantees the carrying through to the end of the great proletarian cultural revolution. To support or not to support, to carry out or not to carry out this policy is itself a matter of principle, a cardinal issue of right and wrong. In allowing yourselves to be incited by those people [Party persons in authority who are taking the capitalist road—*Tr.*] and by deserting your posts in production, whose interests are you serving? By acting in this way, whose hearts, after all, are you gladdening and whose are you saddening? We hope that you will follow Chairman Mao's teachings, that, on this important question of principle, you will see things more clearly, make a clear distinction between right and wrong, stop being deceived, wake up quickly, return to your posts in production, and return to the proletarian revolutionary line. We, comrades of the revolutionary rebel groups, will certainly warmly welcome you back to make revolution along with us and improve production with us. We will certainly not blame you, because we are all close class brothers, and because the overwhelming majority of you are victims of the bourgeois reactionary line, are revolutionary masses who have been hoodwinked by those within the Party who are in authority and taking the capitalist road and by those who are stubbornly following the bourgeois reactionary line.

All revolutionary students and revolutionary government cadres of the city! Let us closely unite with the masses of revolutionary workers, and in order to carry out resolutely **the policy of "taking firm hold of the revolution and promoting production" put forward by Chairman Mao,** let us undertake widespread propaganda work and struggle, open fire fiercely and with still greater resolve at the bourgeois reactionary line, crush all new counter-attacks by the bourgeois reactionary line and launch a new upsurge in the great proletarian cultural revolution in the factories and plants!

In the boundless brilliance of the great thought of Mao Tsetung, we look towards the future and see the magnificent prospect of the revolution. We are the working class, poor and lower-middle peasants, and all working people must unite with the revolutionary students, intellectuals and cadres, must make a common effort, fight shoulder to shoulder and continue our victorious advance so as to carry the great proletarian cultural revolution through to the end!

Long live the great proletarian cultural revolution!
Long live the red sun in our hearts, the greatest leader Chairman Mao and long life, long, long life to him!

> *The Shanghai Workers' Revolutionary Rebel General Headquarters and ten other revolutionary mass organizations*
> *January 4, 1967*

MAO TSE-TUNG*

Excerpts from *Chairman Mao's Speech to the Cultural Revolution Group of the Central Committee*

(January 9, 1967)

The leftists have now seized power at the *Wenhui Pao*. They rebelled on the fourth, and those of the *Chieh-fang Jih-pao* also rebelled on the sixth. This direction is fine. I have read three issues of the *Wenhui Pao* following the sizure of power there. They have selected for publication articles by the Red Guards. Some good articles may be selected for publication. The *Jen-min Jih-pao* can reproduce the *Wenhui Pao's* letter of January 5 to the people of the whole municipality, and the radio stations can also broadcast it.

Internal rebellion is a good thing, and after a few days, things can be summed up in a report. This stands for the overthrow of one class by another; it is a great revolution. In my view, it is better to close down a number of newspapers. However, newspapers must be published, and the question is who should publish them.

---

* Mao Tse-tung, translated in *Current Background*, No. 892 (October 21, 1969), p. 47.

It is good that the *Wenhui Pao* and the *Chieh-fang Jih-pao* have changed their formats. The effect of the publication of these two papers will certainly be felt in East China and all provinces throughout the country. To make revolution, it is first necessary to create public opinion. Following the seizure of power at the *Jen-min Jih-pao* on June 1 and the dispatch of a work group by the Central Committee, the editorial "Sweep Away All Monsters and Demons" was published. I do not agree with the setting up of another *Jen-min Jih-pao,* but power must be seized. When X X X took over from Wu Leng-hsi, the masses at first had no faith in the *Jen-min Jih-pao* because it had hoodwinked people in the past and also did not issue any announcement. The seizure of power in the two papers is a question of national significance, and it is necessary to support their rebellion. Our newspapers must reproduce articles by the Red Guards. These articles are very well written, while ours are too rigid. . . .

The rise of the revolutionary forces in Shanghai has given hope to the whole country. The impact is bound to be felt in the whole of East China and all provinces and municipalities in the whole country. The "Letter to the People of the Whole Municipality" is a good article seldom encountered. It deals with the problems of Shanghai but has national significance.

MAO TSE-TUNG*
Chairman Mao's Instruction to Comrade Lin Piao

(January–February, 1967)

Comrade Lin Piao:
You should send the Liberation Army to support the broad masses of the Left.

* Mao Tse-tung, translated in JPRS No. 90 (February 12, 1970), JPRS 49826.

P.S.

From now on, you should do this whenever any true revolutionary leftists ask for army support and assistance. What is called non-intervention is false since intervention has been going on for some time. Another order should be issued in respect to this matter, and all previous orders should be cancelled. Please consider this.

CHANG CH'UN-CH'IAO*
Talk by Chang Ch'un-ch'iao
to the Anhwei Delegation

Comrade K'ang has asked me to talk about the "January Revolution" in Shanghai and how the seizure of power came to take place. I will try to do so in the hope that it may be of some help to your judgment of the seizure of power and to the solution of your problems. However, because the situation in Shanghai then was not the same, it cannot be wholly applicable in your case.

The mobilization of the masses in the "January Revolution" in Shanghai was the same as in other parts of the country. Because the old Shanghai Municipal Party Committee had misled the masses to a serious extent, the masses there were mobilized a little later than those in other localities. This is particularly true of the workers as only a few of them rose in rebellion until August-September. Even by October, only several thousand rebels stepped forth out of a total of more than a million industrial workers. At a rally of rebel organizations formed throughout the city held in early November, more than a million people attended. Actually, some of the participants were conservatives and people secretly planted by the old municipal Party committee to watch how things were going at the rally; only five thousand were genuine rebels.

During November-December, the mass movement in Shang-

* Chang Ch'un-ch'iao, from SCMP No. 4145 (March 25, 1968), pp. 1–8.

hai appeared to have gained momentum to an appreciable extent. There were fierce struggles between both factions which were equally matched in strength. The main force in Shanghai stemmed from the workers who made up two major factions, namely the rebels called the "Workers' Rebel H.Q."—a force of several thousand people that had grown to fifty to sixty thousand strong, and the "Workers' Red Militia Detachment" which claimed to have a following of eighty thousand strong, a contingent of at least fifty to sixty thousand people. The two factions were equally matched in strength, explaining the reason why massive armed clashes were rife between them. By the end of December, however, the "Workers' Red Militia Detachment" had collapsed. At this juncture, the revolutionaries had the workers as the backbone plus revolutionary Red Guards and cadres of public organs. By the end of December, the revolutionary peasants on the outskirts of Shanghai had also come forward, thus spontaneously forming an alliance with the revolutionary workers.

The situation in Shanghai then was excellent because the "Workers' Red Militia Detachment" and the Red Guards antagonistic to the revolutionary workers had collapsed while the conservatives of public organs had not yet formed an alliance. Under these circumstances, the old municipal Party committee resorted to "economism" [money and material inducements] to corrupt and disintegrate the rebels among the workers.

I recall going to Shanghai with Comrade Yao Wen-yuan on January 4. The old municipal Party committee had then been paralyzed. Many factories, including vital industrial plants, had stopped production. The stoppage of operations of Kao-chiao Chemical Works led many other plants to halt production. The piers and railway stations were also immobilized, causing severe dislocations. Under such circumstances, the revolutionary rebels in Shanghai began to seize power [from those holding power in the old Shanghai Municipal Party Committee].

In the early stage of the seizure of power in Shanghai, we never thought of the "capture of power" nor did we use the words "January Revolution." We proceeded in the main from the Party spirit with no thought of factionalism. This is because we saw with our own eyes stoppages of work in industrial plants, and the piers were in such a state of paralysis that foreign vessels entering Shanghai harbor were unable to unload or load cargoes. Taking advantage of the situation, imperialists lost no time in broadcasting to the world, saying that wharf workers in Shanghai went on strike. They did so with the malicious intention to attack and slander us. Some foreign merchant ships displayed our national flag upside down. This greatly irritated the rebels and wharf workers.

Because large numbers of members of the "Workers' Red Militia Detachment" quit their jobs after drawing their pay, many [revolutionary] workers worked for several days on end without leaving their jobs, instead of working the usual eight-hour shift or sixteen-hour [double] shifts. Railway stations were also manned by a skeleton staff and only two runs were scheduled each day. Sometimes, not even a single train was run.

At the time, we were not motivated by factionalism nor did we think of recapturing power [from the power-holders]. What was uppermost in our minds was what we were going to do [about the widespread dislocations]. After discussing the situation as a whole, we set about putting the vital departments such as the piers, railway stations, waterworks, power plants, broadcasting stations, postal offices and banks under our control. We did so to prevent counter-revolutionary acts of sabotage. Therefore, we mobilized troops and students and the rebels of industrial plants and railway stations to assist the revolutionary workers.

In the case of the Shanghai Railway Bureau, for instance, the rebels of railway stations with the assistance of thousands of college students manned the ticket booths and entry points to platforms, or served as locomotive conductors and train attendants. The students of practically all secondary schools in Shanghai were busy at the piers helping to load or unload cargoes. To get these workers organized, a joint command was set up not for seizing power on behalf of this or that faction, but for the sake of class interests, for the honor of the fatherland, for the socialist economy and for repelling the counterattack of bourgeois "economism."

We submitted a report to the Center on the situation in Shanghai and what steps we had taken. Chairman Mao endorsed our actions, telling us that the seizure of power was wholly necessary and correct. This is how we came to use the term "seizure of power" as suggested by Chairman Mao.

However, at the mention of "seizure of power," we found the resultant evils of factionalism, such as selfishness, obsession with personal gain, the "mountain stronghold" mentality, the "small group" mentality, sectarianism, and so forth. This is because when those people were subjected to oppression or branded as "counter-revolutionary," they hardly noticed these evils. But once the moment for the seizure of power came, some people became obsessed with selfishness and the "mountain stronghold" mentality.

The seizure of power in Shanghai was not just plain sailing because once petit-bourgeois factionalism came to the fore, it was detrimental to the proletarian Party spirit and upset the general orientation of struggle. . . .

. . . As a result of our prodding, meetings were held many times in early February to approve of the professed plans for the seizure of power by the thirty-eight recognized rebel organizations. At these sessions, we made it clear that the seizure of power [from persons in power] in no way involved the seizure of official seals or occupation of the premises of official establishments. Rather, it involved the issues as to whether or not Chairman Mao's revolutionary line was carried out, great alliances forged, the interests of the broad masses of people represented and popular support secured. We also made it clear that the seizure of official seals would be of no avail and in the absence of popular recognition of the Shanghai Municipal Party Committee and the Shanghai Municipal People's Council, occupation of their offices would also be of no avail—merely a manifestation of formalism. We sold them: Sukarno held a baton symbolizing presidential powers: nonetheless, Suharto stripped Sukarno of all his powers. What is the use of carrying the baton again?

In the joint seizure of power by the thirty-eight organizations, the great majority of organizations in Shanghai had in the main formed alliances. The situation was quite favorable because all the prominent rebel organizations in the city took part. At the time when the thirty-eight organizations met to draft a document for the formation of the "Shanghai People's Commune," another twenty-five organizations also met to inaugurate their "New Shanghai People's Commune." They told their rivals: Since you people haven't asked us to join your setup, we call ours "New Shanghai People's Commune"—something newer than yours!

The problem which confronted us then was that two major factions would be formed. The thirty-eight organizations were in the majority, being undisputed rebel groups. On the other hand, the twenty-five organizations were in the minority, having quarreled among themselves by calling one another conservative organizations. What was to be done in such a situation? If we proceeded from factional considerations when tackling the matter, deep rifts would inevitably occur. However, if we proceeded from fundamental class interests, from the interests of socialism, from the interests of all our people, and from considerations of the Party spirit, internal rifts would be avoided.

If the thirty-eight organizations proclaimed their readiness to seize power then and there, opposition would almost certainly arise and the factions in opposition to the thirty-eight organizations would not stop struggling against them, reminding us of what happened in Anhwei and Kiangsu (Comrade K'ang: Rifts will result if the seizure of power is undertaken by one faction and not jointly with other factions).

In these circumstances, we held fast to the general orientation of struggle in accordance with Chairman Mao's established policies and instructions of uniting the majority and relying on the majority. This general orientation must not be abandoned when uniting the revolutionary forces and struggling against the capitalist roaders. This is because once our own ranks were thrown into disarray in an unsuccessful seizure of power, the capitalist roaders would only be too pleased. Therefore, we tackled the matter in two stages, first dealing with the thirty-eight organizations which had formed the "Shanghai People's Commune" because they were backed by solid strength and were numerically superior to other groups.

We told them: Do you people think it is right to do it this way and is the general orientation in order? They replied: Since seizing power from the capitalist roaders is in keeping with the general orientation, it is of course right for us to do so. But can we say we are keeping to the correct general orientation after splitting our own ranks as a result of the seizure of power? What you have said is right. Have they done the right thing by seizing power from the capitalist roaders and forming the "New Shanghai People's Commune"? Who will benefit from this? Some people then said those were smaller organizations which could be smashed to pieces overnight and therefore it really didn't matter much at all.

We told them: If you people do it this way, the power you people have wrested won't last long because nobody will accept you.

Later, we submitted a report to the center and proposed the following measures to the two rival factions:

First, we suggested changing the thirty-eight component units making up the "Shanghai People's Commune" to proposing units, in this way leaving the door open to the other twenty-odd units after subjecting them to gradual stages of screening.

Second, a notice should be inserted in the newspapers tomorrow, but none of the proposing units will identify itself with the inserted announcement so as not to be mixed up with the seizure of power on behalf of a particular unit or with the desire to seek limelight. The first Message to the People of Shanghai which appeared in newspapers was issued by eleven units approved by Chairman Mao. That message made quite an impression on the public. The second Message to the People of Shanghai, however, was not made known to the public until the twenty-odd units which drafted the notice had vehemently wrangled over the order the names of the individual organizations should follow the message. Quarrels went out of hand and at one point the contenders for precedence over others disputed so furiously that they almost closed down the *Wenhui Pao*, indicating the serious extent of factionalism. Therefore, proclamations are not to be inserted in newspapers to avoid fomenting factionalism.

Third, at the inaugural meeting, delegates from organizations big and small or proposing or non-proposing units should be seated in the presidium. This is to unite the majority.

Fourth, regardless of what organizations, conservative or otherwise, they are from, the people of Shanghai (Comrade K'ang: the citizens of Shanghai) have the right to attend celebration rallies or take part in processions. The conservatives are welcome whether they attend celebration rallies or take part in processions. In fact, all are welcome so long as they are not our enemies or landlords, rich peasants, counter-revolutionaries, bad elements and rightists. In this way, the majority is united.

After this was done, dealing with the other twenty-five organizations posed no problems at all. Because the proposing units made allowance for other organizations to join them after screening by stages, no feelings were ruffled. Consequently, steps were not taken to form the "New Shanghai People's Commune."

Of course, it wasn't easy at all to convert these people to our point of view. For instance, some people clamored for inclusion on the next day and considered themselves as proposing units and so had the right to be seated in the presidium. We had to hold repeated negotiations with them. Fortunately, we then had a "trump card" in our hands, for the Center designated myself and Comrade Yao Wen-yuan to be members of the "Shanghai People's Commune." Since there could be only one and not two organs of power in Shanghai, we could only join one. Incidentally, the three services of the army could not possibly support two organs of power because if they were asked to support both organs of power they would certainly lose heart. Of course, that wasn't final and what was a matter of decisive importance was none other than Chairman Mao's revolutionary line. In short, what the editorial of the February issue of *Hung-ch'i* journal stressed was a call to the proletarian revolutionaries to unite and to seize power from the handful of Party persons in authority taking the capitalist road.

In the congratulatory message sent on January 11 to the people of Shanghai by the CCP Central Committee, the State Council, the Central Military Commission and the Central Cultural Revolution Group, there was this line: "You have formed a revolutionary great alliance, thus putting firmly in your hands the destiny of the great proletarian cultural revolution, the destiny of the dictatorship of the proletariat, and the destiny of the socialist economy." . . .

The reason why the situation in Shanghai was under control without showing any serious signs of rift was not that problems did not crop up among proletarian revolutionary organizations;

rather, various mass organizations were able to handle problems correctly whenever they had cropped up in accordance with Chairman Mao's revolutionary line and on the basis of guidelines laid down by the Party Center. Otherwise, Shanghai would have been seriously divided as in other [trouble spots]. Since we made a practice of handling and resolving problems in accordance with Chairman Mao's revolutionary line and the thought of Mao Tse-tung, the question of Shanghai was rather successfully resolved and the situation there stabilized.

Arriving in Shanghai in the course of his inspection tour, Chairman Mao said: Why is Shanghai so stabilized? Well, barring other factors, the relationships between the masses and the cadres and between the masses and the Liberation Army were rather good. Between the masses themselves, between the masses and the cadres, and between the masses and the Liberation Army, the relationship was one of uniting with one another, not in opposition to one another. Under the condition of keeping to the same general orientation, if problems should crop up, people would sit down and discuss them, go over Chairman Mao's writings, make criticism and self-criticism. That is why no serious rifts occurred then and no major problems cropped up. There were occasional rifts on a minor scale as there were cases in which certain individuals turned bad but nothing abnormal. But on the whole there were no problems of consequence.

RED FLAG*

Excerpts from *On the Proletarian Revolutionaries' Struggle to Seize Power*

Proletarian revolutionaries are uniting to seize power from the handful of persons within the Party who are in authority and taking the capitalist road. This is the strategic task for the new

* *Red Flag* (Peking: Foreign Languages Press, 1968), pp. 1–14.

stage of the great proletarian cultural revolution. It is the decisive battle between the proletariat and the masses of working
people on the one hand and the bourgeoisie and its agents in
the Party on the other.

This mighty revolutionary storm started in Shanghai. The
revolutionary masses in Shanghai have called it the great "January Revolution." Our great leader Chairman Mao immediately
gave it resolute support. He called on the workers, peasants,
revolutionary students, revolutionary intellectuals and revolutionary cadres to study the experience of the revolutionary
rebels of Shanghai and called on the People's Liberation Army
actively to support and assist the proletarian revolutionaries in
their struggle to seize power. . . .

The experience of Shanghai, Shansi Province and other places
tells us that in the course of the struggle to seize power, we
must pay great attention to the following questions:

(1)

. . . Chairman Mao teaches us: "Strategically we should
despise all our enemies, but tactically we should take them all
seriously." The handful of Party people in authority and taking
the capitalist road will never succeed in their schemes, which
are doomed to failure. We should despise them. However, we
must deal with them seriously, and must never treat them
casually or lightly.

Proletarian revolutionaries must fully understand that the
struggle to seize power and counter-seize power between us and
the handful of persons within the Party who are in authority
and taking the capitalist road is a life-and-death struggle between the proletariat and the bourgeoisie. It is a contradiction
between ourselves and the enemy.

The general orientation for proletarian revolutionaries is to
form an alliance and seize power from the handful of Party
people in authority and taking the capitalist road. All revolutionary comrades must proceed from this general orientation
and adhere to it in considering and handling all matters. If not,
they will embark on the wrong road and may go over to the
opposite side.

In places and organizations where the mass movement of the great proletarian cultural revolution has been vigorously carried out for more than half a year, the revolutionary masses have become clear as to who are the chief figures among those Party people in authority and taking the capitalist road. In the struggle to seize power, the proletarian revolutionaries must fix their aim on their target and deal the enemy heavy blows. A strict distinction must be made between contradictions between ourselves and the enemy and those among the people. We must not treat contradictions among the people as contradictions between ourselves and the enemy and blast away indiscriminately. Otherwise, the struggle to seize power from the handful of Party people in authority and taking the capitalist road will be hindered and we will commit errors on questions of orientation and will be made use of by the class enemy.

(2)

Resolutely build the great alliance of the proletarian revolutionaries and unite the broad masses. This is the most important condition for victory in the struggle to seize power from the handful of persons within the Party who are in authority and taking the capitalist road.

Now that the great proletarian cultural revolution has reached the stage of the struggle to seize power from the handful of Party people in authority and taking the capitalist road, it is essential for revolutionary mass organizations to forge a great alliance. Without a great alliance of proletarian revolutionaries, the struggle to seize power cannot be completed successfully; even if some power has been seized, it may be lost again. . . .

Once the revolutionary mass organizations have seized power in a particular department, their own position alters. At this time, the bourgeois ideas and petit-bourgeois ideas in the minds of certain comrades readily come to the fore. We must be highly vigilant. We must rid ourselves of all selfish ideas and personal considerations and make a revolution to the depth of our souls. Everything must proceed from the fundamental interests of the proletariat. We must attach the utmost importance to the interests of the whole instead of concerning ourselves with personal prestige and position. We must firmly respond to **Chairman Mao's call to "practice economy in carrying out revolution"** and not show off, spend money without measure and waste state property. We must not fall victim to the "sugar-coated bullets" of the bourgeoisie.

Revolutionary mass organizations which have seized power and the leaders of these organizations should adopt the principle of unity towards the masses and the mass organizations holding different views. They should win over and not exclude the majority. This will help isolate to the maximum the handful of Party people in authority and taking the capitalist road and deal them blows, and help establish the new proletarian revolutionary order.

Everyone, in the course of the struggle to seize power and after coming to power, has to undergo new tests. We hope that the revolutionary path-breakers who have emerged during the movement will always be loyal to the proletariat, to Chairman Mao, and to the proletarian revolutionary line represented by Chairman Mao, and that they will become politically mature in the course of time rather than be like those who just flash across the stage of history. The only way one can live up to this demand is to study Mao Tse-tung's thought conscientiously, to integrate oneself with the masses of workers and peasants and to make serious efforts to remold one's own non-proletarian world outlook. There is no other way.

(3)

Adequate attention must be paid to the role of revolutionary cadres in the struggle to seize power. Leading cadres who have firmly adhered to the proletarian revolutionary line are the treasure of the Party. They can become the backbone of the struggle to seize power and can become leaders in this struggle.

Such leading comrades have, for quite a long time in the past, waged struggles within the Party against the handful of people in authority and taking the capitalist road. They have now stepped out before the masses and openly taken their stand on the side of the proletarian revolutionaries and will integrate themselves with the revolutionary masses and fight together with them. The workers, peasants, revolutionary students and revolutionary intellectuals should trust them. A clear distinction must be drawn between those in authority who belong to the proletariat and those who belong to the bourgeoisie, between those who support and carry out the proletarian revolutionary line and those who support and carry out the bourgeois reactionary line. To regard all persons in authority as untrustworthy is wrong. To oppose, exclude and overthrow all indiscriminately runs counter to the class viewpoint of Marxism-Leninism, Mao Tse-tung's thought.

When the revolutionary leading cadres rise up to join the masses in seizing power from the handful of persons within the Party who are in authority and taking the capitalist road, the revolutionary mass organizations should support them. It must be recognized that they are more experienced in struggle, they are more mature politically and they have greater organizational skill. Their inclusion in the core of leadership will greatly help the seizure and holding of power.

Cadres who have made errors should be treated correctly and should not be overthrown indiscriminately. They should be allowed to correct their errors and be encouraged to make amends for their crimes by good deeds, unless they are anti-Party, anti-socialist elements who persist in their errors and refuse to correct them after repeated education. To learn from past mistakes to avoid future ones and to cure the sickness to save the patient is a long-standing policy of the Party. Only thus will those who commit errors submit willingly; and only thus will the proletarian revolutionaries win hearty support from the great majority of the people and become invincible. Otherwise, there is great danger.

The overwhelming majority of the ordinary cadres in the Party and government organizations, enterprises and undertakings are good and want to make revolution. The proletarian revolutionary rebels among them are the vital force for seizing power in these organizations. This is the point which must not be neglected.

Cadres at all levels have to undergo the test of the great proletarian cultural revolution and make new contributions to the revolution. They should not rest on their past achievements, thinking highly of themselves and slighting the young revolutionary fighters who have now come to the fore. The following concepts are completely wrong and must be corrected: to see only one's own past merits but not the general orientation of the revolution of today and to see only the shortcomings and mistakes of the newly emerged young revolutionary fighters, but not to recognize the fact that their general orientation in the revolution is correct.

(4)

The current seizure of power from the handful of persons within the Party who are in authority and taking the capitalist road is not effected by dismissal and reorganization from above, but by the mass movement from below, a movement called for and supported by Chairman Mao himself. Only in this way can the leading organizations of our Party and state, enterprises and undertakings, cultural organizations and schools be regenerated and the old bourgeois practices be thoroughly eradicated.

Experience proves that in the course of the struggle for the seizure of power, it is necessary, through exchange of views and consultations among leading members of revolutionary mass organizations, leading members of local People's Liberation Army units and revolutionary leading cadres of Party and government organizations, to establish provisional organs of power to take up the responsibility of leading this struggle. These provisional organs of power must **"take firm hold of the revolution and promote production,"** keep the system of production going as usual, direct the existing set-ups in administrative and professional work (they should be readjusted where necessary) to carry on with their tasks, and organize the revolutionary masses to supervise these set-ups. These provisional organs of power must also shoulder the task of giving unified direction in suppressing counter-revolutionary organizations and counter-revolutionaries. To set up such provisional organs of power is justified, necessary and extremely important. Through a period of transition, the wisdom of the broad masses will be brought into full play and a completely new organizational form of political power better suited to the socialist economic base will be created.

A number of units, where a handful of Party people in authority and taking the capitalist road have long entrenched themselves, have become rotten. There these persons have been exercising bourgeois dictatorship, not proletarian dictatorship. The Marxist principle of smashing the existing state machine must be put into practice in the struggle for the seizure of power in these units.

In summing up the experience of the Paris Commune, Marx pointed out that the proletariat must not take over the existing bourgeois state machine but must thoroughly smash it. Practice in the international communist movement has proved that this is an essential truth. Since a number of units, in which a handful of persons within the Party who are in authority and taking the capitalist road have entrenched themselves, have been turned into organs for bourgeois dictatorship, naturally we must not take them over as they are, resort to reformism, combine "two into one" and effect peaceful transition. We must smash them thoroughly.

The great mass movement to seize power from the handful of Party people in authority and taking the capitalist road has begun to create and will continue to create new organizational forms for the state organs of the proletarian dictatorship. Here, we must respect the initiative of the masses and boldly adopt the new vital forms that emerge in the mass movement to replace the old practices of the exploiting classes and in fact to replace all old practices that do not correspond to the socialist economic base. It is absolutely impermissible to merely take over power while letting things remain the same and operating according to old rules.

On June 1 last year, Chairman Mao described the first Marxist-Leninist big-character poster in the country, which came from Peking University, as the Manifesto of the Peking People's Commune of the sixties in the twentieth century. Chairman Mao showed his wisdom and genius in predicting even then that our state organs would take on completely new forms.

As a result of arousing hundreds of millions of people from below to seize power from the handful of Party people in authority and taking the capitalist road, smashing the old practices and creating new forms, a new era has been opened up in the international history of proletarian revolution and of the dictatorship of the proletariat. This will greatly enrich and develop what we have learned from the experience of the Paris Commune, and the experience of the Soviets, and greatly enrich and develop Marxism-Leninism.

(5)

The struggle by the proletarian revolutionaries to seize power from the handful of persons within the Party who are in authority and taking the capitalist road is being carried out under the dictatorship of the proletariat. In the course of the seizure of power, the dictatorship of the proletariat must be strengthened. This is an indispensable condition for the establishment of the new proletarian revolutionary order. . . .

It is a very good thing that all the ghosts and monsters come out into the open. This provides us with an opportunity for a good spring-cleaning to **"sweep away all pests."**

We must be firm in exercising dictatorship over these counter-revolutionaries. . . .

A group of ghosts and monsters have now come out to set up counter-revolutionary organizations and carry out counter-revolutionary activities. These counter-revolutionary groups must be resolutely eliminated. Counter-revolutionaries must be dealt with according to law without hesitation.

Chairman Mao has called on the People's Liberation Army to actively support and assist the genuine proletarian revolutionaries and to oppose the Rightists resolutely. The great People's Liberation Army created by Chairman Mao himself has heartily responded to his call. It is making new, great contributions to the cause of socialism during the great proletarian cultural revolution. This is the glorious task of the People's Liberation Army. . . .

In suppressing counter-revolutionary organizations and counter-revolutionaries, the instruments of dictatorship must work closely with the revolutionary masses. For counter-revolutionaries, this is an escape-proof net. . . .

"The cock has crowed and all under heaven is bright." Let us heartily welcome the decisive victory of the great proletarian cultural revolution!

★ ★ ★ ★ ★

5. LIU SHAO-CH'I—
"CHINA'S KHRUSHCHEV"

"The number-one person in the Party taking the capitalist road."

Mao's fourth stage of the Cultural Revolution opened in the spring of 1967 with an attack on "the number-one Party person in authority taking the capitalist road," at first labeled as "China's Khrushchev" but finally cited by name as Liu Shao-ch'i. It was undoubtedly Mao's hope that by elevating the struggle to an assault against the largest target of all—Liu Shao-ch'i —the unruly factions would unite and submerge their local differences in the greater task involving the "ideological seizure of power from revisionism and the bourgeoisie." This hope was dashed when despite general agreement on the crimes of Liu, during the summer of 1967, criticism of Liu was subordinated to the struggle among the revolutionary leaders themselves, events which are covered in the next section.

Liu Shao-ch'i, a leading figure in the Chinese Revolution since the early 1920's, was elected as First Vice-Chairman of the Chinese Communist Party at the Eighth National Congress of the Party in 1956. Two years later, Liu was made Chairman of the People's Republic when Mao resigned from this position ostensibly for reasons of health and his desire to devote himself to other work. Historical debate continues over whether Mao resigned voluntarily or was compelled to relinquish the Chairmanship of the Republic by the leaders of the Central Committee. In any event, by 1966 Mao was determined to remove Liu Shao-ch'i as his successor and to return to active decision-making in the Chinese Communist Party.

Liu, a capable organizer and administrator, was a respected if not overly popular Chinese leader. Together with Teng Hsiao-p'ing, the First Secretary of the Party, Liu molded the Chinese Communist Party of eighteen million into an efficient and tightly knit organization. Relying on organization and careful planning,

Liu's style undoubtedly ran into conflict with Mao's penchant for learning from experience in the maelstrom of revolutionary mass movements. The two men not only differed in style and method of work, but were at odds over a series of major foreign and domestic policy decisions.

Future historians will undoubtedly do weighty researches on the clash between Mao and Liu, but one thing is already clear: a philosophical chasm separated the two men, revealing that the fault lines between the Yenan and the Soviet traditions of Chinese Communism were bound to open up sooner or later.

The following selections contain examples of the kind of criticisms leveled at Liu Shao-ch'i and show that the policy differences between Liu and Mao were substantive. The main ideological charge against Liu was that he had advocated six revisionist theories which threatened to undermine the revolutionary fiber of the Communist Party. These six fallacious theories were summarized as: the theory of "the dying-out of class struggle," the theory of "docile tools," the theory that "the masses are backward," the theory of "entering the Party in order to be an official," the theory of "inner-Party peace," and the theory of "merging private and public interests."

Liu Shao-ch'i was expelled from the Chinese Communist Party in October 1968 at the Twelfth Plenary Session of the Central Committee. He was labeled as a renegade, a traitor, and a scab.

★   ★   ★

SHANGHAI WENHUI PAO*
Criticizing and Repudiating China's Khrushchev: Two Diametrically Opposed Lines in Building the Economy

There are two diametrically opposed lines in building up a country after the proletariat has gained political power.

One is the Soviet modern revisionist line, which stresses only the material—machinery and mechanization—and goes in for material incentives. It opposes giving prominence to proletarian politics, ignores the class struggle and negates the dictatorship of the proletariat. It can only lead to capitalism, never to socialism. The Soviet Khrushchev renegade clique and its successors are fanatical advocates of this line. In tune with the Khrushchev of the Soviet Union, the Khrushchev of China also vehemently pushed this line in China for the purpose of restoring capitalism. . . .

Ever since New China was founded, there has been a sharp and intense struggle between the two lines on the economic front. This struggle focused on whether or not to give prominence to proletarian politics, whether or not to put it in command and whether or not to build up the country in accordance with the great thought of Mao Tse-tung. In the final analysis, the essence of the struggle is whether China should build a socialist or a capitalist economy, whether it should take the socialist or the capitalist road.

In leading us in building a socialist state Chairman Mao has always given top priority to revolutionizing people's thinking. He teaches: **"Political work is the life-blood of all economic work"; "not to have a correct political point of view is like**

* *Shanghai Wenhui Pao*, August 23, 1967 (translated by New China News Agency, August 25, 1967).

having no soul." Among the innumerable ways of expanding socialist production, carrying out a political and ideological revolution is cardinal. If this is done well, there will be an all-round increase in the production of grain, cotton, oil, iron and steel and coal. Otherwise, production will not rise in any field. The fundamental guarantee for the success of our socialist construction lies in instilling Mao Tse-tung's thought in the minds of the masses.

China's Khrushchev does exactly the opposite. He opposes putting proletarian politics in command and spreads the lie that we are using "ultra-economic methods" to guide the country's economic construction. He advocates "using economic methods to run the economy." Shaking his finger he said fiercely: "Why must we run the economy by administrative methods instead of by economic methods?" There has never been an economy independent of politics. No part of a class society exists in a political vacuum. If proletarian politics is not in command in any department or any field, then bourgeois politics must be in command; if Marxism-Leninism, Mao Tse-tung's thought, is not in command, then revisionism, bourgeois ideology, must be in command. By opposing putting proletarian politics in command and by putting bourgeois politics in command instead, China's Khrushchev seeks to restore capitalism.

Let us now analyze what China's Khrushchev calls "using economic methods to run the economy" and see what sort of stuff it really is.

It is in fact putting profits in command. Everything for profit, and profit is everything. China's Khrushchev openly declared: "A factory must make money. Otherwise, it must close down and stop paying wages to the workers." In other words, in order to make money, one is allowed to ignore the unified state plan and the overall interests and engage in all sorts of selfish, speculative activities detrimental to the socialist economy.

This is simply that notorious "material incentive." In capitalist fashion, China's Khrushchev said: "Give him a good reward if he works honestly"; "if you don't give him more money, there'll be no incentives, and he'll not do a good job for you." He attempted to corrupt the masses by instilling bourgeois egoism, divert people's attention from politics, widen the income gap and create a privileged stratum. This is a crying insult to the revolutionary workers and staff; this is a knife which kills without spilling blood!

This also means shamelessly glorifying capitalism. China's Khrushchev said bare-facedly: "Capitalist economy is flexible and varied"; "We should learn from the experience of capitalism in running enterprises, and especially from the experience of monopoly enterprises." He told our cadres to "learn seriously" from the capitalists, saying that the latter's "ability in management surpasses that of our Party members." In his eyes, money-grabbing capitalists are a hundred times wiser than Communists.

In the last analysis, "using economic methods to run the economy" means letting the capitalist law of value reign supreme, developing free competition, undermining the socialist economy and restoring capitalism. If we acted in accordance with these "economic methods" advocated by China's Khrushchev, the discomfited capitalists would be very happy again, the emancipated working class would again suffer enslavement and a group of new bourgeois elements would build their "paradise" on the corpses of millions of laboring people.

The opposition of China's Khrushchev to putting politics in command also manifests itself in his opposition to the large-scale mass movement. The socialist cause is the revolutionary cause of millions of the masses. We must fully arouse the masses and rely on their revolutionary initiative to build a socialist economy. Whether or not one launches an energetic mass movement is an important gauge of whether or not one carries out the principle of putting proletarian politics in command; it is also an important aspect of the basic antagonism between the two lines in economic construction.

With his reactionary bourgeois standpoint, China's Khrushchev bitterly hated the revolutionary mass movement and did his utmost to boost the one-man-leadership system and the reactionary line of relying on experts. He went to Tientsin in 1949 and told the staff members of state-owned enterprises there that they were "organizers in state-owned factories" and that "reliance should be placed particularly on the directors, engineers and technicians" in construction. In a 1952 speech, he said:

"There are many difficulties in building industry. China has money, manpower and machinery (this can be solved in the main with the help of the Soviet Union and the People's Democracies), but has no engineers." In a still more unbridled way he attacked the surging revolutionary mass movement launched in 1958. He spread around such nonsense as that the movement was brought about "in a rush" "on the basis of some vague news or inaccurate information."

According to China's Khrushchev, in economic construction we can rely only on a few "experts," "rely on directors, engineers and technicians" who give orders while the revolutionary masses are only "manpower" and "ignorant rabble" "rising up in a rush," who can only obediently "carry out other people's orders." In order to exercise a bourgeois dictatorship over the workers, he and his followers racked their brains to work out a series of revisionist regulations that hold the workers' initiative in check and put them in a strait jacket. In doing this they not only dampened the socialist initiative of the masses and obstructed the development of socialist economic construction, but also placed the few cadres, administrative personnel and technicians in a position of antagonism to the workers, turning them into bureaucrats and new bourgeois elements who rode roughshod over the masses. In this way the nature of the socialist enterprises was being gradually changed.

Such is the struggle between two diametrically opposed lines in building China's economy.

Marxism tells us that **politics is the concentrated expression of economics.** The degeneration of the socialist economic base inevitably leads to a restoration of capitalism in politics. The whole set of lines, principles, policies and measures advocated by China's Khrushchev for so many years were aimed at fostering capitalist forces in both the cities and the countryside and undermining the socialist economic base so as to cause the socialist economy to degenerate into a capitalist economy. Once the economy degenerated, our Party and state would inevitably change color step by step and capitalism would be restored throughout the country. The struggle between the two lines in economic construction is, therefore, a struggle between two political lines, two roads and two destinies for China. . . .

REVOLUTIONARY COMMITTEE IN PEKING*
Discrediting the Theory of "Docile Tools"

The arch traitor Liu Shao-ch'i energetically spread the reaction-
tary theory of "docile tools." He shouted himself hoarse crying:
"What will you do if you don't act as a tool? Do you think it's
good to be a tool of the Party? Do you think it's good to be a
docile tool? I think it is very good." Liu Shao-ch'i and his
agents vainly attempted to use the theory of "docile tools" to
smother the proletarian revolutionary spirit of Party members
and make them faithful followers working for the restoration of
capitalism. Liu Shao-ch'i and his agents cultivated and took in
Party members also in accordance with this "theory." Many
good comrades who dared to fight against the revisionist line
were regarded by them as "refractory tools" and were kept out
of the Party for long periods.

Interpreting well the mind of their sinister master, the handful of Liu Shao-ch'i's agents in our mill energetically peddled
his sinister book on "self-cultivation" and the reactionary
theory of "docile tools." They declared that only those who
proved to be "honest and obedient" could enter the Party.
Clearly, their "honesty" requires Party members to coexist
peacefully with class enemies and turn a blind eye to the criminal activities of the handful of enemy agents, renegades and
obdurate capitalist roaders to restore capitalism, while their
"obedience" requires Party members and the revolutionary
masses to follow the handful of capitalist roaders and become
their docile tools for restoring capitalism.

At one time in our mill, under the sway of the reactionary

* Political Work Section of the Revolutionary Committee of the
Peking No. 2 Rolling Mill, in *Peking Review* (December 20, 1968).

theory of "docile tools," on the one hand, some people, who were unfit to be Party members but were good at taking the hints of the handful of the Party capitalist roaders, were admitted into the Party. Others who were enemy agents, renegades and counter-revolutionaries but acted as docile tools of the handful of Party capitalist roaders in their scheme to restore capitalism, were promoted to leading posts in our mill. On the other hand, ideologically good comrades from families of the working people who dared to pit themselves against the capitalist roaders and resist the counter-revolutionary revisionist line, were looked upon as "refractory tools." Finding fault with and blocking these comrades' applications, the capitalist roaders prevented their admission into the Party on one pretext or another.

For instance, one veteran worker in the mill, a man with militant revolutionary spirit, who dared to fight the capitalist roaders, was looked upon as "refractory" by the handful of capitalist roaders there. His application to join the Party was pigeonholed. When Chairman Mao's latest instruction was made public, he said with deep emotion: "Beginning in 1958, I eagerly applied to join the Party. As I dared to struggle against the capitalist roaders and refused to be their docile tool for restoring capitalism, they hated me and put aside my application. Chairman Mao's latest instruction expresses what we of the working class have wanted to say. I am determined to follow closely Chairman Mao's great strategic plan, continuously heighten my level of political consciousness and strive to become as soon as possible a proletarian vanguard fighter boundlessly loyal to Chairman Mao."

These facts all show that the theory of "docile tools" is a vicious means of stifling the revolutionary spirit of Party members. We must do away with this theory completely. Resolutely implementing Chairman Mao's instruction, we will completely eliminate the waste matter, the handful of enemy agents, renegades, obdurate capitalist roaders and the like, and take in as Party members rebel fighters who have a vigorous revolutionary fighting will, so as to build our Party into **"a vigorous vanguard organization capable of leading the proletariat and the revolutionary masses in the fight against the class enemy."**

REVOLUTIONARY COMMITTEE IN PEKING*
Refuting the Theory That "The Masses Are Backward"

Chairman Mao recently pointed out: **"Direct reliance on the revolutionary masses is a basic principle of the Communist Party."**

The arch scab Liu Shao-ch'i, however, looked on the masses as a "mob" and as "ignorant and incapable." He wildly clamored for a "struggle against the backward ideas and backward phenomena among the masses." Using the theory that "the masses are backward," he and the handful of his agents kept out of the Party large numbers of outstanding workers with proletarian revolutionary spirit, and imposed on them a bourgeois dictatorship. What happened to Comrade Tien Wen-liang, a revolutionary worker of our printing house, is a typical instance.

Comrade Tien Wen-liang as a child grew up in the misery of the old society. Three generations from his grandfather down to himself had been workers. His father toiled for a capitalist throughout his life. When he fell ill he was kicked out of the factory by the capitalist and died from cold in the street. When Tien Wen-liang was seven years old, he began begging with his mother from door to door and suffered from the bullying and insults of the capitalists. He cherishes wholehearted love for Chairman Mao and profound gratitude to the Communist Party because it is the Communist Party and Chairman Mao that have led the poor people in liberating themselves. That is why he does his work well.

Nurtured on Mao Tse-tung's thought, he has been constantly

* A Critic's Group of the Revolutionary Committee of the Peking Hsinhua Printing House, in *Peking Review* (December 20, 1968).

raising his level of political consciousness. He is determined to follow Chairman Mao in making revolution. With sincere feelings of ardent love for Chairman Mao, he has on three occasions written and sent in applications eagerly asking to be admitted into the Party. But contrary to his expectations, the handful of capitalist roaders in the printing house slandered him as a "backward element" and his applications one after another were shelved. On the other hand, they opened the door of the Party wide to a handful of renegades, enemy agents and capitalists, glorifying them as "good comrades" and admitting them into the Party. A capitalist, for instance, was admitted by them into the Party and promoted to be deputy director of the printing house. When the workers learnt about this, they were deeply angered.

Personally initiated and led by Chairman Mao, the great proletarian cultural revolution started. Then the masses of revolutionary workers came to understand more fully that Liu Shao-ch'i was the chief behind-the-scene backer of the handful of capitalist roaders in the printing house.

It was precisely the theory that "the masses are backward" advocated by this arch scab that had for a long time kept many outstanding workers out of the Party and exercised a bourgeois dictatorship over them. Fired with deep hatred for the bourgeois reactionary line, and fighting heroically in defense of Chairman Mao's revolutionary line, Comrade Tien Wen-liang rose in rebellion against the handful of capitalist roaders in the Party in our printing house.

Comrade Tien Wen-liang displayed the valuable proletarian revolutionary spirit of a worker with a high level of consciousness. This was noted by everyone and he who had once been regarded as a "backward element" by the capitalist roaders was elected a worker representative of the printing house to attend the National Day celebrations.

CHI LI-KUNG, PEOPLE'S LIBERATION ARMY SOLDIER*
The Theory of "Merging Private and Public Interests" Is Poison Corrupting the Souls of Party Members

What kind of world outlook should a Communist have? In one of his talks Liu Shao-ch'i smugly said: "Under the conditions of socialism, anyone who works solely for his personal interests will not secure them. Serving the people with one mind will satisfy personal interests in return." "The benefits come later and this is a question of world outlook."

"The benefits come later," though only a few words, vividly portrays the rotten soul of Liu Shao-ch'i, the Number 1 capitalist roader in the Party, and his malicious intention to poison Communists.

Chairman Mao teaches us: **"In the matter of world outlook, however, today there are basically only two schools, the proletarian and the bourgeois. It is one or the other, either the proletarian or the bourgeois world outlook."** Every one of us Communists must have a thoroughgoing proletarian world outlook.

The core of the proletarian world outlook is **"to serve the people wholeheartedly," "utter devotion to others without any thought of self,"** that is, devotion to the public interests. The core of the bourgeois world outlook is to fight for personal fame, gain and power, that is, self-interest. The essence of "the benefits come later" is the theory of "merging private and public interests" advocated by Liu Shao-ch'i; it is the bourgeois world outlook of working entirely for self-interest.

What are "benefits"? Different classes have different views. Chairman Mao teaches us to **"proceed in all cases from the**

* Chi Li-kung of the Second Artillery Corps, in *Peking Review* (December 20, 1968).

interests of the people" and to become persons **"very useful to the people."** Armed with the invincible thought of Mao Tsetung, proletarian vanguard fighters regard as the greatest benefit the complete liberation of the Chinese people and all the people of the world and the realization of the grand ideal of communism. They look upon the hard struggles and heroic sacrifices involved in achieving this lofty goal as their greatest glory and happiness. This is precisely the reason why Comrade Li Wen-chung, Model in Helping the Left and Cherishing the People, had no fear of death when saving the young Red Guard fighters in the turbulent Kankiang River. In the last moment of his life, his only thought was of Chairman Mao and Chairman Mao's Red Guards and he uttered the resounding words: "Don't worry about me!"

What are the so-called "benefits" Liu Shao-ch'i talked about? They are "personal interests," that is, the enjoyment of "position and fortune throughout one's life," "excelling others," "becoming the Number 1 or Number 2 person" in China, and so on, all of which he has sought after and talked so much about all his life. In short, they are personal fame, gain and power. This is clearly a replica of the exploiting classes' philosophy of life—"If one does not work for oneself, then one is doomed." Is there the slightest inkling of a proletarian idea here!

But, sometimes Liu Shao-ch'i also pretended to talk about "serving the people." Why did Liu Shao-ch'i, who devotes himself to seeking his personal "benefit," talk so much about "serving the people"? He himself answered: "Serving the people with one mind will satisfy personal interests in return." It reveals that working for the public interest is only a false front and the real thing is to work for one's self-interest; "serving the people" is the means and securing "personal interests" is the aim.

Why did he put "personal interests" at a "later" stage? He said: "Under the conditions of socialism, anyone who works solely for his personal interests will not secure them." This proves that to put "personal interests" at an "earlier" stage exposes everything to the light and so one may get nothing. Only when personal interests are put at a "later" stage, can one get them. Despite all his efforts to disguise himself, Liu Shao-ch'i cannot cover up his true face of ultra-selfishness. To put self-interest at an "earlier" stage means working for one-self; so does putting it at a "later" stage. The latter method is more despicable and scheming.

We Communists will make it our only purpose "to serve the people wholeheartedly" according to the great leader Chairman Mao's teachings. We must creatively study and apply Chairman Mao's works, thoroughly wipe out all the pernicious influence of Liu Shao-ch'i, strive hard to remold our world outlook, re-place self-interest with devotion to the public interest, follow Chairman Mao to make revolution throughout our lives, and become vigorous communist fighters worthy of the name.

HEILUNGKIANG CADRE SCHOOL*
Thoroughly Repudiating Liu Shao-ch'i's Theory of "Entering the Party in Order To Be an Official"

Whether a Communist be an ordinary worker and a servant of the people or become an official and overlord is the watershed between Chairman Mao's line on Party building and Liu Shao-ch'i's revisionist line on Party building.

"We Communists seek not official posts, but revolution. Every one of us must be a thoroughgoing revolutionary in spirit and we must never for a moment divorce ourselves from the masses." Our Communist Party members can always retain a revolutionary youthfulness only when they act in accordance with Chairman Mao's teachings to join the Party for the sake of revolution and always integrate themselves with the workers, peasants, and soldiers.

In order to restore capitalism, Liu Shao-ch'i, however, ener-getically peddled the theory of "entering the Party in order to be an official." He shamelessly publicized his nonsense that "in

* Correspondents' Group of the Liuho "May 7" Cadre School in Heilungkiang Province, in *Peking Review*, December 20, 1968.

the old days when one passed the imperial examination at the county level, one could become an official; now when one joins the Communist Party, one can also become an official. Such a Party member will be included in the list of prospective cadres."

The theory of "entering the Party in order to be an official" is a strong corrosive aimed to poison those who are not firm-willed and so lead them on to the revisionist road where they only seek an official post and not want revolution and where they can only be officials and cannot remain one of the common people.

One veteran cadre in our "May 7" Cadre School joined the revolution during the War of Resistance Against Japan. He had been a shepherd. As a child he tended sheep for a landlord and later braved many dangers for the revolution. But, after taking up leading posts, he embarked step by step on the road of "making revolution" comfortably and becoming an official and overlord. He said with remorse: "I was once in danger of being turned into a capitalist roader by Liu Shao-ch'i's theory of entering the Party in order to be an official'! Fortunately I was saved from the quagmire of revisionism by the great cultural revolution initiated by Chairman Mao!"

Preparing organizationally to subvert the dictatorship of the proletariat, Liu Shao-ch'i, making use of the self-interest in the minds of certain Party members, attempted to use the prospect of "becoming an official" as a bait for training our Party members into members of a privileged stratum with minds set on seeking official posts.

Different lines train up different people. Some cadres in government organizations, who were poisoned by Liu Shao-ch'i's reactionary line, had long been divorced from the masses, from reality and from manual labor. Under the guidance of Chairman Mao's instruction, they have taken the road of going down to do manual labor and moved from the status of an "official" to that of an ordinary worker. As a result, a radical change has taken place in the depths of their being.

We are determined to thoroughly criticize and repudiate the theory of "entering the Party in order to be an official," and to become willing servants of the people. We must always be ordinary workers and proletarian revolutionary fighters.

CENTRAL COMMITTEE OF THE CHINESE COMMUNIST PARTY*

Communiqué Announcing the Expulsion of Liu Shao-ch'i from the Chinese Communist Party

The Enlarged Twelfth Plenary Session of the Eighth Central Committee of the Communist Party of China opened in Peking on October 13, 1968, and was successfully concluded on October 31.

Comrade Mao Tse-tung, Chairman of the Central Committee of the Communist Party of China, presided over this session which is of great historic significance and made a most important speech on the great proletarian cultural revolution movement since the Eleventh Plenary Session of the Eighth Central Committee of the Party in August 1966.

Vice-Chairman Lin Piao, Chairman Mao Tse-tung's close comrade in arms, attended the session and made an important speech.

Attending the session were Members and Alternate Members of the Central Committee.

All members of the Cultural Revolution Group under the Central Committee attended the session.

Principal responsible comrades of the revolutionary committees of the provinces, municipalities and autonomous regions attended the session.

Principal responsible comrades of the Chinese People's Liberation Army attended the session.

The Enlarged Twelfth Plenary Session of the Eighth Central Committee unanimously holds that the great proletarian cultural revolution, personally initiated and led by our great leader Comrade Mao Tse-tung, is a great political revolution made by the proletariat against the bourgeoisie and all other exploiting

* SCMP No. 4293 (November 6, 1968), pp. 12–16.

classes under the conditions of the dictatorship of the proletariat in our country.

The Plenary Session ratified the "Report on the Examination of the Crimes of the Renegade, Traitor and Scab Liu Shao-ch'i" submitted by the special group under the Central Committee of the Party for the examination of his case. The report confirms with full supporting evidence that Liu Shao-ch'i, the Number 1 Party person in authority taking the capitalist road, is a renegade, traitor and scab hiding in the Party and is a lackey of imperialism, modern revisionism and the Kuomintang reactionaries who has committed innumerable crimes. The Plenary Session holds that the exposure of the counter-revolutionary features of Liu Shao-ch'i by the Party and the revolutionary masses in the great proletarian cultural revolution is a tremendous victory for Mao Tse-tung's thought and for the great proletarian cultural revolution. The Plenary Session expressed its deepest revolutionary indignation at Liu Shao-ch'i's counter-revolutionary crimes and unanimously adopted a resolution to expel Liu Shao-ch'i from the Party once and for all, to dismiss him from all posts both inside and outside the Party and to continue to settle accounts with him and his accomplices for their crimes in betraying the Party and the country. The Plenary Session calls on all comrades in the Party and the people of the whole country to carry on deep-going revolutionary mass criticism and repudiation and eradicate the counter-revolutionary revisionist ideas of Liu Shao-ch'i and the handful of other top Party persons in authority taking the capitalist road.

★ ★ ★ ★ ★

6. COUNTERCURRENTS—THE RIGHT AND THE "ULTRA-LEFT"

Every revolution has produced those particular nodal points of crisis which mark turning points in the course of history. In France the flight from Paris of Louis XVI and Marie Antoinette in 1791 alerted the French nation to the threat of counter-revolution, while in North America it was the Boston Massacre and later Lexington and Concord that produced the polarization of the population. The 1917 Kornilov attempted coup had the same effect in radicalizing the Russian masses and turning them against the counterrevolutionaries. The Chinese Cultural Revolution witnessed such a turning point in July of 1967, during the dramatic Wuhan Mutiny, when China reached the brink of civil war.

Wuhan, situated at the confluence of the Yangtze and Han rivers, is one of China's great industrial centers. During May and June, 1967, sporadic fighting broke out between the two main mass organizations. The largest of the factions—familiarly known as the "Million Heroes" and backed by the conservative party organization—was made up of office employees, skilled workers, minor officials, and militiamen, and had the full support of the command of the Ninth Independent Division of the People's Liberation Army. Possessing nearly half a million activists, the "Million Heroes" organization was opposed to the "Wuhan Workers' General Headquarters," a coalition composed of workers from the Wuhan Iron and Steel Company, the bulk of Wuhan's university and middle school students, and a contingent of radical Peking Red Guards.

Ch'en Tsai-tao, the army general in charge of the Wuhan Military Region, supported the conservative "Million Heroes" organization and in June provided trucks from the Wuhan garrison to transport members of the "Million Heroes" for an assault on a radical stronghold in Hankow. Hundreds were killed in the ensuing battles and the city soon approached a state of anarchy. As a result of the mounting casualties and the paralysis of industry, the leaders in Peking telephoned General Ch'en and ordered him to halt the fighting. Ch'en refused, and the leaders of the Cultural Revolution were faced with the first mutiny by a key army commander.

On July 14, two members of the Cultural Revolution Group, Wang Li and Hsieh Fu-chih, arrived in Wuhan to negotiate an end to the violence that had existed in the city for months. The first selection on the Wuhan Incident is one version of what happened after Wang and Hsieh arrived in Wuhan. Typical of the revolutionary journalism of China's Red Guards, this account describes in passionate terms an event that stirred the nation.

Learning of the abduction of its two representatives, Wang Li and Hsieh Fu-chih, the Peking leadership acted decisively on July 20. Three infantry divisions and an airborne division were sent to Wuhan while naval gunboats sailed up the Yangtze to help crush the revolt. Hsieh and Wang dramatically escaped from their kidnappers, returning to Peking on July 22, and the mutiny gradually died out after the capitulation of its leaders. Ch'en Tsai-tao and his military staff were arrested and brought to Peking as the Wuhan Military Region was placed under the command of officers loyal to Mao, Lin Piao, and the leaders of the Cultural Revolution. On July 25, a giant rally, attended by all the top Chinese leaders except Mao, was held in Tien An Men square in Peking to welcome home the heroes and to celebrate the revolutionary victory at Wuhan.

As in other great revolutions, the reaction to the rightist Wuhan Mutiny in China was followed by a leftist wave which swept the country, becoming so extreme that it brought the nation to the brink of civil war. Together with Mao, Lin Piao, and Chou En-lai, the Cultural Revolution Group, acting in the name of the Central Committee of the Party which no longer functioned as a viable political organ, had become the command center of the country. The Cultural Group was led by Ch'en Po-ta, a secretary of Mao and editor of the Party magazine *Red Flag*, and Chiang Ch'ing, Mao's wife. In response to the Wuhan Mutiny and resistance from the right, Chiang Ch'ing proclaimed the new slogan "Attack by reasoning—defend by force," which was turned into an offensive doctrine by the young rebels, who began to arm themselves with whatever weapons were available. This was an interpretation Chiang Ch'ing was later to condemn in her famous September 5 speech, which we have included as the last selection.

Two campaigns were launched in response to the Wuhan Mutiny that produced a crisis and a split in the leadership of the Cultural Revolution. One was the promulgation officially issued by members of the Cultural Revolution Group "to drag out the handful in the army." This campaign brought the political leadership of the movement into collision with army generals throughout the country. The other campaign was led by Wang Li and Ch'i Pen-yü, prominent members of the Cultural Group, to seize power at the Foreign Ministry, Peking Radio, and the press, and to lead an attack on Premier Chou En-lai and other leading Ministers of the State Council.

Thus, one section of the revolutionary coalition at the top— the Cultural Revolution Group—collided with the two other elements of the leadership, represented by the army and representatives of the national government. Chairman Mao, an able politician as well as a theoretician, could not support an attack which threatened the collapse of the remaining structures of national power. The revolution reached its apogee in the final weeks of July, and Mao now threw his weight behind a strategy of consolidation and mediation in an effort to compromise the differences between the warring factions. He called upon Premier Chou En-lai and Lin Piao's army to accomplish this task of mediation, a task that was to occupy the remaining months of the Cultural Revolution.

Wang Li's speech of August 7 to a faction of Peking students represents the provocative effort of the "ultra-left" to seize power at the Foreign Ministry and topple Foreign Minister Ch'en Yi. Both Chou En-lai and Mao himself had made it clear that Ch'en Yi could be criticized but not overthrown. One result of Wang Li's speech was the burning of the British Mission in Peking by radical Peking Red Guards who ignored the commands of Premier Chou and other leaders to refrain from such action. It was during the same period that the "ultra-left" seized control of the Foreign Ministry for about a week until Mao, Chou, and Lin moved against them to return control of the ministry to the State Council. Wang Li, Kuan Feng, Lin Chieh, and Mu Hsin, all members of the Cultural Group, were removed some time in August. They were accused of being behind-the-scene backers of the "May 16 Regiment," which was labeled as a counterrevolutionary, "ultra-left" organization. Ch'i Pen-yü, another leading member of the Cultural Group and the famous author of "Patriotism or National Betrayal?" was also linked to the "ultra-left" faction and ousted in January of 1968.

Our last selection, Chiang Ch'ing's September 5 Speech, reflects the decisive turn in the revolution and the new strategy of Mao, Chou, and Lin to reconcile conflicts and bring about the unity of various factions by turning over leadership of the movement to the army. Chiang Ch'ing probably was chosen to make this speech because as Mao's wife and a leading member of the Cultural Revolution Group, she had the most influence on the young rebels. The Cultural Revolution Group still functioned, but it never again had the high prestige it had once had in the first year of the movement.

★ ★ ★

WUHAN RED GUARDS*
The Wuhan Incident—"The Appalling July Mutiny"

On July 14 our much respected great leader Chairman Mao sent Vice Premier Hsieh Fu-chih and Comrade Wang Li to Wuhan to deal with the question of the cultural revolution in that area. This was the greatest support given by the Party center and Chairman Mao to the proletarian revolutionaries in Wuhan. It was a heavy blow to the anti-Party clique of Wang [Jen-chung] and Ch'en [Tsai-tao], indicating that their doom was approaching. However, these enemies would not be reconciled

*Excerpted from an article in the *Wuhan Kang-erh-ssu* (August 22, 1967). Translated in SCMP No. 4073 (December 5, 1967), pp. 1–18.

to their defeat; they continued to put up a last-ditch struggle before their doom. Thus, a counter-revolutionary military coup long planned by the anti-Party clique of Wang and Ch'en eventually erupted.

Prelude to the counter-revolutionary military coup

"A mountain storm is always preceded by gusts of wind." Upon the arrival of Vice Premier Hsieh Fu-chih and Comrade Wang Li in Wuhan, they were unequivocal in declaring their stand and firm support for the proletarian revolutionaries in Wuhan represented by "San Kang," "San Hsin" and "San Lien." They clearly pointed out that the case of the Workers' General Command of Wuhan would be reopened. On learning this, Ch'en Tsai-tao was so furious that he promptly spread the word, declaring: "While the case of the Workers' General Command may be reopened, the 'One Million Heroic Troops' will not permit this thing to happen. Since the 'One Million Heroic Troops' is in control of Wuhan's economic lifelines such as communications, water supplies and electricity, any attempt at reopening the case of the Workers' General Command may result in the cutting off of power and water supplies."

On the night of July 19 Comrade Wang Li on behalf of the Central Cultural Revolution Group conveyed a four-point directive of the Cultural Revolution Group to military cadres at or above the division level at the Wuhan Military Region Command. He pointed out that the case of the Workers' General Command would be reopened, the "February 8 statement" was on the whole correct in its general orientation and good in its main current, "San Kang," "San Hsin" and "San Lien" were organizations of the revolutionary rebels, the "One Million Heroic Troops" was a conservative organization, and the Military Region committed the error of line and orientation in the task of supporting the Left.

Ch'en Tsai-tao looked pale on hearing the instructions conveyed by Comrade Wang Li. This so enraged Niu Hai-lung, divisional commander of the "8201" unit and capable fighter of the Wang-Ch'en clique, that he promptly stood up to say something against the central directive. However, he was stopped by Comrade Wang Li. In the tense atmosphere which prevailed in the headquarters of the Military Region, the political commissar of the "8201" unit was the first to withdraw from the conference hall, while Niu Hai-lung followed suit. Returning to the "8201" unit, Niu raved at his subordinates, banging the table and pushing the chairs in a hysterical manner. He shouted: "Let's have it!" The coup was touch-and-go; the situation was extremely critical.

Meanwhile, Ch'en Tsai-tao and the like lost no time in spreading rumors among the broad masses and PLA fighters, saying: "The general orientation of 'San Ssu' and 'Erh Ssu' is wrong!" "Hsieh Fu-chih has been expelled." "What is the rank of Wang Li, and can he represent the Party Central Committee?" The loudspeaker system controlled by the "One Million Heroic Troops" even had the nerve to order the central leaders to open negotiations "honestly," otherwise "revolutionary action" would be taken against them. Reactionary slogans saying "Both Wang Li and Hsieh Fu-chih are *personae non gratae.*" "Get out of Wuhan, Wang Li and Hsieh Fu-chih" were pasted up all over the streets. The situation was charged with tension and uninhibited wrath, indicating that Ch'en Tsai-tao would take drastic measures.

Unreasonably kidnapping central leaders

At 9:00 P.M. on July 19 the area surrounding Tunghu, including Tunghu Hospital which was five *li* away, was under the control of the "One Million Heroic Troops," while the approaches to the Tunghu Guest House were also closed by the bandits of the "One Million Heroic Troops." Everyone appeared concerned for the safety of the central leaders.

In the stifling heat which engulfed Wuhan in July, a counter-revolutionary act of abducting central leaders began. In the wee hours of July 20, Lei Jung-hua, the number one leader of the Tunghu detachment of the "One Million Heroic Troops," led other bandits to kidnap the central leaders. When the truck-load of bandits stopped at the entrance to the Tunghu Guest House, the guards of the "8201" unit at first pretended not to let the bandits in. However, these bandits simply surged forward and got through without any difficulty. But both Vice Premier Hsieh Fu-chih and Comrade Wang Li were not caught unawares; they faced the pack of "wolves and jackals" firmly. In a firm voice, Vice Premier Hsieh said to them: "I am Hsieh

Fu-chih. Kidnap or kill me as you please." At this juncture the bandits were taken aback, screaming and gesticulating wildly and viciously, before turning their wrath on Comrade Wang Li. The latter angrily scolded the bandits, telling them in an authoritative voice: "Have you people anything to do here? If not, get out!" Liu Hsien-shih, one of the bandits, shouted: "We are not leaving!" He then brazenly took a seat. A moment later, three trucks carrying the bandits of the "One Million Heroic Troops" from the "Hung Lien" of the heavy machine tools plant stopped at the guesthouse. Shortly afterward, the entire building was surrounded.

Comrade Wang Li's guards promptly drew their revolvers and angrily pointed at the bandits in an effort to protect the safety of the central leaders.

At this moment Ch'en Tsai-tao who was directing behind the scene went into close combat. Arriving hurriedly at the scene of commotion, he told Vice Premier Hsieh and Comrade Wang: "Now all depends on how you two work things out; I don't know what to do!" Grinning jubilantly and maliciously, he was at the height of his arrogance.

A moment later trucks carrying fully armed soldiers of the "8210" unit stopped at the guest house. This was followed by more trucks. Directing the mutiny were army officers carrying revolvers. After entering the guest house, they pointed machine-guns and pistols at the central leaders. To avert bloodshed and loss of lives in the event of an armed clash, the guards of Vice Premier Hsieh and Comrade Wang had to put away their revolvers. Seizing the opportunity, the screaming bandits surged forward and began to take away Comrade Wang Li, Comrade Mao's emissary, a member of the Central Cultural Revolution Group and assistant chief editor of *Hung-ch'i* journal.

Moving swiftly and clamping down on Wuhan by armed force

After Comrade Wang Li was seized, the "One Million Heroic Troops" and other detachments trained by the Wang-Ch'en clique for special operations—together with the small bunch of rotten eggs of the "8201" unit—moved swiftly, mounting machine guns on the trucks and some tall buildings, loading their rifles or unsheathing their swords. Brandishing pistols before the unarmed masses, the killers went on a rampage, throwing spears and other lethal weapons all over the river city. The whistle of sirens of fire engines was mingled with the rumble of nearly a thousand vehicles carrying members of the "One Million Heroic Troops" and the detachments of "San Ssu." The loudspeaker vans of the "One Million Heroic Troops" blared reactionary slogans, plunging the entire city of Wuhan into the horrors of war.

After the sentry posts of the Military Region Command were automatically withdrawn, they were seized by coup participants. Thus, all the streets in the vicinity of the Military Region Command were under the control of the mutineers.

As reactionary slogans and reactionary big-character posters put up by the "One Million Heroic Troops," "San Ssu" and the "8201" unit covered all the streets of Wuhan, the arrogant reactionaries were extremely blatant. Both the Yangtze River Bridge and Chiang Han Bridge were closed, navigation along the Yangtze River was stopped, communications routes, main thoroughfares, major buildings occupied, the airfield surrounded and railway stations were seized, thus gravely threatening the security of the liberated area—universities and secondary schools where the rebels were numerically superior to the mutineers.

Running amuck in Wuhan, members of the "One Million Heroic Troops" and the small bunch of rotten eggs of the "8201" unit did things as they pleased, attacking, kidnapping and brutally beating people and even killing young revolutionary fighters and the revolutionary masses.

As Wuhan was then under the complete control of coup participants, a White Terror reigned in the entire city.

Subjecting Comrade Wang Li to struggle and bombarding the proletarian headquarters

Under the scorching sun there was great confusion in the compound of the military command, with mobs pushing Comrade Wang Li to the balcony of a building in the compound. Below the balcony there was a large crowd of men of the "One Million Heroic Troops," the "8201" unit as well as members of "San Ssu." Comrade Wang Li was surrounded by ranting and raving hooligans of both sexes hurling abuses at their captive. One of the bandits wearing an army cap seized Comrade

Wang Li's cap and threw it to the ground. There was commotion below, some clapping their hands and others applauding. A moment later, Comrade Wang Li's uniform and collar were also torn apart, and once again there was confusion below.

In a firm and solemn tone, Comrade Wang Li said: "Comrades, we have been sent here by Chairman Mao and the Party center!" Before Comrade Wang finished, the crowd of people below shouted abuse: "Down with Wang Li!" "Wang Li in no way can represent the Party center!" "Get out of the Central Cultural Revolution Group, Wang Li!"

Unperturbed, Comrade Wang Li told PLA fighters who took part in the disturbances: "We believe you are Chairman Mao's fighters and you know that. We experienced such a situation in Szechwan before. . . ."

Another outburst of abuse broke out from the crowd gathered below the balcony. There was clapping of hands to prevent Comrade Wang Li from speaking to the gathering. Furiously pointing their fingers at Comrade Wang Li, several bandits wearing military uniforms shouted at him: "Tell us what kind of organization the 'One Million Heroic Troops' is!"

Undaunted, Comrade Wang Li said in a firm tone: "If anyone brands your organization counter-revolutionary, we won't concur." Comrade Wang Li's words exploded like a bomb among the bandits. Some of them ranted, others jumped about. "Hell, he didn't even address us as revolutionary comrades!" Another shout was raised: "Down with Wang Li!" "Hang Wang Li!" How utterly reactionary these bandits were in shouting such reactionary slogans!

At this juncture, one of the bandits furiously came up to Comrade Wang Li, seized his hair, pulled it hard and tore out a handful of the hair. But our Comrade Wang remained erect without moving an inch! A moment later, his left eye was hit by another bandit, and blood began to drip from it. Comrade Wang shed blood in order to protect Chairman Mao and uphold his revolutionary line. Comrade Wang was then soaked with sweat. Several hooligans grabbed Comrade Wang's hands and pulled them backward, subjecting him to a form of torture known as "sitting in an airplane." Another outburst of screams and abuses rose from below the balcony. At this moment, one of the hooligans stepped forward and said: "Let's calm down a little. I have just consulted Division Commander Niu, who has suggested giving Wang Li a little rest so he may answer our demands at eight o'clock tomorrow morning."

"Nothing doing. Let him give an answer right now." "No, Division Commander Niu is not our representative." "Down with Wang Li!" "Hang Wang Li!" How utterly blatant these reactionaries were! They spread the word that they would take comrade Wang Li to the stadium on Hsin Hua Road where he would be subjected to struggle, and from there to Hanyang where he would be paraded in the street. However, neither fists nor abuses could shake Comrade Wang Li's revolutionary will.

A counter-revolutionary coup spread all over Hupeh Province

Since the Wang-Ch'en clique had long planned to foment widespread disturbances throughout Hupeh Province, counter-revolutionary coups erupted in many administrative districts of the province at the time the mutiny occurred in Wuhan.

For instance, reactionary slogans such as "Bombard Premier Chou, down with Hsieh Fu-chih and hang Wang Li" and "Wang Li is guilty and should be condemned to ten thousand deaths" were plastered up in Hsiang-yang by the "May 4 Rebel Detachment" fostered by the Wang-Ch'en clique. Similarly, reactionary slogans such as "Ch'en Tsai-tao is our red commander" and "Long live Ch'en Tsai-tao" were blatantly shouted. On July 22 more than 300 members of "Kung Chien Fa," wearing the armband of "San Tzu Ping," held a counter-revolutionary procession, shouting "Down with Wang Li" and other counter-revolutionary slogans in response to the "July 20" counter-revolutionary coup.

The People's Armed Forces Department of Shashih incited more than fifty thousand misled peasants to hold a counter-revolutionary procession. In the Chinchow area reactionary slogans such as "Get out of Wuhan, Hsieh Fu-chih" were put up in the streets.

Similar counter-revolutionary incidents occurred at Ichang.

The counter-revolutionary coup was spreading throughout Hupeh Province. . . .

PEKING RED GUARDS*
The "Ultra-Left"

Bring to Public Notice Wang X's August 7 Speech,
"Very Big Poisonous Weed"

Hung Wei Pao editor's note: Wang X received Yao Teng-shan and others, representatives of the Foreign Ministry Liaison Center, on the evening of August 7 and made his notorious "August 7" speech.

Certain people of the foreign affairs department were frantically overjoyed with the release of the "August 7" speech. They beat the drum for it and published its full text in their mosquito paper. It was massively printed and distributed. They put up big-character posters everywhere and announced it day and night through loudspeakers.... As a result, the seed of falsehood spread far and wide.

What kind of stuff is the "August 7" speech? If we reflect it in the magic mirror of Mao Tse-tung's thought and compare it with the speeches of the leading comrades of the proletarian headquarters, we will find at a glance that the "August 7" speech is a 100 percent and out-and-out "very big poisonous weed" opposed to the thought of Mao Tse-tung. It is upon release of the "August 7" speech that the criminal "August dark wind" was stirred up in the foreign affairs system, causing serious damage to the great cultural revolution in the foreign affairs department and to the foreign affairs of our country.

"All the erroneous ideas, poisonous weeds and freaks and monsters should be criticized and repudiated and must not be allowed to run wild."

For readers' reference in further criticizing and repudiating

* Taken from the *Peking Red Guard Paper* (October 18, 1967). Translated in SCMP Supplement No. 214 (December 27, 1967).

this big poisonous weed we extract below some passages from the "August 7" speech together with our comments:

1. Wang X Is So Audacious as to Plot Seizure of the Diplomatic Power of the Center

Wang X: "The resistance to the movement is strong in the Ministry of Foreign Affairs. Diplomacy is turned into an awe-inspiring and important affair that is beyond the means of other people. It is so mystified that it seems only a few experts can do it. Is diplomacy really so difficult? To my mind, handling the internal problems of Red Guards is much more complicated than diplomacy. Are Red Guards incompetent to handle diplomacy?"

"How much power did you seize in January? How much functional supervisory power? Can you exercise supervision? You have not touched the setup of the ministry Party committee, have you? Made a revolution without touching the setup?! How could you make such a great revolution without touching the setup? Has not the Premier called for 'three-way alliance'? 'Three-way alliance' of the aged, the middle-aged and the young. Why not forge a 'three-way alliance' for a setup of the Foreign Ministry?"

Representative of the Liaison Center: "At the time of rectification somebody criticized us for going too far in the seizure of power, saying that the functional power belonged to the Center."

Wang X: "You are wrong. . . . If the personnel power of the cadre department [Foreign Ministry] cannot be touched, then it would mean that the Organization Department of the Central Committee must be reinstated!? It wields the biggest personnel power!"

"I think you wield no power now. An awe-inspiring reputation presupposes some power."

"You have fought so long to seize power but have not acquired much power. You have only acquired this signboard. From now on the supervisory group will not merely supervise functions."

"The supervisory group may not serve as a flower vase and decoration."

Comment: Look! Wang X ceaselessly incites the mass organizations under his control to plot seizure of the diplomatic power of the Center, and directs the spearhead against our respected Premier Chou. How mad he is! Without a doubt he knows that Premier Chou is in charge of diplomacy, but with ulterior motive he claims: "The resistance to the movement is strong in the Ministry of Foreign Affairs. Diplomacy is turned into an awe-inspiring affair." What he implies is this: The "resistance" must be crushed; can it be said that Wang X, "expert" in dealing with the Red Guard problems, is incapable of handling diplomacy? He goes a step further and says: "Are Red Guards incompetent to handle diplomacy?" Thus he openly incites Red Guards to seize the power of the proletarian headquarters! On this point, Comrade Ch'en Po-ta made it very clear in his September 1 speech: "Diplomatic activities . . . are state activities. The power is concentrated in the State, and people must listen to what Premier Chou says. Premier Chou is in charge of diplomacy. If you are in charge of it, surely you will make a mess of it."

Similarly, Wang X knows perfectly well that Premier Chou gave this directive repeatedly long ago: "So far as the Foreign Ministry is concerned, seizure of power can only mean seizure of the leadership of the great cultural revolution and the functional supervisory power." Yet, Wang X permits the Foreign Ministry Liaison Center to seize the functional leadership. Comrade K'ang Sheng sternly pointed out on September 1: "The Center said long ago that national defense and diplomatic powers may not be seized for they belong to the Center. It is wrong to seize the power of the Ministry of Foreign Affairs of the People's Republic of China. Premier Chou said many times that a functional supervisory group should be set up. . . . Several months have elapsed and I would suggest that you give up hope! Diplomatic power may not be seized." Premier Chou also said in his September 2 speech: "The power of the Foreign Ministry is greater . . . The supervisory power cannot be considered small and should not be in excess of [the power of the Foreign Ministry]. You should train step by step. I tell you: Acquire the supervisory power first and you will gain a greater strength to forge a three-way alliance later. It is wrong to seize the power of the Foreign Ministry. The seizure of the power of the Foreign Ministry is wrong and has been criticized and repudiated." These words pronounce complete shattering of Wang X's fond dream.

2. **Standing Opposed to the Party Center and Changing "Down With Liu, Teng and T'ao" into "Down With Liu, Teng and Ch'en"**

Wang X: "Some people of the Foreign Ministry have gone so far as to make a complaint. . . . This is something abnormal. . . . After Comrade Yao Teng-shan transmitted the report, mass feelings were stimulated to a high degree. And this has been turned into a criminal charge. To them the slogan of 'Down with Liu, Teng and Ch'en' is a crime. Why not shout this slogan? It is a matter for deep thought that such a strange phenomenon should have appeared one year after the launching of the great cultural revolution."

Comment: Wang X, a personage taking up an important post at that time, could not but know that the slogan of the Center was "Down with Liu, Teng and T'ao." Why did he openly stand opposed to the Center and encourage others to shout the slogan "Down with Liu, Teng and Ch'en"? Why?

3. **Egging on and Supporting the "June 16" of Peking Foreign Languages Institute to Bombard Premier Chou in Violation of the Law and Discipline**

Wang X: "The attitude of 'June 16' toward the Premier is wrong and must be changed. . . . We have always supported the revolutionaries while at the same time educating them."

Comment: Comrade Chiang Ch'ing pointed out on September 1: "There are those who shake the leadership of the Center from the extreme 'left' and extreme right. They are 'May 16.' 'May 16' is divided into several front armies, some of which oppose the Premier and some oppose me and Po-ta. This is an important question. 'May 16' attempts to throw our ranks into disorder. 'May 16' is a counter-revolutionary organization." Peking Foreign Languages Institute "June 16" is the hard-core component and the main body of the counter-revolutionary organization "May 16" and is its important front army in the foreign affairs department. Ever since its establishment Peking Foreign Languages Institute "June 16" has all along directed its spearhead against the Premier and prepared a mass of black materials against the Premier.... Can it be said that such a bombardment of the proletarian headquarters is merely a question of "attitude"? Can the main body of a counter-revolutionary organization be a "revolutionary group" which should be given "support"? Wang X says: "We have always done so." True, only the counter-revolutionary double-dealers of the T'ao Chu type "have always done so."

Wang X: "The 'Red Flag Rebel Regiment' and 'June 16' (Peking Foreign Languages Institute) drag out Ch'en and camp outside the Foreign Ministry. Is their main orientation wrong? It is not wrong at all."

"Is it a counter-revolutionary act rather than a revolutionary act? Blocking the entrance of the Foreign Ministry building is of course a question of approach which is secondary. Don't magnify a question of one's approach into a struggle between two lines and don't exaggerate it so much."

Comment: The Center has time and again emphasized that the important departments like the National Defense Ministry and the Foreign Ministry must remain free from intrusion. But, Wang X represents the act of Peking Foreign Languages Institute "June 16"—blocking the entrance of the Foreign Ministry building with the result that the diplomatic activities were interrupted—merely as a "question of approach" which is secondary. What is it if not an open act to egg on the mass organization to defy and violate the Party discipline and State laws? Premier Chou hit the nail on the head when he pointed out in his August 6 speech: "Your (referring to Peking Foreign Languages Institute Rebel Regiment and 6.16) camping and demonstration outside the Foreign Ministry building are against us." Po-ta and the venerable K'ang were also very angry at this. Yet Wang X yelled: "Don't magnify a question of one's method into a struggle between two lines, and don't exaggerate it so much." "What is wrong with camping outside the Foreign Ministry building so far as the main orientation is concerned? It is not wrong at all." "Is it a counter-revolutionary act rather than a revolutionary act?" It is crystal clear where he directs the spearhead and what his intentions are. Look, how arrogant and mad this man is!

4. **Carrying Out the Bourgeois Reactionary Line: Openly
   Opposing "Rectification" and "Fight Self and
   Repudiate Revisionism"**
   Representative of the Liaison Center: During the past half-year since the establishment of our Center, we have spent three months rectifying the style and carried out self-examination three times.
   Wang X: "How much do you have that needs examination? Their (referring to the Foreign Ministry Headquarters) problems are so grave but what have they done to examine their problems?"
   Comment: These few words depict the typical bourgeois reactionary line: cajole support of one group, attack the other group, and incite the masses to struggle against the masses. Nor is that all. Wang X openly opposes the "rectification" and "fight self and repudiate revisionism" in the mass organizations under his control. Says he preposterously: "How much do you have that needs examination?" In this connection, Comrade K'ang Sheng pointed out seriously on September 1: "You organizations of the foreign affairs department must do a good job to rectify your style. You say you have carried out rectification for several months. You must continue to rectify!" Comrade Chiang Ch'ing gave these instructions: "It is the enemy who exploits the anarchism, factionalism and individualism among the masses. One should direct the revolution not only against others but against oneself as well." Each word spoken by the commanders of the proletarian headquarters is indeed the most forceful refutation and repudiation of the "August 7 speech."

CHIANG CH'ING*
Chiang Ch'ing's Speech to Rival Delegations from Anhwei

(September 5, 1967)

Greetings to you all, comrades! (Loud shouting: Long live Chairman Mao! A long, long life to him!)

I have come rather hurriedly, and I have no idea of what is going on here. Old K'ang [K'ang Sheng] just dragged me here. Nor have I prepared for the few words which I shall say here. If what I am going to say is right, you may use it for reference; if not, you may criticize me. You may even bombard me or burn me!

I want to talk about the current situation. On the question of situation, there are some different views among us. We think that taking the nation as a whole, the situation of the great cultural revolution is excellent. If, however, the present situation is viewed in isolation, then of course it appears to be quite serious in certain areas and individual places. Actually, this is not so. Taking the country as a whole and from the historical point of view, isn't the situation this year greatly different from that at this time of the previous year?

At this time last year, the small handful of top Party capitalist roaders in authority and their jackals in the localities still had considerable strength and were able to carry out activities. What about now? They have been paralyzed. Some of them have been struck down by the revolutionary young fighters. Paralysis itself is a good thing because the capitalist roaders in authority can move no longer. That is why revolutionary committees have been set up in some localities.

* Chiang Ch'ing, translated by SCMP and Joint Publications Research Service, SCMP Supplement No. 209 (November 3, 1967).

What is being done at present? The Central Committee is tackling the problems province by province, and city by city in the case of those large cities. Hasn't this been done in Anhwei, too? Now we have invited you comrades to come, so that both sides of you can sit down to solve the problems. This is also a good situation.

Looking back, from last year up to the present, tremendous changes have taken place. The campaign for mass criticism and repudiation of the top Party capitalist roader in authority is now gradually unfolding in the whole country, and fire is being opened against him on all fronts. It is necessary to pull him down, discredit him, and criticize him thoroughly and penetratingly. To do this, as I have said on many occasions previously, we must make it known to every household that we must criticize him more severely than we did Trotsky of the Soviet Union at that time in order to prevent China from changing color. This is because he has held power for a very long time, is a double-dealer, and has a whole set of cadre lines to protect his erroneous line.

But the moment Chairman Mao gave his order for the great proletarian cultural revolution, the young fighters went to the battleground and dragged these fellows out. To be sure, comrades may say: "Comrade Chiang Ch'ing has said it well, but in our place the struggle is quite severe." Our struggle, too, is rather severe, although we do not use force. Nevertheless, I have let it be known that if some people insist on having a violent struggle with me, I will surely defend myself and strike back. (Loud shouting: Learn from Chiang Ch'ing, and salute her!) Learn from you comrades, and salute to you all!

Comrades, I am not in favor of armed struggle, and you must not think that I like it, because I am firmly opposed to it. I resolutely support Chairman Mao's call for "peaceful struggle, not armed struggle." What I mean is: when the class enemies attack us, how can we afford not to have an inch of iron in our hands [be unarmed]? This is the situation I have in mind, but at present we need not have that kind of armed struggle.

Armed struggle always hurts some people and damages State property. Why, then, should we be prodigal sons? And such a problem as this must be clearly explained. This "attack by words and defend by force" must not be deprived of its class content; it must not be viewed in isolation from definite circumstances and conditions. It would be bad if, on your return, you stir up fights by wearing fighter's caps and raising spears. (Old K'ang interrupted: Not spears. We now have the machine guns.) After firing a round of ammunition, a machine gun will have to be reloaded. On the whole, I feel that the situation is excellent. It has tempered the younger generation and the young fighters. It has also tempered the revolutionary cadres as well as men of the older generation like old K'ang! (Old K'ang interrupted: You people are tempering me every day.)

Comrades, don't think that the question of Anhwei is exceptionally complicated. I, for one, do not think so. Each question has its own peculiarities. The present condition of Anhwei is much better than it was last year. And the situation now is better than it was a moment ago. It is wonderful that we have been able to sit down and talk, instead of fighting things out. This is a favorable situation; it is a good beginning. Now in various provinces the case is generally like this: Talks are being held through arrangements made by the Central Committee, and although there have been reversals in some individual places, reversals are a normal phenomenon. Besides, there are imbalances in the situation, but imbalances are also a normal phenomenon.

On the whole the situation is satisfactory and is developing in a favorable situation. This calls for the following several conditions: Leadership by the Party Central Committee headed by Chairman Mao, which is the most important; the presence of the PLA as the pillar of the proletarian dictatorship to defend the great proletarian cultural revolution; and the gradual establishment of local revolutionary committees to promote revolutionary grand alliance and revolutionary "three-way combination" before we can carry out struggle-criticism-transformation and coordinate it with the nationwide mass criticism.

How do things stand at present in this connection? First, there are the Party capitalist roaders in authority, in addition to the landlords, rich peasants, counter-revolutionaries, wicked people and rightists, in addition to U.S. spies, Soviet spies, Japanese spies, and Kuomintang spies—all of them are bent on destroying us. With so many black hands hidden behind their backs, it is not easy for you to discern them. Appearing either as "ultra-Leftists" or as rightists, they are set to undermine the Party Central Committee headed by Chairman Mao. This shall never be permitted and those who do so are doomed to failure.

Comrades, come to think of it: Do you permit this? (The audience: No, we don't!) At present, let us take Peking as an example. There is a bad thing, and I call it a bad thing because it is a counter-revolutionary organization, called the "May 16" Corps. Numerically it is not a large organization, and superficially the majority of its members are young people, who are actually the hoodwinked. The minority consists of bourgeois elements who nurse deep-seated hatred for us and who make use of the ideological instability of the young people. Those who really pull strings behind the scene are very bad indeed.

What about Anhwei? There are also some people who oppose the Central Committee and its nine-point, five-point, and other decisions. They have failed to carry them out. They have refused to carry them out. If things were done according to the nine-point decision reversals would not have taken place, and when reversals occurred, they would be a good thing. Now that you have come we welcome you. The "May 16" assumes an "ultra-Leftist" appearance; it centers its opposition on the Premier. Actually, it has collected black material to denounce every one of us, and it may throw it out in public at any time. (Old K'ang interrupted: Did you people of Anhwei send any person to collect material concerning the Cultural Revolution Group of the Central Committee? The representatives replied: Yes. He was Liu Hsiu-shan. Old K'ang asked again: To be fair, you of the good group had also sent someone to collect material, as the group of babblers had done. Liu Hsiu-shan had sent someone to collect material, and so had you of the two groups.)

We are not afraid of either group. With a clear conscience, what should we be afraid of? Go ahead and find the material you want! You people just eat and do nothing, so now you have chosen this thing instead of the revolution. Do what you like. I am not afraid. They had collected black material against me in the past, but only now have I discovered this. A case-study group while in Shanghai went to collect the material, saying that Comrade Ch'i Pen-yü had said the material concerned me. They had no choice but to bring out the material. When this material was brought back, I did not ask any questions. You

see, a large trunk of it! Recently it has been found that in some
places the so-called "special parties" have been set up. The
setting up of these special parties is a tactic of the clowns, who
cannot see the light. (Comrade Yao Wen-yüan interrupted:
Clowns.) Clowns. From the right side they stirred up the gust
of wind in February this year in opposition to the great proletarian revolution; while at present those who stir up the
"Leftist" wind to oppose the Central Committee oppose the
Premier as "ultra-Leftists."

The "May 16" is a very typical counter-revolutionary organization, and we must raise our vigilance against it. U.S.-Chiang
spies, Soviet revisionist spies as well as the landlords, rich
peasants, counter-revolutionaries, wicked elements and rightists
will never act honestly but will try all possible means to wage
a death-bed struggle. This requires that we raise our vigilance,
discern them, and do propaganda among the masses, awaken
the masses, and isolate these bad people. They are only a
minority who cannot see the light. This is to say that we oppose
people who oppose the leadership group of the Party Central
Committee headed by Chairman Mao either from the Left, the
extreme Left, or from the right side. I advise you comrades to
be more alert on this question.

This is a question of principle. But you cannot steal weapons
from the Army in this way. On the national defense front we
are going to lay down a stern penalty. The Central Committee
has already passed it. I want to warn soldiers if anyone wanted
to take away my weapons I would certainly retaliate. Of course
opening fire would be wrong. I am that sort of person and I
know whether you are a good person or a bad person, if you
come to steal my weapons.

We should become revolutionaries for Mao Tse-tung's
thought, not members of the Chang or the Li groups. Factionalism is a characteristic of the petite bourgeoisie and is of the
"mountain stronghold" mentality, and anarchism—very serious
anarchism. If both sides would make self-criticism, there will
be no quarrels. For example, if you oppose me I should go to
your place and make self-criticism. Naturally you would feel a
bit ashamed. I would seek out my own mistakes and make
another self-criticism. In this way we could cool down and
have a chat.

I want to discuss the third question of setting up a revolutionary committee. This is a provisional organ of power which has been gradually evolved. There is a gust of evil wind at present and a tendency towards not only attacking the Central Committee headed by Chairman Mao or the PLA, i.e., "dragging out the small handful" but also attacking the revolutionary committees. Inevitably members of the revolutionary committee have made mistakes and have shortcomings. It is even more inevitable that some bad elements should sneak in. The revolutionary committees are newborn things which were produced on the mass foundation. At present there is this tendency to demand that the Central Committee dissolve all the revolutionary committees which they have sanctioned. Is it not a case of some people with ulterior motives creating splits? Comrades, do you know about this or not? (Yes) In the future when you gradually form revolutionary committees, you should keep up your vigilance about this problem. Naturally we are not scared if the problem is a bit complicated.

In the present excellent situation you should be vigilant about three things. This is that people from the extreme "Left" or from the Right are sabotaging the Central Committee headed by Chairman Mao, and undermining the PLA and revolutionary committees. Not only are the people in authority taking the capitalist road behind them but they also have landlords, rich peasants, counter-revolutionaries, bad elements and rightists as well as U.S.-Chiang, Soviet revisionist and Japanese agents on their side. We have some material on them and we have made some criticism.

Draw the boundaries between the reactionaries and the revolutionaries, expose the plots of the reactionaries, bring this to the attention of the revolutionaries, raise your own morale, destroy the prestige of the enemy and then you can isolate the reactionaries, fight on to victory and we shall either beat them or kick them out.

★　　★　　★　　★　　★

7. STRUGGLE FOR UNITY AND THE GREAT ALLIANCE

The following selections represent one year of effort by the Chinese leadership to achieve the great alliance of rebel organizations and the establishment of revolutionary committees in every province. These new revolutionary organs of power were to be made up of representatives from the revolutionary mass organizations, the army, and old party cadres who had passed the test of the Cultural Revolution.

Our first selection indicates the key role played by Premier Chou En-lai during this phase of the Cultural Revolution. Chou's talks with opposing factions from the Northeast are typical of the endless negotiating sessions which occupied his time for more than a year. Often working a twenty-hour day, the Premier devoted all of his considerable diplomatic skills to mediating disputes in every area of the country. This skill was put to a difficult test by groups who frequently resented sitting in the same room with members of an opposing faction.

While the Premier worked with the leaders of mass organizations on a provincial and city level, the army acted as a mediating and educational force on the local level. Armed only with their little red books of Mao quotations, politically experienced army men entered schools, factories, and other organizations to bring about the Great Alliance of mass organizations. The Great Alliance meant that opposing factions were each to be represented on the new revolutionary committees. Disputes soon arose as to the percentage of seats each organization should get on the new organs of power.

Our second selection shows that the entrance of the army into civilian institutions did not mean military control in the Western sense, but that the army men were assigned the role of political conciliation. This process took more than a year to complete, since the army units needed agreement from all sides before solutions to various factional problems could be found.

The new slogan of this phase of the Cultural Revolution was "Struggle against self-interest—Repudiate revisionism." Each individual and organization was urged to conduct self-criticism and refrain from criticizing others. In 1968 the army revised the slogan "Support the left" to read "Support the left, but no particular faction." In other words, the army would support all those who followed the line of "Chairman Mao's Headquarters," no matter what faction they belonged to. An effort was once again being made to centralize control in the hands of the new leadership in Peking.

However, a new major dispute broke out in the spring of 1968 when Yang Ch'eng-wu, Acting Chief of the General Staff of the Army, General Yu Li-ch'in, political commissar of the Air Force, and General Fu Ch'ung-pi, commander of the Peking garrison, were all dismissed from office for having committed "serious mistakes." Representing the Central Cultural Group, Ch'en Po-ta and Chiang Ch'ing both gave speeches during this period, warning of a resurgence of the right. As a result of the renewed struggle at the top, factional struggle once again surged up throughout the country. The struggle concerned the problem of representation on the new revolutionary committees and how many of the old cadres to restore to power.

Mao made one last effort to reconcile the Peking student factions when he called in the five main leaders from the major universities in the city at the end of July. After an all-day meeting with Mao, the student leaders returned to their campuses and opened up a new round of factional struggle; each side proclaimed that Mao had supported their faction. This was the last campaign of the historic Peking Red Guards. Massive worker and army teams were sent in to direct and lead the universities. The mass movement was over; all effort was now made to reconstruct shattered institutions and to transform education and administration of the schools. Yao Wen-yüan's article, included in the selections, announced the end of the student movement and the entry into the scene of the working class, who were now to direct the concluding campaign of the Cultural Revolution.

Premier Chou's speech, the last selection, was given to a mass rally in Peking on September 7, 1968. In this speech, Chou proclaimed the establishment of revolutionary committees in all of the nation's twenty-nine provinces. More struggles ensued at the top and the bottom, but the great rebellion was gradually subsiding.

★   ★   ★

CHOU EN-LAI*
Excerpts from *Premier Chou En-lai's Comment on the Situation in Northeast China*

(September 28, 1967)

How many times have you listened to the recorded speech given by Comrade Chiang Ch'ing on the fifth of September to (representatives from) Anhwei? At least twice? Five times! The September 5 speech should be studied carefully. You may learn much from it, from going back to study class to what to support and what to oppose. You will form your conclusions as to the sort of basis on which to form revolutionary great alliances.

Comrade K'ang Sheng has just appealed for agreement. It is said that in some places agreements were reached but were subsequently scrapped. Why? I think it is a question of understanding. Today we shall begin with the recorded talk given by Comrade Chiang Ch'ing. First of all it is necessary to oppose any attempt to undermine the proletarian headquarters headed by Chairman Mao. All utterances and actions that tend to shake and undermine the proletarian headquarters headed by Chairman Mao must be opposed. Positively speaking, it will be necessary to consolidate, strengthen, and support the proletarian headquarters headed by Chairman Mao. All documents and

_____
* Chou En-lai, translated in SCMP Supplement No. 214, December 27, 1967, pp. 6–9.

appeals issued by this headquarters must be earnestly carried out. Is that not right?

The Central Cultural Revolution Group is the staff headquarters of the Great Proletarian Cultural Revolution. Under the direct leadership of Chairman Mao and Vice-Chairman Lin, it is equal to the former Secretariat of the Central Committee, but the responsibilities it shoulders are even greater than those of the latter. In this proletarian headquarters, sometimes some of us may say or do something wrong while transmitting the instructions of the Central Committee. But rectification will be made as soon as a mistake is pointed out. The Central Committee itself will settle matters.

For example, "Drag out the handful from the Army," which was recently put forward, is an erroneous slogan and has adversely affected some localities. We have talked to all concerned and corrected it by discarding "Drag out the handful from the Army." That, however, does not mean that there are no mistakes in our Army. Individuals in the PLA have made mistakes and even very serious ones or committed crimes. For example, counter-revolutionary Chao Yung-fu is an isolated case. It is good to have him dragged out. . . .

A third example is Wuhan. There Ch'en Tsai-tao and Chung Han-hua carried out a counter-revolutionary rebellion. But as soon as Chairman Mao said a few words, the masses understood, the "Million-Strong Mighty Army" was rendered ineffective, and the rebels rallied with the support of the PLA. This shows that as soon as wicked people in the PLA are dragged out, PLA commanders and fighters will not follow the wicked people any longer.

In some areas the armed forces made errors of orientation and line in supporting the Left. They thought they were right when they were not aware of these mistakes, but once they knew, they would correct the mistakes and admit them. For example, after some self-examination, Yang Te-chih of Tsinan Military Region Command has cooperated very well with Wang Hsiao-yu. The work in Shantung has improved as a result, the great cultural revolution has deepened, most of the mistakes have been rectified, and the Army is playing its role better in giving support to the Left. . . .

Our enemies outside the country are imperialists, revisionists and reactionaries. Would they not have invaded us and carried out war provocations had there not been the PLA? This great PLA is armed with the thought of Mao Tse-tung, an army without match in the world.

On this question young Red Guard fighters must think carefully. You must not refuse to trust and rely on the PLA because you are frustrated in a certain matter or because your demands have not been met. Your demands may be right and may be wrong, and some of them are definitely wrong. When you exceed the limits of the four "extensive democracies," you are guilty of factionalism. Individualism, the "mountain stronghold" mentality, suspecting and overthrowing everything, anarchism, liberalism . . . all this is petty-bourgeois fanaticism, which is sometimes extreme Left and sometimes Right. It tends to be utilized by enemies both inside and outside the country and by the overthrown or not yet completely overthrown capitalist roaders. . . .

Revolutionary committees are newborn organs of power. The power, seized from the hands of bourgeois power-holders, is placed in the hands of proletarian revolutionaries. The Revolutionary Committee of Heilungkiang, approved by the Party Central Committee and Chairman Mao, is one of the first six revolutionary committees.

Why do you now point the spearhead at the Revolutionary Committee (Heilungkiang) which you helped to form and which was approved by the Party Central Committee?

The Revolutionary Committee of Heilungkiang is like a clap of spring thunder in the Northeast. Individual members of the committee may have made mistakes, or some of them may need examination. But you cannot overthrow the whole revolutionary committee because of that. The Revolutionary Committee was approved by our great leader. No matter how many reasons you may have for disrupting the Revolutionary Committee, you must not do it. Instead, we must support and consolidate the Revolutionary Committee. You should think over this question carefully. . . .

You must all examine yourselves first. The "Million-Strong Mighty Army" was hoodwinked and utilized by Ch'en Tsai-tao. Our great leader Chairman Mao said: Even in the case of the

"Million-Strong Mighty Army," it is not necessary to have the three Hsin and three Kang apprehend their leaders. The masses of the "Million-Strong Mighty Army" themselves should be allowed to drag out the bad leaders at their back. This is helpful to achieving unity and forming the great alliance.

Chairman Mao tells us after his tour of inspection that we must combat selfishness and repudiate revisionism. Remove selfishness from the mind of everyone. Like Vice-Chairman Lin, every comrade must be at once a target of revolution and part of the force of revolution. Everyone must eliminate selfishness and foster devotion to public good. Everyone must judge everything in accordance with the thought of Mao Tse-tung and establish the proletarian world outlook. Combat selfishness includes the closing of ranks between two organizations. Contradictions between revolutionary mass organizations are contradictions among the people and should be solved by means of unity-criticism-unity. . . .

The working class knows best the importance of alliance. The workers want alliance. They want to grasp revolution and at the same time stimulate production. The majority faction should welcome the minority faction back into the fold. You must treat others as equals and not discriminate against them. Repudiate revisionism and combat selfishness thoroughly, and don't pay off old scores any more. . . .

Of course there must be some among you young people who are being used by others. You must make self-criticism and regularly examine the actions of your own organizations. You must also heighten your vigilance. Generally speaking, you should trust your comrades, but you must watch out vigilantly for bad things. A communist and revolutionary cadre must never lose his revolutionary vigilance under any circumstances.

In its history of 46 years, the Communist Party of China has been infiltrated many times by the enemy and many renegades have been exposed. Background materials concerning Liu Shao-ch'i and P'eng Chen were found by Red Guards. In Sinkiang a number was found from the prisons. Chao and Lin of Kirin belong to that number.

Your organizations are pure, but you must continually purify our ranks. That is a reflection of the class struggle. Some people passed the democratic revolution well, but turned renegade during the socialist revolution. It is a lesson from history. It takes ten or twenty years to foster a mature revolutionary fighter. Therefore you must learn well. You are in the era of Mao Tse-tung. With Chairman Mao's leadership, you need not take so many detours. You should mature quicker than we did.

Peking's reactionary organization "May 16" also exists in Harbin. But don't enlarge it. It has only some leaders. The young fighters, influenced by the doctrine of suspecting everybody, have made investigations into it out of curiosity. We have put forward four principles for dealing with the problem of the "May 16" Corps:

(1) The problem shall not be enlarged. Only a few bad leaders need be arrested, while the hoodwinked ones should be liberated.

(2) When they are awakened, they should arrest the bad leaders themselves.

(3) Do not let the diehard conservatives vindicate themselves as a result of the opposition against the extreme Left.

(4) The rightists must be prevented from fishing in troubled waters. Accusations against the "May 16" should not be broadened. Don't attach too much importance to the problem of the opposite side. . . .

NEW CHINA NEWS AGENCY*
PLA and Civilians Emulate Model Army
Unit in Supporting the Left

Recent press reports on the valuable experience gained by unit 8341 of the People's Liberation Army, while supporting the left at the Peking General Knitwear Mill, have given impetus to the development of the great proletarian cultural revolution.

* New China News Agency (December 23, 1967).

This experience is inspiring proletarian revolutionaries all over the country, including commanders and men of the PLA and civilians in every field of work. They are closely studying it, to search out and overcome their own shortcomings and by doing so are obtaining strength to break new ground in the revolutionary struggle for the complete ascendancy of Mao Tse-tung's thought.

Everywhere revolutionaries are discussing how to measure their own experiences by the three principles in support of the left as applied by unit 8341.

The three principles are:

Vigorously propagate Mao Tse-tung's thought, and engage in thorough and painstaking ideological and political work;

Do not commit oneself in a hurry, but strive to unite the two opposing groupings step by step if on investigation they both prove to be revolutionary mass organizations;

Learn from the masses. Do not be afraid of making mistakes. Correct any mistakes which are made. Pay attention to the well-being of the masses.

Propaganda teams are going to factories, schools, railway stations, docks and villages to publicize these three principles.

Comrades of the PLA airforce in Peking say that these principles are a guide to their work in supporting the left. They add, "there are numerous ways of supporting the left, the most fundamental is to arm the masses with Mao Tse-tung's thought."

They believe that arduous ideological, political work must be carried out in the manner of unit 8341 in order to insure that Mao Tse-tung's thought is implanted in the heart of the masses. They say that "patience in ideological and political work is the gauge measuring one's own class feeling for the revolutionary masses."

The PLA commanders and fighters who are working in support of the left in Tientsin say, "We must take Chairman Mao's calls as battle orders, and go into action as soon as we receive them. Only in this way can we overcome all constructions, steer in the right direction and become invincible." They say that the personnel supporting the left must themselves keep abreast of the developing situation and have full confidence in Chairman Mao's instructions, because all his instructions represent the fundamental interests of the masses and reflect their aspirations.

Wang Nien-sung, a comrade in the PLA unit helping with the cultural revolution in a woolen mill in Shensi Province, related their experience to the *Chieh-fang-chün Pao*. He says that the fundamental principle in supporting the left is to act according to Mao Tse-tung's thought. He specially emphasizes the need to learn from the masses. The comrades in his unit were at first confronted with a number of problems and found themselves in a difficult situation because of their lack of mental preparedness to be pupils of the masses. Acting on Chairman Mao's instructions they went among the masses, collected their opinions and carefully analyzed them. They then changed their own method of work and were warmly welcomed by the masses, who commented, "You are really sent here by Chairman Mao to make revolution with us."

The army comrades tried in every way to understand those among the masses who were misled. They listened patiently to their views and sincerely and frankly discussed their problems with them. If one discussion failed to resolve the problems, they would discuss it a second and even a third or fourth time. If they failed to arrive at an agreement during a meeting, the army comrades would continue to talk over the matter with the masses in the workshops, in their homes, whenever they had any free time. Through their experiences the army comrades came to realize that the masses are most loyal to Chairman Mao, and that they are most strict in following his teachings. They also found that patient ideological and political work can solve any problem that may arise.

PLA comrades working in Peking's Shihchingshan Middle School wrote to the *Jen-min jih-pao* praising unit 8341, which they describe as a good example in the work of supporting the left. Relating their own experiences, they particularly refer to their "three battles" during the course of their work at the school which had twenty-seven revolutionary mass organizations when they went there eight months ago. The first "battle" was to help the revolutionary students and teachers distinguish the main force and allies of the revolution from the enemy in accordance with Chairman Mao's article "Analysis of the Classes in Chinese Society" and firmly grasp the general orientation of struggle. The second "battle" was to help the students and teachers differentiate between the two kinds of contradictions—those between the enemy and the people and those among the people—and strengthen their own unity in accordance with the principles laid down in Chairman Mao's "On the Correct Handling of Contradictions among the People." The third "battle" was to help the students and teachers study the "three constantly read articles" and "On Correcting Mistaken Ideas in the Party" and conduct a rectification campaign aimed at strengthening the Party spirit and overcoming factionalism and small group mentality. The army comrades went among the masses, made friends with them and actively participated in the campaign to "fight self, repudiate revisionism."

In the last analysis, all experiences serve to prove the truth that the fundamental task in supporting the left is to propagate Mao Tse-tung's thought; that the fundamental attitude one should adopt, is to learn from the masses modestly and the fundamental method is to make thoroughgoing and careful investigation and study, in a sentence, to act according to Chairman Mao's instructions.

*PEOPLE'S DAILY**
"Combat Self-Interest, Criticize and Repudiate Revisionism" Is the Fundamental Principle of The Great Proletarian Cultural Revolution

It is imperative to combat self-interest and criticize and repudiate revisionism." Our great leader Chairman Mao recently gave this great fighting call to the workers, peasants, commanders and fighters of the People's Liberation Army, young Red Guard fighters, revolutionary cadres and revolutionary intellectuals throughout the country.

Comrade Lin Piao, Chairman Mao's close comrade in arms,

* *People's Daily* (October 6, 1967). Translated in *Peking Review*, No. 42 (October 13, 1967), pp. 14–15.

passing on this latest instruction of Chairman Mao at the rally celebrating the 18th anniversary of the founding of the People's Republic of China, pointed out: "By combating self-interest, we mean using Marxism-Leninism, Mao Tse-tung's thought to fight selfish ideas in one's own mind. By criticizing and repudiating revisionism, we mean using Marxism-Leninism, Mao Tse-tung's thought to combat revisionism and struggle against the handful of Party persons in authority taking the capitalist road. These two tasks are interrelated. Only when we have done a good job of eradicating selfish ideas, can we do better in carrying through to the end the struggle against revisionism."

In a highly incisive and scientific way, the phrase **"combating self-interest and criticizing and repudiating revisionism"** summarizes the basic content of the great proletarian cultural revolution and of **"criticism and repudiation of the bourgeoisie"** during the entire historical period of socialism. This is a fundamental principle in ensuring the complete and thoroughgoing victory of China's great proletarian cultural revolution. It is a fundamental principle for preventing the restoration of capitalism, and for strengthening and consolidating the dictatorship of the proletariat and turning the whole country into a great, red school of Mao Tse-tung's thought.

The proletariat's seizure of political power from the bourgeoisie can be completed within a relatively short period. Nor does it require a very long time to overthrow ownership by the exploiting classes. But it takes an extremely long time to eliminate the old ideology handed down by the exploiting classes over thousands of years and to remold people's souls with Marxism-Leninism, Mao Tse-tung's thought.

It is a consistently established concept of Marxism-Leninism, Mao Tse-tung's thought, that thinking has its source in matter. Social ideology originates in social being, in the economic base of society, in the system of ownership in society. Man's social being determines his thinking. But thinking in turn plays a tremendous and dynamic role or, under certain conditions, a decisive role, in the development of the politics and economy of a given society. The old ideology, which reflects the demands of the exploiting classes, serves the old economic base and hampers social development. The new ideology, which reflects the demands of the advanced class, serves the new economic base and promotes and accelerates social progress. Once advanced ideas are grasped by the masses, these ideas turn into a powerful material force which promotes social progress. Therefore, we must make great efforts to destroy the old ideology and foster the new.

In what does the oldness of the old ideology of the exploiting classes lie? It lies essentially in "self-interest," which means looking at the world from the viewpoint of everything for one's self, for self-interest. The selfishness of the exploiting classes is natural soil for the growth of capitalism, an important factor that generates revisionism, an ideological virus that disintegrates the socialist publicly-owned economy and subverts the dictatorship of the proletariat.

This explains why it is necessary to start a great political and ideological revolution to consolidate and strengthen the dictatorship of the proletariat and prevent the restoration of capitalism. The current great proletarian cultural revolution, initiated and led by Chairman Mao himself, is a revolution against revisionism and all old ideas. It is a revolution to remold people to their very souls, to revolutionize their thinking. That is why in the course of this revolution, we must **"combat self-interest and criticize and repudiate revisionism."**

Every proletarian revolutionary, every revolutionary comrade, must regard himself both as a motive force and a target of the revolution; we must act both as the vanguard in criticizing and repudiating revisionism and as a shock force in combating self-interest. If we do not combat self-interest and make revolution against ourselves, we cannot do a good job of criticizing and repudiating revisionism; we may become blind to what is revisionist or even fall into the quagmire of revisionism. Conversely, only by taking an active part in the battle to criticize and repudiate revisionism can we reach into the very depths of our souls and relentlessly combat self-interest.

In organizing study classes for the education of cadres and the masses, it is of prime importance to study Chairman Mao's works diligently, conscientiously and creatively, taking into consideration the various problems which have presented themselves and the ideas current in people's minds in the course of the great proletarian cultural revolution. We must adhere to Chairman Mao's consistent teachings, use the formula **"unity—**

criticism and self-criticism—unity," rely on the masses and let the masses educate themselves. The principal way of correcting our own shortcomings and mistakes is through self-criticism to destroy self-interest and promote devotion to the public interest and by summing up experience and accepting the resulting lessons. This study should enable our old and new cadres and young revolutionary fighters to reach a higher ideological and political level, forge a new unity on the basis of Mao Tse-tung's thought and Chairman Mao's proletarian revolutionary line, and give new meritorious service to the people in the course of **"combating self-interest and criticizing and repudiating revisionism."**

*YAO WEN-YUAN**
Excerpts from *The Working Class Must Exercise Leadership in Everything*

Our country has 700 million people, and the working class is the leading class. It is essential to bring into full play the leading role of the working class in the great cultural revolution and in all fields of work. On its part, the working class should always raise its political consciousness in the course of struggle.
—MAO TSE-TUNG

. . . The important task now confronting the revolutionary committees at all levels is to do the work of struggle-criticism-transformation conscientiously and well, and without losing any time. In order to accomplish this task, it is imperative to persist in leadership by the working class and to **"bring into full play the leading role of the working class in the great cultural revolution and in all fields of work."**
The slogan of replacing the dictatorship of the bourgeoisie

* Yao Wen-yuan, translated in *Peking Review*, No. 35 (August 30, 1968), pp. 3–6.

with the dictatorship of the proletariat was put forth from the very time when Marxism began to take shape in the mid-19th century, one hundred and twenty years ago. Only imperialism, the landlord class, the bourgeoisie and their agents—the revisionists, old and new—are opposed to this thoroughgoing revolutionary slogan. The Communist Party of China takes this slogan as its basic program. In order to realize this slogan, it is essential to unite with the non-worker masses, mainly the peasant masses, the urban petty bourgeoisie and those intellectuals who can be remolded, and to lead them forward.

Throughout the entire process, the great proletarian cultural revolution has been under the sole leadership of one class only, the working class. Our Party is the vanguard of the proletariat. The proletarian headquarters headed by Chairman Mao and with Vice-Chairman Lin Piao as its deputy leader represents in a concentrated way the interests of the working class, the poor and lower-middle peasants, and the masses of laboring people; it is the only center of leadership for the whole Party, the whole army, the whole nation and the masses of revolutionary people. Chairman Mao's proletarian revolutionary line and all his instructions reflect the pressing demands of the working class and of the hundreds of millions of revolutionary people and embody the proletariat's firm and strong leadership of the whole great proletarian cultural revolution. It was the leadership of the proletarian headquaters headed by Chairman Mao that made it possible to launch the great proletarian cultural revolution in which hundreds of millions of revolutionary people are taking part. To persist in working-class leadership it is essential, first and foremost, to ensure that every instruction from Chairman Mao, the great leader of the working class, and every order issued by the supreme fighting command of the working class are carried out swiftly and smoothly. The theory of "many centers," that is, the theory of "no center," mountain-stronghold mentality, sectarianism and other reactionary bourgeois trends undermining working-class leadership must be opposed. The revolutionary committees in all places are organs of power of the dictatorship of the proletariat. All units should accept leadership by the revolutionary committees. It is impermissible to allow in our country the existence of any "independent kingdom," big or small, which is counterposed to

Chairman Mao's proletarian headquaters. The old Peking Municipal Party Committee, this watertight and impenetrable "independent kingdom" which resisted Chairman Mao's instructions, was a means used by the gang of big conspirators, China's Khrushchev and company, to oppose working-class leadership and restore capitalism. This "independent kingdom" was completely smashed by revolutionary storms. This historical lesson in class struggle should be borne in mind by all revolutionaries. The citizens of "independent kingdoms," big or small, under the control of bourgeois elements in various parts of the country should also study this lesson.

The workers' propaganda teams are entering the field of education. This is an earth-shaking event. Schools were the monopoly of the exploiting classes and their children from ancient times. Conditions improved somewhat after liberation, but in the main the schools were still monopolized by bourgeois intellectuals. Some students from these schools have been able for various reasons to integrate themselves with the workers, peasants and soldiers and serve them (generally speaking, because they themselves or their teachers are comparatively good or because of the influence of their families, relatives or friends, but chiefly because of the influence of society). Some others have not. In a state of the dictatorship of the proletariat, there is a serious situation—the bourgeoisie contends with the proletariat for leadership. When the young Red Guard fighters rose in rebellion against the handful of capitalist roaders within the Party during the current great proletarian cultural revolution, the reactionary bourgeois forces in the schools for a while got hard blows. But shortly afterwards, certain people were again active in secret. They incited the masses to struggle against each other, and set themselves to sabotage the great cultural revolution, disrupt struggle-criticism-transformation, undermine the great alliance and the revolutionary "three-in-one" combination and obstruct the work of purifying the class ranks and of Party rectification. All this has aroused dissatisfaction among the masses. The facts show us that under such circumstances it is impossible for the students and intellectuals by themselves alone to fulfill the task of struggle-criticism-transformation and a whole number of other tasks on the educational front; workers and People's Liberation Army fighters must take part, and it is essential to have strong leadership by the working class. Chairman Mao recently pointed out: **"In carrying out the proletarian revolution in education, it is essential to have working-class leadership; it is essential for the masses of workers to take part and, in cooperation with Liberation Army fighters, bring about a revolutionary "three-in-one" combination, together with the activists among the students, teachers and workers in the schools who are determined to carry the proletarian revolution in education through to the end. The workers' propaganda teams should stay permanently in the schools and take part in fulfilling all the tasks of struggle-criticism-transformation in the schools, and they will always lead the schools. In the countryside, the schools should be managed by the poor and lower-middle peasants—the most reliable ally of the working class."**

This instruction of Chairman Mao's indicates the orientation and road for the educational revolution in the schools. It is a sharp weapon for thoroughly destroying the bourgeois educational system. The masses of young students should enthusiastically welcome the taking over of the school front by the working class, its participating in struggle-criticism-transformation and its always leading the schools.

The working class has rich practical experience in the three great revolutionary movements of class struggle, the struggle for production and scientific experiment. It most bitterly hates all counter-revolutionary words and deeds against socialism and against Mao Tse-tung's thought. It utterly hates the old educational system which served the exploiting classes. It most strongly opposes the "civil war" activities of certain intellectuals in damaging state property and obstructing struggle-criticism-transformation. It thoroughly detests the habit of empty talk and the practice of double-dealing, where words and actions do not match. Therefore, when they combine with fighters of the Chinese People's Liberation Army—the main pillar of the dictatorship of the proletariat—the masses of the working class will be most powerful in stopping all erroneous tendencies contrary to Chairman Mao's revolutionary line and most effective in resolving all kinds of problems which have been described as long-standing, big and difficult. Contradictions that the intellectuals have been quarreling over without end and unable to resolve are quickly settled when the workers arrive. As regards the handful of villains who have been hiding behind the scenes and inciting the masses to struggle against each other, only when the workers and Liberation Army fighters take a hand in this matter is it possible to lay their counter-revolutionary features completely bare.

"It's quite enough for the workers to run factories." This is an anti-Marxist viewpoint. The working class understands that it can achieve its own final emancipation only by emancipating all mankind. Without carrying the proletarian revolution in education in the schools through to the end and without rooting out revisionism, the working class cannot achieve its final emancipation, and the danger of capitalist restoration and of the working class being again exploited and oppressed will still exist. It is the bounden duty of the politically conscious working class to take an active part in the great cultural revolution in all fields and to ensure that Mao Tse-tung's thought occupies every front in culture and education.

"Let us liberate ourselves. There is no need for the workers outside school to join in." What the Sixteen-Point Decision states is that the method "is for the masses to liberate themselves." Are the workers not included in the "masses"? Is the working class not your own? All genuine proletarian revolutionaries—not those who pay lip service to deceive people—regard the working class as their own and as the most advanced section of the masses of the people with the highest political consciousness. The "three-in-one" combination of workers, soldiers and the revolutionary activists in the schools is the most reliable guarantee for the masses to liberate themselves. Whoever looks on the workers as a force alien to himself is, if not muddleheaded, himself an element alien to the working class; and the working class then has every reason to exercise dictatorship over him. Some intellectuals who are self-proclaimed "proletarian revolutionaries" oppose the workers whenever the working class touches on the interests of their tiny "independent kingdoms." There are still quite a few people in China like Lord Sheh who was fond of dragons but was frightened out of his wits when a real dragon paid him a visit. These are the people who look down upon the workers and peasants, like to put on airs and think themselves great. As a matter of fact, they are just modern Lord Shehs. It is essential for the workers and People's Liberation Army fighters to go to those places where intellectuals are concentrated, be they schools or other units, to smash the complete domination by intellectuals, occupy the "independent kingdoms," big or small, and take over those places where the advocates of the theory of "many centers," that is, the theory of "no center," are entrenched. In this way, the unhealthy atmosphere, style of work and thinking that exist among intellectuals in concentrated groups can be changed and thus there is the possibility for intellectuals to remold themselves and achieve liberation.

"Workers don't understand education." So say some so-called high-ranking intellectuals. Away with your ugly, bourgeois intellectual airs! There are two kinds of education: bourgeois education and proletarian education. What you "understand" is the pseudo-knowledge of the bourgeoisie. Those who teach science and engineering do not know how to operate or repair machines; those who teach literature do not know how to write essays; those who teach agricultural chemistry do not know how to use fertilizer. Aren't such laughing stocks to be found everywhere? The proletarian educational system under which theory and practice accord with each other can be gradually brought into being only if the proletariat takes a direct part. You are utterly ignorant of this.

"The workers don't know the situation in the schools and the history of the struggle between the two lines." Don't worry, comrades. The workers will get to know them. Compared with those short-sighted intellectuals who see only their small mountain strongholds, the working class stands on a far higher eminence. The workers will not stay in the schools for just a few days; they will keep on working there permanently and always occupy the school front and lead the schools. Everything that exists objectively can be known. The working class will deepen its recognition of the world through its own revolutionary practice and remake the world in its own image.

Workers' propaganda teams should systematically and in a planned way go to universities, middle schools and primary schools, to all areas of the superstructure and to all units in which the struggle-criticism-transformation has not been carried out well. Taking Mao Tse-tung's thought as the guiding principle, they should unite with and help the activists there who are determined to carry the proletarian revolution in education through to the end, unite with the great majority of the masses including those intellectuals who can be remolded and, in the proletarian spirit of thoroughgoing revolution, promote the struggle-criticism-transformation there. This is a great historical mission of the Chinese working class at the present time. In the course of fulfilling this mission, the working class will itself be profoundly steeled in the class struggle and a group of out-standing worker-cadres will emerge, not merely to manage schools but to strengthen every aspect of the state organs and the revolutionary committees at all levels. . . .

Chairman Mao has recently pointed out: **"The struggle-criticism-transformation in a factory, on the whole, goes through the following stages: establishing a revolutionary committee based on the 'three-in-one' combination, mass criticism and repudiation, purifying the class ranks, rectifying the Party organization, simplifying organizational structure, changing irrational rules and regulations and sending people who work in offices to grass-roots levels."**

These words of Chairman Mao's sum up the development of the mass movement during the stage of struggle-criticism-transformation, and clearly point out the road for us to fulfill the task of struggle-criticism-transformation in factories and other enterprises.

The first task is to establish the "three-in-one" revolutionary committee so that leadership in factories and other enterprises is truly in the hands of the proletariat. This is often carried out in combination with the tasks of mass criticism and repudiation and the purifying, by and large, of the class ranks.

. . . In this way, we can do a good job in rectifying the Party organization and can reach the great goal set by Chairman Mao for Party rectification: **"The Party organization should be composed of the advanced elements of the proletariat; it should be a vigorous vanguard organization capable of leading the proletariat and the revolutionary masses in the fight against the class enemy."**

This applies to the movement in industrial and mining enter-prises and, broadly speaking, also to the movement in cultural and educational institutions and in the Party and government organs.

The upsurge in revolution spurs the upsurge in production. Thanks to the efforts of the hundreds of millions of poor and lower-middle peasants, agriculture in our country has produced bumper harvests for a number of years running. Only with a solid socialist position in the countryside has it been possible for the great proletarian cultural revolution to win victory after victory in the cities. We salute the poor and lower-middle peasants, the firm ally of the working class. With the deep-going development of the struggle-criticism-transformation, many new things are coming forth on the industrial front as well. In the course of transformation, a vigorous technical revolution has come into being in many places. The situation is excellent and inspiring. . . .

CHOU EN-LAI*
Premier Chou En-lai's Speech
at Peking Rally of Revolutionary Masses—
September 7, 1968

Comrades, comrade workers, comrade poor and lower-middle peasants, comrade commanders and fighters of the Chinese People's Liberation Army, comrade proletarian revolutionaries, young Red Guard fighters, I extend the militant greetings of the victory of the great proletarian cultural revolution to you! *(The masses shout: Long live Chairman Mao! Long live the all-round victory of the great proletarian cultural revolution!)*

Today Peking is holding a rally here celebrating the establishment of the Revolutionary Committees of the Tibet Autonomous Region and the Sinkiang Uighur Autonomous Region, celebrating the establishment of the revolutionary committees in twenty-nine provinces, municipalities and autonomous regions throughout the country. At this rally, let me first extend

* Chou En-lai, translated in *Peking Review*, No. 37 (September 13, 1968), pp. 6–7.

regards to you and congratulate you on behalf of our great
leader Chairman Mao and his close comrade in arms Vice-
Chairman Lin Piao, the Central Committee of the Chinese Communist Party, the State Council, the Military Commission of the
Party's Central Committee and the Cultural Revolution Group
under the Party's Central Committee! *(Warm applause. The
masses shout: Long live Chairman Mao! A long, long life to
Chairman Mao!)* I also congratulate the people of all nationalities of our country!

We all say that now the whole country is red. Twenty
months have elapsed since the "January Storm" of 1967 when
the Shanghai working class took the initiative to seize power
from the capitalist roaders. Now, revolutionary committees have
been established in our twenty-nine provinces, municipalities
and autonomous regions. Now we can declare that through
repeated struggles during the past twenty months we have
finally smashed the plot of the handful of top Party persons in
authority taking the capitalist road—counter-revolutionary revisionists—renegades, enemy agents and traitors headed by
China's Khrushchev to restore capitalism *(applause)*, and fulfilled the great call issued by our great leader Chairman Mao:
**"Proletarian revolutionaries, unite and seize power from the
handful of Party persons in authority taking the capitalist road!"**
*(Applause. The masses shout: Long live the victory of Chair-
man Mao's proletarian revolutionary line!)* This is a tremendous victory for the great proletarian cultural revolution, a great
victory for the invincible thought of Mao Tse-tung. *(The masses
shout: Long live the invincible thought of Mao Tse-tung!)*

In the meantime, we should firmly bear in mind that apart
from the twenty-nine provinces, municipalities and autonomous
regions, Taiwan Province remains to be liberated. We will
liberate Taiwan without fail. *(Warm applause. The masses
shout: We will liberate Taiwan without fail! We will liberate
Taiwan without fail! We will liberate Taiwan without fail! We
will liberate Taiwan without fail!)*

As you all know, the domestic and foreign enemies will not
take their defeat in China lying down. They are bound to
struggle and to try to stage a counterattack. Therefore, we
should respond to the call of the great leader Chairman Mao
and, under the unified leadership of the proletarian headquar-

ters headed by Chairman Mao and with Vice-Chairman Lin Piao as its deputy leader, unify our understanding, coordinate our steps, and concert our actions. All units should act according to this instruction from our great leader Chairman Mao: **"Struggle-criticism-transformation in a factory, on the whole, goes through the following stages: establishing a three-in-one revolutionary committee; carrying out mass criticism and repudiation; purifying the class ranks; consolidating the Party organization; and simplifying the administrative structure, changing irrational rules and regulations and sending office workers to the workshops."** In all units, that is to say, in such places as enterprises and other undertakings, schools and government offices, the struggle-criticism-transformation should also go through these stages.

In the excellent situation that the whole country is red, we must hold high the great red banner of Mao Tse-tung's thought, be well prepared to meet the new high tide of struggle-criticism-transformation we are now launching, completely discredit and overthrow the handful of top capitalist roaders in the Party and their agents in various places and units. At the same time, under our organizational form of revolutionary great alliance and revolutionary "three-in-one" combination, we should purify the class ranks and uncover the bad elements in all units. It is necessary to continue to criticize and repudiate all reactionary ideas, counter-revolutionary revisionism, reactionary academic authorities and technical authorities, and so on.

It is necessary to simplify the administrative structure in all our units and change all irrational rules and regulations and send those people who are thus spared to grass-roots levels and to production.

Young people should also respond to the call of our great leader Chairman Mao, go to the grass-roots levels, to the masses and to production, settle in the mountainous areas and the countryside, and take part in physical work in factories, mines and villages. *(Applause.)*

Our great leader Chairman Mao recently issued the call that **the working class must exercise leadership in everything.** This is our fundamental principle of Marxism, Leninism, Mao Tse-tung's thought. Our Communist Party is the vanguard of the working class. We should call on the revolutionary people all over the country to accept working-class leadership. So we have begun to organize workers' Mao Tse-tung's thought propaganda teams. Backed by the People's Liberation Army and in coordination with P.L.A. fighters, the propaganda teams have entered colleges and schools to promote the revolutionary great alliance in places where this has not been done. They will combine with the activists among the students, teachers, staff members and workers in colleges, schools and other units, and lead the struggle-criticism-transformation there. It is essential that we should act according to Mao Tse-tung's thought and stand on the side of Chairman Mao's proletarian revolutionary line so as to temper ourselves gradually and continuously into proletarian revolutionaries. We have only one group, that is, the proletarian revolutionary group; we have only one thought, that is, Mao Tse-tung's thought; we have only one line, that is, Chairman Mao's proletarian revolutionary line. *(Applause.)*

We shall be able to carry out our revolution in education well by conducting struggle-criticism-transformation in this way. We should send Mao Tse-tung's thought propaganda teams of the working class and Liberation Army fighters not only to the schools, but to enterprises, undertakings and government offices and all other places where the revolutionary great alliance and revolutionary "three-in-one" combination have not been brought about successfully or the tasks of struggle-criticism-transformation have not been carried out well. The propaganda teams and Liberation men should help people there and lead them. *(Applause.)* Only in this way can we really win the all-round victory in the great proletarian cultural revolution.

Now, internationally, the enemy rots with each passing day while for us things are daily getting better. It is very clear that the imperialist camp headed by U.S. imperialists is disintegrating and is beset with internal and external difficulties; the revisionist countries with the Soviet revisionist renegade clique as their center are distrusting each other and are at mutual strife. Hence the reactionaries of all countries who are following U.S. imperialism and Soviet revisionism are also finding it hard to carry on. We can say with certainty that the old world is going to collapse. *(Applause.)* It is also certain that our proletarian socialist revolution is advancing to worldwide victory. However, before the advent of victory, the enemies throughout the world will surely put up last-ditch struggles and launch counterattacks. Therefore, our present great proletarian cultural revolution is a most extensive, thoroughgoing and all-round political and military mobilization. Should enemies from abroad dare to invade China, we will, in response to the call of our great leader Chairman Mao, wipe them out resolutely, thoroughly, wholly and completely! (*Applause. The masses shout: Down with U.S. imperialism! Down with modern revisionism with the Soviet revisionist leading clique as its center! Down with the reactionaries of all countries! We will liberate Taiwan without fail!*)

★   ★   ★   ★   ★

8. REBUILDING THE PARTY

On March 3, 1969, Russian and Chinese troops clashed in a fire-fight on remote Chenpao Island in the middle of the Ussuri River which marks the boundary between China's northeast provinces and the Soviet far east. Thirty-one Russian soldiers were reported by Moscow to have been killed, while the number of Chinese casualties was never announced. Twelve days later, a battle fought on regimental scale occurred in the same area. Tanks, artillery fire, and aircraft accounted for casualties on both sides, which numbered in the hundreds. It was against this background that the Ninth Congress of the Chinese Communist Party opened in Peking on April 1, 1969.

Proclaimed as the Congress of Unity and Victory, the Party proceedings continued throughout the month of April as the delegates elected a new Central Committee of the Chinese Communist Party and adopted a new Party constitution. Mao Tsetung was elected Chairman of the Central Committee, and Lin Piao, who was elected as Deputy Chairman, was also written into the Party constitution as Chairman Mao's "close comrade in arms and successor." Mao, Lin, Chou En-lai, Ch'en Po-ta and K'ang Sheng were named as members of the Standing Committee of the Political Bureau of the Central Committee. But events were to prove that the new leadership did not represent a united group. Within two and a half years, only Mao and Chou remained as national leaders.

The period from the Ninth Party Congress to the fall of 1971 was a period of struggle among the top leaders over strategy, policy, and line for the reconstituted Party. Fought out at the top, this struggle no longer included the participation of the masses. Ch'en Po-ta was dropped from the top leadership in 1970 and disappeared from public view. K'ang Sheng, for either reasons of health or political causes, disappeared from public life during the same period.

The final and most dramatic page of this last struggle among the leaders of the Cultural Revolution was not officially turned until July 28, 1972. On that date, the Chinese embassy in Algeria issued to the world a cryptic statement stating that Lin Piao had died in a plane crash in Outer Mongolia while fleeing the country after an attempt to assassinate Chairman Mao. This official statement on the "Lin Piao Affair," which we include in our selections, is perhaps the most bizarre and puzzling of any document connected with the Cultural Revolution, and leaves much that is unanswered. Perhaps the most significant paragraph of the statement concerns Lin's opposition to "the revolutionary line of Mao Tse-tung and to the revolutionary foreign policy worked out by him, especially after the Ninth Party Congress." We feel that French journalist Robert Guillain's article from *Le Monde* covering the fall of Lin Piao comes as close to the truth of this dramatic affair as may be possible at this time.

From the evidence available, it would appear that Lin opposed the strategy of Mao and Chou to seek a détente with the United States and elevate the Soviet Union to the position of China's principal enemy. On the domestic front, Lin may have opposed the rapid rehabilitation of thousands of Party cadres who had been under attack during the Cultural Revolution, an approach shared by Ch'en Po-ta and other leftists. Mao and Chou evidently stood for a return to normalcy so that the country could proceed with economic development and take its place in the international system. Differences on such major policies could not be reconciled; victory of one line or the other was inevitable. Overthrown with Lin Piao were Huang Yung-sheng, the Chief of Staff of the army, and other top military leaders in the air force and navy. Thus ended the Cultural Revolution, as China turned outward to take her place in the United Nations; China had become a great nation whose revolutionary legitimacy could no longer be denied.

We think it is fitting that we should end this section on the Cultural Revolution with an assessment of the historic significance of this long political movement by Edgar Snow, whose own life was intimately connected with the history of the Chinese Revolution. The publication of a picture of Mao Tse-tung and Edgar Snow on the front page of the *People's Daily* on December 26, 1970, symbolized the new Maoist world strategy. China's subsequent turn toward the United States seems to have led to the final conflict among the leaders who had carried China through the Cultural Revolution. Edgar Snow died in Switzerland on the eve of President Nixon's trip to the People's Republic of China. By Snow's side at the time of his death were a team of Chinese doctors who had been sent by Peking to ease his last days. Snow had been one of the first to prophesy the victory of the Chinese Communists; his death was the symbol of the end of an era.

★　★　★

CHINESE EMBASSY (ALGIERS)*
Text of Chinese Statement on Lin Piao

> *ALGIERS, July 28, 1972 (Reuters)—Following is the text of a statement issued by the Chinese Embassy here today in response to questions about the fate of former Defense Minister Lin Piao:*

Lin Piao died on September 12, 1971. The Lin Piao affair is a reflection of the war between two lines which had been under way inside the party for a long time.

Lin Piao repeatedly committed errors and Mao Tse-tung had waged many struggles against him.

Sometimes Lin Piao was obliged to quell his arrogance and thus was able to accomplish some useful work.

But he was not able to give up his underhand nature and during the Great Proletarian Cultural Revolution he appeared to support the thought of Mao Tse-tung and made propaganda in favor of this thought. He was thus able to hoodwink the masses to become in their eyes the successor of President Mao Tse-tung.

But he was a double-faced man who was in reality opposed to the revolutionary line of Mao Tse-tung and to the revolu-

* *The New York Times* (July 29, 1972).

tionary foreign policy worked out by him, especially after the Ninth Party Congress.

He undertook antiparty activities in a planned, premeditated way with a well-determined program with the aim of taking over power, usurping the leadership of the party, the Government and the army.

Mao Tse-tung unmasked his plot and blocked his maneuver. Mao Tse-tung made efforts to recover him. But Lin Piao did not change his perverse nature one iota.

He attempted a coup d'état and tried to assassinate Mao Tse-tung.

After his plot was foiled, he fled on September 12 toward the Soviet Union on a plane which crashed in the People's Republic of Mongolia.

ROBERT GUILLAIN*
The Fall of Lin Piao:
Final Chapter of a Power Struggle

Tokyo

If the best-informed Chinese and foreign sources are to be credited, Lin Piao's dramatic demise was only the latest act in a leadership struggle that was being fought out well before either the September 1971 crisis or the conspiracy which is given as the immediate cause of his downfall.

Light is at last being shed on this conflict, which, in contrast to the Cultural Revolution of which it is a sequel, took place in the shadows, hidden from the public by the high red walls sheltering the regime's great men. It was a drama in which the masses were in no way called on to take part, and it thus had

* Robert Guillain, "The Fall of Lin Piao," translated in the *Manchester Guardian* (August 5, 1972).

no effect on a people relieved by the calm following the storm, and glad to get working again.

It began at the party's Ninth Congress, called to put an end to the Cultural Revolution: a congress which was to be of national unity, as Mao pointed out, unity forged even in the central committee after four years of strife.

Lin Piao, as Defense Minister with control of the army, was officially named Mao's successor. Before and during the crisis the Minister had promised Mao the support of the armed forces. The military secured a quarter of the seats in the new central committee, and the congress seemed to be an expression of the army's dominance. It controlled the county committees it had set up, and the Communist Party, theoretically rehabilitated and rebuilt at the summit, remained in eclipse in the provinces.

It soon became clear that the congress had been called prematurely and that unity was no more than an illusion. What really happened was that men still divided by profound disagreements in the wake of the Cultural Revolution were yoked to the same tasks: there were the believers in continuous revolution alongside those who favored a return to order, military men and civilians, supporters of Lin Piao, and backers of Premier Chou En-lai. Clumsy accommodations merely papered over the growing awareness of a latent conflict.

The undercurrent began to make itself felt in the ensuing months. The central committee remained powerless to push ahead with the required political reconstruction, and there was tension between the majority in favor of Lin Piao, including some extreme Leftist elements, and the moderates, composed mainly of civilians and some army men. But the presence of military men in moderate ranks made the struggle far more complex than a straight army-party confrontation.

In the background were President Nixon's policy declarations of July and November 1969 on disengagement in Asia, and the intensification of the Sino-Soviet dispute as reflected in the bloody clashes on the Ussuri. These factors took the controversy into the foreign policy field.

There was no agreement there either, and this paralyzing discord perpetuated the dangerous situation of having "to fight on two fronts"—against the United States and the Soviet Union—

which remained, through inability to reach a decision, China's official policy.

A second plenary session of the central committee was eventually called in September 1970. The hope was for a revised, corrected edition of the Ninth Congress, with some agreement on certain points. But this gathering fared no better than the earlier one. Opposition to Lin Piao was gaining ground. The moderates, who had won some of the Leftists over to their cause, considered that priority should be given to reconstitution of the party committees in the provinces, and definition of their roles in relation to the army-controlled revolutionary committees.

But, unable to reach agreement, the central committee took no decision. Lin Piao's supporters, on the other hand, were determined to call a new National Assembly. Instead of the regular procedure, members were to be elected by "activists committees," organizations formed for the propagation of Mao's thought and inspired by and loyal to Lin Piao.

The Defense Minister thus hoped to rebuild State institutions where he held a strong hand, before those of the party, whose resurgence worried him. The second plenary session in September 1970 had at least one positive result: it gave shape and substance to the various positions and polarized their advocates around two men, Lin Piao and Chou En-lai. It certainly clarified the two rival conceptions on how the Chinese revolution should continue to be conducted.

As Lin Piao saw it, since the Communist Party had been dismantled, there was no point in reconstructing it in its own image, nor in proceeding too quickly. He felt the role of the army as interim replacement of the party should be prolonged, or even perpetuated, since the army, ubiquitous with its multiple cells, had become the guarantor of revolutionary purity. Abroad, Lin Piao called for continuation of militant and revolutionary diplomacy, spreading the flame of Maoism and carrying the class struggle into the international arena.

Chou En-lai sought a return to revolutionary orthodoxy by restoring the party to its leading role, so as to restore stability in a country where the economy required a new impetus and some capacity for government had to be revived. Beyond China's borders he envisaged a more traditional diplomacy, but

a diplomacy that was just as revolutionary in his eyes in that its
goal was the creation of a united front against the twin hegemony of Soviet and American imperialism.

In rather unclear circumstances—the history of this crisis still
awaits complete and coherent chronicling—Lin Piao was finally
checkmated in December 1970, doubtless in the political bureau, and probably following an unfavorable ruling from Mao.
Without making any public ado, the political bureau deferred
calling up the National Assembly and gave priority to the task
of rebuilding the party. The provincial committees thus finally
came into existence. It was not the army that lost the day, however, since soldiers headed most of these committees, which
were inaugurated between December 1970 and August 1971.

Nonetheless Chou En-lai had control of the political bureau,
and this body took a number of decisions which demonstrated
that it had adopted both his domestic programs and, marking a
major shift, his foreign policies. The struggle on two fronts was
to be brought to an end, and there was to be an attempt to
improve relations with the United States so that China would
be in a better position to face intense Soviet pressure on the
northern frontier.

Edgar Snow's interview with Mao Tse-tung on December 18
made it clear that the transformation had been made: Mao was
awaiting President Nixon's visit to Peking. It could safely be
said that Chou En-lai "took power" in December 1970. Nonetheless, Lin Piao, the regime's number two man, retained his
position. Was he going to come around to the new policy?

It remains to be clarified what attitude he adopted to the
thaw in Sino-American relations—the visit of the table tennis
players, the preparations for the secret Kissinger visit, all the
possible motives which drove him to rebel. Was it this drift that
impelled him to engage in "illicit relations with a foreign
power," clearly the Soviet Union, as was said after his fall?

The signs of ill-disguised strife remained. Lin Piao still had
control of the information media. There were pictures and editorials eulogizing him and his (no longer) close relations with
Mao Tse-tung. And on July 1 there appeared an article, inspired
by the Defense Minister, containing a veiled attack on Chou
En-lai. Lin's right-hand man, army Chief of Staff Huang Yung-

sheng, made a number of violent attacks on the United States, including one when Henry Kissinger was actually in China.

There was one very striking sign: the 50th anniversary of the party passed without celebration, even though the reconstruction of its country-wide network was nearing completion. Events were leading rapidly to the tragic September finale.

In Peking it is thought that matters came to a head when Lin Piao and his supporters, recognizing that they were now in the minority, called for a new meeting of the central committee in the vain hope of regaining the majority they so briefly enjoyed in the spring of 1969. For the moment, there is no way to confirm the details or the official theory of a plot against Mao Tsetung. But it does seem that Lin took flight in the ill-fated Trident, most probably with his wife, his son, the army Chief of Staff, and a number of other senior officers, just a few hours after a meeting of the nation's top leaders.

If, as is now commonly believed, this was a central committee meeting, it seems clear that at its close Lin was ousted and outlawed.

EDGAR SNOW*
Essence of the Cultural Revolution

I have referred to Chairman Mao's preoccupation with the problem of rebuilding the Party and the state superstructure. Why should they need rebuilding? That short question requires long answers, touched upon later, but here it may be useful to suggest a few reasons for the Great Proletarian Cultural Revolution, which had the effect of temporarily dissolving the Chinese Communist Party, if not the government itself.

The extensive purge began in mid-1966, led by Mao, and

* Edgar Snow, taken from *The Long Revolution* (New York: Random House, 1972; Vintage paperback), pp. 13–22.

lasted till April, 1969, when the Ninth Party Congress elected a new Central Committee composed of a nucleus of surviving protoplasm reinforced by "new blood." In November, 1970, Chou En-lai told me that something like 95 percent of the former Party members* had by then been reinstated. Reinstated, but not necessarily reassigned; many awaited "liberation" following completion of "struggle-criticism-transformation," the three-stage formula for redemption.

One of Mao's aims was to "simplify the administrative structure" and "eliminate duplication." At provincial and urban centers I found the reductions drastic enough, but in the capital the skeletonizing of the central government superstructure was especially severe. Early in 1971 Premier Chou told me that he was assisted by only two vice-premiers, for example, whereas formerly there were seven.

"In the past there were ninety departments directly under the central government," he said. "Now there will be only twenty-six. They are all run at present by revolutionary committees, and in each committee the Party nucleus is the core of the leadership. Formerly there were more than 60,000 administrative personnel in the central government. Now it is about 10,000.". . .

But such reforms in the superstructure were only one aspect of the national *bouleversement*. Mao's basic aim was no less than to proletarianize Party thinking and, beyond that, to push the proletariat really to take power for themselves, and in the process to create a new culture free of domination by the feudal and bourgeois heritage.

It was for no less than that end that Mao Tse-tung deliberately risked wrecking the Party which he, more than anyone else, had built. At the start Mao's intention was to remove "only a handful" from power. In its sweeping reach the hand gathered in many senior veteran leaders and some of Mao's oldest comrades. Above all, they included Liu Shao-ch'i, who in 1959 had succeeded Mao as titular head of state. . . .

It was Liu Shao-ch'i and his allies in the Central Committee who ran the superstructure, the labor unions, the Party schools,

---

* Early in 1966 Party members were said to number about twenty million and 80 percent of them were post-1949 recruits.

the Communist Youth Leagues, the millions of Party cadres and bureaucrats, all in Mao's name. Probably most cadres considered themselves loyal Maoists. It seemed that Liu and his like-minded comrades were, especially after the economic crisis of 1959-61, tolerating the Mao cult in theory and slighting Mao Thought in performance. They tended to put economics before man, encourage effort by material incentives first and zeal second, push production without class struggle, boost technology by relying on "experts," put economics in command of politics to serve technology, and favor the city over the countryside. They wanted expansion of state credit (and state debt) rather than Great Leaps Forward and ideological faith in building capital by hard collective labor.

Such were the allegations brought forth by the cultural revolution.

The crisis between Mao and Liu had been building up even before the clash over the choice of Lin Piao to replace P'eng Teh-huai, in 1959. That was Mao's first overt move in a struggle he foresaw with the growingly powerful urban-based bureaucracy headed by Liu. Lin Piao was Mao's most faithful army disciple, and vice-chairman of the Party Military Affairs Commission, of which Mao had retained chairmanship ever since 1935. Though Liu might be head of state and control the nonmilitary cadres, even while Mao remained Party chairman, the People's Liberation Army was the trump card in any showdown. With Lin Piao in command that card seemed secure in Mao's hand. But Mao let events determine the outcome, and apparently did not finally give up hope of winning Liu around to initiate the purge of his own followers until much later than many supposed.

"When did you finally decide that Liu had to go?" I asked him during our conversation in December of 1970.

He replied that the moment of decision came in January, 1965. At that time he had put before the Politburo a program for the coming cultural revolution. That program was an outgrowth of the Socialist Education Movement, which was carried out first of all in the army under Lin Piao's direction, spread into the rural communes, and then had faltered in the cities. The first point of the Socialist Education program had specifically denounced and demanded the removal of "those in the Party in authority who are taking the capitalist road." Now it was to be the first point of the new drive, the cultural revolution. Liu had strenuously opposed that first point right at the meeting, said Mao. . . .

"Did Liu Shao-ch'i oppose the sixteen-point decision?" I asked.

He was very ambiguous about it at the plenary session, Mao said, but actually was dead against it. By that time he (Mao) had already put up his *ta tzu-pao*, or big-character poster. Liu was thrown into consternation.

"That was your poster, 'Bombard the Headquarters'? And Liu knew that *he* was Headquarters?"

Yes, at that time the power of the Party, the power over propaganda work, the power of the provincial and local Party committees, power even over the Peking Party Committee, was out of Mao's control. That was why he had said (to me, in January, 1965) that there was no "worship of the individual"—personality cult—to speak of, as yet, but that there was need for it.

Mao frankly began to invoke his enormous personal prestige and popularity, using it as a major weapon in his struggle to recover full authority over the orientation of revolutionary power.

Now there was, in 1970, no such need, and the "cult" would be *cooled down*, he said. His justification was the need to inspire the whole nation with the élan and the ideals of the Yenan period (1937–47), when Mao had written his principal works, and when his leadership had prepared revolutionary followers for final victory.

Now it must be "politics in command"—Mao's teachings—all the way; there was no room for heterodoxy and a Party split if the imperiled nation was to survive the twin threats of war with United States imperialism and/or Soviet "social imperialism." That meant self-reliance on "people's war" strategy and tactics. It meant more decentralization; spurring the masses to initiative and innovation; sending city people to learn from the peasants, and vice versa; priority for the needs of the peasants, 70 to 80 percent of the people; capital created by labor and collectively invested by the peasants themselves; and expunging all remaining bourgeois influences under mentorship of the army, "the great school of the people."

In a word, Mao demanded that the proletarian successors to power reenact the revolutionary life experience of his own generation, and reach its logical conclusions.

Thus the first issue was posed by Mao's conviction that the Party was following the revisionist (Soviet) road to capitalism —creating a new class, an elite of bureaucratic power wielders, a mandarinate of cadres divorced from labor and the people. There was a closely linked issue. That was posed by Liu's search—supported by P'eng Chen and others, according to Chairman Mao's comments to me—for a compromise in the Sino-Soviet impasse.

By 1965 the United States' bombing attacks on Vietnam, close upon China's border, threatened China with invasion. Liu wanted to send a Chinese delegation to the Soviet Twenty-third Party Congress, to reactivate the Sino-Soviet alliance. Mao resolutely refused to be drawn into a position of dependence, as in Korea, and a possible double cross. Instead, he insisted upon a posture of complete self-reliance on a people's war of defense— while continuing to build the Bomb—and heavy support for, but not intervention in, Vietnam. . . .

There were many subissues and specific policies in contradiction but the above two were fundamental. Now it was said that Liu and Mao had always represented "two lines" since the beginning, when both became Communists in 1921. "Two lines" there no doubt were. In Mao's own idiom it was also a case of "nonantagonistic contradictions [gradually] becoming antagonistic" over the forty-five years during which the Party had held both of them. Personal power struggle? Subjective factors cannot be entirely separated from objective political reality, but there could be little doubt that the Mao-Liu struggle was mainly one of irreconcilable differences over means and ends affecting the fate of the great Chinese revolution itself—including, of course, the role of the personality cult.

Much has been written about the events which followed the August, 1966, decisions: the dissolution of the Party committees and para-Party organizations such as the Young Communists and the labor unions, the closing of schools (many had been closed earlier) and release of millions of non-Party youths to form Red Guard detachments and engage in overthrowing the Party elite, the free-for-all struggle for power for new leaders, and the ultimate intervention of the armed forces. In this prefatory comment it is enough to note that Mao's victory—with the help of the army—was so complete that Vice-Chairman and Defense Minister Lin Piao was able to state, at the Ninth Party Congress in 1969 (which named him Mao's constitutional successor), that "whoever opposes Chairman Mao Tse-tung's Thought, at any time or under any circumstances, will be condemned and punished by the whole Party and the whole country."

Mao's Thought had by 1970 permeated the whole nation with these aims: to speed up the erasure of differences between town and countryside; to move toward closer equalization of the material and cultural standards and opportunities of the worker, the peasant, the soldier, the cadre, and the technician-expert; to integrate shop and classroom work in everyone's education and life experience; to smash all bourgeois thought and especially its remnants among intellectuals and officials; to proletarianize higher learning by integrating students and workers and combining labor practice with classroom theory; to bring public health and medical services to the rural masses; to train everyone to bear arms and learn from the army; to create a one-class generation of many-sided, well-educated youths inspired by ideals of service to the people, at home and abroad, contemptuous of personal wealth, and dedicated to a "world outlook" anticipating the final liberation of man from hunger, greed, ignorance, war, and capitalism.

All that? Yes, and much more. I merely paraphrase words heard not just from officials and Maoist activists* but from all those "tempered" by Mao Thought when pinned down to define what the cultural revolution was and is all about.

Ah, but the road is long and the road is hard, and must be covered in stages. There will be more cultural revolutions to come. When eating a meal, as Mao says, one takes it mouthful by mouthful—and there must be time to savor each morsel before attacking the next. . . .

---

* An "activist" is one recognized by his group as one who not only studies and knows the Thought of Mao but "applies it in a living way."

III. China in the World

⋙ In 1966 China plunged into the Cultural Revolution and withdrew from active participation in world affairs. In 1972 China, already a member of the United Nations, received visits from President Nixon of the United States and Premier Tanaka of Japan. In 1966 the conventional American conception of China was that of a country gone mad. In 1972 hard-line American columnists returned from China with lyric descriptions of China's peace and progress, which if written by other hands a few years earlier would have been dismissed as the expected ravings of revolutionary leftists. Nixon's visit to Peking in February was hailed as a step forward to a generation of peace, yet only a little more than a month later, savage fighting erupted all over Indochina. Was it not to stop "Chinese expansionism" that the Vietnam War was all about, as Dean Rusk never tired of saying? In the flood of newspaper articles and books written on China that appeared after the announcement in July 1971 of Nixon's visit to Peking, the only explanation offered for what had changed in China was that somehow "moderates" had come to power. China, so it seemed, had recovered from its convulsions and was now ready to become a responsible member of the international community.

How one country relates to other countries is not an easy matter to understand. In America, some political scientists, following balance-of-power theories, have tried to express great-power relationships in complex mathematical terms. Others, adhering to those ideas of "Communist expansionism" that have governed U.S. foreign policy since 1945, have tried to show how the internal power politics of Communist countries have led to an ebb or a flow of those drives toward expansionism. Most established writers on the subject of foreign affairs have presumed that America's own role has always been reactive, responding to Communist challenges and always only for the purpose of restoring a balance of power. Radical writers have suggested that since 1945 it has been America itself which has been expansionistic and imperialistic. Meanwhile, as the writing on foreign affairs (particularly Vietnam) has also proliferated, the clouds of secrecy around the policies and operations of foreign policy in Washington have become thicker. The American public has been told little more than that Nixon's visits to Peking and Moscow were to inaugurate a generation of peace, and that the war in Vietnam was being fought in the interests of peace with honor.

In the last years, there also has been a proliferation of writing on foreign affairs in China, much of which has been translated into English. While the Marxist-Leninist mode of thinking is strange to most Americans, the ideas presented are clear and straightforward. They are no different from those expressed in the many and widely praised interviews Premier Chou En-lai has granted various foreign visitors. Many of the articles on foreign affairs were written by groups of people and therefore appear under allegorical names. The *People's Daily*, which consists of six pages, regularly devotes two full pages to foreign affairs. There is little difference to be discerned between official Chinese governmental statements and articles written by collectives of ordinary people. We know that the Chinese people are well informed on foreign matters, notably through a digest of the world press (*News for Reference*) which is widely circulated among them. There are differences of opinion among the people. But the articles which are published in the official press do reflect the line of thinking dominant at the time. While most Americans would ascribe this to an absence of a free press, another reason is the conviction of the Chinese that foreign policy is so sensitive a matter that the line put forth must be clear and consistent so that China's friends and enemies know precisely where she stands.

The Chinese, like Marxists generally, believe in world history. They believe that the many disparate events that characterize the day-to-day reality of world affairs are manifestations of a fundamental historical process which links the entire world into an interconnected whole. They hold that this process can be rationally analyzed, and long-range trends in power relationships inferred therefrom. Furthermore, they believe that neither harmony nor balance but struggle is the basic condition of mankind. In that struggle there always is a revolutionary left, a reactionary right, and a "center" which equivocates between the two. They see themselves as part of the revolutionary left, but maintain that successful struggle requires that enemies and allies be discerned with care, for they change with time and circumstances. They call this "world view," and Americans might see it as a kind of systems analysis on a global scale with action implications for one's own side.

The directions of Chinese foreign policy can be understood in conventional terms of relations with other countries and basic interests and commitments. But without an analysis of the Chinese "world view," that understanding would be incomplete and defective. It is this world view which is widely discussed, argued about, lectured on throughout China, and so forms a link between people and government. As in most other countries, the intricacies of specific relations to specific countries are not generally known, nor are the full nature and extent of China's commitments. The Chinese believe that there must be a consonance between commitments, policies, and world view, but since the world is constantly changing, so does each of these. Therefore unremitting work and struggle are required to go from changing reality up to world view and from a suitably readjusted world view back down to action.

We shall therefore analyze China's foreign policy for the period 1966 to 1972 in terms of two broad categories: world view and commitments.

The most dramatic change in the Chinese world view during the period 1966 to 1972 took place in 1966, just before the eruption of the Cultural Revolution. This can be pinpointed with some accuracy, for it was in March of 1966 that the Chinese Communist Party sent its last letter to its erstwhile fraternal Soviet Party, refusing the invitation to attend the Twenty-third Soviet Party Congress (see Volume III, p. 500). From that time on, all party-to-party relations between China and the Soviet Union were broken. No matter how bitter the polemics had been till then, the fact that they were carried on between the two parties implied that somehow the special relationship between the two countries still prevailed. Up to that time, the

Chinese world view held that the world was divided into two great camps, the imperialist and the socialist, with neutrals or "intermediate zones" in between. The Soviet Union, as the Chinese saw it, had committed arch betrayal of the socialist camp by putting its national interests ahead of those of the camp as a whole, and specifically by dealing with the United States in such a manner as to infringe on the interests of other socialist countries, notably China and North Vietnam. The thrust of the Chinese party-to-party polemics till March 1966 was to force the Soviet Union to recommit itself to the entire socialist camp and to demonstrate such a return to the fold by ceasing its evolving special relationship to the United States. But after March 1966 the Chinese not only concluded that the Soviet Union was irreparably "revisionist" and "bourgeois," but abandoned the whole notion of a socialist camp.

As early as the mid-fifties, the Chinese had insisted on the principle of noninterference in each other's internal affairs as the indispensable basis for relations between socialist countries and parties. National sovereignty and integrity could not be violated even for the most urgent requisites of international solidarity or collective defense. Both before and after 1966, the Chinese have repeatedly accused the Soviets of interference in their internal affairs. After March 1966 the Chinese replaced the concept of a socialist camp with one of individual socialist countries that varied in degrees of revisionism. For people outside of China, one of the most perplexing aspects of this changing Chinese world view was their adulation of tiny Albania, on the shores of the Adriatic Sea six thousand miles from China. Virtually the only country which was eulogized in the Chinese press during the Cultural Revolution was Albania. Ever since Albania's final break with the Soviet Union in 1961, China has been her main source of economic supply. But for China, Albania's real meaning was symbolic. Albania was a proud, independent, and rigorously socialist country which defied the Soviet Union and its East European allies while at the same time remaining aloof towards Greece, Yugoslavia, and Italy, its direct neighbors. The Albanian view of the Soviet Union was widely propagated in China and obviously coincided with the changing Chinese view of the Soviet Union. The Soviet Union was portrayed as a rapacious, expansionist, imperialist power no different from the United States.

While the Chinese view of the Soviet Union has changed radically from the days of fraternal friendship and alliance in the 1950's, their view of the United States remained unchanged, and despite President Nixon's visit, did not change thereafter. For the Chinese, the United States remains an imperialist power. As Mao Tse-tung put it to Anna Louise Strong, the American journalist who spent the last years of her long and active life in China, in her August 1946 interview with him: "Now the United States controls more territory in the Pacific than Britain's entire past sphere of power; it controls Japan, Kuomintang-dominated China, half of Korea, and the Southern Pacific; it has long since controlled Central and South America; and now it even aspires to control all of Great Britain and Western Europe." By imperialism, the Chinese mean empire-building by a big country. From 1969 they have added the Soviet Union to the United States as a second imperialist power. While they denounce French and British neocolonialism, Indian expansionism, and Japanese militarism, only the United States and the Soviet Union are regarded as imperialist. But a significant nuance has come into the Chinese view of American imperialism, namely that in contrast to the "rising" imperialism of the Soviet Union, the imperialism of America is "waning." In some ways, this conception of a waning American imperialism is an outgrowth of Mao's view of America as a "paper tiger," ferocious in the short run but eventually doomed to decline.

In the mid-fifties, both Chinese and Russians shared a common world view which held that the fundamental struggle in the world was between the rising forces of socialism and the declining forces of capitalism. The Russian Revolution had demonstrated that a backward, semifeudal country could skip over a capitalist stage and enter directly into socialism. American imperialism as the highest and last stage of world capitalism was making frantic efforts to thwart the rise of revolutionary forces in the poor countries and to prevent the inevitable contradictions of the economy from erupting in the advanced countries. It therefore naturally sought recourse to war. But the socialist camp was the world's greatest bastion of peace, and the might of its leader, the Soviet Union, was the main deterrent force against the aggressive designs of American imperialism.

The Chinese now hold that a revisionism unchecked by "uninterrupted revolution," such as the Chinese themselves experienced in their Cultural Revolution, has turned the world's first socialist country, the Soviet Union, into an imperialist power with exactly those attributes which the Russians themselves ascribe to the United States. If American imperialism is a constant source of war, so is Soviet "social imperialism."

In the early seventies, no slogan relating to the trends of world history was so widely propagated by the Chinese as that "countries want independence, nations want liberation, peoples want revolution." The Chinese regard countries, nations, and peoples as the real social units of world politics, and independence, liberation, and revolution as the real motive forces of their struggles. They take no issue with the fundamental Marxist theoretical notion that class struggles between property-holding and propertyless classes remain the motor force of human history as it moves from lower stages, feudalism, through higher stages, capitalism and socialism, and finally to communism. But theory is too abstract and reality too complex to allow for a mechanical extrapolation from theory to practice and fact. They believe that countries defined by boundaries and characterized by sovereignty are real and inviolable historical entities. Imperialism is a violation of sovereignty and the struggle against imperialism is thus one for independence. They often cite America's own war of independence against Britain as an illustration of this principle. Their support of Pakistan against India can be explained in practical foreign policy terms, but their extreme hostility to the secession of East Pakistan reflects their commitment to the principle of inviolable national sovereignty.

The word "nation" poses problems of understanding for many Americans, but in most other countries it has connotations of ethnicity and race. The Chinese word *min-tsu*, which they render as "nation," means an ethnic group with definable cultural, historical, and linguistic characteristics. As a slogan, "nations want liberation" goes back to the late 1950's when "national liberation movements" were arising in different parts of the world. In practical terms, the Chinese give their support to the national liberation movements of the peoples of Indochina, the Palestinians, and the peoples of Southern Africa. They do not regard the struggle of black people in the United States as a national liberation movement, but rather as a revolutionary movement of the people. National liberation movements occur when nations—like the Vietnamese, the Palestinians, or the Angolans—seek to shake off alien colonial rule. The Chinese are not explicit as to why one ethnic group is a nation that seeks liberation whereas others are not. Why should not the Bengalis be considered a nation that sought liberation from West Pakistani colonialism? Race and nationality are obviously sensitive problems everywhere in the world, China included. The Chinese attitude appears to be that there are, in general, powerful national liberation movements in the world, but that for practical reasons, they have chosen to support only certain ones.

No two words are more widely used in China than "people" and "revolution." By "people," the Chinese mean the vast majority but not all the individual human beings that make up a nation or a country. How the Chinese now understand revolution has been determined by their own Cultural Revolution. Their view appears to be that in every society people separate out into those who have power and those who do not, that the natural tendency of power-holders (the state or the superstructure in Marxist terms) is to become alienated from the people, and that currents of revolution invariably arise against such arbitrary authoritarian power. They believe that their Cultural Revolution was such a revolution, as was the "French Revolution" of May–June 1968. They see a world-wide revolutionary process which erupts here and there, such as the Polish workers' strike in Gdansk, the black power and antiwar movements in the United States, the student rebellions in Japan, and many other instances which are always reported in the Chinese press.

The Chinese thus see the world as made up of many countries, nations, and peoples sandwiched in between the two superpowers, the United States and the Soviet Union. They see the Russians and the Americans at times colluding with each other to extend their respective imperial domains and at other times contesting with each other for supremacy. Seeing the rise of a Soviet navy alongside an already powerful American navy, they make analogies with the situation before 1914, in which Britain and Germany were competing for imperial hegemony, with Germany a rising naval power challenging Britain, the established naval power.

In the mid-fifties, Mao Tse-tung spoke of an "intermediate zone" which lay between the two camps. In the mid-sixties, Mao expanded that notion into two intermediate zones. The first consists of the poor countries of Asia, Africa, and Latin America, and the second of the advanced countries of Western Europe and North America. Subsequently the Chinese have further evolved the concept of intermediate zones to include all countries, nations, and peoples of the world except the United States and the Soviet Union. As an advanced country, Japan is now included in the second intermediate zone, as well as the advanced countries of Eastern Europe. What the Chinese call the first intermediate zone is what we call the Third World. The Chinese situate themselves in the first intermediate zone, but as a rapidly developing country, also see themselves as falling into the second intermediate zone.

Just as ruling classes will always extend their power unless checked, so the Chinese hold that the American and Russian empires will extend their dominions unless checked by the forces of independence, liberation, and revolution. In this global picture, the Chinese see themselves as a prime target on the part of both imperialisms, and therefore in order to escape isolation, they must seek "friends," as it is put in the selection "Unite the People, Defeat the Enemy" (p. 425), among the forces fighting for independence, liberation, and revolution. It is this view of the world which explains why the Chinese see no contradiction in cultivating ties with a country like Iran, whose regime is the target of an active revolutionary movement, and at the same time supporting the Indochinese peoples and the Palestinians. Iran is a country seeking economic and political independence both from the Soviet Union and from U.S.-dominated international oil interests. The Chinese hailed the "French Revolution" of 1968 which was directed against the government of Charles de Gaulle, but at the same time maintained the most cordial of relations with De Gaulle, who had asserted France's independence from American domination. Mao has always taught that in struggle one must distinguish the principal from the secondary contradictions, a contradiction being a major struggle for power between rulers and ruled. For them, now, the principal contradiction in the world is that between the two imperialisms and everything else in the world.

That this world view has caused them difficulties is clear from the case of Bangladesh. Pakistan is a "friend" because it extricated itself from American influence yet remained independent from Russia. That it refused to join America's earlier policy of hostile encirclement of China and instead moved close to China was due to Pakistan's and China's common enmity towards India. But objectively, in Chinese eyes, Pakistan's actions were a blow against imperialism. When Indian troops invaded East Pakistan in support of what many in the world considered a true national liberation movement, the Chinese held this to be an instance of Indian expansionism which served mainly to introduce Russian imperialist power into East Bengal.

To end this brief overview of the Chinese world view, it must be pointed out that Mao Tse-tung also argues that one must make distinctions between "who is the principal enemy, who is the secondary enemy and who are temporary allies and who are indirect allies" (see p. 427). China now sees herself as having two main enemies, the United States and the Soviet Union, but Mao's teachings imply that at any given time successful struggle against them can only be waged if one alone is a principal enemy and the other, temporarily, recedes to second place. In 1966 the Chinese were convinced that both the United States and the Soviet Union had become mortal enemies of China; it was not practical to conclude that one and not the other was the principal enemy. When in the spring of 1966, some leaders in China suggested a patching up of the quarrel with the Soviet Union in the interests of "joint action" to support Vietnam, the Chinese agreed to support Vietnam (for example, by transporting Soviet war matériel across Chinese territory), but refused to patch up the quarrel, an action which, in the Chinese world view, would have signified consigning the Soviet Union to the position of secondary enemy. The Chinese were then, in 1966, convinced that Washington and Moscow were colluding in a "Holy Alliance" to encircle China with hostile countries. The period of Chinese isolationism coincided with the Cultural Revolution but also with a time when they felt mortally threatened on both fronts. From late 1968 on, however, signs began to appear that they were veering toward a stance which regarded the Soviet Union as their principal enemy. There were ups and downs in the evolving view, depending on events in Indochina, on the Sino-Soviet border, and the struggles of various political currents in China itself.

Obviously a decision as to whether the United States or the Soviet Union is China's principal enemy has enormous practical consequences. During the Cultural Revolution, the prevailing line, often expressed by visiting Albanians, was that no decision could be made, that both were mortal enemies, and that China should refrain from any move toward either as a secondary enemy who might prove useful in confronting the principal enemy (see p. 534). Lin Piao had been prominently identified with this line, and when he disappeared from the political scene, it could be concluded that a decision had indeed been made finally to regard the Soviet Union as the principal enemy and the United States as a secondary enemy. By the fall of 1972, the Chinese were openly speaking of the Soviet Union as a "greater danger" than the United States (see October 1, 1972, editorial in the *People's Daily*).

In the future, the Chinese will undoubtedly continue to change their policies and actions, depending on concrete circumstances, but their world view will remain as a framework of analysis on which they can base those policies and actions. The entire Cultural Revolution was fought out over the issue of world view as it applied both domestically and internationally. While the Chinese accept disagreement among leaders and among people as a necessary way of keeping a social system alive and functioning, as Communists they hold that there must be a unity of world view. And if there is not, struggle will go on until such unity is re-created.

The Chinese hold that one must be firm in principle but flexible in practice. Their world view allows them to situate themselves with a long-term perspective in a world they believe will remain in a state of struggle for a long time to come. While their practical policies and actions are guided and informed by this world view, they are also formed by the particular circumstances the Chinese face. Like most nations, China has had to meet three needs in the area of its foreign relations: the need for national security, the need for trade, and the need to fulfill commitments. In the area of defense, this has meant developing capabilities primarily to meet the threat of attack from the United States and the Soviet Union. In the area of trade, this has meant cultivating relations with a broad array of countries with which it could develop mutually profitable import-export relations. In the area of commitments, this has meant extending support to those countries whose national interests they consider vital to their own, primarily North Vietnam, but also Albania, North Korea, Tanzania, and others.

In the fifties, not only did China share its world view with the Soviet Union, but its national security depended on the Soviet "nuclear umbrella," its major trading partner was the Soviet Union, and China's commitments were virtually identical with those of the Soviet Union. It was this which prompted American officials to speak of a "Sino-Soviet bloc." At the same time, the United States was in every respect the principal enemy of China. The United States regarded China as morally and ideologically so beyond the pale that during the Geneva negotiations on Vietnam of 1954 the Secretary of State made the symbolic gesture of refusing to shake Premier Chou En-lai's hand. Americans and Chinese fought during the Korean War, and after the armistice in 1953, the United States ringed China with military bases and deployments of which symbolically and practically the most menacing was the Seventh Fleet, which patrolled the Taiwan Straits. The United States not only embargoed all trade with China but sought to dissuade other nations from trading with China. And some of the deepest commitments the United States had were in regions of utmost sensitivity to China: Taiwan, South Korea, and South Vietnam. In the Soviet world view, China was the most important socialist country after the Soviet Union itself and its most valuable ally. In the world view which then reigned in Washington, China was a rabidly revolutionary and expansionist Communist power intent on dominating all of Asia.

In retrospect, it now appears that the central practical issue of controversy between China and the Soviet Union from the late fifties on was China's insistence on developing an independent nuclear capability and refusing to sacrifice its independence in matters of national security to the broader requisites of a Soviet-American understanding on arms control. The first signs of Sino-Soviet acrimony erupted in September 1959 when Premier Khrushchev visited Peking after having visited President Eisenhower at Camp David. The Chinese claim he unilaterally tore up a nuclear sharing agreement he had concluded with them in October 1957. A second and even more important eruption of acrimony occurred in July 1963 when the Soviet Union and the United States signed the Partial Nuclear Test Ban Treaty and sought China's adherence, which would have meant China's halting its nuclear program before developing an operational capability. The Chinese maintain to have done so would have meant accepting Soviet hegemony in China's own national defense. Between October 16, 1964 (a date coinciding with Khrushchev's ouster), and March 18, 1972, the Chinese have carried out fourteen nuclear tests. On April 25, 1970, they also launched their first earth-orbiting satellite, presumably demonstrating an intercontinental missile delivery capability.

China insists its nuclear weapons are for defensive purposes only. Its overall posture is also defensive. For a population of seven hundred million, China has a small army of only some three million in the People's Liberation Army. From 1959 on, China ceased importing Soviet weaponry and had to develop a modern defense industry virtually from scratch. While it now has an air force, a small navy, and missile defense systems, for its defense it depends on the vastness of its territory, local militias, a decentralized and dispersed industrial capability, and, more recently, a thoroughgoing civil defense and air raid shelter system.

In July 1960 Khrushchev abruptly withdrew all Soviet technicians from China, dealing China's economic development program a severe blow. This was soon followed by a sharp drop in Sino-Soviet trade, reaching a record low of only $45 million in 1970, though it rose again to $154 million in 1971. Where the Soviet Union in the early fifties was China's sole supplier of major capital goods and whole industrial plants, and where in the late fifties it was by far China's chief supplier of all kinds of manufactured products, by the beginning of the Cultural Revolution, it had been reduced to a minor trading partner.

Open Sino-Soviet clashes began in 1962 when the Chinese accused the Russians of provoking unrest in Sinkiang province, where China's nuclear test sites are located, and inciting the flight of thousands of Kazaks into the Soviet Union. But the most serious clashes occurred in the early months of 1969 on the Ussuri River where Manchuria, or as the Chinese call it, "the Northeast," meets the Soviet Far East. Open warfare broke out, with heavy casualties on both sides, ostensibly over the matter of who owned a small shifting island in the Ussuri. What made this clash so serious was that by 1969 over one million Soviet troops armed with modern offensive weapons were strung out along the Sino-Soviet and Sino-Mongolian borders, and the bulk of China's PLA forces were also deployed in her northern regions. As Americans began to pour into China after the "ping-pong breakthrough," they were shown vast underground subway and shelter networks apparently designed for defense against Soviet attack.

While the Russians adamantly deny they have any intention of attacking China and claim to have offered China a non-aggression pact, the Chinese appear to be fearful enough of such an eventuality that they have spent huge sums of scarce resources to build civil defense systems, which, one should note, would serve a purpose if the threat of American attack were to revive. There is a widespread impression in American official circles—reflected in the columns of Joseph Alsop, who visited China in December 1972—that the Chinese fear a preventive attack by the Russians on their nuclear sites before their delivery capabilities reach a point of being able to threaten cities in European Russia.

Even while the Sino-Soviet party-to-party polemics were still going on, the formal matter of dispute in state-to-state relations was the boundaries between the two countries. Because the Chinese have raised the issue of "unequal treaties" by which the Russians, in the late seventeenth and early eighteenth centuries, acquired much of Eastern Siberia, the Soviets accuse them of coveting that territory. The Chinese say they have no designs on Soviet or Mongolian territory but simply wish the Russians to acknowledge the principle of unequally concluded treaties. The border issue has been the ostensible item of discussions by a mixed commission that has been meeting off and on since 1969, but in practice that commission serves much the same function in present Sino-Soviet relations as the ambassadorial talks in Geneva and then Warsaw used to in Sino-American relations.

From the perspective of early 1966, nothing would have seemed more improbable than that a little over five years later the President of the United States would announce acceptance of an invitation to visit the People's Republic of China. In early 1966 it seemed possible that the American air war against North Vietnam might spill over into China. In February 1972 President Nixon visited China and then three months later in May ordered the mining of Haiphong harbor and the bombing of rail lines leading to China (save for a narrow twenty-five-mile buffer zone). In 1966 the official American reason for waging war in Vietnam was to stop "Chinese expansionism." By 1972, Washington had dropped most of its rationales for continuing to wage the war save to achieve "peace with honor." Because of the extreme secrecy which has enveloped the foreign policy-making process in Washington since the 1965 Vietnam escalation, it is not possible, without detailed analysis, to say what Washington's "China policy" has been during the period 1966–1972. But to provide the necessary context for China's own moves toward America, we might note some basic facts about Washington's views, policies, and actions towards China.

As of the end of 1972, official American policy towards China remained what it had been since 1949: Washington recognized the Republic of China on Taiwan as the official government of all of China. It had a defense treaty with the Republic of China. However, from the early sixties subtle signs began to emerge from Washington (too subtle for most ordinary citizens to recognize) that the unofficial or, let us say, ideological view of China had begun to change. In the mid-sixties, officials (though not Dean Rusk) began gradually to say "Peking" rather than "Peiping," the word still used in Taipei, and spoke of the need to "build bridges" to China. A dramatic breakthrough in this changing view of China was marked when President Nixon himself began to speak of the "People's Republic of China." What all this added up to became clearer in President Nixon's Kansas City speech of July 5, 1971, given when Kissinger was on his way to Peking on his initial visit and favorably commented on by Premier Chou En-lai. In that speech, Nixon spoke of five major power centers in the world: the United States, the Soviet Union, China, Japan, and Western Europe. The Chinese interpreted this speech to mean final American recognition of the fact that it was no longer a bipolar world dominated by the United States and the Soviet Union, but one in which other powers, notably China, must be treated as equals to the "Big Two." It therefore followed logically that if the chiefs of state of the great powers engaged in summit diplomacy, then China must be included. In late 1971 President Nixon met with Heath of Great Britain, Pompidou of France, Brandt of Germany, and Sato of Japan to explain his new economic policy. In February 1972 he saw Mao Tse-tung and Chou En-lai in Peking, and in May, the Soviet troika of Brezhnev, Podgorny, and Kosygin in Moscow. Since both Russia and China are still considered potential enemies of America in Washington's global planning, the dual visits by Nixon to both signified that Washington was prepared to approach both on an equal basis.

Again, as of the end of 1972, America's real policies toward China have changed less than its view of China. Politically, Washington continued to adhere to a "Two Chinas" policy, for which Secretary of State William Rogers fought a vigorous if losing battle at the United Nations in the fall of 1971. That meant continued insistence on recognition of the Republic of China but only as the government of Taiwan. There was little difference in principle between the "Two Chinas" policy in regard to China or a "Two Koreas" policy in regard to Korea or a "Two Germanys" policy in regard to Germany. It was also in harmony with Washington's insistence on South Vietnam as a state separate and independent from North Vietnam.

Militarily, Washington continued to regard China, along with Russia, as its major adversary in the Pacific. Washington insisted on maintaining a "defense perimeter" aimed at China, a line of defense stretching from Japan and South Korea through Taiwan deep into Southeast Asia. It was reported to be Washington policy to use nuclear weapons if Chinese forces should intervene in conflicts beyond its borders involving allies of the United States.

American actions directed at China were virtually impossible to discern, for they affected some of the most sensitive areas of the Vietnam War. We know from the *Pentagon Papers* that contingency plans were in existence to strike at China with air power if Chinese forces intervened. We do not know what sorts of communications were addressed to China by Washington as on repeated occasions the air war crept closer and closer to the Chinese border. We know the Chinese held a few American fliers shot down on the Chinese side of the Vietnam-China border. We do not know the extent of pressure on Washington policy-makers to strike at supply lines going over China. We know absolutely nothing about what Peking and Washington said to each other about Vietnam. In the mid-1960's the State Department relaxed travel and trade restrictions on China, implying a policy of seeking better relations. We have every reason to believe that it was the policy of the last three administrations, at least at the White House level, to avoid an armed confrontation with China.

In the wake of President Nixon's visit to China, contacts between Chinese and Americans have greatly expanded. A Chinese UN mission now resides in New York; Chinese scientists, athletes, and journalists have toured the United States. A wide variety of Americans has visited China. Trade has been increasing slowly between the two countries, but is as yet far from significant for either side.

On the Chinese side, no change was discernible in their policies and actions towards the United States until November 1968, when they offered the new Nixon administration an improvement in relations between the two countries. The publication of the full text of Nixon's inaugural speech in their theoretical journal *Red Flag*, while severely critical, implied that they thought something had changed on the Washington political scene. Prior to then, they had rejected all offers of travel and trade contacts which the State Department had been timidly offering. Except for the periodic ambassadorial meetings in Warsaw, there was no known contact between the two governments. On the issue of peace talks on Vietnam, the Chinese made clear their position that such talks would only be a smoke screen for Soviet-American collusion to sell out the Vietnamese. What effect this November 1968 feeler had on the Nixon administration is also not known, but it is reported that early in 1969 the Seventh Fleet was withdrawn from the Taiwan Straits, save for one "patrol boat." Whether the Sino-Soviet clashes on the Ussuri at the same time were related to Soviet fears, openly expressed in their press, that Peking and Washington might collude against Moscow has been a matter of speculation. In 1969 the Chinese dropped their opposition to the Paris peace talks and shifted to a position combining support for the Vietnamese with a desire to see the war ended through negotiations.

In 1970 a new element entered the Sino-American relationship as it concerned Indochina. In March 1970, after being overthrown, Prince Sihanouk of Cambodia formed a government in exile in Peking. Since that time, no foreign leader has received such continuing widespread publicity in the Chinese press as Sihanouk. As in the case of Chinese adulation of Albania, their outspoken support of Sihanouk has symbolic as well as practical significance. On April 24–25, 1970, leaders of North Vietnam, the National Liberation Front for South Vietnam, the Pathet Lao, and the newly formed Cambodian revolutionary union met in southern China to form a unified strategy of action for all of Indochina. On April 30, President Nixon announced the American invasion of Cambodia. On May 20, Mao Tse-tung made one of his rare official pronouncements in the area of foreign affairs which vowed full support for the peoples of Indochina in their struggle against the United States and warned that the danger of a new world war still existed. The symbolic importance of Sihanouk can be inferred from the state of Cambodian affairs. The Lon Nol regime which overthrew Sihanouk is supported by the United States, but is also recognized by the Soviet Union. Sihanouk presides over a coalition government located in Peking but recognized by a number of countries: for example, North Vietnam, North Korea, Yugoslavia, Algeria, and Cuba. That government is supported by a united-front type of revolutionary movement, which by late 1972 had assumed power over virtually all of Cambodia save the major cities. Sihanouk, who has numerous friends in the United States, had traditionally sought a "neutral" course between China and the United States as the two great powers in Southeast Asia. In short, the Chinese appear to regard Cambodia as a concrete testing ground to see how the Sino-American relationship will evolve.

If Mao Tse-tung, on May 20, 1970, implied that China and the United States might yet come to armed confrontation, in

December of that year he gave an interview to the American journalist Edgar Snow—widely publicized in *Life* magazine (April 30, 1971)—that implied just the opposite. Lauding America's decentralized tradition of government, Mao extended an invitation to President Nixon to visit China. A photograph of Chairman Mao and Edgar Snow was prominently displayed in the *People's Daily* on December 25, 1970. In China, publicity about meetings between Mao Tse-tung and prominent foreign leaders or personalities always implies highest support for the policies in question. That the Snow interview had practical consequences became evident in late March 1971 when, as Premier Chou En-lai subsequently stated, on the direct intervention of Mao, an American ping-pong team visiting Japan at the same time as a Chinese team was invited to come to China. With unexpected rapidity, an ever-growing number of Americans began to visit China. On July 15, 1971, President Nixon, in a brief television broadcast, made the momentous announcement that he was to visit the People's Republic of China some time before May 1972. His foreign affairs adviser, Henry Kissinger, had made a secret visit to Peking on July 9 through 11, to arrange the visit. Final announcement of the date of the visit was not made till late November, and the visit itself took place during the week of February 21 through 28, 1972.

In November 1971, the world witnessed the curious spectacle of Secretary of State William Rogers personally leading the fight to keep Chiang Kai-shek's government in the United Nations while Henry Kissinger was in Peking, presumably finishing preparations for Nixon's visit. If Rogers had succeeded, China would have automatically rejected any invitation to join the UN alongside a government it categorically refused to recognize as a legal entity. But the Taipei government was ousted and China entered the UN, as well as all UN special agencies and commissions from which the Taipei delegates were also ousted.

That the new policy toward the United States had aroused bitter opposition within China became evident when Lin Piao, Mao's officially designated successor, fell from power in September 1971, allegedly for having conspired against Mao. At the same time, four of China's most prominent military leaders, the equivalent of America's Joint Chiefs of Staff, disappeared from the political scene. Rumors flew that Lin Piao had been killed in the crash of a Chinese plane on Mongolian territory. Lin Piao had been prominently identified with the foreign policy line current during the Cultural Revolution which insisted on uncompromising hostility toward both superpowers. On the other hand, while Mao Tse-tung was known for his uncompromising hostility to the Soviet Union, he was also, through his interview with Edgar Snow and then the personal meeting with President Nixon, symbolically linked with the new policy toward America. When Premier Kosygin met Mao in February 1965 just after U.S. bombing of North Vietnam began, no publicity was given it in China, nor has Mao thereafter ever been photographed with any Soviet personality.

During the entire history of the Chinese Communist Party the issue of who is the principal enemy at any one time has always aroused bitter internal controversy. In the thirties, the dispute centered around Japan and the Kuomintang regime. The line which finally prevailed was that Japan was the principal enemy and the Kuomintang regime, for all its persisting murderous hostility to the Communists in Yenan, was the secondary enemy. Japan was their common enemy, and though Chiang himself at times flirted with the idea of making peace with the Japanese so he could complete his "bandit extermination" campaigns against the Communists, the Communists' policy line remained one of subordinating conflicts with the Kuomintang to the larger cause of defeating Japan. It seems now that, after the fall of Lin Piao, the Chinese are now moving toward an analogous line for the seventies, where the Soviet Union is their principal enemy and the United States, like the Kuomintang in an earlier period, is their secondary enemy.

While China's relationships to the United States and the Soviet Union are shaped by national security considerations, her relations with the advanced countries of the "second intermediate zone" have been shaped by China's search for friends to counterbalance the pressure on her from the two superpowers and by her growing need to trade. As China is moving into a new stage of accelerated economic development, she has rising needs for capital goods imports which must come from the advanced countries. Determined never again to become dependent on a single main source of supply, the Chinese are diversifying their trade relations among all the countries of the "second intermediate zone." Japan is now China's leading trading partner, and in the wake of Premier Kakuei Tanaka's visit to Peking in the fall of 1972, formal diplomatic relations were established between the two countries. With the normalization of Sino-British relations and the establishment of diplomatic relations between China and West Germany, Chinese ties with the Common Market have strengthened. While ties to the independent countries of Eastern Europe (Albania, Yugoslavia, and Romania) have been close for some time, China has also sought to improve relations with other East European countries more closely linked to the Soviet Union. Interestingly, in 1971 Chinese trade with Eastern Europe, including the Soviet Union, rose sharply.

If China identifies with the Third World in general because of her world view, practical considerations have led her to make major commitments only to certain countries. A commitment by a large country to a small one means that the former provides continuing support for the latter's needs in the area of economic development and defense. If even so powerful countries as the United States and the Soviet Union suffer constraints in their external commitments, this is all the more true of China, still basically a poor country. China's strongest commitments are to Albania, Tanzania, and above all to North Vietnam. When Albania broke with the Soviet Union in 1961, her trade with the East European countries plummeted. Had it not been for China which stepped into the breach, Albania would have been forced to turn to the West as Yugoslavia had to do in 1948 when Tito broke with Stalin. For all their commanding economic presence in Albania, the Chinese are, by all accounts, popular with the Albanians. Unlike the Russians, who in 1959 tried to get the Albanians to grant them naval bases and meddled in Albania's political affairs, the Chinese have sought no military advantage from their aid, except for radio broadcasts, and have not used Albania as a "springboard" for moving into other parts of Europe or the Middle East. Tanzania, a socialist country in eastern Africa, is the recipient of one of the most important foreign aid programs in the world today. The Chinese, with a work force of some 20,000 men, are building a railroad from Dar es Salaam, the Tanzanian capital on the shores of the Indian Ocean, to Lusaka, the capital of mineral-rich Zambia, over some of the most difficult terrain in the world. Once the railroad is finished, Zambia will be free from dependence on shipping outlets in South Africa and Portuguese-ruled Mozambique and from falling into the South African-dominated economic bloc which has been arising in Southern Africa.

No commitment is more vital to China than that to North Vietnam. For years now, only one slogan attributed to Mao himself has been featured on the masthead of the *People's Daily* whenever the subject of Vietnam arises: "The seven hundred million people of China are the firm rear shield of the Vietnamese people; the broad lands of China are the reliable rear area of the Vietnamese people." What this slogan meant concretely became clear from official Pentagon admissions at the time of the mining of Haiphong harbor in May 1972— namely, that during all the years of the Vietnam War military supplies continued to come into North Vietnam, not only those furnished by China but those furnished by the Soviet Union as well. Soviet oil and economic supplies had gone through Haiphong, but military hardware passed over China from the Soviet Union by rail. Thus, paradoxically, though Sino-Soviet relations worsened to the point of war, the two countries continued to collaborate to expedite the shipment of matériel to North Vietnam. For a while after the mining of Haiphong harbor, Soviet, though not East European ships, were reportedly excluded from Chinese ports, but then quietly were allowed to enter them, delivering those goods which they normally would have unloaded directly in Haiphong. North Vietnam has consistently maintained close ties with both China and the Soviet Union, evident in the scrupulous care with which Le Duc Tho has stopped at both capitals during his frequent shuttling between Hanoi and Paris. The Chinese are fully committed to North Vietnam for their own reasons, but they also respect North Vietnam's terms for accepting that commitment, namely that the Sino-Soviet dispute not be allowed to interfere with North Vietnam's military and economic needs as determined by the North Vietnamese themselves.

Since one of the major American military rationales for bombing North Vietnam has been to cut the flow of supplies into North Vietnam and from North Vietnam to fighting forces in the south, the presence of supply "sanctuaries" in China is an irritant to military planners. Obviously, bombing them would lead to an armed confrontation with China. That Washington has tried to persuade both the Soviet Union and China to curtail their supply programs to North Vietnam is easy to infer from the statements of Washington policy makers. That the efforts at persuasion have failed is also obvious. Time and time again American bombing of North Vietnam crept closer and closer to the Chinese border: in late June 1966 when Haiphong was bombed; during the heavy bombing campaign of the winter of 1967–1968; during the Christmas to New Year 1971–1972 bombings; during the bombing of rail lines leading to China in May 1972; and during the B-52 carpet bombings of North Vietnam in late 1972. In early 1972 speculation arose that renewed bombing of North Vietnam might lead to a cancellation of President Nixon's announced visit to Peking. In the latter half of 1972, American bombing took place as hundreds of Americans were touring China and a much smaller but equally steady stream of Americans was visiting North Vietnam. All that is known of Chinese reaction to these bombings is that they have honored their commitments to keep North Vietnam supplied with all the equipment the North Vietnamese deem necessary for their struggle.

On November 7, 1971, General Lavelle began the first of his "unauthorized" raids against a North Vietnamese airfield. On November 17, secret negotiations in Paris between Le Duc Tho and Henry Kissinger were broken off. On November 20, Premier Pham Van Dong of North Vietnam went to Peking, where two days later he was prominently photographed with Mao Tse-tung. Signs were mounting (for example, predictions of a major North Vietnamese offensive) that 1971 would be a year of major and climactic fighting in Indochina. Clearly Pham Van Dong was seeking reaffirmation of China's commitments to North Vietnam in the light of President Nixon's forthcoming visit, and he received it. A film showing Mao and Dong together was widely distributed within China to make clear to the Chinese people that the slogan on the masthead of the *People's Daily* had the force of commitment.

Both before and after Nixon's visit, speculation arose in

American circles that the Chinese, in view of their dispute with the Soviet Union, their desire for a new relationship with the United States, and their growing needs for trade, would be willing to put their commitment to North Vietnam on the back burner. But time and time again, Chinese leaders, from Premier Chou En-lai down, reiterated that no "normalization" of U.S.– China relations is possible until the war in Indochina ends.

As this and the previous volume indicate, China's views, policies, and actions in the world do not proceed in spasmodic jerks but have a consistency and constancy even while changing. Her commitments, interestingly, have changed least during these years. Despite the growing rift with the Soviet Union and the improvement of relations with the United States, China's commitments to North Vietnam (and Albania and Tanzania) are little different from what they were a decade ago. Their relations with the United States and the Soviet Union have changed, but not so much as one might have expected from their changing world view. Despite the rift, China continues to trade actively with the Soviet Union, and still trades little with the United States despite the improvement in relations. But at the highest ideological level of world view, there has been dramatic change, as we have shown. There can be no doubt that their radically changed view of the Soviet Union is linked to the great internal changes which occurred in China during the Cultural Revolution, changes which have seen the extirpation of those Soviet influences which were so important in reshaping China in the fifties. China's relationship to the Soviet Union in the seventies seems much like her relationship to America in the fifties, and in fact, Premier Chou has likened the Soviet leaders to John Foster Dulles.

It has become common in some American circles to speak of a triangle of great powers: the United States, the Soviet Union, and China. But President Nixon in his Kansas City speech spoke of five great power centers, including Western Europe and Japan. The triangular notion is essentially a military notion, for the United States, the Soviet Union, and China are the world's three major military powers. A pentagonal notion is essentially economic, in that the power of Western Europe and Japan is predominantly economic. Whether the world will continue to remain in a militarized state in the seventies and beyond, or whether economic concerns come to supersede military confrontation, is as yet an undecided issue. But whether the world moves toward war or peace, the Chinese are saying there is a third issue which is more important than either of these two, and that is whether the poor countries of the world can achieve independence, liberation, and revolution, which the Chinese regard as the prerequisite of all healthy socioeconomic development.

NOTE ON SELECTIONS

We have chosen three kinds of selections for "China in the World": pieces which expound China's world view, those which state China's major foreign policies, and writings by foreigners on China's foreign policies. While Chou En-lai's interviews with Julio Scherer and James Reston are readily understandable, most of the other Chinese selections are written in that Marxist-Leninist style which seems strange to outsiders. We must remember that the Chinese are not only thoroughly versed in the works of Mao Tse-tung, but virtually the entire corpus of writing of Marx, Engels, and Lenin is now available in Chinese translation and widely read in China. Having a long philosophical history, the Chinese are accustomed to expressing themselves in terms of general principles. They also have a tradition of history which allows them to make ample use of historical examples, particularly drawing on the experiences of the Chinese Communists during the last half-century of their struggle.

The Chinese do not just read articles. They are discussed in study sessions, which constitute a learning process in which people acquire a broad education much as they would in a classroom. During the Cultural Revolution, study sessions dealt almost exclusively with internal affairs. But in 1972, as one can see from the content of the *People's Daily*, foreign affairs have become the chief subject of discussion. Americans might argue that what is called "study" is really indoctrination, but rather than learning fixed doctrine by rote memorization, what people actually learn are the frameworks and concepts of analysis. Their learning process is not so different from that of our own schools, where we learn to analyze using the concepts of sociology, economics, or the natural sciences. One of the main purposes of all education is to enable us to think systematically about the reality around us. The Chinese believe that Marxism-Leninism and Mao Tse-tung Thought enable them to do just that, from the problems of life and work to the broad realm of international affairs. If people are interested in how the Chinese see the world, then they must make the effort to try to understand that thinking.

A few pointers may help the reader along. Though the Chinese occasionally use peculiarly "Chinese" expressions ("paper tiger," for instance), by and large the terms they use come out of the Marxist tradition and thus are "Western." While the Chinese use a lot of ritualistic expressions, readers should try to get through to the main argument—there always is an argument. As we have indicated in the introduction to this section, the Chinese hold to the Marxist notion that history has direction and purpose, that its course is marked by never-ending struggles between the classes of people who have power and those who do not, and that the short- and long-run trends of that struggle can be rationally analyzed. Class, struggle, and leadership are the essential components of all Chinese analyses of foreign affairs. Class means that the contending parties in struggle have their roots in some segment of society. Struggle means there always are two sides ("we and the enemy") and "friends" of one side or the other. Leadership means that the contending forces are guided, as in war, by people who formulate goals, strategies, and tactics.

While outsiders can view China with detachment, the Chinese are all "involved." That all their writing serves the purpose of advancing their own side in the struggle does not automatically invalidate the analysis and turn it into "propaganda." The Chinese hold whether an analysis is correct or incorrect will eventually be demonstrated in practice as people act in terms of that analysis. In the West, we do all kinds of analyses and generally collect "data" to support or refute the analyses. In both instances, reality is the final arbiter.

1. WORLD VIEW

MAO TSE-TUNG'S STATEMENT OF MAY 20, 1970

As already noted, this is one of the rare official declarations of
Mao in the area of foreign policy. On April 30, 1970, President
Nixon announced the American invasion of Cambodia. On May
4, the "Royal Government of National Union under the Leadership of the United Front of Kampuchea" was formally proclaimed in Peking and immediately recognized by China. The
last sentence of the opening paragraph is one of the most often
quoted statements of Mao on the subject of a new world war.
It is generally paired with another quote: "Regarding the question of world war, there are only two possibilities: one is that
war will lead to revolution, and the other is that revolution will
prevent war." Since May 1970, Mao Tse-tung has prominently
appeared with Prince Sihanouk and the Chinese press has given
wide publicity to all his activities.

★　★　★

MAO TSE-TUNG*
People of the World, Unite and Defeat the
U.S. Aggressors and All Their Running Dogs

A new upsurge in the struggle against U.S. imperialism is now
emerging throughout the world. Ever since World War II, U.S.
imperialism and its followers have been continuously launching
wars of aggression and the people in various countries have
been continuously waging revolutionary wars to defeat the ag-

* Mao Tse-tung, translated in *Peking Review* (May 23, 1970).

gressors. The danger of a new world war still exists, and the
people of all countries must get prepared. But revolution is the
main trend in the world today.

Unable to win in Vietnam and Laos, the U.S. aggressors
treacherously engineered the reactionary coup d'état by the Lon
Nol-Sirik Matak clique, brazenly dispatched their troops to invade Cambodia and resumed the bombing of North Vietnam,
and this has aroused the furious resistance of the three Indochinese peoples. I warmly support the fighting spirit of Samdech Norodom Sihanouk, Head of State of Cambodia, in opposing U.S. imperialism and its lackeys. I warmly support the Joint
Declaration of the Summit Conference of the Indochinese Peoples. I warmly support the establishment of the Royal Government of National Union Under the Leadership of the National
United Front of Kampuchea. Strengthening their unity, supporting each other and persevering in a protracted people's war, the
three Indochinese peoples will certainly overcome all difficulties
and win complete victory.

While massacring the people in other countries, U.S. imperialism is slaughtering the white and black people in its own
country. Nixon's fascist atrocities have kindled the raging flames
of the revolutionary mass movement in the United States. The
Chinese people firmly support the revolutionary struggle of the
American people. I am convinced that the American people
who are fighting valiantly will ultimately win victory and that
the fascist rule in the United States will inevitably be defeated.

The Nixon government is beset with troubles internally and
externally, with utter chaos at home and extreme isolation
abroad. The mass movement of protest against U.S. aggression
in Cambodia has swept the globe. Less than ten days after its
establishment, the Royal Government of National Union of
Cambodia was recognized by nearly twenty countries. The situation is getting better and better in the war of resistance
against U.S. aggression and for national salvation waged by the
people of Vietnam, Laos and Cambodia. The revolutionary
armed struggles of the people of the Southeast Asian countries,
the struggles of the people of Korea, Japan and other Asian
countries against the revival of Japanese militarism by the U.S.
and Japanese reactionaries, the struggles of the Palestinian and
other Arab peoples against the U.S.-Israeli aggressors, the na-

tional-liberation struggles of the Asian, African and Latin American peoples, and the revolutionary struggles of the peoples of North America, Europe and Oceania are all developing vigorously. The Chinese people firmly support the people of the three Indo-Chinese countries and of other countries of the world in their revolutionary struggles against U.S. imperialism and its lackeys.

U.S. imperialism, which looks like a huge monster, is in essence a paper tiger, now in the throes of its death-bed struggle. In the world of today, who actually fears whom? It is not the Vietnamese people, the Laotian people, the Cambodian people, the Palestinian people, the Arab people or the people of other countries who fear U.S. imperialism; it is U.S. imperialism which fears the people of the world. It becomes panic-stricken at the mere rustle of leaves in the wind. Innumerable facts prove that a just cause enjoys abundant support while an unjust cause finds little support. A weak nation can defeat a strong, a small nation can defeat a big. The people of a small country can certainly defeat aggression by a big country, if only they dare to rise in struggle, dare to take up arms and grasp in their own hands the destiny of their country. This is a law of history.

People of the world, unite and defeat the U.S. aggressors and all their running dogs!

★   ★   ★   ★   ★

"Principal and Secondary Enemies"

This piece appeared in *Red Flag* and the *People's Daily* in mid-August 1971, a month after Kissinger's visit and a month before Lin Piao's disappearance from the political scene. It should be read in the context of the controversy within Chinese political circles on Nixon's proposed visit and, more broadly, on which of the great powers, the United States or the Soviet Union, is China's principal enemy. As is common to many Chinese articles on current political issues, this one is couched in historical allegories. Mao's essay "On Policy" was written in December 1940, only weeks before one of the bloodiest battles between the Nationalists and the Communists since the implementation of their anti-Japan united front policy. Caught in an ambush, virtually the entire Communist Fourth Route Army was annihilated. Yet before and after the "incident," as the Chinese euphemistically call it, the Communists adhered to the united front policy which subordinated their struggle with the Nationalists to the larger struggle against Japan. Insisting on the need for defining who the principal enemy at any one time is, the piece criticizes both right tendencies which advocate "all alliance and no struggle" and ultra-left tendencies which advocate "all struggle and no alliance." It notes that "the winning over of the middle forces is an extremely important task for us." In a section of the article omitted in the abridgment published in the *Peking Review*, the piece states: "We must never allow sentiment to replace policy."

★   ★   ★

PEOPLE'S DAILY*
Unite the People, Defeat the Enemy
—A study of "On Policy"

Our great leader Chairman Mao wrote the brilliant work "On Policy" in December 1940 in the critical period when China's War of Resistance Against Japan entered the stage of a strategic stalemate and there was a high tide of anti-Communist attacks by the Kuomintang reactionaries.

Using dialectical and historical materialism, Chairman Mao scientifically analyzed in this work the social contradictions and class relations of the time, penetratingly criticized the Right and "Left" erroneous lines and policies pushed by the renegades Ch'en Tu-hsiu, Wang Ming and others, systematically summed up our Party's rich experience in protracted struggle against the Kuomintang reactionaries, incisively explained the change and development of the Party's policies during the War of Resistance, and drew up for our Party the tactical principles and the various concrete policies in the Anti-Japanese National United Front. This enabled our Party to keep a clear head in the extremely complex struggle and ensured the implementation of Chairman Mao's correct line and victory in the War of Resistance Against Japan.

The tactical principles and different policies drawn up by Chairman Mao reflect the objective laws of class struggle and manifest the thoroughgoing revolutionary spirit of the proletariat and flexibility in the art of struggle. They enrich and develop the Marxist-Leninist ideas of tactics and have played a powerful part in defeating the enemy and winning victory in the various

* The Writing Group of the Hupeh Provincial Committee of the Communist Party of China, from the *Peking Review*, No. 35 (August 27, 1971), pp. 10–13. Originally published in the journal *Hongqi*, No. 9 (1971).

historical stages of revolutionary struggle. They are always a powerful proletarian weapon for uniting the people and defeating the enemy.

I

In "On Policy," Chairman Mao repeatedly spelled out the importance of policy and tactics and, in terms of the situation at the time, emphatically pointed out from the very start that **"the policy we adopt is of decisive importance."** Chairman Mao has always attached great importance to the decisive role of proletarian policy and tactics. He pointed out: **"The proletariat has to depend for its victory entirely on the correct and firm tactics of struggle of its own party, the Communist Party."** (*Oppose Book Worship.*) In every historical period, Chairman Mao not only drew up the general line and the general policy for the Party but also laid down the tactical principles and various concrete policies for struggle. Chairman Mao's revolutionary tactics and policies are concrete expressions of his revolutionary line while the erroneous policies pushed by such political charlatans as Ch'en Tu-hsiu, Wang Ming and Liu Shao-ch'i are precisely to serve the realization of their "Left" or Right opportunist lines. In this sense, the various aspects of the struggle between the two lines are concretely revealed through the struggle between the two different kinds of policy. **"Policy is the starting-point of all the practical actions of a revolutionary party and manifests itself in the process and the end-result of that party's actions."** ("On the Policy Concerning Industry and Commerce," *Selected Works*, Vol. IV.) As their starting point is wrong, all Right or "Left" policies can never have a correct orientation and if they are not corrected in time but are continued, errors in orientation and line inevitably will be committed.

II

To fully comprehend and correctly implement Chairman Mao's proletarian policies, it is necessary to clearly understand the basis for drawing up and setting forth the tactical principles and policies. The great teacher Lenin pointed out: **"Only an objective consideration of the sum total of the relations between absolutely all the classes in a given society, and consequently a consideration of the objective stage of development reached by that society and of the relations between it and other societies, can serve as a basis for the correct tactics of an advanced class."** ("Karl Marx," *Collected Works*, Vol. 21.) This tells us that Marxist tactical principles and policies are all drawn up on the basis of correct observations and a concrete analysis of the situation in class struggle internationally and domestically, the relations between the various classes and the changes and developments in them.

Without making distinctions, there can be no policy. Marxists must concretely analyze concrete contradictions. Chairman Mao pointed out: **"To understand their** [the different social classes] **interrelations, to arrive at a correct appraisal of class forces and then to formulate the correct tactics for the struggle, defining which classes constitute the main force in the revolutionary struggle, which classes are to be won over as allies and which classes are to be overthrown."** *(Oppose Book Worship.)* The tactical principles and policies Chairman Mao put forth based on class analysis are precisely for correctly handling the relations between the enemy, ourselves and our friends, to unite all forces that can be united, isolate and attack the most stubborn enemy, which consists of a handful, and constantly lead the revolution to victory.

Since the national contradiction between China and Japan during the War of Resistance heightened and became the principal contradiction, the domestic class contradictions subsided to a secondary and subordinate position and the resultant changes in international relations and domestic class relations formed a new stage in the developing situation. On the basis of a scientific analysis of the basic characteristics of the situation in class struggle, Chairman Mao in "On Policy" made very profound and concrete distinctions concerning the complex international and domestic class relations in the historical conditions of that period and built **our policy on these distinctions** to consolidate and expand the Anti-Japanese National United Front and defeat Japanese imperialism.

In analyzing the relations between the various classes at home and their different political attitudes, Chairman Mao first of all emphatically pointed out that "**within the united front our policy must be one of independence and initiative, i.e., both unity and independence are necessary,**" "**all people favoring resistance (that is, all anti-Japanese workers, peasants, soldiers, students and intellectuals, and businessmen) must unite in the Anti-Japanese National United Front**" to defeat the principal enemy of that time, Japanese imperialism, and its running dogs, the traitors and pro-Japanese elements.

What attitude did the Party take towards the various classes in the country in the course of the War of Resistance Against Japan? Chairman Mao clearly pointed out: "**With regard to the alignment of the various classes within the country, our basic policy is to develop the progressive forces, win over the middle forces and isolate the anti-Communist die-hard forces.**"

To educate the whole Party to implement this guiding principle, Chairman Mao concretely pointed out the class content of the progressive forces, the middle forces and the die-hard forces.

Developing the progressive forces meant building up the forces of the proletariat, the peasantry and the urban petty bourgeoisie, boldly expanding the Eighth Route and New Fourth Armies, establishing anti-Japanese democratic base areas on an extensive scale, building up Communist organizations throughout the country and boldly developing mass movements of the workers, peasants, youth, women and children, etc. In criticizing the Right opportunist viewpoint of being afraid to boldly develop the revolutionary anti-Japanese forces, Chairman Mao pointed out: "**Steady expansion of the progressive forces is the only way to prevent the situation from deteriorating, to forestall capitulation and splitting, and to lay a firm and indestructible foundation for victory in the War of Resistance.**" ("Current Problems of Tactics in the Anti-Japanese United Front," *Selected Works*, Vol. II.) This is the guiding principle of making the work of developing the people's forces the basic thing. It has always been our Party's fundamental starting point in defeating all enemies.

By also pointing out that "**the winning over of the middle forces is an extremely important task for us in the period of the anti-Japanese united front**" ("Current Problems of Tactics in the Anti-Japanese United Front," *Selected Works*, Vol. II), Chairman Mao criticized the "Left" viewpoint of neglecting to win over the middle forces and gave us a profound analysis of the various conditions for doing this. These were: we have ample strength, we respect the interests of the middle forces, we resolutely struggle against the die-hard elements and steadily win victories.

To isolate the die-hard forces, Chairman Mao made a profound and concrete analysis and made distinctions between the different social forces and political groupings in the enemy camp and within the middle forces. He pointed out that the pro-Japanese big landlords and big bourgeoisie who were against resistance to Japan must be distinguished from the pro-British and pro-American big landlords and big bourgeoisie who were for resistance; similarly the ambivalent big landlords and big bourgeoisie who wanted to resist but vacillated, and who were for unity but were anti-Communist, must be distinguished from the national bourgeoisie, the middle and small landlords and the enlightened gentry, the duality of whose character was less pronounced.

"We deal with imperialism in the same way." The Communist Party opposes all imperialism but we distinguished between Japanese imperialism which was committing aggression against China and the imperialist powers which were not doing so, and we also made distinctions between the various imperialist countries which adopted different policies under different circumstances and at different times. The scientific distinctions made by Chairman Mao with regard to the enemy camp by using the revolutionary dialectics of one dividing into two most clearly pointed out who was the principal enemy, who was the secondary enemy, and who were temporary allies or indirect allies. Such a concrete and careful differentiation isolated to the greatest extent the Chinese people's principal enemy at the time— the Japanese imperialists who were then invading China.

During the War of Resistance, it was precisely because the whole Party carried out Chairman Mao's tactical principles and policies on the fundamental question of who to rely on, who to unite with and who to attack, that we overcame interference from the erroneous lines, organized millions of people, brought into play a mighty revolutionary army, expanded the people's revolutionary forces, won the sympathy and support of the world's people, hurled back the attacks of the anti-Communist die-hards, thoroughly defeated the principal enemy of the time,

Japanese imperialism, and won great victory in the War of Resistance.

III

On the basis of a profound analysis of the relations between the various classes, Chairman Mao in "On Policy" clearly set forth the important tactical principle in struggling against the enemy: **"To make use of contradictions, win over the many, oppose the few and crush our enemies one by one."** This principle armed the whole Party and played a tremendous role not only in the struggle against the enemy in the past, but in the practical struggle of today it is still a sharp weapon for us to defeat the enemy and win victory.

To preserve their reactionary force and exploit and oppress the people, the imperialist countries and the various class strata, cliques and factions in all enemy camps are bound to collude and work hand in glove. But, as determined by their class nature, they are bound to have many contradictions and contentions. That these contradictions are an objective reality means they are independent of the subjective wishes of any reactionary. The view that all enemies are the same, that they are one monolithic bloc, is not in accord with objective reality. Moreover, with the development of the situation and with the people's revolutionary forces daily expanding, the enemies' contradictions will become more and more acute. The proletariat and its party must learn to concretely analyze the situation in class struggle in the international and domestic spheres at different historical periods and be good at seizing the opportunity to **"turn to good account all such fights, rifts and contradictions in the enemy camp and turn them against our present main enemy."** ("On Tactics Against Japanese Imperialism," *Selected Works*, Vol. I.)

Chairman Mao's analysis of the enemy camp completely conforms to the objective laws governing the development of things. There are four major contradictions in the world today: between the oppressed nations on the one hand and imperialism and social-imperialism on the other; between the proletariat and the bourgeoisie in the capitalist and revisionist countries; between imperialist and social-imperialist countries and among the imperialist countries; and between socialist countries on the one hand and imperialism and social-imperialism on the other. All these contradictions are irreconcilable. Their existence and development are bound to give rise to revolution. For example, U.S. imperialism and social-imperialism are colluding and contending with each other and they are stepping up the expansion of their aggressive forces in the vast intermediate zones trying to redivide the world. This has aroused the people of the world to rise and attack them. To put down the revolution of the world's oppressed nations and people, U.S. imperialism and social-imperialism collude with each other; but to satisfy their own imperialist interests, they are in bitter contention. This includes their contention over the Middle East, Europe and the Mediterranean Sea. Such contentions are growing sharper and sharper. And their collusion and contention will continue to arouse strong opposition from the oppressed people of the world. Therefore, the analysis of the enemy camp contained in this work by Chairman Mao is also of great guiding significance for us to correctly understand today's international situation.

The tactical principles in the struggle against the enemy drawn up by Chairman Mao are the dialectical unity of firm principle and high flexibility. Using flexible tactics in struggle is to realize a firm revolutionary principle. Chairman Mao teaches us: **"We should be firm in principle; we should also have all the flexibility permissible and necessary for carrying out our principles."** ("Report to the Second Plenary Session of the Seventh Central Committee of the Communist Party of China," *Selected Works*, Vol. IV.) The nature of imperialism and all reactionaries will never change. Inevitably, their subjective wish at all times is to oppress and exploit the revolutionary people of the whole world and to oppose the revolutionary cause of the people of all countries. But this is only one side of the coin. There is another side, that is, there are objectively many difficulties for them to realize their counter-revolutionary wishes. Proceeding from their reactionary nature and counter-revolutionary needs, they inevitably and ceaselessly switch their counter-revolutionary tactics and resort to counter-revolutionary dual tactics. On our part, we must seize and make use of all enemy contradictions and difficulties, wage a tit-for-tat struggle against him, strive to gain as much as possible for the people's fundamental interests and seize victory in the struggle against him. To smash the enemy's counter-revolutionary dual policy, we must adopt a revolutionary dual policy. While persisting in armed struggle as the main form of struggle, we must also engage in various forms of struggle with the enemy on many fronts. The different forms of flexible tactics in struggle are required by the proletariat in the fight against the enemy.

IV

To consolidate and develop the revolutionary united front, the proletariat must have a correct policy. In "On Policy," Chairman Mao concisely summed up the policy for the Anti-Japanese National United Front. He pointed out that in such a united front it **"is neither all alliance and no struggle nor all struggle and no alliance, but combines alliance and struggle."**

Alliance and struggle—the relationship between the two is one of dialectical unity. Such a dual-nature policy of combining alliance and struggle is built on the basis that those to be united with in the united front have a dual nature. In the War of Resistance period, it was to unite all social strata that opposed Japanese imperialism and form a united front with them. But we carried out various forms of struggle against them according to the degree of their capitulationist and anti-Communist and anti-popular vacillations. In dealing with the relation between alliance and struggle in the anti-Japanese united front, Chairman Mao pointed out: **"Struggle is the means to unity and unity is the aim of struggle. If unity is sought through struggle, it will live; if unity is sought through yielding, it will perish."** ("Current Problems of Tactics in the Anti-Japanese United Front," *Selected Works*, Vol. II.) If it is only all struggle and no alliance, we will not be able to unite all the forces that can be united and consolidate and develop the revolutionary united front. We will also not be able to push the principal enemy into a narrow and isolated position and therefore will not be able to win victory in the struggle against the enemy. If it is only all alliance and no struggle, we will lose our revolutionary, principled stand, relinquish the Party's revolutionary leadership in the united front, the Party will disintegrate ideologically, politically and organizationally, and the revolution will fail.

Chairman Mao sharply pointed out: **"Both extremist policies** [all alliance and no struggle and all struggle and no alliance] **caused great losses to the Party and the revolution.**" The lessons in blood from these two erroneous policies in our Party's history are extremely profound. Ch'en Tu-hsiu, Wang Ming, Liu Shao-ch'i and their like wildly pushed their "Left" or Right opportunist lines. They never made a scientific class analysis, always negated class differentiation and reversed the relations between the enemy and ourselves. Whether it was in the period of the democratic revolution or during the period of the socialist revolution, they always opposed class analysis and class differentiation and set themselves against Chairman Mao's proletarian revolutionary line and policies formulated on the basis of revolutionary, scientific class analysis. History has proved that the two extremist policies of all alliance and no struggle and all struggle and no alliance are out-and-out opportunist policies and that only the policy of forming a broad united front through alliance and struggle is Marxist-Leninist policy. The victory of the Chinese revolution is the victory of Chairman Mao's proletarian revolutionary line and the victory of Chairman Mao's great tactical thinking.

V

In "On Policy," Chairman Mao summed up our Party's historical experience and fully explained the importance of raising the level of tactical thinking in the whole Party. He emphatically pointed out: **"To correct the lopsided views of many Party cadres on the question of tactics and their consequent vacillations between 'Left' and Right, we must help them to acquire an all-round and integrated understanding of the changes and developments in the Party's policy, past and present."** Chairman Mao's teaching clearly points out the direction for us to better our tactical thinking and raise our level of understanding and carrying out of policy. In restudying "On Policy" today, a fundamental problem for us is to arm our minds with dialectical and historical materialism, acquire an all-round and integrated understanding of our Party's policies and tactics and overcome the erroneous "Left" and Right tendencies while carrying out policy.

Chairman Mao's tactical principles and policies reflect both the fundamental laws of proletarian revolution and the specific laws of various historical stages. They are the dialectical unity of the universality and particularity of contradiction, and it is necessary to acquire an all-round and integrated understanding of them. If we use the idealist and metaphysical viewpoint to comprehend the Party's tactical principles and various policies in a one-sided, isolated and static way, completely affirming or negating complicated matters, then we will inevitably go to the extreme "Left" or the extreme Right in the course of implementing policy. We must persevere in the Marxist scientific method advocated by Chairman Mao of investigating and studying social conditions; conscientiously observe, analyze and study the complicated international and domestic class struggles, the relations between the various classes and their changes and development; correctly distinguish and handle the two different types of contradictions; be good at grasping and exploiting the various contradictions in the enemy camp; and differentiate in dealing with different people and different conditions. By doing this, we will not be saddled with subjectivism, one-sidedness or superficiality when we observe and handle problems; we will overcome thinking in absolute terms, and enable our thinking to constantly fit in with changes in the objective situation. Thus, we can remain firm, overcome vacillation, do away with blindness and raise our consciousness in implementing the Party's policies.

★ ★ ★ ★ ★

Chinese View of World History

The following piece appeared, in several installments, in *Red Flag* at a time when the Chinese people were undergoing a veritable leap forward in the study of foreign affairs. Thus a reader of the *People's Daily* would find about three quarters of the six-page daily devoted to foreign affairs by the latter part of 1972. "Shih Chün" is not a real name but a designation for a collective of writers, reportedly at Peking University, who wrote this piece together. *Shih* means history and *chün* means army. The phrase in the original Chinese version, "study a little world history," apparently from Mao, is a suggestion to the people to learn about foreign things as much as they can with the material available. The Chinese people are now being widely urged to cultivate the acquaintance of foreigners and to study foreign languages.

The opening paragraphs state in capsule form the prevalent Chinese world view. Since the theme of the piece is on the inevitable decline of imperialism, it can be read as an exposition of the theme of "waning" American imperialism. The frequent references to Britain are meant to apply allegorically to the United States, and the stress on maritime rivalry among imperialist powers can also be read as allegorical reference to present-day Soviet-American naval rivalry. The phrase of Mao's that "a weak nation can defeat a strong nation, a small nation can defeat a big nation" is one of the most widely quoted phrases of Mao's today. It not only alludes to the Indochina conflict but to China's own relatively weak position vis-à-vis the two superpowers. The statement that "the characteristic feature of the world situation today is 'upheaval'" has been repeated many times by the Chinese delegates to the United Nations.

★   ★   ★

*"SHIH CHÜN"**

Excerpts from *Why It Is Necessary to Study World History and Some History about Imperialism*

CHARACTERISTIC FEATURE OF WORLD SITUATION

The era in which we live today is **"a great era of radical change in the social system throughout the world, an earth-shaking era."** Countries want independence, nations want liberation and the people want revolution—this has become an irresistible histori-

* "Shih Chün," *Peking Review*, Nos. 21, 24, 25, 26 (May 26, June 16, June 23, and June 30, 1972).

cal tide. The time has gone for ever when two superpowers could dominate the world. Living in such an era, we must be prepared to engage in great struggles which will have many features that are different in form from those of the past.

Victorious in revolution, socialist China must strive to make greater contributions to mankind. Since the Chinese revolution is part of the world revolution, all the revolutionary tasks we undertake are closely linked to the revolutionary struggles of the world's people. To have the world at heart, it is necessary to understand it. The world today is a development of the world yesterday. The contemporary struggles of the world's people against imperialism and its lackeys are a continuation and development of their past and long struggles against class oppression, oppression by foreign invaders and colonial rule. To study world history will enable us, by acquiring a knowledge of the entire process of world history and drawing on historical experience, to better understand the special feature of the present world situation, foresee its general trend, strengthen our confidence in the victory of the proletariat and the revolutionary people and raise our consciousness of proletarian patriotism and internationalism. This will benefit the promotion of mutual support between the people of China and other countries in revolutionary struggles and thus help in the still greater development of world revolution.

The characteristic feature of the world situation today is "upheaval," or "global upheaval." This "upheaval" which has a class nature is an expression of the sharpening basic world contradictions. What accounts for the "global upheaval"? Is it a good or a bad thing? How should this complicated international phenomenon be assessed? Reading world history will tell us that to overthrow the old social system and establish a new one is a great revolution marked by soul-stirring class struggles and earth-shaking changes. This has been the case in every great turning point in human history. The course of the collapse of the Western slave system was filled with recurrent slave uprisings in the ancient Roman Empire and unending foreign invasions, with civil wars going hand in hand with external wars. In the course of the collapse of the world feudal system, the bourgeois world revolution swept Europe and America; there were frequent civil and international wars, attempts at a come-back and opposing it and the alternate emergence of systems of monarchy and republic—a great up-heaval lasting almost two hundred years.

In the more than one hundred years since the birth of Marxism, when the proletariat appeared on the world scene, the revolutionary struggle to overthrow the bourgeoisie and other exploiting classes and the liberation struggles of the oppressed people have rolled on with full force and rocked the whole world. Therefore, the great upheaval in the world situation is a normal occurrence in the great era of revolution and in accord with the objective law governing the development of history. Today's world "upheaval" reflects the life-and-death struggle between contemporary revolutionary forces and counter-revolutionary forces—an "upheaval" by which the imperialist-ruled old world is headed for collapse and a socialist new world is advancing to victory.

GRASPING THE OBJECTIVE LAW OF SOCIAL DEVELOPMENT

Chairman Mao has pointed out: **"Classes struggle, some classes triumph, others are eliminated. Such is history, such is the history of civilization for thousands of years."** Reading world history will help us to know and grasp the objective law governing the development of human society in the light of the concrete historical course of the world-wide class struggle and gain still greater initiative in the struggle. Modern and contemporary world history is a record of the criminal acts of capitalism, colonialism and imperialism in exploitation and aggression at home and abroad and also one of the heroic struggle of the world's revolutionary people and the oppressed colonial people against exploitation, aggression and oppression. In the long course of struggle, capitalism, colonialism and imperialism have changed from strong to weak in moving step by step towards their extinction, while the revolutionary people and the oppressed colonial people have grown from weak to strong in advancing to victory. This is what historical dialecticism means. The historical course of the rise and fall of any once rampant colonial empire in world history, be it tsarist Russian or fascist

Germany which were thrown off the historical stage, or the rapidly declining British Empire, has vividly demonstrated the objective law of historical development that capitalism is bound to perish while socialism is sure to triumph.

An unrivaled maritime overlord in the nineteenth century, the British Empire, by gunboat policy and power politics, became a vast colonial empire which spread across five continents and on which "the sun never sets." But instead of solving the deep contradictions inherent in capitalism, the policy of expansion only deepened and widened them. With the steady progress of the proletarian socialist revolution and the vigorous development of the liberation movement of the oppressed people of the colonies, the British Empire has been irrevocably and rapidly declining. The rise and decline of the British Empire throws light on how to look at modern imperialism and social-imperialism. Throwing their weight about everywhere in the world, the two superpowers today look like huge monsters. But, sitting on the volcano of the people's revolution, they are in fact plunged into the depths of inextricable crises. Like the star over the British Empire, the stars over them are falling.

The course of imperialism heading for doom is also one in which the revolutionary forces of the whole world constantly expand and develop. Though invariably weak and small at the beginning, the people's revolutionary forces are in essence invincible because they represent the orientation of historical development. They will grow from small to big and from weak to strong so long as they dare to struggle and are good at waging unyielding struggles to the end despite any setback. The revolutionary truth that **a weak nation can defeat a strong, a small nation can defeat a big** has not only been confirmed by the Chinese revolution, the Albanian people's revolution and the Korean people's war against U.S. aggression and for national salvation but also by the war of the Vietnamese, Cambodian and Lao peoples against U.S. aggression and for national salvation. This has also been repeatedly borne out by many previous facts in world history. The 1775–83 American War of Independence is a case in point. Then the world's biggest industrial country with a population of almost thirty million, the British Empire sent 90,000 troops to its northern American colony which had a population of only three million. The latter had only a small number of out-of-date guns, a few guerrilla bands and some militia groups. At the start of the war, it lost many battles to the British aggressor troops who thereby occupied much of its territory. But supported by the people and progressive forces in European countries, the mobilized masses launched guerrilla warfare, persisting to the end in their war of independence, a war of justice. Their protracted struggle culminated in a defeat for the British Empire and the winning of independence. Countless historical facts tell us that in the present struggle against the policy of aggression pursued by U.S. imperialism and social-imperialism, the only way for us is to be guided by a correct revolutionary line, **"dare to fight, defy difficulties, and advance wave upon wave. Then the whole world will belong to the people. Monsters of all kinds shall be destroyed."**

LEARNING FROM STRONG POINTS OF THE PEOPLE OF ALL COUNTRIES

World history shows that Asia and Africa are the cradle of civilization. Because of their splendid ancient civilizations, Asia, Africa and Latin America have made great contributions to human progress. As a result of Western colonialist invasion after the late fifteenth century, vast areas of three continents were reduced to colonies or semi-colonies and subjected to ruthless exploitation and enslavement by the Western colonialists. The vicious slave trade and various forms of cruel plunder by the Western colonialists changed Africa from a land of wealth, beauty and traditional civilization to a "dark" continent. Four centuries of plunder by the colonialists reduced the African population by 100 million. After throwing African Negroes into the abyss of unprecedented suffering, the slave traders came to China to trick large numbers of Chinese laboring people and shipped them to America as "coolies." Like African Negroes and American working people, hundreds of thousands of Chinese laborers lived in deep misery; they sweated and shed their blood together with them. Where there is oppression, there is resistance. Fighting shoulder to shoulder against the Western colonialists, they cemented their militant friendship in blood. The British colonialist bandit and butcher Gordon who took part in suppressing the Chinese Taiping Revolution was killed by the Sudanese people when he went to Africa to repress them. A common historical experience has helped the people of Asia, Africa and Latin America to take the road of mutual support and close unity in struggle. Though they are separated by mountains and rivers, the common struggle against colonialist aggression has bound together the oppressed people and nations of the three continents.

A knowledge of this history enables us to realize profoundly that the Chinese people and the oppressed nations and people of Asia, Africa and Latin America are class brothers and comrades in arms who are as closely linked as flesh and blood and share weal and woe and that China and the overwhelming majority of the Asian, African and Latin American countries belong to the Third World. Therefore, the Chinese people regard victory in the anti-imperialist struggle by the people of Asia, Africa and Latin America as their own and give warm sympathy and support to all their anti-imperialist and anti-colonialist struggles.

Guided by Chairman Mao's proletarian revolutionary line in foreign affairs, the Chinese people have steadily developed friendly contacts with the people of other countries and modestly learned from their strong points. Redoubling efforts to learn from one another conforms to the world historical trend. World history shows that it is the millions and millions of slaves who propel the progress of history as well as science and culture. The masses are the masters of history and the true makers and successors of the outstanding cultures of mankind. The people of all countries, big or small, have made their contributions to mankind; they have both strong and weak points, as well as things from which others can learn or draw lessons. Through long years of friendly exchanges with other peoples, we Chinese people in the past learned many useful things from them to enrich and develop our own national culture. The proletariat should adopt the Marxist analytical attitude towards all things. Blind worship of foreign things and the slavish comprador philosophy are manifestations of the shameless servile features of the comprador class in semi-colonial countries, and must be thoroughly criticized. The metaphysical attitude of refusing to come into contact with foreign things, and not studying and analyzing them, is also completely wrong. The correct principle we should follow is to **"make the past serve the present and foreign things serve China."** . . .

THREE STAGES

If we start counting from England's bourgeois revolution of 1640, modern and contemporary world history covers a span of over three hundred years. It can be divided into three stages. The first, from 1640 to the eve of the 1871 revolution of the Paris Commune, is the period of "free" capitalism, in which capitalism through protracted struggles replaced feudalism in a number of countries in Europe and America. The second stage, from the 1871 Paris Commune to immediately before the 1917 October Socialist Revolution, is one in which "free" capitalism was going over to imperialism until imperialism finally took shape. In this period, the socialist revolutionary movement of the proletariat and the national-democratic revolutionary movement were on the rise and making onslaughts against capitalism, colonialism and imperialism. Led by Lenin, the 1917 October Socialist Revolution in Russia opened a new epoch in world history. Modern world history thereby entered its third stage, the period of contemporary history. As Chairman Mao has pointed out, this is **"the historic epoch in which world capitalism and imperialism are going down to their doom and world socialism and people's democracy are marching to victory."**

Modern-contemporary history covers the inception, growth and decline of capitalism and the inception, growth and advance to victory of socialism. The struggle of the proletariat and all other exploited toilers against the capitalist class, the struggle of the colonial and semi-colonial peoples against colonialism and imperialism, and the united struggle of a growing number of medium-sized and small countries against aggression, interference, subversion and plunder by the two superpowers are the main contents in the annals of modern-contemporary world history. In the final analysis, the complex contradictions of the present world are expressions of the various contradictions of the old world as they develop and interact in new historical circumstances. . . .

STRUGGLE FOR HEGEMONY BETWEEN IMPERIALIST COUNTRIES

One of the basic contradictions in modern-contemporary world history is the conflict and contention among imperialist countries. Capitalism developed to the stage of imperialism towards the end of the nineteenth and at the beginning of the twentieth century. In this stage, the contradictions inherent in capitalism become ever more acute and broader in scope. The contradictions, in essence, are the contentions among imperialists for world domination and spheres of influence in colonies. Imperialism is monopolistic, parasitic, moribund capitalism. Lenin said: **"An essential feature of imperialism is the rivalry between several Great Powers in the striving for hegemony"** *(Imperialism, the Highest Stage of Capitalism)*, and **" 'world domination' is, to put it briefly, the substance of imperialist policy."** *(A Caricature of Marxism and Imperialist Economism)*

Rivalry among the big colonialist and imperialist powers has never ceased in modern-contemporary world history. In the seventeenth century, it was mainly contention for maritime hegemony between Britain and the Netherlands. In the eighteenth century, there was fierce rivalry between Britain and France for maritime and European hegemony. In the nineteenth century, a complicated situation arose on the European continent, with Britain, Russia, France, Germany and Austria locked in strife for supremacy at different times. Rivalries became sharper when world capitalism entered the stage of imperialism. At the beginning of the twentieth century, the contradictions between the two overlords, Britain and Germany, became the main imperialist contradictions of the time. A latecomer among the imperialist pirates, Germany went all out in expansion in the Middle East and elsewhere. It attempted to realize its ambition for world domination by occupying the Middle East, the hub of communication between Europe, Asia and

Africa and an important strategic area leading to the Mediterranean and the Indian Ocean, and seizing British and French colonies. The Middle East thus became an important area for which the imperialist powers contended with one another. Britain, the old-line colonial empire, planned to defeat its powerful rival Germany in war, wrest Mesopotamia and Palestine from Turkey, enslave the Arab people and consolidate its colonial rule in Africa. Several other imperialist countries also had their sinister designs for dividing up the world. The rapid sharpening of their contradictions led to World War I of 1914–18, bringing mankind unprecedented suffering. But war gave rise to revolution and the outbreak of the revolutions in Russia, Germany, Hungary, Turkey and other countries spelled the end of tsarist Russia, the German Empire and the Austro-Hungarian Empire—the seemingly powerful colossi who were aggressive by nature.

The study of modern-contemporary world history will enable us to see the deep historical background of today's contention between two superpowers for world domination. As imperialist and social-imperialist countries, they are bound to be governed by the laws of imperialism, to take the beaten path of hegemonism. This is dictated by the nature of imperialism and their downfall is also inevitable.

One of the latecomers among the imperialist countries, U.S. imperialism in its early period seldom became involved in the scramble for supremacy among the European powers because of conditions peculiar to the development of capitalism in the United States. Its first step was aggression and expansion in Latin America. Starting and winning the 1898 Spanish-American War, the first war to redivide colonies in world history, U.S. imperialism became overnight the overlord in the Western Hemisphere. In the short period of thirty years after entering the stage of imperialism, the United States was involved in thirty-three military invasions and interventions in Latin America.

Moreover, the United States lost no time in contending with other imperialist countries for hegemony in the Pacific region and in Asia. There were both contention and collusion over the years between U.S. imperialism and Japanese imperialism in their complicated scramble for hegemony in the Pacific. Their deep, irreconcilable contradictions culminated in the surprise raid on Pearl Harbor by Japanese militarism in 1941 and the Pacific War of 1941–45. U.S. imperialism amassed vast wealth in the two world wars. As the Number One imperialist country after World War II, the United States stretched its tentacles everywhere around the world. While plundering other peoples economically, it resorted to the big-stick policy of undisguised armed interference in the internal affairs of other countries, starting a new scramble for world hegemony. But times have changed. The unprecedented upsurge in the revolution of the Asian, African and Latin American peoples in the postwar period, the drastic decline of world capitalism, the sharpening of different contradictions in and outside the United States and growing contradictions among the imperialist countries—all these very soon sent U.S. imperialism tumbling from the peak of its strength.

The modern history of Russia also tells us about tsarist Russia's **"never changed and neglected aim—Russia's world hegemony."** (Engels: *The Foreign Policy of the Tsarist Government of Russia*) By suppressing the revolution in Poland and Hungary, occupying large tracts of Chinese territory and engaging in expansion in West and Central Asia, the old tsars built a huge colonial empire astride Europe and Asia towards the end of the nineteenth century. Tsarist Russia always regarded hegemony in the Middle East and the Balkan Peninsula as the first strategic objective to achieve. Doing its utmost to expand its navy and contending for an outlet from the Baltic Sea, it tried to clear the way through the Black Sea Strait and control the Mediterranean Sea to build up its maritime hegemony. To realize this global strategy of aggression and expansion, it unleashed wars abroad. Its contention with Japan for supremacy over East Asia led to the Russo-Japanese War of 1904. Defeated, it divided and shared with Japan their spheres of influences in East Asia at the expense of the sovereignty of China and Korea, in addition to supporting Japan in its aggression against the two countries. Meanwhile, it worked together with Britain in the West. The two concluded secret treaties for dividing up spheres of influence in Iran, Afghanistan and China's

Tibet and jointly sent forces to put down the revolution in Iran. But all the schemes between the imperialist countries could in no way stop the tide of revolution. It was during World War I, an imperialist war, that the revolutionary situation in Russia developed rapidly until tsarist Russia, the main bulwark of the reactionary forces in Europe, was changed into the source of the storm of the socialist revolution and the Russian proletariat won the world's first victory in socialist revolution. History thus proclaimed the end of the dream of a huge tsarist empire. Completely betraying the road of the October Socialist Revolution and fully inheriting the old tsar's mantle of expansionism, the Soviet revisionist renegade clique now entrenched in the Kremlin has restored capitalism and pushed social-imperialism. It can be said with certainty that it is only a pipe dream for the Soviet revisionists to try to reestablish a big colonial empire in the era when the imperialist system is heading for collapse.

Looking back on the history of the imperialist countries contending for world domination and suffering continuous defeats and of U.S. imperialism and tsarist Russian imperialism is of great help in observing today's contention for world hegemony by the two superpowers and some other international problems. The nature of imperialism determines that while frequently colluding, the imperialist countries have no way of reconciling their conflicts in contending for world hegemony. Their collusion means greater suppression of the peoples, whereas their bitter rivalry provides favorable conditions for the victory of the revolutionary people. The revolutionary people must regard the contradictions among imperialists as an inevitable historical phenomenon as capitalism heads towards its doom, and concretely analyze and correctly handle them from a class standpoint. Plunder and aggression by the imperialist powers and the strife for hegemony among them, particularly between the two superpowers, account for the complex conflicts in some areas and also give birth to the tempestuous anti-imperialist struggle of the people in the intermediate zones. Only by overthrowing imperialism, colonialism and neocolonialism can these peoples solve their problems in their own interests, independently and with the initiative in their own hands.

WHERE THERE IS OPPRESSION
THERE IS RESISTANCE

Where there is oppression there is resistance. Modern-contemporary world history is also the history of the unceasing heroic struggles of the proletariat and the oppressed nations and people of the world against capitalism, colonialism and imperialism. The great truth **"The people, and the people alone, are the motive force in the making of world history"** has been proved by many historical facts—from the first great trial of strength between the proletariat and the bourgeoisie of France in June 1848 to the hoisting of the red flag of the Paris Commune—the world's first dictatorship of the proletariat—in 1871; from the monumental triumph of the October Socialist Revolution to the great victory of the Chinese people's revolution and on to the new development of the current international communist movement. All these are a magnificent epic written by the proletariat and other laboring people of various countries and declare the bankruptcy of modern revisionism.

Side by side with the vigorous advance of the revolutionary movement of the world's proletariat, the oppressed nations' liberation movements have developed into a violent historical trend. Asia, Africa and Latin America have become an arena seething with revolutionary storms that hit directly at imperialism. This is the outcome of the acute development of the contradictions between the oppressed nations in the colonies and semi-colonies on the one hand and imperialism and colonialism on the other. It has undergone a long historical process. The revolution always advances according to this law: The more the oppression, the greater the resistance; long suppressed, resistance is bound to break out rapidly. In the few hundred years since the end of the fifteenth century, the people of Asia, Africa and Latin America have suffered all sorts of plunder and oppression by Western colonialism and imperialism and have set into motion one revolutionary storm after another in fierce offensives against colonialism and imperialism.

Large-scale wars for independence and liberation of the colonies broke out in Latin America at the end of the eighteenth century and the beginning of the nineteenth century. Taking the lead were the hundreds of thousands of Negro slaves in Haiti who in more than ten years of fierce fighting routed 60,000 colonial troops of France and Spain and forced the arrogant Napoleon's aggressor troops to surrender; in 1804 they founded Latin America's first independent state of blacks freed from colonial rule and the slave system. This was followed by the uprisings of the people of many Latin American countries which destroyed the colonial system of Spain and Portugal on the continent. In the mid-nineteenth century when the Asian people became politically awakened, the first revolutionary tide against colonialism and feudalism in Asia swept from the Persian Gulf and India to China. Marx and Engels hailed these great new things with great revolutionary enthusiasm. Engels predicted that **"the opening day of a new era for all Asia"** *(Persia and China)* would come before long. A new source of great world storms opened up in India, Vietnam, Korea, the Philippines and China in the early twentieth century and especially after the October Socialist Revolution in Russia. This turned Asia into a vast battlefield against imperialism. In Africa, the enslaved black people, armed with such primitive weapons as bows and arrows and shotguns, have fought heroically for several centuries against the Western colonialist aggressors armed to the teeth with advanced weapons. Since World War II, Asia, Africa and Latin America have become the focal point of the contradictions of the present-day world and are seething with struggles on an unprecedented scale against imperialism and colonialism and neo-colonialism. The ever-growing national-democratic revolutionary movements in the heartland of capitalism, such as the struggle of the Afro-Americans against racial discrimination and the struggle of the people of Northern Ireland for national independence, all have profound historical origins. The U.S. bourgeoisie for generations has been the class enemy of the Afro-Americans whose ancestors were black slaves shipped from Africa to America by Western colonialists. More than twenty million Afro-Americans in the United States are fighting ruthless exploitation and oppression by the monopoly capitalists. In his statement supporting their struggle against racial discrimination, Chairman Mao penetratingly pointed out: **"The evil system of colonialism and** imperialism arose and throve with the enslavement of Negroes and the trade in Negroes, and it will surely come to its end with the complete emancipation of the black people."

REVOLUTION WILL TRIUMPH

The advance of history shows that the great trend of our era— countries want independence, nations want liberation, and the people want revolution—is an outcome of the logical development of modern history. The rise of the Third World is not accidental but an inevitable result of the struggle against imperialism and colonialism by the people of Asia, Africa and Latin America. Chairman Mao pointed out: **"Imperialism has pushed the great masses of the people throughout the world into the historical epoch of the great struggle to abolish imperialism."**

The people invariably want revolution and the revolution is bound to win. But the road of revolution is tortuous, progressing in the course of struggle which is full of twists and turns. This is the dialectical law of historical development. In modern world history, the bourgeois revolution in England beginning in 1640 went through a zigzag course of struggle for nearly half a century. So did the bourgeois revolution in the United States beginning in 1775 for nearly a century and the bourgeois revolution in France beginning in 1789 for more than eighty years. It was after such protracted struggles that the bourgeoisie in these countries consolidated their domination. The people in the colonies have been doing the same in their struggle for independence. The colonialists and imperialists never quit their colonies of their own accord. They are bound to create all kinds of troubles for the people's revolution. It was not until they had fought wars of independence for almost twenty years in the early nineteenth century that the people of Latin American countries freed themselves from Spanish and Portuguese colonial rule. After their independence, however, many countries were turned into "commercial colonies" by British imperialism as a result of economic infiltration. Under the signboard of "pan-Americanism," U.S. imperialism imposed the chains of neo-colonialism on many Latin American countries by combining the big stick and carrot tactics.

These historical experiences show us that there has never been a genuine revolution without going through a tortuous course of hard struggle, or a revolution that has advanced without a hitch after victory was won and does not have to undergo the protracted struggle between those attempting a comeback and those opposing it. Since this is true for the bourgeois revolution, the socialist revolution led by the proletariat has to go through an even sharper and more tortuous struggle in order to win final victory. Chairman Mao pointed out: **"The correctness or incorrectness of the ideological and political line decides everything."** The proletariat and the revolutionary people are able to overcome all difficulties on their road of advance, speed up the pace of revolution and promote historical advance provided they have a correct Marxist-Leninist line. The study of world history will enable us to have a still deeper understanding of Chairman Mao's great theory of continuing the revolution under the dictatorship of the proletariat and his proletarian revolutionary line and politics, and spur us to continually raise our consciousness of class struggle and the struggle between the two lines and our consciousness of continuing revolution, so as to carry the socialist revolution through to the end.

The whole course of modern-contemporary world history vividly proves that socialism is certain to replace capitalism, just as capitalism replaced feudalism. This is an irresistible law of history. The tide of world revolution is pushing ahead today precisely in accordance with this law. Countries want independence, nations want liberation, and the people want revolution—the world situation is excellent. Aggression and oppression by the two superpowers are arousing the people of the world to a new awakening and promoting unity among the large number of developing countries. No force in the world can prevent the inevitable downfall of imperialism, nor can any force hold back the sure victory of the revolutionary cause of the people.

Lenin pointed out long ago: **"But the morrow of world history will be a day when the awakening peoples oppressed by imperialism are finally aroused and the decisive long and hard**

struggle for their liberation begins." *(Question of Nationalities or "Autonomisation")* This great day has now come! In such an earth-shaking great era, it is most useful for every revolutionary to read some modern-contemporary world history and draw on the rich experience accumulated by the people of all countries in their revolutionary struggles, military or political, economic or cultural, with or without bloodshed, positive or negative. . . .

★ ★ ★ ★ ★

The Chinese View of Russia

This is one of the most vehement and comprehensive indictments of the Soviet Union ever published in China. It constitutes a final step in the transformation of the Chinese world view of the Soviet Union from that of fraternal socialist ally to one of imperialist revisionist enemy. The article was published just three days before the Chinese launched their first earth-orbiting satellite, two days before the summit conference of the Indochina leaders in southern China, and eight days before President Nixon announced the American invasion of Cambodia. The article was jointly published by the *People's Daily, Red Flag,* and the army newspaper *Liberation Army Daily* in order to demonstrate the highest policy-making sanction for the views expressed. As is customary, the publication in *Red Flag* was preceded by selected phrases of Chairman Mao designed to set the overall tone of the article. The first slogan reads:

> Things are getting worse for the enemy day by day. Things are getting better for us day by day.

> We too must make an artificial satellite.

> The Chinese people have determination and ability. They certainly will, in the not too distant future, catch up with and surpass world standards of progress.

The first paragraph of the second slogan reads:

> The rise to power of revisionism is in effect the rise to power of the capitalist class . . . The present Soviet Union is a dictatorship of the capitalist class, is a dictatorship of the big capitalist class, is a German–fascist-type dictatorship, is a Hitler-type dictatorship.

The first slogan alludes to the United States, the "waning imperialism." Not the invasion of Cambodia nor the even more ferocious intervention of American power in Indochina thereafter changed the basic Chinese view of American imperialism as "waning." The second slogan makes clear that the references within the article to the Soviet Union's "Hitlerite policies" are not casual but directly express the main argument.

Though the ostensible reason for the publication was the celebration of the hundredth anniversary of Lenin's birth on April 22, the real reason was to state again China's basic perceptions of her two great enemies, the Soviet Union and the United States, during a time of mushrooming crisis. The launching of China's satellite demonstrated a potential missile delivery capability which both her enemies perceived as a threat. The Indochina summit conference and signs of an American move into Cambodia heralded another major crisis in the Indochina war.

The article gives the most explicit rationale, in Marxist terms, of what "revisionism" is in the Soviet Union. It notes that in socialist societies power is the key question of the class struggle. It maintains that a bureaucratic monopoly capitalist class has come to power in the Soviet Union which possesses the instruments of state power and all the wealth of the society. The Chinese maintain that, had it not been for their Cultural Revolution, the same would have occurred in China.

In its greed for profits, in order to maintain its rule, and to exploit and oppress, this new capitalist class seeks expansion abroad in the manner of international imperialism. Every instance of Soviet activity beyond its borders is denounced as serving the interests of imperialist control. Of particular note is the article's imputation to the Soviet Union of a persistent drive for war: "They are frenziedly increasing their military expenditures, intensifying their mobilization and preparations for aggressive war, and plotting to unleash a Hitler-type blitzkrieg."

The article also expends a considerable number of words on a subject which some people consider one of the most sensitive in the Soviet Union: the nationalities. The article accuses the Russians, who are a minority in the Soviet Union, of reverting to Pan-Slav policies and suppressing the other nationalities.

With their comparison of the present-day Soviet Union to Hitlerite Germany, it is not difficult to see why the Chinese regard the Soviet Union as a "rising" imperialism.

★   ★   ★

PEOPLE'S DAILY*
Leninism or Social Imperialism?

I. THE BANNER OF LENINISM IS INVINCIBLE

The centenary of the birth of the great Lenin falls on April 22 this year.

Throughout the world, the Marxist-Leninists, the proletariat and the revolutionary people are commemorating this date of historic significance with the highest respect for the great Lenin.

After the death of Marx and Engels, Lenin was the great leader of the international communist movement and the great teacher of the proletariat and oppressed people of the world.

In 1871, the year after Lenin was born, the uprising of the Paris Commune occurred; this was the first attempt of the proletariat to overthrow the bourgeoisie. The world was entering the era of imperialism and proletarian revolution late in the nineteenth and early in the twentieth centuries when Lenin began his revolutionary activities. In his struggles against imperialism and opportunism of every kind, and especially against

---

* *People's Daily* (April 22, 1970). The article was translated and published as a pamphlet, *Leninism or Social Imperialism?* (Peking: Foreign Languages Press, 1970).

the revisionism of the Second International, Lenin inherited, defended and developed Marxism and brought it to a new and higher stage, the stage of Leninism. As Stalin put it, **"Leninism is Marxism of the era of imperialism and of the proletarian revolution."**

Lenin analyzed the contradictions of imperialism, revealed the law governing it and solved a series of major questions of the proletarian revolution in the era of imperialism and settled the question of socialism **"achieving victory first in one or several countries."** He expounded the thesis that the proletariat must assume leadership in the bourgeois-democratic revolution and led the Russian proletariat in staging a general rehearsal in the revolution of 1905. Under his leadership the Great October Socialist Revolution brought about the fundamental change from the old world of capitalism to the new world of socialism, opening up a new era in the history of mankind.

Lenin's theoretical and practical contributions to the cause of the proletarian revolution were extremely great.

After the death of Lenin, Stalin inherited and defended the cause of Leninism in his struggles against domestic and foreign class enemies and against the Right and "Left" opportunists in the Party. He led the Soviet people in continuing the advance along the socialist road and in winning great victories. During World War II the Soviet people under the command of Stalin became the main force in defeating fascist aggression and made magnificent contributions which will live forever in the history of mankind.

We Chinese Communists and the Chinese people will never forget that it was precisely in Leninism that we found our road to liberation. Comrade Mao Tse-tung says: **"The salvos of the October Revolution brought us Marxism-Leninism."** **"They** [the Chinese—*Tr.*] **found Marxism-Leninism, the universally applicable truth, and the face of China began to change."** He points out: **"The Chinese people have always considered the Chinese revolution a continuation of the Great October Socialist Revolution."**

Applying the theory of Marxism-Leninism, Comrade Mao Tse-tung creatively solved the fundamental problems of the Chinese revolution and led the Chinese people in waging the most protracted, fierce, arduous and complicated revolutionary struggles and revolutionary wars ever known in the history of the world proletarian revolution and in winning victory in the people's revolution in China, this large country in the East. This is the greatest victory in the world proletarian revolution since the October Revolution.

We are now living in a great new era of world revolution. The international situation has undergone world-shaking changes since Lenin's time. The development of the entire world history has proved that Lenin's revolutionary teachings are correct and that the banner of Leninism is invincible.

But history has its twists and turns. Just as Bernstein-Kautsky revisionism emerged after the death of Engels, so did Khrushchev-Brezhnev revisionism after the death of Stalin.

Eleven years after Khrushchev came to power, a split occurred within the revisionist clique and he was replaced by Brezhnev. More than five years have elapsed since Brezhnev took office. And now it is this Brezhnev who is conducting the "commemoration" of the centenary of Lenin's birth in the Soviet Union.

Lenin once said: **"It has always been the case in history that after the death of revolutionary leaders who were popular among the oppressed classes, their enemies have attempted to appropriate their names so as to deceive the oppressed classes."**

This is exactly what the renegade Brezhnev and his ilk are doing to the great Lenin. In their so-called Theses on the Centenary of the Birth of Vladimir Ilyich Lenin, they have the impudence to distort the great image of Lenin, the revolutionary teacher of the proletariat, and pass off their revisionist rubbish as Leninism. They pretend to "commemorate" Lenin, but in reality they are appropriating the name of Lenin to press forward with their social-imperialism, social-fascism and social-militarism. What an outrageous insult to Lenin!

Today our fighting tasks are thoroughly to expose the betrayal of Leninism by the Soviet revisionist renegades, to lay bare the class nature of Soviet revisionist social-imperialism, point out the historical law that social-imperialism, like capitalist imperialism, will meet its inevitable doom, and further promote the great struggle of the people of the world against U.S. imperialism, Soviet revisionism and all reaction. Here is the tremendous significance of our commemoration of the centenary of the birth of the great Lenin.

II. THE FUNDAMENTAL QUESTION OF LENINISM IS THE DICTATORSHIP OF THE PROLETARIAT

In his struggles against opportunism and revisionism, Lenin repeatedly pointed out that the fundamental question in the proletarian revolution is that of using violence to seize political power, smash the bourgeois state machine, and establish the dictatorship of the proletariat.

He said: **"The latter** [the bourgeois state—*Tr.*] *cannot* **be superseded by the proletarian state (the dictatorship of the proletariat) in the process of 'withering away'; as a general rule, this can happen only by means of a violent revolution."**

He added that Marx's theory of the dictatorship of the proletariat **"is inseparably bound up with all he taught on the revolutionary role of the proletariat in history. The culmination of this role is the proletarian dictatorship."**

The victory of the October Revolution led by Lenin was a victory for the Marxist theory of the proletarian revolution and the dictatorship of the proletariat. The road of the October Revolution is the road of the proletariat achieving the dictatorship of the proletariat through violent revolution.

Around the time of the October Revolution, Lenin summed up the new revolutionary practice and further developed the Marxist theory of the dictatorship of the proletariat. He pointed out that the socialist revolution covers **"a whole epoch of intensified class conflicts"** and that **"until this epoch has terminated, the exploiters inevitably cherish the hope of restoration, and this** *hope* **is converted into** *attempts* **at restoration."** Therefore, he maintained that the dictatorship of the proletariat **"is necessary . . . not only for the** *proletariat* **which has overthrown the bourgeoisie, but for the entire** *historical period* **between capitalism and 'classless society,' communism."**

Today, as we commemorate the centenary of Lenin's birth, it is of vital practical significance to study anew these brilliant ideas of Lenin's.

As is well known, it is precisely on the fundamental question of the proletarian revolution and the dictatorship of the proletariat that the Soviet revisionist renegade clique has betrayed Leninism and the October Revolution.

Far back, when Khrushchev began to reveal his revisionist features, Comrade Mao Tse-tung acutely pointed out: **"I think there are two 'swords': One is Lenin and the other Stalin. The sword of Stalin has now been abandoned by the Russians."** **"As for the sword of Lenin, has it too now been abandoned to a certain extent by some leaders of the Soviet Union? In my view, it has been abandoned to a considerable extent. Is the October Revolution still valid? Can it still be the example for all countries? Khrushchev's report at the Twentieth Congress of the C.P.S.U. says it is possible to gain political power by the parliamentary road, that is to say, it is no longer necessary for all countries to learn from the October Revolution. Once this gate is opened, Leninism by and large is thrown out."**

III. COUNTER-REVOLUTIONARY COUP D'ÉTAT BY THE KHRUSHCHEV-BREZHNEV RENEGADE CLIQUE

How was it possible for the restoration of capitalism to take place in the Soviet Union, the first socialist state in the world, and how was it possible for the Soviet Union to become social-imperialist? If we examine this question from the standpoint of Marxism-Leninism, and especially in the light of Comrade Mao Tse-tung's theory of continuing the revolution under the dictatorship of the proletariat, we shall be able to understand that this was mainly a product of the class struggle in the Soviet Union, the result of the usurpation of Party and government leadership by a handful of Party persons in power taking the capitalist road there, in other words, the result of the usurpation of the political power of the proletariat by the Soviet bourgeoisie. At the same time, it was the result of the policy of "peaceful evolution" which world imperialism, in trying to save itself from its doom, has pushed in the Soviet Union through the medium of the Soviet revisionist renegade clique.

Comrade Mao Tse-tung points out: **"Socialist society covers** a considerably long historical period. In the historical period of socialism, there are still classes, class contradictions and class struggle, there is the struggle between the socialist road and the capitalist road, and there is the danger of capitalist restoration." In socialist society the class struggle still focuses on the question of political power. Comrade Mao Tse-tung points out: "Those representatives of the bourgeoisie who have sneaked into the Party, the government, the army and various spheres of culture are a bunch of counter-revolutionary revisionists. Once conditions are ripe, they will seize political power and turn the dictatorship of the proletariat into a dictatorship of the bourgeoisie."

Classes and class struggle continued to exist in the Soviet Union long after the October Revolution, although the bourgeoisie had been overthrown. Stalin cleared out quite a gang of counter-revolutionary representatives of the bourgeoisie who had wormed their way into the Party—Trotsky, Zinoviev, Kamenev, Radek, Bukharin, Rykov and the like. This showed that sharp class struggle was going on all the time and that there was always the danger of capitalist restoration.

Being the first state of the dictatorship of the proletariat, the Soviet Union lacked experience in consolidating this dictatorship and preventing the restoration of capitalism. In these circumstances and after Stalin's death, Khrushchev, a capitalist roader in power hiding in the Soviet Communist Party, came out with a surprise attack in his "secret report" viciously slandering Stalin and by every kind of treacherous maneuver usurped Party and government power in the Soviet Union. This was a counter-revolutionary coup d'état which turned the dictatorship of the proletariat into the dictatorship of the bourgeoisie and which overthrew socialism and restored capitalism.

Brezhnev was Khrushchev's accomplice in the counter-revolutionary coup d'état and later replaced him. Brezhnev's rise to power is, in essence, the continuation of Khrushchev's counter-revolutionary coup. Brezhnev is Khrushchev the Second.

Comrade Mao Tse-tung points out: "The rise to power of revisionism means the rise to power of the bourgeoisie." "The Soviet Union today is under the dictatorship of the bourgeoisie, a dictatorship of the big bourgeoisie, a dictatorship of the German fascist type, a dictatorship of the Hitler type."

This brilliant thesis of Comrade Mao Tse-tung's most penetratingly reveals the class essence and social roots of Soviet
revisionist social-imperialism and its fascist nature.

Since the Soviet revisionist renegade clique usurped Party
and government power in the Soviet Union, the Soviet bourgeois privileged stratum has greatly expanded its political and
economic power and has occupied the ruling position in the
Party, the government, and the army as well as in the economic
and cultural fields. And from this stratum there has emerged a
bureaucrat monopoly capitalist class, namely, a new type of big
bourgeoisie which dominates the whole state machine and controls all the social wealth.

Utilizing the state power under its control, this new-type
bureaucrat monopoly capitalist class has turned socialist ownership into ownership by capitalist roaders and turned the socialist economy into a capitalist economy and a state monopoly
capitalist economy. In the name of the "state," it unscrupulously plunders the state treasury and embezzles at will the
fruits of the labor of the Soviet people in every possible way.
Indulging in luxury and debauchery, it rides roughshod over the
people.

This new-type bureaucrat monopoly capitalist class is a bourgeoisie that has turned **the hope of restoration** into *attempts* at
restoration. It has suppressed the heroic sons and daughters of
the October Revolution, is lording it over the people of different
nationalities in the Soviet Union and has set up its own small
counter-revolutionary tsarist court. Therefore, it is reactionary
in the extreme and mortally hates and fears the people.

Like all other reactionary and decadent classes, this new-type
bureaucrat monopoly capitalist class is riddled with internal
contradictions. In their desperate efforts to keep the power they
have usurped, the members of this class are both working hand
in glove with each other and scheming and struggling against
one another. The greater their difficulties, the fiercer their strife,
open and secret.

In order to extort maximum profits and maintain its reactionary rule, this new-type bureaucrat monopoly capitalist class not
only exploits and oppresses the people of its own country, but
it necessarily engages in rabid expansion and aggression, joins
the company of world imperialism in redividing the world and
pursues the most vicious social-imperialist policies.

This new-type bureaucrat monopoly capitalist class constitutes the class basis of Soviet revisionist social-imperialism. At present the general representative of this class is Brezhnev. He has frantically pushed and developed Khrushchev revisionism and is completing the evolution from capitalist restoration to social-imperialism, which was already begun when Khrushchev was in power.

Since Brezhnev took office, he has pushed the so-called new economic system in an all-round way and established the capitalist principle of profit in a legal form, thus intensifying the exploitation of the working people by the oligarchy of bureaucrat monopolists. He and his like extort exorbitant taxes in total disregard of the lives of the people, follow Hitler's policy of "guns instead of butter" and accelerate the militarization of the national economy to meet the needs of social-imperialism for arms expansion and war preparation.

The perverse acts of the Soviet revisionist renegade clique have caused immense damage to the social productive forces and brought about grave consequences: the decline of industry, the deterioration of agriculture, the reduction in livestock, inflation, shortages of supplies, the unusual scarcity of commodities on state markets, and the increasing impoverishment of the working people. The Soviet revisionist renegades have not only squandered a vast amount of the wealth accumulated by the Soviet people through decades of hard work, but have also humbly begged for loans from West Germany, a country defeated in World War II, and are even selling out the country's natural resources and inviting Japanese monopoly capital into Siberia. The economy of the Soviet Union is already in the grip of an inextricable crisis. As friends of the Soviet people, we the Chinese people, along with the people of the world, are extremely indignant with the Soviet revisionist renegades who have brought so much damage and disgrace to the homeland of Leninism; we feel deep sympathy for the broad masses of the Soviet people who are suffering enormously from the all-round restoration of the capitalist system.

The Soviet revisionist renegade clique once said that the dictatorship of the proletariat "has ceased to be indispensable in the U.S.S.R." and that the Soviet Union "has . . . become a state of the entire people." But now they are slapping their own faces and asserting that the "state of the entire people continues the cause of the proletarian dictatorship" and that "the state of the whole people" and "the state of proletarian dictatorship" are "of one and the same type." They are also making a hullabaloo about "strengthening party leadership," "strengthening discipline," "strengthening centralism" and so on. "A state of the entire people" and at the same time a "proletarian dictatorship" —they lump together these two diametrically opposed concepts for no other purpose than to deceive the masses and camouflage the dictatorship of the big bourgeoisie. By "party leadership" they actually mean political control over the broad masses of the party members and the people by the handful of social-fascist oligarchs. By "discipline" they mean suppression of all who are dissatisfied with their rule. And by "centralism" they mean further centralizing the political, economic and military power in the hands of their gang. In short, they are putting all these signboards up for the purpose of strengthening their fascist dictatorship and preparing for wars of aggression.

Beset with difficulties at home and abroad, the Soviet revisionist renegade clique is resorting more and more openly to counter-revolutionary violence to buttress its reactionary rule which betrays Lenin and the October Revolution. In the Soviet Union of today, special agents and spies run amuck and reactionary laws and decrees multiply. Revolution is a crime, and people are everywhere being jailed on false charges; counter-revolution is a merit, and renegades congratulate each other on their promotion. Large numbers of revolutionaries and innocent people have been thrown into concentration camps and "mental hospitals." The Soviet revisionist clique even sends tanks and armored cars brutally to suppress the people's resistance.

Lenin pointed out: **"Nowhere in the world is there such an oppression of the majority of the country's population as there is in Russia,"** and nationalities other than Russians were regarded **"as** *inorodtsi* **(aliens)."** National oppression **"turned the nationalities without any rights into great reservoirs of fierce hatred for the monarchs."** Now the Soviet revisionist new tsars have restored the old tsars' policy of national oppression, adopted such cruel measures as discrimination, forced migration, splitting and imprisonment to oppress and persecute the minority nationalities and turned the Soviet Union back into the **"prison of nations."**

The Soviet revisionist renegade clique exercises comprehensive bourgeois dictatorship throughout the ideological sphere. It wantonly suppresses and destroys the proletariat's socialist ideology and culture while opening the floodgates to the rotten bourgeois ideology and culture. It vociferously preaches militarism, national chauvinism and racism and turns literature and art into tools for pushing social-imperialism.

In denouncing the dark rule of the tsarist system, Lenin indicated that police tyranny, savage persecution and demoralization had reached such an extent that "**the very stones cry out!**" One can just as well compare the rule of the Soviet revisionist renegade clique with the tsarist system castigated by Lenin.

In staging the counter-revolutionary coup d'état, the Khrushchev-Brezhnev renegade clique played a role which no imperialist or reactionary was in a position to play. As Stalin said, "**The easiest way to capture a fortress is from within.**" The fortress of socialism, which had withstood the fourteen-nation armed intervention, the Whiteguard rebellion, the attack of several million Hitlerite troops and imperialist sabotage, subversion, blockade and encirclement of every kind, was finally captured from within by this handful of renegades. The Khrushchev-Brezhnev clique are the biggest renegades in the history of the international communist movement. They are criminals indicted by history for their towering crimes.

IV. SOCIALISM IN WORDS, IMPERIALISM IN DEEDS

Lenin denounced the renegades of the Second International as "**socialism in words, imperialism in deeds,** *the growth of opportunism into imperialism.*"

The Soviet revisionist renegade clique, too, has grown from revisionism into social-imperialism. The difference lies in the fact that the social-imperialists of the Second International such as Kautsky did not hold state power; they only served the imperialists of their own countries to earn a few crumbs from the super-profits plundered from the people of other countries. The Soviet revisionist social-imperialists, however, directly plunder and enslave the people of other countries by means of the state power they have usurped.

The historical lesson is: Once its political power is usurped by a revisionist clique, a socialist state will either turn into social-imperialism, as in the case of the Soviet Union, or be reduced to a dependency or a colony, as in the case of Czechoslovakia and the Mongolian People's Republic. Now one can see clearly that the essence of the Khrushchev-Brezhnev renegade clique's rise to power lies in the transformation of the socialist state created by Lenin and Stalin into a hegemonic social-imperialist power.

The Soviet revisionist renegade clique talks glibly about Leninism, socialism and proletarian internationalism, but it acts in an out-and-out imperialist way.

It talks glibly about practicing "internationalism" towards its so-called fraternal countries, but in fact it imposes fetter upon fetter, such as the "Warsaw Treaty Organization" and the "Council for Mutual Economic Assistance," on a number of East European countries and the Mongolian People's Republic, thereby confining them within its barbed-wire "socialist community" and freely ransacking them. It uses its overlord position to press its "international division of labor," "specialization in production" and "economic integration," to force these countries to adapt their national economies to the Soviet revisionist needs and turn them into its markets, subsidiary processing workshops, orchards, vegetable gardens and ranches, all so that outrageous super-economic exploitation can be carried on.

It has adopted the most despotic and vicious methods to keep these countries under strict control and stationed massive numbers of troops there, and it has even openly dispatched hundreds of thousands of troops to trample Czechoslovakia underfoot and install a puppet regime at bayonet point. Like the old tsars denounced by Lenin, this gang of renegades bases its relations with its neighbors entirely **"on the feudal principle of privilege."**

The Soviet revisionist renegade clique talks glibly about its "aid" to countries in Asia, Africa and Latin America, but in fact, under the guise of "aid," it is trying hard to bring a number of these countries into its sphere of influence in contending with U.S. imperialism for the intermediate zone. Through the export of war matériel and capital and through unequal trade, Soviet revisionism is plundering their natural resources, interfering in their internal affairs and looking for chances to grab military bases.

Lenin pointed out: **"To the numerous 'old' motives of colonial policy, finance capital has added the struggle for the sources of raw materials, for the export of capital, for 'spheres of influence,' . . . for economic territory in general."** Soviet revisionist social-imperialism is moving along precisely this orbit of capitalist imperialism.

The Soviet revisionist renegade clique talks glibly about its "full support" for the revolutionary struggles in other countries, but in fact it is collaborating with all the most reactionary forces in the world to undermine the revolutionary struggles of various peoples. It wildly vilifies the revolutionary masses in the capitalist countries as "extremists" and "mobs" and tries to split and disintegrate the people's movements there. It has supplied money and guns to the reactionaries of Indonesia, India and other countries and thus directly helped them massacre revolutionaries, and is scheming night and day to put out the flames of the people's armed struggles in Asia, Africa and Latin America, and suppress the national-liberation movements. Like U.S. imperialism, it is acting as a world gendarme.

The Soviet revisionist renegades clique talks glibly about its approval of "struggle against imperialism," mouthing a few phrases scolding the United States now and then, but in fact, Soviet revisionism and U.S. imperialism are both the biggest imperialists vainly attempting to dominate the world. There is absolutely nothing in common between the Soviet revisionists' so-called opposition to the United States and the struggles of the people of the various countries against U.S. imperialism. In order to redivide the world, Soviet revisionism and U.S. imperialism are contending and colluding with each other at the same time. What Soviet revisionism has done on a series of major issues, such as the questions of Germany, the Middle East, Southeast Asia, Japan and nuclear weapons, is evidence of its crimes in contending and colluding with U.S. imperialism. Both of them are playing imperialist power politics at the expense of the interests of the people of all countries. Whatever compromises may be reached between Soviet revisionism and U.S. imperialism are mere temporary agreements between gangsters.

Lenin pointed out: **"Contemporary militarism is the result of capitalism."** Contemporary war **"arises out of the very nature of imperialism."**

Since Brezhnev came to power, the Soviet revisionist renegade clique has gone farther and farther down the road of
militarism. It has taken over Khrushchev's military strategic
principle of nuclear blackmail and energetically developed
missile-nuclear weapons, and at the same time redoubled its
efforts to expand conventional armaments, comprehensively
strengthening its ground, naval and air forces, and carried out
the imperialist "gunboat policy" throughout the world.

On the question of war, formerly Khrushchev hypocritically
advocated a world "without weapons, without armed forces
and without wars" to cover up actual arms expansion and war
preparation. Today, Brezhnev and company have somewhat
changed their tune. They have gone all out to stir up war fanaticism, clamoring that the present international situation is
"fraught with the danger of a new world war," brazenly threatening to "forestall the opponent" and bragging about their
"strategic missiles" being "capable of destroying any target at
any place." They have been increasing military expenditures
still more frantically, stepping up their mobilization and preparation for wars of aggression and plotting to unleash a blitzkrieg of the Hitler type.

The Soviet revisionist renegade clique has occupied Czechoslovakia by surprise attack, encroached upon Chinese territories
such as Chenpao Island and the Tiehliekti area and made
nuclear threats against our country. All this fully reveals the
aggressive and adventurous nature of Soviet revisionist social-
imperialism. Like the U.S. imperialists, the handful of oligarchs
of Soviet revisionist social-imperialism have become another
arch-criminal preparing to start a world war.

V. THE "BREZHNEV DOCTRINE" IS AN
OUTRIGHT DOCTRINE OF HEGEMONY

In order to press on with its social-imperialist policy of expansion and aggression, the Brezhnev renegade clique has developed Khrushchev revisionism and concocted an assortment of
fascist "theories" called the "Brezhnev doctrine."

Now let us examine what stuff this "Brezhnev doctrine" is
made of.

First, the theory of "limited sovereignty." Brezhnev and company say that safeguarding their so-called interests of socialism means safeguarding "supreme sovereignty." They flagrantly declare that Soviet revisionism has the right to determine the destiny of another country "including the destiny of its sovereignty."

What "interests of socialism"! It is you who have subverted the socialist system in the Soviet Union and pushed your revisionist line of restoring capitalism in a number of East European countries and the Mongolian People's Republic. What you call the "interests of socialism" are actually the interests of Soviet revisionist social-imperialism, the interests of colonialism. You have imposed your all-highest "supreme sovereignty" on the people of other countries, which means that the sovereignty of other countries is "limited," whereas your own power of dominating other countries is "unlimited." In other words, you have the right to order other countries about, whereas they have no right to oppose you; you have the right to ravage other countries, but they have no right to resist you. Hitler once raved about "the right to rule." Dulles and his ilk also preached that the concepts of national sovereignty "have become obsolete" and that "single state sovereignty" should give place to "joint sovereignty." So it is clear that Brezhnev's theory of "limited sovereignty" is nothing but an echo of imperialist ravings.

Secondly, the theory of "international dictatorship." Brezhnev and company assert that they have the right to "render military aid to a fraternal country to do away with the threat to the socialist system." They declare: "Lenin had foreseen" that historical development would "transform the dictatorship of the proletariat from a national into an international one, capable of decisively influencing the entire world politics."

This bunch of renegades has completely distorted Lenin's ideas.

In his article "Preliminary Draft of Theses on the National and Colonial Questions," Lenin wrote of **"transforming the dictatorship of the proletariat from a national one (i.e., existing in one country and incapable of determining world politics) into an international one (i.e., a dictatorship of the proletariat covering at least several advanced countries and capable of exercising decisive influence upon the whole of world politics)."**

Lenin meant here to uphold proletarian internationalism and propagate proletarian world revolution. But the Soviet revisionist renegade clique has emasculated the proletarian revolutionary spirit embodied in this passage of Lenin's and concocted the theory of "international dictatorship" as the "theoretical basis" for military intervention in or military occupation of a number of East European countries and the Mongolian People's Republic. The "international dictatorship" you refer to simply means the subjection of other countries to the new tsars' rule and enslavement. Do you think that by putting up the signboard of "aid to a fraternal country" you are entitled to use your military force to bully another country, or send your troops to overrun another country as you please? Flying the flag of "unified armed forces," you invaded Czechoslovakia. What difference is there between this and the invasion of China by the allied forces of eight powers in 1900, the fourteen-nation armed intervention in the Soviet Union, and the "sixteen-nation" aggression organized by U.S. imperialism against Korea!

Thirdly, the theory of "socialist community." Brezhnev and company shout that "the community of socialist states is an inseparable whole" and that the "united action" of "the socialist community" must be strengthened.

A "socialist community" indeed! It is nothing but a synonym for a colonial empire with you as the metropolitan state. The relationship between genuine socialist countries, big or small, should be built on the basis of Marxism-Leninism, on the basis of the principles of complete equality, respect for territorial integrity, respect for state sovereignty and independence and of noninterference in each other's internal affairs, and on the basis of the proletarian internationalist principle of mutual support and mutual assistance. But you have trampled other countries underfoot and made them your subordinates and dependencies. By "united action" you mean to unify under your control the politics, economies and military affairs of other countries. By "inseparable" you mean to forbid other countries to free themselves from your control and enslavement. Are you not brazenly trying to enslave the people of other countries?

Fourthly, the theory of "international division of labor." Brezhnev and company have greatly developed this nonsense spread by Khrushchev long ago. They have not only applied "international division of labor" to a number of East European countries and the Mongolian People's Republic as mentioned above, but have extended it to other countries in Asia, Africa and Latin America. They allege that the Asian, African and Latin American countries cannot "secure the establishment of an independent national economy," unless they "cooperate" with Soviet revisionism. "This cooperation enables the Soviet Union to make better use of the international division of labor. We shall be able to purchase in these countries increasing quantities of their traditional export commodities—cotton, wool, skins and hides, dressed nonferrous ores, vegetable oil, fruit, coffee, cocoa beans, tea and other raw materials, and a variety of manufactured goods."

What a list of "traditional export commodities"!

It is a pity that this list is not complete. To it must be added petroleum, rubber, meat, vegetables, rice, jute, cane sugar, and so forth.

In the eyes of the handful of Soviet revisionist oligarchs, the people of the Asian, African and Latin American countries are destined to provide them with these "traditional export commodities" from generation to generation. What kind of "theory" is this? The colonialists and imperialists have long maintained that it is they who are to determine what each country is to produce in the light of its natural conditions, and they have forcibly turned Asian, African and Latin American countries into sources of raw materials and kept them in a state of backwardness so that industrial capitalist countries can carry on the most savage colonial exploitation at their convenience. The Soviet revisionist clique has taken over this colonial policy from imperialism. Its theory of "international division of labor" boils down to "industrial Soviet Union, agricultural Asia, Africa and Latin America" or "industrial Soviet Union, subsidiary processing workshop Asia, Africa and Latin America."

Mutual and complementary exchange of goods and mutual assistance on the basis of equality and mutual benefit between genuine socialist countries and Asian, African and Latin American countries are conducted for the purpose of promoting the growth of an independent national economy in these countries keeping the initiative in their own hands. However, the theory of "international division of labor" is preached by the handful of Soviet revisionist oligarchs for the sole purpose of infiltrating, controlling and plundering the Asian, African and Latin

American countries, broadening their own spheres of influence and putting these countries under the new yoke of Soviet revisionist colonialism.

Fifthly, the theory that "our interests are involved." Brezhnev and company clamor that "the Soviet Union which, as a major world power, has extensive international contacts, cannot regard passively events that, though they might be territorially remote, nevertheless have a bearing on our security and the security of our friends." They arrogantly declare: "Ships of the Soviet Navy" will "sail . . . wherever it is required by the interests of our country's security"!

Can a country regard all parts of the world as areas involving its interests and lay its hands on the whole globe because it is a "major power"? Can a country send its gunboats everywhere to carry out intimidation and aggression because it "has extensive international contacts"? This theory that "our interests are involved" is a typical argument used by the imperialists for their global policy of aggression. When the old tsars engaged in foreign expansion, they did it under the banner of "Russian interests." The U.S. imperialists too have time and again shouted that the United States bears responsibility "not only for our own security but for the security of all free nations," and that it will "defend freedom wherever necessary." How strikingly similar are the utterances of the Soviet revisionists to those of the old tsars and the U.S. imperialists!

The Soviet revisionist renegade clique which has long gone bankrupt ideologically, theoretically and politically cannot produce anything presentable at all; it can only pick up some trash from imperialism and, after refurbishing, come out with "Brezhnevism." This "Brezhnevism" is imperialism with a "socialist" label; it is outright hegemonism, naked neo-colonialism.

VI. THE SOVIET REVISIONISTS' DREAM
OF A VAST EMPIRE

A hundred years ago, in exposing tsarist Russia's policy of aggression, Marx pointed out: **"Its methods, its tactics, its maneuvers may change, but the guiding star of this policy—world hegemony—will never change."**

Tsar Nicholas I once arrogantly shouted: "The Russian flag should not be taken down wherever it is hoisted." Tsars of several generations cherished the fond dream, as Engels said, of setting up a vast "Slav empire" extending from the Elbe to China, from the Adriatic Sea to the Arctic Ocean. They even intended to extend the boundaries of this vast empire to India and Hawaii. To attain this goal, they **"are as treacherous as they are talented."**

The Soviet revisionist new tsars have completely taken over the old tsars' expansionist tradition, branding their faces with the indelible stigma of the Romanov dynasty. They are dreaming the very dream the old tsars failed to make true and they are far more ambitious than their predecessors in their designs for aggression. They have turned a number of East European countries and the Mongolian People's Republic into their colonies and dependencies. They vainly attempt to occupy more Chinese territory, openly copying the old tsars' policy towards China and clamoring that China's northern frontier "was marked by the Great Wall." They have stretched their arms out to Southeast Asia, the Middle East, Africa and even Latin America and sent their fleets to the Mediterranean, the Indian Ocean, the Pacific and the Atlantic in their attempt to set up a vast Soviet revisionist empire spanning Europe, Asia, Africa and Latin America.

The "Slav empire" of the old tsars vanished like a bubble long ago and tsardom itself was toppled by the Great October Revolution led by Lenin in 1917. The reign of the old tsars ended in thin air. Today too, in the era when imperialism is heading for total collapse, the new tsars' mad attempt to build a bigger empire dominating the whole world is nothing but a dream.

Stalin said: **"Lenin called imperialism 'moribund capitalism.' Why? Because imperialism carries the contradictions of capitalism to their last bounds, to the extreme limit, beyond which revolution begins."**

Since Soviet revisionism has embarked on the beaten track of imperialism, it is inevitably governed by the law of imperialism and afflicted with all the contradictions inherent in imperialism.

Comrade Mao Tse-tung points out: **"The United States is a**

paper tiger. Don't believe in the United States. One thrust and it's punctured. Revisionist Soviet Union is a paper tiger too."

In carrying out rabid expansion and aggression, Soviet revisionist social-imperialism is bound to go to the opposite of what it expects and create the conditions for its own downfall. Soviet revisionism treats the other countries of the "socialist community" as its fiefs, but it can never succeed in perpetuating its colonial rule over the people of these countries, nor can it alleviate its contradictions with these countries. East Europe today is just like a powder keg which is sure to go off. The intrusion of the Soviet revisionist tanks into Prague does not in the least indicate the strength of Soviet revisionist social-imperialism; on the contrary it marks the beginning of the collapse of the Soviet revisionist colonial empire. With its feet deep in the Czechoslovak quagmire, Soviet revisionist social-imperialism cannot extricate itself.

By its expansion and plunder in Asia, Africa and Latin America, Soviet revisionism has set itself against the people of these regions. It has so overreached itself and become so burdened that it is swollen all over like a man suffering from dropsy. Even the U.S. imperialist press says: "We've discovered that they [the Russians] blunder as badly as we do—if not worse."

With Soviet revisionist social-imperialism joining the company of world imperialism, the contradictions among the imperialists have become more acute. Social-imperialism and imperialism are locked in a fierce rivalry to broaden their respective spheres of influence. The strife between social-imperialism and imperialism, which are encircled ring upon ring by the world's people, must inevitably accelerate the destruction of the entire imperialist system.

At home the rule of Soviet revisionist social-imperialism also rests on a volcano. During the period of the Stolypin reaction, Lenin wrote that the upsurge of the struggle of the Russian working class **"may be rapid, or it may be slow," "but in any case it is leading to a revolution."** In the Soviet Union today the conflict and antagonism between the new-type bureaucrat monopoly capitalist class on the one hand and the enslaved proletariat, laboring peasants and revolutionary intellectuals on the other are becoming increasingly acute. Class struggle develops independently of man's will and must lead to revolution sooner or later.

The Soviet Union was originally a union of multinational socialist states. Such a union can be built, consolidated and developed only under socialist conditions and on the basis of equality and voluntary affiliation. The Soviet Union, as Stalin indicated, **"had before it the unsuccessful experiments of multinational states in bourgeois countries. It had before it the experiment of old Austria-Hungary, which ended in failure."** Nevertheless, the union of Soviet multinational states was **"bound to stand every and any test,"** because **"real fraternal cooperation among the peoples has been established"** by the socialist system **"within the system of a single federated state."** Now the Soviet revisionist renegade clique has subverted the socialist system, exercised a bourgeois dictatorship and substituted national oppression for national equality and the jungle law of the bourgeoisie for mutual help and fraternity among the nationalities. Now that the proletarian basis, the socialist basis, of the original union has been discarded, will not the huge multinational "union" under the rule of the bourgeoisie of a new type one day undergo the same crisis and end in failure as the Austro-Hungarian empire did in the past?

To extricate itself from its impasse at home and abroad, Soviet revisionist social-imperialism, like U.S. imperialism, feverishly engages in missile-nuclear blackmail and seeks a way out through military adventures and large-scale war of aggression. But will war bring a new lease of life to imperialism and social-imperialism in their death throes? No. Just the opposite. History irrefutably proves that, far from saving imperialism from its impending doom, war can only hasten its extinction.

Chairman Mao points out: **"With regard to the question of world war, there are but two possibilities: One is that the war will give rise to revolution and the other is that revolution will prevent the war."**

Chairman Mao also says: **"People of the world, unite and oppose the war of aggression launched by any imperialism or social-imperialism, especially one in which atom bombs are used as weapons! If such a war breaks out, the people of the world should use revolutionary war to eliminate the war of aggression, and preparations should be made right now!"**

This great call made by Chairman Mao on the basis of the present international situation indicates the orientation of struggle for the proletariat and the revolutionary people throughout the world. The people of the world must maintain high vigilance, make every preparation and be ready at all times to deal resolute crushing blows to any aggressor who dares to unleash war!

In recent years, the Soviet revisionist renegade clique, inheriting the old tricks of the old tsars, has been backing and engineering, half openly, half secretly, a new "Movement for Pan-Slavism" and publicizing the "sacredness of the national spirit" of the Russians in a futile attempt to poison the minds of the Soviet labouring masses and younger generation with this reactionary trend of thought and induce the Soviet people to serve as tools for the policies of aggression and war of the handful of Soviet revisionist oligarchs. In all sincerity, we would like to remind the fraternal Soviet people never to be taken in by "Pan-Slavism."

What is "Pan-Slavism"?

In exposing the old tsars, Marx and Engels pointed out incisively: **"Pan-Slavism is an invention of the St. Petersburg Cabinet."** Engels said that the old tsars used this swindle in preparation for war **"as the last sheet anchor of Russian tsarism and Russian reaction."** Therefore, **"Pan-Slavism is the Russians' worst enemy as well as ours."**

Like Hitler's "Aryan master race," the "Pan-Slavism" of the Soviet revisionist new tsars is exceedingly reactionary racism. They publicize these reactionary ideas only to serve expansion abroad by the handful of reactionary rulers of their "superior race." For the broad masses of the people, this only spells catastrophe.

Lenin once pointed out: **"The oppression of 'subject peoples' is a double-edged weapon. It cuts both ways—against the 'subject peoples' and against the Russian people."** It is precisely under the smoke screen of "Pan-Slavism" that the handful of Soviet revisionist oligarchs are now working against time both to plot wars of aggression and to step up their attacks on the Soviet people, including the Russian people.

The interests of the proletariat and the broad masses in the Soviet Union are diametrically opposed to those of the Soviet revisionist new tsars but are in accord with the interests of the revolutionary people the world over. If the Soviet revisionist new tsars launch a large-scale war of aggression, then, in accordance with Lenin's principle in dealing with imperialist wars of aggression, the proletariat and the revolutionary people of the Soviet Union will surely refuse to serve as cannon fodder for the unjust war unleashed by Soviet revisionist social-imperialism. They will carry forward the cause of the heroic sons and daughters of the Great October Revolution and fight to overthrow the new tsars and reestablish the dictatorship of the proletariat.

Two hundred years ago, eulogizing the "achievements" of the wars of aggression of Tsarina Catherine II, a Russian poet wrote: "Advance, and the whole universe is thine!" Now the Soviet revisionist new tsars have mounted the horse of the old tsars and "advanced." They are dashing about recklessly, unable to rein in and completely forgetting that their ancestors were thrown from this same horse and that thus the Russian empire of the Romanov dynasty came to an end. It is certain that the new tsars will come to no better end than the old tsars. They will surely be thrown from their horse and dashed to pieces.

VII. PEOPLE OF THE WORLD, UNITE AND FIGHT
TO OVERTHROW U.S. IMPERIALISM, SOVIET
REVISIONISM, AND ALL REACTION

Comrade Mao Tse-tung points out: **"The Soviet Union was the first socialist state and the Communist Party of the Soviet Union was created by Lenin. Although the leadership of the Soviet Party and state has now been usurped by revisionists, I would advise comrades to remain firm in the conviction that the masses of the Soviet people and of Party members and cadres are good, that they desire revolution and that revisionist rule will not last long."**

The Chinese people cherish deep feelings for the people of the Soviet Union. During the Great October Revolution led by Lenin, Chinese laborers in Russia fought shoulder to shoulder with the Russian proletarians. The people of our two countries have supported each other, helped each other and forged a close friendship in the course of protracted revolutionary struggles. The handful of Soviet revisionist oligarchs are perversely

trying to sow dissension and undermine the relations between
the Chinese and Soviet peoples, but in the end they will be lift-
ing a rock only to drop it on their own feet.

The Soviet people are a great people with a glorious revolutionary tradition who were educated by Lenin and Stalin. They
will under no circumstances allow the new tsars to sit on their
bottoms for long. Though the fruits of the October Revolution
have been thrown away by the Soviet revisionist renegades, the
principles of the October Revolution are eternal. Under the
great banner of Leninism, the mighty current of people's revolution is bound to break through the ice of revisionist rule, and
the spring of socialism will surely return to the land of the
Soviet Union!

Comrade Mao Tse-tung points out: **"Whether in China or in
other countries of the world, to sum up, over 90 per cent of the
population will eventually support Marxism-Leninism. There
are still many people in the world who have not yet awakened
because of the deceptions of the social-democrats, revisionists,
imperialists and the reactionaries of various countries. But anyhow they will gradually awaken and support Marxism-Leninism.
The truth of Marxism-Leninism is irresistible. The masses of
the people will eventually rise in revolution. The world revolution is bound to triumph."**

In commemorating the centenary of the birth of the great
Lenin, we are happy to see that, under the guidance of Marxism-Leninism-Mao Tse-tung Thought, the cause of the world
proletarian revolution is advancing from victory to victory. The
genuine Marxist-Leninist forces are steadily growing throughout
the world. The liberation struggles of the oppressed nations and
people are vigorously forging ahead. All countries and people
subjected to aggression, control, intervention or bullying by
U.S. imperialism and Soviet revisionism are forming the broadest united front. A new historical period of struggle against U.S.
imperialism and Soviet revisionism has begun. The death knell
is tolling for imperialism and social-imperialism.

Invincible Marxism-Leninism-Mao Tse-tung Thought is the
powerful weapon of the proletariat for knowing and changing
the world, the powerful weapon for propelling history forward.
Marxism-Leninism-Mao Tse-tung Thought, integrated with the

revolutionary masses in their hundreds of millions and with the concrete practice of people's revolution in all countries, will certainly bring forth inexhaustible revolutionary strength to smash the entire old world to smithereens!

Long live great Marxism!
Long live great Leninism!
Long live great Mao Tse-tung Thought!

★　　★　　★　　★　　★

The heading on the map reads: "Peoples of the World Unite. Defeat the American aggressors and all their running dogs."

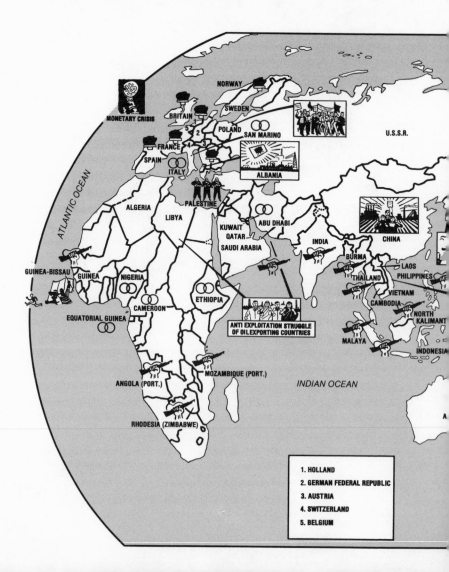

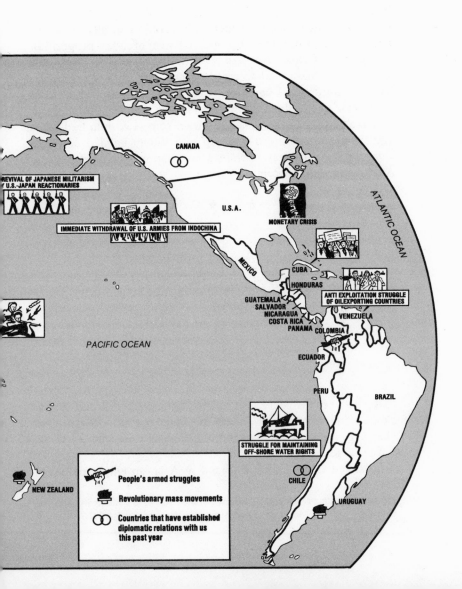

CANADA

REVIVAL OF JAPANESE MILITARISM
Y U.S.-JAPAN REACTIONARIES

IMMEDIATE WITHDRAWAL OF U.S. ARMIES FROM INDOCHINA

U.S.A.

MONETARY CRISIS

ATLANTIC OCEAN

MEXICO

CUBA

HONDURAS

ANTI EXPLOITATION STRUGGLE
OF OIL EXPORTING COUNTRIES

GUATEMALA
SALVADOR
NICARAGUA
COSTA RICA
PANAMA

COLOMBIA

VENEZUELA

PACIFIC OCEAN

ECUADOR

PERU

BRAZIL

STRUGGLE FOR MAINTAINING
OFF-SHORE WATER RIGHTS

CHILE

URUGUAY

NEW ZEALAND

People's armed struggles

Revolutionary mass movements

Countries that have established
diplomatic relations with us
this past year

CHOU EN-LAI SPEAKS

This interview with Mr. Julio Scherer García, which we present in slightly abridged form, was held early in September 1971 at a time when the events surounding Lin Piao were approaching a climax. While the interview speaks for itself, noteworthy are Chou's concern with the role of the armed forces in any society and the debates in China on a new constitution. While "China watchers" would naturally look for hints on the Lin Piao question, Chou's broader proposition that any chief executive, like Allende, who does not have full control over his armed forces does not have full power in his hands applies to all countries, our own included. While little is known about the constitution-making process in China, it seems to be similar to America's own some two hundred years ago. Since America also built up rather than handed down its Constitution, this may explain Mao's expressed interest in the American federal system.

★ ★ ★

*JULIO SCHERER GARCÍA**
Interview with Chou En-Lai

PEKING (September 6, 1971)

As between democratic election and armed violence, China chooses the second path, since she believes the vote can provide a government, but only the gun, the forces of an army, can provide the power.

So stated Chou En-lai, a legend in Asia, an enigmatic celeb-

---

* Julio Scherer García (Editor-in-chief of the Mexican journal *Excelsior*), in the Mexico City *El Mercurio*, September 7, 1971.

rity for the rest of the world, member of the Politburo of the
Central Committee of the Communist Party, and premier of
the People's Republic of China, in an exclusive two-and-one-
half-hour interview that took place in the Kiangsu room of the
Great Hall of the People above the Grand Avenue of Eternal
Peace.

The seventy-three-year-old revolutionary and diplomat,
descendant of a mandarin educated in Confucian philosophy,
founder in Paris in 1920 of a Communist section for China [of
the Comintern], one of the 30,000 survivors of the 300,000
who began the Long March, negotiator of an end to the civil
war and the establishment of a united front against Japan in
1936, who made the first public break with the U.S.S.R. when
Khrushchev attacked the Albanian Communist Party, and
most recently the liaison for the Mao Tse-tung–Richard Nixon
talks planned for May 1972, declared to *Excelsior*: "President
Allende is right when he recognizes that he has conquered the
government but not the power. Elections or voting are transitory, passing phenomena. As we see it in terms of our conceptions, it is impossible for a democratic government to achieve
consolidation without the support of the armed forces. Every
government should be sure of its own democratic and proletarian forces so that it be assured in its power." . . .

SERVE THE PEOPLE

Like every soldier of the People's Army of China, like
everyone who holds state or party office, Chou En-lai wears
over his heart a small gold button with the profile of Mao
Tse-tung in relief and some characters meaning "Serve the
people."

His extraordinary eyes impress one, as do the jet-black eyebrows. The eyes speak. The eyebrows speak. It seems impossible to escape the careful observation of a man who measures
and calculates, who knows and decides right from the beginning.

Closed as a circle, basic as unity, Chou En-lai seems absolute
at the moment of concentration. When he smiles, the furrows
in his forehead soften, the tension in his chin muscles relaxes,

and his face communicates in a thousand small ways that express comprehension and good will.

His clothing is his uniform, his uniform is his clothing— straight; five buttons in line, the first on the collar; the pockets superimposed like an attachment. This is known as the Sun Yat-sen style because it was used for the first time back in 1920 by the founder and leader of the Kuomintang, later president of the Republic. In this way, Sun Yat-sen showed his opposition to the traditional dress, the long gowns that stylized the body and constrained movement: "Heritage of the mandarins, of the exploiting classes."

The Kiangsu room is dedicated, as is every room in the Great Hall of the People, to a province of China. The ceiling rises many meters above a row of chairs set for visitors. Enormous windows filter the light of a tranquil sunset. In dimensions, the Kiangsu room is like a temple; in its austerity, with only a rug and some ink sketches with the profile of the province, it suggests a place of work.

Chou En-lai appeared at exactly five o'clock in the afternoon, his right hand offered in greeting. Without losing a moment, he showed me the right place to pose for a picture and immediately guided me to a seat and sat by my side. Hardly had I indicated that I wanted to ask him why he invariably appeared with his right arm bent against his body and his left arm rigid and martial, than he said: "I fell off a horse. People say it happened during the Long March, but that is not true. I fell many times during the Long March but with no bad results. It happened to me as it did to many others. But once on a peaceful outing, I fell from a horse, and suffered the results: a fracture from which I never completely recovered."

If sounds permit one to distinguish betwen an indication and an order there is no doubt that Chou En-lai's rough powerful voice is that of a commander. Charged with electricity, more than vigorous, the Prime Minister seems free from any kind of private amusement. Being the man for his job, he does not waste time with formalities nor twist and turn in his answers. If he does not want to touch a subject, he says so. If he wants to continue on a subject he is involved in, or if he wants to get involved in a subject, he indicates it. "Permit me to continue," he says. And he cuts short any interruption. Chou

En-lai does not waste time with compliments and perhaps for this reason is so engaging.

He touched on, among others, the following themes:

1. Revolutions can neither be exported nor imported. Only the people are responsible for the destiny of their nation.

2. Geographical boundaries are the final frontier of all revolutions, but this has nothing to do with the diffusion of revolutionary ideas. Their realm is the world.

3. China will not fail in her duty to support national liberation movements. "Why not?" was his response to the question, one of the two times he used English, a language he knows, as well as French, German, and Russian.

4. China has never had nor has pretensions to turn herself into a center of the world revolution. Chairman Mao has made categorical declarations to this effect.

5. It is not impossible a military coup could occur in Chile.

6. The perpetrators of the latest coup d'état in Bolivia were trained abroad.

7. Mexico is admirable because, for other reasons, she defends her national independence. The *chicanos* are an expression of this spirit.

8. China would never accept, "not even as a gift," American or English-style democracy.

9. A few monopolize everything in the United States; so also is the Constitution of the country accessible only to scholars as well as the secret of the death of President Kennedy.

10. If President Nixon does not come to Peking in May 1972 with clear intentions, he will have unmasked himself before the conscience of the world. It is not to be taken for granted that his visit to China will benefit him.

11. China reiterates: she will not traffic in principles nor sell out her comrades in arms.

There was much of the monologue in the interview. Always linking the subject discussed to political aims, the Prime Minister showed himself full of passion which was the knot that tied all his words together. When I said that often he would not allow me to say something, with all resources on one side alone, he answered: "What do you want? Our knowledge about China is not the same." His chuckle was even more engaging than the reply.

REVOLUTIONARY PRACTICE

Question: "What implications does the thesis of Chairman Mao that the center of the world revolution has moved to China have for Latin America?"

Chou answered: "Chairman Mao has never said that, nor does it correspond with anything else he has said. Chairman Mao has unswervingly maintained that in terms of world view, Marxism-Leninism is a universal truth for the proletariat, but only when this universal truth is combined with the revolutionary practice of the people of each individual country can one find the revolutionary line which will be successful.

"When some individuals say that China is the center of the world revolution, they are making these statements on their own personal responsibility. That is their affair, not ours. It is possible that during the Cultural Revolution some elements of ultra-left tendency made statements of this sort. But we censure such a point of view.

"If you want a demonstration of what I have just told you, I can offer you the following, an inscription that Chairman Mao recently presented to a delegation from Japan. In it, he says: 'The Japanese revolution will beyond a doubt be victorious, as long as the universal truth of Marxism-Leninism be really integrated with the concrete practice of the Japanese revolution.' This thought of Chairman Mao is reflected in many of his writings.

"We have spoken of action as a limited form that is subject to the decision of each people in each country, but the case is different with thought as well as ideas. It is clear that ideas can be spread throughout the world. The bourgeoisie has spread its world view throughout the world. *The New York Times,* the London *Times,* and *Le Monde* are examples. The ideology of the proletariat has also spread everywhere.

"Religion has done the same. Thought does not have limitations nor frontiers of any kind. But as far as actions are concerned, I say again, they must always be carried out by the people in each country. There are no exceptions to this. No one can impose them from the outside with any chances for lasting success. For this reason revolution can not be exported. Chairman Mao is very clear on this in his writings and maintains that no one can try to impose his ideas on anyone else."

ALLENDE—ONLY NOMINAL POWER

Question: "Before the Ninth Party Congress of China in 1969, Vice-president Lin Piao stated 'the fundamental Marxist-Leninist principle of seizing power by armed force.' What do you think of Salvador Allende, who chose the road of the ballot box in order to gain the presidency of Chile? And of Fidel Castro, who opted for armed force? What kind of future does China see for socialism by the electoral route?"

Chou replied: "Elections or voting are transitory, passing phenomena. President Salvador Allende is able to head his party of 'Popular Unity' and gain a relative but not absolute majority. But he must take into account that in the second vote the decisive factor was the attitude of a centrist party, the Christian Democrats. But what most helped Salvador Allende, what was really decisive, was a counterrevolutionary bullet, an assassin's bullet which killed General Schneider. Do you remember? General Schneider respected the results of the elections and supported Allende. It was this bullet which aroused and angered the Chilean people, who realized that the crime was the result of maneuvers by insidious elements. The assassin's bullet also powerfully influenced the Christian Democratic Party. For that reason the voting majority favored Allende. But let us remember that in the beginning it did not seem that events would develop in this manner.

"I should also like to call your attention to another fact that seems important to me. If a small portion of the Chilean armed forces become subject to the influence of foreign aggressive forces, if extreme care is not taken on this problem, then something very serious could happen in the country. That something is a possible military coup.

"Of course, we hope that all the officers and soldiers of the Chilean armed forces are patriotic. By patriotism we mean the sovereignty of Chile, the defense of her full national independence. By patriotism we also mean support of the two-hundred-mile limit of territorial waters advocated by Chile, Peru, and ten other Latin-American countries. By patriotism we mean the struggle for nationalization, step by step, of foreign firms. All this constitutes the policies of the democratic revolution proclaimed by President Allende.

"All this is good from our point of view, but if the strictest

care is not given to the armed forces, it is not impossible that
some unfortunate troubles could take place. You have seen
what has happened in Bolivia. It certainly was no accidental
event, some extraordinary phenomenon."

BOLIVIA, CHILE, CASTRO—POWER

There are voices, like bearings, that seem like steel. The voice
of Chou En-lai is one of them.

Question: "The forces that carried out the military coup in
Bolivia were trained abroad. What do you think?"

I had read some press digests, incomplete and clearly insufficient for the problem, here in China. I was especially interested
in Chou En-lai's version.

The Prime Minister responded: "What I offer you is reliable
information. The Bolivians themselves have recognized that
the elements that carried out the coup were prepared abroad.
But, turning back to Chile, the government of President Allende
is democratic. But as far as we are concerned, according to our
conceptions, it is impossible for a democratic government to
achieve consolidation without the support of the armed forces.
In Latin America, governments with progressive tendencies
have been overthrown on numerous occasions. Isn't that so?"

Question: "Why do you say that elections are transitory, passing phenomena?"

Chou answered: "Because elections do not consolidate power
in and of themselves. Every government must reckon with its
own armed forces, whether democratic or proletarian, for they
assure it in its power."

P'eng Hua, an official from the Department of Information
of the Foreign Ministry, intervened: "President Allende himself has recognized this and said so: 'I have conquered the
government, but not the power.' "

Chou En-lai, in a definitive tone: "President Allende is right!"

Question: "Therefore, Fidel Castro was more effective than
Allende in seizing power through armed force?"

Chou: "Relatively speaking, yes, in the conditions of his own
country. Castro overthrew the reactionary and traitor Batista,
disarmed Batista's army, and took power."

MEXICO AND CHICANOS—
CHINA AND MINORITIES

Question: "Do you see any future for socialism via the electoral path?"

Chou: "We do not believe in struggle via the parliamentary path. We make no secret of this principle of ours. We have seen no case where through parliamentary practice any country has succeeded in achieving the expulsion of foreign forces of aggression, full national independence, and true, authentic democratic practice. The countries of Latin America achieved their national independence through armed struggle. Unfortunately in the twentieth century new aggressive forces have again penetrated these countries."

Question: "I would like to ask you some concrete questions about Mexico."

Chou: "México (Chou En-lai seized on the word and spoke it that way)—I have little knowledge about Mexico, and hardly any ideas. I have never done any studying about Mexico, studies worthy of the name. But there are four reasons which call my attention to Mexico and make me admire her. Mexico is a country with a very ancient civilization. Relics unearthed in Mexico have shown that some date from 7,000 years ago. Your country is more ancient than ours. Relics unearthed in China date from 4,000 years ago. Relics from Pang Su in Thailand may be some 5,000 years old, but this has not yet been conclusively proven. Ceramic relics are available for conjecture, but nothing definitive. Another thing I admire about Mexico: the Europeans who intermarried with the natives. Really, I admire this fact. It has not happened elsewhere, where, as we know, the Europeans refused to intermarry with the indigenous people. Not only that, they even drove them out of the fertile zones. I also admire Mexico because in order to seize and maintain democratic power it defends its national independence. It has achieved this through many wars against the foreigner. There is a fourth fact which attracts me powerfully about your country: the struggle of the *chicanos* who work for the equality of their rights outside of their country."

Someone present did not understand the word *chicano*. Obviously it was not in his vocabulary nor even in his dictionary. The Prime Minister made jokes at his expense, saying, "Yankee, Yankee," pretending to chase him away. "He's a pro-Yankee," he said to the English journalist. His naturalness, his easy, free humor were contagious.

Before Chou En-lai resumed the discussion, someone asked: "If you do not believe in the parliamentary struggle, can you say something about disaffected minorities in China?"

Chou: "Are you referring to minorities who oppose socialism or to those who hold different opinions about the revolution and socialist construction under the dictatorship of the proletariat? These are two kinds of minorities. The minority which opposes socialism and wants to restore capitalism is intolerable in China, and we consider such an antagonistic contradiction between the enemy and ourselves. We openly criticize that minority among the masses. With the aid of the masses we isolate them. If this minority carries out counterrevolutionary activities, we apply the dictatorship of the proletariat against them and punish its members under the law. Punishment by law in China takes the form of labor and of reeducation. Few are imprisoned, and even fewer executed. We do not believe in the effectiveness of execution. We do not stay in power through slaughter. There is another very distinct type of minority. It exists within the people themselves who support the socialist revolution and the dictatorship of the proletariat but maintain different opinions about the revolution and socialist construction. Differences of opinion not only occur among the masses, of workers, peasants, and soldiers, but within the Party itself.

"Not only do we admit differences of opinion in this area, but theoretically and philosophically we consider contradictions of this sort beneficial. If there did not exist this type of contradictions among the people, as well as within the Party, society would cease to move forward and the Party would die. The existence of these two types of contradictions different by their nature (that between the enemy and ourselves, and that which develops within the people themselves) is an objective fact of society. Only when we have recognized this objective phenomenon, can we find a solution. If you should wish to study the Thought of Chairman Mao, I recommend to you one of his works: 'On the Correct Handling of Contradictions Among the People.' "

Subsequently he talked about the struggle in the factories for the raising of production, how different principles could prevail on this matter, and how these contradictions are brought under discussion between the technical and working masses and the managers in order finally to resolve them.

There is no way to hold back Chou En-lai. His is the only voice. "I'll give you a concrete example in the political realm. In order to revise our constitution, we mobilized for a full discussion amongst the people. The discussion began in 1970. Participating in the discussion were workers in the factories, peasants in the communes, educational centers, stores, neighborhood groups, as well as democratic personages (from the minority parties). Some were in favor of a very detailed Constitution, and others wanted it to be brief, concise, dealing only with matters of principle. Those who were in favor of a complex constitution, who wanted it complete and detailed, said that was the only way to know how to obey the law without violating it. But the opponents thought that if the constitution be too complicated, all kinds of problems and difficulties would arise. First, they said, this could restrict the initiative of the people because each person would explain it individually in his own way. It would be like a voluminous book in which many opinions would be fitted in. And the judges facing such a juxtaposition of points of view would never be able to achieve unanimity in their verdicts."

THE ASSASSINATION OF PRESIDENTS

Each pause forms a unity with the words that preceded it. Words and breaths support each other and are solidly integrated with each other like the stone and cement of a fortification. There is no way to storm the fort and introduce a question. Chou: "The Constitution of the United States has lasted some two hundred years and still it is not possible to change it, even though in many cases it is no longer applicable. They have had to resort to amendments, but nobody knows how many amendments there have been. And despite so many, there still are gaps, empty spaces. For example, *The New York Times* which published some secret documents. There was much discussion on the subject, recourse was taken to the law, and finally the Supreme Court had to intervene. Most lawyers were in favor of publication of the documents. But a correspondent of this newspaper told me that even among the advocates of publication there were aspects on which they contradicted each other.

"But there are instances that are even more serious: the assassination of presidents. No one has satisfactorily explained them. According to our experience, the Constitution of China should not be like that of the United States. There are lots of difficulties when one gets caught up in details; it complicates things. We believe that a constitution should speak only of principles, in such a way that concrete cases can be resolved according to a principle of justice. A foreign correspondent said there exists no democracy in China. Since he was so accustomed to bourgeois democracy, he was shocked by ours. What he wanted was American or British democracy in our country. But in our judgment that is not worthwhile learning nor striving for.

"The decline of the British Empire confirms what I have said. Nixon himself admitted on July 6 past, in a press conference, that twenty-five years ago it would not have been possible to imagine that the prestige of the United States could fall so dramatically as he sees it has. Twenty some years after the Second World War, the United States is suffering a loss of prestige so serious that it surprises even the President. The origin of these problems, this loss of prestige is due to the fact that the United States wants to dominate the world."

Could Chou En-lai's rhythm be that of a motor?

He continues: "We do not believe in such policies and therefore have no wish to learn from them. The truth about the assassination of President Kennedy still has not been revealed. When they subvert a foreign government. they dare not admit it. We are not in agreement with that kind of democracy.

"Our democracy is proletarian, is socialist. The bourgeoisie does not like it and calls it a dictatorship. That is right. Chairman Mao has said it is a dictatorship, but a popular democratic dictatorship—that is, the dictatorship of the proletariat—and it is applied only against counterrevolutionaries and exploiters. We will not tolerate that landowners recover their lands nor that rich peasants buy land and hire laborers. We will not tolerate capitalists trafficking in production, nor those who steal work tools or raw materials in order to start up an illegal business. Nor do we tolerate speculation and even less counter-revolutionary assassination or robbery by violence. Toward this kind of people, we apply the dictatorship.

"The fact of debates about our constitution in itself explains many things. The new constitution, after discussions among the people and within the party, will be simpler than the previous ones, for it will have the following advantages: it will be easy to memorize and all can learn it, principle by principle.

"We are in favor of the workers being able to learn the articles of the constitution by heart. When the masses know something, they will apply it. The constitution is explanation and comprehension, not form. The constitution should not be monopolized by a few jurists, lawyers, and judges, as happens in the United States. That is dangerous. Our constitution will not be the privilege of scholars like over there.

"Your democracy? We don't want it."

We interrupted. We wanted to ask him about Latin America. Chou: "Latin America? We have had only limited opportunity to establish contacts with Latin America. But let me conclude. We shall consecrate in our constitution these liberties: the full and frank expression of opinions, the full use of *ta-tzu-pao* (wall newspapers) and debates. These are liberties for the people so they can criticize the government, the leaders, the party so all can see. But in the newspapers of the United States and Britain, however voluminous they may be, full of the advertising of the capitalists so they can expand their profits, you won't find the opinion of the people. If you don't believe what I say about China and if you should pass through Hong Kong on your way back home, go and look through the huge collections of posters they have there which were circulated throughout China with criticisms of the government. Even the CIA has put together its collection. Japanese newspapermen collected even more of them. There were correct and incorrect criticisms, but the fact is the people were able to express themselves through these big posters. They say here we have no democracy, but they, in the United States and Britain, do not have that kind of democracy.

"Speaking of proletarian liberty, our constitution also stipulates the freedom to strike. In addition to freedom of speech and of publication, there is the freedom to strike. We allow that workers go on strike if the factories are not well managed; we accept the strike as a sign of protest.

"In the eyes of Western journalists, there is no freedom under a socialist system. But looking at it from the point of view of the proletariat, it is there that there exists no freedom for the people. There only exists real, true liberty for the bourgeoisie, for the minority, not for the majority. Our liberty is of the proletariat, of the masses. That is the difference. They, in their democracy, want everything for the minority; we want it for the majority.

"If anyone wants to make us a gift of English or North American democracy, we won't accept it. Our liberty is much broader than theirs. In our judgment, freedom rests in the interests of the collectivity and of the individual. We believe that their interests are identical and not contradictory. In capitalist society, personal freedom contradicts society's freedom.

"I respect your freedom and I wish you feel you have the right to publish or not to publish what I have said to you."

The Prime Minister looks at his watch. It is clear the interview is coming to an end. Almost standing, he says: "How is it possible that the champion of anticapitalism, Chairman Mao Tse-tung, should meet with the champion of anticommunism, President Richard Nixon? Why should China invite her mortal enemy into her home?

"Because the United States has imposed a blockade against China and has shown hostility towards us these last twenty-two years. The discussions at the ambassadorial level in Geneva and Warsaw have gone on for sixteen years without any results. Now Nixon wishes to raise the level of the negotiations and is knocking at our door. Why should we not open the door for him? Besides, there is no war between China and the United States. Why should we not begin to talk at the highest level? Even if there should be war, there are instances where negotiations have gone on in the midst of full military conflict. When we fought Chiang Kai-shek, we also negotiated with him. During the Korean War there were negotiations. That war lasted more than three years and negotiations went on for two.

"The United States invaded Vietnam more than ten years ago. Nonetheless, talks between Vietnamese and North Americans have gone on for three years, since 1968. The only difference is at what level. Could the people lose anything from that? I am certain not."

Question: "Do you think President Nixon would come to China if he did not think the trip would be of advantage to him?"

Chou: "There are two possibilities for his visit to China. If the negotiations should be successful, the peoples of the East and of the entire world would benefit therefrom. That is the main thing. But if they should not be successful, President Nixon would have unmasked himself. If he arrives in Peking without any desire to resolve problems, the whole world will see it and take note of it. We only foresee this: China will not traffic in principles and will not sell out its comrades in arms. Never!"

Question: "And the United States would?"

Chou: "Draw your own conclusions. I think they are pretty clear." Then Chou said jokingly: "My bourgeois influence." Already standing, a last question managed to get thrown in: "Does China support movements of national liberation?"

Chou: "Why not? The destiny of each nation is the responsibility of its people. We are against aggression, interventions, subversions, and other abuses. But we do support liberation movements."

"In what fashion?"

"If a people wants to rise up against a reactionary government, they have full right to do so. There are many classic examples: the case of Nasser against the dynasty of Farouk, the case of Fidel Castro against Batista. When Castro asked us for weapons to prevent aggression from abroad, we sent them to him. We also support the Palestinian people. But in each country what is important and what is truly decisive are the domestic forces, not external aid. Revolution cannot be imported, while revolutionary ideas cannot be blockaded. We are people of principle, and one principle of our policies is that each people must make its own revolution in its own country, never outside of it."

★　　★　　★　　★　　★

2. COMMITMENTS

CHOU EN-LAI SPEAKS

Despite its length, we include this interview between Premier Chou En-lai and James Reston, vice-president and columnist of *The New York Times*, because of its importance at the time. Although Reston implies in his remark "we can talk philosophy and that is interesting" that Chou En-lai discussed the Chinese world view, a comparison with other selections in this reader and even the interview with Julio Scherer García quickly shows that Chou was talking not "philosophy" or world view but policies and commitments. Therefore the interview forms a fitting transition to this section. Chou En-lai obviously made an effort not to bring ideology into the conversation but to remain "practical" so that the real differences between China and the United States could be explored.

A look at the Chinese press from March till September 1971 shows a pronounced emphasis on the need to oppose American imperialism throughout the world, reflected in the publication of the revolutionary map of the world on May 22, 1971 (see p. 474). Clearly the debate on the changing relationship between China and the United States was in full swing. Reston's reference to General Huang's call for a full U.S. withdrawal from all Southeast Asia relates to Huang Yung-sheng, chief of staff of the Chinese Army, who, along with Lin Piao, disappeared from the political scene in September. After September 1971 this emphasis wanes but is accompanied by a gradually rising emphasis on China's commitments to and support of the peoples of Indochina against the United States. If the United States was no longer a principal enemy, then it is specific issues which are the principal matter of contention between them. And as Chou En-lai said in the interview with Reston, "at present the most urgent question still is Vietnam."

A large part of the interview was taken up with Japan directly, and indirectly through the discussion on Korea. Chou's references to the "three pillars" of the Nixon Doctrine give the essence of his view on Japan: that Japan and other Asian partners of the United States are to be armed under the American nuclear umbrella. The very opening of the interview indicates Chou's conviction that it was collusion between the Satō government and the Taipei regime that played a major role in Secretary of State Rogers' vigorous advocacy for the retention of the Chiang government in the General Assembly of the UN. What Chou thus indicated to Reston was a triangular link between the United States, Japan, and the Chiang regime under the Nixon Doctrine which the Chinese perceived as a direct threat to themselves.

Obviously something has changed since the Reston interview. China was admitted to the UN and the Chiang regime was ousted. Premier Satō was replaced, unexpectedly, by Kakuei Tanaka, who visited Peking, established diplomatic relations with Peking, and broke with Taipei. Since Tanaka came to power in the wake of the "Nixon shock," as the Japanese call Nixon's August 15, 1971 "new economic policy," directed more against Japan than any other country, the Chinese have presumably concluded that the Japan-America link has been seriously weakened. That accounts for a remarkable change in the tone of the Chinese press from one of vehement denunciation of rising Japanese militarism to one of cautious friendliness.

The interview constitutes neither an exposition of the Chinese world view nor a comprehensive statement of their policies, but rather an exchange of views as both China and America were gearing up for Nixon's announced visit in 1972. Chou En-lai avoided some of the pessimistic remarks about the possibility of failure of the Nixon visit which he voiced to Scherer García, but the general Chinese attitude of the time, widely expressed within China and by Chinese representatives abroad, was that the visit "would succeed or it would fail."

★   ★   ★

JAMES RESTON*
Interview with Chou En-Lai

MR. CHOU—Have you recovered your health completely?

MR. RESTON—I am a kind of an old dog, you know. And I've never been sick in my life, and I was rather surprised to be struck away from home.

MR. CHOU—Perhaps you had this trouble before, but because of your good health you didn't quite feel it.

MR. RESTON—There are specific things, particularly in the last few days. I wanted to be sure that we understood the clarity of your thought. The first thing in my mind was whether you were surprised by Secretary Rogers's statement. In the Chinese news agency—sorry, it was said that the United States Government was saying one thing and doing another, and therefore I wondered whether you were not only surprised but perhaps felt deceived, whether you have been led to believe something by Dr. Kissinger other than what was in the Rogers statement.

MR. CHOU—I do not plan now to make a comparison for you on this. The position of the Chinese Government has all along been clear. That has been the case throughout the sixteen years of the Sino-U.S. ambassadorial talks, first in Geneva and then in Warsaw. And that has also been the case with the whole series of statements we have recently made.

This statement issued by the U.S. Secretary of State was a self-contradictory formula worked out under the pressure of the talks betwen the Japanese Government and the Chiang Kai-shek representative in Tokyo. This, of course, must be pointed out by our press.

As for the position of our Government, it has never changed. It is possible that you already heard about this from the French

* James Reston, "Interview with Chou En-lai, August 5, 1971," from *The New York Times* (August 10, 1971).

friends because I had a talk with the French parliamentary delegation, and I also had a talk with some American friends from the Committee of Concerned Asian Scholars. And do you want me to reiterate our position?

MR. RESTON—The central question that is in my mind is whether you felt that the statement by Rogers in any way interfered with the movement which I believe was taking place toward a normalization of relations between the United States and China?

MR. CHOU—At least it is not a step forward. And what is more, a confused debate is bound to take place in the United Nations and in the international arena, in which case we are compelled to speak out.

MR. RESTON—I thought that there was a misjudgment here, frankly, in what it was that Rogers and President Nixon were doing. I thought that the President, by seeking a conference with you before the UN, was saying to members of the UN who had wavered in past years or followed our line in past years: We have now changed, we want to see the People's Republic seated in New York. And by that process he had started a procedure which inevitably would lead to the seating of your Government in the UN, particularly on his third point, which clearly implied that he would not use the veto in the Security Council, yet as I interpreted the news agency's remark, this was not taken into account at all.

MR. CHOU—The central point of that statement is to retain the Chiang representative in the United Nations, and that means that it would be impossible for us to go in.

MR. RESTON—Perhaps this is not a subject that lends itself to useful conversation at this time. Maybe it's too delicate. And if it is, I hope you will tell me so and we'll go on to other things.

MR. CHOU—You are not planning to make clear our position in an all-round way?

MR. RESTON—I want to do that. I mean—

"We Are Seeing Some Changes"

MR. CHOU—As I have seen from your talk with our friends, your proposition is that since the United States is to recognize the People's Republic of China, then it should give up the Taiwan representative.

MR. RESTON—I believe very frankly that we've come to an unusual moment in the history of the world that neither in your life nor in mine will we see again. In my own country there are great changes taking place, philosophical and political. In Europe we are seeing a transformation, with the British coming into the Common Market. In the Middle East we see more evidence, I think, that force does not prevail for anybody. The only place where force seems to have prevailed is for Russia in Czechoslovakia. And therefore what I've come here to do is to find out, during this long period when China had not been actively participating in these affairs of the UN and elsewhere, how you see the world of this great transformation? Do you really believe that the United States is ready for change, as I do, or do you feel that we are engaged again in maneuvers and manipulations for imperialist purposes, as you seem to be saying in your press?

MR. CHOU—We admit we also are seeing some changes. As you said to our friends, you are also seeing changes taking place in China. But there is one question and that is we will not barter away principles. And so once this question is raised, there is bound to be a dispute.

As for Taiwan, who occupied Taiwan? And so if you want to have a change, then you should act according to a Chinese saying, that is, it is for the doer to undo the knot.

The latest discussions between Japan and Taiwan were obviously designed to create an obstacle so that it would not be possible for us to get into the UN. After Rogers's statement, the Japanese Acting Foreign Minister, Kimura, and the Secretary General of the ruling Japanese Liberal Democratic party, Hori Shigoru, made similar statements.

Both Kimura and Hori Shigoru said that this basic policy of the United States was determined after many consultations between the United States and Japan. And Japan's demand was put forward after two secret talks held between the Chiang representative and Satō in the latter part of July and on August 1.

And so the statement made by the so-called Foreign Ministry of Chiang Kai-shek did not touch on Roger's statement at all but concentrated on attacking the Albanian resolution.

Japan has ambitious designs with regard to Taiwan. Japan wants to control Taiwan in her hands. So it's not a simple matter that Japan is supporting Taiwan in the United Nations.

In fact, we can even go further from there. That is, not only will there be a question of two Chinas or one China, one Taiwan—it's even conceivable that they are trying to separate Taiwan from China and, under the direction of Japan and also possibly with support from some quarters in the United States, to bring about a so-called independent Taiwan.

And because of this, we cannot but make our attitude very clear. We have stated very clearly that should a state of two Chinas or one China, one Taiwan appear in the UN, or a similar absurd state of affairs take place in the UN designed to separate Taiwan from China to create a so-called independent Taiwan, we will firmly oppose it and under those circumstances we will absolutely not go into the UN.

It is indeed true that the world is undergoing changes. But these changes must not cause further damage to the Chinese people. Over the past twenty years and more, it's not we who have caused harm to others, but the U.S. Government who have been causing harm to other countries and other peoples. We have waited already for more than twenty years and we can wait for another year. That doesn't matter. But there must be a just solution.

Will Chou Attend UN Himself?

MR. RESTON—May I ask whether, in the event that your present position proves to be too pessimistic and the General Assembly and the Security Council without any veto by the United States decide to seat China, will you at this meeting of the Security Council go to New York yourself and represent China at this meeting of the General Assembly?

MR. CHOU—Will Chiang Kai-shek still be there or not?

MR. RESTON—No, on the assumption that he is not.

MR. CHOU—He has left?

MR. RESTON—Yes.

MR. CHOU—Only if he has really left can I express an attitude, and Taiwan must be a part of China. But if in the UN resolution there is anything to the effect that the status of Taiwan remains to be determined, then we will not go in.

MR. RESTON—I understand that. But I am assuming by my question that the Albanian resolution will have been put up and voted to your satisfaction in the General Assembly, and that you will go on and be voted into the Security Council, at which time Taiwan will be expelled, and my question is: Would you at that time personally go to New York?

MR. CHOU—But I was asking the question that would they still consider the status of Taiwan undetermined and the status of Taiwan an outstanding question? You cannot answer that question now, nor can I.

MR. RESTON—I don't see that that question would be a question for the UN at all. At that time it's a question between you and the Taiwanese. As early as 1955 I believe that you said that this was an internal question and it should be settled between the Government of the People's Republic and the local authorities, I believe you called them at that time, on Taiwan. Is it still your view, that it should be settled in that way? And second, is there anything to Edgar Snow's remark that he believes there already has been contact between the People's Republic and officials on Taiwan?

"No Foreign Interference"

MR. CHOU—I've said on many occasions that the liberation of Taiwan is China's internal affair, which brooks no foreign interference. That is still our position now. At the same time, I've said that the United States has committed aggression against and occupied China's Taiwan Province and the Taiwan Strait, so we are willing to sit down and enter into negotiations with the U.S. Government for a settlement of this question.

This has been going on for sixteen years, first in Geneva and then in Warsaw. And what is more, I've said that the Chinese people are friendly to the American people, the two peoples have been friendly with each other in the past, and in the future they should all the more live together in friendship, because the Chinese people have now stood up.

That was said far back in 1955 at the Bandung conference. Afterwards, we tried to accept the visit of some American correspondents to China, but John Foster Dulles's State Department did not approve of that. And so, since the way was blocked by the U.S. Government, then we on our side would no longer want any such contacts. We have thus been cut off for more than twenty years, but it doesn't matter.

But now since there are some changes in the world, then we should see to it no damage is done to anyone, that concern should be shown to the wronged party and the wronged party should not continue to be wronged. Therefore, the question of Taiwan is not merely an internal question. If it were merely an internal matter, then we will be able to settle it ourselves. The solution of this internal problem has been obstructed now for already twenty-one years, and so changes are taking place. And in this process some country has started to harbor ambitions. That is quite evident.

MR. RESTON—You mean by that Japan?

MR. CHOU—Yes.

MR. RESTON—May I ask you to state the principles again. You have been very clear about this in the past, you have told Snow, in 1960, I believe. Principle one was nothing between us on Taiwan shall be settled by force or the threat of force. Principle two, there is only one China. Now are these the two and only two principles to be settled? What about withdrawal of forces, what about the question of the treaty between Washington and Taipei?

MR. CHOU—When you say us, you mean China and the United States?

MR. RESTON—Yes, the United States and China.

MR. CHOU—If Taiwan is to be returned to the motherland, the U.S. forces must withdraw, because otherwise how can it be returned to the motherland? And since the United States is to withdraw all their troops and military installations from Taiwan and the Taiwan Strait area, then as a matter of course the so-called U.S.-Chiang mutual defense treaty, which we had all along considered to be illegal, would become invalid.

Preliminary Talks "Possible"

MR. RESTON—I understand. It is clear, I think, since the differences over Rogers's statement, that there is a lot of underbrush to be cleared away before you and the President are to

meet. I wondered what ideas you have about whether preliminary technical talks at a lower level should take place and
where, between now and the President's arrival?

MR. CHOU—It is possible. But if these questions are to be
solved, they can only be solved when the President himself
comes. He expressed a desire to come and we have invited
him to come.

MR. RESTON—Could I ask one final question about the UN
and China? In your mind, is there a conflict between the basic
principle of the UN, namely, that all disputes between nations
shall be resolved without the use of force or the threat of
force, and the principle of revolution and support for national
liberation movements in the world as espoused by your Government in the past? Is there a conflict between these two things?

MR. CHOU—No. Who has committed aggression against other
countries? China hasn't. Over the twenty-two years of the history of our People's Republic, we only went abroad to assist
Korea, but that was under certain conditions. We made it very
clear to the so-called UN Command composed of sixteen countries led by the U.S. We said to them that if they press toward
the Yalu River, then we will not sit idly by, although at that
time our Taiwan and Taiwan Strait area had already been
occupied by the U.S. Seventh Fleet and the U.S. Air Force. It
was the U.S. which first committed aggression against China,
and not vice versa. It was only after the U.S. forces had reached
the Yalu River that we sent our C.P.V. [Chinese People's
Volunteers] to resist American aggression and aid Korea.

Chinese People's Volunteers

As for our help to other countries of the world, that is in the
case when they are subjected to aggression. And in the view of
the UN itself, aggression is wrong and should be stopped. So
we are merely helping them to resist aggression. And in the
view of the UN itself, they should be given support. And a
striking instance is Vietnam.

As for Vietnam, we will continue to give them assistance to
the end, until the complete withdrawal of the U.S. forces. At
present the most urgent question is still Vietnam. You wondered
very much why I said to the Committee of Concerned Asian
Scholars that it was our position that first of all the question

of Vietnam and Indochina should be solved, and not the
question of Taiwan or other questions.

Because the status quo of Taiwan has remained for twenty-
one years. There is no war there. That is because of restraint
on our part. But this is not the case with Vietnam. Not only
did the U.S. send troops to commit aggression there, but the
U.S. is expanding the war there. When President Nixon took
office, he started withdrawing troops from Vietnam, that is
anyhow changing the former situation. But in March last year,
the peaceful role of Samdech Norodom Sihanouk in Cambodia
was subverted and then the U.S. troops went in. Even your
New York Times criticized that action.

MR. RESTON—Especially *The New York Times.*

MR. CHOU—And then this year there was the attack on
Route 9. Isn't that an expansion of the war?

MR. RESTON—Yes, I think so.

The Cost of the Vietnam War

MR. CHOU—And so that has brought even greater harm to
the Vietnamese people and the Indochinese people as a whole.
Such a small place as Indochina with a small population. Yet
such a huge sum has been spent. The American Government
itself admitted that in ten years' time it spent $120 billion and
suffered such heavy casualties. And the American people are
unhappy about the American casualties. We on our side feel
they are needless casualties. But the Vietnamese people have
suffered even greater casualties.

MR. RESTON—I agree.

MR. CHOU—Just take a look there and you can see that.
Shouldn't we sympathize with them?

MR. RESTON—Absolutely. It's a tragedy.

MR. CHOU—So why shouldn't the United States end its
aggression?

MR. RESTON—Yes. Now what do you think we should do to
stop it? I went straight there from Panmunjom in 1953, and I
have been fighting against our involvement in that war ever
since. As a matter of act, when I went to Saigon in 1953 I saw
the British brigadier who was the observer there at that time
and I asked, was there any way in which the West can possibly
deal with the Vietminh, as they were then called. And he said,

yes, there may be one way: If you would give foreign aid, military program to the Vietminh, especially tanks, then you might be able to find them. That will be the only way, said he, the West will ever win a war in this part of the world.

MR. CHOU—You did some work, your *New York Times*, by making public some of the secret Pentagon papers.

MR. RESTON—Yes.

MR. CHOU—Indeed, back in the time of Truman, the U.S. Government started helping the French in their aggression and colonial war in Indochina. And after Dulles took over from Acheson, this further developed.

Aid to Vietnamese Described

MR. RESTON—Are there some Peking papers on that period on the war that have not been published? If there are, then *The New York Times* would like to accommodate you and publish them.

MR. CHOU—We have no secret papers like that. But we did send some weapons to the Vietnamese people to help them in their resistance. The French Government is aware of that. Within less than half a year after the founding of our People's Republic, we recognized the DRVN [Democratic Republic of Vietnam] headed by President Ho Chi Minh. Actually the French Government was prepared to recognize the P.R.C. [People's Republic of China], but because of that matter, France put off the recognition until the time of General de Gaulle. So if you are interested in secret documents, this is a document but not a secret one.

MR. RESTON—Yes. Your commentator the other day made it quite clear that your Government is opposed to the Geneva conference for a settlement of the Indochina war. Now, do you see the Laotian and the Cambodian questions being settled separately from the Vietnam question?

MR. CHOU—This is a matter within the sovereignty of the Government of the DRVN, of the provisional revolutionary government of the Republic of SVN [South Vietnam], of the royal government of national union of Cambodia, and of the Laotian Patriotic Front. It is within their sovereignty to decide whether the Indochina question is to be settled together or separately.

Judging from the present situation, negotiations are going on now only on Vietnam. And so maybe the Vietnam question will be first solved. As for Cambodia, the U.S. refuses to recognize Prince Sihanouk's Government, and Prince Sihanouk has clearly stated his just position in his message No. 24 to his compatriots. I haven't heard anyone say anything more on that score. As for Laos, they are planning to discuss among themselves. And there is correspondence between Souvanna Phouma and Prince Souphanouvong, and the Laotian Patriotic Front has put forward a five-point proposal, one of which is cease-fire throughout Laos.

We support this five-point proposal of the Laotian Patriotic Front. As for the summit conference of the Indochinese peoples, the four sides of the three countries issued a joint statement in April last year and they put forward a common proposition. They demand all troops from countries outside of Indochina to completely withdraw and let the three peoples of Indochina solve their question by themselves. And we support this principle.

MR. RESTON—You are not interested in mediating this struggle between the U.S. and the North Vietnamese and Liberation Front?

MR. CHOU—We don't want to be a mediator in any way. And we were very badly taken in during the first Geneva conference. If you are interested, I can go into it now. If not, we can discuss it at the dinner table.

MR. RESTON—Yes, but I want to hear all about your confrontation with John Foster Dulles at dinner. You know, nothing has surprised me quite so much since coming here as the vehemence of your feeling about Japan.

MR. CHOU—You too were victims of Japanese militarism. But you said the Americans are more forgetful. But I know you still recall the Pearl Harbor incident.

MR. RESTON—Yes, but this is one of—in my view—the endearing qualities of the American people: They have no memory. They have every reason to be aggrieved, if not full of hatred, about Japan and about Germany. There is no hatred in our country toward Japan or Germany. And if there is one thing that has troubled me a bit since I have come here, it is a sense that, while you are, in your domestic policy, looking

forward toward the twenty-first century, in your foreign policy
I think you are looking backward to the old disputes. And that
saddens me. Now am I being unfair to you? Because I don't
want to be.

MR. CHOU—It is unfair. Because you didn't have any direct
talk with us about our foreign policy, you just heard about
some of our slogans.

Why is there such sentiment among the Americans? Because
the U.S. benefitted from both World Wars, and the U.S. losses
were rather small. Why is it that the American people have a
rather deep impression about the present U.S. war of aggression
against Vietnam? Because they have really suffered. And so the
American people demand the withdrawal of the American
troops. It is not that the American people don't summarize their
experience.

So I don't quite agree with your estimate that the American
people are easily forgetful. Any nation is bound to summarize
its own historical experience. Just yesterday I met a friend who
had come from the U.S. some time ago, and he said that among
the Americans there are now some changes toward the black
people and that is a good thing. And it shows that many white
people in the U.S. are becoming awakened to the fact that it is
not right to continue the exploitation and oppression of the
black people left over from history. So isn't that a summary
of historical experience? And it is very good.

MR. RESTON—Yes.

Japanese "Reactionaries" Opposed

MR. CHOU—We oppose the Japanese reactionaries. It is not
that we have any hatred for the Japanese people. After the end
of the Pacific war, we have not stopped our contacts with the
Japanese people. New China has never imposed a blockade
against them. The Japanese people have kept on visiting China,
and we are also willing to go there.

The Japanese people are a diligent and brave people and a
great nation. And it was the U.S. Government which after the
war strengthened the Japanese reactionaries. And when they
have developed to the present stage they are bound to develop
militarism.

Just look at the economic development of Japan. According

to your President, the steel output of Japan is about to catch up to that of the U.S., as he said in Kansas City on July 6. Why is it that Japan has developed so quickly? I've heard that you also admit that the reason was that not only was no indemnity exacted from Japan, but Japan was protected and provided with raw materials, markets, investments and technology.

And then there is another thing. That is, the U.S. has promoted the development of Japan toward militarism by the indefinite prolongation of the Japan-U.S. security treaty. The Japanese people are opposed to this treaty. And according to the report of the American congressmen who went to Japan to study the matter, Japan does not need such a huge defense budget for its fourth defense plan for the purpose of self-defense.

The budget for the fourth defense plan reached the amount of more than $16 billion. And Defense Secretary Laird himself admits that according to Japan's present economic strength and industrial and technical ability, she will not need five years (1972–1976) to complete that plan, and two to two and a half years will be sufficient.

In Japan, in South Korea and when he returned to Washington, Laird said that there were three pillars to the Nixon doctrine. The first is to arm your partners, and of these partners, the principal one will be Japan. The second is nuclear protection, and only thirdly is negotiation. And what is more, he made it clear that these negotiations have to proceed from a position of strength. And without the previous two pillars, there would not be the third.

MR. RESTON—Could I ask you, sir, what you want us to do about Japan? Because it seems to me there is a dilemma here. If we stay allied to Japan, with some control over her, particularly in the nuclear field, that is one thing. If we end the security pact with Japan, is it in your view that it is more likely then that Japan will become more militaristic or less militaristic?

It seems to me that, confronted by two nuclear powers in the Pacific, both China and the Soviet Union, and freed from us and our pact, she would almost certainly have to go nuclear, would she not? Therefore I find myself puzzled by your desire to see this pact with the United States broken.

MR. CHOU—That argument is quite a forced argument. Despite this treaty, Japan with her present industrial capabilities is fully able to produce all the means of delivery, she is able to manufacture ground-to-air, ground-to-ground missiles, and sea-to-ground missiles. As for bombers, she is all the more capable of manufacturing them. The only thing lacking is the nuclear warhead.

Japan's output of nuclear power is increasing daily. The United States supply of enriched uranium to Japan is not enough for her requirement, and she is now importing enriched uranium from other countries. And so her nuclear weapons can be produced readily. She cannot be prevented from doing so merely by the treaty. You have helped her develop her economy to such a level. And she is bound to demand outward expansion.

Economic expansion is bound to bring about military expansion. And that cannot be restrained by a treaty. Look at all your nuclear bases in Japan. Even if you are to withdraw your nuclear weapons, the nuclear bases are still there, and they can make use of them.

When you said that there is no militarism, well, I'll argue with you on that score. This is borne out by the film which we have shown you and by the activities of Mishima, who had committed suicide.

Just when you were ill in Peking, you probably heard of the incident of a Japanese fighter colliding with a Boeing civil airliner, causing heavy casualties. Why? Because the air corridor in Japan is very narrow.

You have been to Japan. You know that the Japanese air corridors are divided into several levels, the higher for the Boeings, the lower for the propeller-driven aircraft. And with the Japanese Air Force being equipped with more and more planes, they just fly everywhere with them at will for training. And the pilot of that fighter parachuted to safety but let his fighter collide with the Boeing. And when asked why they did that, the trainer just said there was no place for training. What could they do?

That of course gave rise to public indignation. And among those voicing indignation were the opposition within the ruling Liberal-Democratic party itself, who said this is one of the harms of militarism. It is not something said by the Chinese alone; they themselves are saying that.

MR. RESTON—You are really worried about Japan, aren't you?

Fifty Years of Suffering

MR. CHOU—Because you know we suffered a long time, for fifty years. Such calamities can be prevented by opposition from us and from the Japanese people together.

Of the four opposition parties in Japan, only the Japanese Communist party has differing views with China; that part supports Sato on this.

The Japanese Socialist party admits the revival of Japanese militarism. The Komeito party admits that Japanese militarism is being revived, the Democratic Socialist party does not deny this fact, and the opposition wing of the Liberal-Democratic party also admits this fact.

When you oppose a danger, you should oppose it when it is only budding. Only then can you arouse public attention. Otherwise, if you are to await until it has already developed into a power, it will be too strenuous. If the Far East situation is really to move towards relaxation, and if Japan gives up its ambitions of aggression against Korea and China's Taiwan, then it will be possible for China and Japan to conclude a mutual non-aggression treaty on the basis of the five principles of peaceful coexistence.

MR. RESTON—Could I ask you at that point whether you can foresee an expansion of such a pact to include the United States and the Soviet Union?

MR. CHOU—That must go through a whole series of steps and I cannot at the present time give an immediate answer. Because at the present time the two superpowers, the U.S. and the Soviet Union, are involving themselves in affairs throughout the world. And it is not an easy thing to bring about a solution of world problems, so we would rather like to have a discussion with your President.

MR. RESTON—On this subject—

MR. CHOU—Various questions can be discussed. This question, too, may be discussed.

MR. RESTON—This is too serious a question to be dismissed lightly. Could you define as you have done so often in the past and so helpfully in the past, what are the principles that must precede such a far-sighted move as such a four-power non-aggression pact?

MR. CHOU—This question can be thought about only after we come to it because international questions are too complicated. It is easy to say the five principles of peaceful coexistence which we advocate. But to go into an examination to see whether or not these principles are observed, then many problems will arise.

For instance, it was with India that we had first reached an agreement on the five principles of peaceful coexistence. Because both China and India are two big countries, and in history there was no aggression by either against the other, with the sole exception of Genghis Khan's descendants, who went to the subcontinent but then stayed here and intermarried with the local inhabitants.

As for the two peoples, we had lived together in friendship for generations. As for the boundary question, it was something left over by British imperialism. But precisely over this boundary question, they fell out with us.

On this question, it was India which occupied Chinese territory. They even crossed the so-called McMahon Line. As for us, we did not press forward and were ready to solve the question by negotiations. As for Aksai Chin, in the western sector, that had all along been Chinese territory, there was never a boundary dispute over that territory before, but suddenly they raised the question about the western sector.

I went to India to negotiate this boundary question with the Indians on three occasions, and no solution was reached. What is more, they want to further occupy our territory north of the so-called McMahon Line. You didn't know much about this. Now you should know about it. A very good proof of the facts about this situation was a book written by a British author, Mr. Maxwell.

MR. RESTON—Yes.

MR. CHOU—That book is similar to the Pentagon papers which you published. They did not make use of a single Chinese document. All are from Indian sources.

Control of Nuclear Arms

MR. RESTON—May I ask you, sir, how you view the control of nuclear arms? You are now one of the nuclear powers.

MR. CHOU—No, we are not a nuclear power. We are only in the experimental stage. And what is more, that has been the case throughout the period from 1964 to the present, seven years already. We will not test when there is no need. We know it is quite expensive and a waste. And it is not beneficial to the improvement of the livelihood of the people.

It is quite clear, we can see, that the two big powers, the United States and the Soviet Union, having embarked on the mass production of nuclear weapons—cannot get down from the horse, so to speak. But can they thereby monopolize nuclear weapons. No, they cannot.

We produced nuclear weapons by ourselves. We manufacture nuclear weapons because we are forced to do so in order to break the nuclear monopoly. And our aim is the complete prohibition and thorough destruction of nuclear weapons. And so every time we make a test, we declare that we will never be the first to use nuclear weapons. You will see what we Chinese say counts.

MR. RESTON—Do you want to see a world conference on this question? How can this ghastly problem be solved when the world is now spending about $220 billion a year on arms? It is a disgrace to the intelligence of the human family. What are we to do about this question, and what can China do to help?

MR. CHOU—We do not agree with the Soviet proposal for a conference of the five nuclear powers. They want to lasso us by that means. We have expressed our disapproval, Britain said that she would not take part in the conference, and France too now says that she would not take part either.

We are calling for the convening of a conference of all countries of the world, big or small—because all the countries of the world, regardless of their size, should be equal—for the purpose of reaching an agreement on the complete prohibition and thorough destruction of nuclear weapons, and as a first step, on the nonuse of nuclear weapons. Once everyone agrees on the nonuse of nuclear weapons then what will be the need for the production of nuclear weapons?

508   *PEOPLE'S CHINA*

"How Can We Sign Them?"

MR. RESTON—Why do you use the word "lasso"?

MR. CHOU—When I said "lasso," it means if they want to drag us into such an affair. They will, first of all, demand that we sign on the partial nuclear test ban treaty, on the nonproliferation treaty and so on. How can we sign them?

But we undertake not to be the first to use nuclear weapons. The people of the world have indeed noted the fact that these two big powers are using so much money on nuclear weapons. Your Defense Secretary, Laird, himself admits that with so many nuclear weapons it is not possible for the United States and the Soviet Union to fight a nuclear war. The two peoples will oppose such a war.

MR. RESTON—True.

MR. CHOU—Since you do not want to have a nuclear war, then the United States and the Soviet Union should first undertake forthrightly that neither of them will be the first to use nuclear weapons, and then to go on to the next business. Because by reaching such an agreement, people will feel at ease. Secretary Laird said, now the United States should be prepared for conventional warfare. So Laird is telling Japan to strengthen the modernization of conventional weapons in Japan.

MR. RESTON—Is there a conflict between the so-called Nixon doctrine or Guam doctrine and our efforts to reach an accommodation with China? The thought I have in mind is this: I am afraid there is a puzzling and troubling point here that as we try to reduce our commitments in the Pacific, we encourage Japan and other countries to assume a larger military role, and that, in turn, leads to a greater dismay and anxiety on the part of China. Is there a conflict here? Is this one of the things to talk about with President Nixon when he comes to Peking?

MR. CHOU—You put it well. It is indeed a contradiction. I also discovered this contradiction because this is to encourage the militarization of Japan. There should be an effort at relaxation by all parties concerned. Indeed, there are a lot of questions. And as you know, your President spoke to the correspondents on the fourth after Rogers made his statement. We have not yet seen the full text of his interview, we have read only a partial text. Have you seen it?

MR. RESTON—You mean the Rogers?

MR. CHOU—No, Nixon's.

MR. RESTON—No, I have not seen it.

MR. CHOU—I have only received very fragmentary reports, and probably I might get the full text tonight. President Nixon said that there were no preconditions for the forthcoming talks with China. Neither side has made any commitments. That is, there was no tacit understanding previously reached between the two sides.

MR. RESTON—I think it is useful to clarify this point because I think your allies and ours have both been a bit suspicious on this point.

MR. CHOU—China is a country which was blockaded by the United States for more than twenty years. Now since there is a desire to come and look at China, it's all right. And since there is a desire to talk, we are also ready to talk. Of course, it goes without saying that the positions of our two sides are different. And there are a lot of differences between our points of view. To achieve relaxation, there must be a common desire for it, so various questions must be studied, and all these questions may be placed on the table for discussion. We do not expect a settlement of all questions at one stroke. That is not possible. That would not be practicable. But by contacting each other, we may be able to find out from where we should start in solving these questions.

Prospects for a Settlement

MR. RESTON—We are a very impatient people, you know, Mr. Prime Minister. In the old grocery stores up in our country-side there used to be little signs which said the improbable we do today, the impossible tomorrow. How long do you antici-pate that is will take for reasonable men to resolve these prob-lems of Taiwan, Vietnam and get the principles solved and get down to diplomatic relations between these two countries?

MR. CHOU—We hope that the Indochina question will be solved first because the war is still going on there. I have read some of your articles, and you said in one of your articles that you felt that your President lacked courage. But of course, in deciding to come to China this time, it is something which even the opposition party say others dare not do. So on this point he has some courage. Mr. Mansfield himself said that.

MR. RESTON—Courage or lack of courage, those are fighting words. What I was trying to say is that I do not think that he is a bold-minded man in the sense that de Gaulle was when de Gaulle said, "I was wrong about Algeria, therefore, I stop it, and I move to change it now."

I think the trend of the President's thought is bold and even right on both Vietnam and China. His timing and his politics are rather ambiguous. That was what I meant, not a lack of courage—it is not a lack of courage, it's a lack of clarity and definition and boldness to cut and end the killing and end the stupidity of isolation of China.

You asked me before about what did I mean by favoring China and the end of the Taiwan relationship. It's very simple. We cannot resolve the problems in the world without China. It's just that simple. We can resolve the problems of the world without Taiwan. It's not a question of sentiment, it's a question of reality and power.

That is why I want to see this resolved, and resolved at a moment when the country is ready for it. That is why I am worried about the China news agency and their story of the other night. If we leave it to journalists, the world will be in a mess. It has to get down to quiet diplomacy.

MR. CHOU—Well, some things can be dealt with quietly, but when some things have been openly declared by the other party for several times, then it must be openly answered in the press.

I agree to your estimate of the character of President Nixon, and of course there is also the question of the position he is now in. The then position of General de Gaulle in France was a bit different. But as there are going to be conversations between us, I hope he will clearly see the future, as you said, to look forward.

For instance, a complete withdrawal from Vietnam will be quite an honorable thing. What is there dishonorable about their withdrawal from Vietnam? I think that is most honorable. When General de Gaulle withdrew from Algeria, the whole world expressed their approval, and the Algerian people expressed approval, too. The relations between France and Algeria improved in de Gaulle's time.

MR. RESTON—I should say one thing to you privately about

this. I think it is very important that you say you should look forward. I think the President does look forward. I think there are two things about him that are particularly interesting.

One, he is a Californian and he looks to the Pacific in the way that we who live on the other side of the continent do not. Second, he has one ambition. His ambition is to preside over the 200th anniversary of the Declaration of Independence in 1976. There is one small barrier in the way of that, which is he must get reelected in 1972. And beyond that, I think he is a romantic, and I think he is dead serious about China.

I think he sees an historic opportunity here to repair the damage that has been done and even the injustice that has been done to China, and also perhaps in his own sense, a certain rebuke to his own past and a feeling that the role he has played in the cold war is something that might be altered by a great and generous move to unify the peoples of the Pacific before he ends his term.

MR. CHOU—Thank you for providing me with this information. And you are motivated by your concern about the overall world situation.

MR. RESTON—Yes, one doesn't come abroad to criticize one's own President, and I don't do that. It is true and it is still part of the mythology of America—I believe it's true—that the White House—you know, Woodrow Wilson once said that in the White House a man either grows or he swells, but most men are ennobled by it, and I think President Nixon is focusing on China, where he sees a historic role. This I think is terribly important psychologically.

MR. CHOU—We've noted this.

Demand for Withdrawal

MR. RESTON—May I, because I don't want to impose on or weary you. There is one thing I want to have you clarify for me if you will. You see we can talk philosophy, and that is interesting. But when we get down to it and I listen to all the specific conditions to which I've heard since I have come to Peking, I get rather depressed. The condition on Vietnam I understand, and I can see that it can be met. The conditions and the principles of Chou En-lai on Taiwan, I think, can be met. But when I hear General Huang say that we must withdraw from the Philippines, we must withdraw from Japan, we must withdraw from Thailand, I think this is asking us, in a way, to withdraw from the Pacific, and I get depressed at that point because this doesn't seem to me to be a realistic basis which any President could accept.

MR. CHOU—If one really wants to achieve a relaxation throughout the world and not the aggravation of tension, then the troops of all foreign countries, not only the U.S. troops, should be withdrawn from the territories of the countries they have occupied and let the peoples of various countries solve their own problems by themselves.

This is a question of principle. But as to when and where these withdrawals are to take place first, and how to discuss and reach agreement with the governments concerned, they are concrete matters.

When the principle has been put forward, and if one really goes in this direction, there are many specific details which have to be discussed for the implementation of this principle.

MR. RESTON—I have a feeling that perhaps we'd better end on this point. There are two great movements in the world today. There is a movement of withdrawal by the U.S. in Vietnam and a retrenchment of its commitment overseas, and, on the other hand, the most visible movement it seems to me is the enlargement and the expansion of Soviet power across the Middle East and along the southern shore of the Mediterranean, and once the Suez is opened, into the Indian Ocean and the Pacific. Is one justified in being troubled by this Soviet movement in your view? Are you bothered by it?

MR. CHOU—Of course, for us it is an even more urgent matter. The assistant managing editor of your paper, Mr. [Harrison] Salisbury had been to Mongolia. He testified to the fact that there are massive troops concentrated on our borders in the north. So, in general, we stand for the withdrawal of all foreign troops back to their own countries so that the people of various countries may settle their own questions by themselves.

This is a matter of principle. But to put that into concrete form, of course, requires a process. In a word, in the past twenty-five years, first the U.S. tried to manage affairs of the whole globe, and then after Khrushchev took office it was a matter of striving for hegemony between the two superpowers.

The so-called disarmament conference is in fact a conference for arms expansion. Although there has been no world war, yet small wars have never ceased. We are not for demanding only the U.S. withdrawal and not the Soviet withdrawal, because that would be unfair. We say so in general terms, and specific matters will be dealt with concretely.

So if you say one should relax the situation, it is indeed not an easy matter. The reason is they have a few more atom bombs. But we Chinese are not afraid of atom bombs. We are prepared against their attack, against their launching a pre-emptive attack on us. That is why we are digging underground tunnels. You probably heard about this.

A Network of Tunnels

MR. RESTON—Yes, I did. As a matter of fact, you have a great network of tunnels under Peking.

MR. CHOU—Not only Peking. The great majority of our big and medium cities now have a network of underground tunnels.

[*At this point the formal interview broke for dinner, but after dinner, though it was then past midnight, Mr. Chou asked that the formal discussion be resumed. The official transcript was renewed.*]

MR. CHOU—There is one thing I've forgotten to mention. We have just discussed the question of Japan without discussing the question of Korea. As you know, there is still only an armistice agreement in Korea, and there has been no peace treaty. In this connection, we have to revert to John Foster Dulles.

In the Geneva conference, the first stage was devoted to the Korean question. As for the armistice in Korea, on your side it was a result of the decision taken by President Eisenhower. One of your generals admitted that the Korean war was a wrong war fought at a wrong time at a wrong place.

MR. RESTON—General Omar Bradley.

MR. CHOU—At the 1954 Geneva conference there should have been a result on the Korean question, at least a decision should have been made to continue the conference in the future. But even that was disrupted by Dulles. And so even now there is a demilitarized zone, a Military Armistice Commission which meets once every one or two weeks in Panmunjom.

On your side there is an American representative and a representative from what we call the puppet Government in South Korea. And on the northern side is a representative of the Democratic People's Republic of Korea and a representative of the Chinese People's Volunteers. So the state of war has not ended. And you may recall the two incidents caused by your side, one of the Pueblo spy ship and the other a spy plane which was downed.

"Situation Remains Tense"

MR. RESTON—Yes.

MR. CHOU—And so the situation remains tense. And this is a matter which should be discussed.

MR. RESTON—Yes. If you could give me your views about that, I would be very happy to report them.

MR. CHOU—Our people's volunteers were withdrawn back in 1958. And the troops of other countries under the so-called U.N.C. have also been withdrawn. Only American troops remain there. And of the 60,000 troops or more in Korea at that time, 20,000 troops have been withdrawn and 40,000 and more still remain. And the American troops should all be withdrawn.

To solve the Korean question, a way should be found to bring about a rapprochement between the two sides in Korea and to move toward a peaceful unification of Korea. That of course requires time. But this demand is reasonable.

Now in the UN there is still a so-called commission for the unification and rehabilitation of Korea which is completely unilateral, composed of those countries of the so-called U.N.C. participating in the Korean war, and not a commission of both sides.

That presents a problem too. And so the Korean question is also linked up with the problem of Japanese militarism. If things do not go well, Japan may use the treaty it has concluded with South Korea, i.e., the Japan-R.O.K. treaty, to get into South Korea immediately upon the withdrawal of the U.S. forces.

MR. RESTON—It is extremely useful to have this view because, for one thing we have not been able to do is to define those questions, of which I presume is one, that really should be on the agenda when the President comes here.

MR. CHOU—The Korean question also involves a question

of preventing the rise of Japanese militarism. If Japanese militarism is to expand outward, it will first aim at these two wings, Taiwan and this wing. I only deal with Taiwan. This is just what I would like to add.

MR. RESTON—Prime Minister, thank you very much for your kindness. I would like to ask the Prime Minister while I am here, would it be presumptuous for me to ask whether it is at all possible to see the Chairman?

MR. CHOU—Not very possible this time, because the Chairman is preoccupied with other matters. But of course you can come with your President next time.

MR. RESTON—No, I don't think I'll do that. I'll worry about him from now till then, and let you worry about him after he gets here.

★   ★   ★   ★   ★

NUCLEAR WEAPONS

The nuclear bomb exploded on December 27, 1968 was China's eighth test detonation since the first on October 16, 1964. This press communiqué not only announces the test, but restates basic Chinese policy on nuclear matters. The key policy is given in the last paragraph, particularly in the declaration that China will never be the first to use nuclear weapons. The Chinese have repeatedly urged the United States and the Soviet Union to make a similar no-first-use pledge. The thinking behind her nuclear policy is given toward the end of the preceding paragraph where it is described as a counter to "the policy of nuclear threat and nuclear blackmail" practiced by the United States and the Soviet Union. The United States had been generally considered the source of nuclear threat and the Soviet Union the source of nuclear blackmail. The reference to the Vietnam War is not casual, for the Chinese had always been aware of the possibility that nuclear weapons might be used, and called particular attention to this possibility in February 1971.

★   ★   ★

CHINESE GOVERNMENT*
Hydrogen Bomb Test

In the advance to the all-round victory of her great proletarian cultural revolution and under the tremendous inspiration
of the Communiqué of the Enlarged 12th Plenary Session of
the Eighth Central Committee of the Chinese Communist Party,
China exploded another hydrogen bomb over her western region on December 27, 1968, and thereby successfully conducted
a new thermonuclear test.

This is another great victory for the invincible thought of
Mao Tse-tung, another fruitful result of the great proletarian
cultural revolution and a significant gift to the forthcoming
Ninth National Congress of the Party. We hail with great joy
the success of this hydrogen bomb test which marks a new leap
forward in the development of China's nuclear weapons.

Our great leader Chairman Mao teaches us: **"We cannot just
take the beaten track traversed by other countries in the development of technology and trail behind them at a snail's pace.
We must break away from conventions and do our utmost to
adopt advanced techniques in order to build our country into a
powerful modern socialist state in not too long a historical
period."**

The success of this hydrogen bomb test is the result of the
all-out efforts in grasping revolution and promoting production
with vigor and militancy by the Chinese workers, People's
Liberation Army men and scientific and technical personnel
engaged in the research, manufacture and testing of nuclear
weapons, who, by holding aloft the great red banner of Marxism, Leninism, Mao Tse-tung's thought, have closely followed
Chairman Mao's great strategic plan and resolutely responded
to Chairman Mao's great call to **"carry out the task of struggle-**

* Hsinhua News Agency, Peking (December 28, 1968). Translated in
Peking Review, No. 1 (January 3, 1969).

criticism-transformation conscientiously." In the course of the research, manufacture and testing, they made a penetrating study of the history of the struggle between the two lines, forcefully repudiated the counter-revolutionary revisionist line pushed by the renegade, traitor and scab Liu Shao-ch'i and his agents, and resolutely defended the proletarian revolutionary line represented by Chairman Mao. They brought into full play the leading role of the working class and carried out the principle of integrating the scientific and technical personnel with the workers and of integrating theory with practice. Pooling their wisdom and relying on their own efforts, they boldly undertook scientific experiments, overcame all kinds of difficulties and solved a series of new problems, thus ensuring the complete success of this new hydrogen bomb test.

The Central Committee of the Communist Party of China, the Cultural Revolution Group under the Party's Central Committee, the State Council, and the Military Commission of the Central Committee of the Party extend warm congratulations to the workers, the commanders and fighters of the People's Liberation Army, the engineers, technicians and scientists and other people who are engaged in the research, manufacture and testing of nuclear weapons! It is hoped that they will guard against conceit and impetuosity and continue to exert themselves and that, under the leadership of the proletarian headquarters with Chairman Mao as the leader and Vice-Chairman Lin as the deputy leader, they will hold still higher the great red banner of Marxism, Leninism, Mao Tse-tung's thought, energetically give prominence to proletarian politics, implement Chairman Mao's latest instructions in an all-round way, and raise to a new level the mass movement for the creative study and application of Chairman Mao's works. They should further promote the revolutionization of their thinking, constantly strengthen their revolutionary spirit, scientific approach and sense of organization and discipline, work hard to fulfill the tasks set by Chairman Mao for the various stages of struggle-criticism-transformation, carry the great proletarian cultural revolution through to the end, and make new and still greater contributions to accelerating the development of our country's national defense science and technology and to realizing the modernization of our national defense!

At present, **the world revolution has entered a great new era.**

Riddled with contradictions and beset with difficulties both at home and abroad, the imperialists headed by the United States and the modern revisionists with the Soviet revisionist renegade clique as their center are disintegrating; they are at the end of their tether and are becoming increasingly isolated. In order to save themselves from doom, U.S. imperialism and Soviet revisionism are both colluding and struggling with each other and are stepping up arms expansion in a vain attempt to redivide the world. On the question of nuclear weapons, they concocted a so-called nuclear nonproliferation treaty and are plotting to make a new deal on "limitation and reduction of strategic nuclear weapons systems" in an effort to maintain their nuclear monopoly—which has already been broken—and to push nuclear colonialism. But their counter-revolutionary collusion only serves as a negative example to educate the revolutionary people all over the world and promote the latter's great struggle against imperialism headed by the United States, modern revisionism with the Soviet revisionist renegade clique as its center, and all reaction. The success of China's new hydrogen bomb test is another blow at the policy of nuclear threat and nuclear blackmail pursued by U.S. imperialism and Soviet revisionism. It is a great inspiration and support to the heroic Vietnamese people in carrying their war against U.S. aggression and for national salvation through to the end and to the people of all countries in their revolutionary struggles.

The Chinese Government reiterates once again that the conducting of necessary and limited nuclear tests and the development of nuclear weapons by China are entirely for the purpose of defense and for breaking the nuclear monopoly, with the ultimate aim of abolishing nuclear weapons. We solemnly declare once again that at no time and in no circumstances will China be the first to use nuclear weapons. We always mean what we say. As in the past, the Chinese people and Government will continue to make common efforts with the other revolutionary people and other countries in the world which uphold independence and cherish peace in striving to achieve the lofty aim of complete prohibition and thorough destruction of nuclear weapons.

★   ★   ★   ★   ★

VIETNAM

The following two selections relate to the time of the U.S.-backed South Vietnamese invasion of Laos in early 1971, when the Chinese press, for the first time in the history of the escalated Vietnam War, openly discussed the possibility that the United States might resort to nuclear weapons. The communiqué, signed jointly by Premiers Chou En-lai and Pham Van Dong, was issued at the conclusion of a three-day visit to Hanoi (March 5–8, 1971) by a large and high-ranking Chinese delegation including military men. While neither the *People's Daily* editorial nor the joint communiqué, for obvious security reasons, spelled out the details of China's commitments to North Vietnam, both, as well as every single statement made by a Chinese leader before and after, made clear that the commitment was so deep that the Chinese were prepared for war if it came to that. As the communiqué says, "The Chinese people will never allow U.S. imperialism to run amuck and do whatever it pleases in Indochina . . . and are determined to take all necessary measures, not flinching even from the greatest national sacrifices." While there was speculation in the American press that China's commitments to North Vietnam might have changed in the wake of the Nixon visit, there was no evidence to indicate such was the case. In 1966 René Dabernat, a French journalist, presumably relying on information supplied by French governmental circles, indicated that the Chinese would enter the war if China herself were attacked, if North Vietnam were invaded, or if the United States tried to destroy North Vietnam's physical existence. In Volume III of this reader (p. 580) we indicated similar conditions. China's stance on negotiations changed after 1968, as we have pointed out. As a *People's Daily* editorial of October 30, 1972, when the draft accord between North Vietnam and the United States appeared to have been "complete," put it: "The people of the world ardently hope that the Vietnam problem can be quickly resolved." But while the language of the Chinese on Vietnam became calmer, there were no indications that the substance of the Chinese commitment had changed.

★   ★   ★

PEOPLE'S DAILY COMMENTATOR*
Don't Lose Your Head, Nixon

U.S. imperialist chieftain Richard Nixon made a speech reeking with gunpowder at his February 17 press conference. Keeping silent for about ten days after the massive invasion of Laos by U.S. imperialism, Nixon finally came forward with wild war cries, openly revealing his diabolical warmonger features.

Nixon minced no words in making several points clear:

1) To achieve their goal of aggression, the U.S.-puppet troops invading Laos on a massive scale "will stay" there "if it takes a longer time."

2) The Saigon puppets themselves can "make decisions" on invading North Vietnam.

3) As long as he considers the U.S. forces in South Vietnam "threatened," he will "take strong action" and is not going to "place any limitation upon the use of air power" of the United States.

4) "There will be Americans in South Vietnam and enough Americans," as long as the so-called U.S. prisoner-of-war issue is not settled.

In this way, Nixon in fact told the whole world that he is willfully continuing to carry out the criminal plan of persisting in and expanding the war of aggression in Indochina. He is not only prepared to stick to its mad course in Laos, but also plans to step up bombing raids on North Vietnam further, and even unleash the Saigon puppet troops to mount, with the coordination of the U.S. aggressor troops, surprise attacks on the Democratic Republic of Vietnam, thus expanding the war of aggression in Vietnam and the rest of Indochina to a still larger scale.

---

* *People's Daily Commentator* (February 20, 1971). Translated in *Peking Review*, No. 9 (February 20, 1971), p. 6.

Showing his ferocious features, Nixon has indeed reached the height of arrogance.

Nixon's mad talk has again proved to the world that U.S. imperialism wants to hang on in South Vietnam, and the so-called "troop withdrawal from Vietnam" is only a ruse aimed at deception. By using this ruse, U.S. imperialism yesterday extended the flames of the war of aggression to Cambodia; and resorting to the same ruse again, it spreads the flames of aggressive war to Laos today. Nixon had the cheek to say that this rotten trick was the fixed policy of his government and declared that he would continue to pursue it. This only shows that the Nixon government is bent on going down the road of expanding its war of aggression in Indochina.

For the Nixon government to willfully "escalate" the war in Indochina in a big way is highly dangerous. The U.S. bourgeois press has pointed out that he is taking the road the Truman administration took in Korea many years ago. But Nixon claimed that U.S. imperialist actions of enlarging the aggression "present no threat" to China and said: "I do not believe" that China has "any reason . . . to react to it." Nixon's attempt to tie the hands of the Chinese people in supporting the Laotian people and the other peoples in Indochina in their war against U.S. aggression and for national salvation can never succeed.

Laos is not in Northwest Europe or South America, but in north Indochina. She and China are linked by the same mountains and rivers and have a common boundary of several hundred kilometers. Nixon should not lose his head and forget such common knowledge of geography. By spreading the flames of aggressive war to the door of China, U.S. imperialism certainly poses a grave threat to China. The Chinese people cannot be indifferent to such rabid acts of aggression on the part of U.S. imperialism. The Chinese people have rich experience in struggle against U.S. imperialism and we know very well how to deal with the U.S. aggressors. We must warn Nixon once again that the 700 million Chinese people will never let you run amuck in Indochina.

Though it shows its teeth and claws and adopts an insolent air, U.S. imperialism is in reality only a paper tiger putting up a death-bed struggle. The Nixon government's reactionary pol-

PEOPLE'S CHINA

icy of persisting in expanding the war in Indochina **started with the aim of injuring others only to end up by ruining itself,** as the law of development which governs all reactionary policies shows. U.S. imperialism will certainly suffer the consequences of its frantic war adventures.

GOVERNMENTS OF CHINA AND NORTH VIETNAM*
Joint Communiqué

...U.S. imperialism has now dispatched tens of thousands of U.S. troops and Saigon puppet troops to carry out a massive invasion of Laos in collusion with the Laotian Rightist forces and Thai mercenaries. At the same time, it has employed U.S. and puppet troops to launch a large-scale attack on the area along Route 9 in South Vietnam and slaughter the South Vietnamese people. It has concentrated large numbers of U.S. troops and Saigon puppet troops in areas close to the 17th Parallel, dispatched many warships of the Seventh Fleet to prowl about in the Bac Bo Gulf and used aircraft and warships to intensify raids against many densely inhabited areas of the Democratic Republic of Vietnam. It has sent additional Saigon puppet troops to Cambodia to step up its war of aggression against Cambodia in collusion with the Lon Nol puppet troops. What is more, the Nixon government has blatantly declared that it will not place any limitation upon the use of U.S. air power anywhere in Indochina.

This is a new and extremely grave war escalation by U.S. imperialism aimed at intensifying its aggression against South Vietnam, Laos and Cambodia, which directly menaces the security of the Democratic Republic of Vietnam and at the same time menaces the security of the People's Republic of China, thus creating a dangerous situation to peace in Asia and the

* *Peking Review*, No. 11 (March 12, 1971), pp. 18–21.

world. All this shows that although U.S. imperialism has suffered disastrous defeats, it remains very obstinate and will not give up its wild design of aggression against Vietnam and the other countries of Indochina. This fully reveals the Nixon government's repeated professions about "peace," "negotiations" and "troop withdrawal" as nothing but a smoke screen for its war expansion.

In the two years since the Nixon government assumed office, the United States has done its utmost to push its plan of "Vietnamizing" the war, which in essence is to prolong the U.S. imperialist war of aggression and perpetuate the U.S. military occupation of South Vietnam. However, this plan is meeting with failure. In order to remedy this situation, the United States has committed aggression against Cambodia and expanded its war of aggression against Laos and is wildly attempting to launch new military adventures against the Democratic Republic of Vietnam.

The U.S. expansion of its war of aggression to Laos and Cambodia has turned Indochina into one battlefield. The Chinese and Vietnamese sides have noted with great pleasure that since the Summit Conference of the Indochinese Peoples, the militant unity of the Indochinese peoples has witnessed important development. The peoples of Vietnam, Laos and Cambodia have formed a powerful united front for the common cause of opposing U.S. imperialist aggression and winning national liberation. Coordinating with each other, uniting closely together and fighting shoulder to shoulder, they have won brilliant victories on all battlefronts and brought about an excellent situation through their fight. At present, in accordance with President Ho Chi Minh's behest and under the wise leadership of the Vietnam Workers' Party, the heroic Vietnamese people, holding high the glorious banner of **"firm resolve to fight and win,"** are forging ahead victoriously and fighting courageously to smash the U.S. imperialist scheme of "Vietnamizing" its war of aggression against Vietnam and to realize the great cause of liberating the south, defending the north and proceeding to the peaceful reunification of their fatherland. Under the wise leadership of the Head of State of Cambodia Samdech Norodom Sihanouk and the National United Front of Cambodia, the heroic Cambodian people's struggle against U.S. imperialism is developing vigorously and, within less than a year, they have liberated large tracts of their territory, dealing heavy blows at the U.S. aggressors, the Saigon puppets and the Phnom Penh traitorous clique. Under the wise leadership of the Laotian Patriotic Front headed by Prince Souphanouvong, the heroic Laotian patriotic armed forces and people have fought courageously and tenaciously, smashing many "encroachment" attacks by the U.S. aggressors and their lackeys and have thus consolidated and expanded the liberated areas. The two sides warmly hail the splendid victories won by the three Indochinese peoples.

The two sides strongly condemn the Nixon government for its criminal acts of expanding the war of aggression in Indochina and have studied the resultant grave situation there. The two sides have taken full account of the recklessness and madness of the Nixon government and held discussions on questions as to how to deal with possible military adventures by U.S. imperialism and have reached completely identical views.

The Government of the Democratic Republic of Vietnam solemnly declares that acting upon the will of respected and beloved President Ho Chi Minh, the Vietnamese people will resolutely frustrate the policy of aggression and any war escalation by U.S. imperialism and its lackeys and carry the cause of resisting U.S. aggression and saving the nation to final victory. Together with the fraternal Laotian and Cambodian peoples, the Vietnamese people will resolutely drive U.S. imperialism out of the Indochinese Peninsula. No brute force or truculent threat can shake the strong will of the three peoples of Indochina to fight to the finish for the defense of their sacred national rights.

The Chinese Government and people firmly support the statement of the Government of the Democratic Republic of Vietnam dated February 10, 1971 and the statement of the National Assembly of the Democratic Republic of Vietnam dated March 4, 1971, which strongly condemn U.S. imperialism for its expansion of the war of aggression in Indochina. The Chinese side declares that it is the firm and unshakable principle of the Chinese Communist Party and the Chinese Government as well as the unshirkable internationalist duty of the Chinese people to give support and assistance to the Vietnamese people and all the three peoples of Indochina in their war against U.S. aggression and for national salvation. The Chinese people will never allow U.S. imperialism to run amuck and do whatever it pleases in Indochina. Should U.S. imperialism go down the road of expanding its war of aggression in Indochina, the Chinese people are determined to take all necessary measures, not flinching even from the greatest national sacrifices, to give all-out support and assistance to the Vietnamese and other Indochinese peoples for the thorough defeat of the U.S. aggressors.

The two sides strongly condemn U.S. imperialism for its crimes of frantically expanding its war of aggression against Vietnam. The Vietnam question must be settled on the basis of the "ten-point over-all solution" and the "eight-point clarifications" put forward by the South Vietnam National Front for Liberation and the Provisional Revolutionary Government of the Republic of South Vietnam. The U.S. aggressor troops and vassal troops must wholly and unconditionally withdraw from South Vietnam and let the Vietnamese people settle their own questions by themselves.

The two sides strongly condemn U.S. imperialism and its lackeys in Saigon and Bangkok for their grave crimes of massive invasion of Laos and firmly support the fraternal Laotian people in their war against U.S. aggression and for national salvation. U.S. imperialism must immediately stop its intervention and aggression against Laos, must unconditionally stop its bombing of Laos and must withdraw all the U.S. aggressor troops and vassal troops from Laotian territory. The Laotian question should be settled by the Laotian people themselves in accordance with the "five-point political solution" put forward by the Laotian Patriotic Front on March 6, 1970.

The two sides strongly condemn U.S. imperialism and its lackeys for their barbarous crimes of intensifying their aggression against Cambodia, firmly support the Cambodian people's war against U.S. aggression and for national salvation and firmly support the just stand put forward in the "five-point declaration" issued on March 23, 1970 by Samdech Norodom Sihanouk, Head of State of Cambodia. U.S. imperialism and its lackeys must immediately and unconditionally stop all their acts of aggression against Cambodia and withdraw all their aggressor troops.

The two sides express their firm belief that the peoples of

Vietnam, Laos and Cambodia, holding high the militant banner of the Summit Conference of the Indochinese Peoples, strengthening their unity, persevering in and pushing forward the people's war, will certainly drive all the U.S. aggressors out of the Indochinese Peninsula. Victory surely belongs to the three heroic peoples of Indochina! . . .

The Vietnamese people will never forget the enthusiastic and powerful support and gigantic and effective aid rendered by the Communist Party of China, the Chinese Government and the fraternal Chinese people in the noble spirit of proletarian internationalism both during their past long revolutionary struggles against imperialism and for national independence and in the present cause of resisting U.S. aggression and saving the nation and of socialist construction. Respected and beloved Chairman Mao Tse-tung's statement of May 20, 1970 has greatly inspired the Vietnamese people in forging ahead valiantly together with the Laotian and Cambodian peoples to thoroughly defeat the U.S. aggressor bandits.

The Vietnam Workers' Party, the Government of the Democratic Republic of Vietnam and the Vietnamese people express their sincere and profound thanks to respected and beloved Chairman Mao Tse-tung, the Chinese Communist Party, the Chinese Government and people for their extremely valuable support and assistance.

The Chinese side holds that the Vietnamese and other Indochinese peoples, standing at the forefront of the struggle against U.S. imperialism, working hard and fighting the enemy courageously, have given the greatest encouragement and support to the Chinese people and are a model and example for the Chinese people to learn from. The Chinese Communist Party, the Chinese Government and people are sincerely grateful to the fraternal Vietnamese and other Indochinese peoples. It is the Chinese people's unshirkable internationalist duty to give support and assistance to the Vietnamese people in their war against U.S. aggression and for national salvation and in their socialist construction, and this is simply what the Chinese people should do. . . .

★   ★   ★   ★   ★

TAIWAN

No policy has been more unswervingly maintained by China than its absolute and total opposition to any form of a "Two Chinas" arrangement on the world scene. This editorial of the *People's Daily* appeared during the maneuvers preceding the vote on China's membership in the United Nations. The Chinese position, unchanged since 1949, is that they will not establish diplomatic relations with any country that also recognizes the Taipei government or sit in any international body or agency that also contains delegates from that government. The large numbers of countries which established relations with China in the wake of the Sino-American détente all broke their ties with Taipei, though a face-saving formula was invoked. Perhaps the most important breakthrough for China was Japan's recognition of China and break with Taipei; note the editorial's accusation against the "reactionary Satō government" as being behind the U.S. "Two Chinas" resolution.

★   ★   ★

*PEOPLE'S DAILY COMMENTATOR**
*Resolutely Oppose U.S. Scheme of
Creating "Two Chinas"*

After many difficulties and prolonged, painstaking maneuvering, the U.S. Government, in league with the reactionary Sato government of Japan, on September 22 finally trotted out in the United Nations two resolutions on so-called Chinese representation by inducing and dragging a number of countries into its scheme. One is the so-called "important question" resolution

* *People's Daily* Commentator (September 25). Translated in the *Peking Review*, No. 40 (September 30, 1971), pp. 5–6.

which calls for a two-thirds majority vote for the expulsion of the Chiang Kai-shek clique; the other is the so-called "dual representation" resolution which "affirms the right of representation of the People's Republic of China" and "affirms" at the same time "the continued right of representation" of the Chiang Kai-shek clique. This further reveals that U.S. imperialism is persisting in its hostility to the Chinese people and is openly pushing its "two Chinas" scheme in the United Nations. The Chinese Government and people are most indignant at and firmly oppose this criminal U.S. imperialist plot.

The U.S. so-called "important question" resolution is wholly unjustifiable. Expulsion of the Chiang Kai-shek clique and restoration of the legitimate rights of the People's Republic of China in the United Nations are two aspects of the same thing. This is purely a simple procedural matter and has nothing to do with the provision concerning important questions under Article 18 of the U.N. Charter. The United States itself has had to admit that its past insistence on regarding the restoration of China's legitimate seat in the U.N. as an "important question" was "unpracticable." But now it asserts that the Chiang Kai-shek clique's expulsion is an "important question." Is this not self-contradictory?

The U.S. so-called "dual representation" resolution is also entirely untenable. The U.S. resolution alleges "having regard for the existing factual situation." But the living reality is: There is only one China in the world, namely, the People's Republic of China; and there is only one Chinese Government in the world, namely, the Government of the People's Republic of China. Taiwan is an inalienable part of the territory of the People's Republic of China. The Chiang Kai-shek clique is a reactionary gang overthrown long ago by the Chinese people. It is utterly illegal that the Chiang Kai-shek clique has usurped China's seat in the United Nations. All the legitimate rights of China in the U.N. can be enjoyed only by the Government of the People's Republic of China, the sole legal Government of the Chinese people. To restore the legitimate rights of the People's Republic of China in the U.N., it is necessary to expel the Chiang Kai-shek clique which is usurping China's seat from the U.N. and all its organs. Without expelling the Chiang Kai-shek clique, restoration of the legitimate rights of the People's Republic of China is totally out of the question. How can one "affirm" the right of representation of the People's Republic of China while "affirming" at the same time "the continued right of representation" of the Chiang Kai-shek clique? What is this if not flagrant interference in China's internal affairs? The U.S. resolution also says that it "recommends" that the People's Republic of China "be seated as" one of the permanent members of the Security Council. This is the height of absurdity! China is one of the founding members of the United Nations and has always been a permanent member of the U.N. Security Council. Restoration of the rights of the People's Republic of China in the U.N. means the return to it of all seats in all U.N. organs, including the Security Council seat usurped by the Chiang Kai-shek clique. There is no need for any U.S. "charity" at all. The United States can mislead nobody with such a hoax which it contrived when it found its obstruction to the restoration of the legitimate rights of the People's Republic of China in the United Nations getting increasingly unpopular.

It is crystal clear that in putting up its two resolutions, the United States not only aims to continue to obstruct the restoration of the legitimate rights of the People's Republic of China in the United Nations, but also vainly hopes to create a "two Chinas" situation in the United Nations so as to realize its scheme of permanently occupying China's sacred territory Taiwan Province and severing Taiwan from China. George Bush, chief U.S. representative to the United Nations, went in for sophistry when he argued that the two resolutions submitted by the United States do not "represent a 'two Chinas' policy." However, it is this self-same George Bush who openly announced that the U.S. "dual representation" resolution was to avoid "the question of who's the sole government of China." This is an open confession that the essence of the U.S. resolutions is nothing other than to create "two Chinas" in the United Nations. The U.S. Government has openly trumpeted the fallacy that "the status of Taiwan remains to be determined" and recently has redoubled its efforts to engineer the so-called "Taiwan independence movement." On the eve of the opening of the current General Assembly session the United States even instigated a handful of elements trying to create "an independent Taiwan" to stage a ludicrous farce in New York. Thus the criminal schemes of U.S. imperialism to carve out Chinese territory and create "two Chinas" or "one China, one Taiwan" have been further exposed.

The stand of the Chinese Government and the Chinese people is always very clear and unshakable. We resolutely oppose "two Chinas," "one China, one Taiwan" or any other similar absurdities, firmly oppose the fallacy that "the status of Taiwan remains to be determined" and firmly oppose the scheme of creating an "independent Taiwan." The Chinese people are determined to liberate their sacred territory Taiwan Province. All the legitimate rights of the People's Republic of China in the United Nations must be completely restored. The Chiang Kai-shek clique must be expelled from the United Nations and all its organs. Should a situation of "two Chinas," "one China, one Taiwan," or "the status of Taiwan remaining to be determined" or any other similar situation occur in the United Nations, the Government of the People's Republic of China will have absolutely nothing to do with the United Nations. As long as the United States does not give up its schemes, the Chinese people will resolutely fight it to the end. No matter what tricks U.S. imperialism plays they will be futile and will only land it in a more isolated and passive position.

Albania, Algeria and nineteen other countries have submitted a draft resolution to the United Nations demanding the restoration to the People's Republic of China of all her legitimate rights in the United Nations and immediate expulsion of the Chiang Kai-shek clique's representatives from the United Nations and all its organs. This correct and reasonable stand reflects the general demand of many U.N. member countries, expresses the common desire of the people of various countries, and has won support from more and more countries. We are convinced that the struggle of all friendly countries in upholding justice is bound to win.

Our great leader Chairman Mao has pointed out: **"The present situation in which the United States controls a majority in the United Nations and dominates many parts of the world is a temporary one, which will eventually be changed."** Facts have proved and will continue to prove that it has become increasingly difficult for the United States to manipulate the United Nations. It can be said with certainty that all the schemes hostile to the Chinese people resorted to by U.S. imperialism in the United Nations will certainly end in ignominious failure.

★   ★   ★   ★   ★

ALBANIA

One aspect of the Sino-Albanian relationship which is virtually unknown abroad is that Albanians and Chinese genuinely like each other. This is evident to those who have lived in China, and also has been reported by visitors to Albania, including many old-fashioned Albanian-Americans who only went back to visit relatives. The phrases about friendship and brotherhood may appear ceremonially effusive to grim intelligence analysts, but they happen to be sincere. In Albania, the thousands of Chinese technicians live simply, do their work, and refrain from interfering in Albanian politics. If anything infuriated the Albanians against the Russians, it was Khrushchev's blithe assumption he could push the Albanians around. Historians might find some cultural reasons for this Sino-Albanian affinity. The Albanians are predominantly Muslims in a Christian ocean, and for all the differences between Islam and Confucianism, they have in common a simple rationalist approach to life, different from the more expansive aspects of Orthodox or Catholic Christianity.

Again, the material on the Sino-Albanian relationship can be measured in megatonnage. But the short selection we have chosen (two excerpts of speeches by senior military men) are meant not only to underscore the warmth of the friendship, but a divergence in Chinese and Albanian perceptions of their mutual enemies. We have italicized certain important sentences in Yeh Chien-ying's and Beqir Balluku's speeches. In short, while Yeh states clearly that the Soviet Union is a more dangerous enemy than the United States, Balluku states the view current until the Sino-American rapprochement, namely that "one is as dangerous as the other."

While Albania no longer has quite the symbolic importance it had in the sixties, Sino-Albanian ties remain strong, and the Chinese press continues to carry lengthy accounts of developments in Albania. Albania herself has emerged from isolation, having restored relations with her two land neighbors, Yugoslavia and Greece. Albania's socialism has much of the simple, rigorous, puritanical quality of China's, and there are no signs the Albanians are ready for the delights of Frankfurt, Belgrade, or Moscow. Whatever misgivings they might privately have about China's foreign policy, their admiration for the new society the Chinese have built seems deep and sincere.

★   ★   ★

YEH CHIEN-YING AND BEQIR BALLUKU*

Yeh Chien-ying: The friendship military delegation from the People's Republic of Albania led by Comrade Beqir Balluku has traveled thousands of miles for a friendly visit to China, bringing us the profound revolutionary comradeship of the Albanian People and Army. Comrade Balluku is an old comrade in arms of ours and familiar to us all. It fills us with joy and warmth to meet him again. Please allow me, on behalf of the Chinese people and all commanders and fighters of the Chinese People's Liberation Army, to extend our warmest welcome to the glorious envoys of the Albanian people and army. . . .

The present international situation is changing more and more in favor of the people of various countries in the world. The struggles to win national liberation and safeguard national independence have deepened in various parts of the world. The attempts of superpowers to manipulate international affairs at will and shape the destiny of other countries are going bankrupt. Countries want independence, nations want liberation, and the people want revolution—this has become an irresistible

* Yeh Chien-ying and Beqir Balluku, from *People's Daily*, translated in *Survey of China Mainland Press*, November 7, 1972.

historical trend. But Soviet revisionist social-imperialism and U.S. imperialism have not restrained their ambition for world hegemony.

While flaunting a signboard of socialism, social-imperialism is actually engaged in acts of imperialism, flagrantly carrying out expansion everywhere. It is more deceptive than old-line imperialism, and therefore more dangerous. Soviet revisionist social-imperialism and U.S. imperialism both contend and collude with each other, so that the world is far from peaceful. However, no matter how tortuous the road ahead may be, the law of historical development, we believe, is independent of the will of one or two superpowers. Victory surely belongs to the people of the world.

Comrades, comrades in arms, the peoples and armies of China and Albania are closest comrades and comrades in arms. Comrade Enver Hoxha says: "We shall always be together like blood brothers, in sunny days or in difficult times." Chairman Mao says: "China and Albania are separated by thousands of mountains and rivers but our hearts are closely linked." Our two parties, countries and armies always support and encourage each other and act in close cooperation in our protracted common struggles. . . .

Beqir Balluku: This is not the first time we visit your great and beautiful country. Each and every time we come to the great People's China and live among you, we feel at home as if we are in the midst of our brothers and most esteemed and closest friends. . . .

The Chinese people are a heroic people, an industrious and talented people. Under the leadership of the Communist Party of China and Chairman Mao Tse-tung, they got rid of the darkness in which they were subjected to oppression from generation to generation and remained backward, and saw the light of socialism after years of endeavor. Today, the People's Republic of China has become a true socialist giant with powerful modern industry that embraces all branches, with advanced socialist agriculture, proletarian education and culture, very advanced science and technology, and invincible defense capability. All this inspires us with boundless joy and pride.

Because of the victory of the Great Proletarian Cultural Revolution personally initiated and led by Chairman Mao Tse-tung, the People's Republic of China has become stronger; it has further emancipated and brought into play the inexhaustible strength of the Chinese people, carried forward the militant spirit and revolutionary enthusiasm of the people in their hundreds of millions, and frustrated all plots of imperialism and revisionism and their agents in the country.

Under the leadership of Chairman Mao Tse-tung, the Communist Party of China has defeated the plots of enemies of all shades who attempted from both right and ultra-left to stop China from building socialism, and is leading the great China in advancing victoriously along the socialist road. *The People's Republic of China stands in the forefront of the struggle against imperialism headed by the United States, against modern revisionism headed by the Soviet revisionist renegade clique, and against all reaction in the world, and always pursues a correct and revolutionary foreign policy.* As a result, all attempts of imperialism and revisionism to contain and isolate the People's Republic of China have burst like bubbles. . . .

Our two parties, governments and countries always pursue correct Marxist-Leninist policies and make an objective assessment of the current international situation and the trend in its development. *We base ourselves on the following principle: imperialism and revisionism are the source of war of aggression, one is as dangerous as the other. People of all countries must not harbor the slightest illusion about them.* The people of our two countries and other countries should heighten their vigilance and strengthen preparedness against war so as to *smash any plot and attempt of aggression by the two superpowers.*

Dear comrades and brothers, the people of our two countries, our two parties and our two armies are linked by a great, sincere, and unbreakable revolutionary friendship. This friendship is profound, pure and sincere, and its manifestations of comradeship and mutual respect, and the all-round internationalist support and assistance to each other are unprecedented. Our friendship is our greatest pride. It is forged by our two Marxist-Leninist parties and our two great leaders—Comrade Mao Tse-tung and Comrade Enver Hoxha. No force in the world could harm it in the least. It is tempered and daily strengthened in our struggle for the noble ideal of building and defending socialism, in our common struggle for the victory of the revolutionary cause and against imperialism headed by the United States and modern revisionism headed by the Soviet Union. . . .

★　★　★　★　★

SINO-SOVIET BOUNDARIES

The one concrete issue that has become discernible amidst the furor of the Sino-Soviet dispute is that of boundaries. The Soviets maintain that China covets huge tracts of territory in Eastern Siberia. The Chinese retort that they do not covet any territory and are willing to negotiate a boundary treaty on the basis of the present frontiers. However, they demand that the Russians admit in principle that they acquired those territories as the result of Czarist expansionism beginning in the seventeenth century and unequal treaties imposed on China in the nineteenth century. In effect, the Chinese are demanding an apology from the Russians for their past imperialist behavior, and by implication, for their "unequal" treatment of China after 1949. Obviously, the Chinese see the boundary issue as the manifestation of an even more serious issue: the deployment of huge numbers of Soviet troops along the Sino-Soviet and Sino-Mongolian borders, troops ready for offensive action. In early 1969 the two countries fought a small-scale war ostensibly over who owned a small shifting island in the Ussuri River (Chenpao Island to the Chinese, and Damanskii Island to the Russians). The Chinese have concluded boundary agreements with all countries on their borders, save the Soviet Union and India. Such treaties are designed to signify basic peaceful intent by both contracting parties. If the Sino-Indian conflict is serious, the Sino-Soviet conflict is menacing. As the selection states, "neither a small war, nor a big war, nor a nuclear war can ever intimidate the Chinese people."

The selection consists of Part Six of a long statement sent to the Soviet Government by the Chinese Government as an invitation to start negotiations. Since its issuance in May 1969, a Sino-Soviet boundary commission has met intermittently, but with no known results. The first five parts of the statement are a detailed exposition of the Chinese case, culminating in an accusation that "it is the Soviet Government that expands its territory everywhere."

★   ★   ★

PEKING REVIEW*
Statement of the Government of the People's Republic of China

(May 24, 1969)

THE CHINESE GOVERNMENT STANDS FOR PEACEFUL NEGOTIATIONS AND IS AGAINST RESORT TO THE USE OF FORCE

The Chinese Government has consistently stood and worked for the settlement of boundary questions with its neighboring countries through negotiations and for the maintenance of the status quo of the boundary pending a settlement. As early as August 22 and September 21, 1960, the Chinese Government twice took the initiative in proposing to the Soviet Government that negotiations be held. Furthermore, on August 23, 1963, the Chinese Government put forward to the Soviet Government a six-point proposal for maintaining the status quo of the boundary and averting conflicts. Sino-Soviet boundary negotiations finally took place in Peking in 1964. During the negotiations, the Chinese side took the reasonable stand that the treaties relating to the present Sino-Soviet boundary should be taken as the basis for settling the boundary question, and it made the maximum efforts and showed the greatest sincerity

* *Peking Review,* No. 22 (May 30, 1969), pp. 3, 7–9.

for the settlement of the Sino-Soviet boundary question. If the Soviet Government had the slightest sincerity, it would not have been difficult to settle the Sino-Soviet boundary question. What Premier Chou En-lai said in answering the provocative question of an American correspondent at a press conference held in Kathmandu on April 28, 1960 precisely expressed this idea of the Chinese Government. However, the Soviet Government clung to its big-power chauvinist and territorial expansionist stand; it not only wanted to keep under its forcible occupation the Chinese territory which tsarist Russia had seized by means of the unequal treaties, but also insisted that China recognize as belonging to the Soviet Union all the Chinese territory which it had occupied or attempted to occupy in violation of the treaties, and as a result the negotiations were disrupted. Hence, while China has now settled boundary questions with many of her neighboring countries, only the boundary questions between China and the Soviet Union and between China and India remain unsettled.

While expressing willingness to resume "consultations" in its statement of March 29, the Soviet Government tried hard to deny the existence of a boundary question between China and the Soviet Union, which actually amounts to saying that there is nothing to discuss at all.

While indicating in its statement that "urgent practical measures should be taken to normalize the situation on the Soviet-Chinese border," the Soviet Government has continued to direct Soviet troops to open fire with light and heavy machine guns and heavy artillery on China's Chenpao Island and areas deep within Chinese territory, and to this day the firing has not ceased; at the same time, it is carrying out provocations in other sectors of the Sino-Soviet boundary. Reading from a prepared text, the Soviet frontier representative even brazenly threatened on April 3: "The Soviet Union will not cease fire unless the Chinese Government holds negotiations with the Soviet Government, nor will it cease fire unless the Chinese withdraw from Damanskii Island" (N.B. China's Chenpao Island) .

Furthermore, the Soviet Government has canvassed among the imperialist countries headed by the United States, begging for their support. Meanwhile, setting in motion all its propaganda machines, it has done its utmost to spread lies and slanders, tried to fan up national chauvinist sentiments, made war clamors and brandished nuclear weapons at China.

The above series of facts show that it is highly doubtful as to how much sincerity the Soviet Government has, after all, for negotiations.

The development of the Sino-Soviet boundary question to its present state is not the responsibility of the Chinese side. Nevertheless, the Chinese Government is still ready to seek an overall settlement of the Sino-Soviet boundary question through peaceful negotiations and is against resort to the use of force.

The Chinese Government holds that it must be confirmed that the treaties relating to the present Sino-Soviet boundary are all unequal treaties imposed on China by tsarist Russian imperialism. But taking into consideration the fact that it was tsarist Russian imperialism which compelled China to sign these treaties when power was in the hands of neither the Chinese people nor the Russian people and the Soviet people bear no responsibility and that large numbers of Soviet laboring people have lived on the land over a long period of time, the Chinese Government, out of the desire to safeguard the revolutionary friendship between the Chinese and Soviet peoples, is still ready to take these unequal treaties as the basis for determining the entire alignment of the boundary line between the two countries and for settling all existing questions relating to the boundary. Any side which occupies the territory of the other side in violation of the treaties must, in principle, return it wholly and unconditionally to the other side, and this brooks no ambiguity. The Chinese Government maintains that what should be done is to hold negotiations for the overall settlement of the Sino-Soviet boundary question and the conclusion of a new equal treaty to replace the old unequal ones, and not to hold "consultations" for "clarification on individual sectors of the Soviet-Chinese state border line."

Of course, on the premise that the treaties relating to the present Sino-Soviet boundary are taken as the basis, necessary adjustments at individual places on the boundary can be made in accordance with the principles of consultation on an equal footing and of mutual understanding and mutual accommodation. But it is absolutely impermissible to take such a truculent attitude: What the tsars occupied is yours, and what you want to occupy is yours, too.

In order to bring about a peaceful settlement of the Sino-Soviet boundary question, the Soviet Government must stop all its provocations and armed threats on the Sino-Soviet border. Neither a small war, nor a big war, nor a nuclear war can ever intimidate the Chinese people. The Chinese Government once again proposes: Each side ensures that it shall maintain the status quo of the boundary and not push forward by any means the line of actual control on the border, and that in sectors where a river forms the boundary, the frontier guards of its side shall not cross the central line of the main channel and of the main waterway; each side ensures that it shall avert conflicts and that under no circumstances shall the frontier guards of its side fire at the other side; there should be no interference in the normal productive activities carried out by the border inhabitants of both sides according to habitual practice.

The Chinese Government holds that negotiations are intended for settling questions and not for deceiving the people. To make serious negotiations possible, it is essential to adopt an honest attitude, and not a hypocritical attitude. In its note of April 11 to the Chinese Government, the Soviet Government suggested that "consultations" start right on April 15 in Moscow and, without waiting for a reply from the Chinese Government, it published the note on the following day. This attitude of the Soviet Government's is far from being serious, to say the least. The Chinese Government proposes that the date and place for the Sino-Soviet boundary negotiations be discussed and decided upon by both sides through diplomatic channels.

The Chinese Government hopes that the Soviet Government will make a positive response to the above proposals.

The Soviet Government will have completely miscalculated if it should take the Chinese Government's stand for a peaceful settlement of the boundary question as a sign that China is weak and can be bullied, thinking that the Chinese people can be cowed by its policy of nuclear blackmail and that it can realize its territorial claims against China by means of war.

Armed with Mao Tse-tung Thought and tempered through the Great Proletarian Cultural Revolution, the 700 million Chinese people are not to be bullied. The Chinese people's great leader Chairman Mao has taught us: **"We will not attack unless we are attacked; if we are attacked, we will certainly counter-attack."** "As far as our own desire is concerned, we don't want **to fight even for a single day. But if circumstances force us to fight, we can fight to the finish."** This is the answer of the Chinese Government and people to the Soviet Government's policies of war and nuclear blackmail.

★ ★ ★ ★ ★

INDIA—PAKISTAN—SRI LANKA

No Chinese external policy in recent years has aroused more bafflement than their vehement support of Pakistan against India in the events that led to the formation of Bangladesh. Since 1959, as Sino-Indian relations worsened, Sino-Pakistani relations became close and cordial. When Indian troops invaded East Pakistan in late 1971, the Chinese not only supported Pakistan but subsequently showed their continuing opposition to Bangladesh by vetoing its acceptance for membership in the United Nations. The first selection, particularly in the third paragraph, gives the nub of the Chinese view: Bangladesh is a "puppet" state created by Indian arms and Soviet collusion.

The second selection indicates China's views on what many see as a growing Soviet-American naval competition in the Indian Ocean. China's policies toward the Bangladesh issue cannot be dissociated from her overall policies towards the three countries of the South Asian subcontinent, nor from the even larger triangle of relationships between the United States, the Soviet Union, and China.

★ ★ ★

PEOPLE'S DAILY COMMENTATOR*
Refuting the TASS Statement

The Soviet news agency TASS issued a statement on December 5, 1971. On the Indo-Pakistan situation, the statement stands truth on its head, confuses right and wrong, flagrantly interferes in the internal affairs of Pakistan, and instigates with utmost effort the Indian Government to enlarge its armed aggression against Pakistan. At a time when tension is rapidly mounting in the Indo-Pakistan subcontinent, the TASS statement which smells strongly of gunpowder warrants serious attention.

In its statement, TASS started off by saying that "the Pakistan Government's actions" in East Pakistan were "the main cause of the tension" between India and Pakistan. This is sheer nonsense. The East Pakistan question is entirely Pakistan's internal affair. How can the internal affair of one country become the main cause of tension between states? TASS has glossed over the fundamental fact, that is, the Indian Government's interference, subversion and aggression in Pakistan. Indian troops have since the latter half of last month launched large-scale armed attacks on Pakistan and occupied its territory. Why did TASS pretend not to see this? The Indian Prime Minister openly clamored for the withdrawal of Pakistan troops from their own territory, East Pakistan. The Indian Minister of Defense flagrantly cried that the Indian troops which have crossed the border and invaded Pakistan may "go across as far as necessary." Why did TASS pretend not to hear this? Facts show quite clearly that "the main cause of the tension" is none other than the support and encouragement given by Soviet re-

* *People's Daily Commentator* (December 7, 1971). Translated in the *Peking Review* (December 10, 1971), p. 11.

visionist social-imperialism to the Indian reactionaries in their aggression and expansion against Pakistan.

Pakistan is an independent and sovereign state. No country is entitled to interfere in its internal affairs. Nevertheless, the TASS statement, in the tone of an overlord, told Pakistan that it must do this and do that. This is another performance of Soviet revisionist social-imperialism in trampling on the norms of international relations at will and grossly interfering in other country's internal affairs. In so doing, it is flagrantly supporting the Indian reactionaries to create a puppet "Bangladesh." In the thirties, Japanese imperialism rigged up a puppet "Manchukuo" in northeast China, and, acting in close coordination, the German and Italian fascists "recognized" it. Now, the so-called "Bangladesh" has not yet been thrust into Pakistan, yet at the U.N. Security Council meeting the Soviet representative wanted to "invite" the representative of "Bangladesh" to the meeting. This shows how eager and impatient Soviet revisionist social-imperialism is!

The TASS statement advertised the Soviet Government as "consistently coming out for the preservation of peace in the Hindustan Peninsula" and that it "comes out for the speediest ending of the bloodshed." This is 100 percent hypocrisy. In the same statement, TASS declared with ulterior motives that the "Soviet Union cannot remain indifferent to the developments, considering also the circumstance that they are taking place in direct proximity of the U.S.S.R.'s borders and, therefore, involve the interests of its security." This is really an unheard-of absurdity! It is crystal clear that you, the superpower, in collusion with the Indian expansionists, have been bullying Pakistan. How could it be said to the contrary that the security of the Soviet Union is threatened? You occupied by armed force your neighbor Czechoslovakia several years ago by flaunting the banner of so-called defending "security." Now, by making special mention about "in direct proximity of the U.S.S.R.'s borders," are you going to take action? This is barefaced blackmail and intimidation.

While paying lip service to "peace," Soviet revisionist social-imperialism is actually doing its utmost to stir up trouble and pour oil on fire by instigating the Indian Government to proceed unscrupulously along the road of military venture. One of the main aims of the Soviet-Indian treaty of military alliance concluded last August is to support India in committing aggression and expansion and annexing East Pakistan. This has been fully borne out by the development of events.

The TASS statement exposes once again the ugly features of the Soviet revisionist renegade clique. People can see from this that this superpower is trying, by taking advantage of the aggravation of the Indo-Pakistan situation, to further control India and expand its sphere of influence in the Subcontinent and the Indian Ocean. But its scheme will never succeed. The Pakistani people are waging a just struggle to defend their state sovereignty and territorial integrity. The Indian people will eventually see through Soviet revisionist social-imperialism as their false friend. All peace-loving and justice-upholding countries and peoples demand that India's armed aggression against Pakistan be checked. It can be said with certainty that Soviet revisionism will come to no good end in pushing the policy of social-imperialism in the Indo-Pakistan situation.

PEKING REVIEW*
U.S.–Soviet Scramble for Hegemony in South Asian Subcontinent and Indian Ocean

The two superpowers have beefed up their military strength in the Indian Ocean. The Soviet revisionists see India's war of aggression against Pakistan as a good opportunity to expand and consolidate their sphere of influence in the South Asian subcontinent and Indian Ocean. The scramble for this area between the United States and the Soviet Union will become ever fiercer in the days to come.

U.S. imperialism is planning to reinforce its military power in the Indian Ocean in the wake of the armed invasion and occupation of East Pakistan by the Indian reactionaries with the

* *Peking Review*, No. 2 (January 14, 1972), pp. 16–17.

support of Soviet revisionist social-imperialism. There are indications that these two overlords are stepping up their maneuvers in their scramble for the South Asian subcontinent and the Indian Ocean.

U.S. IMPERIALISM STRENGTHENS POWER

U.S. imperialism has constantly sent warships into the Indian Ocean and, in collusion with Britain, has speeded up construction of military installations on the strategic Island of Diego Garcia. When the Indian reactionaries launched the war of aggression against Pakistan with Soviet revisionist social-imperialism's support last November, the United States regarded this as a major "challenge" to its "interests" in the area and sent warships, including "the world's largest nuclear-powered aircraft carrier *Enterprise*," to "show the flag" in the Bay of Bengal.

U.S. Defense Department spokesman Jerry Friedheim announced on January 6 that the U.S. Navy task force built around the nuclear-powered aircraft carrier *Enterprise* will remain indefinitely in the Indian Ocean. Asked how long that naval force would remain there, he said, "An end date does not exist at the moment." He added that one of the reasons in keeping the taks force there was to enable the ships of the U.S. Seventh Fleet to get more "experience" operating in the Indian Ocean.

The Pentagon spokesman emphasized that the U.S. military authorities have "always regarded the Indian Ocean as an important and strategic part of the world." He added, "We are interested in the area. I think it could be anticipated that Seventh Fleet naval vessels would operate more frequently there."

Friedheim also announced that beginning January 1, "responsibility" for the Indian Ocean was switched from the U.S. Navy's Atlantic Command to the Pacific Command. He pointed out emphatically that "this particular deployment of forces there was obviously related to the international situation on the (South Asian) subcontinent."

Friedheim also confirmed reports that the United States has taken over parts of the British naval station at Bahrain in the Persian Gulf area, where the U.S. Middle East task force is based. A U.S. Navy announcement said that these actions "manifest the continuing strong interest of the United States in the (Persian) Gulf." A UPI dispatch said, "All these actions appeared part of a new determination to strengthen the U.S. naval presence in the Indian Ocean, prompted in part by British withdrawal from east of Suez and in part by the Soviet Union's constant presence of twelve to fifteen ships in the area."

William Mack, Commander of the U.S. Seventh Fleet, said on January 6 that his fleet will "keep in a high state of readiness" and will increase its shadowing of Soviet ships in the Pacific and Indian Ocean.

SOVIET REVISIONISTS DON OLD TSARS' MANTLE

The Russian tsars had dreamt of sending their navy into the Indian Ocean to ensure for Russia "free sea lanes" to the various oceans. Russian Tsar Peter I had said, "Water space—that is what Russia needs." Donning the mantle of the old tsars, the Soviet revisionist leading clique ambitiously set out on its expansionist activities in the Indian Ocean long ago with the aim of establishing a sea lane arch stretching from the Black Sea to the Japan Sea through the Mediterranean, the Red Sea, the Indian Ocean and the West Pacific, linking Europe, Asia and Africa, in order to attain sea hegemony. Since Brezhnev took office, Soviet revisionism has tried to get hold of the right to use naval bases and ports of certain countries on the shores of the Indian Ocean by providing "economic aid" and "military aid" and other bait.

The Soviet Union's Pacific Fleet and Black Sea Fleet began intruding into the Indian Ocean in 1965 under the signboard of "visits."

Since 1968, Soviet fleets have "visited" almost every country on the Arabian Gulf, Gulf of Aden, West Indian Ocean and Red Sea. Soviet naval vessels, disguised as fishing boats, and electronic spy ships, made up as trawlers or oceanic scientific research ships, were often sent to certain countries along the coast of the Indian Ocean to engage in criminal activities— stealing military and oceanic information.

A Soviet fleet, which took part in Soviet global naval maneuvers in 1970, began to be stationed permanently in the Indian Ocean in 1969.

A formation of cruisers of the Soviet Pacific Fleet showed up in the Indian Ocean and carried out a military exercise there in 1971.

To turn India into an important base for its expansion in the Indian Ocean, Soviet revisionism has been hard at work bolstering up the Indian reactionaries for years. In 1968, the Soviet Union purchased with a number of aircraft the right for the Soviet Pacific Fleet to sail to Madras and Bombay and, at the same time, gave India several naval vessels in exchange for the right to use some of her naval bases.

To meet its design for expansion in the Indian Ocean, Soviet revisionism, by making use of India's expansionist ambitions, has abetted the Indian reactionaries in constantly carrying out armed provocations against other Asian countries.

Soviet revisionism regarded India's recent war of aggression against Pakistan as a good opportunity to further its control of India and step up its expansion in the Indian Ocean and its contention with U.S. imperialism for hegemony. The Japanese paper *Yomiuri Shimbun* reported that the Soviet Union considers "the prevailing Indo-Pakistan situation a golden opportunity to realize its Indian Ocean strategy," which is to use India as a "pawn" to "ensure a passage through the Indian Ocean for expansion in Southeast Asia." "The Soviet Union has acquired the possibility of establishing political and military operational bases in India," opening a "wide lane" for Soviet fleets in their "expansion from the Mediterranean to the Indian Ocean," the paper added. A Western news agency noted that Soviet revisionism's backing for India's armed occupation of East Pakistan "could give Moscow a privileged position in the Bay of Bengal."

When U.S. imperialism dispatched an aircraft carrier and other warships from the Seventh Fleet to the Bay of Bengal, the Soviet social-imperialists countered by also moving cruisers and other warships from their Pacific Fleet into the bay. Kyodo

News Agency in Japan reported that some twenty-seven Soviet warships have been deployed in the Indian Ocean, reinforced by three of the four missile warships in the Soviet Pacific Fleet. This is a Soviet "show of force," it said. The *Times of India* reported on December 16 that the Soviet Union had moved "units of its powerful naval fleet into the Bay of Bengal" and that "the Soviet move is obviously a response" to the U.S. action "in sending out a task force of its Seventh Fleet into the area."

Soviet revisionism recently accused U.S. imperialism of pursuing a "gunboat policy," declaring that "the Indian Ocean is not an American lake." But at the same time it regards the Indian Ocean as a Soviet "lake" and frantically followed a social-imperialist "gunboat policy" by sending its own task force there. The reason is that the scramble between U.S. imperialism and Soviet revisionism for domination over the Indian Ocean has intensified.

VOICE OF MEDIUM-SIZED AND SMALL COUNTRIES

Aggression and expansion in the Indian Ocean by U.S. imperialism and Soviet revisionism have long aroused strong discontent and opposition from the medium-sized and small countries of Asia and Africa. The leaders of Ceylon, Pakistan and Zambia have strongly denounced the superpowers for increasing their military forces and establishing military bases in the Indian Ocean, thereby threatening the security of the countries in the region. Ceylon's Prime Minister Mrs. Bandaranaike has advanced a program for a peace zone in the Indian Ocean. She pointed out in her proposal, "Recent reports point to an increasing naval presence of Soviet and U.S. fleets in the Indian Ocean. Another disturbing development is militarization of the Indian Ocean." She criticized "direct or indirect intervention by superpowers in the internal affairs of states." This proposal of Ceylon's Prime Minister is supported by other countries.

As our great leader Chairman Mao teaches us, **"The imperialist wolves must remember that gone forever are the days when they could rule the fate of mankind at will and could do what-**

ever they liked with the Asian and African countries." The affairs of the South Asian subcontinent can only be handled by the peoples of the subcontinent, and the Indian Ocean area affairs can only be handled by the peoples of the area. No domination or carving up of the area by U.S. imperialism and Soviet revisionism will be tolerated. Their interference and aggression in the area will only arouse the people of the area to rise against them, and their schemes of aggression and expansion are bound to end in utter defeat.

★　　★　　★　　★　　★

THE MIDDLE EAST

If the other areas of Chinese commitment are to specific countries, this cannot be the case in the Middle East, for geographical reasons alone. The Middle East, a concept developed by the British in World War II, encompasses, in Chinese as well as Western understanding, a region stretching from Pakistan into the Mediterranean. China's ties to Middle Eastern countries date from the 1950's, when Nasser's Egypt became the first Arab country to brave Dulles' embargo and recognize China. From that time, too, the Chinese became strong supporters of the Palestinian cause, regularly describing it as one of the major national liberation movements in the world. The importance of the Middle East in China's eyes is indicated by the fact that during the Cultural Revolution only one ambassador remained abroad, Huang Hua, then ambassador to Cairo and now China's ambassador to the United Nations.

Since China's return to the world diplomatic scene, the press has stressed three main themes concerning the Middle East: the U.S.-U.S.S.R. rivalry, the rapid development of China's relations with the countries of the Middle East, and unremitting attacks against Israel in support of the Arab and Palestinian cause. The two selections reflect two of these themes. Neither are remarkable in themselves, but are typical of what one could read in the Chinese press in 1972. The warmth of the Sino-Iranian relationship may seem surprising, but can be explained in terms of Iran's strategic location in Western Asia, and above all, its vast oil-producing capabilities. The character of the

Chinese and Iranian delegations mentioned in our selection says much about the developing relationship.

The brief commentary on Israeli attacks against Syria and Lebanon appeared after the Munich massacre of Israeli athletes. While the phrases are standard, the thrust of the "Commentator's" remarks is that the Arab states must not abandon the Palestinian cause for the sake of peace with Israel nor to accommodate the two superpowers.

★　★　★

PEOPLE'S DAILY*
"Friendly Relations Between China and Iran Are Uninterruptedly Developing"

China and Iran had historical relationships and traditional friendship for a long time. In recent years, the friendly relations between the two countries have been able to develop on a new basis.

According to records in the ancient Chinese "Veritable Records," during the Western Han Dynasty in the second century B.C., the general Chang Ch'ien was sent as ambassador to the western territories, and dispatched his own deputy ambassador to visit the Parthian Kingdom in Persia; there he received a good welcome. This was the beginning of diplomatic ties between the two countries. In the first century A.D., during the Western Han Dynasty, Pan Ch'ao was sent as ambassador to the western regions, and his deputy also got as far as Persia. During the subsequent period of the Southern and the Northern Dynasties, there are more than ten known instances of Persia having sent embassies to the court of the Northern Wei Dynasty. During the Ming, the great maritime explorer Cheng Ho seven times visited the Hormuz region of Persia.

Persia in ancient and medieval times was a key juncture on

* *People's Daily*, September 19, 1972.

the land routes stretching across Asia. From the second century B.C. to the sixth century A.D., large quantities of Chinese silk crossed Persia to reach the Mediterranean and various parts of Rome. This was the famous "silk route" of history. China and Persia, through this "silk route," carried on economic and cultural exchanges.

The peoples of both countries, China and Iran, have suffered aggression and oppression from abroad, and therefore have the common task of opposing imperialism and maintaining state sovereignty and national independence. However, in recent times, particularly since the Second World War, due to the harassment and hostility of imperialism, the contacts between our two countries have been few. During the last years, China and Iran have established new relations on an historical basis of mutual friendship. In April and May, 1971, the younger sisters of Shah Muhammad Reza Pahlevi, Princesses Ashraf and Fatima, carried out a friendly visit to our country in response to an invitation from our country. This was a contribution to the mutual understanding between our two peoples and friendly relations between our two countries. That same year in August, Iran formally established diplomatic relations with our country, thereby indicating that the friendly relations between our two countries had entered a new phase. In October of that same year, our country sent emissaries to participate in the activities at Persepolis for the 2500th anniversary of the founding of Persia. During the 26th session of the United Nations, Iran supported the proposals of Albania and Algeria to restore to our country their legitimate rights in the UN and expel the Chiang Kai-shek clique. Last year in November, an Iranian trade delegation led by Abdullah Ali Farman-farmayan, deputy chairman of the United Iranian Council of Industry, Commerce, and Mining visited our country. This year a Chinese civil aviation technical team led by Ma Jen-hui, deputy director of the general department of civil aviation; a Chinese government trade delegation led by Ch'en Chi, deputy director of the Ministry of Foreign Trade; a Chinese ping-pong team led by Wang Fu-yung; an oil research team led by Chang Wen-pin, manager of the China Oil Exploration and Development Company—all visited Iran at various times. An Iranian government civil aviation delegation led by Hassan Alababi, deputy minister of transportation and director of the department of civil aviation, also visited China. The present visit of Empress Farah Pahlevi to China will further increase the friendship of our two peoples, and the friendly relations of our two countries will be further developed.

PEOPLE'S DAILY COMMENTATOR*
"A New Crime of the Israeli Aggressors"

Recently, the Israeli Zionists launched large numbers of planes to bomb peaceful villages and Palestinian refugee camps in Syria and Lebanon. This newest crime of the Israeli aggressors aroused boundless anger amongst the Arab peoples and the peoples of the entire world. The Chinese people express the strongest censure of the warlike provocations of the Israeli aggressors.

The Israel aggressors proclaim that their "security" is threatened. Their bombings of Syria and Lebanon supposedly occurred out of the requirements of "self-defense" and "security." This is entirely the logic of robbers. Everyone knows that for the last twenty years, it has been the Israeli Zionists who under the guise of "self-defense" and "security" have three times carried out aggressive war against the Arab and Palestinian peoples. She occupies large parts of the territories of Palestine, Egypt, and Syria. She has forced over a million Palestinians and Arabs to flee, to suffer oppression, to be killed. It is clear that those whose right to exist and whose security is threatened are not Israel, but the Palestinian people and the peoples of the Arab countries. However much the Israeli Zionists might shout and yell, they can never cover up their aggressive crimes.

The Israeli aggressors also shout that if only the Arab peoples would no longer help and support the Palestinian guerrillas,

* *People's Daily* Commentator, September 13, 1972.

then "peace" could "ripen." These are all lies aiming at something else. The objectives of the struggle of the Palestinian people are the recovery of their lost country and the restoration of their stolen national rights. Their struggle is inseparable from that of the Arab countries and peoples for the recovery of their lost territories. The Palestinian and Arab peoples with their common sufferings naturally must feel for and support each other. The "peace" that the Israeli Zionists talk about is in fact accompanied by the threat of war, their aim being none other than to destroy the solidarity of the peoples of the various Arab countries with the Palestinian people, thereby to keep the things they have stolen. This reveals the true nature of the aggressor.

The peoples of the various Arab countries and the Palestinian people, in their common struggle to oppose aggression, know they must strengthen their solidarity. The superpowers in the Middle East are maintaining and using a situation of no peace and no war in order to carry out intrigues for carving out spheres of influence. They have met with censure and opposition from the broad masses of the Arab and Palestinian peoples. At present, meetings of the Arab League now underway in Cairo have strongly condemned the recent attacks of the Israeli aggressors against Syrian and Lebanese territory and the Palestinian refugee camps, calling for a further strengthening of solidarity, and supporting Syria, Lebanon, and the Palestinians in their struggle against aggression. This is a strong response to the intrigues of imperialism and the new Israeli attacks.

The Arab peoples and the Palestinian peoples are great peoples, who have a long tradition of struggle. The armed threats and barbaric provocations of the Israeli Zionists can never impede their forward march. We are confident that the Arab and Palestinian peoples will resolutely maintain their independence, their solidarity, and their struggle. Their righteous cause will triumph.

★   ★   ★   ★   ★

3. VIEWS ON CHINA—FRANCE, TANZANIA, ZAMBIA, U.S.S.R., U.S.A.

FRENCH VIEW ON CHINA

Robert Guillain is one of the leading writers for *Le Monde, The New York Times* of France. Based in Tokyo, he has observed the East Asian scene for two decades. He has written extensively on China in the past, but rarely with the positive tone he shows in this selection. The team of writers on the *Le Monde* staff who cover Eastern Asia are perhaps the finest in the Western newspaper world: Jacques Decornoy, Alain Bouc, Claude Julien, Philippe Devillers, Jean-Claude Pomonti, and others. The French have a tradition of newspaper writing which combines reporting, scholarly analysis, and individual opinion with clarity and conciseness of style. In the case of China and Indochina, the French have the additional advantage of a long cultural association with that part of the world (and in the case of People's China, a special relationship dating back to the early 1960's). Since the eighteenth century, the French have been fascinated by China and while they cruelly oppressed Vietnam, they also loved it, creating a cultural affinity between Vietnamese (North and South) and French which remains to this day.

One other interesting fact must be mentioned: Paris has become a central focus not just for Indochina negotiations, but for the Sino-American relationship. What role the French played as intermediaries between Peking and Washington remains a mystery.

★　　★　　★

ROBERT GUILLAIN*
Asia Seen From Peking

"LEAVE THE ENEMY A WAY OUT"

Prosperous fields beautifully cultivated by a peasant people who seem happy with their lives—orderly cities, clean, well-kept, intensely alive, enlivened by working multitudes properly dressed, well-fed, united behind leaders who stay close to the people. That is what a dozen French journalists were able to see in People's China who, for the first time in six or seven years, had the chance to crisscross the country along with the French parliamentary delegation led by Alain Peyrefitte.

Since the end of the 1950's, China has undergone a series of internal challenges: the Great Leap Forward, and the launching of the rural people's communes, the crisis caused by the Russian withdrawal and the natural calamities, the first struggles against "revisionism," and finally the explosion of the "proletarian cultural revolution." All that is part of the past. No longer are there any traces today of these storms of yesterday. With that amazing gift of knowing how to heal and restore herself very rapidly, People's China of 1971 gives an impression of ease, order, and peace.

And that is undoubtedly one of the main reasons why problems of foreign policy are now at the top level of concern, and —something not seen in ten years—have superseded domestic policy. But another reason is obviously the international situation itself. For the first time in years, China seems to be on the verge of success in the long struggle she has waged to break the circle of hostility and injustice that tried to hold her prisoner. What is even more remarkable about that is that these last years China seemed threatened by all kinds of catas-

* Robert Guillain, in *Le Monde*, August 10, 11, and 12, 1971.

trophes. The fires of war were at her frontiers. The American enemy was just about at her doorstep. On the other side, alarums were sounding also on the Soviet frontier. She would have to fight on two fronts at the same time and at the worst time, a time when violent internal shocks were weakening the entire country.

Anyone else but Mao Tse-tung would have suffered shipwreck. But instead, the recovery of China's well-being carried out under Mao's leadership has been spectacular. In the international game where China appeared to be losing, she held off the attack and now is winning. The Indochina conflagration is receding, and the United States is withdrawing. The Cultural Revolution rid Mao of his adversaries. The Sino-American thaw which is now beginning could put an end to the dangerous acrobatics of a struggle on two fronts. The triple dangers of yesterday are followed today by a triple euphoria. A great turning point is becoming apparent, an important historical moment has come. On the world scene, as one sees it from Peking, People's China is advancing and rising, while the United States is withdrawing and declining.

"FIRM AS TO PRINCIPLES"

In the dialectics of Mao Tse-tung, astute flexibility in practical action always goes together with rigorous firmness on principles. People's China announces this firmness and stresses it as the game begins, from the very beginning of the negotiations which are to replace resolution by "the barrel of a gun." That is obviously what Premier Chou En-lai wanted to demonstrate from the beginning, as soon as we got to Peking. The sensational announcement about the forthcoming visit by President Nixon was immediately followed by the revelation made by the Prime Minister himself to Alain Peyreffite and repeated to a group of American Sinologists of a whole series of very pressing "points" which China intended to stress in the forthcoming dialogue.

No peace in Indochina without the complete withdrawal of the Americans; no solution on Taiwan without a similar departure of American forces; China will not enter the UN if Taiwan stays there; no resumption of diplomatic relations with Washington if it does not reject the fiction of the legitimacy and the very existence of a so-called "Chinese government" of Chiang Kai-shek. These are some, among others, of the "points" on which it would be futile to expect accommodation or compromise by Peking.

The Peking press makes quite clear that it is absolutely necessary that realities be substituted for the fictions which, for twenty-five years, constituted the China policy of the United States. The entire international press, in turn, has emphasized, quite correctly, this rigidity in regard to positions of principle on the part of People's China. One might conclude that the American negotiators will soon stumble against insurmountable obstacles. Nevertheless it is noteworthy that among Western China specialists and particularly among diplomatic observers in Peking, as I have been able to note, optimism is clearly predominant over skepticism or pessimism as to the chances for the dialogue now begun.

"CAN NIXON SAVE FACE?"

"Leave the enemy a way out"—in the military arts of ancient China that was a rule that no victorious general ever forgot as he faced his enemy holed up in a surrounded city. That is also a precept which the New China practices. One can find it in Marshal Lin Piao's report to the Ninth Party Congress (April 1969), and many signs indicate it could be applied to the American enemy. Chinese firmness on the settlement of the Indochina question and of the Taiwan problem does not exclude the possibility—though the Chinese give no hint of it—that President Nixon might be allowed "to save face," as the Chinese say, in regard to American public opinion.

Face-saving, as far as Indochina is concerned, means simply that a South Vietnam continue to exist even after the departure of the last American; in other words, that the Americans, on withdrawing, will leave behind two distinct Vietnams, that of the North and that of the South. For that, it will be necessary to constitute a coalition government of progressive tendencies which will be joined by members of the present Provisional

Revolutionary Government of South Vietnam. The survival of a South Vietnam could last for a long while. Immediate reunification with the North would cause too many problems. Reunification will be postponed to a time when the two Vietnams can negotiate.

The United States thus faces a choice. If it withdraws its forces without having reached an agreement with its adversaries in Indochina, and by implication, with China, the fires of war and insurgency will rapidly flare up again, and Vietnamization will end in catastrophe. But if it leaves with an agreement, there will be no explanation and face will have been saved. The new Indochina will come into being without shocks through a gradual pulling together in accordance with the people's wishes and in a manner acceptable to the American public.

As far as Taiwan is concerned, face-saving seems possible. China demands that the Americans take away their forces and remove their military and naval protection of the island. But they do not ask to take their place and put in their own troops. Implicitly, China could agree not to use force to resolve the question of the "liberation" of the island. Here too, China would accept that things do not happen right away, nothing tragic for the Taiwanese, nor anything compromising or unacceptable for the Americans.

Above all else, a great possibility is being offered to Mr. Nixon to "save the face" of the United States, at least in the eyes of American public opinion, by the possibility of compensating for the loss of Indochina by a very important gain, namely the Sino-American thaw. The cruel defeat in Indochina would seem to be softened by the success of the new China policy. The final accounting would thus not be all negative.

China is even more inclined to this because she herself can reap major benefits. She could score a double hit which was one of her objectives and so long seemed impossible: to get the Americans to extend the Indochina settlement to a settlement of the Taiwan problem. The Americans' retreat from these two sectors would constitute a single "package," one single operation, which might take some time, but which would guarantee China that all along its southeastern periphery the ending of the encirclement would be complete.

However, the game has yet to be played, and People's China, while waiting, is careful not to celebrate its triumph. The forthcoming visit of Mr. Nixon to Peking was revealed to the Chinese public with only the minimum of publicity. At the present time, the official line is being laid out only behind closed doors, in "study" and information sessions of the Party, of cadres, and of mass organizations. One has to explain to Chinese public opinion why they are negotiating after having talked so much about fighting on indefinitely and why the head of a country so often vilified is now being invited to Peking.

The explanation given is simple: Mr. Nixon is coming to China because the Americans have been defeated. As Mr. Chou En-lai recently confided to one of his visitors, Chairman Mao Tse-tung believes there is a profound and long crisis in the United States, a belief he arrived at after giving his entire attention for some time now to the situation in America. As far as the leader of China and his prime minister are concerned, Mr. Nixon in trouble is ripe for some big concessions.

But these views are not stated in public. They know they have to handle the Americans gingerly, avoid humiliating them, and helping them bring about their great turnabout. One has also to feed positive and favorable arguments to that growing mass of friends and sympathizers which People's China has succeeded in gaining in the United States, helping them in their campaign for peace in Indochina and the recognition of the Peking government.

It is not just tactical astuteness that makes Mao's China so careful to avoid all arrogance. Her moderation is dictated by her deep convictions, by her views of the world, and her own role in that world—that is one of the keys to her strategy.

"CHINA DOES NOT WANT TO BE A SUPERPOWER"

"China is not and never will be a superpower"—that is the slogan which Peking constantly repeats at the hour of her success and her return to the stage. She has no intention, she explains, of getting into the international game as the third thief. She has no intention of replacing the detestable system of two-power domination (the U.S. and the U.S.S.R.) by one of three. Her mission is just the reverse. It is to encourage the small powers to defend themselves against the demands and aggressions of the two superpowers. She wants to teach them, as Chairman Mao said in a declaration widely publicized in May 1970, how a small country can defeat a big country and that a united front of the small can checkmate the hegemony of the big.

Self-reliance and safety from interference by the superpowers —that is the only prescription for peace. That applies everywhere where people are fighting for their freedom—in Latin America, in Africa, in the Middle East, in Asia. The peace in Indochina must be arranged among Indochinese. The fate of Taiwan can only be settled by the Chinese themselves.

"ENCIRCLEMENT BROKEN"

There will not be any "new Geneva." At Geneva, in 1954, Britain, the Soviet Union, France, Canada, Poland, the United States and who knows how many other non-Asian powers mixed themselves into the affairs of Indochina. But the world seen from Peking seems quite different today. Asia in 1971 is very different from Asia in 1954. The colonial powers have been driven out. Thus it is unacceptable that they make pretensions of wishing to return to the stage. The most that one can imagine is that certain countries, if they are directly involved, and that is the case of China, might bring their own guarantees to the new equilibrium.

As Premier Chou En-lai put it on July 18 to the American Sinologists whom he received in Peking, the new Indochina will be based "on the revolutionary position of the peoples and of the revolutionary governments of the three countries: the Democratic Republic of Vietnam, the Provisional Revolutionary Government of the Republic of South Vietnam, the government of national union under the leadership of the United National Front of Kampuchea, and the Patriotic Front of the Pathet Lao." That makes, one might note in passing, three countries and four governments, a new indication that the bringing together of the two Vietnams, as we said, will not come about right away.

Back in April 1970, the heads of the four above-mentioned revolutionary governments held a "summit" conference at a secret location, probably Canton in South China. The importance of that conference is more apparent today, and one can begin to see the outlines of a settlement among Asians. Mr. Chou En-lai appeared at the conference just before it ended to congratulate the participants for having united their four struggles into a single war and to offer them the support of China for their independence and a guarantee of their frontiers.

It is also significant that China's sponsorship of the Canton "summit" was the first important diplomatic initiative which she undertook since the end of the Cultural Revolution. Thus since Chinese foreign policy has got going again, it is the preparation for a solution in Indochina that demands her priority attention.

"THE INDOCHINA ARRANGEMENT"

Transform the Indochina peninsula into a solid and unified whole which would form a friendly bloc on the southeastern flank of China—that is the aim. And to achieve that, China is concerned that those involved solve the problems of the region by themselves through arrangements among themselves, and commit themselves, particularly, to respect mutually those frontiers they will have recognized. The task will not be easy, if one keeps in mind particularly that China must be the first not to interfere in the affairs of Indochina. China knows Hanoi is ferociously committed to its independence. She also knows that the Laotians and the Cambodians fear the appearance, in Hanoi, of a new tendency toward hegemony on the peninsula. China thus has the delicate task of helping the various parties reach understandings with each other and to organize themselves, to defend and guarantee their independence, and to make certain that the rule of equality between the strong and the weak operates in Indochina as elsewhere. As a more distant aim, there are reasons for thinking that in the eyes of the Chinese a reconstruction of Indochina will not be complete until Thailand, in turn, at the right time and of its own accord, decides to integrate itself into the new system.

But is it not difficult to explain to the Indochina fighters this reorientation of China's policies which suddenly advocates negotiating with the enemy after having for so long called for a struggle to the finish? In actuality, the formula about a struggle to the finish can be explained, according to the best observers of the Chinese scene, by the fact that both Hanoi and Peking fear being tricked again in a final settlement, an incomplete solution like the formation of a South Vietnamese government which would remain as an American economic and political bridgehead. The Vietnamese believe they have already been tricked twice: once by the French in 1946 after Fontainebleau and then by the Americans after 1954 and the false Geneva peace. Struggling militarily to the finish meant fighting to that point where the enemy is sufficiently distraught to eliminate any possibility of a wobbly solution and make a final and genuine resolution certain. That moment has arrived, so goes the thinking in Peking.

One might ask, lastly, whether this new Chinese position has not brought about a malaise, even some tension in the relations between Hanoi and Peking? These same observers are convinced the contrary is the case. The facts are, they say, that relations between the two never have been tighter. Their commonalty of views was affirmed in striking terms in the important communiqué of March 8 after the visit of Premier Chou En-lai to Hanoi which was followed soon thereafter by the unleashing of the "ping-pong diplomacy." The solidarity between Hanoi and Peking has continued to tighten since the "summit" of Canton, and moreover has become apparent during an entire decisive period when the Soviet Union lost influence in Indochina (we shall return to this matter).

"TAIWAN—RECOVERY WITH A LIGHT TOUCH"

The logic of Chinese politics makes for a rather striking parallelism between its positions on Indochina and its positions on Taiwan. Just as it is among Indochinese that the Indochina conflict must be settled, so it is among Chinese that the final liberation of Taiwan must be settled. Just as in the case of Indochina, the precondition is the withdrawal of American forces, after which China will refuse all foreign powers, including the United Nations, any right to mix themselves into the final solution of the Taiwan question. China wants this solution discussed around a table and not acquired by force. But she will reject in an absolutely intransigent fashion any attempt, under whatever form or whatever subterfuge, that might be presented to impose the inadmissible notion that there are two Chinas or that there is a second Chinese government facing the only legitimate government in Peking.

But that having been said, a new factor appeared in the issue when the ping-pong players came to Peking. That gave Premier Chou En-lai an opportunity for the first time to make clear the views of the Chinese government on the fate of that big island after its eventual reattachment to China. The astute Prime Minister directly confronted that point which offends American opinion, namely its disinclination to envisage the abandonment of an unhappy old friend Chiang Kai-shek and the turning over of 14 million Taiwanese to what it imagines as the political and economic horrors of Chinese Communism.

In an interview with Seymour Topping of *The New York Times,* amongst others, Premier Chou En-lai repeated reassuring words. Speaking beyond his visitor, he declared in essence to the Taiwanese that their living conditions would not deteriorate; on the contrary, incomes and salaries would be maintained and not taxed—China has no income tax. To those refugees from the mainland now on Taiwan who would want to return, he promised them not only amnesty, but compensation. He reminded the officials of Chiang Kai-shek that his government has always been generous with KMT defectors of whom there are many in Peking. And finally he told the people of the Taiwan independence movement that to them China would be pitiless. They are no more than agents in the pay of Washington or Tokyo. China will never accept a plebiscite on the possible independence of Taiwan, because the issue does not exist—the Taiwanese are Han, that is, Chinese.

Chou En-lai added, "Is not Chiang Kai-shek also opposed, like us, to the so-called doctrine of two Chinas? At one time, we were allies of his before we became enemies, but on this issue we have something in common with him." From there to invite Chiang Kai-shek to Peking like Mr. Nixon is no longer so great a distance—it is hard to be surprised at anything any longer. After all, Marshal Ch'en Yi proposed it in a famous press conference of September 1965. The explosion of the Cultural Revolution shortly thereafter made one forget this episode. Is it not curious that once the Cultural Revolution had ended, the matter seems to have been resumed at the point where it had been?

Whatever the case, the Chinese leaders, speaking through Chou En-lai, obviously wanted to put a promise on the record to bring about the recovery of Taiwan with a light touch. Moreover, China is not in a hurry. Events are working for her, so believe the Chinese. The deterioration of the nationalist regime can only accelerate. Half-abandoned by its American allies, it is in danger in the United Nations and internally undermined by the prospect of the death of Chiang Kai-shek, which can not be too far off. It will surely be by gnawing away that People's China hopes to break that link in the chain of anti-China encirclement so long solid and formidable—Taiwan.

There was a time in the Pacific, said a Western diplomat in Peking, when the United States placed their defense perimeter at a longitude running through Hawaii. That was too far back and they had occasion to regret it. After the second war, they put it on land, on the Asian continent. That was too far in advance and the mistake was disastrous. They found themselves fatally and dangerously involved in the conflicts and storms of a yellow world profoundly different from their own. That perimeter no longer is defensible and has become a line of insecurity.

Will that perimeter, one might add, be reconstituted somewhere else and where will it be? Will it retain the character it has hitherto had, namely a chain to contain and isolate People's China? But the great event at this beginning of the decade is that China has more than half succeeded, on its southern frontiers, to break the ring that encircled her. She will never accept easily that the encirclement reconstitute itself and continue somewhere further north.

And it now will be toward the north that China can turn its attention: toward Japan, who she fears might in turn take up

America's policies, and toward the Soviet Union, whose own encirclement of China, on its land frontiers, seems to her to be the most loathsome and the most menacing.

"CONCERN ABOUT THE NORTH"

"Hardening Toward Japan and Korea"

Till now, Peking's policies toward Japan consisted above all in separating its public opinion from its government, and to dangle in front of the eyes of the *zaikai*, the Japanese businessmen, the bait of increased trade if the two countries should get together.

Is China now going to play a more active and tougher game toward Tokyo? Already the invitation to Mr. Nixon dealt a severe blow to Japan and especially to Mr. Sato, whose position is very shaken. This is probably a result Peking assumed in its calculations before extending the invitation to Nixon. But in a more long-range sense, it is possible China hopes to undo the Japan-U.S.A. front and convince the Americans that they have common interests with China to put the brakes on the growing power of Japan.

For the moment, Peking is certainly counting on the impending fall from power of Mr. Sato and is already working on a "post-Sato period." Some important approaches are not out of the question. Possibly a trip to Tokyo by an important Chinese personality. Or possibly an invitation to whoever succeeds Sato as soon as he accedes to power. Or perhaps the offer of a nonaggression treaty between China and Japan, about which Premier Chou En-lai talked to several visitors from Tokyo recently. At the same time, Peking is hardening its position in regard to Korea. The rapprochement with Kim Il Sung's Korea was recently strengthened when on July 11, on the occasion of the tenth anniversary of the mutual assistance treaty between Peking and Pyöngyang, Li Hsien-nien, China's vice-premier, stated here that in case of aggression against North Korea, "the Chinese people will take up arms without the slightest hesitation," to fight together with the Koreans. This is the first time the Chinese have committed their support in so clear-cut a fashion.

Without doubt, from Peking one sees more clearly than ever that Japan faces a choice: either it makes itself the heir and continuer of an anti-Chinese containment policy and accepts an extended confrontation, or it could profit from the fact that it is supplanting the position of the Americans to throw into the junkyard their old policies (as Nixon himself may be doing), and for better or worse, and with perseverance in the face of difficulties, replaces them by new policies, Japanese policies which will in their own way seek a détente with China and maybe even collaboration.

"Facing the Soviet Union"

There is another eventuality about which People's China is extremely hostile, and that would be, given the present changes in roles, a rapprochement between Tokyo and Moscow. For Peking that would be, as far as Japan is concerned, a grave mistake and a very hostile maneuver. The Japanese danger, today still remediable, would under such circumstances become absolute and mixed up with the Soviet danger. From China's point of view, Japan would have passed into the enemy camp.

The Soviet Union is really China's number one menace and enemy. The big attraction in a détente with the United States is the possibility of ending "the struggle on two fronts," which they cannot continue indefinitely. To oppose and resist the Soviet Union in all domains and in all places has become the principal thrust of Chinese foreign policy since the ending of the Cultural Revolution. That is a struggle in which China has certainly gained points, as the Indochina situation, particularly, indicates.

The Russians seem to be in full retreat on the Indochina peninsula, just as the Americans are in full military retreat. China has always bitterly challenged any justification for a Russian presence in this region. The only reason they are there is because the Americans brought them in. Peking certainly will refuse them any right to participate in a final solution. It is a Russo-American solution to the conflict which has now been completely routed, one where Moscow said to Washington: "You can have the South, and we keep the North, and all will be well if no one touches the 17th parallel which cuts

Indochina in two, because that is our frontier, that of the
Soviet world." Kosygin shared with the Americans a common
ignorance of the deep realities of the Indochina peninsula.
These realities are, on the other hand, at the basis of the solution which China is in the process of making prevail in order
to reconstruct Indochina, because the Chinese have always
understood the geopolitics of the region.

The struggle against the Soviet Union is also at the root of
a phenomenon which would have seemed incredible a few
years ago, namely China's entry into the European political
game. China seems to have three aims. First, that East Europe
rebel against the Sovet Union or, as Peking puts it, weaken
the colonial domination of "social imperialism." Second, that
at the same time Western Europe become a force which counts
for more and more at the rear of a Soviet Union that wants to
turn its attention toward Asia. Long live the Common Market
and Britain's entry because a Europe enlarged and reinforced
will contain the Russians and also put an end to the Soviet-
American duopoly. And third, that this Europe place no trust
in any agreement on Berlin or on any détente with the U.S.S.R.
to the extent that its hands would be freed for the East.

"MISSILES ON THE FRONTIER"

The fact is that toward the north and the northwest of China's
vastness, the Soviet encirclement remains a permanent menace
in the eyes of the rulers in Peking, all along the endless frontier
with the USSR and its Mongolian satellite. The Soviet deployment in Asia is something to be worried about, so say Western
observers. There are one million soldiers forming forty-five
divisions, half right on the frontier and the others in the rear.
Offensive arms with tanks and a powerful air capability, plus
missile and nuclear weapons bases. China, for her part, probably has the same number of men, ten armies of fifty thousand
each, along the frontier and farther back. Her deployments are
purely defensive, and she counts, above all else, on the armed
resistance of the entire population, in case of an invasion. Mao
Tse-tung and Chou En-lai take pains to tell their visitors that

China's nuclear capability remains weak and is still in an experimental stage. But nevertheless it is believed that China will soon have a missile with a range of from 8,000 to 10,000 kilometers, and the launching of two Chinese satellites has shown that she can probably strike at Moscow.

Her growing strength in the area of missiles and nuclear weapons is, in any case, just a matter of time. Can China reach the point where she will be truly strong without anything irreparable having happened from the Russians? That is the question foreign observers are asking in Peking.

In the meantime, China, as any visitor can see, is keeping remarkably cool. There is no war hysteria. There is no visible military training either in the cities or the countryside. No propaganda about the foreign danger, and not a word in public about the Sino-Russian tension.

Only one strange sight upsets the picture of peace and confidence which People's China everywhere presents: that is the piles of earth or stones which one sees along the broad avenues of the cities and even in the small narrow streets, all along densely populated habitations. They have been freshly dug out of the soil. Across the entire country, in the big and little cities, the Chinese are ready to go underground.

★　★　★　★　★

ZAMBIAN AND TANZANIAN VIEWS ON THE TANZAM RAILROAD PROJECT

The fame of China, of its revolution, ideology, and socialist construction, is widespread throughout the Third World. Since the early 1950's, streams of visitors from Asia, Africa, and Latin America have toured China. But as with many Western admirers of China, many Third World people tend to have idealized notions of China because they lack concrete contact with the Chinese. This is not true of Tanzania and Zambia, two countries of Southern Africa, where 20,000 Chinese engineers, workers, and technicians are building the great Tanzam Railroad which when it is finished will be called the Uhuru

(Freedom) Railroad. Nor is it true of the two presidents of those countries, Kaunda and Nyerere, who not only have visited China, but have been considerably influenced by that country. Tanzania in particular is building a socialist system which, while considerably different from that of China, has accepted one of its main premises: that a predominately agricultural country must develop workable, productive, yet non-oppressive and broadly accepted forms of rural cooperation. Thus Nyerere's program of organizing *ujamaa* or cooperative villages throughout his country.

The other premise which Nyerere and Kaunda have accepted from China and which forms the rationale for the railroad is self-reliance. Both countries are rich in minerals. Aside from Zambia's immense copper resources, both countries also have iron, coal, manganese, gold, diamonds, and uranium. Like all other poor Third World countries, Tanzania and Zambia must export their raw materials in order to earn the foreign exchange they need to buy capital and necessary consumer goods. But until the railway is finished, the only rail connection to the sea is through Portuguese-ruled Mozambique. While much of the world has been unaware of it, a powerful economic bloc dominated by South Africa has been arising in the southern half of that continent. Abetted by the Portuguese and Ian Smith's Rhodesia, that bloc is arising on the foundation of economic dependence of the poorer Black African nations on the rich areas. Once the railroad is completed in 1974, as seems likely from unexpectedly rapid progress, Zambia, Tanzania, and the Katanga region of Zaïre (formerly the Congo) will be economically independent of South Africa.

The agreement to build the railroad was concluded in 1967 (during the Cultural Revolution!), and China made an interest-free loan of over 400 million U.S. dollars to both countries, with payment deferred for fifteen years. Construction on the 1,859-kilometer-long line began in October 1970, when the inauguration speeches we here present were given. By the end of 1971, 500 kilometers had been completed. The Tanzanian press regularly contains stories about the railroad. The Tanzam project is, since the completion of the Aswan Dam, the single largest foreign aid project in the world in the early 1970's. The Chinese agreed to do it after other countries refused on grounds it was impossible and not worth it. But the Chinese stepped in as part of a long-range policy toward Black Africa.

★ ★ ★

DR. KENNETH KAUNDA*
Another Link is Forged:
Inauguration of the Zambia-Tanzania
Railway Project

Comrades, this is a proud and historical moment for Tanzania and Zambia and indeed for the rest of East and Central Africa.

Last week was a period of celebrations in Zambia—celebrations of the sixth anniversary of our independence.

The rejoicing was certainly about our past achievements—achievements of which we are justly proud.

To us this ceremony today here in Tanzania—the inauguration of the construction of the Tanzania-Zambia railway line—is the crowning and most important event of all the celebrations of our sixth national birthday.

It ushers in the seventh year of our Independence as an era of consolidation of the foundations of our nationhood and of our economic base to guarantee accelerated development in every sector in order to increase the benefits of real independence in economic and social terms.

There are many reasons why we should rejoice on this occasion.

FIRST

> We have waited for many years for an idea conceived before Independence to materialize. We invested so much in terms of time and energy. We staked the unity and strength of

* Dr. K. D. Kaunda, Zambian government pamphlet (Lusaka, 1970) pp. 1–8.

TANU and UNIP and their respective Governments, whose unity was threatened by the enemies of the railway, in order that we might secure for ourselves a better future.

SECOND

The railway, the construction of which we inaugurate today, is perhaps one of the most opposed schemes in the world. This ceremony today puts the final seal to doubts and uncertainties, although it does not necessarily end the threats being issued against its construction.

THIRD

The completion of the railway line will have tremendous significance to Zambia's future as a strong, prosperous and truly independent nation; to the economies of Tanzania and Zambia; to the growing fraternal relations between neighboring and brotherly nations in Eastern Africa and to the friendly ties between us in this part of the world and the Chinese people.

Many things have been said against our railway. It has been called an ideological railway, a 1,000-mile "blood" railway and many other labels, all indicating total and stiff opposition to it or its construction.

The second element of opposition comes from vested interests in white-ruled Southern Africa and their supporters elsewhere in the world. Campaigning against the railway has been wide and intense. The railway would be uneconomic, it was argued. We refused to listen. The railway would be too expensive in relation to economic returns, we were advised. We rejected the advice. The railway would take too long to build, it was emphasized rather discouragingly. We ignored the warning. Above all, it was argued that Zambia did not need the railway after all as UDI, with all the hardships to Zambia, would end in a matter of months.

Consequently would-be Western investors were discouraged —indeed advised—against the formation of a consortium to construct the railway line. But we are fortunate to have friends among them. Indeed, we are not without friends in Western governments who revealed the efforts in some Western capitals designed to sabotage our efforts in bringing this project to reality.

The old imperial idea that Tanzania and Zambia lay in the British sphere of influence was a determining factor. Governments, prepared to participate in the project, were discouraged because the British Government did not think the project necessary.

Zambia was to remain dependent on the white-ruled south for the transportation of her exports and imports. We were to be subservient to white domination for as long as it was in the interests of Western governments regardless of our objectives and interests.

This is not strange since historically the then Northern Rhodesia was organized within a framework designed to create a big sphere of influence for Britain and other Western countries. South Africa's ambition is to create a greater Southern Africa under her sphere of influence with Pretoria as the capital. Zambia and other countries north of the Zambezi are still targets.

Our determination to be independent from the south has paid off. The grand design of imperialist and neo-colonialist forces happily lies in the dust bin of history. The railway line from Dar es Salaam to Kapiri Mposhi in Zambia is well under way.

This marks the beginning of the end of our struggle for a more reliable and secure transportation of our commodities to and from the sea.

Another opposition has been based on a rather psychopathic fear of the intentions and objectives of the Chinese in offering to build the railway amidst campaigns in other nations against investing in it.

However, the fact is that it was not Western investors as such who refused to participate in the project but Western governments who objected.

Their objection was not based on poor economic returns, as this had been cleared already in a survey report submitted in August, 1966, in which the survey team declared: "We believe that the railway is a feasible and economic proposition." It was based on political and ideological grounds.

All these pressures we ignored. To date, the campaigns against the railway, and particularly its construction by the Chinese, continue.

We have learned one important lesson, namely, what other peoples and nations say about us is not the most important thing in the world. What is vital to our future success in building our nations is what we decide to be in the best interests of Man and what our people and Governments do to realize their hopes and desires; to secure a peaceful and more stable, prosperous future. So we decided to have the Tanzam railway.

We accepted the generous offer of the Chinese friends—true friends at that—to construct it when all other nations not only stood aloof hoping to force upon landlocked Zambia more dependence on the minority regimes, but to sabotage any efforts in favor of successful diversification of our economy and to reduce our dependence on the south.

My friends, the construction of our railway is a fact. It started some weeks ago on the route covering slightly more than 1,000 miles. It will be completed.

Having reached thus far, despite stiff opposition, we cannot afford to fail. We will not fail. The railway line will reach Kapiri Mposhi.

Tanzania and Zambia are two independent nations committed to a policy of good neighborliness, brotherly love and cooperation. We want peace, and peace there will be provided other states can leave us alone. Progress there will be, provided we are allowed possession of economic instruments such as the Tanzam railway.

The cooperation of the Chinese Government and people with the Tanzanian and Zambian Governments is based, *inter alia*, strictly on mutual respect and noninterference in the internal affairs of other independent nations.

The Chinese people and their Government respect our evolving economic and social systems. This respect is reciprocated. They respect our goals as nations. We also respect their goals. There is, therefore, no reason for apprehension on our part. We reject this as arrogance. Geography may not allow us to choose neighbors, but we can at least choose our friends and our enemies. The Chinese people are our friends and they will remain so as long as it is to the benefit of our respective peoples.

This railway will have a tremendous impact on the future of this part of the world. It will increase our capacity to diversify our economy and trade. Already, even with the present capacity of the port of Dar es Salaam, we have done so much.

Our exports via Dar es Salaam have risen from 39 tons in 1966 to 189,000 tons in 1967, 220,000 tons in 1968 and 231,-000 tons in 1969—an increase of 590 per cent in four years.

The volume of traffic between Dar es Salaam and Zambia has, therefore, increased. Indeed, a lot more remains except for the capacity of the road, which is at present our lifeline.

While the road traffic has increased so much, there is still a very large quantity of goods which can most easily and cheaply be carried by rail, and these comprise the bulk of our trade goods.

When once the Tanzam railway is completed, immediate benefits will accrue both to Tanzania and Zambia. The line is designed to have a carrying capacity of over 7,000,000 tons in both directions.

This capacity will be built gradually over a period. Consequently, the railway has a tremendous significance to both countries, as it will lead to the opening of the parts of Tanzania and Zambia which hitherto have lagged behind in development as a result of lack of transportation facilities.

We very much welcome this endeavor as opening a new chapter for millions of our people to improve their economic and social conditions, apart from the employment which both the construction and operation of the railway system will provide. The objective of self-reliance will be brought nearer.

The impact of this railway will be felt in a political sense. Tanzania and Zambia—countries sharing not only common boundaries but common interests and sharing in the principles which should underline not only African unity but world peace and security and also committed to the policy of nonalignment —will, through this railway line, add to the ties that have brought them together into a fellowship so fundamental to the unity of peoples.

We have now the East African Shipping Line, the pipeline, Tanzam Road Services, as well as the new railway, which we inaugurate today, as concrete expressions of the ties that bind us together as one people with one destiny.

I am pleased that this is happening between neighboring countries in Africa, for African countries will not achieve the goals of African unity unless we are prepared to work out concrete plans to make this a practical possibility.

Let us build our unity on a firm, economic infrastructure as the best foundation for our future. We cannot do anything without roads; we cannot do anything without railway lines.

We will continue to be dependent on other people. Hence the significance of the Tanzam railroad.

For this reason, for making the new railway to be constructed a practical possibility, we thank the Chinese people, their party and Government.

We thank Chairman Mao Tse-tung, Vice Chairman Lin Piao, Prime Minister Chou En-Lai and their colleagues and all their people for this gesture of genuine friendship and cooperation in the world for peace and development.

I can only say, as you give so shall you receive, and for the moment we return this gesture of comradeship with a fountain of goodwill.

We know the efforts against the completion of the railway will continue, but we remain undaunted by threats or criticism.

All we want is a railway line from Dar es Salaam to Lusaka, and all we want is friendship and cooperation among all peoples, provided these are based on mutual respect and non-interference in the internal affairs of independent nations.

We therefore ask those who may be tempted to sabotage our efforts, to keep off the route and let the people—our people—work out a destiny that is theirs and their children's.

We therefore, once again, pay tribute to Chairman Mao Tse-tung and his colleagues. We pay tribute and express deep appreciation for the exemplary and outstanding manner in which the People's Republic of China has made a tremendous contribution to this historic railway project.

This project is a symbol of international cooperation for peace, independence, development and cooperation among independent nations.

We know it to be your international obligation to assist, without strings, other nations which accept your friendship. We are confident that you will continue to show the same genuine concern and regard for the interests of your friends.

On our part, we pledge to fight malicious campaigns being waged against the railway by the detractors. We are confident that the standards of engineering and construction of the railway will defy those who are opposed to it.

We reaffirm our conviction that the Tanzam railway will forge permanent bonds of brotherhood and partnership not only between Tanzania and Zambia on the one hand and China on the other, but between the whole of the Eastern and Central African region and the rest of the world—a decisive contribution to the universal goal of African unity.

The battle for the construction of this railway has been uphill and difficult. Today we have reached the pinnacle. Victory is in sight, if not won already.

This is a proud moment for Zambia and for the people of Tanzania whom it is my greatest honor to pay tribute to on this occasion. They have been very helpful in the past.

They made a tremendous contribution to our efforts to survive the UDI crisis. The pipeline begins from Dar es Salaam; so will the railway—both the lifeblood of Zambia.

Talking of the contribution of the Tanzania people to the development of the people of Zambia reminds us of the need to develop on a firm permanent basis a people's cooperation, not only cooperation between leaders.

The Tanzania-Zambia road and the airlines have in the past been the main arteries for developing this type of cooperation. Their capacity has been limited for our purposes. Construction and completion of the Tanzam railway will facilitate the promotion of the cooperation between not only the people of Tanzania and Zambia but between the peoples of Central Africa and East Africa and, indeed, the world as a whole.

It must not, therefore, be surprising when, on the occasion of the closing of our sixth anniversary independence celebrations, I should derive greatest pleasure and honor in laying the foundation stone of this magnificent Tanzania-Zambia railway project with a fervent hope that, in a short time, we will see our life's ambition of traveling by rail from Dar es Salaam to Lusaka being fulfilled in the full measure. Thank you.

DR. JULIUS NYERERE*

This is an important day for Zambia, for Tanzania, and for Africa. For today we conduct the second part of a twin ceremony: we are marking the beginning of the actual construction of a railway which will link Kapiri Mposhi to Dar es Salaam. We have worked for a long time to make this day possible. For now we are sure that in the future we shall celebrate the completion of the railway link between Zambia and the whole of East Africa. The work has started.

In fact, it has been left to the independent states of Zambia and Tanzania to bring to fruition a project which has been talked about for many years. For it was in 1947 that the idea of a railway linking what was then Northern Rhodesia and what was then Tanganyika was first considered. As early as 1952, preliminary economic and engineering reports were completed; one of these was prepared by the East African Railways and Harbours administration and showed this link to be both possible and worthwhile. Yet nothing happened. Only under pressure from the nationalist movements of our two countries, and after Tanganyika had become independent, was there any progress at all. Then, when it became clear that a UNIP Government would soon be able to act on this matter, the colonial government of Northern Rhodesia asked for a World Bank Report on the question. The World Bank Commission, however, was given terms of reference which virtually prejudged the issue; the result was the only adverse report there has ever been on the economic feasibility of this project.

Fortunately, neither Tanzania nor Zambia has ever faltered in the conviction that a railway link between our two countries is of the utmost importance. Our two governments were determined that it should be constructed. We knew that, in the

* Dr. J. Nyerere, Zambian government pamphlet (1970), pp. 17–22.

long run, the unity of Africa required that our continent should be linked by railway lines from north to south. We know also that linking Zambia with the north is vital for the security of free Africa—and especially vital for our two frontier states.

Developments in Southern Africa, and particularly the unilateral declaration of independence by the Smith regime in Rhodesia, did, however, make this project very urgent indeed. For a railway link with the port of Dar es Salaam is vital for the full implementation of Zambia's policy of linking herself to the free African states to the north. In colonial times Zambia had communications only with the countries of Southern Africa. Despite the fact that Tanganyika was also administered by the British Government, no links at all had been created between our two countries; even the road was designed only for light traffic during dry weather. Consequently, when the Smith rebellion of November, 1965, was met by a policy of economic sanctions, the most immediate result was grave problems for the newly independent Zambia.

For despite all the difficulties of its economic and communications inheritance, Zambia responded wholeheartedly to the African decision to boycott Rhodesia. Of course, Zambia could not make her boycott immediately and 100 per cent effective. Of course, the immediate effect of reducing imports from Rhodesia to the very minimum had to be a temporary increase in the importation of goods from South Africa. But the people of this country, under the leadership of President Kaunda and UNIP, did more than anyone had believed possible, and made sacrifices which few outsiders understand even now. Indeed, I am disgusted by those who were mainly responsible for Zambia's predicament and who now, from thousands of miles away, dare to criticize the Government and people of this country for their actions at that time and since. No one could have done more without causing chaos and collapse in Zambia: only a fierce determination for freedom enabled this country to do as much as it did.

President Kaunda, those who dare to criticize what has been done by the people of your country towards the isolation of Rhodesia, and of South Africa, are beneath contempt. And when they not only ignore, but also oppose all the efforts which Zambia is making to overcome the effects of its inheritance, and use Zambia's residual trade with Southern Africa as an excuse for actions which will strengthen the enemies of this country and of African freedom, then words cannot express our feelings.

Of course it is not only Zambia which will benefit when this railway line is completed. Tanzania will receive immediate and direct benefit too. It will gain—as well as Zambia will—by the increased trade which will be possible. It will gain through Zambia's use of Dar es Salaam harbor; rather than Portuguese-controlled Beira. It will also gain because this railway will reinforce the alliance for freedom which exists between our two countries, and which helps us both to withstand the pressures exerted upon us by the enemies of African dignity and African freedom.

Nor is this all. The whole of Africa will benefit from this railway. We shall benefit because it will strengthen Zambia and therefore strengthen the forces of African freedom. We shall benefit because trade between different African countries will become easier, and thus the development of us all will increase. And, in particular, the countries of Eastern Africa will benefit by the closer contact the railway will make possible. I would add that I believe this railway will make Zambia's membership of the East African Community even more natural—and mutually beneficial—than it already is.

Yet despite all these advantages, I have noticed one very odd thing about the international reactions to this railway project. It is that some of those nations which have had the effrontery to criticize Zambia for her residual trade with nations to the south, also criticize us for building this railway! They make it clear that they admit our right to build the railway. They sometimes even admit the obvious fact that only when the railway exists will Zambia be in a position to choose for herself with whom she trades, and through which country her goods pass. Thus—under pressure—they admit that a railway to the north will increase the reality of Zambia's freedom. Yet some of them also suggest that, by building this railway now, Tanzania and Zambia are coming under Chinese influence!

I can only respond to this suggestion with some amazement. First is the fact that from 1918 to 1961 a Western country controlled both Tanzania and Zambia—surely that was long enough for them to have at least begun the railway they were talking about from 1942 onwards? Indeed, Western countries could have acceded to our requests for help with this project right up until 1965 and after. They failed to do so. But more interesting—and in a way more frightening—is the self-revelation which this Western criticism implies. For this criticism implies that in their view aid is always an instrument of domination. And this criticism comes from those who dominated Africa and, in varying degrees, are still dominating Africa now. The Chinese have no colonies in Africa or anywhere else in the world; and their present leadership, at least, is genuinely and fervently anti-imperialist; and so are we.

Therefore, let me make it absolutely clear—and in this I know I speak for the Governments and peoples of all our countries. We are extremely grateful to the Chinese People's Republic for their help in this matter, the railway project; we are grateful for the spirit in which the offer of assistance was made, and for the manner in which this assistance is being given. A railway is a railway; and that is what we want, and that is what we are being given. But there is something more; this railway will be our railway. It will not be a Chinese railway, because the Chinese are not building a Chinese railway!

What is happening is that the People's Republic of China is giving us an interest-free loan of 2,865,000,000 shillings—that is, 286,500,000 Kwacha—for the construction of the railway and the provision of railway stock. Tanzania and Zambia will jointly repay this loan when it becomes due—but that will not be for some time after the railway has begun to contribute to the development of our economies. For, under the agreement, we only begin repayment in 1985; we then continue to pay gradually until repayment is completed in the year 2012! These terms are more than generous; an interest-free loan, with a grace period of fifteen years from 1968, and then payment over fifty years—this is real "aid." Thus, to say the very least, the Chinese people are not planning to make a profit from this railway. Indeed, they are making a gift to us, for it would be very expensive to borrow this amount of money at commercial rates of interest.

Let me state quite clearly that we appreciate this loan, and we appreciate the fact that it is interest-free. We greatly appreciate all this help with the building of our railway. And—I repeat—the Chinese people have not asked us to become communists in order to qualify for this loan! They know that we would not sell our independence, even for the railway; and they have never at any point suggested that we should change any of our policies—internal or external—because of their help with this railway. They have simply offered us generous terms in money and in men.

For there will be about 7,000 Chinese technicians working in either Tanzania or Zambia by December of this year. More than 4,000 are already working here. I would like to express our welcome to these men and women—who have already shown us an example of hard work and dedication in the fulfillment of the jobs they have undertaken. Because of this number of technicians, the 1,900 kilometers of line will be built within six years, despite all the physical difficulties of the route.

I said that we welcome these technicians, and I want to emphasize that. For we are not afraid of the Chinese people who will be working with our people. Despite all the indoctrination we have had over a long period, we believe that the Chinese people are human beings, and not ogres.

Of course we shall learn from the Chinese technicians who will be working in Tanzania and Zambia. We hope to learn their technical skills—and experience in Tanzania has shown us that they are willing to teach these technical skills to our people. Further, we hope to learn something of the history and the ideas of the Chinese people. For the world needs unity in its diversity; and it needs international understanding between peoples of different backgrounds, different political beliefs, different religions and different histories. Indeed, we believe that the peoples of Zambia and Tanzania, and the Chinese people who are working here, will all learn from each other. And we believe that friendship between a great nation and two small nations will be increased because of this contact. Certainly I hope that this will happen, for we need friendship between Africa and the people of China, just as we do between Africa and the peoples of other continents.

To suggest, as it has been suggested, that this means Tanzania and Zambia are going to be hostile to Western countries is absurd. The railway has, and will have, nothing whatever to do with our attitude to the countries of Europe and America. Our attitude towards each country in the world is determined only by its actions toward Africa and toward world peace. It is not determined by our need for aid, nor by the help that we got from any country. As we in Tanzania and Zambia have said many times, we want to be friendly with all nations, and we allow no one to choose our enemies for us.

Yet we in Africa do have an enemy—our enemy is the racialism and colonialism which now exist in Southern Africa. Our hostility to the apartheid regime of South Africa, and that of Rhodesia, and our hostility towards the Portuguese colonialism, is neither increased nor decreased by the building of this railway. Of course, the fact that Southern Africa is not free does make one important difference to this railway project. For if the peoples of Southern Africa were governing themselves, they would be represented at this meeting today, and they would be joining in our happiness at this development. As it is, we know that the regimes to the south bitterly oppose the building of this railway, because of the strength its completion will give to Zambia, to Tanzania, and to Africa as a whole. For they do not want us to become strong; they want us to remain their puppets. . . .

★   ★   ★   ★   ★

Russian View of China

It is ironic that the one selection bitterly hostile to China in Volume IV of the *China Reader* should come from a Russian source. In fact, except for the Russian press and that of its allies, by and large the treatment of People's China in the world press has been warm and friendly. How extraordinary the contrast with the world press in the early 1950's, when it was virtually only the Russian press and that of its allies and sympathizers that portrayed the new China in a favorable light!

While Pavlov's article deals specifically with China's policies toward Europe, the analysis perfectly reflects the official Russian view of China. Put in its simplest terms, the Russians hold that all Chinese policies are governed by only one criterion: hostility to the Soviet Union. The Russians regard Mao's rule as a "military-bureaucratic dictatorship" with chauvinist and expansionist pretensions. However, they also hold, as the selection indicates, that the proper division of the world remains one between capitalism and socialism, and so—in theory, anyway— the Russians still see China as being a part of the socialist part of the world. Just as the Chinese imply that Russia could recover from revisionism if the renegade leadership of Brezhnev et al. were removed, so the Russians imply that China's deviations are all the fault of what they call the "Mao clique."

In regard to Europe, the Russians accuse the Chinese of seeking a revival of West European political and military unity directed against Russia, and at the same time trying everything to break up the "socialist community" in Eastern Europe. A fairly common balance-of-power explanation of both Chinese and Russian policies toward Western Europe is that the Chinese want a strong Western Europe to deflect Russian attention away from their borders, and the Russians want a settlement with Western Europe (mutual force reductions) so they can concentrate on those borders.

Over a quarter century ago, Stalin was furious at Roosevelt for trying to give China a voice in European affairs; he saw it as a devious Roosevelt machination to double America's voice through his Chinese puppet Chiang Kai-shek. But from the mid-1950's, China began to play an active role in the affairs of Eastern Europe, and by the early 1970's was playing a similarly active role in Western Europe. The Chinese are now, for example, building a large dry dock in Malta, now independent, with diplomatic relations with China. China has now directly and indirectly become a part of European politics. Given the extreme hostility between China and Russia, the Russians can hardly be blamed for having paranoiac feelings about Chinese activities in Europe. The Chinese maintain the warmest ties with Rumania, noted for its own nationalist hostility to the Soviet Union. The warming relations between Peking and Belgrade went proportionate to Yugoslav fury against the Soviet Union because of the invasion of Czechoslovakia. Naturally, if Sino-American relations develop further in a positive direction, then V. Pavlov's suspicions about Chinese support of Britain's role in the Common Market will grow even more. For years, the French had assumed that British entry into the Common Market was in fact an American Trojan Horse and opposed it. Pavlov implies that the Chinese are now abetting these old American schemes.

The selection should be carefully read as a standard Russian line on China.

★ ★ ★

V. PAVLOV*
Europe in the Plans of Peking

In the subversive, splitting, adventurist foreign policy of Peking, Europe occupies an increasingly larger place. As a counterbalance to the peace-loving policy of the U.S.S.R. and the other countries of the socialist community, who are striving to create on the European continent a system of collective security based on awareness of the territorial and political realities which arose as a result of World War II, the Maoists are trying in every way to prevent the lessening of tension and the development of equitable cooperation between the countries of Europe.

Coming forth with an openly great-power stance, the Chinese leadership is striving, in Europe as well as in other areas of the world, to preserve tensions and maintain positions from which to broaden their influence. They are embarking along a path of the most diverse political and diplomatic combinations, setting some countries against others, increasingly often coming out in a united front with the most reactionary circles of the imperialist powers.

The interest of the Chinese leadership in European affairs is growing along with Peking's hegemonistic pretensions. It has

* V. Pavlov, "Europe in the Plans of Peking," in· *Mezhdunarodnaia Zhizn'*, No. 2 (1972).

been especially active in recent years, when, in European public opinion, the conviction began to ripen that, in the interests of lasting peace, and of arranging all-European cooperation, it was necessary to normalize the relationships of all countries, to overcome the division of the continent into military-political groupings, to strengthen the security of nations, and most of all to eliminate the use of force or threatening with force in reciprocal relations between the governments.

The changes in China's position on problems of European security, as well as on other international problems, reflect the evolution of the P.R.C. foreign policy during the years of its existence, and in many ways are explained by Peking's present anti-Soviet, anti-socialist line.

In the fifties, the Chinese People's Republic completely shared the cause undertaken by the Soviet Union and other socialist countries of safeguarding the peace and cooperation of the European nations. They exposed the schemes of revanchist and militaristic circles, opponents of the lessening of tension on the continent. In an April 1955 statement made by the government of the P.R.C. concerning cessation of the state of war with Germany, it was noted that the P.R.C. supported the G.D.R. and the whole German nation, as well as the U.S.S.R. and all peace-loving countries and nations, in their struggle for collective European security.

In January 1957, in a joint communiqué issued by the governments of Poland and China, approval was expressed for Soviet proposals to safeguard the peace in Europe; they warned against the revival of revanchist elements in the F.R.G., and stated that the western border of Poland along the Oder-Neisse was a border of peace and served the interests of security in Europe.

"Both sides"—it was emphasized in the joint Soviet-Chinese communiqué of January 18, 1957—"feel that all the self-enclosed military groupings should be replaced by a system of collective peace and collective security. The Warsaw Pact is a defensive military alliance which the socialist countries of Europe were compelled to create after the conclusion of the aggressive military North Atlantic Treaty. The countries participating in the Warsaw Pact consequently recommend the liquidation of the North Atlantic Treaty and the Warsaw Pact and replacing them with a treaty for collective security in Europe."

At the beginning of the sixties, however, after coming out with its own particular line in the international communist movement, the Chinese leadership began to depart from the positions on the problems of European security which had been drawn up jointly with the other socialist countries. On February 4, 1960, at a meeting of the Political Advisory Committee of the governments participating in the Warsaw Pact, an observer from the P.R.C., before stating his position on the German question, announced that China would not consider herself bound by any agreements concluded without her participation. From 1961 on, the P.R.C. stopped sending its observer to participate in the work of the organs of the Warsaw Pact.

Since the mid-sixties, Peking has been taking a sharply negative position in respect to proposals made by the socialist countries intended to get the matter of European settlement rolling along practical rails, to safeguard the real prerequisites for creating a system of collective security and the development of cooperation among the countries of the continent. The leaders of the P.R.C. did everything to discredit the program put forth by the socialist countries to safeguard European security, thereby impeding and tearing down a European settlement.

Documents from the meetings of the socialist government leaders and communist parties of Europe, at which proposals had been worked out to strengthen peace and security, were exposed to malicious attacks. Chinese propaganda strove to represent these historic documents and proposals from the socialist countries and the European communist parties as an attempt to "scrape together a counter-revolutionary 'Holy Alliance,' to suppress the revolutionary movement in Europe, to stabilize the order in the capitalist world." The outburst against the program for order in Europe was "justified" by demagogic and slanderous discourses on the aspirations of the Soviet Union and the other socialist countries to "engage in anti-Chinese, anti-communist and anti-national intrigues."

The Chinese leaders are striving to place mines under the edifice for safeguarding peace in Europe and under its foundation —acknowledgment of the stability and invulnerability of the existing European boundaries. As early as 1964, in a conversation with a group of Japanese socialists, Mao Tse-tung openly expressed doubt about the boundaries which had appeared in Europe as a result of World War II, and declared the necessity for changing them. In December 1969 *Jen-min jih-pao* was distressed over the fact that the idea of European security was aimed at "preserving the status quo in Europe."

Such a position was one of the most important reasons for Peking's attacks on the treaty between the U.S.S.R. and the F.R.G., which specifically supports the position, obligatory at the level of international law, of recognizing existing boundaries, principally the boundaries along the Oder-Neisse, and between the G.D.R. and the F.R.G. On September 13, 1970, *Jen-min jih-pao* printed an article which depicted the treaty as a "betrayal of the interests of the German people, the Soviet people and the people of all Europe," "the encouragement of West German militarism," and so forth. Peking also "assessed" the four-party agreement on West Berlin in analogous fashion. The Chinese leadership gave a hostile reception to these treaties and agreements, mainly because they were already contributing toward improvement of the political climate in relations between the governments on the continent, and turning out to be a positive influence in the course of European affairs. "Peking does not touch the English Crown Colony of Hong Kong"—wrote *Neues Deutschland*, à propos of this—"but is shedding crocodile tears, when, thanks to the U.S.S.R., tension in Europe is easing in one of the most dangerous breeding grounds—West Berlin."

In its attempts to tear down or at least to impede the process of relaxation in Europe, Peking made no small effort to ruin the very idea of convocation of an all-European conference on questions of security and cooperation, which the Soviet Union and the other socialist governments advanced five years ago. In 1969, the vice-premier of the P.R.C., Li Hsien-nien, attacked the all-European conference, representing the initiative of the socialist countries, as an attempt to "share the spheres of influence with American imperialism, to control and enslave Eastern Europe." A similar "interpretation" of the program of the socialist governments continues even to this day. By means of behind-the-scenes machinations, the Chinese leadership is attempting to sow seeds of doubt as to the appropriateness and potential of the conference, hinting that, as they say, the time is not yet ripe for this.

Using the contradictions between socialism and capitalism in Europe and the active operations of circles which are striving to reverse the process of relaxation in Europe, the Peking government has as its object the aggravation of tension on the continent, so that, in this way, they may maximally intensify the confrontation between the U.S.A. and the U.S.S.R., switch the chief attention of the United States onto Europe, and thereby facilitate the implementation of their own plans in Asia.

On November 8, 1968, when commenting on Nixon's victory in the U.S.A. presidential elections, the Hsinhua agency spoke approvingly of his pre-election promise to reduce the commitment of the U.S.A. in areas where they had "overextended their activity"—that is, in Asia—and to "lay greater stress on the primary areas." The official Hsinhua agency, voicing the plans of the Maoists, who were thinking of kindling the fires of international tension a little farther away from China, implies that such a "primary area" should, first of all, be Europe. On November 26 of the same year, Peking proposed to Washington that they conclude an agreement on the peaceful coexistence of the two countries, based on five principles. Peaceful coexistence with the U.S.A. in exchange for transferring the center of gravity of American aggressive policy from Asia to Europe—such was the intention of the Chinese leaders.

At the present time, the Chinese government, preserving unchanged its strategic goals, is resorting to tactical maneuvers and demagoguery, in order to give its policy a "peace-loving" aspect. On this level, Peking's European policy is assuming an increasingly more crafty, refined, and therefore still more dangerous character. The Maoists today are not restricting themselves to propagandistic outbursts against all efforts in the sphere of establishing order in Europe, but are trying to push the countries of the continent along paths which would correspond to Chinese doctrines, and to enlist in this the support of the most reactionary circles of NATO. China is stimulating such tendencies in the policy of the European countries, especially the capitalist ones, the development of which, in Peking's opinion, should in the end assure the division of the continent into military-political blocs.

In recent months, the Chinese leaders have begun to come forth with certain new ideas on Europe's future development. Peking has begun to promote and spread the idea of the so-called "five centers" of world policy. In an interview published on December 5, 1971, given by the premier of the P.R.C. State Council to a correspondent from the English newspaper the *Sunday Times*, these centers were named: U.S.S.R., U.S.A., Western Europe—"the third power," located "in the second intermediate zone," "confronting the United States and acting as a rival to it," Japan, "the fourth power," and China, the fifth, "potential power," which "in a few decades will turn into a strong and flourishing country." (We note that such a division of the world into five centers in the Chinese interpretation is, essentially, borrowed from the speech of the president of the U.S.A. in Kansas City on July 6, 1971.)

In this scheme, as in the well-known Peking doctrine of "struggle against the monopoly of the two superpowers," the nonclass approach to current events is openly revealed. The Chinese leaders, ignoring the existence of two opposing socio-political systems, are trying to present the world as a conglomerate of countries, to depict today's basic conflict not as a struggle between these systems, but as a clash of narrow governmental interests. The path along which Peking is pushing the people and states of the world is the path of rivalry, of a fierce struggle for hegemony, the path of political combinations to the detriment of the third countries, a path dangerous, and as history shows, fraught with serious and grave consequences for the world and for international security.

According to Peking's intentions, the "third power" (Western Europe) must also be forged in this struggle. The Maoists are proposing to create it by means of "strengthening unity and cooperation," which is presented as the only possible way for the countries of Western Europe to "preserve their position," "to continue to exist."

It is not by chance that the idea of Western Europe as a "third power" is put forward by Peking—in unison with the U.S.A. In turning this part of the continent into a self-contained political, economic, and military unit, the Chinese leaders see an alternative to all-European cooperation. The realization of Peking's intentions would signify Europe's return to the period of the "cold war," the preservation of splits, the replacement of regulatory cooperation between the countries—both socialist and capitalist—by the growth of antagonism and tension.

The goal of preserving splits in Europe is also served by the "idea," advanced by the Maoists, of creating micro-European associations, various groupings in the form of a "Mediterranean Alliance," a "Balkan Bloc," and others. In their great-power fever, the Chinese leadership has even worked out formulas for the countries of the Mediterranean basin, since these, they say, "are not in condition to oppose the fact that the U.S.A. and the U.S.S.R. are contending for their hegemony here," and thus, according to the advice of the Maoists, the limits of the territorial waters should be extended two hundred miles out, which would "automatically remove all foreign fleets from the Mediterranean Sea."

The press in many countries has turned its attention to China's diplomatic activity toward several Balkan governments, which, as the *Berliner Zeitung* wrote, is developing just at the the moment when Peking has begun to intensify its contacts with U.S.A. imperialism. "The suspicion arises," notes the paper, "that the activity recently displayed by the Chinese People's Republic is aimed at scraping together in the Balkans a bloc opposed to the socialist countries . . . Inasmuch as Peking's attitude toward all world political powers is dictated exclusively by its own aspirations to dominate, then today's efforts on the Balkan peninsula must also be regarded as part of the great-power chauvinism of Mao's group . . . the aim of this policy is to drive a wedge between the Socialist countries, and to bring about disagreements."

Peking's "theoretical" findings in regard to Europe as a "third power" are accompanied and fortified by practical activities aimed at activating P.R.C. connections with the governments of Western Europe, especially with the NATO countries. Just since October 1970 China has established diplomatic relations with five more NATO members. In determining the principle for its relations with them, Peking takes into consideration their commitments ensuing from participation in the North Atlantic bloc. Also scrupulously calculated is the position occupied by the various countries on problems of European security and cooperation, and how relations with the Soviet Union are taking

shape. It is precisely on the basis of England's known position
on the questions mentioned that a considerable enlivening of
Anglo-Chinese contacts is taking place.

Peking's relations with the F.R.G. are taking a rather distinc-
tive form. The Kiesinger government's policy of aggravating tensions in Europe, of revanchist pretensions toward neighboring
countries, and of provocations in respect to socialist friendship
were undoubtedly quite convenient for the Chinese leaders. In
that period, Chinese-West German relations were becoming
yearly more intimate and many-sided. Clearly not at all to Peking's liking, however, was the predominance of realism in the
policy of the new F.R.G. government, and the treaties which it
concluded with the U.S.S.R. and Poland. As a result, the development of Chinese-West German relations has slowed down in
the last two years.

Against a background of Peking's concern for the "unity" of
West European capitalist countries, their praise of "tendencies
toward solidarity" is in stark contrast to the open hostility of
the Chinese leadership toward socialist friendship, its attempts
to "put on a theoretical basis" the subversive, splitting actions
against the socialist countries, and their collective organizations
—The Council for Mutual Economic Assistance and the Warsaw Pact Organization. Convinced that to wage a frontal attack
against the whole socialist alliance is not within their power,
the Maoists are attempting to approach the socialist countries
differentially, to broaden the channels for their own ideological
penetration into these countries, to make them the instrument of
their policy, and in the last analysis, to undermine or weaken
the unity and power of the socialist system.

The Chinese leaders are trying to prevent the development of
world socialism as a single, integrated system. Hailing the
"unity" of the capitalist governments of Western Europe, they
are at the same time imposing the idea that the "basic course
in the building of socialism" must be the course of "self-
reliance."

Similar motifs—"Capitalist countries, unite," "Socialist governments, separate"—shine through quite persistently in the
numerous talks of Chinese officials with representatives of Western governments and in material from the Chinese press. The
"recipe" for separation is also foisted off on various forces of
the workers' revolutionary movement. In a conversation with

Nenni, Premier Chou advised uniting the capitalist countries of Western Europe and the governments of the Mediterranean basin, but when it came to the question of revolutionary forces, he announced: "We think and hope that the various revolutionary movements will rely on their own forces." All this confirms the fact that the Chinese government is not interested in the development of the working-class movement in the capitalist countries of Western Europe, since the growth and success of this movement would signify the consolidation of world socialism.

The attitude of the Chinese leaders toward the "Common Market," this international union of monopoly capital, again graphically testifies to their own unscrupulousness and opportunistic leaps.

In 1957, after the signing of the Rome Treaty, China's assessment of the "Common Market" did not essentially differ from the general conclusions of the Soviet Union and the other socialist countries, which regarded this economic union as an appendage of NATO, promoting the revival of West German militarism, and directed against the socialist governments. The press of the P.R.C. noted that the forming of the "Common Market" created an obstacle to all-European cooperation and that "the plans of the six countries of Western Europe will lead only to widening the division."

In the beginning of the sixties, when the Peking government launched a polemic on many international questions, the Chinese press, in characterizing the European economic association, stressed the fact that the "Common Market" was a clear manifestation of the "death rattle of imperialism and the break-up of imperialism." The organ of the Chinese Communist Party Central Committee, the journal *Red Flag*, emphasized: "The point of view that the creation of the 'Common Market' signifies an intensification of the imperialist countries' tendency toward unification is completely incorrect. Such a view designates the adoption of the Kautsky theory of ultra-imperialism." Chinese theoreticians at that time still acknowledged, although quite hollowly, that the "Common Market" was a means of attacking the interests of the working class of the six countries, of struggling against the socialist countries, and was the instrument of neo-colonialism.

In January 1964 the Maoists brought forth and renovated the

so-called "theory of intermediate zones," which had been worked out as far back as 1946. According to the new interpretation, the second "intermediate zone" consisted of the industrially developed capitalist countries (except the U.S.A.) which allegedly had "something in common with the socialist countries and peoples of various other states." Similar "theoretical" findings were called upon to justify the policy of reorienting P.R.C. ties with the capitalist world, the policy of cooperation with the governing circles of the imperialist states, on the basis of the allegedly "anti-imperialist" position of the monopolistic bourgeoisie and also to interest the monopolistic bourgeoisie in the prospect of an anti-socialist alliance with Peking.

The P.R.C. policy with respect to the "Common Market" in its present form was formulated in the last two years, when Peking tried to emerge from the foreign policy of isolation of the Cultural Revolution period, principally with an eye to developing relations with the capitalist countries, and took as a weapon the new tactic of its global strategy of struggle against the Soviet Union and socialist cooperation. Moreover, in the "Common Market," the leaders of the P.R.C. are supporting the very thing that was dictated by the class aims of the struggle of the imperialist powers against socialist cooperation and by the aims of consolidating the capitalist system in Western Europe.

"The 'Common Market,' as the first step on the path to an independent Europe, is, possibly, a positive fact," stated the premier of the P.R.C. State Council. Peking justifies the attitude of approval toward the EEC by the fact that the "Common Market" permits a more effective waging of the "struggle against the monopoly of the two superpowers." "The new situation in Western Europe," wrote the weekly *Peking Review* in connection with England's entry into the EEC, "is a serious obstacle for the United States and the Soviet Union in carrying out their policy of hegemony in Europe." From this and other Chinese articles it is clear that in the unification of the major monopolies around the "Common Market," the Maoists see a force for opposing the Soviet Union and the other socialist countries, a key factor by means of which it would be possible to undermine the struggle to normalize the situation in Europe and in the whole world.

Peking is drawing attention to itself with its persistent

attempts to instill in the capitalist countries the idea that they will not achieve their aims if they confine themselves to economic and political collaboration alone, that the "tendency to consolidate the cooperation and unity of Western Europe" should also be extended in a military direction. "The entry of England and three other countries into the 'Common Market,' " writes *Jen-min jih-pao*, "will signify the further development of the economic, and then of the *defensive* and diplomatic union of the countries of Western Europe (italics mine—V.P.)."

The Chinese leadership approves the creation in Europe of its own center for "nuclear terror." As early as the beginning of the sixties, the P.R.C. press wrote that counterbalancing the efforts of the U.S.A. to "strengthen its nuclear monopoly," the Western European countries did not intend to "play the role of pawns in nuclear power strategy," and would like to join the "nuclear club" and occupy an equal position with the U.S.A. Even today Chinese leaders are continuing to support the point of view that the more the "other atomic states," the better.

Finally, the Maoists' interest in and support of the "Common Market" have also been aroused by Peking's clear aspiration toward making the member-countries of the EEC China's donors in economic and scientific-technical respects. The trade of the P.R.C. with capitalist governments occupies about 80 per cent of its foreign trade turnover, of which a considerable portion goes to Western Europe. China has, in the last few years, also been receiving strategic goods, including items the export of which is forbidden to socialist countries. According to press reports from overseas, Peking is undertaking practical steps toward establishing closer ties with the EEC and its staff headquarters in Brussels.

The position of the Chinese leaders with respect to the "Common Market," this international union of monopolistic capital, again confirms their breaking away from a class analysis of events and phenomena. They approve integration in the capitalist world, and take up arms against socialist economic integration, trying to undermine this process. The "Common Market," the Maoists maintain, "is an instrument of unity and cooperation," and the CMEA [Comecon]—"fetters" put on the socialist countries.

Peking is openly encouraging the spread of the "Common

Market" through England's entry, thereby playing into the hands of big business, the major banks, and the industrial monopolies of Great Britain, which are bursting onto the continent in the hope of new markets and big profits. And at the same time, the Maoists are deliberately closing their eyes to the fact that strengthening the union of monopolies signifies a further attack on the vital interests of the working class, intensifying the exploitation of laborers, and lowering their standard of living. The Chinese government leaders do not share the estimate of the EEC made by the English communists at the 32nd Congress of the Communist Party of Great Britain: "The Common Market is a closed economic bloc, perpetuating the division of Europe. It is an institution of the cold war, an anti-socialist and anti-worker institution." But on the other hand, as the Maoists' policy shows, they fully approve the point of view of the EEC, stated at the yearly conference of the Conservatives in Brighton. "In the eyes of the Chinese," notes the *Times* with satisfaction, "the Tory policy of drawing England into the Common Market is a progressive one."

Peking's benevolent attitude toward England's entry into the "Common Market," under the pretense that it will allegedly facilitate "a sharp drop in the hegemony of American imperialism in the Western world," in reality plays into the hands of the United States. The latter is pushing England into the EEC, trying to open a broader road to Western Europe's huge monopolies, to bind the West European governments more closely to Washington's "Atlantic" policy. The U.S.A. regards the Maoists' opinions concerning the "economic and defensive union" of the West European countries no less favorably. After all, it is precisely the reactionary circles of the United States which are interested in the need for "increasing the military investment" of the Western European countries in NATO and are fighting for an acceleration of the armaments race, frightening these states with the mythical "Soviet threat."

Peking thus proves to be on the side of the advocates of the notorious "Atlantism," the horizons of which are formed by the boundaries of blocs, of the perpetuation of splits in Europe and the whole world into opposing military-political groupings, which threatens the interests of common peace and international security with fatal consequences.

The European people know through their own experience how dangerous is the path along which Peking is pushing them into a "united front" with the advocates of the "cold war." The hopelessness of the Maoists' policy is all the more obvious in that it runs counter to the vital interests of the peoples of Europe, of all peace-loving powers. And there is no doubt that the future belongs to those powers who are struggling to strengthen all-European security, to bring order and develop cooperation, which is of prime significance for the strengthening of peace in the whole world.

★   ★   ★   ★   ★

AMERICA AND CHINA

Unlike Volume III, where we presented several selections from official and academic American sources, in this present Volume IV we have generally chosen to let the Chinese speak for themselves, particularly in the matters of domestic politics and foreign policy. Our introductions, while obviously presenting analyses, have nevertheless tried to guide readers into the selections so that in the end they could make their own judgments.

But at the very end of this volume, we faced the choice of presenting some American opinions, views, and analyses of China. The inclusion of the Joint Communiqué seemed obvious, but what criteria were to be used to make selections from the megatonnage of recent American writing on China? The outpouring after the ping-pong breakthrough of April 1971 by far dwarfs the American writing on Russia after the "thaw" of 1956. Traditionally, Americans have been far more interested in China than in Russia, and so this cultural fact helped a proliferation sparked by a desire to see what that China so long barred to Americans was like. In addition, there is a substantial amount of academic writing on China, ranging from the abstruse to the popular. Clearly we would have to use some criteria in making selections.

We believe that President Nixon's Kansas City speech of July 6, 1971 and Chou En-lai's reaction to it, as communicated to James Reston, indicates that changing relationships amongst the five great power centers of the world were the main factor in the Sino-American breakthrough. We further believe that the Sino-Soviet conflict was a major factor on the Chinese side, and that Washington's perception of that conflict similarly was a major factor on the American side. Many people in America have written on the triangular relationship between America, China, and Russia, but not all opinions, no matter how well informed, carry the same weight.

Under the Nixon Administration, the Navy has become the dominant of the three armed services. Navy opinions have played a much larger role in the formation of American foreign policy, particularly in East Asia, than one might think. Until recently, China was regarded as a grave threat to American national security. Navy opinions, as expressed in *Sea Power,* or on occasion in the *U.S. News and World Report,* were extremely hostile and often came close to advocating preventive war. However, as the selection by Lawrence Griswold, who contributes frequently to *Sea Power* on Asian subjects, indicates, the Navy view on China has changed. Not only does Griswold stress the warmth of the reception Nixon received in Peking, but he offers his own explanation for China's new stance: China is weak, threatened with fragmentation, and unstable. She is threatened by a vastly more powerful Soviet Union which also poses the chief threat to the United States, and specifically to the U.S. Navy. Griswold's views are undoubtedly widely held within U.S. military circles and therefore play a far greater role in the policy-making process than, say, an academic or a journalistic analysis.

Joseph Alsop is one of America's most renowned journalists. President Kennedy used to dine regularly with Alsop, and as regularly but at different times, with Walter Lippmann. Most American journalistic products blow away in the wind, as those of academics are buried in deep libraries, but Joseph Alsop is a different matter. His opinions count, perhaps in ways somewhat similar to those of "Observer" and "Commentator" in the *People's Daily.* During World War II, Alsop, after a brief captivity in Hong Kong under the Japanese, made his way to Chungking, where he was closely associated with Claire Chennault. Alsop shared Chennault's enthusiasm for Chiang-Kai-shek, and during the fifties and the sixties he expressed his views about "Red China" with his usual stridency and alarums of impending catastrophe. In 1960 he wrote of a "descending spiral" in China, implying collapse could come soon. On Vietnam, he has been an uncompromising hawk.

But from the early seventies on, Alsop, like many of his military friends, began to take the Sino-Soviet conflict seriously —if one million troops are deployed on either side, it must be for real. In 1971 he began writing about the horrendous possibilities of a Soviet preventive strike against China. With drumbeat regularity, he pounded home that theme. In the fall of 1972 American newspaper readers were surprised to read that Alsop had been invited to People's China. While still there, he began a series of pieces he himself called the most important reporting in his life. His pieces were unabashedly pro just about everything he saw, with none of the qualifications other American journalists often put in their writing to show they were not duped. He explained his conversion with a retort that he was not converted: if the Kuomintang had won, they could have done it too! Alsop, who regards himself as a China scholar, has always been pro-Chinese. He has just switched "his" Chinese from Taiwan to all of China.

The formal communiqué states the official and bureaucratically permissible formulation of U.S. policy toward People's China as it was in February 1972. Such documents should not be disregarded, for they often indicate the limits which restrain more adventuresome thrusts. Whatever Nixon actually wished to do when he was in Peking, his bureaucracies set limits. But as the impetus toward policy changes, the limits get worn down. The direction new policies are striving for are often spelled out in writings by people who are outside of but close to the power centers involved. The thrust of Griswold's and Alsop's pieces is the same: the United States should seek closer ties to China to counterbalance the Soviet threat.

★　　★　　★

GOVERNMENTS OF CHINA AND THE UNITED STATES*
Joint U.S.–China Communiqué

The Chinese and U.S. sides reached agreement on a joint communiqué on February 27 in Shanghai. Full text of the communiqué is as follows:

Joint Communiqué

President Richard Nixon of the United States of America visited the People's Republic of China at the invitation of Premier Chou En-lai of the People's Republic of China from February 21 to February 28, 1972. Accompanying the President were Mrs. Nixon, U.S. Secretary of State William Rogers, Assistant to the President Dr. Henry Kissinger, and other American officials.

President Nixon met with Chairman Mao Tse-tung of the Communist Party of China on February 21. The two leaders had a serious and frank exchange of views on Sino-U.S. relations and world affairs.

During the visit, extensive, earnest and frank discussions were held between President Nixon and Premier Chou En-lai on the normalization of relations between the United States of America and the People's Republic of China, as well as on other matters of interest to both sides. In addition, Secretary of State William Rogers and Foreign Minister Chi Peng-fei held talks in the same spirit.

President Nixon and his party visited Peking and viewed cultural, industrial and agricultural sites, and they also toured Hangchow and Shanghai where, continuing discussions with Chinese leaders, they viewed similar places of interest.

The leaders of the People's Republic of China and the United

* *Peking Review*, No. 9 (March 3, 1972), pp. 4–5.

States of America found it beneficial to have this opportunity, after so many years without contact, to present candidly to one another their views on a variety of issues. They reviewed the international situation in which important changes and great upheavals are taking place and expounded their respective positions and attitudes.

The Chinese side stated: Wherever there is oppression, there is resistance. Countries want independence, nations want liberation and the people want revolution—this has become the irresistible trend of history. All nations, big or small, should be equal; big nations should not bully the small and strong nations should not bully the weak. China will never be a superpower and it opposes hegemony and power politics of any kind. The Chinese side stated that it firmly supports the struggles of all the oppressed people and nations for freedom and liberation and that the people of all countries have the right to choose their social systems according to their own wishes and the right to safeguard the independence, sovereignty and territorial integrity of their own countries and oppose foreign aggression, interference, control and subversion. All foreign troops should be withdrawn to their own countries. The Chinese side expressed its firm support to the peoples of Vietnam, Laos and Cambodia in their efforts for the attainment of their goal and its firm support to the seven-point proposal of the Provisional Revolutionary Government of the Republic of South Vietnam and the elaboration of February this year on the two key problems in the proposal, and to the Joint Declaration of the Summit Conference of the Indochinese Peoples. It firmly supports the eight-point program for the peaceful unification of Korea put forward by the Government of the Democratic People's Republic of Korea on April 12, 1971, and the stand for the abolition of the "U.N. Commission for the Unification and Rehabilitation of Korea." It firmly opposes the revival and outward expansion of Japanese militarism and firmly supports the Japanese people's desire to build an independent, democratic, peaceful and neutral Japan. It firmly maintains that India and Pakistan should, in accordance with the United Nations resolutions on the India-Pakistan question, immediately withdraw all their forces to their respective territories and to their own sides of the cease-fire line in Jammu and Kashmir and firmly supports

the Pakistan Government and people in their struggle to preserve their independence and sovereignty and the people of
Jammu and Kashmir in their struggle for the right of self-
determination.

The U.S. side stated: Peace in Asia and peace in the world
requires efforts both to reduce immediate tensions and to eliminate the basic causes of conflict. The United States will work
for a just and secure peace: just, because it fulfills the aspirations of peoples and nations for freedom and progress; secure,
because it removes the danger of foreign aggression. The United
States supports individual freedom and social progress for all
the peoples of the world, free of outside pressure or intervention. The United States believes that the effort to reduce tensions is served by improving communication between countries
that have different ideologies so as to lessen the risks of confrontation through accident, miscalculation or misunderstand-
ing. Countries should treat each other with mutual respect and
be willing to compete peacefully, letting performance be the
ultimate judge. No country should claim infallibility and each
country should be prepared to reexamine its own attitudes for
the common good. The United States stressed that the peoples
of Indochina should be allowed to determine their destiny without outside intervention; its constant primary objective has been
a negotiated solution; the eight-point proposal put forward by
the Republic of Vietnam and the United States on January 27,
1972 represents a basis for the attainment of that objective; in
the absence of a negotiated settlement the United States envis-
ages the ultimate withdrawal of all U.S. forces from the region
consistent with the aim of self-determination for each country
of Indochina. The United States will maintain its close ties with
and support for the Republic of Korea; the United States will
support efforts of the Republic of Korea to seek a relaxation of
tension and increased communication in the Korean peninsula.
The United States places the highest value on its friendly relations with Japan; it will continue to develop the existing close
bonds. Consistent with the United Nations Security Council
Resolution of December 21, 1971, the United States favors the
continuation of the cease-fire between India and Pakistan and
the withdrawal of all military forces to within their own territories and to their own sides of the cease-fire line in Jammu

and Kashmir; the United States supports the right of the peoples of South Asia to shape their own future in peace, free of military threat, and without having the area become the subject of great-power rivalry.

There are essential differences between China and the United States in their social systems and foreign policies. However, the two sides agreed that countries, regardless of their social systems, should conduct their relations on the principles of respect for the sovereignty and territorial integrity of all states, non-aggression against other states, noninterference in the internal affairs of other states, equality and mutual benefit, and peaceful coexistence. International disputes should be settled on this basis, without resorting to the use or threat of force. The United States and the People's Republic of China are prepared to apply these principles to their mutual relations.

With these principles of international relations in mind the two sides stated that:

—progress toward the normalization of relations between China and the United States is in the interests of all countries;

—both wish to reduce the danger of international military conflict;

—neither should seek hegemony in the Asia-Pacific region and each is opposed to efforts by any other country or group of countries to establish such hegemony; and

—neither is prepared to negotiate on behalf of any third party or to enter into agreements or understandings with the other directed at other states.

Both sides are of the view that it would be against the interests of the peoples of the world for any major country to collude with another against other countries, or for major countries to divide up the world into spheres of interest.

The two sides reviewed the long-standing serious disputes between China and the United States. The Chinese side reaffirmed its position: The Taiwan question is the crucial question obstructing the normalization of relations between China and the United States; the Government of the People's Republic of China is the sole legal government of China; Taiwan is a province of China which has long been returned to the motherland; the liberation of Taiwan is China's internal affair in which no other country has the right to interfere; and all U.S. forces and military installations must be withdrawn from Taiwan. The Chinese Government firmly opposes any activities which aim at the creation of "one China, one Taiwan," "one China, two governments," "two Chinas," an "independent Taiwan" or advocate that "the status of Taiwan remains to be determined."

The U.S. side declared: The United States acknowledges that all Chinese on either side of the Taiwan Strait maintain there is but one China and that Taiwan is a part of China. The United States Government does not challenge that position. It reaffirms its interest in a peaceful settlement of the Taiwan question by the Chinese themselves. With this prospect in mind, it affirms the ultimate objective of the withdrawal of all U.S. forces and military installations from Taiwan. In the meantime, it will progressively reduce its forces and military installations on Taiwan as the tension in the area diminishes.

The two sides agreed that it is desirable to broaden the understanding between the two peoples. To this end, they discussed specific areas in such fields as science, technology, culture, sports and journalism, in which people-to-people contacts and exchanges would be mutually beneficial. Each side undertakes to facilitate the further development of such contacts and exchanges.

Both sides view bilateral trade as another area from which mutual benefit can be derived, and agreed that economic relations based on equality and mutual benefit are in the interest of the peoples of the two countries. They agree to facilitate the progressive development of trade between their two countries.

The two sides agreed that they will stay in contact through various channels, including the sending of a senior U.S. representative to Peking from time to time for concrete consultations to further the normalization of relations between the two countries and continue to exchange views on issues of common interest.

The two sides expressed the hope that the gains achieved during this visit would open up new prospects for the relations between the two countries. They believe that the normalization of relations between the two countries is not only in the interest of the Chinese and American peoples but also contributes to the relaxation of tension in Asia and the world.

President Nixon, Mrs. Nixon and the American party expressed their appreciation for the gracious hospitality shown them by the Government and people of the People's Republic of China.

LAWRENCE GRISWOLD*
The Eagle and the Dragon:
Washington-Peking Contact Has
Broad Naval Implications

One of the major, if invisible, products of President Nixon's visit to Peking was the strengthening of continental China, a country as seriously menaced by internal fragmentation as by its ancient external enemies, Russia and Japan. If, as appeared increasingly likely during recent years, that country were again to slide into the chaos of warlordism and political disintegration, the future of all Korea, both North and South, as well as Taiwan, would inevitably become prime targets of the Kremlin. Within too few years, the western Pacific, including the Philippines, even Japan, could be gathered up, however reluctantly, into a Russian-ruled East Asian political sphere. This prospect, recognized independently by Peking and Washington, directed the tentative probings by both sides leading to Nixon's announcement of his trip in his speech of July 15, 1971. Only the American leader could leave his country without jeopardizing his Government.

Contrary to the impression conveyed by the press and pontificated by TV's instant experts, President Nixon was warmly greeted by China's Chou En-lai, who rose from a sickbed to welcome his American guest at the airport. A broadcast by the BBC's men in Peking, on the eve of Nixon's departure from Hawaii, predicted that Chou's recent illness—an item ignored by the American press—would prevent his attendance. Another

* Lawrence Griswold, "The Eagle and the Dragon" in *Sea Power* (April 1972), pp. 28–32.

broadcast from Hamburg echoed that opinion. Nevertheless the Chinese premier was there. The fact that there was "no enthusiastic welcome" by cheering mobs was dwelt upon. Except for the long Guard of Honor, the large military band, the group of high Chinese officials standing with the Premier (and, doubtless, other large groups behind the television cameras) and a few busy functionaries, the airport was indeed deserted. That fact underscored the evident sincerity of the welcome. "Cheering mobs" or "hostile mobs" must be carefully organized, as TV newsmen should be well aware. At least, it showed no stage effects at the normally empty airport.

And there were other, more personal, indications of warmth apparently unrecognized by reporters, commencing with the firm and protracted handshake of the Premier—a significant gesture to the meticulous Chinese who even as Communists retain a Confucian nicety. Then, there was the careful, if laborious, rendering of *The Star-Spangled Banner* by the Red Army Band; the ostentatious display of the American and Chinese flags, end to end on the sides of the banquet hall; the near intimacy shown by Chou En-lai when he selected morsels of food from his own plate and deftly transferred them to Nixon's— a gesture common enough between close friends or to a highly esteemed guest, but by no means a casual courtesy—and then, to mention one other, there was Chou's personal collection and delivery of the glasses when he invited the President to join him in a toast to their two countries.

TERRITORIAL INTEGRITY

Despite his physical indisposition, Chou remained with his guests after the conferences in a tour to Hangchow's ancient palaces and up to the final leave-taking at the Shanghai airport —all demonstrable evidence of his wish for a closer relationship. Insofar as inherited national policies permitted them, the American and Chinese leaders expressly created the basis of an eventual rapprochement by their statements that a *modus vivendi* ("peaceful coexistence") was both possible and desirable.

Nixon's visit could not solve Chou's internal problems, but

it gave "face" to an administration suffering from the blunders of the recent past and it gave warning to external enemies of Washington's deep concern with the territorial integrity of all eastern Asia.

Eurasian monolithic communism, as directed by the Moscow-Peking Axis, had shown its first structural fault in 1955 with a Manchurian revolt against Mao's "running dog alliance" with Moscow, an alliance as cynically unrealistic and almost as short-lived as the Ribbentrop-Molotov Pact of 1939. By 1962, Peking had found a more congenial ally in Indonesia's Sukarno, but when the formative Jakarta-Peking Axis collapsed in 1965, China was an isolated and friendless country, committed to internal and external policies, including the export of Maoist Communism, which it was simply incapable of fulfilling. And, despite Peking's suppressive efforts, older Chinese revolutionaries had outgrown the undigested slogans of the late 1940's and were backsliding into non-communistic traditional patterns of existence. Mao's ill-advised attempts to reverse the process by massive social experimentation, such as the "Hundred Flowers" and "Great Leap Forward" programs, simply enlarged and expedited it.

Mao's final desperate expedient, the "Great Cultural Revolution," an attempt to reincarnate the ideological exaltation of his own generation among the teen-agers of China's great cities, succeeded only in destroying the remnants of internal cohesion. The excesses of youthful Red Guards aimed at the extirpation of the threatening "Four Olds"—old ideas, old habits, old customs, old culture—boomeranged. Already suffering from cerebral sclerosis, Mao Tse-tung was forced into retirement and Chou En-lai, a better-informed and far more moderate leader, assumed direction of China's government.

HANGOVER IN PEKING

Since the frenzied bloodshed of the "Cultural Revolution," China's situation, to put it mildly, has been unstable. Open rebellion against Peking and "centralism" erupted generally among the southern provinces late in 1967 and by the following year had spread to the far northern province of Heilungkiang, bordering the Amur River and Siberia. In the south, from Kwangtung (Canton) to Sinkiang's common frontier with Russia, revitalized provincialism sprang up and threatened a revival of the ancient Sung Empire in a modern South Chinese Federation, an impracticable union of the provinces south of the Yangtze River. But each of the provinces held potential warlords, such as Sinkiang's General Wang En-mao, and the specter of provincial armies overrunning the villages, as during the 1920's and 1930's, could not be exorcised. Only the fighting at Canton was observable to the crystal-gazers in Hong Kong, but Peking was conscious enough of their generality and Peking's armies had all they could do to check them. By the summer of 1970, reports from Peking announced that the rebellion had been successfully suppressed. But the embers remain.

Since 1965, when the still-formative Peking-Jakarta Axis fell apart, the Kremlin has been awaiting just such an opportunity. In 1948, under heavy international pressure, the Russian army of occupation was withdrawn from Manchuria (leaving industrial ruin in its wake). But that vast and rich area, bulging vulnerably northward between Soviet-satellite Mongolia and Russia's Maritime (Primorskiy Kray) Province with the major naval base and city of Vladivostok at its southern tip, and extending eastward to North Korea and the Sea of Japan, is as alluring as ever. If Peking's large but ill-equipped armies should be dispersed throughout continental China in another widespread campaign of suppression, or should suffer internal disorganization through provincial secessions, another Russian occupation of Manchuria would be protested only by Japan. Until late last February, mutual Sino-American aloofness, even enmity, would have inhibited official interference by Washington. Then, following the pattern expressed by the ancient Chinese proverb, "Who rules Manchuria rules China," Russian influence, predictably, would expand southward.

As this is written, Russian armies are poised along Sinkiang's frontiers from Mongolia to Tibet and Kashmir and, at the north, from Chita and Lake Baikal to Khabarovsk and down to Vladivostok; about 44 to 50 divisions, all well-supported by military and naval aircraft on many air bases. About the same number of Chinese troops, but deficient in tanks, aircraft, artillery and ammunition, confront them. The opposing forces are not equal and if Peking must withdraw troops to cope with internal insurrections, the road before the Russian Army would be open.

In terms of air power and sea power, Russia has no‿challengers anywhere in Asia. Army air bases are judiciously distributed everywhere along the Sino-Russian frontier but the weight of their force is centered along the Amur to its meeting with the Ussuri River, dividing Manchuria and the Maritime Province. Within both Khabarovsk and Komsomolsk are not only major air force bases but manufacturers of military aircraft, and both are important industrially.

PEKING AND THE STATUS QUO

As a competitor with Moscow for the political profits accruing from the aggrandizement of North Vietnam, Peking's China has served as a reluctant transmission line for Russian-made military hardware destined for Hanoi, especially those carried by railway from Khabarovsk. On several occasions, entire trainloads have been hijacked by southern Chinese. On other occasions, the destruction of railroad bridges within Vietnam by American bombers has required Chinese assistance for repairs, even reconstruction. Nevertheless, statistics show a drop in Hanoi-bound munitions since the peak year of 1967, the year preceding the Tet offensive, when Russian deliveries approximated $500 million and the contribution of Peking amounted to, roughly, a third of that total. At the end of 1970, the last year recorded statistically, the value of supplies, military and economic, had fallen to $75 million from China and $100 million from Russia. How much military help arrived at Haiphong by sea is less easy to calculate. However, during the six-month period ending last Feb. 29, 1972, nearly 100 merchant ships *of all flags* were listed as having arrived in North Vietnam from Chinese ports. And an undisclosed number of those ships bore the flags of NATO members.

Since 1968 and the retirement of Mao's aggressive leadership, Peking's dilemma has been even more acute than that of Washington. A truculent North Vietnam lies just below southern China's most intransigent provinces. For Peking to terminate Mao's commitments to Hanoi would amount to, in effect, handing over North Vietnam to Russia and so completing a Russian encirclement of continental China. With Moscow abetting and arming the warlords of the still-simmering southern provinces, Peking's necessity for national unity would be heavily mortgaged, if not fatally compromised.

Peking's situation is precarious. Even if Chou En-lai were imbued with the reckless aggressiveness of Mao Tse-tung, China lacks the capability of competing with Russia. It has only token numbers of modern tanks, insufficient aircraft and artillery for its own needs; no sophisticated antiaircraft missilery at all and no exportable electronic equipment. Few, if any, of those items now pass through China; they are delivered to North Vietnam by sea from Vladivostok and the important nearby port of Nakhodka. For the present, at least, Peking's ability to rule continental China is as important to the United States as it is to Chou En-lai. If his control were to collapse in revolution, Russia's ambitions in East Asia would be easily gained. China's overrated nuclear strength lies well in the future, in terms of real capability.

Because the preservation of the legal status quo in East Asia, from Vietnam to Korea, is essential to the security of the United States, it must also include the territorial integrity of China and Japan because expansionist Russia is still persistently maneuvering for domination of the western Pacific coast.

THE VIEW FROM VLADIVOSTOK

Until October, 1945, except for the long, icy route to the North Atlantic around the North Cape of Norway and past Iceland into Denmark Strait, Russia was still a land-locked nation. Geographically barred from the Atlantic by the narrow passage of Ore Sund, between Denmark and Sweden, and from the Mediterranean by the Turkish Bosporus and Dardanelles Straits, Russian egress from its usable, ice-free (with the help of ice-breakers in winter) ports of Vladivostok and Nakhodka, only nominally Pacific Ocean ports, was restricted to the Strait of Korea, between the southern tip of Korea and the Japanese main islands of Honshu and Kyushu, a strait divided by the

Japanese island of Tsushima where Admiral Rodzhesvenski's unwieldy armada came to its final grief at the guns of the Japanese Navy in 1905. In wartime, the Strait of Japan—as long as Japan is free to act in its own defense—would be useless. Accordingly, after its Seven Day War with Japan in August 1945, the Russian Navy made other arrangements for an uncertain future.

By the terms of their surrender, the Japanese ceded the Chishima (Kuriles) to Russia, along with southern Sakhalin, the large island lying in the Sea of Okhotsk off the Siberian coast. However—and this is an important point now in dispute—the cession of the Kuriles did not include the two long islands extending north from Hokkaido called Kunashiri and Etorofu, separated by a relatively ice-free and highly navigable strait named after La Perouse, the eighteenth-century French navigator who discovered it. In October 1945, Kunashiri and Etorofu were summarily occupied by the Russian Navy, which promptly staked out its own establishments along the lands adjacent to the straits and claimed them for the U.S.S.R.

The Japanese were outraged but helpless, and whatever appeals were made to General Douglas MacArthur appeared to end in futility. La Perouse Strait, widely opening on the waters of the North Pacific, was renamed Proliv Yekateriniy by the Soviets, and the Russian Navy based at Vladivostok and other ports higher on the Maritime Province and in the Sea of Okhotsk is now free to range wherever it wishes regardless of the political climate. If Proliv Yekateriniy is within range of Japanese military airfields, the airfields are also within range of Russian air bases in and around the Maritime Province, and in this as in ASW submarines, the Russians have the advantage.

But Tokyo has not yet thrown in the sponge. Technically, a state of war between Japan and Russia still exists. True, an "arrangement" has permitted an exchange of "ambassadors," but a Treaty of Peace formalizing Japanese concessions has yet to be signed, and ownership of the two strategic islands of Kunashiri and Etorofu is certain to be a major obstacle to agreement. The United States, having failed to seize the strategic islands in August 1945 as the Japanese fully expected, is offi-

cially neutral but, unofficially, it supports Japanese ownership.
Obviously, American interests are not served by Russian own-
ership. And Japan can cite its recovery of Okinawa from the
United States as a precedent.

THE KURILES AND KAMCHATKA

The Kuriles are bleak, a closely linked chain of jagged volcanic
mountain peaks dropping from the tip of the peninsula of
Kamchatka to Japanese-claimed Etorofu. Stormy, foggy, ice-clad
and separated by seething, treacherous currents, studded with
uncharted rocks, with the Kamchatka Peninsula they enclose
the ice-packed Sea of Okhotsk and, excepting La Perouse, constitute a nearly impenetrable barrier to shipping. Surrounded
by drifting packs of seaweed, an unnecessarily additional obstacle to navigation, they are sparsely populated by people of
mixed Ainu and Aleut stock. The solitary asset of the northern
Kuriles is fish. The Japanese, for centuries, have mined the
rich sulphur deposits of Etorofu and Kunashiri. The adjacent
Habomai Group and Shikotan, now occupied by Russia, are
also only a few miles from Hokkaido. The length of the Kuriles
chain, from the southern tip of Kamchatka to Hokkaido, is
about 800 nautical miles. With the Japanese and Ryukyu
islands, the barrier east of Siberia extends almost to Taiwan.
    Without almost continuous use of icebreakers, the Kamchatka
Peninsula, with its naval base for the Russian Fifth Fleet—the
northern division of the Vladivostok-based Pacific Fleet—at the
usually ice-bound port of Petropavlovsk on its southeastern
coast, is a dreary wasteland of glacial rock and stunted conifers.
Open to the extreme northern Pacific and the Bering Strait
during July and August, it can be made an operational base for
submarines throughout the year. Petropavlovsk also contains a
naval air base, with repair and docking facilities for submarines,
ASW frigates, patrol craft and icebreakers. Minelayers and
sweepers also form a substantial part of the northern Fifth
Fleet.
    Centering upon the westward approaches to La Perouse
Strait, the sea-distance from Vladivostok is over 800 miles;
from the auxiliary base at Magadan, to the north on the Sea

of Okhotsk, it exceeds 1,100 miles. For several years, an oil refinery at Vladivostok has been the major source of fuel for the Russian Navy, and the refineries located among the Russian Maritime Province cities have been forced to rely on tankers transporting the fuel, in company with icebreakers, across the Northern (Arctic) Ocean route from Murmansk. As the Russian Pacific Fleet increases in strength, demands for fuel and lubricants surpass the total capacity of the local refineries and, some years ago, Russian engineers commenced the construction of a pipeline from Tyumen, not far from Sverdlovsk in the south central Urals, across Siberia to Khabarovsk for distribution to storage tanks at Vladivostok and Nakhodka and to naval stations to the north, such as Nikolaevsk, at the mouth of the Amur River for surface transportation to Petropavlovsk. Now the T-K (Tyumen-Khabarovsk) pipeline—originally planned to cut through north China from Mongolia through Manchuria to Komsomolsk—means a shorter and more economical route, and one less vulnerable to interruption.

RUSSIA'S MAIN TARGET

Completion of the 48-inch T-K pipeline, with its annual capacity of 50 to 90 million metric tons, could signal a more rapid build-up of the Russian Pacific Fleet's surface components than has taken place since 1968. Less than half of the 150 submarines now attached to the Pacific Fleet are nuclear-fueled. All of the surface fleet's 320 warships, including patrol boats and minesweepers, and headed by at least 10 KRESTA, KRIVAK, KYNDA and KASHIN missile-armed "heavies," are conventionally powered. Driven by gas-turbine and diesel engines, Moscow's surface navy needs petroleum products for propulsion. And so do the Army and naval aircraft now crowding the airports of the Maritime Province and Kamchatka.

The main target of the Russian drive to the Eastern Asian coast has been blunted by the recent U.S.-Chinese talks and the Russians may be expected to try to reverse or alter the results to their advantage when President Nixon goes to Moscow next month.

Though the growing encirclement of China, clear enough in

mid-July last year when the President first announced his forth-coming trip to Peking, has almost certainly been accelerated by the addition of Bangladesh to Moscow's clientele, including India, Japan's legal claim to Kunashiri, La Perouse Strait and Etorofu must also share in the timing. Following years of ex-ploratory preliminaries, the Russo-Japanese Peace Treaty is scheduled for negotiation by September, and Japan intends to put up a fight for the repossession of those islands and their vital strait.

And for Americans who recall the "Day of Infamy," Etorofu should have a special meaning because it was from Etorofu's wide and secure anchorage that the Japanese Battle Fleet set forth through La Perouse Strait to attack Pearl Harbor.

JOSEPH ALSOP*
The Soviet Buildup
On China's Frontier

PEKING, CHINA

During the earlier part of my stay here, I had a constant sense of being carefully pretested, both politically and intellectually.

The tests took the form of a series of conversations with offi-cials in an ascending order of importance. They included a long luncheon with the leading men of the *People's Daily* and the even more important Chinese official news agency, Hsinhua. They culminated in three fascinating hours of talk with the brilliant vice-minister of Foreign Affairs, Chiao Kuan-hua, who is known to be particularly close to Prime Minister Chou En-lai.

My sense of being tested was confirmed when the Prime Minister finally sent for my wife and me. Things I had said earlier somehow cropped up, even though I had not yet said

* Joseph Alsop, "The Soviet Buildup on China's Frontier," in the *San Francisco Chronicle* (December 6, 1972).

them to Chou En-lai himself. Thus this trying-out process must be seen as having genuine meaning.

The meaning was reasonably bleak, too; for the central subject of the tryers-out was the triangular relationship between the United States, China and the Soviet Union. And the main sub-theme was the danger of a Soviet preventive attack on China.

One does not want to be too simplistic. The delay in the Vietnamese cease-fire was certainly raised, although not so vigorously as when Chou En-lai received me. Again, the Helsinki talks about force reductions in Europe also recurred with even greater regularity. But here it was obvious that the Chinese were deeply concerned lest mutual force reductions in Europe should permit the Russians to deploy even more divisions on China's frontier.

In a later talk, I was criticized for "judging everything by weapons." I could only reply that the basic problem seemed to me to be political, in the sense that the Russians still had to decide "what to do about China." I then asked whether the growth of China's nuclear strength would not control the timing of this vital decision. "I'm afraid you are probably right," was the answering comment.

There were other striking aspects of this series of talks, too. Although Nikita Khrushchev was the man who pulled out the Soviet experts and began the break with China, the government headed by Leonid Brezhnev was invariably decribed as "much worse."

The growing influence of the Soviet military caste on Soviet political decisions was treated as a known fact. The "unmasking" and death of Lin Piao was also treated as most important to the Russians, because it had "removed their only hope" of a differently oriented Chinese government.

In sum, this remarkable series of political talks made one thing perfectly clear to me. The people at home are deluding themselves, who comfortably suppose that Chinese policy is chiefly influenced by such currently unalarming factors as "fear of Japanese Militarism." The unending Soviet military buildup on China's frontier is the true mainspring.

Peking's Awesome
*Underground City**

PEKING, CHINA

This busy city has few busier commercial streets than Ta Sha La. Besides a whole series of specialty shops, the short street has two department stores, an opera house, two movie houses and a couple of hotels, altogether employing about 1800 people.

Ta Sha La also has a secret. I learned of it in a bustling store where they sell the padded coats Peking people wear against the cold. Ta Sha La's Gloria Steinem, fair but formidable, dramatically revealed the secret by stepping on a hidden spring.

Whereupon a section of the store's flooring slid back. A concrete staircase appeared steeply descending into the earth. And so our party went down to inspect one section of Peking's all but incredible system of air-raid shelters.

Ta Sha La, it must be understood, is only one of countless districts into which Peking is divided. The shelters are tunnels, all brick and concrete built, and all wide and high enough for three tall men to walk abreast. Ta Sha La alone has a couple of kilometers of these tunnels all connecting, in turn, with similar tunnels in neighboring districts.

All this was begun in 1969 when the Russians came so close to launching a preventive nuclear attack on China. Under a full-time staff of four, the Ta Sha La tunnels were built by the employees of the street's enterprises.

Nowadays, in fact, there are two complete cities of Peking, one above ground and another underground. The theory of the

* Joseph Alsop, "Peking's Awesome Underground City," in the *San Francisco Chronicle* (December 1, 1972).

shelter system is that of the Soviet Civil-Defense System—to move the people safely out of the city in case of threatened attack.

Peking has this enormous network of underground tunnels, while Moscow solely depends on early warning for timely evacuation. In sum, the Peking Civil-Defense System is ten times better than that of Moscow.

All this is pretty awesome and every other major city in China today, and almost all the smaller ones, too, have close to identical shelter systems.

In order to perceive the true cost here, you have only to consider how Peking people live. Fairly highly placed officials with wives and two children must be content with two-room flats. The same holds true for workers. For the investment put into the underground city, every family in Peking could surely have been provided with one more room of precious living space.

No government in its senses could have ordered such enormous sacrifices and burdensome investments without a grimly serious, grimly urgent motive. There is no doubt at all about the motive, either. It was the fear of Soviet surprise attack which became acute when the Soviet government vainly asked for U.S. support for such an attack in 1969.

APPENDIX

The Tenth National Congress
of the Communist Party of China

As we noted in the introduction to this reader, our main work was completed by the end of 1972. It was obvious by that time that the Ninth Congress of the Chinese Communist Party, far from placing the capstone on the Cultural Revolution, was only the prelude to another major political struggle among China's leaders to establish a stable coalition of forces which could carry the nation into the post-Mao Tse-tung era. This final struggle took more than four years and has been labeled by the Chinese as "the tenth major struggle between the two lines" in the fifty-year history of the Chinese Communist Party. It is therefore the Tenth National Congress of the Chinese Party, held from August 24 to 28, 1973, that will probably be considered by historians as the last act and consolidation of the Great Proletarian Cultural Revolution. The question which only the future can decide is the extent to which the Tenth Congress either consolidated and incorporated, or compromised and retracted, the values, goals, and world outlook of the Cultural Revolution.

Perhaps the most dramatic change in Chinese policy since the Ninth Congress has been in foreign affairs. The détente with the United States, the elevation of the Soviet Union to the position of China's main enemy, and the emergence of China as a major power within the international system were all confirmed and established as official policy by the Tenth Congress.

There was a certain logic to the fact that the two men who had simultaneously founded the Chinese Communist Party in Shanghai and Paris in 1921, more than a half century later, presided over the Congress which laid the basis for turning over the revolution to a new generation. Mao Tse-tung and Chou En-lai, the two great statesmen produced by the Chinese Revolution, represent the dialectic and the combination of social forces and organizational efficiency that made the victory of the Chinese Revolution possible. In political terms, Mao and Chou put together a coalition of power at the Tenth Congress which represented the major social groupings of a vast nation. This coalition included representatives of the corps of trained Party functionaries, the army, the workers, peasants, intellectuals, youth, and women. The overthrow of Lin Piao and Ch'en Po-ta indicated that the army and the radicals were not capable of providing the broad base of leadership necessary to unite the vast population of China. The election of Wang Hung-wen, a thirty-eight-year-old Shanghai worker, to the third highest position in the nation was a sign that the Cultural Revolution had in fact generated some new leaders who emerged from the masses. And the election of Chang Ch'un-ch'iao, one of the most capable leaders of the Cultural Revolution, to the post of Secretary-General of the Party further established Shanghai as one of the most progressive bastions of power in the nation.

The Tenth Congress once again proved the remarkable ability of the Chinese to create harmony out of chaos. But the lack of policy pronouncements on the economy, education, and other vital internal matters pointed to continued struggle among groups over many unresolved issues created by the Cultural Revolution. One thing was made clear by the Congress, and that was that these conflicts would now be fought out inside the Party. After the resolution of the Lin Piao question, involving both foreign policy and the rehabilitation of the old Party cadres, the resurrection of the Party as the leading organization in the nation stands as the fundamental action of the Tenth Congress. After years of experimentation with new organs of power, such as the three-in-one revolutionary committees, China has returned to the concept of the vanguard party which "must exercise leadership in everything." Nevertheless, the Cultural Revolution has left its mark on the organization and ideology of the reconstituted Party. Eight million new members were taken into the Party from the activists produced by the Cultural Revolution, to bring the total membership of the Party up to twenty-eight million. And the institution of the cultural revolution was written into the new Party Constitution: "Revolutions like this will have to be carried out many times in the future." It remains to be seen whether the Party in the future will call upon the masses to supervise Party leaders and pull out new capitalist roaders.

We have included the complete text of the Party Constitution approved by the Tenth Congress in our selections, since it will presumably govern Chinese political life for the foreseeable future. For reasons of space we have not included the full texts of Premier Chou En-lai's report to the Congress or Wang Hung-wen's report on the revision of the Party Constitution. Instead, we have chosen those excerpts that have proved most interesting to us, and do not intend that our selections be understood either as summaries of the complete reports or substitutes for the whole. Readers who wish to study the full texts will find them in the combined issues of *Peking Review* 35 and 36, published on September 7, 1973.

CHOU EN-LAI*
Report to the Tenth National Congress of The Communist Party of China

ON THE LINE OF THE NINTH NATIONAL CONGRESS

. . . As we all know, the political report to the Ninth Congress was drawn up under Chairman Mao's personal guidance. Prior to the congress, Lin Piao had produced a draft political report in collaboration with Chen Po-ta. They were opposed to continuing the revolution under the dictatorship of the proletariat, contending that the main task after the Ninth Congress was to develop production. This was a refurbished version under new conditions of the same revisionist trash that Liu Shao-chi and Chen Po-ta had smuggled into the resolution of the Eighth Congress, which alleged that the major contradiction in our country was not the contradiction between the proletariat and the bourgeoisie, but that "between the advanced socialist system and the backward productive forces of society." Naturally, this draft by Lin Piao and Chen Po-ta was rejected by the Central Committee. Lin Piao secretly supported Chen Po-ta in the latter's open opposition to the political report drawn up under Chairman Mao's guidance, and it was only after his attempts were frustrated that Lin Piao grudgingly accepted the political line of the Central Committee and read its political report to the congress. However, during and after the Ninth Congress, Lin Piao continued with his conspiracy and sabotage in spite of the admonishments, rebuffs and efforts to save him by Chairman Mao and the Party's Central Committee. He went further to start a counter-revolutionary coup d'état, which was aborted, at the Second Plenary Session of the Ninth Central

* Chou En-lai, report delivered on August 24 and adopted on August 28, 1973. Reprinted in *Peking Review*, Nos. 35–36 (September 7, 1973), pp. 17–25.

Committee in August 1970. Then in March 1971 he drew up
the plan for an armed counter-revolutionary coup d'état entitled *Outline of Project "571"*, and on September 8, he
launched the coup in a wild attempt to assassinate our great
leader Chairman Mao and set up a rival central committee.
On September 13, after his conspiracy had collapsed, Lin Piao
surreptitiously boarded a plane, fled as a defector to the Soviet
revisionists in betrayal of the Party and country, and died
in a crash at Undur Khan in the People's Republic of Mongolia. . . .

ON THE VICTORY OF SMASHING THE
LIN PIAO ANTI-PARTY CLIQUE

. . . As early as January 13, 1967, when the Great Proletarian
Cultural Revolution was at high tide, Brezhnev, the chief of
the Soviet revisionist renegade clique, frantically attacked
China's Great Proletarian Cultural Revolution in his speech
at a mass rally in Gorky Region and openly declared that
they stood on the side of the Liu Shao-ch'i renegade clique,
saying that the downfall of this clique was "a big tragedy
for all real communists in China, and we express our deep
sympathy to them." At the same time, Brezhnev publicly announced continuation of the policy of subverting the leadership
of the Chinese Communist Party, and ranted about "struggling
. . . for bringing it back to the road of internationalism."
(*Pravda*, January 14, 1967) In March 1967 another chief of
the Soviet revisionists said even more brazenly at mass rallies
in Moscow that "sooner or later the healthy forces expressing
the true interests of China will have their decisive say . . . and
achieve the victory of Marxist-Leninist ideas in their great
country." (*Pravda*, March 4 and 10, 1967) What they called
"healthy forces" are nothing but the decadent forces representing the interests of social-imperialism and all the exploiting
classes; what they meant by "their decisive say" is the usurpation of the supreme power of the Party and the state; what
they meant by "victory of ideas" is the reign of sham Marxism-
Leninism and real revisionism over China; and what they
meant by the "road of internationalism" is the road of reduc-

ing China to a colony of Soviet revisionist social-imperialism. The Brezhnev renegade clique has impetuously voiced the common wish of the reactionaries and blurted out the ultra-Rightist nature of the Lin Piao anti-Party clique.

Lin Piao and his handful of sworn followers were a counter-revolutionary conspiratorial clique "who never showed up without a copy of *Quotations* in hand and never opened their mouths without shouting 'Long Live' and who spoke nice things to your face but stabbed you in the back." The essence of the counter-revolutionary revisionist line they pursued and the criminal aim of the counterrevolutionary armed coup d'état they launched were to usurp the supreme power of the Party and the state, thoroughly betray the line of the Ninth Congress, radically change the Party's basic line and policies for the entire historical period of socialism, turn the Marxist-Leninist Chinese Communist Party into a revisionist, fascist party, subvert the dictatorship of the proletariat and restore capitalism. Inside China, they wanted to reinstate the land-lord and bourgeois classes, which our Party, Army and people had overthrown with their own hands under the leadership of Chairman Mao, and to institute a feudal-comprador-fascist dictatorship. Internationally, they wanted to capitulate to Soviet revisionist social-imperialism and ally themselves with imperialism, revisionism and reaction to oppose China, communism and revolution. . . .

In the last fifty years our Party has gone through ten major struggles between the two lines. The collapse of the Lin Piao anti-Party clique does not mean the end of the two-line struggle within the Party. Enemies at home and abroad all understand that the easiest way to capture a fortress is from within. It is much more convenient to have the capitalist roaders in power who have sneaked into the Party do the job of subverting the dictatorship of the proletariat than for the landlords and capitalists to come to the fore themselves; this is especially true when the landlords and capitalists are already quite odious in society. In the future, even after classes have disappeared, there will still be contradictions between the superstructure and the economic base and between the relations of production and the productive forces. And there will still be two-line struggles reflecting these contradictions, i.e., struggles between the advanced and the backward and between the correct and the erroneous. Moreover, socialist society covers a considerably long historical period. Throughout this historical period, there are classes, class contradictions and class struggle, there is the struggle between the socialist road and the capitalist road, there is the danger of capitalist restoration and there is the threat of subversion and aggression by imperialism and social-imperialism. For a long time to come, there will still be two-line struggles within the Party, reflecting these contradictions, and such struggles will occur ten, twenty or thirty times. Lin Piaos will appear again and so will persons like Wang Ming, Liu Shao-chi, Peng Teh-huai and Kao Kang. This is something independent of man's will. Therefore, all comrades in our Party must be fully prepared mentally for the struggles in the long years to come and be able to make the best use of the situation and guide the struggle to victory for the proletariat, no matter how the class enemy may change his tactics. . . .

Chairman Mao has constantly taught us: It is imperative to note that one tendency covers another. The opposition to Chen Tu-hsiu's Right opportunism which advocated "all alliance, no struggle" covered Wang Ming's "Left" opportunism which advocated "all struggle, no alliance." The rectification of Wang Ming's "Left" deviation covered Wang Ming's Right deviation. The struggle against Liu Shao-chi's revisionism covered Lin Piao's revisionism. There were many instances in the past where one tendency covered another and when a tide came, the majority went along with it, while only a few withstood it. Today, in both international and domestic struggles, tendencies may still occur similar to those of the past, namely, when there was an alliance with the bourgeoisie, necessary struggles were forgotten and when there was a split with the bourgeoisie, the possibility of an alliance under given conditions was forgotten. It is required of us to do our best to discern and rectify such tendencies in time. And when a wrong tendency surges towards us like a rising tide, we must not fear isolation and must dare to go against the tide and brave it through. Chairman Mao states, **"Going against the tide is a Marxist-Leninist principle."** In daring to go against the tide and adhere to the correct line in the ten struggles between the two lines within the Party, Chairman Mao is our example and teacher. Every one of our comrades should learn well from Chairman Mao and hold to this principle.

Under the guidance of the correct line represented by Chairman Mao, the great, glorious and correct Communist Party of China has had prolonged trials of strength with the class enemies both inside and outside the Party, at home and abroad, armed and unarmed, overt and covert. Our Party has not been divided or crushed. On the contrary, Chairman Mao's Marxist-Leninist line has further developed and our Party grown ever stronger. Historical experience convinces us that **"this Party of ours has a bright future."** Just as Chairman Mao predicted in 1966, **"If the Right stage an anti-Communist coup d'état in China, I am sure they will know no peace either and their rule will most probably be short-lived, because it will not be tolerated by the revolutionaries, who represent the interests of the people making up more than 90 per cent of the population."** So long as our whole Party bears in mind historical experience, and upholds Chairman Mao's correct line, all the schemes of the bourgeoisie for restoration are bound to fail. No matter how many more major struggles between the two lines may occur, the laws of history will not change, and the revolution in China and the world will eventually triumph.

ON THE SITUATION AND OUR TASKS

. . . The present international situation is one characterized by great disorder on the earth. "The wind sweeping through the tower heralds a rising storm in the mountains." This aptly depicts how the basic world contradictions as analyzed by Lenin show themselves today. Relaxation is a temporary and superficial phenomenon, and great disorder will continue. Such great disorder is a good thing for the people, not a bad thing. It throws the enemies into confusion and causes division among them, while it arouses and tempers the people, thus helping the international situation develop further in the direction favorable to the people and unfavorable to imperialism, modern revisionism and all reaction.

The awakening and growth of the Third World is a major event in contemporary international relations. The Third

World has strengthened its unity in the struggle against hegemonism and power politics of the superpowers and is playing an ever more significant role in international affairs. The great victories won by the people of Vietnam, Laos and Cambodia in their war against U.S. aggression and for national salvation have strongly encouraged the people of the world in their revolutionary struggles against imperialism and colonialism. A new situation has emerged in the Korean people's struggle for the independent and peaceful reunification of their fatherland. The struggles of the Palestinian and other Arab peoples against aggression by Israeli Zionism, the African peoples' struggles against colonialism and racial discrimination and the Latin American peoples' struggles for maintaining 200-nautical-mile territorial waters or economic zones all continue to forge ahead. The struggles of the Asian, African and Latin American peoples to win and defend national independence and safeguard state sovereignty and national resources have further deepened and broadened. The just struggles of the Third World as well as of the people of Europe, North America and Oceania support and encourage each other. Countries want independence, nations want liberation, and the people want revolution—this has become an irresistible historical trend.

Lenin said that **"an essential feature of imperialism is the rivalry between several Great Powers in the striving for hegemony."** Today, it is mainly the two nuclear superpowers—the U.S. and the U.S.S.R.—that are contending for hegemony. While hawking disarmament, they are actually expanding their armaments every day. Their purpose is to contend for world hegemony. They contend as well as collude with each other. Their collusion serves the purpose of more intensified contention. Contention is absolute and protracted, whereas collusion is relative and temporary. The declaration of this year as the "year of Europe" and the convocation of the European Security Conference indicate that strategically the key point of their contention is Europe. The West always wants to urge the Soviet revisionists eastward to divert the peril towards China, and it would be fine so long as all is quiet in the West. China is an attractive piece of meat coveted by all. But this piece of meat is very tough, and for years no one has been able to bite into it. It is even more difficult now that Lin Piao the "super-spy" has fallen. At present, the Soviet revisionists are "making a feint to the east while attacking in the west," and stepping up their contention in Europe and their expansion in the Mediterranean, the Indian Ocean and every place their hands can reach. The U.S.-Soviet contention for hegemony is the cause of world intranquillity. It cannot be covered up by any false appearances they create and is already perceived by an increasing number of people and countries. It has met with strong resistance from the Third World and has caused resentment on the part of Japan and West European countries. Beset with troubles internally and externally, the two hegemonic powers—the U.S. and the U.S.S.R.—find the going tougher and tougher. As the verse goes, "Flowers fall off, do what one may," they are in a sorry plight indeed. This has been further proved by the U.S.-Soviet talks last June and the subsequent course of events.

"The people, and the people alone, are the motive force in the making of world history." The ambitions of the two hegemonic powers—the U.S. and the U.S.S.R.—are one thing, but whether they can achieve them is quite another. They want to devour China, but find it too tough even to bite. Europe and Japan are also hard to bite, not to speak of the vast Third World. U.S. imperialism started to go downhill after its defeat in the war of aggression against Korea. It has openly admitted that it is increasingly on the decline; it could not but pull out of Vietnam. Over the last two decades, the Soviet revisionist ruling clique, from Khrushchev to Brezhnev, has made a socialist country degenerate into a social-imperialist country. Internally, it has restored capitalism, enforced a fascist dictatorship and enslaved the people of all nationalities, thus deepening the political and economic contradictions as well as contradictions among nationalities. Externally, it has invaded and occupied Czechoslovakia, massed its troops along the Chinese border, sent troops into the People's Republic of Mongolia, supported the traitorous Lon Nol clique, suppressed the Polish workers' rebellion, intervened in Egypt, causing the expulsion of the Soviet experts, dismembered Pakistan and carried out subversive activities in many Asian and African countries. This series of facts has profoundly exposed its ugly features as the new Czar and its reactionary nature, namely, **"socialism in words, imperialism in deeds."** The more evil and foul things it does, the sooner the time when Soviet revisionism will be relegated to the historical museum by the people of the Soviet Union and the rest of the world.

Recently, the Brezhnev renegade clique has talked a lot of nonsense on Sino-Soviet relations. It alleges that China is against relaxation of world tension and unwilling to improve Sino-Soviet relations, and so forth. These words are directed to the Soviet people and the people of other countries in a vain attempt to alienate their friendly feelings for the Chinese people and disguise the true features of the new Czar. These words are above all meant for the monopoly capitalists in the hope of getting more money in reward for services in opposing China and communism. This was an old trick of Hitler's, only Brezhnev is playing it more clumsily. If you are so anxious to relax world tension, why don't you show your good faith by doing a thing or two—for instance, withdraw your armed forces from Czechoslovakia or the People's Republic of Mongolia and return the four northern islands to Japan? China has not occupied any foreign countries' territory. Must China give away all the territory north of the Great Wall to the Soviet revisionists in order to show that we favor relaxation of world tension and are willing to improve Sino-Soviet relations? The Chinese people are not to be deceived or cowed. The Sino-Soviet controversy on matters of principle should not hinder the normalization of relations between the two states on the basis of the Five Principles of Peaceful Coexistence. The Sino-Soviet boundary question should be settled peacefully through negotiations free from any threat. **"We will not attack unless we are attacked; if we are attacked, we will certainly counter-attack"**—this is our consistent principle. And we mean what we say.

We should point out here that necessary compromises between revolutionary countries and imperialist countries must be distinguished from collusion and compromise between Soviet revisionism and U.S. imperialism. Lenin put it well: **"There are compromises and compromises. One must be able to analyze the situation and the concrete conditions of each compromise, or of each variety of compromise. One must learn** to distinguish between a man who gave the bandits money and firearms in order to lessen the damage they can do and facilitate their capture and execution, and a man who gives bandits money and firearms in order to share in the loot." *("Left-Wing" Communism, an Infantile Disorder)* The Brest-Litovsk Treaty concluded by Lenin with German imperialism comes under the former category; and the doings of Khrushchev and Brezhnev, both betrayers of Lenin, fall under the latter.

Lenin pointed out repeatedly that imperialism means aggression and war. Chairman Mao pointed out in his statement of May 20, 1970: **"The danger of a new world war still exists, and the people of all countries must get prepared. But revolution is the main trend in the world today."** It will be possible to prevent such a war, so long as the peoples, who are becoming more and more awakened, keep the orientation clearly in sight, heighten their vigilance, strengthen unity and persevere in struggle. Should the imperialists be bent on unleashing such a war, it will inevitably give rise to greater revolutions on a world-wide scale and hasten their doom.

In the excellent situation now prevailing at home and abroad, it is most important for us to run China's affairs well. Therefore, on the international front, our Party must uphold proletarian internationalism, uphold the Party's consistent policies, strengthen our unity with the proletariat and the oppressed people and nations of the whole world and with all countries subjected to imperialist aggression, subversion, interference, control or bullying, and form the broadest united front against imperialism, colonialism and neo-colonialism, and in particular, against the hegemonism of the two superpowers—the U.S. and the U.S.S.R. We must unite with all genuine Marxist-Leninist Parties and organizations the world over, and carry the struggle against modern revisionism through to the end. On the domestic front, we must pursue our Party's basic line and policies for the entire historical period of socialism, persevere in continuing the revolution under the dictatorship of the proletariat, unite with all the forces that can be united and work hard to build our country into a powerful socialist state, so as to make a greater contribution to mankind.

We must uphold Chairman Mao's teachings that we should **"be prepared against war, be prepared against natural disasters, and do everything for the people"** and should **"dig tunnels deep, store grain everywhere, and never seek hegemony,"** maintain high vigilance and be fully prepared against any war of aggression that imperialism may launch and particularly against surprise attack on our country by Soviet revisionist social-imperialism. Our heroic People's Liberation Army and our vast militia must be prepared at all times to wipe out any enemy that may invade.

Taiwan Province is our motherland's sacred territory, and the people in Taiwan are our kith and kin. We have infinite concern for our compatriots in Taiwan, who love and long for the motherland. Our compatriots in Taiwan can have a bright future only by returning to the embrace of the motherland. Taiwan must be liberated. Our great motherland must be unified. This is the common aspiration and sacred duty of the people of all nationalities of the country, including our compatriots in Taiwan. Let us strive together to attain this goal. . . .

Constitution of the Communist Party of China*

Chapter I
General Program

The Communist Party of China is the political party of the proletariat, the vanguard of the proletariat.

The Communist Party of China takes Marxism-Leninism-Mao Tse-tung Thought as the theoretical basis guiding its thinking.

The basic program of the Communist Party of China is the complete overthrow of the bourgeoisie and all other exploiting classes, the establishment of the dictatorship of the proletariat in place of the dictatorship of the bourgeoisie and the triumph of socialism over capitalism. The ultimate aim of the Party is the realization of communism.

Through more than fifty years of arduous struggle, the Communist Party of China has led the Chinese people in winning complete victory in the new-democratic revolution, great victories in socialist revolution and socialist construction and great victories in the Great Proletarian Cultural Revolution.

Socialist society covers a considerably long historical period. Throughout this historical period, there are classes, class contradictions and class struggle, there is the struggle between the socialist road and the capitalist road, there is the danger of capitalist restoration, and there is the threat of subversion and aggression by imperialism and social imperialism. These contradictions can be resolved only by depending on the theory of continued revolution under the dictatorship of the proletariat and on practice under its guidance.

Such is China's Great Proletarian Cultural Revolution, a great political revolution carried out under the conditions of socialism by the proletariat against the bourgeoisie and all other exploiting classes to consolidate the dictatorship of the

---

*Adopted at the Tenth National Congress of the Communist Party of China on August 28, 1973. Reprinted in *Peking Review*, Nos. 35–36 (September 7, 1973), pp. 26–29.

proletariat and prevent capitalist restoration. Revolutions like this will have to be carried out many times in the future.

The Party must rely on the working class, strengthen the worker-peasant alliance and lead the people of all the nationalities of our country in carrying on the three great revolutionary movements of class struggle, the struggle for production and scientific experiment; lead the people in building socialism independently and with the initiative in our own hands, through self-reliance, hard struggle, diligence and thrift and by going all out, aiming high and achieving greater, faster, better and more economical results; and lead them in preparing against war and natural disasters and doing everything for the people.

The Communist Party of China upholds proletarian internationalism and opposes great-power chauvinism; it firmly unites with the genuine Marxist-Leninist Parties and organizations the world over, unites with the proletariat, the oppressed people and nations of the whole world, and fights together with them to oppose the hegemonism of the two superpowers —the United States and the Soviet Union—to overthrow imperialism, modern revisionism and all reaction, and to abolish the system of exploitation of man by man over the globe, so that all mankind wil be emancipated.

The Communist Party of China has strengthened itself and grown in the course of the struggle against both Right and "Left" opportunist lines. Comrades throughout the Party must have the revolutionary spirit of daring to go against the tide, must adhere to the principles of practicing Marxism and not revisionism, working for unity and not for splits, and being open and aboveboard and not engaging in intrigues and conspiracy, must be good at correctly distinguishing contradictions among the people from those between ourselves and the enemy and correctly handling them, must develop the style of integrating theory with practice, maintaining close ties with the masses and practicing criticism and self-criticism, and must train millions of successors for the cause of proletarian revolution, so as to ensure that the Party's cause will advance forever along the Marxist line.

The future is bright, the road is tortuous. Members of the Communist Party of China, who dedicate their lives to the struggle for communism, must be resolute, fear no sacrifice and surmount every difficulty to win victory!

Chapter II
Membership

Article 1. Any Chinese worker, poor peasant, lower-middle peasant, revolutionary army man or any other revolutionary element who has reached the age of eighteen and who accepts the Constitution of the Party, joins a Party organization and works actively in it, carries out the Party's decisions, observes Party discipline and pays membership dues may become a member of the Communist Party of China.

Article 2. Applicants for Party membership must go through the procedure for admission individually. An applicant must be recommended by two Party members, fill out an application form for Party membership and be examined by a Party branch, which must seek the opinions of the broad masses inside and outside the Party. Application is subject to acceptance by the general membership meeting of the Party branch and approval by the next higher Party committee.

Article 3. Members of the Communist Party of China must:

(1) Conscientiously study Marxism-Leninism-Mao Tse-tung Thought and criticize revisionism;

(2) Work for the interests of the vast majority of people of China and the world;

(3) Be able at uniting with the great majority, including those who have wrongly opposed them but are sincerely correcting their mistakes; however, special vigilance must be maintained against careerists, conspirators and double-dealers so as to prevent such bad elements from usurping the leadership of the Party and the state at any level and guarantee that the leadership of the Party and the state always remains in the hands of Marxist revolutionaries;

(4) Consult with the masses when matters arise;

(5) Be bold in making criticism and self-criticism.

Article 4. When Party members violate Party discipline, the Party organizations at the levels concerned shall, within their functions and powers and on the merits of each case, take appropriate disciplinary measures—warning, serious warning, removal from posts in the Party, placing on probation within the Party, or expulsion from the Party.

The period for which a Party member is placed on probation shall not exceed two years. During this period, he has no right to vote or elect or be elected.

A Party member whose revolutionary will has degenerated and who does not change despite repeated education may be persuaded to withdraw from the Party.

When a Party member asks to withdraw from the Party, the Party branch concerned shall, with the approval of its general membership meeting, remove his name from the Party rolls and report the matter to the next higher Party committee for the record.

Proven renegades, enemy agents, absolutely unrepentent persons in power taking the capitalist road, degenerates and alien-class elements must be cleared out of the Party and not be readmitted.

Chapter III
Organizational Principle of the Party

Article 5. The organizational principle of the Party is democratic centralism.

The leading bodies of the Party at all levels shall be elected through democratic consultation in accordance with the requirements for successors to the cause of the proletarian revolution and the principle of combining the old, the middle-aged and the young.

The whole Party must observe unified discipline: The individual is subordinate to the organization, the minority is subordinate to the majority, the lower level is subordinate to the higher level, and the entire Party is subordinate to the Central Committee.

Leading bodies of Party at all levels shall regularly report on their work to congresses or general membership meetings, constantly listen to the opinions of the masses both inside and outside the Party and accept their supervision. Party members have the right to criticize organizations and leading members of the Party at all levels and make proposals to them. If a Party member holds different views with regard to the decisions or directives of the Party organizations, he is allowed to reserve his views and has the right to bypass the immediate leadership and report directly to higher levels, up to and including the Central Committee and the Chairman of the Central Committee. It is absolutely impermissible to suppress criticism and to retaliate. It is essential to create a political situation in which there are both centralism and democracy, both discipline and freedom, both unity of will and personal ease of mind and liveliness.

Article 6.   The highest leading body of the Party is the National Party Congress and, when it is not in session, the Central Committee elected by it. The leading bodies of Party organizations in the localities, in army units and in various departments are the Party congresses or general membership meetings at their respective levels and the Party committees elected by them. Party congresses at all levels are convened by Party committees at their respective levels. The convening of Party congresses in the localities, in army units and in various departments and their elected Party committee members are subject to approval by the higher Party organizations.

Party committees at all levels shall set up their working bodies or dispatch their representative organs in accordance with the principles of close ties with the masses and simple and efficient structure.

Article 7.   State organs, the People's Liberation Army and the militia, labor unions, poor and lower-middle peasant associations, women's federations, the Communist Youth League, the Red Guards, the Little Red Guards and other revolutionary mass organizations must all accept the centralized leadership of the Party.

Party committees or leading Party groups may be set up in state organs and popular organizations.

Chapter IV
Central Organizations of the Party

Article 8.   The National Party Congress shall be convened every five years. Under special circumstances, it may be convened before its due date or postponed.

Article 9.   The plenary session of the Central Committee of the Party elects the Political Bureau of the Central Committee, the Standing Committee of the Political Bureau of the Central Committee, and the Chairman and Vice-Chairman of the Central Committee.

The plenary session of the Central Committee of the Party is convened by the Political Bureau of the Central Committee.

When the Central Committee is not in plenary session, the Political Bureau of the Central Committee and its Standing

Committee exercise the functions and powers of the Central Committee.

Under the leadership of the Chairman, Vice-Chairmen and the Standing Committee of the Political Bureau of the Central Committee, a number of necessary organs, which are compact and efficient, shall be set up to attend to the day-to-day work of the Party, the government and the Army in a centralized way.

Chapter V
Party Organizations in the Localities
And the Army Units

Article 10. Local Party congresses at the county level and upwards and Party congresses in the People's Liberation Army at the regimental level and upwards shall be convened every three years. Under special circumstances, they may be convened before their due date or postponed.

Party committees at all levels in the localities and the army units elect their standing committees, secretaries and deputy secretaries.

Chapter VI
Primary Organizations of the Party

Article 11. Party branches, general Party branches or primary Party committees shall be set up in factories, mines and other enterprises, people's communes, offices, schools, shops, neighborhoods, companies of the People's Liberation Army and other primary units in accordance with the requirements of the revolutionary struggle and the size of the Party membership.

Party branches and general Party branches shall hold elections once a year and primary Party committees shall hold elections every two years. Under special circumstances, the election may take place before its due date or be postponed.

Article 12. The main tasks of the primary organizations of the Party are:

(1) To lead the Party members and non-Party members in studying Marxism-Leninism-Mao Tse-tung Thought conscientiously and criticizing revisionism;

(2) To give constant education to the Party members and non-Party members concerning the ideological and political line and lead them in fighting resolutely against the class enemy;

(3) To propagate and carry out the policies of the Party, implement its decisions and fulfill every task assigned by the Party and the state;

(4) To maintain close ties with the masses, constantly listen to their opinions and demands and wage an active ideological struggle so as to keep Party life vigorous;

(5) To take in new Party members, enforce Party discipline and constantly consolidate the Party organizations, getting rid of the stale and taking in the fresh, so as to maintain the purity of the Party ranks.

WANG HUNG-WEN*

Report on the Revision of the Party Constitution

. . . One. Concerning the Great Proletarian Cultural Revolution. The Great Proletarian Cultural Revolution is a great political revolution carried out under the conditions of socialism by the proletariat against the bourgeoisie and all other exploiting classes, and it is also a deep-going Party consolidation movement. During the Great Proletarian Cultural Revolution the whole Party, Army and people, under the leadership of Chairman Mao, have smashed the two bourgeois headquarters, the one headed by Liu Shao-chi and the other by Lin Piao, thus striking a hard blow at all domestic and international reactionary forces. **The current Great Proletarian Cultural Revolution is absolutely necessary and most timely for consolidating the dictatorship of the proletariat, preventing capitalist restoration and building socialism.** The draft fully affirms the great victories and the tremendous significance of this revolution and has the following statement explicitly written into it: "Revolutions like this will have to be carried out many times in the future." Historical experience tells us that not only will the struggle between the two classes and the two roads in society at home inevitably find expression in our Party, but imperialism and social-imperialism abroad will inevitably recruit agents from within our Party in order to carry out aggression and subversion against us. In 1966 when the Great Proletarian Cultural Revolution was just rising, Chairman Mao already pointed out: **"Great disorder across the land leads to great order. And so once again every seven or eight years. Monsters and demons will jump out themselves. Determined by their own class nature, they are bound to jump out."** The living reality of class struggle has confirmed and will continue to confirm this objective law as

* Wang Hung-wen, report delivered at the Tenth National Congress of the Communist Party of China on August 24 and adopted on August 28, 1973. Reprinted in *Peking Review*, Nos. 35–36 (September 7, 1973), pp. 29–33.

revealed by Chairman Mao. We must heighten our vigilance and understand the protractedness and complexity of this struggle. In order to constantly consolidate the dictatorship of the proletariat and seize new victories for the socialist cause, it is necessary to deepen the socialist revolution in the ideological, political and economic spheres, to transform all those parts of the superstructure that do not conform to the socialist economic base and carry out many great political revolutions such as the Great Proletarian Cultural Revolution. . . .

Three. We must have the revolutionary spirit of daring to go against the tide. Chairman Mao pointed out: **Going against the tide is a Marxist-Leninist principle.** During the discussions on the revision of the Party Constitution, many comrades, reviewing the Party's history and their own experiences, held that this was most important in the two-line struggle within the Party. In the early period of the democratic revolution, there were several occasions when wrong lines held sway in our Party. In the later period of the democratic revolution and in the period of socialist revolution, when the correct line represented by Chairman Mao has been predominant, there have also been lessons in that certain wrong lines or wrong views were taken as correct for a time by many people and supported as such. The correct line represented by Chairman Mao has waged resolute struggles against those errors and won out. When confronted with issues that concern the line and the overall situation, a true Communist must act without any selfish considerations and dare to go against the tide, fearing neither removal from his post, expulsion from the Party, imprisonment, divorce nor guillotine.

Of course, in the face of an erroneous trend there is not only the question of whether one dares go against it but also that of whether one is able to distinguish it. Class struggle and the two-line struggle in the historical period of socialism are extremely complex. When one tendency is covered by another, many comrades often fail to note it. Moreover, those who intrigue and conspire deliberately put up false fronts, which makes it all the more difficult to discern. Through discussion, many comrades have come to realize that according to the dialectic materialist point of view, all objective things are knowable. **"The naked eye is not enough, we must have the aid of the telescope and** the microscope. **The Marxist method is our telescope and microscope in political and military matters.**" So long as one diligently studies the works of Marx, Engels, Lenin and Stalin and those of Chairman Mao, takes an active part in the actual struggle and works hard to remold one's world outlook, one can constantly raise the ability to distinguish genuine from sham Marxism and differentiate between correct and wrong lines and views.

In waging struggle, we must study Chairman Mao's theory concerning the struggle between the two lines and learn from his practice; we must not only be firm in principle, but also carry out correct policies, draw a clear distinction between the two types of contradictions of different nature, make sure to unite with the vast majority and observe Party discipline.

Four. We must train millions of successors for the cause of the proletarian revolution in the course of mass struggles. Chairman Mao said, **"In order to guarantee that our Party and country do not change their color, we must not only have a correct line and correct policies but must train and bring up millions of successors who will carry on the cause of proletarian revolution."** As stated above, those to be trained are not just one or two persons, but millions. Such a task cannot be fulfilled unless the whole Party attaches importance to it. In discussing the revision of the Party Constitution, many elder comrades expressed the strong desire that we must further improve the work of training successors, so that the cause of our proletarian revolution initiated by the Party under the leadership of Chairman Mao will be carried forward by an endless flow of succesors. Many young comrades on their part warmly pledged to learn modestly from the strong points of veteran cadres who have been tempered through long years of revolutionary war and revolutionary struggle and have rich experience, to be strict with themselves and to do their best to carry on the revolution. Both veteran and new cadres expressed their determination to learn each other's strong points and overcome their own shortcomings. In the light of the views expressed, a sentence about the necessity of training successors has been added to the general program of the draft, and another sentence about the application of the principle of combining the old, the middle-aged and the young in leading bodies at all levels has been added to the articles. We must, in accordance with the five requirements Chairman Mao has laid down for successors to the cause of the proletarian revolution, lay stress on selecting outstanding persons from among the workers and poor and lower-middle peasants and placing them in leading posts at all levels. Attention must also be paid to training women cadres and minority nationality cadres.

Five. We must strengthen the Party's centralized leadership and promote the Party's traditional style of work. The political party of the proletariat is the highest form of the organization of the proletariat, and the Party must exercise leadership in everything; this is an important Marxist principle. The draft has incorporated suggestions from various units on strengthening the Party's centralized leadership. It is laid down in the articles that state organs, the People's Liberation Army and revolutionary mass organizations "must all accept the Party's centralized leadership." Organizationally, the Party's centralized leadership should be given expression in two respects: First, as regards the relationship between various organizations at the same level, **of the seven sectors—industry, agriculture, commerce, culture and education, the Army, the government and the Party—it is the Party that exercises overall leadership;** the Party is not parallel to the others and still less is it under the leadership of any other. Second, as regards the relationship between higher and lower levels, the lower level is subordinate to the higher level, and the entire Party is subordinate to the Central Committee. This has long been a rule in our Party and it must be adhered to. We must strengthen the Party's centralized leadership, and a Party committee's leadership must not be replaced by a "joint conference" of several sectors. But at the same time, it is necessary to give full play to the role of the revolutionary committees, the other sectors and organizations at all levels. The Party committee must practice democratic centralism and strengthen its collective leadership. It must unite people "from all corners of the country" and not practice mountain-stronghold sectionalism. It must "let all people have their say" and not "let one person alone have the say." The most essential thing about the Party's centralized leadership is leadership through a correct ideological and political line. Party committees at all levels must, on the basis of Chairman Mao's revolutionary line, achieve **unity in thinking, policy, plan, command and action.**

The style of integrating theory with practice, maintaining
close ties with the masses and practicing criticism and self-
criticism has been written into the general program of the
draft. Communists of the older generations are familiar with
this fine tradition of our Party as cultivated by Chairman
Mao; however, they still face the question of how to carry
it forward under new historical conditions, whereas for the
many new Party members, there is the question of learning,
inheriting and carrying it forward. Chairman Mao often educates us with accounts of the Party's activities in its years of
bitter struggle, asking us to share the same lot, rough or smooth,
with the broad masses. We must beware of the inroads of
bourgeois ideology and the attacks by sugar-coated bullets; we
must be modest and prudent, work hard and lead a plain life,
resolutely oppose privilege and earnestly overcome all such
unhealthy tendencies as "going in by the back door."

Now, I would like to discuss with special emphasis the question of accepting criticism and supervision from the masses. Ours
is a socialist country under the dictatorship of the proletariat.
The working class, the poor and lower-middle peasants and the
masses of working people are the masters of our country. They
have the right to exercise revolutionary supervision over cadres
of all ranks of our Party and state organs. This concept has
taken deeper root throughout the Party, thanks to the Great
Proletarian Cultural Revolution. However, there are still a
small number of cadres, especially some leading cadres, who
will not tolerate differing views of the masses inside or outside
the Party. They even suppress criticism and retaliate, and it is
quite serious in some individual cases. In handling problems
among the people, Party discipline absolutely forbids such
wrong practices as resorting to "suppression if unable to persuade, and arrest if unable to suppress." In the draft, the
sentence that "it is absolutely impermissible to suppress criticism and to retaliate" has been added to the articles. We should
approach this question from the high plane of two-line struggle
to understand it, and resolutely fight against such violations of
Party discipline. We must have faith in the masses, rely on
them, constantly use the weapons of arousing the masses to air
their views freely, write big-character posters and hold great
debates and strive **"to create a political situation in which there**

are both centralism and democracy, both discipline and freedom, both unity of will and personal ease of mind and liveliness, so as to facilitate our socialist revolution and socialist construction, make it easier to overcome difficulties, enable our country to build a modern industry and modern agriculture at a fairly rapid pace, consolidate our Party and state and make them better able to weather storm and stress."

Six. It is our Party's consistent principle to uphold proletarian internationalism. This time we have further included "Oppose great-power chauvinism" in the draft. We will forever stand together with the proletariat and the revolutionary people of the world to oppose imperialism, modern revisionism and all reaction, and at present to oppose especially the hegemonism of the two superpowers—the U.S. and the U.S.S.R. The danger of a new world war still exists. We must, without fail, prepare well against any war of aggression and guard against surprise attack by imperialism and social-imperialism.

Chairman Mao says: **"In our international relations, we Chinese people should get rid of great-power chauvinism resolutely, thoroughly, wholly and completely."** Our country has a large population, vast territory and abundant resources. We must make our country prosperous and strong and we are fully capable of doing it. However, we must persist in the principle of **"never seek hegemony"** and must never be a superpower under any circumstances. All Party comrades must firmly bear in mind Chairman Mao's teachings that we must never be conceited, not even after a hundred years, and never be cocky, not even after the twenty-first century. At home, too, we must oppose every manifestation of "great-power" chauvinism, and further strengthen the revolutionary unity of the whole Party, the whole Army and the people of all the nationalities of the country to speed up our socialist revolution and socialist construction and strive to fulfill our due international obligations.

Comrades! Ours is a great, glorious and correct Party. We are confident that the whole Party acting according to the political line defined by the Tenth Congress and the new Party Constitution adopted by it, can surely build our Party into a stronger and more vigorous one. Let us, under the leadership of the Party's Central Committee headed by Chairman Mao, **unite to win still greater victories!**

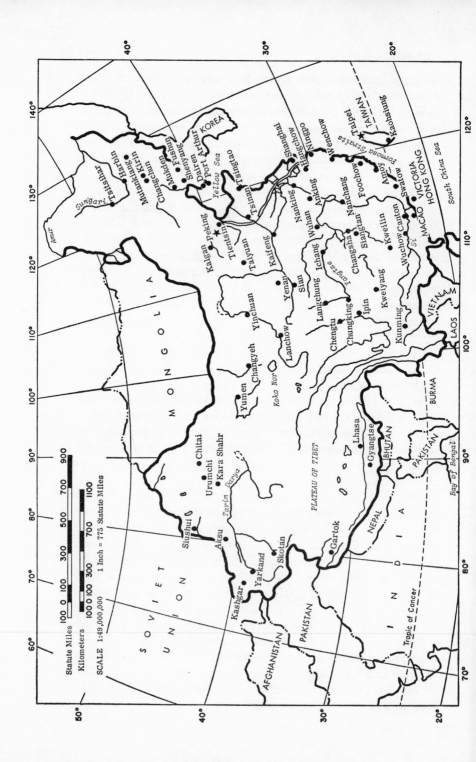

CHRONOLOGY

[*1966*]

February:	Five-member "Cultural Revolution Group" led by P'eng Chen
March 4–April 19:	Liu Shao-ch'i visits Pakistan, Afghanistan, Burma
May 7:	May 7 directive from Mao Tse-tung and Lin Piao on educational revolution
May 9:	Thermonuclear detonation
May 10:	Beginning of public attack on "demons and monsters"
May 12:	Five U.S. planes penetrate Yünnan Province
May 16:	May 16 directive—formation of new Cultural Revolution Group
May 25:	Nieh Yüan-tzu's wall poster launches attack in Peking University
May 29:	First Red Guards formed in Tsinghua University
June 3:	Expulsion of P'eng Chen
June 13:	Suspension of all entrance exams to universities
June 16:	Chou En-lai visits Albania, Rumania
June 29:	U.S. attacks Hanoi, Haiphong
July 16:	Mao swims Yangtze, signifying resumption of power
July 22:	Million people demonstrate for Vietnam in Peking
August 1:	Eleventh Plenum of Central Committee, C.C.P.
August 5:	Mao Tse-tung's "Bombard the Headquarters" Wall Poster
August 8:	Sixteen-Point resolution of Central Committee; Mao, Lin, Chou designated top leaders
August 18:	One million people demonstrate in T'ien An Men Square—Mao greets Red Guards
September 20:	Sino-French aviation agreement
Fall:	Red Guards mass-march through China to spread Cultural Revolution
October 23:	Central Committee working session criticizes Liu Shao-ch'i and Teng Hsiao-p'ing
October 27:	Detonation of missile with nuclear warhead
December 28:	Fifth thermonuclear detonation

[*1967*]

January 3:	January revolutionary seizure of power begins in Shanghai
January 12:	Criticism of "economism" (bribery of workers by wage increases); revolutionary rebel headquarters set up in Shansi
January 25:	Fight between Russian police and Chinese students in Moscow's Red Square
January 31:	First provincial revolutionary committee established in Heilungkiang
February 3:	Chinese embassy personnel attacked in Moscow
February 22:	National meeting of Red Guards at Peking University
February (late):	Beginning of February "counter-current" by capitalist roaders
March 7:	Mao's March 7 appeal for reopening of schools
March 18:	Central Committee call to workers, managers, revolutionary cadres to maintain production
April 1:	Beginning of comprehensive attacks against Liu Shao-ch'i
April 20:	Peking city revolutionary committee established
May 6:	Strikes, demonstrations, clashes in Hong Kong
May 27:	Chinese embassy in Ulan Bator (Mongolia) attacked
June 17:	Hydrogen bomb detonated
June 21:	President Kaunda visits China
July 20:	Hsieh Fu-chih and Wang Li detained by conservative military in Wuhan
July–August:	Ultra-left wave—attack on PLA, Foreign Ministry, British Consulate
August:	Preliminary agreement reached between Tanzania, Zambia, and China to build Tanzam railroad
August 5:	China-North Vietnam economic assistance agreement
September 2:	Mass meeting in Peking to support PLA propaganda teams entering Cultural Revolution
September 15:	McNamara announces "anti-China" ABM
September:	Russians carry out first anti-China military maneuvers (code name *Dniepr*)
October 27:	Chinese Embassy blockaded in New Delhi
October 31:	Chinese experts leave Burma

[*1968*]

January–September	Revolutionary Committees set up throughout China

January 7:	U.S. planes bomb Chinese ships in North Vietnam port
January 31:	Wang Li, Ch'i Pen-yü expelled from Cultural Revolution Group
March 24:	Acting Chief of Staff Yang Ch'eng-wu removed from office
May:	Revolutionary upheaval in France; mass support demonstrations in Peking
June 13:	Paris peace talks begin
June 18:	President Nyerere visits China
August 20:	U.S.S.R. invades Czechoslovakia
September 5:	With Tibet, revolutionary committees now established in all twenty-nine provinces save Taiwan
September 13:	Albania formally withdraws from Warsaw Pact
September 16:	Soviet planes intrude into Heilungkiang air space
October 1:	Yangtze River railroad bridge formally inaugurated
October 13–31:	Twelfth Plenum of Central Committee—Liu Shao-ch'i expelled from Party
October 31:	Johnson's bombing halt
December 22:	Call for city youth to go to countryside
December 27:	New nuclear test; China announces all external and internal debts repaid

[*1969*]

March 2:	Sino-Soviet military clashes over Chenpao island
March 3:	Mass anti-Soviet demonstrations in China
March 7–8:	Anti-China demonstrations in Moscow
April 1:	Ninth Party Congress; Lin Piao written into Party Constitution as Mao's successor
May 28:	Significant work with acupuncture reported at PLA hospitals
July 24–28:	Bumper summer crops reported from throughout South China
September 4:	Ho Chi Minh dies
September 11:	Chou En-lai–Kosygin talks at Peking airport
September 23:	First underground nuclear test
September 29:	Thermonuclear test
October 19:	Soviet border talks delegation arrives in Peking
November 14:	Zambia, Tanzania, China railroad agreement signed
December 27–31:	Year-end record industrial output reported

[*1970*]

January 9:	Record textile output reported
March 18:	Cambodia coup—Sihanouk establishes government in Peking
April 24:	China launches earth-orbiting satellite
April 24–25:	Indochina summit conference
April 30:	U.S. invades Cambodia
May 20:	Mao statement on danger of new world war
August 14:	Edgar Snow visits China
October 13:	Diplomatic relations established with Canada
November 6:	Diplomatic relations with Italy established
November 8:	Relations with Burma renewed after three-year break
November 12:	Soviet trade delegation arrives in China
November 29:	Sino-Soviet trade agreement signed
December 6:	Mexican president Echeverria raises possibility of diplomatic relations

[*1971*]

January 1:	Record food harvests reported
February:	U.S.-supported South Vietnamese invasion of Laos; China warns of possible use of nuclear weapons
March 5–8:	Chou En-lai and large delegation conclude major agreements in Hanoi.
April 10–14:	American ping-pong team visits China; Chou En-lai greets American ping-pong team
April 30:	Mao says Nixon welcome to China in December 1970 interview with Snow published in *Life* magazine
May:	Committee of Concerned Asian Scholars and American journalists visit China
July 9–11:	Kissinger visits Peking
July 15:	Nixon visit announced
July 27:	U.S. halts spy flights over China
August 26:	Party committees completely reestablished throughout China
September 12:	All flights suspended in China; Lin Piao dies; major military leaders ousted
October 5:	Second Kissinger visit to Peking
October 12:	Nixon visit to Moscow announced
October 25:	China voted into UN
November 15:	Chinese delegation arrives at UN
November 29:	China attacks Indian invasion of East Pakistan

[*1972*]

February 15:	Edgar Snow dies
February 20:	Head of Soviet border talks delegation Ilychev returns to Peking
February 21–28:	Nixon in Peking
March (end):	Liberation forces offensive begins in Vietnam
April–May:	Massive U.S. bombing of North Vietnam—Hanoi bombed, Haiphong harbor mined
May 22–29:	Nixon in Moscow
June 24–July 5:	Sri Lanka prime minister Bandaranaike visits China
July 18:	U.S. planes bombing North Vietnam violate China air space
July 24:	China agrees to buy Concorde supersonic planes
July 28:	Lin Piao death officially confirmed
August 25:	China vetoes Bangladesh membership in UN
Fall:	Certain top leaders attacked during Cultural Revolution rehabilitated
September 1:	Japan–U.S. summit talks
September 9:	China buys Boeing jets
September 25–29:	Premier Tanaka visits China
October 27:	Purchase of U.S. corn announced
November:	Trade agreements and talks with Mexico, Japan, Britain, Nigeria, Canada, Brazil, Algeria, Venezuela
November 25:	Urban exodus to rural areas reduced

GLOSSARY

As those who read writings from China, even in English translation, soon discover, there are many terms which seem curious to the average reader. Since these terms occur frequently in this book, we have decided to furnish a brief glossary. Our own definitions are preliminary and the glossary is but a minimal list of Chinese political terms. There are specialized studies and small lexica of these terms available in any academic library of materials on China.

CADRE: Most commonly used in reference to a full-time functionary of the Party or the Government. Also used to designate anyone exercising leadership in an ordinary political or working situation. The Chinese word is *kan-pu* (old romanization) or *gan-bu* (new romanization). The preferred pronunciation in China of the English word is *káh-der*.

CAPITALIST ROADERS: Term applied during the Cultural Revolution to those in power who, by persisting in Soviet-type policies and practices, were turning into a new ruling elite and encouraging trends in society toward bourgeois ways (for example, profits and bonuses in industry, and private plots on farms).

CULTURAL REVOLUTION GROUP: Chairman Mao's operational headquarters from which key directives to guide the Cultural Revolution were issued. Mao, Lin Piao, and Chou En-lai together with the Cultural Group constituted the de facto leadership of the country until the fall of 1967 when, after the expulsion of the ultra-leftist members, the group itself declined in power.

DAZIBAO (TA-TZU-PAO), WALL POSTER: A bill of particulars, written by individuals, groups, or organizations, posted publicly, which expresses citizens' opinions about certain cadres, issues, and problems, often of a critical nature. *Dazibao* are one of the chief vehicles for expressing public opinion in China.

DICTATORSHIP OF THE PROLETARIAT: Marx's term for the direct exercise of power by the working class after the seizure of power in a revolution. It implies both a dictatorial use of force to prevent the overthrown classes from returning to power as well as direct and participatory democracy on the part of the overwhelming majority of the people.

ECONOMISM: Term coined by Lenin to designate such trade-unionistic and vulgar Marxist thinking that assumed the workers' sole and highest interest was to increase their share of the economic surplus and that therefore all issues of power were reducible to economic terms. During the Cultural Revolution, it designated the practice of capitalist roaders, notably in Shanghai, who bribed workers with wage increases to gain their support in the struggle for power.

GREAT ALLIANCE: The term used for the formula by which two or more revolutionary organizations united to jointly agree upon and elect representatives to the new revolutionary committees in their administrative unit. The formula opposed the exclusion of any revolutionary mass organization from representation on the revolutionary committees.

PARTY COMMITTEE: The body of leading cadres who are members of the Communist Party in a particular organization functioning to implement higher Party policy as well as reflect the conditions and opinions of the masses to higher Party echelons.

PROPAGANDA TEAMS: Teams made up of workers and soldiers, sent into various organizations, particularly higher schools rent by factional quarreling, in order to lead the contending groups to unite, form the Great Alliance, recognize general policy and interests, and resolve their particular disputes.

RECTIFICATION: Periodic movements to identify, attack, and transform erroneous tendencies in the Communist Party. Such movements range from criticism to expulsion of Party members.

REVISIONISM: Term applied by Lenin to such German Social Democrats at the turn of the century as Eduard Bernstein, who argued that the proletariat could gain power through peaceful, evolutionary, and reformist means. From the early 1960's on, the Chinese have used the term (first indirectly and then directly) to designate the ideology and policies of the Soviet leaders, notably their elevation of the thesis of peaceful coexistence and peaceful transition to socialism above that of revolution. Used in China to designate tendencies opposed to Mao's concept of uninterrupted revolution under socialism and espousing a Soviet-type line in domestic and foreign affairs.

REVOLUTIONARY COMMITTEE: A representative body of workers or members of a particular organization that arose during the Cultural Revolution as its leading policy-making and supervisory body. The revolutionary committees went through several transformations and continue to function alongside the newly reconstituted Party committees.

SOCIAL IMPERIALISM: Term originally coined by Lenin to charac-

terize Social Democratic supporters of various national imperialisms, particularly those socialists who supported their national
governments during World War I. Now widely used by the Chinese to designate the imperialistic character of the Soviet Union.

STRUGGLE–CRITICISM–TRANSFORMATION (TOU-P'I-KAI): A slogan
designating the three stages through which the Cultural Revolution should be carried out in each organization. The first stage
was to identify and struggle against capitalist roaders in power;
the second stage involved criticism and self-criticism of all groups
and individuals participating in the movement; and the final
stage was to transform all organizations, institutions, and practices which did not conform to revolutionary socialism. This
transformation involving various new experimental institutional
reforms is still under way.

SUPERPOWER: Term borrowed by the Chinese from the West to
designate the United States and the Soviet Union whom they
regard as the world's two imperialisms seeking to impose their
control on all other countries.

SUPERSTRUCTURE: Marxist term for the state, which includes government, education, law, culture, and the army contrasted with
society (the substructure or base, notably the economy).

THREE-IN-ONE ALLIANCE: The practical approach toward reconstituting power when revolutionary committees were being set up.
"Three-in-one" meant representative activists who had risen from
the masses during the Cultural Revolution, old cadres who had
been managers and administrators in the organization (including
Party cadres who were considered as still revolutionary), and
PLA soldiers. Together they formed the revolutionary committees.

TWO LINES (BOURGEOIS REACTIONARY LINE; PROLETARIAN REVOLU-
TIONARY LINE): Following Mao Tse-tung's famous conception
that in all revolutionary struggles there are "we" and the
"enemy," the struggle during the Cultural Revolution was seen
as between two lines. While individuals could and did shift
(sincerely or not) from one line to the other, the issues always
remained. The bourgeois reactionary line related to those who
were against rebellion by the masses, repressed the masses, and
opposed revolution; the proletarian revolutionary line, which
Mao expressed in his poster "Bombard the Headquarters," called
for rebellion by the masses to criticize, struggle against, and
remove from power bourgeois rightists and capitalist roaders.

ULTRA-LEFT: Term to designate a persistent tendency for left revolutionary action to go to extremes, seeking the complete destruction

of all constituted authority, often stated by the Chinese to include the incorrect view which sought to oppose all and overthrow all.

WORK TEAM: A work team is a group of cadres and other political people sent by some central headquarters to "trouble-shoot" different problems, to lead a mass movement, or bring people into line with higher policy. During the early period of the Cultural Revolution, it designated the teams sent out by "royalist" Party headquarters to take over and suppress the mass movement of the Cultural Revolution.

NOTE ON ROMANIZATION

While the Wade-Giles system has been standard for transliterating Chinese into English since the early part of this century, the Chinese have developed their own system of romanization which is standard in China, universally taught in the schools, and also used as the script for many minority languages.

Wade-Giles	Chinese Romanization	Pronunciation
a	a	father
ai	ai	aye
ang	ang	ahng
ao	ao	cow
ch	zh	juice
ch'	ch	check
ch'	q	chit
ê	e	uh
ei	ei	table
erh	er	girl
f	f	fine
h	h	hat
hs	x	between seat and sheet
i	i	bee
ia	ia	eeyah
iao	iao	eeyow
ieh	ie	eeyeh
ih	i	turn
in	in	in
ing	ing	being
iu	iu	you
j	r	red
k	g	guard
k'	k	kin
l	l	land
m	m	man
n	n	no
o	e	girl
ou	ou	go

p	b	*b*all
p'	p	*p*ut
s	s	*s*and
sh	sh	*sh*ut
ssu	si	*sssuh*
t	d	*d*og
t'	t	*t*own
ts	z	e*du*cate
ts'	c	ca*ts*
tz	z	a*dz*e
tz'	c	ca*ts*
u	u	g*oo*se
u	i	m*i*rth
ü	u	*ü*ber (German)
üeh	ue	*üeh*
ui	ui	*way*
w	w	*w*ater
y	y	*y*ou

BIBLIOGRAPHY

There is a wealth of material in English on China since 1966 from a variety of perspectives. Books and articles on China generally fall into three categories: (1) publications of the left and Third World press; (2) journalistic analyses and reports; and (3) academic and policy-oriented studies. There is wide disagreement within and between each of these perspectives on the meaning of the Cultural Revolution and on China's new world role since then. Readers who live in large cities or academic centers can often find left and Third World material on China in radical bookshops. Serious journalistic reports and analyses can be found in major newspapers, notably *The New York Times* (and the Sunday magazine), the *Wall Street Journal,* the *Christian Science Monitor,* and other papers (including British and Canadian). Academic studies are scattered in learned journals with the London-based *China Quarterly* exclusively devoted to contemporary China. The Hong Kong-based *Far Eastern Economic Review* and *Eastern Horizon* provide continuing coverage on issues and events in China.

The following bibliography consists of some major recent books on China:

I. *Cultural Revolution*

Gurtov, Melvin: *The Foreign Ministry and Foreign Affairs in China's Cultural Revolution.* Rand Corporation: Santa Monica, 1969.
Hinton, William: *Turning Point in China: An Essay on the Cultural Revolution.* Monthly Review Press: New York, 1972.
————: *Hundred Day War: The Cultural Revolution at Tsinghua University.* Monthly Review Press: New York, 1972. By the author of *Fanshen,* a long–time friend of the Chinese Revolution.
Hunter, Neale: *Shanghai Journal.* Beacon Press: New York, 1969. Hunter taught in China during the beginning of the Cultural Revolution.
Karnow, Stanley: *Mao and China: From Revolution to Revolution.* Viking Press: New York, 1972. The perspective of a Hong Kong-based journalist.
Nee, Victor: *The Cultural Revolution at Peking University.* Monthly Review Press: New York, 1969.
Nee, Victor, and Peck, James (eds.): *Essays on the Cultural Revolu-*

tion. Pantheon: New York, 1974. An analytical view from the left.

Rice, Edward E.: *Mao's Way*. University of California Press: Berkeley and Los Angeles, 1972. The view of a Hong Kong-based diplomat.

Robinson, Thomas: *The Cultural Revolution in China*. University of California Press: Berkeley and Los Angeles, 1971. The view of a RAND Corporation analyst.

Solomon, Richard: *Mao's Revolution and the Chinese Political Culture*. University of California Press, 1971. Professor at the University of Michigan, and staff member of the National Security Council.

II. *General*

Alley, Rewi: *Travels in China 1966–1971*. Peking: New World Press, 1973. New Zealand engineer resident in China for forty years.

Barnstone, Willis (in collaboration with Ko Ching-po): *The Poems of Mao Tse-tsung*. Harper's: New York, 1972.

Buchanan, Keith: *The Transformation of the Chinese Earth*. Praeger: New York, 1971. New Zealand geographer of China.

Chen, Jack: *A Year in Upper Felicity*. Macmillan: New York, 1973. Long-time Peking resident.

Chen, Jerome: *Mao Papers, a New Anthology and Bibliography*. Oxford University Press: New York, 1970. The author is a biographer of Mao and a professor at York University, Canada.

Cheng, Peter: *A Chronology of the People's Republic of China from October 1, 1949*. Totowa, New Jersey: Littlefield, Adams & Co., 1972.

Clubb, Edmund O.: *Sino-Russian Relations from the Thirteenth Century to the Present*. Columbia University Press: New York, 1971. The author was a U.S. diplomat and teacher serving until McCarthyite period.

Cohen, Jerome (ed.): *The Dynamics of China's Foreign Relations*. Harvard University Press: Cambridge, Mass., 1970. The author is a professor of Chinese law at Harvard.

Committee of Concerned Asian Scholars: *China! Inside the People's Republic*. Bantam, 1972.

Geoffroy-Dechaume, Francois: *China Looks at the World*. Pantheon: New York, 1967. French diplomat and Sinologist.

Gittings, John: *The Role of the Chinese Army*. Oxford University Press: New York, 1967. The author is a United Kingdom scientist and an observer of Sino-Soviet scene.

Gray, Jack: *Modern China's Search for a Political Form*. Oxford University Press: New York, 1969. The author is a United Kingdom economist specializing on China.

Han Suyin: *China in the Year 2001.* Basic Books, Inc.: New York, 1967. Doctor, novelist, journalist, and author of many books on China.

————: *The Morning Deluge: Mao Tse-tung and the Chinese Revolution.* Little, Brown and Co.: Boston, 1972.

Horn, Joshua: *Away With All Pests.* Monthly Review Press: New York, 1971. The author, an English surgeon, spent fourteen years in China.

Johnson, Chalmers (ed.): *Ideology and Politics in Contemporary China.* University of Washington Press: Seattle, 1973. Professor of Political Science, University of California at Berkeley.

Karol, K. S.: *China and the Other Communism.* Hill and Wang: New York, 1967. View of a left pro-China European.

Macciocchi, Maria Antonietta: *Daily Life in Revolutionary China.* Monthly Review Press: New York, 1972. View of an Italian leftist.

Mehnert, Klaus: *China Returns.* E. P. Dutton: New York, 1972. View of a long-time German observer of the Russian and Chinese scenes.

Melby, John F.: *The Mandate of Heaven: Record of a Civil War, China 1945–49.* University of Toronto Press, 1968. Former State Department officer in the 1940's.

Myrdal, Jan, and Kessel, Gun: *China: The Revolution Continued.* Pantheon, 1970. A view from Swedish friends of China.

Neville, Maxwell: *India's China War.* Pantheon, 1970. A different view of the 1962 Sino-Indian border clashes, by the London *Times* New Delhi correspondent.

The New York Times *Report From Red China.* Quadrangle Press: New York, 1971. Collection of articles by the first *New York Times* correspondents to go to China in 1971.

Rand McNally: *China: An Illustrated Atlas.* Rand McNally: Skokie, Illinois, 1972.

Richman, Barry: *Industrial Society in Communist China.* Random House: New York, 1968. View of a specialist in industrial management and a student of the Soviet scene.

Schell, Orville, and Esherick, Joseph: *Modern China: The Story of a Revolution.* Knopf: New York, 1972. A left popular history of China.

Sidel, Ruth: *Women and Child Care in China.* Hill and Wang: New York, 1972. The author is a social work supervisor at the Albert Einstein School of Medicine.

Salisbury, Harrison: *To Peking and Beyond.* Quadrangle Press: New York, 1973. The author is a long-time Moscow correspondent for *The New York Times.*

Selden, Mark: *The Yenan Way in Revolutionary China.* Harvard University Press: Cambridge, 1971. Professor of History at Washington University, St. Louis.

Snow, Edgar: *The Long Revolution.* Random House: New York, 1972.

Spence, Jonathan: *To Change China: Western Advisers in China, 1620–1960.* Little, Brown and Co.: Boston, 1969. Teaches at Yale University.

Syboldt, Peter J.: *Revolutionary Education in China: Documents and Commentary.* International Arts and Sciences Press: White Plains, New York, 1973.

Terrill, Ross: *800,000,000—The Real China.* Little, Brown and Co.: Boston, 1971. The author is an Australian Sinologist.

Topping, Seymour: *Journey Between Two Chinas.* Harper and Row: New York, 1972. The author is *The New York Times* correspondent who served in Moscow and Hong Kong.

Vogel, Ezra: *Canton Under Communism, 1949–1968.* Harper Torch Books, 1969. The author is a professor of sociology at Harvard.

Wakeman, Frederick, Jr.: *History and Will: Philosophical Perspectives of Mao Tse-tung's Thought.* University of California Press, 1973. Professor of History at University of California, Berkeley.

Wheelright, E. L., and McFarland, Bruce J.: *Chinese Road to Socialism.* Monthly Review Press: New York, 1970. A left economists' view.

Whitson, William (with Chen Hsia-huang): *A History of Chinese Communist Military Politics 1927–1961.* Praeger: New York, 1973. View of an American military man with long East Asian experience.

INDEX

About the Editors

FRANZ SCHURMANN is a Professor of Sociology and History at the University of California, Berkeley, and a member of the Bay Area Institute, San Francisco. Born in New York City in 1926, he received his bachelor's degree from Trinity College and his doctorate from Harvard University; he served in the United States Army after World War II. He is the author of *Ideology and Organization in Communist China,* and co-author of *The Politics of Escalation in Vietnam.* Professor Schurmann writes on the current history of China, on American foreign policy, and on the Indochina War. He makes his home in San Francisco.

DAVID MILTON, who was born in Chicago, was a merchant seaman during World War II and was active in the trade union movement during the late 1940's and the 1950's. A graduate of San Francisco State University, he is presently engaged in graduate work in sociology at the University of California at Berkeley. From 1964 to 1969, he taught at the First Foreign Languages Institute in Peking. He is a contributor to the forthcoming *Essays on the Chinese Cultural Revolution* (Pantheon, 1974) and with Nancy Milton is writing a book on the Cultural Revolution. His articles on China have appeared in *The New York Times* and *The Chicago Sun Times.*

NANCY MILTON, a native Californian, is a graduate in creative writing from Stanford, with an M.A. in English from San Francisco State University. She taught at the Peking First Foreign Languages Institute in the People's Republic of China from 1964 through 1969 and now teaches in the San Francisco Community College District. She is co-editor of *Fragment from a Lost Diary* (Pantheon, 1973), a contributor to the forthcoming *Essays on the Chinese Cultural Revolution* (Pantheon, 1974), and with David Milton has a book in progress on China's Cultural Revolution.